10th Edition

# Web Development & Design Foundations with HTML5

10th Edition

# Web Development & Design Foundations with HTML5

Terry Ann Felke-Morris, Ed.D.

Professor Emerita
Harper College

 Pearson

ISBN 10:  0-13-668154-9
ISBN 13: 978-0-13-668154-0

# Preface

*Web Development & Design Foundations with HTML5* is intended for use in a beginning web development course. This textbook introduces HTML and CSS topics such as text configuration, color configuration, and page layout, with an enhanced focus on the topics of design, accessibility, and Web standards. The text covers the basics that web developers need to build a foundation of skills:

- Internet concepts
- Creating web pages with HTML5
- Configuring text, color, and page layout with Cascading Style Sheets (CSS), including the new CSS Flexbox and CSS Grid Layout Systems
- Web design best practices
- Accessibility standards
- The web development process
- Using media and interactivity on web pages
- Website promotion and search engine optimization
- E-commerce and the Web
- JavaScript

A special feature of this text is the *Web Developer's Handbook*, which is a collection of appendixes that provide resources including an HTML5 Reference, Special Entity Character List, CSS Property Reference, WCAG 2.1 Quick Reference, FTP Tutorial, and web-safe color palette.

## New to This Edition

Building on this textbook's successful ninth edition, new features for the tenth edition include the following:

- Updated coverage of HTML5 elements and attributes
- Updated code samples, case studies, and web resources
- Expanded treatment of page layout design and responsive web design techniques
- Chapter 7 has been renamed **Responsive Page Layout,** takes a mobile first approach, and has an expanded focus on new layout systems including CSS Flexible Layout Module (Flexbox) and CSS Grid Layout
- Form layout with the CSS Flexbox and Grid Layout Systems
- Updated reference sections for HTML5 and CSS
- Additional Hands-On Practice exercises

Student files are available for download from the companion website for this textbook at www.pearson.com/felke-morris. These files include solutions to the Hands-On Practice exercises, the Website Case Study starter files, and access to the book's companion VideoNotes. See the access card in the front of this textbook for further instructions.

## Organization of the Text

This textbook is designed to be used in a flexible manner; it can easily be adapted to suit a variety of course and student needs. Chapter 1 provides introductory material, which may be skipped or covered, depending on the background of the students. Chapters 2 through 4 introduce HTML and CSS coding. Chapter 5 discusses web design best practices and can be covered anytime after Chapter 3 (or even along with Chapter 3). Chapters 6 through 9 continue with HTML and CSS.

Any of the following chapters may be skipped or assigned as independent study, depending on time constraints and student needs: Chapter 10 (Web Development), Chapter 11 (Web Multimedia and Interactivity), Chapter 12 (E-Commerce Overview), Chapter 13 (Web Promotion), and Chapter 14 (A Brief Look at JavaScript and jQuery). A chapter dependency chart is shown in Figure P.1.

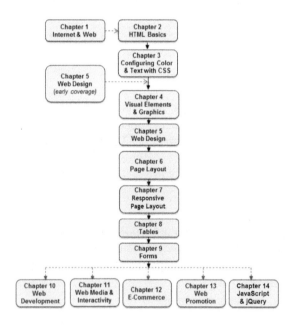

Figure P.1 This textbook is flexible and can be adapted to individual needs

## Brief Overview of Each Chapter

**Chapter 1: Introduction to the Internet and World Wide Web** This brief introduction covers the terms and concepts related to the Internet and the Web with which Web developers need to be familiar. For many students, some of this will be a review. Chapter 1 provides the base of knowledge on which the rest of the textbook is built.

**Chapter 2: HTML Basics**  As HTML5 is introduced, examples and exercises encourage students to create sample pages and gain useful experience. Students use a variety of structural, grouping, and text-level HTML elements to create web pages with hyperlinks. Solution pages for the Hands-On Practice are available in the student files.

**Chapter 3: Configuring Color and Text with CSS**  The technique of using Cascading Style Sheets to configure the color and text on web pages is introduced. Students are encouraged to create sample pages as they read through the text. Solutions for the Hands-On Practice are available in the student files.

**Chapter 4: Visual Elements and Graphics**  This chapter discusses the use of graphics and visual effects on web pages, including image optimization, CSS borders, CSS image backgrounds, CSS visual effects, and HTML5 visual elements. Students are encouraged to create web pages as they read through the text. Sample solutions for the Hands-On Practice are available in the student files.

**Chapter 5: Web Design**  This chapter focuses on recommended web design practices and accessibility. Some of this is reinforcement because tips about recommended website design practices are incorporated into the other chapters.

**Chapter 6: Page Layout**  This chapter has been greatly revised for the 10th ediition. It continues the study of CSS begun earlier and introduces techniques for positioning and floating web page elements, including CSS two-column page layouts. Coding techniques for CSS sprites, configuring for print, a fixed position navigation bar, a single page website, and parallax scrolling are also introduced. Students are encouraged to create web pages as they read through the text. Sample solutions for the Hands-On Practice are available in the student files.

**Chapter 7: Responsive Page Layout**  This chapter has undergone a huge revision for the 10th edition. Chapter 7 has increased in-depth coverage of CSS Flexible Box Layout (Flexbox) and CSS Grid Layout. Chapter 7 continues to introduce CSS media queries and responsive image techniques along with CSS feature queries. Students are encouraged to create pages as they read through the text. Sample solutions for the Hands-On Practice are available in the student files.

**Chapter 8: Tables**  This chapter focuses on the HTML elements used to create tables. Methods for configuring a table with CSS are introduced. Students are encouraged to create pages as they read through the text. Sample solutions for the Hands-On Practice are available in the student files.

**Chapter 9: Forms**  This chapter focuses on the HTML elements used to create forms. Methods for configuring the form with CSS are introduced, including using CSS Grid Layout. HTML5 form control elements and attribute values are introduced. Students are encouraged to create sample pages as they read through the text. Sample solutions for the Hands-On Practice are available in the student files.

**Chapter 10: Web Development**  This chapter focuses on the process of website development, including the job roles needed for a large-scale project, the web development process, and web hosting. The topic of file organization is also addressed. A web host checklist is included in this chapter.

**Chapter 11: Web Multimedia and Interactivity** This chapter offers an overview of topics related to adding media and interactivity to web pages. These topics include HTML5 video and audio, CSS transform, transition, and animation properties, interactive drop-down menu, interactive image gallery, JavaScript, jQuery, Ajax, and HTML5 APIs. Students are encouraged to create pages as the topics are discussed. Sample solutions for the Hands-On Practice are available in the student files.

**Chapter 12: E-Commerce Overview** This chapter introduces e-commerce, security, and order processing on the Web.

**Chapter 13: Web Promotion** This chapter discusses site promotion from the web developer's point of view and introduces search engine optimization. A solution for the Hands-On Practice is available in the student files.

**Chapter 14: A Brief Look at JavaScript and jQuery** This chapter provides an introduction to client-side scripting using JavaScript and jQuery. Sample solutions for the Hands-On Practice are available in the student files.

***Web Developer's Handbook* Appendixes:** This handbook contains appendixes that include resources and tutorials that are useful for students, such as an HTML5 Quick Reference, Special Entity Characters, CSS Property Reference, a WCAG 2.1 Quick Reference, FTP Tutorial, ARIA Landmark Roles, and web-safe color palette.

## Features of the Text

**Well-Rounded Selection of Topics** This text includes both "hard" skills such as HTML5, CSS, and JavaScript (Chapters 2, 3, 4, 6, 7, 8, 9, and 14) and "soft" skills such as web design (Chapter 5), website promotion (Chapter 13), and e-commerce (Chapter 12). This well-rounded foundation will help students as they pursue careers as web professionals. Students and instructors will find classes more interesting because they can discuss, integrate, and apply both hard and soft skills as students create web pages and websites.

**Hands-On Practice** Web development is a skill and skills are best learned by hands-on practice. This text emphasizes hands-on practice through exercises within the chapters, end-of-chapter exercises, and the development of websites through ongoing real-world case studies. The variety of exercises provides instructors with a choice of assignments for a particular course or semester.

**Website Case Studies** There are four case studies that continue throughout most of the text (starting with Chapter 2). An additional case study starts in Chapter 5. The case studies serve to reinforce the skills discussed in each chapter. Instructors can cycle assignments from semester to semester or allow students to choose the case study that most interests them. Sample solutions to the case studies are available for download from the Instructor Resource Center at www.pearson.com.

**Web Research** Each chapter offers web research activities that encourage students to further study the topics introduced in the chapter.

**Focus on Web Design** Most chapters offer additional activities that explore the web design topics related to the chapter. These activities can be used to reinforce, extend, and enhance the course topics.

**FAQs** In the author's web development courses, she is frequently asked similar questions by students. They are included in this textbook and are marked with the identifying FAQ logo.

**Checkpoints** Each chapter contains two or three Checkpoints, which are groups of questions to be used by students to self-assess their understanding of the material. A special Checkpoint icon appears with each group of questions.

**Focus on Accessibility** Developing accessible websites is more important than ever and this textbook is infused with accessibility techniques throughout. The special icon shown here makes accessibility information easy to find.

Focus on Accessibility

**Focus on Ethics** Ethics issues related to web development are highlighted throughout the textbook and are marked with the special ethics icon shown here.

Focus on Ethics

**Reference Materials** The appendixes in the *Web Developer's Handbook* offer reference materials, including the HTML5 Quick Reference, Special Entity Characters, CSS Property Reference, a WCAG 2.1 Quick Reference, FTP Tutorial, ARIA Landmark Roles, and Web-Safe Color Palette.

**VideoNotes** These short step-by-step videos demonstrate how to solve problems from design through coding. VideoNotes allow for self-placed instruction with easy navigation including the ability to select, play, rewind, fast-forward, and stop within each VideoNote exercise.

VideoNote

Margin icons in your textbook let you know when a VideoNote video is available for a particular concept or homework problem.

## Supplemental Materials

**Student Resources** The student files for the web page exercises, Website Case Study assignments, and access to the book's VideoNotes are available to all readers of this textbook at its companion website www.pearson.com/felke-morris. A complimentary access code for the companion website is available with a new copy of this textbook. Subscriptions may also be purchased online.

**Instructor Resources** The following supplements are available to qualified instructors only. Visit the Pearson Instructor Resource Center (www.pearson.com) for information on how to access them:

- Solutions to the end-of-chapter exercises
- Supplemental Design Activities
- Solutions for the case study assignments
- Test questions
- PowerPoint® presentations
- Sample syllabi

**Author's Website**  In addition to the publisher's companion website for this textbook, the author maintains a website at https://www.webdevfoundations.net. This website contains additional resources, including review activities and a page for each chapter with examples, links, and updates. This website is not supported by the publisher.

## Acknowledgments

Very special thanks go to all the folks at Pearson, especially Michael Hirsch, Tracy Johnson, Erin Sullivan, Scott Disanno, Carole Snyder, and Robert Engelhardt.

Thank you to the following people who provided comments and suggestions that were useful for this tenth edition and previous editions:

Carolyn Andres—*Richland College*
James Bell—*Central Virginia Community College*
Ross Beveridge—*Colorado State University*
Karmen Blake—*Spokane Community College*
Jim Buchan—*College of the Ozarks*
Dan Dao—*Richland College*
Joyce M. Dick—*Northeast Iowa Community College*
Elizabeth Drake—*Santa Fe Community College*
Mark DuBois—*Illinois Central College*
Genny Espinoza—*Richland College*
Carolyn Z. Gillay—*Saddleback College*
Sharon Gray—*Augustana College*
Tom Gutnick—*Northern Virginia Community College*
Jason Hebert—*Pearl River Community College*
Sadie Hébert—*Mississippi Gulf Coast College*
Lisa Hopkins—*Tulsa Community College*
Barbara James—*Richland Community College*
Nilofar Kadivi—*Richland Community College*
Jean Kent—*Seattle Community College*
Mary Keramidas—*Sante Fe College*
Karen Kowal Wiggins—*Wisconsin Indianhead Technical College*
Manasseh Lee—*Richland Community College*
Nancy Lee—*College of Southern Nevada*
Kyle Loewenhagen—*Chippewa Valley Technical College*
Michael J. Losacco—*College of DuPage*
Les Lusk—*Seminole Community College*
Will Mahoney-Watson—*Portland Community College*
Mary A. McKenzie—*Central New Mexico Community College*
Bob McPherson—*Surry Community College*
Cindy Mortensen—*Truckee Meadows Community College*
John Nadzam—*Community College of Allegheny County*
Teresa Nickeson—*University of Dubuque*
Brita E. Penttila—*Wake Technical Community College*
Anita Philipp—*Oklahoma City Community College*
Jerry Ross—*Lane Community College*
Noah Singer—*Tulsa Community College*
Alan Strozer—*Canyons College*

Lo-An Tabar-Gaul—*Mesa Community College*
Jonathan S. Weissman—*Finger Lakes Community College*
Tebring Wrigley—*Community College of Allegheny County*
Michelle Youngblood-Petty—*Richland College*

A very special thank you also goes to Jean Kent, North Seattle Community College, and Teresa Nickeson, University of Dubuque, for taking time to provide additional feedback and sharing student comments about the book.

Thanks are in order to colleagues at William Rainey Harper College for their support and encouragement, especially Ken Perkins, Enrique D'Amico, and Dave Braunschweig.

Most of all, I would like to thank my family for their patience and encouragement. My wonderful husband, Greg Morris, has been a constant source of love, understanding, support, and encouragement. Thank you, Greg! A big shout-out to my children, James and Karen, who grew up thinking that everyone's Mom had their own website. Thank you both for your understanding, patience, and timely suggestions! And, finally, a very special dedication to the memory of my father who is greatly missed.

## About the Author

Terry Ann Felke-Morris is a Professor Emerita of Computer Information Systems at William Rainey Harper College in Palatine, Illinois. She holds a Doctor of Education degree, a Master of Science degree in information systems, and numerous certifications, including Adobe Certified Dreamweaver 8 Developer, WOW Certified Associate Webmaster, Microsoft Certified Professional, Master CIW Designer, and CIW Certified Instructor.

Dr. Felke-Morris has been honored with Harper College's Glenn A. Reich Memorial Award for Instructional Technology in recognition of her work in designing the college's Web Development program and courses. In 2006, she received the Blackboard Greenhouse Exemplary Online Course Award for use of Internet technology in the academic environment. Dr. Felke-Morris received two international awards in 2008: the Instructional Technology Council's Outstanding e-Learning Faculty Award for Excellence and the MERLOT Award for Exemplary Online Learning Resources—MERLOT Business Classics.

With more than 25 years of information technology experience in business and industry, Dr. Felke-Morris published her first website in 1996 and has been working with the Web ever since. A long-time promoter of Web standards, she was a member of the Web Standards Project Education Task Force. Dr. Felke-Morris is the author of the popular textbook *Basics of Web Design: HTML5 & CSS*, currently in its fifth edition. She was instrumental in developing the Web Development certificate and degree programs at William Rainey Harper College. For more information about Dr. Terry Ann Felke-Morris, visit https://terrymorris.net.

# Contents

# CHAPTER **6**

Page Layout   245

# CHAPTER 7

## Responsive Page Layout   311

# CHAPTER 8

Tables   385

# CHAPTER 9

Forms   413

# CHAPTER 10

Web Development   469

## CHAPTER 11

## Web Multimedia and Interactivity 493

## CHAPTER 12

## E-Commerce Overview 537

**VideoNotes are available at www.pearson.com/felke-morris**
**LOCATION OF VIDEONOTES IN THE TEXT** ▶

A series of videos have been developed as a companion for this textbook. VideoNote icons indicate the availability of a video on a specific topic.

| | |
|---|---|
| **Chapter 1** | Evolution of the Web, p. 2 |
| **Chapter 2** | Your First Web Page, p. 29<br>HTML Validation, p. 61 |
| **Chapter 3** | External Style Sheets, p. 107<br>CSS Validation, p. 117 |
| **Chapter 4** | CSS Background Images, p. 156<br>Rounded Corners with CSS, p. 171 |
| **Chapter 5** | Principles of Visual Design, p. 209 |
| **Chapter 6** | Interactivity with CSS pseudo-classes, p. 265<br>Linking to a Named Fragment, p. 282 |
| **Chapter 7** | CSS Grid Layout, p. 326 |
| **Chapter 8** | Configure a Table, p. 386 |
| **Chapter 9** | Connect a Form to Server-Side Processing, p. 438 |
| **Chapter 10** | Choosing a Domain Name, p. 482 |
| **Chapter 11** | HTML5 Video, p. 501 |
| **Chapter 12** | E-Commerce Benefits and Risks, p. 538 |
| **Chapter 13** | Configure an Inline Frame, p. 580 |
| **Chapter 14** | JavaScript Message Box, p. 592 |

# Introduction to the Internet and World Wide Web

## Chapter Objectives — In this chapter, you will learn how to . . .

- Describe the evolution of the Internet and the Web
- Explain the need for web standards
- Describe universal design
- Identify benefits of accessible web design
- Identify reliable resources of information on the Web

- Identify ethical use of the Web
- Describe the purpose of web browsers and web servers
- Identify networking protocols
- Define URIs and domain names
- Describe HTML, XHTML, and HTML5

**The Internet and the Web are parts of our daily lives.** How did they begin? What networking protocols and programming languages work behind the scenes to display a web page? This chapter provides an introduction to some of these topics and is a foundation for the information that web developers need to know. You'll be introduced to Hypertext Markup Language (HTML), the language used to create web pages.

# 1.1 The Internet and the Web

## The Internet

The **Internet**, the interconnected network of computer networks that spans the globe, seems to be everywhere today. It has become part of our lives. You can't watch television or listen to the radio without being urged to visit a website. Even newspapers and magazines have a place on the Internet.

## Birth of the Internet

The Internet began as a network to connect computers at research facilities and universities. Messages in this network would travel to their destination by multiple routes, or paths. This configuration allowed the network to function even if parts of it were broken or destroyed. In such an event, the message would be rerouted through a functioning portion of the network while traveling to its destination. This network was developed by the Advanced Research Projects Agency (ARPA)—and the ARPAnet was born. Four computers (located at UCLA, Stanford Research Institute, University of California Santa Barbara, and the University of Utah) were connected by the end of 1969.

## Growth of the Internet

As time went on, other networks, such as the National Science Foundation's NSFnet, were created and connected with the ARPAnet. Use of this interconnected network, or Internet, was originally limited to government, research, and educational purposes. The number of individuals accessing the Internet continues to grow each year. According to Internet World Stats (https://www.internetworldstats.com/emarketing.htm), the percentage of the global population that used the Internet was 0.4% in 1995, 5.8% in 2000, 15.7% in 2005, 28.8% in 2010, 45% in 2015, and 56.1% in 2019.

The lifting of the restriction on commercial use of the Internet in 1991 set the stage for future electronic commerce: Businesses were now welcome on the Internet. However, the Internet was still text based and not easy to use. The next set of developments solved this issue.

## Birth of the Web

**VideoNote**
**Evolution of the Web**

While working at CERN, a research facility in Switzerland, **Tim Berners-Lee** envisioned a means of communication for scientists by which they could easily "hyperlink" to another research paper or article and immediately view it. Berners-Lee created the World Wide Web to fulfill this need. In 1991, Berners-Lee posted the code for the Web in a newsgroup and made it freely available. This version of the World Wide Web used **Hypertext Transfer Protocol (HTTP)** to communicate between the client computer and the web server, used **Hypertext Markup Language (HTML)** to format the documents, and was text based.

## The First Graphical Browser

In 1993, Mosaic, the first graphical web browser became available. Marc Andreessen and graduate students working at the National Center for Supercomputing Applications (NCSA) at the University of Illinois Urbana–Champaign developed Mosaic. Some individuals in this group later created another well-known web browser—Netscape Navigator—which is an ancestor of today's Mozilla Firefox browser.

## Convergence of Technologies

By the early 1990s, personal computers with easy-to-use graphical operating systems (such as Microsoft's Windows, IBM's OS/2, and Apple's Macintosh OS) were increasingly available and affordable. Online service providers such as CompuServe, AOL, and Prodigy offered low-cost connections to the Internet. Figure 1.1 depicts this convergence of available computer hardware, easy-to-use operating systems, low-cost Internet connectivity, the HTTP protocol and HTML language, and a graphical browser that made information on the Internet much easier to access. The **World Wide Web**—the graphical user interface to information stored on computers running web servers connected to the Internet—had arrived!

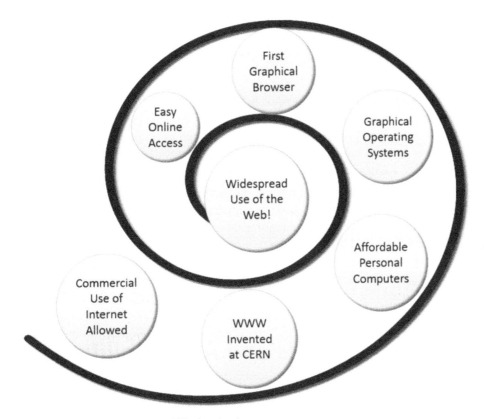

Figure 1.1 Convergence of Technologies

## Who Runs the Internet?

You may be surprised that there is no single person "in charge" of the global interconnected network of computer networks known as the Internet. Instead, Internet infrastructure standards are overseen by groups, such as the **Internet Engineering Task Force (IETF)** and the **Internet Architecture Board (IAB)**. The IETF is the principal body engaged in the development of new Internet protocol standard specifications. It is an open international community of network designers, operators, vendors, and researchers concerned with the evolution of Internet architecture and the smooth operation of the Internet. The actual technical work of the IETF is completed in its working groups. These working groups are organized into areas by topic, such as security and routing.

The IAB is a committee of the IETF and provides guidance and broad direction to the IETF. As a function of this purpose, the IAB is responsible for the publication of the **Request for Comments (RFC)** document series. An RFC is a formal document from the IETF that is drafted by a committee and subsequently reviewed by interested parties. RFCs are available for online review at https://www.ietf.org/standards/rfcs/. Some RFCs are informational in nature, while others are meant to become Internet standards. In the latter case, the final version of the RFC becomes a new standard. Future changes to the standard must be made through subsequent RFCs.

The **Internet Corporation for Assigned Numbers and Names (ICANN)**, https://www.icann.org, was created in 1998 and is a nonprofit organization. Its main function is to coordinate the assignment of Internet domain names, IP address numbers, protocol parameters, and protocol port numbers. Prior to 1998, the **Internet Assigned Numbers Authority (IANA)** coordinated these functions. IANA still performs certain functions under the guidance of ICANN and maintains a website at https://www.iana.org.

## Intranets and Extranets

Recall that the Internet is an interconnected network of computer networks that is globally available. When an organization needs the communication capabilities of the Internet, but doesn't want its information to be available to everyone, either an intranet or extranet is appropriate.

An **intranet** is a private network that is contained within an organization or business. Its purpose is to share organizational information and resources among coworkers. When an intranet connects to the outside Internet, usually a gateway or firewall protects the intranet from unauthorized access.

An **extranet** is a private network that securely shares part of an organization's information or operations with external partners such as suppliers, vendors, and customers. Extranets can be used to exchange data, share information exclusively with business partners, and collaborate with other organizations. Privacy and security are important issues in extranet use. Digital certificates, encryption of messages, and virtual private networks (VPNs) are some technologies used to provide privacy and security for an extranet. Digital certificates and encryption used in e-commerce are discussed in Chapter 12.

# 1.2  Web Standards and Accessibility

Just as with the Internet, no single person or group runs the World Wide Web. However, the **World Wide Web Consortium** (https://www.w3.org), referred to as the **W3C,** takes a proactive role in developing recommendations and prototype technologies related to the Web. Topics that the W3C addresses include web architecture, standards for web design, and accessibility. In an effort to standardize web technologies, the W3C produces specifications called recommendations.

## W3C Recommendations

The W3C Recommendations are created in working groups with input from many major corporations involved in building web technologies. These recommendations are not rules; they are guidelines. Major software companies that build web browsers, such as Microsoft, do not always follow the W3C Recommendations. This makes life challenging for web developers because not all browsers will display a web page in exactly the same way. The good news is that there is a convergence toward the W3C Recommendations in new versions of major browsers. You'll follow W3C Recommendations as you code web pages in this book. Following the W3C Recommendations is the first step toward creating a website that is accessible.

## Web Standards and Accessibility

The **Web Accessibility Initiative (WAI)** (https://www.w3.org/WAI), is a major area of work by the W3C. Since the Web has become an integral part of daily life, there is a need for all individuals to be able to access it.

**Focus on Accessibility**

The Web can present barriers to individuals with visual, auditory, physical, and neurological disabilities. An **accessible website** provides accommodations that help individuals overcome these barriers. The WAI has developed recommendations for web content developers, web authoring tool developers, web browser developers, and developers of other user agents to facilitate use of the Web by those with special needs. An overview of the WAI's **Web Content Accessibility Guidelines (WCAG)** is available at https://www.w3.org/WAI/standards-guidelines/wcag/glance/. The most recent version of WCAG is WCAG 2.1, which extends WCAG 2.0 and introduces additional success criteria including requirements for increased support of mobile device accessibility, low vision accessibility, and cognitive and learning disability accessibility.

## Accessibility and the Law

The **Americans with Disabilities Act (ADA)** of 1990 is a federal civil rights law that prohibits discrimination against people with disabilities. The ADA requires that business, federal, and state services are accessible to individuals with disabilities.

**Focus on Accessibility**

**Section 508 of the Federal Rehabilitation Act** was amended in 1998 to require that U.S. government agencies give individuals with disabilities access to information technology that is comparable to the access available to others. This law requires developers creating information technology (including web pages) for use by the federal government to provide for accessibility. The GSA Government-wide IT Accessibility Initiative (https://www.section508.gov) provides accessibility requirement resources for information technology developers. As the Web and Internet technologies developed, it became necessary to review the original Section 508 requirements. New Section 508 requirements, commonly referred to as the Section 508 Refresh, were aligned to WCAG 2.0 guidelines and published in 2017. This textbook focuses on WCAG 2.0 guidelines to provide accessibility.

In recent years, state governments have also begun to encourage and promote web accessibility. The Illinois Information Technology Accessibility Act (IITAA) standards (http://www.dhs.state.il.us/page.aspx?item=96985) are an example of this trend.

## Universal Design for the Web

**Universal design** is a "strategy for making products, environments, operational systems, and services welcoming and usable to the most diverse range of people possible" (https://www.dol.gov/odep/topics/UniversalDesign.htm). Examples of universal design are all around us. The cutouts on curbs that make it possible for people in wheelchairs to access the street also benefit a person pushing a stroller or riding a Segway Personal Transporter (Figure 1.2). Doors that open automatically for people with mobility challenges also benefit

Figure 1.2  A smooth ride is a benefit of universal design

people carrying packages. A ramp is useful for a person in a wheelchair, a person dragging a rolling backpack or carry-on bag, and so on.

Awareness of universal design by web developers has been steadily increasing. Forward-thinking web developers design with accessibility in mind because it is the right thing to do. Providing access for visitors with visual, auditory, and other challenges should be an integral part of web design rather than an afterthought.

A person with visual difficulties may not be able to use graphical navigation buttons and may use a screen reader device to provide an audible description of the web page. By making a few simple changes, such as providing text descriptions for the images and perhaps providing a text navigation area at the bottom of the page, web developers can make the page accessible. Often, providing for accessibility increases the usability of the website for all visitors.

**Focus on
Accessibility**

Accessible websites, with alternative text for images, headings used in an organized manner, and captions or transcriptions for multimedia features, are more easily used not only by visitors with disabilities, but also by visitors using a browser on a mobile device such as a phone or tablet. Finally, accessible websites may be more thoroughly indexed by search engines, which can be helpful in bringing new visitors to a site. As this text introduces web development and design techniques, corresponding web accessibility and usability issues are discussed.

# 1.3  Information on the Web

These days anyone can publish just about anything on the Web. In this section we'll explore how you can tell if the information you've found is reliable and how you can use that information.

## Reliability and Information on the Web

There are many websites—but which ones are reliable sources of information? When visiting websites to find information, it is important not to take everything at face value (Figure 1.3).

Questions to ask about web resources are listed as follows:

- **Is the organization credible?**

  Anyone can post anything on the Web! Choose your information sources wisely. First, evaluate the credibility of the website itself. Does it have its own domain name, such as http://terrymorris.net, or is it a free website consisting of just a folder of files hosted on a free web hosting site (such as weebly.com, awardspace.com, or 000webhost.com)? The URL of a free website usually includes part of the free web host's domain name. Information obtained from a website that has its own domain name will usually (but not always) be more reliable than information obtained from a free website.

  Evaluate the type of domain name: Is it for a nonprofit organization (.org), a business (.com or .biz), or an educational institution (.edu)? Businesses may provide information in a biased manner, so be careful. Nonprofit organizations and schools will sometimes treat a subject more objectively.

**Figure 1.3** Who really updated that web page you are viewing?

- **How recent is the information?**

  Another item to look at is the date the web page was created or last updated. Although some information is timeless, very often a web page that has not been updated for several years is outdated and may not be the best source of information.

- **Are there links to additional resources?**

  Hyperlinks indicate websites with supporting or additional information that can be helpful to you in your research as you explore a topic. Look for these types of hyperlinks to aid your studies.

- **Is it Wikipedia?**

  Wikipedia (https://wikipedia.org) is a good place to begin research, but don't accept what you read there for fact, and avoid using Wikipedia as a resource for academic assignments. Why? Well, except for a few protected topics, anyone can update Wikipedia with anything! Usually it all gets sorted out eventually—but be aware that the information you read may not be valid.

  Feel free to use Wikipedia to begin exploring a topic, but then scroll down to the bottom of the Wikipedia web page and look for "References"—and then explore those websites and others that you may find. As you gather information on these sites, also consider the other criteria: credibility, domain name, timeliness, and links to additional resources.

## Ethical Use of Information on the Web

This wonderful technology called the World Wide Web provides us with information, graphics, and music—all virtually free (after you pay your Internet service provider, of course). Let's consider the following issues relating to the ethical use of this information:

**Focus on Ethics**

- Is it acceptable to copy someone's graphic to use on your own website?

- Is it acceptable to copy someone's website design to use on your own site or on a client's site?

- Is it acceptable to copy an essay that appears on a web page and use it, or parts of it, as your own writing?

- Is it acceptable to insult someone on your website or link to that person's site in a derogatory manner?

The answer to all of these questions is no. Using someone's graphic without permission is the same as stealing it. In fact, if you link to it, you are actually using up some of the site's bandwidth and may be costing the owner money. Instead, ask the owner of the website for permission to use the graphic. If permission is granted, store the graphic on your own website and be sure to indicate the source of the graphic when you display it on your web page. The key is to request permission before using someone else's resources. Copying the website design of another person or company is also a form of stealing. Any text or graphic on a website is automatically copyrighted in the United States, regardless of whether a copyright symbol appears on the site or not. Insulting a person or company on your website or linking to the person's or company's website in a derogatory manner could be considered a form of defamation.

Issues like these, related to intellectual property, copyright, and freedom of speech, are regularly discussed and decided in courts of law. Good Web etiquette requires that you ask permission before using others' work, give credit for what you use ("fair use" in the U.S.

copyright law), and exercise your freedom of speech in a manner that is not harmful to others. The **World Intellectual Property Organization (WIPO)**, https://wipo.int, is dedicated to protecting intellectual property rights internationally.

What if you'd like to retain ownership, but make it easy for others to use or adapt your work? **Creative Commons**, https://creativecommons.org, is a nonprofit organization that provides free services that allow authors and artists to register a type of a copyright license called a Creative Commons license. There are several licenses to choose from, depending on the rights you wish to grant. The Creative Commons license informs others as to exactly what they can and cannot do with your creative work.

 **Checkpoint 1.1**

1. Describe the difference between the Internet and the Web.

2. Explain three events that contributed to the commercialization and exponential growth of the Internet.

3. Is the concept of universal design important to web developers? Explain your answer.

# 1.4 Network Overview

A **network** consists of two or more computers connected for the purpose of communicating and sharing resources. Common components of a network are shown in Figure 1.4 and include the following:

- Server computer(s)
- Client workstation computer(s)
- Shared devices such as printers
- Networking devices (routers, hubs, and switches) and the media that connect them

Figure 1.4 Common components of a network

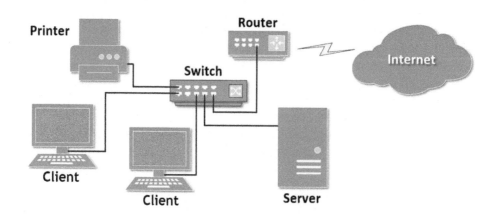

The **clients** are the computer workstations used by individuals, such as a personal computer (PC) on a desk. The **server** receives requests from client computers for resources such as files. Computers used as servers are usually kept in a protected, secure area and are accessed only by network administrators. Networking devices, such as hubs and switches, provide network connections for computers, and routers direct information from one network to another. The media connecting the clients, servers, peripherals, and networking devices may consist of copper cables, fiber optic cables, or wireless technologies.

Networks vary in scale. A **local area network (LAN)** is usually confined to a single building or group of connected buildings. Your school computer lab may use a LAN. If you work in an office, you probably use a computer connected to a LAN. A **wide area network (WAN)** is geographically dispersed and usually uses some form of public or commercial communications network. For example, an organization with offices on both the East and West coasts of the United States probably uses a WAN to provide a link between the LANs at each of the offices.

A **backbone** is a high-capacity communication link that carries data gathered from smaller links that interconnect with it. On the Internet, a backbone is a set of paths that local or regional networks connect to for long-distance interconnection. The Internet is a group of interconnected networks with very high-speed connectivity provided by the Internet backbones.

## 1.5 The Client/Server Model

The term **client/server** dates from the 1980s and refers to personal computers joined by a network. "Client/server" can also describe a relationship between two computer programs—the client and the server. The client requests some type of service (such as a file or database access) from the server. The server fulfills the request and transmits the results to the client over a network. While both the client and the server programs can reside on the same computer, typically they run on different computers (Figure 1.5). It is common for a server to handle requests from multiple clients.

The Internet is a great example of client/server architecture at work. Consider the following scenario: An individual is at a computer using a web browser client to access the Internet. The individual uses the web browser to visit a website, let's say https://www.yahoo.com. The server is the web server program running on the computer with an IP address that corresponds to yahoo.com. It is contacted, locates the web page and related resources that were requested, and responds by sending them to the individual.

Figure 1.5 Web client and web server

Here's how to distinguish between web clients and web servers:

**Web Client**

- Connected to the Internet when needed
- Usually runs web browser (client) software such as Google Chrome or Microsoft Edge
- Uses HTTP or HTTPS
- Requests web pages from a server
- Receives web pages and files from a server

**Web Server**

- Continually connected to the Internet
- Runs web server software such as Apache or Internet Information Services (IIS)
- Uses HTTP or HTTPS
- Receives a request for the web page
- Responds to the request and transmits the status code, web page, and associated files

When clients and servers exchange files, they often need to indicate the type of file that is being transferred; this is done through the use of a MIME type. **Multipurpose Internet Mail Extensions (MIME)** are rules that allow multimedia documents to be exchanged among many different computer systems. MIME was initially intended to extend the original Internet e-mail protocol, but it is also used by HTTP. MIME provides for the exchange of seven different media types on the Internet: audio, video, image, application, message, multipart, and text. MIME also uses subtypes to further describe the data. The MIME type of a web page is text/html. MIME types of GIF and JPEG images are image/gif and image/jpeg, respectively.

A web server determines the MIME type of a file before the file is transmitted to the web browser. The MIME type is sent along with the document. The web browser uses the MIME type to determine how to display the document.

How does information get transferred from the web server to the web browser? Clients (such as web browsers) and servers (such as a web server) exchange information through the use of communication protocols such as HTTP, TCP, and IP, which are introduced in the next section.

# 1.6 Internet Protocols

**Protocols** are rules that describe how clients and servers communicate with each other over a network. There is no single protocol that makes the Internet and Web work; a number of protocols with specific functions are needed.

## File Transfer Protocol (FTP)

**File Transfer Protocol (FTP)** is a set of rules that allow files to be exchanged between computers on the Internet. Unlike HTTP, which is used by web browsers to request web pages and their associated files in order to display a web page, FTP is used simply to move files from one computer to another. Web developers commonly use FTP to transfer web page files from their computers to web servers. FTP is also commonly used to download programs and files from other servers to individual computers.

## E-mail Protocols

Most of us take e-mail for granted, but there are two servers involved in its smooth functioning: an incoming mail server and an outgoing mail server. When you send e-mail to others, **Simple Mail Transfer Protocol (SMTP)** is used. When you receive e-mail, **Post Office Protocol** (POP; currently **POP3**) and **Internet Message Access Protocol (IMAP)** can be used.

## Hypertext Transfer Protocol (HTTP)

**HTTP** is a set of rules for exchanging files such as text, images, audio, video, and other multimedia on the Web. Web browsers and web servers usually use this protocol. When the user of a web browser requests a file by typing a website address or clicking on a hyperlink, the browser builds an HTTP request and sends it to the server. The web server in the destination machine receives the request, does any necessary processing, and responds with the requested file and any associated files (such as image files, media files, and other related files).

## Hypertext Transfer Protocol Secure (HTTPS)

**Hypertext Transfer Protocol Secure (HTTPS)** combines HTTP with a security and encryption protocol. Using HTTPS provides a more secure transaction because the information passed between the browser and the web server is encrypted. See Chapter 12 for more information on HTTPS.

## Transmission Control Protocol/Internet Protocol (TCP/IP)

**Transmission Control Protocol/Internet Protocol (TCP/IP)** has been adopted as the official communication protocol of the Internet. TCP and IP have different functions that work together to ensure reliable communication over the Internet.

### TCP

The purpose of **TCP** is to ensure the integrity of network communication. TCP starts by breaking files and messages into individual units called **packets**. These packets (see Figure 1.6) contain information such as the destination, source, sequence number, and checksum values used to verify the integrity of the data.

**Figure 1.6** TCP packet

TCP is used together with IP to transmit files efficiently over the Internet. IP takes over after TCP creates the packets, using IP addressing to send each packet over the Internet via the best path at the particular time. When the destination address is reached, TCP verifies the integrity of each packet by using the checksum, requests a resend if a packet is damaged, and reassembles the file or message from the multiple packets.

### IP

Working in harmony with TCP, **IP** is a set of rules that controls how data is sent between devices on the Internet. IP routes a packet to the correct destination address. Once sent, the packet gets successively forwarded to the next closest router (a hardware device designed to move network traffic) until it reaches its destination.

Each device connected to the Internet has a unique numeric **IP address**. These addresses consist of a set of four groups of numbers called octets. The current version of IP, **Internet Protocol Version 4 (IPv4)**, uses 32-bit (binary digit) addressing. This results in a decimal number in the format of xxx.xxx.xxx.xxx, where each xxx is a value from 0 to 255. Theoretically, this system allows for at most 4 billion possible IP addresses (although many potential addresses are reserved for special uses). However, even these many addresses will not be enough to meet the needs of all of the devices expected to be connected to the Internet in upcoming years.

**IP Version 6 (IPv6)**, intended to replace IPv4, was designed as an evolutionary set of improvements and is backwardly compatible. Service providers and Internet users can update to IPv6 independently without having to coordinate with each other. IPv6 provides for more Internet addresses because the IP address is lengthened from 32 bits to 128 bits. This means that there are potentially $2^{128}$ unique IP addresses possible, or 340,282,366,920,938,463,463,347,607,431,768,211,456 addresses. (Now there will be enough IP addresses for everyone's PC, notebook, cell phone, tablet, toaster, and so on!)

The IP address of a device may correspond to a domain name. The **Domain Name System (DNS)** associates these IP addresses with the text-based URLs and domain names you type into a web browser address box. For example, at the time this book was written, an IP address for Google was 216.58.194.46. You can enter this number in the address text box in a web browser (as shown in Figure 1.7), press Enter, and the Google home page will display. Of course, it's much easier to type "google.com," which is why domain names such as google.com were created in the first place! Since long strings of numbers are difficult for humans to remember, the Domain Name System was introduced as a way to associate text-based names with numeric IP addresses.

Figure 1.7 Entering an IP address in a web browser

**FAQ    What is HTTP/2?**

HTTP/2 is the first major update to HTTP, which was first developed in 1999. As websites have become more image and media intensive, the number of requests needed to display a web page and its related files have increased. A major benefit of HTTP/2 will be quicker loading of web pages by processing multiple concurrent HTTP requests. Visit https://http2.github.io for more information about HTTP/2.

# 1.7 Uniform Resource Identifiers and Domain Names

## URIs and URLs

A **Uniform Resource Identifier (URI)** identifies a resource on the Internet. A **Uniform Resource Locator (URL)** is a type of URI which represents the network location of a resource such as a web page, a graphic file, or an MP3 file. The URL consists of the protocol, the domain name, and the hierarchical location of the file on the web server.

The URL http://www.webdevfoundations.net/chapter1/index.html, shown in Figure 1.8, denotes the use of HTTP protocol and the web server named www at the domain name of webdevfoundations.net. In this case, the root file (usually index.html or index.htm) in the directory named chapter1 will be displayed.

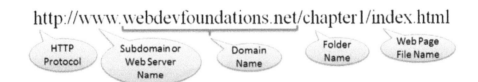

Figure 1.8 URL Describing a file within a folder

## Domain Names

A **domain name** locates an organization or other entity on the Internet. The purpose of the Domain Name System (DNS) is to divide the Internet into logical groups and understandable names by identifying the exact address and type of the organization. The DNS associates the text-based domain names with the unique numeric IP address assigned to a device.

Let's consider the domain name www.google.com. The portion "google.com" is the domain name that is registered to Google. The ".com" is the top-level domain name. The "google" is considered a second-level domain name. The "www" is the name of the web sever (sometimes called the host) at the google.com domain.

A **subdomain** can be configured to house a separate website located at the same domain. For example, Google's Gmail can be accessed by using the subdomain "gmail" in the domain name (gmail.google.com). Google Maps can be accessed at maps.google.com, and Google News Search is available at news.google.com. A list of the top 40 Google subdomains is available at https://www.labnol.org/internet/popular-google-subdomains/5888/. The combination of a host/subdomain, second-level domain, and top-level domain name (such as www.google.com or mail.google.com) is called a **fully qualified domain name (FQDN)**.

## Top-Level Domain Names

A **top-level domain (TLD)** identifies the rightmost part of the domain name, starting with the final period. A TLD is either a **generic top-level domain (gTLD)**, such as .com for commercial, or a **country-code top-level domain**, such as .fr for France. The **Internet Assigned Numbers Authority (IANA)** website has a complete list of TLDs (https://www.iana.org/domains/root/db).

## Generic Top-Level Domain Names (gTLDs)

The Internet Corporation for Assigned Names and Numbers (ICANN) administers gTLDs. Table 1.1 shows several common gTLDs and their intended use.

Table 1.1 Top-level domains

| Generic TLD | Used By |
| --- | --- |
| .aero | Air-transport industry |
| .asia | Pan-Asia and Asia Pacific community |
| .biz | Businesses |
| .cat | Catalan linguistic and cultural community |
| .com | Commercial entities |
| .coop | Cooperative |
| .edu | Restricted to accredited degree-granting institutions of higher education |
| .gov | Restricted to government use |
| .info | Unrestricted use |
| .int | International organization (rarely used) |
| .jobs | Human resources management community |
| .mil | Restricted to military use |
| .museum | Museums |
| .name | Individuals |
| .net | Entities associated with network support of the Internet, usually Internet service providers or telecommunication companies |
| .org | Nonprofit entities |
| .post | Universal Postal Union, an agency of the United Nations |
| .pro | Professionals such as accountants, physicians, and lawyers |
| .tel | Contact information for individuals and businesses |
| .travel | Travel industry |

The .com, .org, and .net TLD designations are currently used on the honor system, which means that, for example, an individual who owns a shoe store (not related to networking) can register shoes.net if the domain name is not already taken.

Expect the number and variety of gTLDs to increase. As of 2017, there were over 1,500 TLDs. The new gTLDs include place names (.quebec, .vegas, and .moscow), retail terms (.blackfriday), financial terms (.cash, .trade, and .loans), technology terms (.systems, .technology, and .app), and whimsical, fun terms (.ninja, .buzz, and .cool). ICANN has set a schedule to periodically launch new gTLDs. A list of the newest gTLDs can be found at  https://newgtlds.icann.org/en/program-status/delegated-strings.

## Country-Code Top-Level Domain Names

Two-character country codes have also been assigned as TLD names. These codes were originally intended to be meaningful by designating the geographical location of the individual or organization that registered the name. Table 1.2 lists some popular country codes used on the Web.

Table 1.2 Country codes

| Country Code TLD | Country |
| --- | --- |
| .au | Australia |
| .de | Germany |
| .es | Spain |
| .eu | European Union (a group of countries rather than a single country) |
| .in | India |
| .jp | Japan |
| .ly | Libya |
| .nl | The Netherlands |
| .us | United States |
| .ws | Samoa |

Visit https://icannwiki.org/Country_code_top-level_domain#Current_ccTLDs for a complete list of country-code TLDs. Domain names with country codes are often used for municipalities, schools, and community colleges in the United States. For example, the domain name www.harper.cc.il.us denotes, from right to left, the United States, Illinois, community college, Harper, and the web server named "www" as the site for Harper College in Illinois.

Although country-code TLD names were intended to designate geographical location, it is fairly easy to obtain a domain name with a country-code TLD that is not local to the registrant. Examples of non-geographical use of country-code TLDs include domain names such as mediaqueri.es, webteacher.ws, and bit.ly.

## Domain Name System (DNS)

The DNS associates domain names with IP addresses. The following happens each time a new URL is typed into a web browser:

1. The DNS is accessed.
2. The corresponding IP address is obtained and returned to the web browser.

3. The web browser sends an HTTP request to the destination computer with the corresponding IP address.

4. The HTTP request is received by the web server.

5. The necessary files are located and sent by HTTP responses to the web browser.

6. The web browser renders and displays the web page and associated files.

We all get impatient sometimes when we need to view a web page. The next time you wonder why it is taking so long to display a web page, think about all of the processing that goes on behind the scenes before the browser receives the files needed to display the web page (Figure 1.9).

Figure 1.9
Accessing a
web page

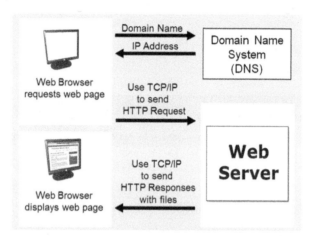

# 1.8  Markup Languages

**Markup languages** consist of sets of directions that tell the browser software (and other user agents such as mobile phones) how to display and manage a web document. These directions are usually called tags and perform functions such as displaying graphics, formatting text, and referencing hyperlinks.

## Standard Generalized Markup Language (SGML)

**SGML** is a standard for specifying a markup language or tag set. SGML in itself is not a document language, but a description of how to specify one and create a document type definition (DTD). When Tim Berners-Lee created HTML, he used SGML to create the specification.

## Hypertext Markup Language (HTML)

**HTML** is the set of markup symbols or codes placed in a file intended for display on a web browser. The web browser renders the code in the HTML file and displays the web page document and associated files. The W3C sets the standards for HTML.

## Extensible Markup Language (XML)

**XML** was developed by the W3C as a flexible method to create common information formats and share the format and the information on the Web. It is a text-based syntax designed to describe, deliver, and exchange structured information. It is not intended to replace HTML, but to extend the power of HTML by separating data from presentation. Using XML, developers can create whatever tags they need to describe their information.

## Extensible Hypertext Markup Language (XHTML)

**XHTML** uses the tags and attributes of HTML4 along with the more rigorous syntax of XML. XHTML was used on the Web for over a decade and you'll find many web pages coded with this markup language. At one point the W3C was working on a new version of XHTML, called XHTML 2.0. However, the W3C stopped development of XHTML 2.0 because it was not backward compatible with HTML4. Instead, the W3C decided to move forward with HTML5.

## HTML5—the Newest Version of HTML

**HTML5** is the successor to HTML4 and replaces XHTML. HTML5 incorporates features of both HTML and XHTML, adds new elements, provides new features such as form edits and native video, and is intended to be backward compatible. The W3C approved HTML5 for final Recommendation status in late 2014. The W3C continued its development of HTML and added more new elements, attributes, and features in an update to HTML5 called HTML5.1. In late 2017, HTML 5.2 reached final Recommendation status. At the time this was written, HTML5.3 was in working draft status.

 **Checkpoint 1.2**

    **1.** Describe the components of the client/server model as applied to the Internet.

    **2.** Identify two protocols used on the Internet to convey information that use the Internet, but do not use the Web.

    **3.** Explain the similarities and differences between a URL and a domain name.

# 1.9 Popular Uses of the Web

## E-Commerce

Continued growth is expected for **e-commerce**, which is the buying and selling of goods and services on the Internet. The statistics portal Statista reports that United States retail e-commerce sales will increase from $446.8 billion in 2017 to over $700 billion in 2022 (https://www.statista.com/statistics/272391/us-retail-e-commerce-sales-forecast/). A study by PEW Research Center indicates that about 80% of American adults shop online (http://www.pewinternet.org/2016/12/19/online-shopping-and-e-commerce). E-commerce can be done not only from desktop computers, but also from a variety of other devices including tablets, smartphones, and devices with voice-enabled personal assistant software (such as Google Assistant and Amazon Alexa).

## Mobile Access

Accessing the Web with devices other than the standard desktop or notebook computers has become commonplace. The PEW Research Center reported in 2018 that 77% of Americans own a smartphone and 53% own a tablet (http://www.pewresearch.org/fact-tank/2017/01/12/evolution-of-technology/). Twenty percent of American adults depend only on smartphone access to the Internet and do not have broadband access in their home (http://www.pewinternet.org/fact-sheet/internet-broadband). Web designers must consider how their pages will display and function not only on desktop and notebook computers, but also on smartphones, tablets, and other mobile devices.

## Blogs

A **blog** is a journal that is available on the Web; it is a frequently updated page with a chronological list of ideas and links. Blog topics range from politics to technical information to personal diaries. Blogs can focus on one subject or range across a diverse group of topics—it's up to the person, called a blogger, who has created the blog and maintains it. Bloggers usually update their blogs daily with easy-to-use software designed to allow people with little or no technical background to update and maintain a blog. Many blogs are hosted at blog communities such as https://www.wordpress.com. Others are hosted at individual websites, such as the blog kept by the web designer Eric Meyer at https://meyerweb.com. Businesses have noted the value of blogs as communication and customer relationship tools. Companies such as TechSmith (https://www.techsmith.com/blog/) and IBM (https://developer.ibm.com/dwblog/) utilize blogs in this manner.

## Wikis

A **wiki** is a website that can be updated immediately at any time by visitors, using a simple form on a web page. Some wikis are intended for a small group of people, such as the members of an organization. The most powerful wiki is Wikipedia, an online encyclopedia, which can be updated by anyone at any time. Wikis are a form of social software in action—visitors sharing their collective knowledge to create a resource freely used by all. While there have been isolated incidents of practical jokes, and inaccurate information has occasionally been posted at Wikipedia, the given information and linked resources are a good starting point when exploring a topic.

## Social Networking

Blogs and wikis provide web visitors with new methods for interacting with websites and other people—a use referred to as **social networking**. A trendy activity these days is participating in a social networking sites such as Facebook, Twitter, Pinterest, LinkedIn, or Instagram. Pew Research Center reports that in 2019, 70% of American adults use at least one social media site (https://www.pewinternet.org/fact-sheet/social-media/). If it seems to you as if most of your friends are on Facebook, that may be the case: As of 2019, Facebook had over two billion monthly active users (http://newsroom.fb.com/company-info). While LinkedIn was created with professional and business networking in mind, businesses often also use other social media sites to promote their products and services.

Twitter is a social networking site for **microblogging**, or frequently communicating with a brief message (280 characters or less) called a **tweet**. Twitter users (called twitterers) tweet to update a network of friends and followers about their daily activities and observations. Twitter is not limited to personal use. The business world has also discovered the marketing reach that Twitter can provide. Visit https://business.twitter.com/basics for insights on how to use Twitter to promote your business and communicate with customers.

## Cloud Computing

Document collaboration sites like Google Drive and Microsoft OneDrive, blogs, wikis, and social networking sites are all accessed via the Internet (the "cloud") and are examples of **cloud computing**. The National Institute of Standards and Technology (NIST) defines cloud computing as the on-demand use of software and other computing resources hosted at a remote data center (including servers, storage, services, and applications) over the Internet. Expect to see more public and private use of cloud computing in the future.

## RSS

**Really Simple Syndication,** or **Rich Site Summary (RSS)** is used to create newsfeeds from blog postings and other websites. The RSS feeds contain a summary of new items posted to the site. The URL to the RSS feed is usually indicated by the letters XML or RSS in white text within an orange rectangle. A **newsreader** is needed to access the information. Some browsers, such as Firefox and Safari, can display RSS feeds. Commercial and shareware newsreader applications are also available. The newsreader polls the feed URL at intervals and displays the new headlines when requested. RSS provides web developers with a method to push new content to interested parties and (hopefully) generate return visits to the site.

## Podcasts

**Podcasts** are audio files on the web that take the format of an audio blog, radio show, or interview. Podcasts are typically delivered by an RSS feed, but can also be made available by providing the link to a recorded MP3 file on a web page. These files can be saved to your computer or to an MP3 player (such as an iPod) for later listening.

## Constant Change

Internet and web-related technologies are in a constant state of development and improvement. If constant change and the opportunity to learn something new excite you, web development is a fascinating field. The skills and knowledge you gain in this book should provide a solid foundation for your future learning.

 FAQ   **What is the next big thing on the Web?**

The Web is changing by the minute. Check the textbook's companion website at https://www.webdevfoundations.net for a blog that will help you stay current about web trends.

# Chapter Summary

This chapter has provided a brief overview of Internet, Web, and introductory networking concepts. Much of this information may already be familiar to you.

Visit the textbook's website at http://www.webdevfoundations.net for links to the URLs listed in this chapter and to view updated information.

## Key Terms

accessible website
Americans with Disabilities Act (ADA)
backbone
blog
client/server
clients
cloud computing
country-code top-level domain
Creative Commons
domain name
Domain Name System (DNS)
e-commerce
extranet
File Transfer Protocol (FTP)
fully qualified domain name (FQDN)
generic top-level domain (gTLD)
HTML5
Hypertext Markup Language (HTML)
Hypertext Transfer Protocol (HTTP)
Hypertext Transfer Protocol Secure (HTTPS)
Internet
Internet Architecture Board (IAB)
Internet Assigned Numbers Authority (IANA)
Internet Corporation for Assigned Numbers and Names (ICANN)

Internet Engineering Task Force (IETF)
Internet Message Access Protocol (IMAP)
intranet
IP
IP address
IP Version 4 (IPv4)
IP Version 6 (IPv6)
local area network (LAN)
markup languages
microblogging
Multipurpose Internet Mail Extensions (MIME)
network
newsreader
packets
podcasts
Post Office Protocol (POP3)
protocols
Really Simple Syndication or Rich Site Summary (RSS)
Request for Comments (RFC)
Section 508 of the Federal Rehabilitation Act
server
Simple Mail Transfer Protocol (SMTP)
social networking

Standard Generalized Markup Language (SGML)
subdomain
TCP
Tim Berners-Lee
top-level domain (TLD)
Transmission Control Protocol/Internet Protocol (TCP/IP)
tweet
Uniform Resource Identifier (URI)
Uniform Resource Locator (URL)
universal design
Web Accessibility Initiative (WAI)
Web Content Accessibility Guidelines (WCAG)
web host server
wide area network (WAN)
wiki
World Intellectual Property Organization (WIPO)
World Wide Web
World Wide Web Consortium (W3C)
XHTML
XML

## Review Questions

### Multiple Choice

1. What is a unique text-based Internet address corresponding to a computer's unique numeric IP address called?
   a. IP address
   b. domain name
   c. URL
   d. user name

2. Select the item below that indicates the top-level domain name for the URL http://www.mozilla.com.
   a. mozilla
   b. com
   c. http
   d. www

3. Of the following organizations, which one coordinates applications for new TLDs?
   a. Internet Assigned Numbers Authority (IANA)
   b. Internet Engineering Task Force (IETF)
   c. Internet Corporation for Assigned Numbers and Names (ICANN)
   d. World Wide Web Consortium (W3C)

4. Which of the following is a network that covers a small area, such as a group of buildings or campus?
   a. LAN
   b. WAN
   c. Internet
   d. WWW

5. Which of the following organizations takes a proactive role in developing recommendations and prototype technologies related to the Web?
   a. World Wide Web Consortium (W3C)
   b. Web Professional Standards Organization (WPO)
   c. Internet Engineering Task Force (IETF)
   d. Internet Corporation for Assigned Numbers and Names (ICANN)

## True or False

6. _____ A URL is one type of URI.

7. _____ Markup languages contain sets of directions that tell the browser software how to display and manage a web document.

8. _____ The World Wide Web was developed to allow companies to conduct e-commerce over the Internet.

9. _____ A domain name that ends in .net indicates that the website must be for a networking company.

10. _____ An accessible website provides accommodations that help individuals overcome barriers such as visual, auditory, physical, and neurological disabilities.

## Fill in the Blank

11. _____ is the set of markup symbols or codes placed in a file intended for display on a web browser.

12. A _____ can be configured to house a separate website located at the same domain.

13. A standard language used for specifying a markup language or tag set is _____.

14. Frequently communicating by posting brief messages at a social networking site is called _____.

15. The purpose of _____ is to ensure the integrity of network communication.

# Hands-On Exercise

1. Twitter (https://www.twitter.com) is a social networking website for microblogging, or frequently communicating with a brief message (280 characters or less) called a tweet. Twitter users (referred to as twitterers) tweet to update a network of friends and followers about their daily activities, observations, and information related to topics of interest. A hashtag (the #symbol) can be placed in front of a word or term within a tweet to categorize the topic, such as typing the hashtag #SXSWi in all tweets about the SXSW Interactive Conference for the web design industry. The use of a hashtag makes it easy to search for tweets about a category or event in Twitter.

   If you don't already use Twitter, sign up for free account. Use your Twitter account to share information about websites that you find useful or interesting. Post at least three tweets. You might tweet about websites that contain useful web design resources. You might describe sites that have interesting features, such as compelling graphics or easy-to-use navigation. After you begin to develop your own websites, you could tweet about them, too!

Your instructor may direct you to include a distinctive hashtag (for example, something like #CIS110) in your tweets that are related to your web design studies. Searching Twitter for the specified hashtag will make it easy to collect all the tweets posted by the students in your class.

2. Create a blog to document your learning experiences as you study web development. Visit one of the many sites that offer free blogs, such as https://www.blogger.com, https://www.wordpress.com, or https://www.tumblr.com. Follow the site's instructions to establish your own blog. Your blog could be a place to note websites that you find useful or interesting. You might report on sites that contain useful web design resources. You might describe sites that have interesting features, such as compelling graphics or easy-to-use navigation. Write a few sentences about each site that you find intriguing. After you begin to develop your own sites, you could include the URLs and reasons for your design decisions. Share this blog with your fellow students and friends. Display your page in a browser, and print the page. Hand in the printout to your instructor.

## Web Research

1. The World Wide Web Consortium creates standards for the Web. Visit its site at https://www.w3c.org and then answer the following questions:

   a. How did the W3C get started?

   b. Who can join the W3C? What does it cost to join?

   c. The W3C home page lists a number of technologies. Choose one that interests you, click on its link, and read the associated pages. List three facts or issues you discover.

2. The Internet Society takes an active leadership role in issues related to the Internet. Visit its site at https://www.internetsociety.org and then answer the following questions:

   a. Why was the Internet Society created?

   b. Determine which local chapter is closest to you. Visit its website. List the website's URL and an activity or service that the chapter provides.

   c. How can you join the Internet Society? What does it cost to join? Would you recommend that a beginning Web developer join the Internet Society? Why or why not?

3. HTTP/2 is the first major update to HTTP, which was first developed in the late 1990s. As websites have become more image and media intensive, the number of requests needed to display a web page and its related files have increased. A major benefit of HTTP/2 will be quicker loading of web pages.

   HTTP/2 Resources:

   - https://readwrite.com/2015/02/18/http-update-http2-what-you-need-to-know
   - https://http2.github.io
   - https://www.engadget.com/2015/02/24/what-you-need-to-know-about-http-2
   - https://tools.ietf.org/html/rfc7540

   Use the resources listed above as a starting point as you research HTTP/2 and answer the following questions.

   a. Who developed HTTP/2?

   b. When was the HTTP/2 proposed standard published?

   c. Describe three methods used by HTTP/2 intended to decrease latency and provide for quicker loading of web pages in browsers.

## Focus on Web Design

1. Visit a website that interests you. Print the home page or one other pertinent page from the site. Write a one-page summary of the site that addresses the following topics:

   a. What is the URL of the site?

   b. What is the purpose of the site?

   c. Who is the intended audience?

   d. Do you think that the site reaches its intended audience? Why or why not?

   e. Is the site useful to you? Why or why not?

   f. Does this site appeal to you? Why or why not? Consider the use of color, images, multimedia, organization, and ease of navigation.

   g. Would you encourage others to visit this site? Why or why not?

   h. How could this site be improved?

# 2

# HTML Basics

## Chapter Objectives    In this chapter, you will learn how to . . .

- Describe HTML, XHTML, and HTML5
- Identify the markup language in a web page document
- Use the html, head, body, title, and meta elements to code a template for a web page
- Configure the body of a web page with headings, paragraphs, line breaks, divs, lists, and blockquotes
- Configure text with phrase elements
- Configure special characters

- Configure a web page with HTML5 structural elements: header, nav, main, footer, section, and article
- Use the anchor element to link from page to page
- Create absolute, relative, and e-mail hyperlinks
- Code, save, and display a web page document
- Test a web page document for valid syntax

**This chapter gets you started on your very first web page.** You'll be introduced to Hypertext Markup Language (HTML), the language used to create web pages. The chapter begins with an introduction to the syntax of HTML5; continues with sample web pages; and introduces HTML structural, phrase, and hyperlink elements as more example web pages are created. You will learn more if you work along with the sample pages in the text. Coding HTML is a skill, and every skill improves with practice.

# 2.1 HTML Overview

**Markup languages** consist of sets of directions that tell the browser software (and other user agents such as mobile phones) how to display and manage a web document. These directions are usually called tags and perform functions such as displaying graphics, formatting text, and referencing hyperlinks.

The World Wide Web is composed of files containing **Hypertext Markup Language (HTML)** and other markup languages that describe web pages. Tim Berners-Lee developed HTML using Standard Generalized Markup Language (SGML). SGML prescribes a standard format for embedding descriptive markup within a document and for describing the structure of a document. SGML is not in itself a document language, but rather a description of how to specify one and create a document type definition (DTD). The W3C sets the standards for HTML and its related languages. Like the Web itself, HTML is in a constant state of change.

## HTML

HTML is the set of markup symbols or codes placed in a file that is intended for display on a web page. These markup symbols and codes identify structural elements such as paragraphs, headings, and lists. HTML can also be used to place media (such as graphics, video, and audio) on a web page and describe fill-in forms. The browser interprets the markup code and renders the page. HTML permits the platform-independent display of information across a network. No matter what type of computer a web page was created on, any browser running on any operating system can display the page.

Each individual markup code is referred to as an **element** or a **tag**. Each tag has a purpose. Tags are enclosed in angle brackets, the < and > symbols. Most tags come in pairs: an opening tag and a closing tag. These tags act as containers and are sometimes referred to as container tags. For example, the text that is between the `<title>` and `</title>` tags on a web page would display in the title bar on the browser window. Some tags are used alone and are not part of a pair. For example, a `<br>` tag that configures a line break on a web page is a stand-alone, or self-contained, tag and does not have a closing tag. Most tags can be modified with **attributes** that further describe their purpose.

## XML

**XML (eXtensible Markup Language)** was developed by the W3C to create common information formats and share the format and the information on the Web. It is a text-based syntax designed to describe, deliver, and exchange structured information, such as RSS feeds. XML is not intended to replace HTML, but to extend the power of HTML by separating data from presentation. Using XML, developers can create any tags they need to describe their information.

## XHTML

**eXtensible HyperText Markup Language (XHTML)** uses the tags and attributes of HTML4 along with the syntax of XML. XHTML was used on the Web for over a decade and you'll find many web pages coded with this markup language. At one point the W3C was working on a new version of XHTML, called XHTML 2.0. However, the W3C stopped development of XHTML 2.0 because it was not backward compatible with HTML4. Instead, the W3C decided to move forward with HTML5.

## HTML5

**HTML5** is the successor to HTML4 and replaces XHTML. HTML5 incorporates features of both HTML and XHTML, adds new elements of its own, provides new features such as form edits and native video, and is intended to be backward compatible.

The W3C approved HTML5 for final Recommendation status in late 2014. This markup language is constantly changing and evolving. New versions HTML5.1 and HTML5.2 have reached final Recommendation status and HTML 5.3 is currently in working draft status. Recent versions of popular browsers offer good support for HTML5, including its newest official version, HTML5.2, which you'll learn to use as you work through this textbook. W3C HTML5.2 documentation is available at https://www.w3.org/TR/html52/.

In 2019, the W3C and the **WHATWG (Web Hypertext Application Technology Working Group)** agreed to collaborate on the development of HTML specifications. The WHATWG is an open group founded by individuals working at many leading technology organizations including Apple, the Mozilla Foundation, and Opera Software. The WHATWG plans to prepare a Review Draft of the HTML Standard every six months.

 FAQ   **What software do I need?**

No special software is needed to create a web page document; all you need is a text editor. The Notepad text editor is included with Microsoft Windows. TextEdit is distributed with the Mac OS X operating system. An alternative to the operating system's basic text editor is one of the many free or shareware editors that are available, such as Notepad++ (http://notepad-plus-plus.org/download), BBEdit (http://www.barebones.com/products/bbedit/index.html), Brackets (http://brackets.io), and Visual Studio Code (https://code.visualstudio.com). Another commonly used alternative is a commercial web-authoring tool, such as Adobe Dreamweaver. Regardless of the software or program you use, having a solid foundation in HTML will be useful.

You will need to test your web pages in the most popular browsers, such as Microsoft Edge, Mozilla Firefox, Apple Safari, and Google Chrome. Access a free download of Firefox at https://www.mozilla.org/en-US/firefox/new/. A free download of Google Chrome is available at https://www.google.com/chrome.

You will also find the Web Developer Extension for Firefox (https://addons.mozilla.org/en-us/firefox/addon/web-developer) to be useful.

# 2.2 Document Type Definition

Because multiple versions and types of HTML and XHTML exist, the W3C recommends identifying the type of markup language used in a web page document with a **Document Type Definition (DTD)**. The DTD identifies the version of HTML contained in your document. Browsers and HTML code validators can use the information in the DTD when processing the web page. The DTD statement, commonly called a **doctype** statement, is the first line of a web page document. The DTD for HTML5 is:

```
<!DOCTYPE html>
```

**Figure 2.1** It's what is under the hood that matters.

# 2.3 Web Page Template

You already know that the HTML markup language tells browsers how to display information on a web page. Let's take a closer look at what's "under the hood" (Figure 2.1) of every web page you create. Every single web page you create will include the DTD and the html, head, title, meta, and body elements. We will follow the coding style to use lowercase letters and place quotes around attribute values. A basic HTML5 web page template (see chapter2/template.html in the student files) is as follows:

```
<!DOCTYPE html>
<html lang="en">
<head>
<title>Page Title Goes Here</title>
<meta charset="utf-8">
</head>
<body>
... body text and more HTML tags go here ...
</body>
</html>
```

With the exception of the specific page title, the first seven lines will usually be the same on every web page that you create. Review the code above and notice that the document type definition statement has its own formatting and that the HTML tags all use lowercase letters. Next, let's explore the purpose of the html, head, title, meta, and body elements.

# 2.4 HTML Element

The purpose of the html element is to indicate that the document is HTML formatted. The html element tells the browser how to interpret the document. The opening **<html>** tag is placed on a line below the DTD. The closing </html> tag indicates the end of the web page and is placed after all other HTML elements in the document.

The html element also needs to indicate the spoken language, such as English, of the text in the document. This additional information is added to the <html> tag in the form of an attribute, which modifies or further describes the function of an element. The **lang attribute** specifies the spoken language of the document. For example, lang="en" indicates the English language. Search engines and screen readers may access this attribute.

# 2.5 Head, Title, Meta, and Body Elements

There are two sections on a web page: the head and the body. The **head section** contains information that describes the web page document. The **body section** contains the actual tags, text, images, and other objects that are displayed by the browser as a web page.

## The Head Section

Elements that are located in the head section include the title of the web page, meta tags that describe the document (such as the character encoding used and information that may be accessed by search engines), and references to scripts and styles. Many of these features do not show directly on the web page.

### The Head Element

The **head element** contains the head section, which begins with the **<head>** tag and ends with the **</head>** tag. You will always code at least two other elements in the head section: a title element and a meta element.

### The Title Element

The first element in the head section, the **title element**, configures the text that will appear in the title bar of the browser window. The text between the **<title>** and **</title>** tags is called the title of the web page and is accessed when web pages are bookmarked and printed. Popular search engines, such as Google, use the title text to help determine keyword relevance and even display the title text on the results page of a search. A descriptive title that includes the website or organization name is a crucial component for establishing a brand or presence on the Web.

### The Meta Element

The **meta element** describes a characteristic of a web page, such as the character encoding. **Character encoding** is the internal representation of letters, numbers, and symbols in a file such as a web page or other file that is stored on a computer and may be transmitted over the Internet. There are many different character-encoding sets. However, it is common practice to use a character-encoding set that is widely supported, such as utf-8, which is a form of Unicode (https://home.unicode.org). The meta tag is not used as a pair of opening and closing tags. It is considered to be a stand-alone, or self-contained, tag (referred to as a **void element** in HTML5). The meta tag uses the **charset attribute** to indicate the character encoding. An example meta tag is as follows:

```
<meta charset="utf-8">
```

## The Body Section

The body section contains text and elements that display directly on the web page in the browser window, also referred to as the browser viewport. The purpose of the body section is to configure the contents of the web page.

### The Body Element

The **body element** contains the body section, which begins with the **<body>** tag and ends with the **</body>** tag. You will spend most of your time writing code in the body of a web page. Text and elements typed between the opening and closing body tags will display on the web page in the browser viewport.

# 2.6 Your First Web Page

## Hands-On Practice 2.1

VideoNote
**Your First
Web Page**

Now that you're familiar with basic elements used on every web page, it's your turn to create your first web page, shown in Figure 2.2.

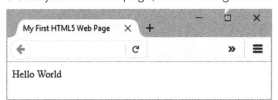

**Figure 2.2** Your first webpage

## Create a Folder

You'll find it helpful to create folders to organize your files as you develop the web pages in this book and create your own websites. Use your operating system to create a new folder named mychapter2 on your hard drive or a portable flash drive.

To create a new folder on a Mac:

1. Launch Finder, and select the location where you would like to create the new folder.
2. Choose File > New Folder to create an untitled folder.
3. To rename the folder, select the folder and click on the current name. Type a name for the folder, and press the Return key.

To create a new folder with Windows:

1. Launch File Explorer (formerly called Windows Explorer):

   a. Display the Desktop.

   b. Right-click on the Start button and select File Explorer.

2. Navigate to the location where you would like to create the new folder, such as Documents, your C: drive, or an external USB drive.
3. Select the Home tab. Select New Folder.
4. To rename the New Folder, right-click on it, select Rename from the context-sensitive menu, type in the new name, and press the Enter key.

 **FAQ**   **Why should I create a folder? Why not just use the desktop?**

Folders will help you to organize your work. If you just use the desktop, it would quickly become cluttered and disorganized. It's also important to know that websites are organized on web servers within folders. By starting to use folders right away to organize related web pages, you are on your way to becoming a successful web designer.

## Your First Web Page

Now you are ready to create your first HTML5 web page. Launch Notepad or another text editor. Type in the following code:

```
<!DOCTYPE html>
<html lang="en">
<head>
<title>My First HTML5 Web Page</title>
<meta charset="utf-8">
</head>
<body>
Hello World
</body>
</html>
```

Notice that the first line in the file contains the doctype. The HTML code begins with an opening `<html>` tag and ends with a closing `</html>` tag. The purpose of these tags is to indicate that the content between them makes up a web page. The head section is delimited by `<head>` and `</head>` tags and contains a pair of title tags with the words "My First HTML5 Web Page" in between, along with a **<meta>** tag to indicate the character encoding.

The body section is delimited by `<body>` and `</body>` tags. The words "Hello World" are typed on a line between the body tags. See Figure 2.3 for a screenshot of the code as it would appear in Notepad. You have just created the source code for a web page document.

```
index.html - Notepad                    —   □   ×
File  Edit  Format  View  Help
<!DOCTYPE html>
<html lang="en">
<head>
<title>My First HTML5 Web Page</title>
<meta charset="utf-8">
</head>
<body>
Hello World
</body>
</html>
```

**Figure 2.3** Code displayed in Notepad. Courtesy of Microsoft Corporation.

 **FAQ  Do I have to start each tag on its own line?**

No, you are not required to start each tag on a separate line. A browser can display a page even if all the tags follow each other on one line with no spaces. Humans, however, find it easier to write and read web page code if line breaks and indentation are used.

## Save Your File

You will save your file with the name of index.html. A common file name for the home page of a website is index.html or index.htm. Web pages use either a .htm or a .html file extension. The web pages in this book use the .html file extension. Display your file in Notepad or another text editor. Select File from the menu bar, and then select Save As. The Save As dialog box will appear. Navigate to your mychapter2 folder. Using Figure 2.4 as an example, type the file name. Click the Save button after you type the file name. Sample solutions for the exercises are available in the student files. If you like, you can compare your work with the solution in the student files at chapter2/index.html before you test your page.

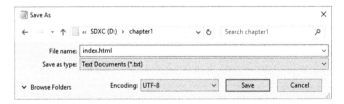

**Figure 2.4** The Save As dialog box. Courtesy of Microsoft Corporation.

**FAQ** **Why does my file have a .txt file extension?**

In some older versions of Windows, Notepad will automatically append a .txt file extension. If this happens, type the name of the file within quotation marks ("index.html"), and save your file again.

## Test Your Page

There are two ways to test your page:

1. Launch File Explorer or Finder (Mac). Navigate to your index.html file. Double-click index.html. The default browser will launch and will display your index.html page.
2. Launch a web browser. Select File > Open, and navigate to your index.html file. Double-click index.html and click OK. The browser will display your index.html page.

   Examine your page. If you are using Microsoft Edge, your page should look similar to the one shown in Figure 2.5. A display of the page using Firefox is shown in Figure 2.2. Look carefully at the browser window. Notice how the browser title bar or browser tab displays the title text, "My First HTML5 Web Page." Some search engines use the text enclosed within the `<title>` and `</title>` tags to help determine the relevancy of keyword searches, so make certain that your pages contain descriptive titles. The title element is also used when viewers bookmark your page or add it to their Favorites. An engaging and descriptive page title may entice a visitor to revisit your page. If your web page is for a company or an organization, it's a best practice to include the name of the company or organization in the title.

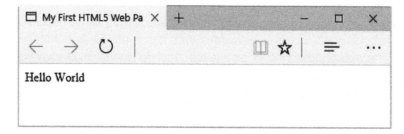

**Figure 2.5** Web page displayed by Microsoft Edge. Courtesy of Microsoft Corporation.

**FAQ** **When I viewed my page in a browser, the file name was index.html.html–why did this happen?**

This usually happens when your operating system is configured to hide file extension names. You will correct the file name, using one of the following two methods:

- Use the operating system to rename the file from "index.html.html" to "index.html".

OR

- Open the index.html.html file in your text editor and save it with the name "index.html".

It's a good idea to change the settings in your operating system to show file extension names. Access the system help for your operating system or the resources below for information about how to configure your operating system to show file extension names:

- *Windows:* http://www.file-extensions.org/article/show-and-hide-file-extensions-in-windows-10

- *Mac:* http://www.fileinfo.com/help/mac_show_extensions

 **Checkpoint 2.1**

**1.** Describe the origin, purpose, and features of HTML.

**2.** Describe the software needed to create and test web pages.

**3.** Describe the purpose of the head and body sections of a web page.

## 2.7  Heading Element

**Heading elements** are organized into six levels: h1 through h6. The text contained within a heading element is rendered as a "block" of text by the browser (referred to as **block display**) and displays with empty space (sometimes called "white space") above and below. The size of the text is largest for **<h1>** (called the heading 1 tag) and smallest for **<h6>** (called the heading 6 tag). Depending on the font being used (more on font sizes in Chapter 3), the text contained within **<h4>**, **<h5>**, and **<h6>** tags may be displayed smaller than the default text size. All text contained within heading tags is displayed with bold font weight. Figure 2.6 shows a web page document with six levels of headings.

 **FAQ** **Why doesn't the heading tag go in the head section?**

It's common for students to try to code the heading tags in the head section of the document, but doing this is not valid and will cause issues with the way the browser displays the web page. Even though "heading tag" and "head section" sound similar, always code heading tags in the body section of the web page document.

**Figure 2.6** Sample headings

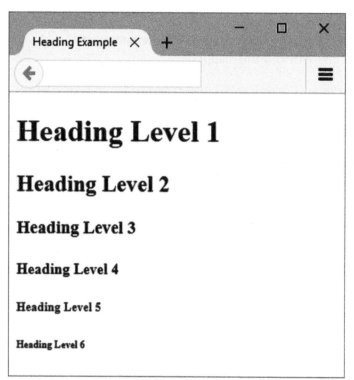

## Hands-On Practice 2.2

To create the web page shown in Figure 2.6, launch Notepad or another text editor. Select File > Open to edit the HTML5 template file located at chapter2/template.html in the student files. Modify the title element and add heading tags to the body section as indicated by the following code:

```
<!DOCTYPE html>
<html lang="en">
<head>
<title>Heading Example</title>
<meta charset="utf-8">
</head>
<body>
<h1>Heading Level 1</h1>
<h2>Heading Level 2</h2>
<h3>Heading Level 3</h3>
<h4>Heading Level 4</h4>
<h5>Heading Level 5</h5>
<h6>Heading Level 6</h6>
</body>
</html>
```

Save the document as heading.html on your hard drive or flash drive. Launch a browser such as Microsoft Edge or Firefox to test your page. It should look similar to the page shown in Figure 2.6. You can compare your work with the solution found in the student files (chapter2/heading.html).

## Accessibility and Headings

Heading tags can help to make your pages more accessible and usable. It is good coding practice to use heading tags to outline the structure of your web page content. To indicate areas within a page hierarchically, code heading tags numerically as appropriate (h1, h2, h3, and so on), and include page content in block display elements such as paragraphs and lists. In Figure 2.7, the `<h1>` tag contains the name of the website in the logo header area at the top of the web page, the `<h2>` tag contains the topic or name of the page in the content area, and other heading elements are coded in the content area as needed to identify major topics and subtopics.

**Focus on Accessibility**

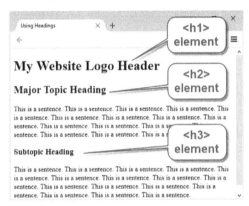

Figure 2.7 Heading tags outline the page

Visually challenged visitors who are using a screen reader can direct the software to display a list of the headings used on a page to focus on the topics that interest them. Your well-organized page will be more usable for every visitor to your site, including those who are visually challenged.

## 2.8 Paragraph Element

A **paragraph element** groups sentences and sections of text together. Text within `<p>` and `</p>` tags display as a "block" (referred to as block display) and will appear with empty space above and below it. Figure 2.8 shows a web page document with a paragraph after the first heading.

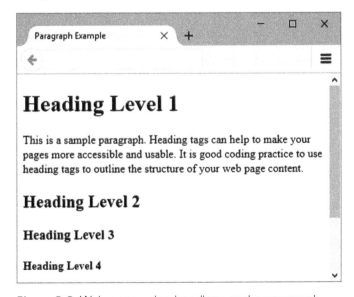

Figure 2.8 Web page using headings and a paragraph

# Hands-On Practice 2.3

To create the web page shown in Figure 2.8, launch a text editor. Select File > Open to edit the file located at chapter2/heading.html in the student files. Modify the page title, and add a paragraph of text to your page below the line with the `<h1>` tags and above the line with the `<h2>` tags. Use the following code as an example:

```
<!DOCTYPE html>
<html lang="en">
<head>
<title>Paragraph Example</title>
<meta charset="utf-8">
</head>
<body>
<h1>Heading Level 1</h1>
<p>This is a sample paragraph. Heading tags can help to make your
pages more accessible and usable. It is good coding practice to use
heading tags to outline the structure of your web page content.
</p>
<h2>Heading Level 2</h2>
<h3>Heading Level 3</h3>
<h4>Heading Level 4</h4>
<h5>Heading Level 5</h5>
<h6>Heading Level 6</h6>
</body>
</html>
```

Save the document as paragraph.html on your hard drive or flash drive. Launch a browser to test your page. It should look similar to the page shown in Figure 2.8. You can compare your work with the solution (chapter2/paragraph.html) found in the student files. Notice how the text in the paragraph wraps automatically as you resize your browser window.

## Alignment

As you tested your web pages, you may have noticed that the headings and text begin near the left margin. This placement is called **left alignment** and is the default alignment for web pages. There are times when you want a paragraph or heading to be centered or right aligned. The align attribute can be used for this purpose. Note that the align attribute is obsolete in HTML5, which means that the attribute has been removed from the W3C HTML5 specification, even though it is still supported by browsers. You'll learn techniques to configure alignment with Cascading Style Sheets (CSS) in Chapters 6 and 7.

# 2.9  Line Break Element

The **line break element** causes the browser to advance to the next line before displaying the next element or portion of text on a web page. The line break tag is not coded as a pair of opening and closing tags. It is a stand-alone, or void element, and is coded as **<br>**. Figure 2.9 shows a web page document with a line break after the first sentence in the paragraph.

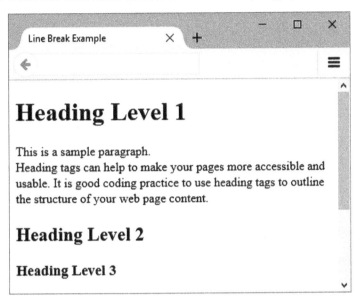

**Figure 2.9**
Notice the line break after the first sentence

## Hands-On Practice 2.4

To create the web page shown in Figure 2.9, launch a text editor. Select File > Open to edit the file located at chapter2/paragraph.html in the student files. Modify the text contained between the title tags to be "Line Break Example". Place your cursor after the first sentence in the paragraph (after "This is a sample paragraph."). Press the Enter key. Save your file. Test your page in a browser, and notice that even though your source code showed the "This is a sample paragraph." sentence on its own line, the browser did not render it that way. A line break tag is needed to configure the browser to display the second sentence on a new line. Edit the file in a text editor, and add a <br> tag after the first *sentence* in the paragraph, as shown in the following code snippet:

```
<body>
<h1>Heading Level 1</h1>
<p>This is a sample paragraph. <br> Heading tags can help to make your
pages more accessible and usable. It is good coding practice to use
heading tags to outline the structure of your web page content.
</p>
<h2>Heading Level 2</h2>
<h3>Heading Level 3</h3>
<h4>Heading Level 4</h4>
<h5>Heading Level 5</h5>
<h6>Heading Level 6</h6>
</body>
```

Save your file as linebreak.html. Launch a browser to test your page. It should look similar to the page shown in Figure 2.9. You can compare your work with the solution found in the student files (chapter2/linebreak.html).

**FAQ    Why does my web page still look the same?**

Often, students make changes to a web page document, but get frustrated because their browser shows an older version of the page. The following troubleshooting tips are helpful when you know you modified your web page, but the changes do not show up in the browser:

1. Make sure you save your page after you make the changes.
2. Verify the location that you are saving your page to—a specific folder on the hard drive or removable storage.
3. Verify the location that your browser is requesting the page from—a specific folder on the hard drive or removable storage.
4. Be sure to click the Refresh or Reload button in your browser.

Figure 2.10 The text within the blockquote element is indented

# 2.10  Blockquote Element

In addition to organizing text in paragraphs and headings, sometimes you need to add a quotation to a web page. The **blockquote element** is used to display a block of quoted text in a special way—indented from both the left and right margins. A block of indented text begins with a **<blockquote>** tag and ends with a **</blockquote>** tag. Figure 2.10 shows a web page document with a heading, a paragraph, and a blockquote.

## Hands-On Practice 2.5

To create the web page shown in Figure 2.10, launch a text editor. Select File > Open to edit the template file located at chapter2/template.html in the student files. Modify the title element. Add a heading tag, a paragraph tag, and a blockquote tag to the body section as indicated by the following code:

```
<!DOCTYPE html>
<html lang="en">
<head>
<title>Blockquote Example</title>
<meta charset="utf-8">
</head>
<body>
<h1>The Power of the Web</h1>
<p>According to Tim Berners-Lee, the inventor of the World Wide Web,
at https://www.w3.org/WAI/:</p>
<blockquote>
The power of the Web is in its universality. Access by everyone
regardless of disability is an essential aspect.
</blockquote>
</body>
</html>
```

Save the document as blockquote.html on your hard drive or flash drive. Launch a browser to test your page. It should look similar to the page shown in Figure 2.10. You can compare your work with the solution (chapter2/blockquote.html) found in the student files.

You have probably noticed how convenient the `<blockquote>` tag could be if you need to indent an area of text on a web page. You may have wondered whether it would be okay to use the blockquote element anytime you would like to indent text or whether the blockquote element is reserved only for long quotations. The semantically correct use of the blockquote element is only for displaying large blocks of quoted text within a web page. Avoid using a blockquote element just to indent text. You will learn modern techniques to configure margins and padding on elements in Chapters 6 and 7.

# 2.11 Phrase Elements

**Phrase elements** indicate the context and meaning of the text between the container tags. It is up to each browser to interpret that style. Phrase elements are displayed right in line with the text (referred to as **inline display**) and can apply to a section of text or even just a single character of text. For example, the **`<strong>`** element indicates that the text associated with it has strong importance and should be displayed in a "strong" manner in relation to normal text on the page. Table 2.1 lists common phrase elements and examples of their use. Notice that some tags, such as `<cite>` and `<dfn>`, result in the same type of display (italics) as the `<em>` tag in popular browsers. These tags semantically describe the text as a citation or definition, but the physical display is usually italics in both cases.

Table 2.1 Phrase elements

| Element | Example | Usage |
|---|---|---|
| `<abbr>` | WIPO | Identifies text as an abbreviation; configure the title attribute with the full name |
| `<b>` | **bold** text | Text that has no extra importance, but is styled in bold font by usage and convention |
| `<cite>` | *cite* text | Identifies a citation or reference; usually displayed in italics |
| `<code>` | code text | Identifies program code samples; usually a fixed-space font |
| `<dfn>` | *dfn* text | Identifies a definition of a word or term; usually displayed in italics |
| `<em>` | *emphasized* text | Causes text to be emphasized in relation to other text; usually displayed in italics |
| `<i>` | *italicized* text | Text that has no extra importance, but is styled in italics by usage and convention |
| `<kbd>` | kbd text | Identifies user text to be typed; usually a fixed-space font |
| `<mark>` | mark text | Text that is highlighted in order to be easily referenced |
| `<samp>` | samp text | Shows program sample output; usually a fixed-space font |
| `<small>` | small text | Legal disclaimers and notices ("fine print") displayed in small font size |
| `<strong>` | **strong** text | Strong importance; causes text to stand out from surrounding text; usually displayed in bold |
| `<sub>` | sub text | Displays a subscript as small text below the baseline |
| `<sup>` | sup text | Displays a superscript as small text above the baseline |
| `<var>` | *var* text | Identifies and displays a variable or program output; usually displayed in italics |

Each phrase element is a container element, so an opening and a closing tag must be used. As shown in Table 2.1, the `<strong>` element indicates that the text associated with it has "strong" importance. Usually, the browser (or other user agent) will display `<strong>` text in bold font type. A screen reader, such as JAWS or Window-Eyes, might interpret `<strong>` text to indicate that the text should be more strongly spoken. In the following line, the phone number is displayed with strong importance:

```
Call for a free quote for your web development needs:   888.555.5555
```

The corresponding code is:

```
<p>Call for a free quote for your web development needs:
<strong>888.555.5555</strong></p>
```

Notice that the opening `<strong>` and closing `</strong>` tags are contained within the paragraph tags (`<p>` and `</p>`). This code is properly nested and is considered to be **well formed**. When improperly nested, the `<p>` and `<strong>` tag pairs overlap each other instead of being nested within each other. Improperly nested code will not pass validation testing (see Section 2.18, "HTML Validation") and may cause display issues.

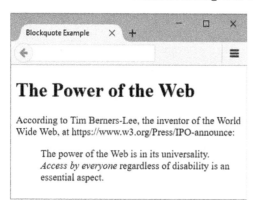

Figure 2.11 shows a web page document (also found in the student files at chapter2/em.html) that uses the `<em>` tag to display the emphasized phrase "Access by everyone" in italics. The code snippet is

```
<blockquote>
The power of the Web is in its universality.
<em>Access by everyone</em>
regardless of disability is an essential aspect.
</blockquote>
```

Figure 2.11 The `<em>` tag in action

## 2.12 Ordered List

Lists are used on web pages to organize information. When writing for the Web, headings, short paragraphs, and lists can make your page more clear and easy to read. HTML can be used to create three types of lists—description lists, ordered lists, and unordered lists. All lists are rendered as block display with an empty space above and below.

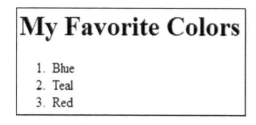

Figure 2.12 Sample ordered list

This section focuses on the **ordered list**, which displays a numbering or lettering system to itemize the information contained in the list. Ordered lists can be organized by the use of numerals (the default), uppercase letters, lowercase letters, uppercase Roman numerals, and lowercase Roman numerals. See Figure 2.12 for a sample ordered list.

Ordered lists begin with an **<ol>** tag and end with an **</ol>** tag. Each list item begins with an **<li>** tag and ends with an **</li>** tag. The code to configure the heading and ordered list shown in Figure 2.12 follows:

```
<h1>My Favorite Colors</h1>
<ol>
      <li>Blue</li>
      <li>Teal</li>
      <li>Red</li>
</ol>
```

## The Type, Start, and Reversed Attributes

The purpose of an **attribute** is to modify the properties of an HTML element. The **type attribute** configures the symbol used for ordering the list. For example, to create an ordered list organized by uppercase letters, use <ol type="A">. Table 2.2 documents the type attribute and its values for ordered lists.

Table 2.2   The type attribute for ordered lists

| Value | Symbol |
|-------|--------|
| 1 | Numerals (the default) |
| A | Uppercase letters |
| a | Lowercase letters |
| I | Roman numerals |
| i | Lowercase Roman numerals |

The **start attribute** is useful when you need a list to begin with an integer value other than 1 (for example, start="10"). Use the HTML5 **reversed attribute** (set reversed="reversed") to configure the list markers to display in descending order.

## Hands-On Practice 2.6

In this Hands-On Practice, you will use a heading and an ordered list on the same page. To create the web page shown in Figure 2.13, launch a text editor. Select File > Open to edit the template file located at chapter2/template.html in the student files. Modify the title element and add h1, ol, and li elements to the body section as indicated by the following code:

```
<!DOCTYPE html>
<html lang="en">
<head>
<title>Heading and List</title>
<meta charset="utf-8">
</head>
```

```
<body>
<h1>My Favorite Colors</h1>
<ol>
    <li>Blue</li>
    <li>Teal</li>
    <li>Red</li>
</ol>
</body>
</html>
```

Save your file as ol.html. Launch a browser and test your page. It should look similar to the page shown in Figure 2.13. You can compare your work with the solution in the student files (chapter2/ol.html).

Figure 2.13 An ordered list

Take a few minutes to experiment with the type attribute. Configure the ordered list to use uppercase letters instead of numerals. Save your file as ola.html. Test your page in a browser. You can compare your work with the solution in the student files (chapter2/ola.html).

## 2.13  Unordered List

An **unordered list** displays a bullet, or list marker, before each entry in the list. This bullet can be one of several types: disc (the default), square, and circle. See Figure 2.14 for a sample unordered list.

Unordered lists begin with a **<ul>** tag and end with a **</ul>** tag. Each list item begins with an **<li>** tag and ends with an **</li>** tag. The code to configure the heading and unordered list shown in Figure 2.14 is

**My Favorite Colors**

- Blue
- Teal
- Red

Figure 2.14 Sample unordered list

```
<h1>My Favorite Colors</h1>
<ul>
    <li>Blue</li>
    <li>Teal</li>
    <li>Red</li>
</ul>
```

## Hands-On Practice 2.7

In this Hands-On Practice, you will use a heading and an unordered list on the same page. To create the web page shown in Figure 2.15, launch a text editor. Select File > Open to edit the template file located at chapter2/template.html in the student files. Modify the title element and add h1, ul, and li tags to the body section as indicated by the following code:

Figure 2.15 An unordered list

```
<!DOCTYPE html>
<html lang="en">
<head>
<title>Heading and List</title>
<meta charset="utf-8">
</head>
<body>
<h1>My Favorite Colors</h1>
<ul>
    <li>Blue</li>
    <li>Teal</li>
    <li>Red</li>
</ul>
</body>
</html>
```

Save your file as ul.html. Launch a browser and test your page. It should look similar to the page shown in Figure 2.15. You can compare your work with the solution in the student files (chapter2/ul.html).

 ## FAQ   Can I change the "bullet" in an unordered list?

Back in the day before HTML5, the type attribute could be included with a <ul> tag to change the default list marker to a square (type="square") or open circle (type="circle"). However, be aware that using the type attribute on an unordered list is considered obsolete in HTML5 because it is decorative and does not convey meaning. No worries, though—you'll learn techniques to configure list markers (bullets) in Chapter 6 to display images and shapes.

# 2.14 Description List

A **description list** can be used to organize terms and their descriptions. The terms stand out, and their descriptions can be as long as needed to convey your message. Each term begins on its own line at the margin. Each description begins on its own line and is indented. Description lists are also handy for organizing Frequently Asked Questions (FAQs) and their answers. The questions and answers are offset with indentation. Any type of information that consists of a number of corresponding terms and longer descriptions is well suited to being organized in a description list. See Figure 2.16 for an example of a web page that uses a description list.

Figure 2.16
A description list

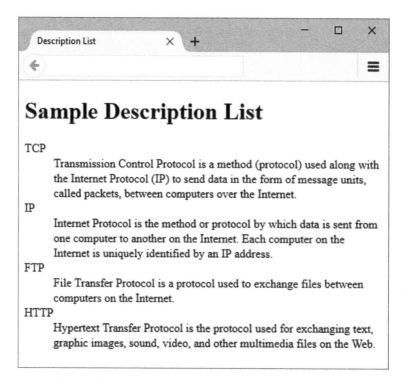

Description lists begin with the **<dl>** tag and end with the **</dl>** tag. Each term or name in the list begins with the **<dt>** tag and ends with the **</dt>** tag. Each description begins with the **<dd>** tag and ends with the **</dd>** tag.

 Hands-On Practice 2.8

In this Hands-On Practice, you will use a heading and a description list on the same page. To create the web page shown in Figure 2.16, launch a text editor. Select File > Open to edit the template file located at chapter2/template.html in the student files. Modify the title element and add h1, dl, dd, and dt tags to the body section as indicated by the following code:

```
<!DOCTYPE html>
<html lang="en">
<head>
<title>Description List</title>
```

```html
<meta charset="utf-8">
</head>
<body>
<h1>Sample Description List</h1>
<dl>
    <dt>TCP</dt>
        <dd>Transmission Control Protocol is a method (protocol) used
along with the Internet Protocol (IP) to send data in the form of
message units, called packets, between computers over the Internet.</dd>
    <dt>IP</dt>
        <dd>Internet Protocol is the method or protocol by which data
is sent from one computer to another on the Internet. Each computer on
the Internet is uniquely identified by an IP address.</dd>
    <dt>FTP</dt>
        <dd>File Transfer Protocol is a protocol used to exchange
files between computers on the Internet.</dd>
    <dt>HTTP</dt>
        <dd>Hypertext Transfer Protocol is the protocol used for
exchanging text, graphic images, sound, video, and other multimedia
files on the Web.</dd>
</dl>
</body>
</html>
```

Save your file as description.html. Launch a browser and test your page. It should look similar to the page shown in Figure 2.16. Don't worry if the word wrap is a little different; the important formatting is that each `<dt>` term should be on its own line and the corresponding `<dd>` description should be indented under it. Try resizing your browser window, and notice how the word wrap on the description text changes. You can compare your work with the solution in the student files (chapter2/description.html).

### FAQ   Why is the HTML code in the Hands-On Practice examples indented?

Actually, it doesn't matter to the browser if web page code is indented, but humans find it easier to read and maintain code when it is logically indented. Review the description list created in Hands-On Practice 2.8. Notice how the `<dt>` and `<dd>` tags were indented. This makes it easier for you or another web developer to understand the source code in the future. There is no rule as to how many spaces to indent, although your instructor or the organization you work for may have a standard. Consistent indentation helps to create more easily maintainable web pages.

## Checkpoint 2.2

**1.** Describe the features of a heading element and how it configures the text.

**2.** Describe the difference between ordered lists and unordered lists.

**3.** Describe the purpose of the blockquote element.

# 2.15 Special Characters

In order to use special symbols such as quotation marks, the greater-than sign (>), the less-than sign (<), and the copyright symbol (©) in your web page document, you need to use **special characters**, sometimes called **entity characters**. For example, if you wanted to include a copyright line on your page as follows:

© Copyright 2020 My Company. All rights reserved.

Use the special character code **&copy;** to display the copyright symbol, as shown in the following code:

&copy; Copyright 2020 My Company. All rights reserved.

Another useful special character code is ** **, which stands for nonbreaking space. You may have noticed that web browsers treat multiple spaces as a single space. If you need a small number of spaces in your text, you may use   multiple times to indicate multiple blank spaces. This practice is acceptable if you simply need to tweak the position of an element a little. However, if you find that your web pages contain many   special characters in a row, you should use a different method, such as configuring the padding or margin with Cascading Style Sheets (see Chapters 4 and 6). Table 2.3 and Appendix B, "Special Entity Characters," provide descriptions of special characters and their corresponding code.

Table 2.3  Common special characters

| Character | Entity Name | Code |
| --- | --- | --- |
| " | Quotation mark | &quot; |
| ' | Apostrophe | &#39; |
| © | Copyright symbol | &copy; |
| & | Ampersand | &amp; |
| Empty space | Nonbreaking space |   |
| — | Long dash | &mdash; |
| \| | Vertical Bar | &#124; |

## Hands-On Practice 2.9

Figure 2.17 shows the web page you will create in this Hands-On Practice. Launch a text editor. Select File > Open to edit the template file located at chapter2/template.html in the student files. Save your file as design.html. Modify the title of the web page by changing the text between the <title> and </title> tags to "Web Design Steps."

The sample page shown in Figure 2.17 contains a heading, an unordered list, and copyright information. Configure the heading "Web Design Steps" as a Level 1 heading (<h1>) as follows:

```
<h1>Web Design Steps</h1>
```

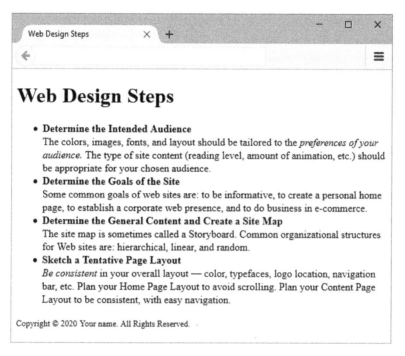

Figure 2.17  The design.html web page

Now create the unordered list. The first line of each bulleted item is the title of the web design step, which should be strong or stand out from the rest of the text. The code for the beginning of the unordered list is as follows:

```
<ul>
  <li><strong>Determine the Intended Audience</strong><br>
The colors, images, fonts, and layout should be tailored to the
<em>preferences of your audience.</em> The type of site content
(reading level, amount of animation, etc.) should be appropriate for
your chosen audience.</li>
```

Now code the entire unordered list in your design.html file. Remember to code the closing </ul> tag at the end of the list. Don't worry if your text wraps a little differently; your screen resolution or browser window size may be different from what is displayed in Figure 2.17.

Finally, configure the copyright information with the small element. Use the special character &copy; for the copyright symbol. The code for the copyright line is as follows:

```
<p><small>Copyright &copy; 2020 Your name. All Rights Reserved.
</small></p>
```

How did you do? Compare your work to the sample in the student files (chapter2/design.html).

## 2.16 Structural Elements

HTML5 introduces a number of semantic structural elements that can be used to configure specific areas on a web page. These new HTML5 header, nav, main, and footer elements are intended to be used in conjunction with div and other elements

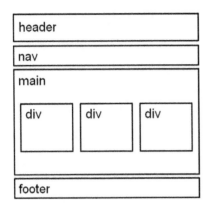

Figure 2.18 Structural elements

to structure web page documents in a more meaningful manner that indicates the purpose of each structural area. Figure 2.18 shows a diagram of a page (called a wireframe) that indicates how the structure of a web page could be configured with the header, nav, main, div, and footer elements.

## Div Element

The **div element** has been used for many years to configure a generic structural area or "division" on a web page as a block display with empty space above and below. A div element begins with a **`<div>`** tag and ends with a **`</div>`** tag. Use a div element when you need to format an area of a web page that may contain other block display elements such as headings, paragraphs, unordered lists, and even other div elements. You'll use Cascading Style Sheets (CSS) later in this book to style and configure the color, font, and layout of HTML elements.

## Header Element

The purpose of the **header element** is to contain the headings of either a web page document or an area within the document such as a section or article element. The header element begins with the **`<header>`** tag and ends with the **`</header>`** tag. The header element is block display and typically contains one or more heading level elements (h1 through h6).

## Nav Element

The purpose of the **nav element** is to contain a section of navigation links. The block display nav element begins with the **`<nav>`** tag and ends with the **`</nav>`** tag.

## Main Element

The purpose of the **main element** is to contain the main content of a web page document. The block display main element begins with the **`<main>`** tag and ends with the **`</main>`** tag.

## Footer Element

The purpose of the **footer element** is to contain the footer content of a web page or section of a web page. The block display footer element begins with the **`<footer>`** tag and ends with the **`</footer>`** tag.

## Hands-On Practice 2.10

In this Hands-On Practice you will use structural elements as you create the Trillium Media Design home page, shown in Figure 2.19. Launch a text editor, and open the template.html file from the chapter2 folder in the student files. Edit the code as follows:

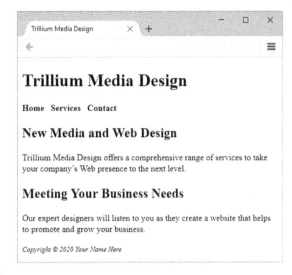

1. Modify the title of the web page by changing the text between the `<title>` and `</title>` tags to Trillium Media Design.

2. Position your cursor in the body section and code the header element with the text, "Trillium Media Design" contained in an h1 element:

```
<header>
  <h1> Trillium Media Design</h1>
</header>
```

**Figure 2.19** Trillium home page

3. Code a nav element to contain text that will indicate the main navigation for the website. Configure bold text (use the b element) and use the ` ` special character to add extra blank space:

```
<nav>
  <b>Home   Services   Contact</b>
</nav>
```

4. Code a main element that contains the h2 and paragraph elements:

```
<main>
  <h2>New Media and Web Design</h2>
  <p>Trillium Media Design offers a comprehensive range of
services to take your company&#39;s Web presence to the next
level.</p>
  <h2>Meeting Your Business Needs</h2>
  <p>Our expert designers will listen to you as they create a
website that helps to promote and grow your business.</p>
</main>
```

5. Configure the footer element to contain a copyright notice displayed in small font size (use the small element) and italic font (use the i element). Be careful to properly nest the elements as shown here:

```
<footer>
  <small><i>Copyright &copy; 2020 Your Name Here</i></small>
</footer>
```

Save your page as structure.html. Test your page in a browser. It should look similar to Figure 2.19. You can compare your work to the sample in the student files (chapter2/structure.html).

Coding HTML is a skill and skills are best learned by practice. You'll get more practice coding a web page using structural elements in this section.

## Hands-On Practice 2.11

In this Hands-On Practice you will use the wireframe shown in Figure 2.20 as a guide as you create the Casita Sedona Bed & Breakfast web page, shown in Figure 2.21.

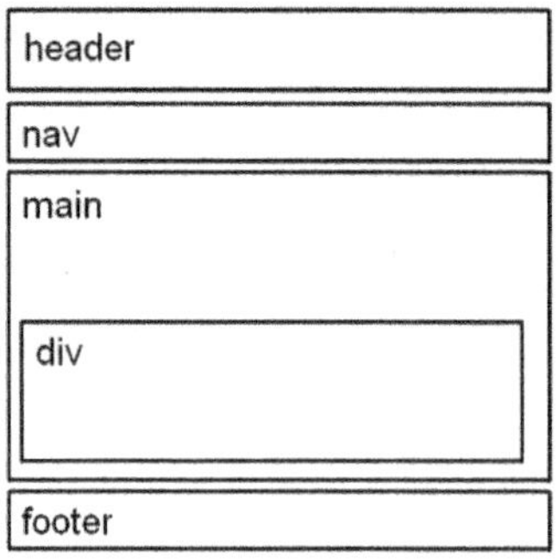

```
header
nav
main

    div

footer
```

**Figure 2.20** Wireframe for Casita Sedona

Launch a text editor, and open the template.html file from the chapter2 folder in the student files. Edit the code as follows:

**1.** Modify the title of the web page by changing the text between the `<title>` and `</title>` tags to Casita Sedona.

**2.** Position your cursor in the body section and code the header element with the text, "Casita Sedona Bed &amp; Breakfast" contained in an h1 element. Be sure to use the special character &amp; for the ampersand.

```
<header>
  <h1>
  Casita Sedona Bed &amp;
   Breakfast
  </h1>
</header>
```

**3.** Code a nav element to contain text that will indicate the main navigation for the website. Configure bold text (use the b element) and use the   special character to add extra blank space:

```
<nav>
  <b>
    Home  
    Rooms  
    Events  
    Contact
  </b>
</nav>
```

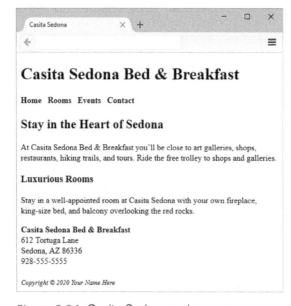

**Figure 2.21** Casita Sedona web page

**4.** Code the content within a main element. Start with the h2 and paragraph elements:

```
<main>
<h2>Stay in the Heart of Sedona</h2>
  <p>At Casita Sedona Bed &amp; Breakfast you&#39;ll be close to art
galleries, shops, restaurants, hiking trails, and tours. Ride the
free trolley to shops and galleries.</p>
  <h3>Luxurious Rooms</h3>
```

```
    <p>Stay in a well-appointed room at Casita Sedona with your own
    fireplace, king-size bed, and balcony overlooking the red rocks.</p>
    </main>
```

5. Configure the company name, address, and phone number within a div element. Code the div element *within* the main element before the closing main tag. Use line break tags to display the name, address, and phone information on separate lines and to create extra empty space before the footer.

```
<div>
  <strong>Casita Sedona Bed &amp; Breakfast</strong><br>
  612 Tortuga Lane<br>
  Sedona, AZ 86336<br>
  928-555-5555<br><br>
</div>
```

6. Configure the footer element to contain a copyright notice displayed in small font size (use the small element) and italic font (use the i element). Be careful to properly nest the elements as shown here:

```
<footer>
  <small><i>Copyright &copy; 2020 Your Name Here</i></small>
</footer>
```

Save your page as casita.html. Test your page in a browser. It should look similar to Figure 2.21. You can compare your work to the sample in the student files (chapter2/casita.html). Older browsers (such as Internet Explorer 8 and earlier) do not support the new HTML5 structural elements. In Chapter 6, we'll explore coding techniques that will force older browsers to correctly display HTML5 structural elements. For now, be sure to use a current version of any popular browser to test your pages.

You've just worked with the HTML5 header, nav, main, and footer elements. These HTML5 elements are used along with div and other elements to structure web page documents in a meaningful manner that defines the purpose of the structural areas. Next, you'll explore the section, article, aside, and time elements.

## Section Element

The purpose of a **section element** is to indicate a "section" of a document, such as a chapter or topic. This block display element begins with the **<section>** tag, ends with the **</section>** tag, and could contain header, footer, section, article, aside, figure, div, and other elements needed to configure the content.

## Article Element

The **article element** is intended to present an independent entry, such as a blog posting, comment, or e-zine article that could stand on its own. This block display element begins with the **<article>** tag, ends with the **</article>** tag, and could contain header, footer, section, aside, figure, div, and other elements needed to configure the content.

## Aside Element

The **aside element** indicates a sidebar or other tangential content. This block display element begins with the **`<aside>`** tag, ends with the **`</aside>`** tag, and could contain header, footer, section, aside, figure, div, and other elements needed to configure the content.

## Time Element

The **time element** represents a date or a time. The time element is not a structural element, but it is included here because it is useful to identity the date of content, such as an article on a web page or a blog entry. The inline display time element begins with the **`<time>`** tag, ends with the **`</time>`** tag. An optional `datetime` attribute can be used to specify a calendar date and/or time in machine-readable format. Use YYYY-MM-DD for a date. Use a 24-hour clock and HH:MM for time.

# Hands-On Practice 2.12

In this Hands-On Practice, you'll edit a web page document and apply the section, article, aside, and time elements to create the page with blog postings shown in Figure 2.22.

Launch a text editor and open the starter.html file from the chapter2 folder in the student files. Save the file as blog.html. Examine the source code.

1. Locate the title tag in the head section. Change the text within the title tags to "Lighthouse Bistro Blog."

2. Locate the opening main tag. Delete the HTML elements and text between the opening and closing main tags.

3. Code an aside element with the following content below the opening main tag. The HTML follows:

```
<aside>
  <p><i>Watch for the March
  Madness Wrap next month!</i></p>
</aside>
```

4. Code an opening section tag followed by an h2 element. The HTML follows:

```
<section>
<h2>Bistro Blog</h2>
```

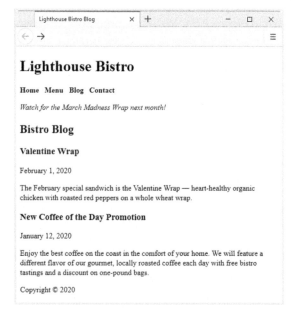

Figure 2.22  The blog page.

5. Code two blog articles as shown below. Note the use of the header, h3, time, and paragraph elements. Also, code a closing section tag. The HTML follows:

```
<article>
  <header><h3>Valentine Wrap</h3></header>
  <time datetime="2020-02-01">February 1, 2020</time>
  <p>The February special sandwich is the Valentine Wrap &mdash;
  heart-healthy organic chicken with roasted red peppers on a
  whole wheat wrap.</p>
</article>
<article>
  <header><h3>New Coffee of the Day Promotion</h3></header>
  <time datetime="2020-01-12">January 12, 2020</time>
  <p>Enjoy the best coffee on the coast in the comfort of your
  home. We will feature a different flavor of our gourmet,
  locally roasted coffee each day with free bistro tastings and a
  discount on one-pound bags.</p>
</article>
</section>
```

Save your file. Display your blog.html page in a browser. It should look similar to the page shown in Figure 2.22. A sample solution is in the student files (chapter2/blog.html).

# 2.17  Hyperlinks

## The A Element

Use the **a element** (commonly called the **anchor element**) to specify a **hyperlink**, often referred to as a *link*, to another web page or file that you want to display. Each anchor element begins with an **<a>** tag and ends with a **</a>** tag. The opening and closing anchor tags surround the text to click to perform the hyperlink.

## The Href Attribute

Use the **href attribute** to configure the hyperlink reference, which identifies the name and location of the file to access. Figure 2.23 shows a web page document with an anchor tag that configures a hyperlink to this book's website, http://webdevfoundations.net.

Figure 2.23  Sample hyperlink

The code for the anchor tag in Figure 2.23 is as follows:

```
<a href="http://webdevfoundations.net">Web Development &amp; Design
  Foundations</a>
```

Notice that the href value is the URL for the website. The text that is typed between the two anchor tags displays on the web page as a hyperlink and is underlined by most browsers. When you move the mouse cursor over a hyperlink, the cursor changes to a pointing hand, as shown in Figure 2.23.

## Hands-On Practice 2.13

To create the web page shown in Figure 2.23, launch a text editor. Select File > Open to edit the template file located at chapter2/template.html in the student files. Modify the title element and add anchor tags to the body section as indicated by the following code:

```
<!DOCTYPE html>
<html lang="en">
<head>
<title>Anchor Example</title>
<meta charset="utf-8">
</head>
<body>
<a href="http://webdevfoundations.net">Web Development &amp; Design
Foundations</a>
</body>
</html>
```

Save the document as anchor.html on your hard drive or flash drive. Launch a browser to test your page. It should look similar to the page shown in Figure 2.23. You can compare your work with the solution found in the student files (chapter2/anchor.html).

## FAQ   Can images be hyperlinks?

Yes. Although we'll concentrate on text hyperlinks in this chapter, it's also possible to configure an image as a hyperlink. You'll get practice with image links in Chapter 4.

## Absolute Hyperlinks

An **absolute hyperlink** indicates the absolute location of a resource on the Web. Use absolute hyperlinks when you need to link to resources on other websites. The href value for an absolute hyperlink to the home page of a website includes the `http://` protocol and the domain name. The following hyperlink is an absolute hyperlink to the home page of this book's website:

```
<a href="http://webdevfoundations.net">Web Development &amp; Design
Foundations</a>
```

Note that if we want to access a web page other than the home page on the book's website, we could also include a specific folder name and file name. For example, the following anchor tag configures an absolute hyperlink for a file named chapter1.html located in a folder named 10e on this book's website:

```
<a href="http://webdevfoundations.net/10e/chapter1.html">Web Development
&amp; Design Foundations Chapter 1</a>
```

## Relative Hyperlinks

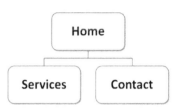

When you need to link to web pages within your site, use a **relative hyperlink**. The href value for a relative hyperlink does not begin with the http:// and does not include a domain name. For a relative hyperlink, the href value will contain only the file name or file name and folder of the web page you want to display. The hyperlink location is relative to the page currently being displayed. For example, if you were coding a home page (index.html) for the website whose site map is illustrated in Figure 2.24 and wanted to link to a page named contact.html located in the same folder as index.html, you would use the following code sample:

Figure 2.24 Site map

```
<a href="contact.html">Contact Us</a>
```

## Site Map

A **site map** represents the structure, or organization, of pages in a website in a visual manner. Each page in the website is represented by a box on the site map. Figure 2.24 displays the site map for a website that contains a Home page and two content pages: a Services page and a Contact page. Review Figure 2.24 and notice that the Home page is at the top of the site map. The second level in a site map shows the other main pages of the website. In this very small three-page website, the other two pages (Services and Contact) are included on the second level. The main navigation of a website usually includes hyperlinks to the pages shown on the first two levels of the site map.

## Hands-On Practice 2.14

The best way to learn how to code web pages is by actually doing it! Let's practice and create three pages in the website shown in Figure 2.24: home page (index.html) with two content pages: services page (services.html) and contact page (contact.html).

1. **Create a Folder.** If you had printed papers to organize you would probably store them in a paper folder. Web designers store and organize their computer files by creating a folder on a hard drive (or portable storage such as an SD card or Flash drive) for each website. This helps them to be efficient as they work with many different websites. You will organize your own web design work by creating a new folder for each website and storing your files for that website in the new folder. Use your operating system to create a new folder named mypractice for your new website.

2. **Create the Home Page.** Use the Trillium Media Design web page (Figure 2.19) from Hands-On Practice 2.10 as a starting point for your new home page (shown in Figure 2.25). Copy the sample file for Hands-On Practice 2.10 (chapter2/structure.html) into your mypractice folder. Change the file name of structure.html to index.html. It's common practice to use the file name index.html for the home page of a website.

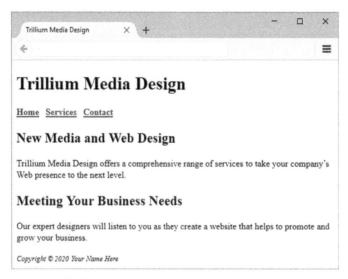

Figure 2.25  New index.html web page

Launch a text editor, and open the index.html file.

a. The navigation hyperlinks will be located within the nav element. You will edit the code within the nav element to configure three hyperlinks:

- The text "Home" will hyperlink to index.html
- The text "Services" will hyperlink to services.html
- The text "Contact" will hyperlink to contact.html

Modify the code within the nav element as follows:

```
<nav>
        <b><a href="index.html">Home</a>    
           <a href="services.html">Services</a>    
           <a href="contact.html">Contact</a>
        </b>

</nav>
```

b. Save the index.html file in your mypractice folder. Test your page in a browser. It should look similar to Figure 2.25. You can compare your work to the sample in the student files (chapter2/2.14/index.html).

3. **Create the Services Page.** It is common practice to create a new web page based on an existing page. You will use the index.html file as a starting point for the new services page, shown in Figure 2.26.

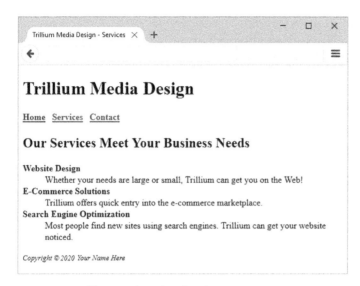

Figure 2.26 The services.html web page

Open your index.html file in a text editor and save the file as services.html. Edit the code as follows:

**a.** Modify the title of the web page by changing the text between the `<title>` and `</title>` tags to "Trillium Media Design - Services". In order to create a consistent header, navigation, and footer for the web pages in this website, do not change the code within the header, nav, or footer elements.

**b.** Position your cursor in the body section and delete the code and text between the opening and closing main tags. Code the main page content (heading 2 and description list) for the services page between the main tags as follows:

```
<h2>Our Services Meet Your Business Needs</h2>
  <dl>
    <dt><strong>Website Design</strong></dt>
      <dd>Whether your needs are large or small, Trillium can
      get you on the Web!</dd>
    <dt><strong>E-Commerce Solutions</strong></dt>
      <dd>Trillium offers quick entry into the e-commerce
      marketplace.</dd>
    <dt><strong>Search Engine Optimization</strong></dt>
      <dd>Most people find new sites using search engines.
      Trillium can get your website noticed.</dd>
  </dl>
```

**c.** Save the services.html file in your mypractice folder. Test your page in a browser. It should look similar to Figure 2.26. You can compare your work to the sample in the student files (chapter2/2.14/services.html).

**4. Create the Contact Page.** Use the index.html file as a starting point for the new Contact page, shown in Figure 2.27. Open your index.html file in a text editor and save the file as contact.html. Edit the code as follows:

**a.** Modify the title of the web page by changing the text between the `<title>` and `</title>` tags to "Trillium Media Design – Contact". In order to create a consistent header, navigation, and footer for the web pages in this website, do not change the code within the header, nav, or footer elements.

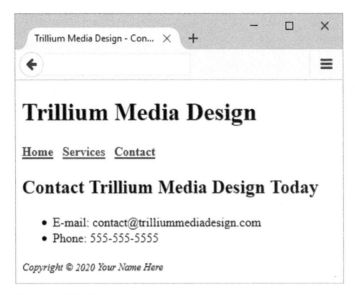

Figure 2.27    The contact.html web page

**b.** Position your cursor in the body section and delete the code and text contained between the opening main tag and the closing main tag. Code the main page content for the contact page between the main tags:

```
<h2>Contact Trillium Media Design Today</h2>
   <ul>
      <li>E-mail: contact@trilliummediadesign.com</li>
      <li>Phone: 555-555-5555</li>
   </ul>
```

**c.** Save the contact.html file in your mypractice folder. Test your page in a browser. It should look similar to Figure 2.27. Test your page by clicking each link. When you click the "Home" hyperlink, the index.html page should display. When you click the "Services" hyperlink, the services.html page should display. When you click the "Contact" hyperlink, the contact.html page will display. You can compare your work to the sample in the student files (chapter2/2.14/contact.html).

 **FAQ**   **What if my relative hyperlink doesn't work?**

Check the following:

- Did you save files in the specified folder?

- Did you save the files with the names as requested? Use Windows File Explorer or Finder (Mac users) to verify the actual names of the files you saved.

- Did you type the file names correctly in the anchor tag's href attribute? Check for typographical errors.

- When you place your mouse over a link, the file name of a relative link will display in the status bar in the lower edge of the browser window. Verify that this is the correct file name. On many operating systems, such as UNIX or Linux, the use of uppercase and lowercase letters in file names matters—make sure that the file name and the reference to it are in the same case. It's a good practice to always use lowercase for file names used on the Web.

## The Target Attribute

You may have noticed as you have coded hyperlinks that when a visitor clicks on a hyperlink, the new web page will automatically open in the same browser window. You can configure the **target attribute** on an anchor element with `target="_blank"` to open a hyperlink in a new browser window or browser tab. For example, the following HTML will open Google's home page in a new browser window or tab:

```
<a href="http://google.com" target="_blank">Search Google</a>
```

Note that you cannot control whether the web page opens in a new window or opens in a new tab; this is dependent upon your visitor's browser configuration. See an example in the student files (chapter2/target.html).

## Block Anchor

It's typical to use anchor tags to configure phrases or even just a single word as a hyperlink. HTML5 provides a new function for the anchor element—the block anchor. A block anchor can configure one or more entire elements (even those that display as a block, such as a div, h1, or paragraph) as a hyperlink. See an example in the student files (chapter2/block.html).

## E-Mail Hyperlinks

The anchor tag can also be used to create **e-mail hyperlinks**. An e-mail hyperlink will automatically launch the default mail program configured for the browser. It is similar to an external hyperlink with the following two exceptions:

- It uses `mailto:` instead of `http://`.
- It launches the default e-mail application for the visitor's browser with your e-mail address as the recipient.

For example, to create an e-mail hyperlink to the e-mail address help@terrymorris.net, code the following:

```
<a href="mailto:help@terrymorris.net">help@terrymorris.net</a>
```

It is good practice to place the e-mail address both on the web page and within the anchor tag. Not everyone has an e-mail program configured with his or her browser. By placing the e-mail address in both places, you increase usability for all of your visitors.

 ## Hands-On Practice 2.15

In this Hands-On Practice you will modify the contact page (contact.html) of the website you created in Hands-On Practice 2.14 and configure an e-mail link in the page content area. Launch a text editor, and open the contact.html file from your mypractice folder. This example uses the contact.html file found in the student files in the chapter2/2.14 folder.

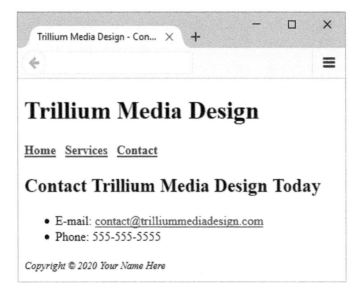

Figure 2.28 An e-mail hyperlink on the contact page

Configure the e-mail address as an e-mail hyperlink as follows, but type the entire anchor element on a single line.:

```
<li>E-mail:
<a href="mailto:contact@trilliummediadesign.com">
contact@trilliummediadesign.com</a>
</li>
```

Save and test the page in a browser. The browser display should look similar to the page shown in Figure 2.28. You can compare your work with the sample in the student files (chapter2/2.15/contact.html).

FAQ **Won't displaying my actual e-mail address on a web page increase spam?**

Yes and no. While it's possible that some unethical spammers may harvest web pages for e-mail addresses, the chances are that your e-mail application's built-in spam filter will prevent your inbox from being flooded with messages. When you configure an easily readable e-mail hyperlink you increase the usability of your website for your visitors in the following situations:

- The visitor may be at a public computer with no e-mail application configured. In this case, when the e-mail hyperlink is clicked, an error message may display, and the visitor will have difficulty contacting you using the e-mail link.

- The visitor may be at a private computer but may prefer not to use the e-mail application (and address) that is configured by default to work with the browser. Perhaps he or she shares the computer with others, or perhaps he or she wishes to preserve the privacy of the default e-mail address.

If you prominently displayed your actual e-mail address in both of these situations, the visitor can still access your e-mail address and use it to contact you (in either their e-mail application or via a web-based e-mail system such as Google's Gmail). The result is a more usable website for your visitors.

## Accessibility and Hyperlinks

Visually challenged visitors who are using a screen reader can configure the software to display a list of the hyperlinks in the document. However, a list of links is useful only if the text describing each link is actually helpful and descriptive. For example, on your college website, a "Search the course schedule" link would be more useful than a link that simply says, "More information."

### FAQ    What are some tips for using hyperlinks?

- Make your link names descriptive and brief to minimize possible confusion.

- Avoid using the phrase "Click here" in your hyperlinks. In the early days of the Web, this phrase was needed because clicking links was a new experience for web users. Now that the Web is a daily part of our lives, this phrase is slightly redundant, and even archaic.

- Try not to bury hyperlinks within large blocks of text; use lists of hyperlinks instead. Be aware that it is more difficult to read web pages than printed pages.

- Be careful when linking to external websites. The Web is dynamic, and it's possible that the external site may change the name of the page, or even delete the page. If this happens, your link will be broken.

## Checkpoint 2.3

**1.** Describe the purpose of special characters.

**2.** Describe when to use an absolute link. Is the http protocol used in the href value?

**3.** Describe when to use a relative link. Is the http protocol used in the href value?

# 2.18  HTML Validation

The W3C's free Markup Validation Service, available at http://validator.w3.org, will validate your HTML code and check it for syntax errors. HTML **validation** provides students with quick self-assessment—you can prove that your code uses correct syntax. In the working world, HTML validation serves as a quality assurance tool. Invalid code may cause browsers to render the pages slower than otherwise.

## Hands-On Practice 2.16

In this Hands-On Practice, you will use the W3C Markup Validation Service to validate a web page file. This example uses the page completed in Hands-On Practice 2.9 (located in the student files at chapter2/design.html). Open design.html in a text editor. Add an error to the design.html page by deleting the first closing `</strong>` tag. This modification should generate several error messages.

Next, attempt to validate the design.html file. Launch a browser and visit the W3C Markup Validation Service file upload page at http://validator.w3.org/#validate_by_upload. Click the Browse button, and select the chapter2/design.html file from your computer. Click the Check button to upload the file to the W3C site (Figure 2.29).

VideoNote
**HTML Validation**

**Figure 2.29** Validating a page with the W3C Markup Validation Service. Screenshots of W3C. Courtesy of W3C (World Wide Web Consortium).

An error page will display. Notice the "Errors found while checking this document" message. You can view the errors by scrolling down the page, as shown in Figure 2.30.

Notice that the first message indicates line 12, which is after the missing closing `</strong>` tag. HTML error messages often point to a line that follows the error. The text of the message, "End tag li seen, but there were open elements," lets you know that something is wrong. It is up to you to figure out what it is. A good place to start is to check your container tags and make sure they are in pairs. In this case, that is the problem. You can scroll down to view the other errors. However, since multiple error messages are often displayed after a single error occurs, it is a good idea to fix one item at a time and then revalidate.

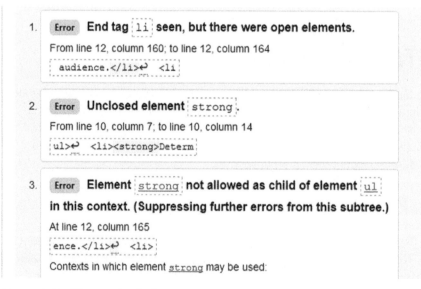

**Figure 2.30** The service indicates errors. Screenshots of W3C. Courtesy of W3C (World Wide Web Consortium).

Edit the design.html file in a text editor, and add the missing `</strong>` tag. Save the file. Launch a browser, and visit http://validator.w3.org/#validate_by_upload. Select your file, select More Options, and verify that the Show Source and Verbose Output check boxes are checked. Click the Check button to begin the validation.

Your display should be similar to that shown in Figure 2.31. Notice the "Document checking completed. No errors or warnings to show." message. This means that your page passed the validation test. Congratulations, your design.html page is valid! You may also notice a warning message, which you can overlook, indicating that the HTML5 conformance checker is in experimental status.

It is good practice to validate your web pages. However, when validating code, use common sense. Since web browsers still do not completely follow W3C recommendations, there will be situations, such as when adding multimedia to a web page, in which HTML code configured to work reliably across a variety of browsers and platforms will not pass validation.

---

**Document checking completed. No errors or warnings to show.**

The Content-Type header specified text/html. Used the HTML parser.
Total execution time 1 milliseconds.

---

**Figure 2.31** The page has passed the validation test. Screenshots of W3C. Courtesy of W3C (World Wide Web Consortium).

 **FAQ** **Are there other ways to validate my HTML?**

In addition to the W3C validation service, there are other tools that you can use to check the syntax of your code. Explore the HTML5 validator at https://html5.validator.nu and the HTML & CSS Validator / Linter at https://www.freeformatter.com/html-validator.html.

# Chapter Summary

This chapter has provided an introduction to HTML, XHTML, and HTML5. The basic elements that are part of every web page were demonstrated. HTML elements including div, paragraph, blockquote, header, nav, main, and footer were presented. Additional topics included configuring lists and using special characters, phrase elements, and hyperlinks. You have practiced testing your HTML5 code for valid syntax. If you worked along with the samples in the chapter, you should be ready to create some web pages on your own. The Hands-On Exercises and Web Case Studies that follow will provide some additional practice.

Visit this textbook's website at https://www.webdevfoundations.net for links to the URLs listed in this chapter and to view updated information.

## Key Terms

&copy;
 
<a>
<abbr>
<article>
<aside>
<b>
<blockquote>
<body>
<br>
<cite>
<code>
<dd>
<dfn>
<div>
<dl>
<dt>
<em>
<footer>
<h1>
<h6>
<head>
<header>
<html>
<i>
<kbd>
<li>
<main>
<mark>
<meta>
<nav>
<ol>
<p>
<samp>
<section>

<small>
<strong>
<sub>
<sup>
<time>
<title>
<ul>
<var>
a element
absolute hyperlink
anchor element
article element
aside element
attribute
block anchor
block display
blockquote element
body element
body section
character encoding
description list
div element
doctype
Document Type Definition (DTD)
element
e-mail hyperlinks
entity element
eXtensible HyperText Markup Language (XHTML)
footer element
head element
head section
header element
heading element
href attribute

HTML5
hyperlink
Hypertext Markup Language (HTML)
inline display
lang attribute
left alignment
line break element
main element
markup languages
meta element
nav element
ordered list
paragraph elements
phrase elements
relative hyperlink
reversed attribute
section element
site map
special characters
stand-alone
start attribute
tag
target attribute
time element
title element
type attribute
unordered list
validation
void element
Web Hypertext Application Technology Working Group (WHATWG)
well-formed
XML (eXtensible Markup Language)

## Review Questions

### Multiple Choice

1. Which tag pair configures a structural area on a web page?
   a. `<area> </area>`
   b. `<div> </div>`
   c. `<cite> </cite>`
   d. `<strong> </strong>`

2. Which tag configures the next element or portion of text to display on a new line?
   a. `<line>`
   b. `<nl>`
   c. `<br>`
   d. `<new>`

3. Which tag pair is used to link web pages to each other?
   a. `<link> </link>`
   b. `<hyperlink> </hyperlink>`
   c. `<a> </a>`
   d. `<body> </body>`

4. Which tag pair is used to create the largest heading?
   a. `<h1> </h1>`
   b. `<h9> </h9>`
   c. `<h type="largest"> </h>`
   d. `<h6> </h6>`

5. What is the default horizontal alignment for elements on a web page?
   a. center
   b. left
   c. right
   d. wherever you type them in the source code

6. When do you need to use a fully qualified URL in a hyperlink?
   a. always
   b. when linking to a web page file on the same site
   c. when linking to a web page file on an external site
   d. never

7. Which of the following is a reason that the text contained by the title tag should be descriptive and include the name of the business or organization?
   a. The title is saved by default when a visitor bookmarks a web page.
   b. The title may be printed when a visitor prints a web page.
   c. The title may be listed in search engine results.
   d. All of the above are reasons that the text contained by the title tag should be descriptive and include the name of the business or organization.

8. Which type of HTML list will automatically number the items for you?
   a. numbered list
   b. ordered list
   c. unordered list
   d. definition list

9. Which of the following is an HTML5 element used to indicate navigational content?
   a. main
   b. nav
   c. header
   d. a

10. What does an e-mail link do?
    a. automatically sends you an e-mail message with the visitor's e-mail address as the reply-to field
    b. launches the default e-mail application for the visitor's browser, with your e-mail address as the recipient
    c. displays your e-mail address so that the visitor can send you a message later
    d. links to your mail server

### Fill in the Blank

11. Use the _____ element to configure text to have strong importance and display in a bold font weight.

12. The _____ element is intended to present an independent entry such as a blog posting.

13. The `<meta>` tag can be used to _____.

14. The _____ is used to place a non-breaking space on a web page.

15. Use the _____ element to configure text to be emphasized and displayed in an italic font style.

## Short Answer

**16.** Explain why it is good practice to place an e-mail address on the web page and within an anchor element when creating an e-mail link.

## Apply Your Knowledge

**1. Predict the Result.** Sketch out and briefly describe the web page that will be created with the following HTML code:

```
<!DOCTYPE html>
<html lang="en">
<head>
  <title>Predict the Result</title>
  <meta charset="utf-8">
</head>
<body>
  <header><h1><i>Favorite Sites</i></h1></header>
  <main>
    <ol>
      <li><a href="http://facebook.com">Facebook</a></li>
      <li><a href="http://google.com">Google</a></li>
    </ol>
  </main>
  <footer>
    <small>Copyright &copy; 2020 Your name here</small>
  </footer>
</body>
</html>
```

**2. Fill in the Missing Code.** The web page defined by the given code should display a heading and a description list, but some HTML tags, indicated by **<_>**, are missing. Fill in the missing code.

```
<!DOCTYPE html>
<html lang="en">
<head>
  <title>Door County Wildflowers</title>
  <meta charset="utf-8">
</head>
<body>
  <header><_>Door County Wild Flowers<_></header>
  <main>
  <dl>
    <dt>Trillium<_>
      <_>This white flower blooms from April through June in
      wooded areas.<_>
    <_>Lady Slipper<_>
      <_>This yellow orchid blooms in June in wooded areas.</dd>
  <_>
  </main>
</body>
</html>
```

3. **Find the Error**. All the text on the web page defined by the given code displays in large and bold font typeface. Explain why this is happening.

```html
<!DOCTYPE html>
<html lang="en">
<head>
  <title>Find the Error</title>
  <meta charset="utf-8">
</head>
<body>
  <h1>My Web Page<h1>
  <p>This is a sentence on my web page.</p>
</body>
</html>
```

## Hands-On Exercises

1. Write the HTML to display your name with the largest heading element.

2. Write the HTML to create an absolute link to your school's website.

3. Write the HTML for an unordered list to display the days of the week.

4. Write the HTML for an ordered list that uses uppercase letters to order the items. This ordered list should display the following phrases: wake up, eat breakfast, and go to school.

5. Think of a favorite quotation by someone you admire. Write the HTML code to display the person's name in a heading and the quotation in a blockquote element.

6. Modify the following code snippet to indicate that the term "site map" should have strong importance:

```html
<p>A diagram of the organization of a website is called a site map.
A site map represents the structure, or organization, of pages in
a website in a visual manner. Creating the site map is one of the
initial steps in developing a website.</p>
```

7. Modify the blockquote.html web page you created in Hands-On Practice 2.5. Configure the URL https://www.w3.org/WAI/ as a hyperlink. Save the file as blockquote2.html.

8. Create a web page that uses a description list to display three network protocols (see Chapter 1) and their descriptions. Include a hyperlink to a website that provides information about the protocols. Add an appropriate heading to the page. Save the page as network.html.

9. Create a web page about your favorite musical group. Include the name of the group, the individuals in the group, a hyperlink to the group's website, your favorite three (or fewer if the group is new) album releases, and a brief review of each album.

   • Use an unordered list to organize the names of the individuals.
   • Use a description list for the names of the albums and your reviews.

   Save the page as band.html.

10. Create a web page about your favorite recipe. Use an unordered list for the ingredients and an ordered list to describe the steps needed to prepare the food. Include a hyperlink to a website that offers free recipes. Save the page as recipe.html.

11. Create a web page with two blog posts about websites that could be useful to you in your web development studies. Each blog post should contain a hyperlink to the home page of the website, a description of the type of information provided at the website, and the date you accessed the website. Use the article and time elements for each blog post. Save the page as myblog.html.

## Web Research

There are many HTML5 tutorials on the Web. Use your favorite search engine to discover them. Choose two that are helpful. For each, print out the home page or other pertinent page and create a web page that contains the answers to the following questions:

**a.** What is the URL of the website?

**b.** Is the tutorial geared toward the beginner level, intermediate level, or both levels?

**c.** Would you recommend this site to others? Why or why not?

**d.** List one or two concepts that you learned from this tutorial.

## Focus on Web Design

You are learning the syntax of HTML5. However, coding alone does not make a web page; design is also very important. Surf the Web and find two web pages, one that is appealing to you and one that is unappealing to you. Print each page. Create a web page that answers the following questions for each of your examples:

**a.** What is the URL of the website?

**b.** Is the page appealing or unappealing? List three reasons for your answer.

**c.** If the page is unappealing, what would you do to improve it?

# WEBSITE CASE STUDY

Each of the case studies in this section continues throughout most of the text. This chapter introduces each website scenario, presents the site map, and directs you to create two pages for the site.

## JavaJam Coffee Bar

Julio Perez is the owner of the JavaJam Coffee Bar, a gourmet coffee shop that serves snacks, coffee, tea, and soft drinks. Local folk music performances and poetry readings are held a few nights during the week. The customers of JavaJam are mainly college students and young professionals. Julio would like a web presence for his shop that will display his services and provide a calendar for the performances. He would like a home page, menu page, music performance schedule page, and job opportunities page.

A site map for the JavaJam Coffee Bar website is shown in Figure 2.32. The site map describes the architecture of the website, which consists of a "Home" page with three main content pages: "Menu," "Music," and "Jobs."

**Figure 2.32** JavaJam site map

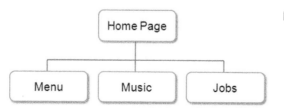

Figure 2.33 displays a wireframe sketch of the page layout for the website. It contains a header area, a navigation area, a main content area, and a footer area for copyright information.

You have three tasks in this case study:

1. Create a folder for the JavaJam website.

2. Create the Home page: index.html.

3. Create the Menu page: menu.html.

## Hands-On Practice Case Study

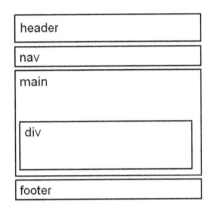

**Figure 2.33**  JavaJam wireframe

**Task 1: The Website Folder.** Create a folder on your hard drive or portable storage device (thumb drive or SD card) called "javajam" to contain your JavaJam website files.

**Task 2: The Home Page.** You will use a text editor to create the Home page for the JavaJam Coffee Bar website. The Home page is shown in Figure 2.34.

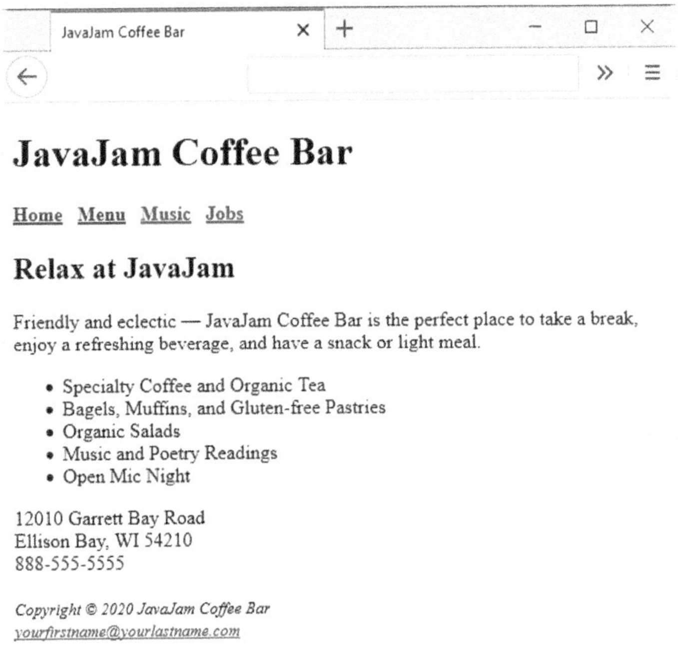

---

JavaJam Coffee Bar   ×   +   —  □  ×

←

# JavaJam Coffee Bar

<u>Home</u>  <u>Menu</u>  <u>Music</u>  <u>Jobs</u>

## Relax at JavaJam

Friendly and eclectic — JavaJam Coffee Bar is the perfect place to take a break, enjoy a refreshing beverage, and have a snack or light meal.

- Specialty Coffee and Organic Tea
- Bagels, Muffins, and Gluten-free Pastries
- Organic Salads
- Music and Poetry Readings
- Open Mic Night

12010 Garrett Bay Road
Ellison Bay, WI 54210
888-555-5555

*Copyright © 2020 JavaJam Coffee Bar*
*yourfirstname@yourlastname.com*

**Figure 2.34**  JavaJam index.html

---

Launch a text editor, and create a web page with the following specifications:

1. **Web Page Title.** Use a descriptive page title. The company name is a good choice for the home page of a business website. On pages other than the home page, the title typically contains both the company name and a word or a phrase that describes the purpose of the page.

2. **Wireframe Header.** Code the header element with the text, "JavaJam Coffee Bar" contained within a heading 1 element.

3. **Wireframe Navigation.** Place the following text within a nav element with bold text (use the <b> element):

Home Menu Music Jobs

Code anchor tags so that "Home" links to index.html, "Menu" links to menu.html, "Music" links to music.html, and "Jobs" links to jobs.html. Add extra blank spaces between the hyperlinks with the   special character as needed.

4. **Wireframe Main Content.** Code the main page content within a main element. Use Hands-On Practice 2.10 as a guide.

   a. Code the following text within an h2 element:

   Relax at JavaJam

   b. Configure the following content within a paragraph.

   Friendly and eclectic — JavaJam Coffee Bar is the perfect place to take a break, enjoy a refreshing beverage, and have a snack or light meal.

   c. Configure the following content in an unordered list:

   Specialty Coffee and Organic Tea

   Bagels, Muffins, and Gluten-free Pastries

   Organic Salads

   Music and Poetry Readings

   Open Mic Night

   d. Code the following address and phone number contact information within a div element. Use line break tags to help you configure this area and add extra space between the phone number and the footer area.

   12010 Garrett Bay Road

   Ellison Bay, WI 54210

   888-555-5555

5. **Wireframe Footer.** Configure the following copyright and e-mail link information within a footer element. Format it with small text size (use the <small> tag) and italics font style (use the <i> tag).

Copyright © 2020 JavaJam Coffee Bar

Place your name in an e-mail link on the line under the copyright.

The page in Figure 2.34 may seem a little sparse, but don't worry; as you gain experience and learn to use more advanced techniques, your pages will look more professional. White space (blank space) on the page can be added with <br> tags where needed. Your page does not need to look exactly the same as the sample. Your goal at this point should be to practice and get comfortable using HTML.

Save your page in the javajam folder, and name it index.html.

**Task 3: The Menu Page.** Create the Menu page shown in Figure 2.35. A technique that improves productivity is to create new pages based on existing pages so that you can benefit from your previous work. Your new Menu page will use the index.html page as a starting point.

**JavaJam Coffee Bar**

Home  Menu  Music  Jobs

**Coffee at JavaJam**

**Just Java**
 Regular house blend, decaffeinated coffee, or flavor of the day.
 Endless Cup $3.50
**Cafe au Lait**
 House blended coffee infused into a smooth, steamed milk.
 Single $4.00 Double $5.00
**Iced Cappuccino**
 Sweetened espresso blended with icy-cold milk and served in a chilled glass.
 Single $5.00 Double $6.50

*Copyright © 2020 JavaJam Coffee Bar*
*yourfirstname@yourlastname.com*

Figure 2.35  JavaJam menu.html

Open the index.html page for the JavaJam website in a text editor. Select File > Save As, and save the file with the new name of menu.html in the javajam folder. Now you are ready to edit the page.

1. **Web Page Title.** Modify the page title. Change the text contained between the `<title>` and `</title>` tags to the following:

   JavaJam Coffee Bar Menu

2. **Wireframe Main Content.**

   a. Delete the Home page content paragraph, unordered list, and contact information.

   b. Replace the text in the h2 element with the following:

      Coffee at JavaJam

   c. Use a description list to add the menu content to the page. Use the `<dt>` tag to contain each menu item name. Configure the menu item name to have strong importance and display in bold font weight with the `<strong>` tag. Use the `<dd>` tag to contain the menu item description. Configure line break tags as needed to display two lines of information within each dd element. The menu item names and descriptions are as follows:

      **Just Java**

      Regular house blend, decaffeinated coffee, or flavor of the day.

      Endless Cup $3.50

      **Cafe au Lait**

      House blended coffee infused into a smooth, steamed milk.

      Single $4.00 Double $5.00

      **Iced Cappuccino**

      Sweetened espresso blended with icy-cold milk and served in a chilled glass.

      Single $5.00 Double $6.50

Save your page, and test it in a browser. Test the hyperlink from the menu.html page to index.html. Test the hyperlink from the index.html page to menu.html. If your links do not work, review your work, paying close attention to these details:

- Verify that you have saved the pages with the correct names in the correct folder.

- Verify your spelling of the page names in the anchor elements.

Test again after you make changes.

## Fish Creek Animal Clinic

Magda Patel is a veterinarian and owner of the Fish Creek Animal Clinic. Her customers are local pet owners who range from children to senior citizens. Magda would like a website to provide information to her current and potential customers. She has requested a home page, a services page, a page for advice from a veterinarian, and a contact page.

A site map for the Fish Creek Animal Clinic website is shown in Figure 2.36. The site map describes the architecture of the website, which consists of a "Home" page with three main content pages: "Services," "Ask the Vet," and "Contact."

Figure 2.36  Fish Creek site map

Figure 2.37 displays a wireframe sketch of the page layout for the website. It contains a header area, a navigation area, a main content area, and a footer area for copyright information.

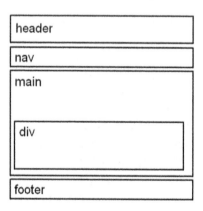

Figure 2.37  Fish Creek wireframe

You have three tasks in this case study:

1. Create a folder for the Fish Creek website.

2. Create the Home page: index.html.

3. Create the Services page: services.html.

## Hands-On Practice Case Study

**Task 1: The Website Folder.** Create a folder on your hard drive or portable storage device (thumb drive or SD card) called "fishcreek" to contain your Fish Creek website files.

**Task 2: The Home Page.** You will use a text editor application to create the Home page for the Fish Creek Animal Clinic website. The Home page is shown in Figure 2.38.

**Figure 2.38** Fish Creek index.html

Launch a text editor, and create a web page with the following specifications:

1. **Web Page Title.** Use a descriptive page title. The company name is a good choice for the home page of a business website. On pages other than the home page, the title typically contains both the company name and a word or a phrase that describes the purpose of the page.

2. **Wireframe Header.** Code the header element with the text, "Fish Creek Animal Clinic" contained within a heading 1 element.

3. **Wireframe Navigation.** Place the following text within a nav element with bold text (use the `<b>` element)

   Home Services Ask the Vet Contact

   Code anchor tags so that "Home" links to index.html, "Services" links to services.html, "Ask the Vet" links to askvet.html, and "Contact" links to contact.html. Add extra blank spaces between the hyperlinks with the ` ` special character as needed.

4. **Wireframe Main Content.** Code the main page content within a main element. Use Hands-On Practice 2.10 as a guide.

   a. Code the following text within an h2 element:

   Professional, Compassionate Care for your Pet

   b. Code the following text within a paragraph element:

   The caring doctors and staff at Fish Creek Animal Clinic understand the special bond you share with your cherished pet.

   c. Code the following content in a description list. Configure the text in each dt element to have strong importance and display in bold font weight:

   **Years of Experience**

   Fish Creek Veterinarians have provided personalized and compassionate care since 1984.

**Open Door Policy**

We welcome owners to stay with their pets during any medical procedure.

**Always Available**

Our professionals are on duty 24 hours a day, 7 days a week.

**d.** Configure the following address and phone number contact information within a div element below the description list. Use line break tags to help you format this area.

Fish Creek Animal Clinic

800-555-5555

1242 Grassy Lane

Fish Creek, WI 55534

5. **Wireframe Footer.** Code the following copyright and e-mail link information within a footer element. Format it with small text size (use the `<small>` tag) and italics font style (use the `<i>` tag).

Copyright © 2020 Fish Creek Animal Clinic

Place your name in an e-mail link on the line under the copyright.

The page in Figure 2.38 may seem a little sparse, but don't worry; as you gain experience and learn to use more advanced techniques, your pages will look more professional. White space (blank space) on the page can be added with `<br>` tags where needed. Your page does not need to look exactly the same as the sample. Your goal at this point should be to practice and get comfortable using HTML.

Save your page in the fishcreek folder, and name it index.html.

**Task 3: The Services Page.** Create the Services page shown in Figure 2.39. A technique that improves productivity is to create new pages based on existing pages so that you can benefit from your previous work. Your new Services page will use the index.html page as a starting point.

Open the index.html page for the Fish Creek website in a text editor. Select File > Save As, and save the file with the new name of services.html in the fishcreek folder. Now you are ready to edit the page.

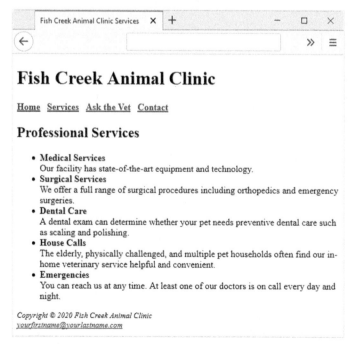

Figure 2.39  Fish Creek services.html

1. **Web Page Title.** Modify the page title. Change the text contained between the `<title>` and `</title>` tags to the following:

   Fish Creek Animal Clinic Services

2. **Wireframe Main Content.**

   a. Delete the Home page content paragraph, description list, and contact information.

   b. Replace the text in the h2 element with the following:

   Professional Services

   c. Use an unordered list to add the services content to the page. Configure the name of each services category to use bold font weight and have strong emphasis. (Use the <strong> tag.) Use line break tags to help you configure this area. The service categories and descriptions are as follows:

   **Medical Services**

   Our facility has state-of-the-art equipment and technology.

   **Surgical Services**

   We offer a full range of surgical procedures including orthopedics and emergency surgeries.

   **Dental Care**

   A dental exam can determine whether your pet needs preventive dental care such as scaling and polishing.

   **House Calls**

   The elderly, physically challenged, and multiple pet households often find our in-home veterinary service helpful and convenient.

   **Emergencies**

   You can reach us at any time. At least one of our doctors is on call every day and night.

Save your page, and test it in a browser. Test the hyperlink from the services.html page to index.html. Test the hyperlink from the index.html page to services.html. If your links do not work, review your work, paying close attention to these details:

- Verify that you have saved the pages with the correct names in the correct folder.
- Verify your spelling of the page names in the anchor elements.

Test again after you make changes.

## Pacific Trails Resort

Melanie Bowie is the owner of Pacific Trails Resort, located on the California North Coast. The resort offers a quiet getaway, with luxury camping in yurts along with an upscale lodge for dining and visiting with fellow guests. The target audience for Pacific Trails Resort is couples who enjoy nature and hiking. Melanie would like a website that emphasizes the uniqueness of the location and accommodations. She would like the website to include a home page, a page about the special yurt accommodations, a reservations page with a contact form, and a page to describe the activities available at the resort.

A site map for the Pacific Trails Resort website is shown in Figure 2.40. The site map describes the architecture of the website, which consists of a "Home" page with three main content pages: "Yurts," "Activities," and "Reservations."

Figure 2.40 Pacific Trails Resort site map

Figure 2.41 displays a wireframe sketch of the page layout for the website. It contains a header area, a navigation area, a main content area, and a footer area for copyright information.

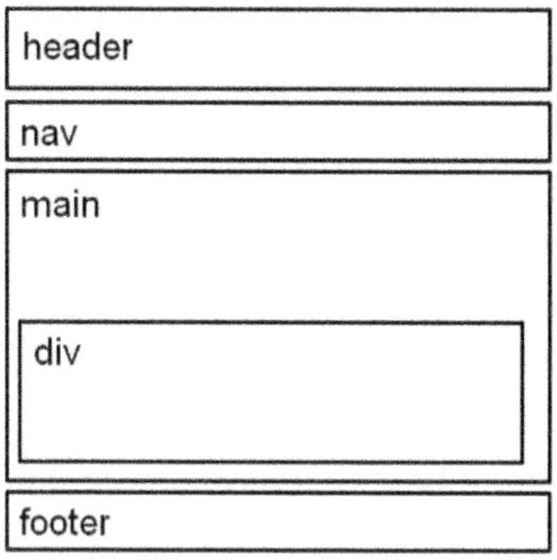

| header |
| --- |
| nav |
| main |
| div |
| footer |

Figure 2.41 Pacific Trails Resort wireframe

You have three tasks in this case study:

1. Create a folder for the Pacific Trails website.

2. Create the Home page: index.html.

3. Create the Yurts page: yurts.html.

## Hands-On Practice Case Study

**Task 1: The Website Folder.** Create a folder on your hard drive or portable storage device (thumb drive or SD card) called "pacific" to contain your Pacific Trails Resort website files.

**Task 2: The Home Page.** You will use a text editor to create the Home page for the Pacific Trails Resort website. The Home page is shown in Figure 2.42.

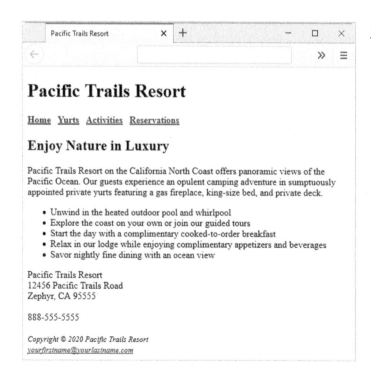

Figure 2.42 Pacific Trails Resort index.html

Launch a text editor, and create a web page with the following specifications:

1. **Web Page Title.** Use a descriptive page title. The company name is a good choice for the home page of a business website. On pages other than the home page, the title typically contains both the company name and a word or a phrase that describes the purpose of the page.

2. **Wireframe Header.** Code the header element with the text, "Pacific Trails Resort" contained within a heading 1 element.

3. **Wireframe Navigation.** Place the following text within a nav element with bold text (use the `<b>` element):

   Home Yurts Activities Reservations

   Code anchor tags so that "Home" links to index.html, "Yurts" links to yurts.html, "Activities" links to activities.html, and "Reservations" links to reservations.html. Add extra blank spaces between the hyperlinks with the ` ` special character as needed.

4. **Wireframe Main Content.** Code the main page content within a main element. Use Hands-On Practice 2.10 as a guide.

   **a.** Code the following text within an h2 element:

   Enjoy Nature in Luxury

   **b.** Configure the following sentences in a paragraph:

   Pacific Trails Resort on the California North Coast offers panoramic views of the Pacific Ocean. Our guests experience an opulent camping adventure in sumptuously appointed private yurts featuring a gas fireplace, king-size bed, and private deck.

   **c.** Code the following content in an unordered list:

   Unwind in the heated outdoor pool and whirlpool

   Explore the coast on your own or join our guided tours

   Start the day with a complimentary cooked-to-order breakfast

   Relax in our lodge while enjoying complimentary appetizers and beverages

   Savor nightly fine dining with an ocean view

   **d.** Configure the following address and phone number contact information within a div element below the unordered list. Use line break tags to help you format this area.

   Pacific Trails Resort

   12010 Pacific Trails Road

   Zephyr, CA 95555

   888-555-5555

5. **Wireframe Footer.** Configure the following copyright and e-mail link information within a footer element. Format it with small text size (use the `<small>` tag) and italics font style (use the `<i>` tag).

   Copyright © 2020 Pacific Trails Resort

   Place your name in an e-mail link on the line under the copyright.

The page in Figure 2.42 may seem a little sparse, but don't worry; as you gain experience and learn to use more advanced techniques, your pages will look more professional. White space (blank space) on the page can be added with `<br>` tags where needed. Your page does not need to look exactly the same as the sample. Your goal at this point should be to practice and get comfortable using HTML.

Save your page in the pacific folder, and name it index.html.

**Task 3: The Yurts Page.** Create the Yurts page shown in Figure 2.43. A technique that improves productivity is to create new pages based on existing pages so that you can benefit from your previous work. Your new Yurts page will use the index.html page as a starting point.

**Figure 2.43** Pacific Trails Resort yurts.html

Open the index.html page for the Pacific Trails Resort website in a text editor. Select File > Save As, and save the file with the new name of yurts.html in the pacific folder. Now you are ready to edit the page.

1. **Web Page Title.** Modify the page title. Change the text contained between the `<title>` and `</title>` tags to the following:

   Pacific Trails Resort :: Yurts

2. **Wireframe Main Content.**

   **a.** Replace the text in the h2 element with the following:

   The Yurts at Pacific Trails

   **b.** Delete the Home page content paragraph, unordered list, and contact information.

   **c.** Add the yurts content to the page as a FAQs (frequently asked questions) list by using a description list. Configure each question to have strong importance and bold font weight (use the `<strong>` phrase element) within a dt element. Configure each answer within a dd element. The text is shown as follows:

   **What is a yurt?**

   Our luxury yurts are permanent structures four feet off the ground. Each yurt has canvas walls, a wooden floor, a roof dome that can be opened, and a private deck.

### How are the yurts furnished?

Each yurt is furnished with a gas fireplace, king-size bed with down quilt, comfy couch, dining table and chairs, mini-fridge, microwave, and coffee maker. Your luxury camping experience includes a sink with hot and cold running water. Shower and restroom facilities are located in the lodge.

### What should I bring?

Most guests pack comfortable walking shoes and plan to dress for changing weather with light layers of clothing. It's also helpful to bring a flashlight and a sense of adventure!

Save your page, and test it in a browser. Test the hyperlink from the yurts.html page to index.html. Test the hyperlink from the index.html page to yurts.html. If your links do not work, review your work, paying close attention to these details:

- Verify that you have saved the pages with the correct names in the correct folder.

- Verify your spelling of the page names in the anchor elements.

Test again after you make the changes.

## Path of Light Yoga Studio

Path of Light Yoga Studio is a small, recently opened yoga studio. The owner, Ariana Starrweaver, would like a website to showcase her yoga studio and provide information for both new and current students. Ariana would like a home page, a classes page that contains information about the types of yoga classes offered, a schedule page, and a contact page.

A site map for the Path of Light Yoga Studio website is shown in Figure 2.44. The site map describes the architecture of the website, which consists of "Home" page with three main content pages: "Classes," "Schedule," and "Contact."

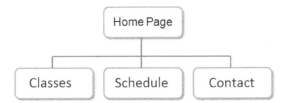

Figure 2.44  Path of Light Yoga Studio site map

Figure 2.45 displays a wireframe sketch of the page layout for the website. It contains a header area, a navigation area, a main content area, and a footer area for copyright information.

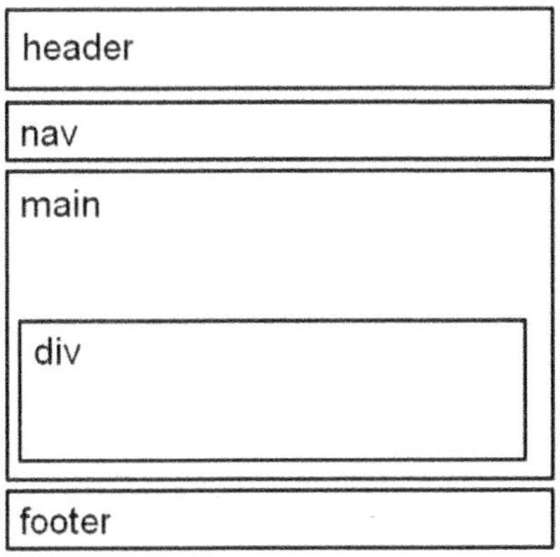

Figure 2.45  Path of Light Yoga Studio wireframe

| header |
|---|
| nav |
| main |
| div |
| footer |

You have three tasks in this case study:

1. Create a folder for the Path of Light Yoga Studio website.

2. Create the Home page: index.html.

3. Create the Classes page: classes.html.

## Hands-On Practice Case Study

**Task 1: The Website Folder.**  Create a folder on your hard drive or portable storage device (thumb drive or SD card) called "yoga" to contain your Path of Light Yoga Studio web page files.

**Task 2: The Home Page.**  You will use a text editor to create the Home page for the Path of Light Yoga Studio website. The Home page is shown in Figure 2.46.

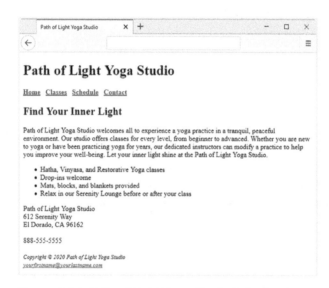

**Figure 2.46**  Path of Light Yoga Studio index.html

Launch a text editor, and create a web page with the following specifications:

1. **Web Page Title.**  Use a descriptive page title. The company name is a good choice for the home page of a business website. On pages other than the home page, the title typically contains both the company name and a word or a phrase that describes the purpose of the page.

2. **Wireframe Header.**  Code the header element with the text, "Path of Light Yoga Studio" contained within a heading 1 element.

3. **Wireframe Navigation.**  Place the following text within a nav element with bold text (use the <b> element):

   Home Classes Schedule Contact

   Code anchor tags so that "Home" links to index.html, "Classes" links to classes.html, "Schedule" links to schedule.html, and "Contact" links to contact.html. Add extra blank spaces between the hyperlinks with the   special character as needed.

4. **Wireframe Main Content.**  Code the main page content within a main element. Use Hands-On Practice 2.10 as a guide.

   a. Code the following text within an h2 element:

      Find Your Inner Light

**b.** Configure the following sentences in a paragraph:

Path of Light Yoga Studio welcomes all to experience a yoga practice in a tranquil, peaceful environment. Our studio offers classes for every level, from beginner to advanced. Whether you are new to yoga or have been practicing yoga for years, our dedicated instructors can modify a practice to help you improve your well-being. Let your inner light shine at the Path of Light Yoga Studio.

**c.** Configure the following content in an unordered list:

Hatha, Vinyasa, and Restorative Yoga classes

Drop-ins welcome

Mats, blocks, and blankets provided

Relax in our Serenity Lounge before or after your class

**d.** Code the following address and phone number contact information within a div element. Use line break tags to help you configure this area and add extra space between the phone number and the footer area.

Path of Light Yoga Studio

612 Serenity Way

El Dorado, CA 96162

888-555-5555

5. **Wireframe Footer.** Configure the following copyright and e-mail link information within a footer element. Format it with small text size (use the <small> tag) and italics font style (use the <i> tag)

Copyright © 2020 Path of Light Yoga Studio

Place your name in an e-mail link on the line under the copyright information.

The page in Figure 2.46 may seem a little sparse, but don't worry; as you gain experience and learn to use more advanced techniques, your pages will look more professional. White space (blank space) on the page can be added with <br> tags where needed. Your page does not need to look exactly the same as the sample. Your goal at this point should be to practice and get comfortable using HTML.

Save your page in the yoga folder, and name it index.html.

**Task 3: The Classes Page.** Create the Classes page shown in Figure 2.47. A technique that improves productivity is to create new pages based on existing pages so that you can benefit from your previous work. Your new Classes page will use the index.html page as a starting point.

Open the index.html page for the Path of Light Yoga Studio website in a text editor. Select File > Save As, and save the file with the new name of classes.html in the yoga folder. Now you are ready to edit the page.

1. **Web Page Title.** Modify the page title. Change the text contained between the <title> and </title> tags to the following:

Path of Light Yoga Studio :: Classes

2. **Wireframe Main Content.**

**a.** Delete the Home Page content paragraphs, unordered list, and contact information.

**b.** Configure the following text in the heading 2 element:

Yoga Classes

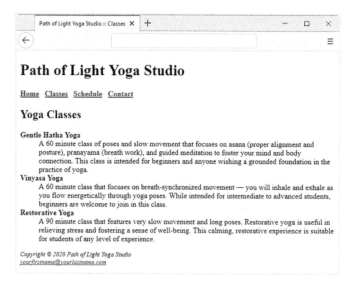

Figure 2.47  Path of Light Yoga Studio classes.html

c. Use a description list to configure information about the yoga classes. Configure the name of each class to have strong importance and bold font weight (use the `<strong>` phrase element) within a dt element. Configure `<dd>` elements for the class descriptions. The information follows:

Gentle Hatha Yoga

A 60 minute class of poses and slow movement that focuses on asana (proper alignment and posture), pranayama (breath work), and guided meditation to foster your mind and body connection. This class is intended for beginners and anyone wishing a grounded foundation in the practice of yoga.

Vinyasa Yoga

A 60 minute class that focuses on breath-synchronized movement — you will inhale and exhale as you flow energetically through yoga poses. While intended for intermediate to advanced students, beginners are welcome to join in this class.

Restorative Yoga

A 90 minute class that features very slow movement and long poses. Restorative yoga is useful in relieving stress and fostering a sense of well-being. This calming, restorative experience is suitable for students of any level of experience.

Save your page and test it in a browser. Test the hyperlink from the classes.html page to index.html. Test the hyperlink from the index.html page to classes.html. If your links do not work, review your work with close attention to these details:

- Verify that you have saved the pages with the correct names in the correct folder.

- Verify your spelling of the page names in the anchor elements.

Test again after you make the changes.

# Configuring Color and Text with CSS

**Chapter Objectives**  In this chapter, you will learn how to . . .

- Describe the evolution of style sheets from print media to the Web
- List advantages of using Cascading Style Sheets
- Configure background and text color on web pages
- Create style sheets that configure common color and text properties
- Apply inline styles
- Use embedded style sheets
- Use external style sheets
- Configure element, class, id, and descendant selectors
- Utilize the "cascade" in CSS
- Validate CSS

**Now that you have been introduced to HTML,** let's explore **Cascading Style Sheets (CSS).** Web designers use CSS to separate the presentation style of a web page from the information on the web page. CSS is used to configure text, color, and page layout. CSS is not new—it was first proposed as a standard by the W3C in 1996. In 1998, additional properties for positioning web page elements were introduced to the language with CSS level 2 (CSS2), which was used for over a decade before reaching official "recommendation" status in 2011. CSS level 3 (CSS3) properties support features such as embedding fonts, rounded corners, and transparency. The CSS specification is divided into modules, each with a specific purpose. These modules move along the approval process independently. The W3C continues to evolve CSS, with proposals for many types of properties and functionality currently in draft form. This chapter introduces you to the use of CSS on the Web as you explore how to configure color and text.

# 3.1  Overview of Cascading Style Sheets

For years, style sheets have been used in desktop publishing to apply typographic styles and spacing instructions to printed media. CSS provides this functionality (and much more) for web developers. CSS allows web developers to apply typographic styles (typeface, font size, and so on) and page layout instructions to a web page. The CSS Zen Garden, http://www.csszengarden.com, exemplifies the power and flexibility of CSS. Visit this web site for an example of CSS in action. Notice how the content looks dramatically different depending on the design (CSS style rules) you select. Although the designs on the CSS Zen Garden are created by CSS masters, at some point these designers were just like you—starting out with CSS basics.

CSS is a flexible, cross-platform, standards-based language developed by the W3C. The W3C's description of CSS can be found at https://www.w3.org/Style/CSS. Be aware that even though CSS has been in use for many years, it is still considered an emerging technology, and different browsers do not support it in exactly the same way. We concentrate on aspects of CSS that are well supported by popular browsers.

## Advantages of Cascading Style Sheets

There are several advantages to using CSS (see Figure 3.1):

- **Typography and page layout can be better controlled.** These features include font size, line spacing, letter spacing, indents, margins, and element positioning.

- **Style is separate from structure.** The format of the text and colors used on the page can be configured and stored separately from the body section of the web page document.

- **Styles can be stored.** You can store styles in a separate document and associate them with the web page. When the styles are modified, the HTML remains intact. This means, for example, that if your client decides to change the background color of a set of web pages from red to white, you only need to change one file that contains the styles, instead of modifying each web page document.

- **Documents are potentially smaller.** The formatting is separate from the document; therefore, the actual documents should be smaller.

- **Site maintenance is easier.** Again, if the styles need to be changed, then it is possible to complete the modifications by changing the style sheet only.

**Figure 3.1** The power of a single CSS file

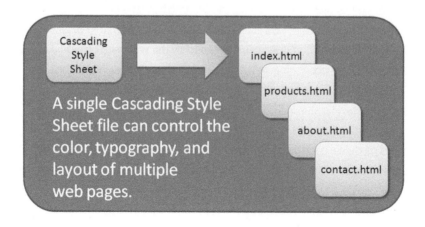

Cascading Style Sheet

index.html

products.html

about.html

contact.html

A single Cascading Style Sheet file can control the color, typography, and layout of multiple web pages.

## Configuring Cascading Style Sheets

Web developers use four methods to incorporate CSS technology: inline, embedded, external, and imported.

- **Inline styles** are coded in the body of the web page as an attribute of an HTML tag. The style applies only to the specific element that contains it as an attribute.

- **Embedded styles** (also referred to as **internal styles**) are defined within a style element in the head section of a web page. These style instructions apply to the entire web page document.

- **External styles** are coded in a separate text file. This text file is associated with the web page by configuring a link element in the head section.

- **Imported styles** are similar to external styles in that they can connect styles coded in a separate text file with a web page document. An external style sheet can be imported into embedded styles or into another external style sheet by using the @import directive.

## CSS Selectors and Declarations

Style sheets are composed of style rules that describe the styling to be applied. Each **rule** has two parts: a **selector** and a **declaration**:

- **CSS Style Rule Selector**  The selector can be an HTML element name, a class name, or an id name. In this section, we will focus on applying styles to element name selectors. We will work with class selectors and id selectors later in this chapter.

- **CSS Style Rule Declaration**  The declaration indicates the CSS **property** you are setting (such as color) and the value you are assigning to the property.

For example, the CSS rule shown in Figure 3.2 would set the color of the text used on a web page to blue. The selector is the body tag, and the declaration sets the color property to the value of blue.

**Figure 3.2**
Using CSS to set the text color to blue

## The background-color Property

The CSS **background-color property** configures the background color of an element. The following style rule will configure the background color of a web page to be yellow. Notice how the declaration is enclosed within braces and how the colon symbol (:) separates the declaration property and the declaration value.

```
body { background-color: yellow }
```

## The color Property

The CSS **color property** configures the text (foreground) color of an element. The following CSS style rule will configure the text color of a web page to be blue:

```
body { color: blue }
```

## Configure Background and Text Color

Figure 3.3 displays a web page with a white text and an orchid background. To configure more than one property for a selector, use a semicolon (;) to separate the declarations as follows:

```
body { color: white; background-color: orchid; }
```

**Figure 3.3**
A web page with orchid background color and white text color

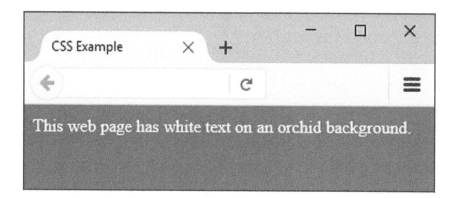

The spaces in these declarations are optional. The ending semicolon (;) is also optional, but useful in case you need to add additional style rules at a later time. The following code samples are also valid:

```
body {color:white;background-color:orchid}
body { color: white;
       background-color: orchid; }
body {
    color: white;
    background-color: orchid;
}
```

You might be asking yourself how you would know what properties and values can be used. See the CSS Property Reference in Appendix C for a detailed list of CSS properties. This chapter introduces you to some of the CSS properties commonly used to configure color and text, shown in Table 3.1. In the next sections, we'll take a look at how color is used on web pages.

Table 3.1 CSS properties introduced in this chapter

| Property | Description | Values |
|---|---|---|
| background-color | Background color of an element | Any valid color |
| color | Foreground (text) color of an element | Any valid color |
| font-family | Name of a font or font family | Any valid font or a font family such as serif, sans-serif, fantasy, monospace, or cursive |
| font-size | Size of the font | Varies; a numeric value with pt (standard font **point** sizes) or px (**pixels**) units or the unit em (which corresponds to the width of the uppercase M of the current font); a numeric percentage; and the text values xx-small, x-small, small, medium, large, x-large, and xx-large |
| font-style | Style of the font | normal, italic, or oblique |
| font-weight | The "boldness" or weight of the font | Varies; the text values normal, bold, bolder, and lighter and the numeric values 100, 200, 300, 400, 500, 600, 700, 800, and 900 |
| letter-spacing | The space between characters | A numeric value (px or em) or normal (default) |
| line-height | The spacing allowed for the line of text | It is most common to use a percentage for this value; for example, a value of 200% would correspond to double-spacing. |
| margin | Shorthand notation to configure the margin surrounding an element | A numeric value (px or em); for example, body {margin: 10px} will set the page margins in the document to 10 pixels. When eliminating the margin, do not use the px or em unit—for example, body {margin:0} |
| margin-left | Configures the space in the left margin of the element | A numeric value (px or em), auto, or 0 |
| margin-right | Configures the space in the right margin of the element | A numeric value (px or em), auto, or 0 |
| text-align | The alignment of text | center, justify, left, or right |
| text-decoration | Determines whether text is underlined; this style is most often applied to hyperlinks | The value "none" will cause a hyperlink not to be underlined in a browser that normally processes in this manner |
| text-indent | Configures the indentation of the first line of text | Numeric value (px or em) or percentage |
| text-shadow | Configures a drop shadow on the text displayed within an element. This CSS3 property is not supported in all browsers. | Two to four numerical values (px or em) to indicate horizontal offset, vertical offset, blur radius (optional), spread distance (optional), and a valid color value. |
| text-transform | Configures the capitalization of text | none (default), capitalize, uppercase, or lowercase |
| white-space | Configures the display of whitespace | normal (default), nowrap, pre, pre-line, or pre-wrap |
| width | The width of the content of an element | A numeric value (px or em), numeric percentage, or auto (default) |
| word-spacing | The space between words | A numeric value (px or em) or normal (default) |

# 3.2 Using Color on Web Pages

Monitors display color as a combination of different intensities of red, green, and blue, a concept known as **RGB color**. RGB intensity values are numerical from 0 to 255. Each RGB color has three values, one each for red, green, and blue. These values are always listed in the same order (red, green, blue) and specify the numerical value of each color

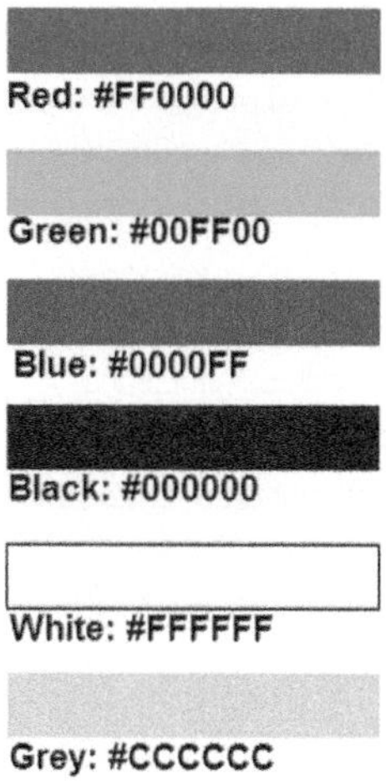

Red: #FF0000

Green: #00FF00

Blue: #0000FF

Black: #000000

White: #FFFFFF

Grey: #CCCCCC

Figure 3.4 Color swatches and hexadecimal color values

used (see the examples in Figure 3.4). You will usually use hexadecimal color values to specify RGB color on web pages.

## Hexadecimal Color Values

Hexadecimal is the name for the base-16 numbering system, which uses the characters 0, 1, 2, 3, 4, 5, 6, 7, 8, 9, A, B, C, D, E, and F to specify numeric values. **Hexadecimal color values** specify RGB color with numeric value pairs ranging from 00 to FF (0 to 255 in base 10). Each pair is associated with the amount of red, green, and blue displayed. Using this notation, one would specify the color red as #FF0000 and the color blue as #0000FF. The # symbol signifies that the value is hexadecimal. You can use either uppercase or lowercase letters in hexadecimal color values; #FF0000 and #ff0000 both configure the color red.

Don't worry—you won't need to do calculations to work with web colors. Just become familiar with the numbering scheme. See Figure 3.5 for an excerpt from the color chart at http://webdevfoundations.net/color.

| | | | | | |
|---|---|---|---|---|---|
| #FFFFFF | #FFFFCC | #FFFF99 | #FFFF66 | #FFFF33 | #FFFF00 |
| #FFCCFF | #FFCCCC | #FFCC99 | #FFCC66 | #FFCC33 | #FFCC00 |
| #FF99FF | #FF99CC | #FF9999 | #FF9966 | #FF9933 | #FF9900 |
| #FF66FF | #FF66CC | #FF6699 | #FF6666 | #FF6633 | #FF6600 |
| #FF33FF | #FF33CC | #FF3399 | #FF3366 | #FF3333 | #FF3300 |
| #FF00FF | #FF00CC | #FF0099 | #FF0066 | #FF0033 | #FF0000 |

Figure 3.5 Partial color chart

## Web-Safe Colors

Back in the day of 8-bit color monitors, web page color could be problematic and it was important to use one of the 216 **web-safe colors**, which display in a similar manner on both the Mac and PC platforms. The hexadecimal color values of web-safe colors use the numerals 00, 33, 66, 99, CC, and FF. The 216 web-safe colors make up the **Web-Safe Color Palette**, found in the Appendix (also at http://webdevfoundations.net/color). Now that most monitors display millions of colors, using web-safe colors is less important. The Web-Safe Color Palette is rather limited, and it is common for today's web designers to choose colors creatively rather than select them only from the palette.

## CSS Color Syntax

CSS syntax allows you to configure colors in a variety of ways:

- color name
- hexadecimal color value
- hexadecimal shorthand color value
- decimal color value (RGB triplet)
- HSL (Hue, Saturation, and Lightness) color value notation (see Chapter 4)

We'll typically use hexadecimal color values in this book. Table 3.2 shows CSS syntax examples that configure a paragraph with red text.

Table 3.2 CSS color syntax examples

| CSS Syntax | Color Type |
| --- | --- |
| p { color: red; } | Color name |
| p { color: #FF0000; } | Hexadecimal color value |
| p { color: #F00; } | Shorthand hexadecimal (one character for each hexadecimal pair; used only with web-safe colors) |
| p { color: rgb(255,0,0); } | Decimal color value (RGB triplet) |
| p { color: hsl(0, 100%, 50%); } | HSL color values |

**FAQ    How do I choose a color scheme for a web page?**

There's a lot to consider when you select a color scheme for a website. The colors that you choose set the tone and help to create a web presence for the company or organization that appeals to the target audience. The colors you choose for text and background need to have good contrast in order to be readable. We'll explore techniques for choosing a color scheme in Chapter 5.

# 3.3  Inline CSS with the Style Attribute

Recall that there are four methods for configuring CSS: inline, embedded, external, and imported. In this section, we focus on inline CSS using the style attribute.

## The Style Attribute

Inline styles are coded as an attribute on an HTML tag using the **style attribute**. The value of the style attribute is set to the style rule declaration that you need to configure. Recall that a declaration consists of a property and a value. Each property is separated from its value with a colon (:). The following code will use inline styles to set the text color of an <h1> tag to a shade of red:

```
<h1 style="color:#cc0000">This is displayed as a red heading</h1>
```

If there is more than one property, they are separated by a semicolon (;). The following code configures the heading with a red text color and a gray background color:

```
<h1 style="color:#cc0000;background-color:#cccccc">
This is displayed as a red heading on a gray background</h1>
```

# Hands-On Practice 3.1

In this Hands-On Practice, you will configure a web page with inline styles. The inline styles will specify the following:

- Global body tag styles for an off-white background with teal text. These styles will be inherited by other elements by default. For example:

```
<body style="background-color:#F5F5F5;color:#008080;">
```

- Styles for an h1 element with a teal background with off-white text. This style will override the global styles configured on the body element. For example:

```
<h1 style="background-color:#008080;color:#F5F5F5;">
```

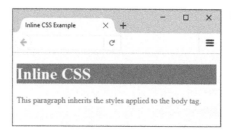

**Figure 3.6** Web page using inline styles

A sample is shown in Figure 3.6. Launch a text editor. Select File > Open to edit the template file located at chapter3/template.html in the student files. Modify the title element, and add heading tags, paragraph tags, style attributes, and text to the body section as indicated by the following code:

```
<!DOCTYPE html>
<html lang="en">
<head>
<title>Inline CSS Example</title>
<meta charset="utf-8">
</head>
<body style="background-color:#F5F5F5;color:#008080;">
<h1 style="background-color:#008080;color:#F5F5F5;">Inline CSS</h1>
<p>This paragraph inherits the styles applied to the body tag.</p>
</body>
</html>
```

Save the document as inline.html on your hard drive or flash drive. Launch a browser to test your page. It should look similar to the page shown in Figure 3.6. Note that the inline styles applied to the body tag are inherited by other elements on the page (such as the paragraph) unless more-specific styles are specified (such as those coded on the `<h1>` tag). You can compare your work with the solution found in the student files (chapter3/inline.html).

Let's continue and add another paragraph, with the text color configured to be dark gray:

```
<p style="color:#333333">This paragraph overrides the text color style
applied to the body tag.</p>
```

Figure 3.7 The second paragraph's inline styles override the global styles configured on the body tag

Save the document as inlinep.html. It should look similar to the page shown in Figure 3.7. You can compare your work with the solution found in the student files (chapter3/inlinep.html). Note that the inline styles applied to the second paragraph override the global styles applied to the body of the web page.

## FAQ    **Are inline styles recommended?**

While inline styles can sometimes be useful, you'll find that you won't use this technique much in practice—it's inefficient, adds extra code to the web page document, and is inconvenient to maintain. However, inline styles can be quite handy in some circumstances, such as when you post an article to a content management system or blog and need to tweak the sitewide styles a bit to help get your point across.

# 3.4 Embedded CSS with the Style Element

In the previous Hands-On Practice, you added inline styles for one of the paragraphs. To do so, you coded a style attribute on the paragraph element. But what if you needed to configure the styles for 10 or 20 paragraphs instead of just one? Using inline styles, you might be doing a lot of repetitive coding! While inline styles apply to one HTML element, embedded styles apply to an entire web page.

## Style Element

The opening `<style>` tag and the closing `</style>` tag contain the list of embedded style rules. Embedded styles apply to the entire document and are typically placed within a style element located in the head section of a web page. Note that while HTML 5.2 also allows the style element in the body section, we'll always code the style element in the head section.

The web page in Figure 3.8 uses embedded styles to set the text color and background color of the web page document with the body element selector. See the example in the student files at chapter3/embed.html. The code follows:

Figure 3.8 Web page with embedded styles

```
<!DOCTYPE html>
<html lang="en">
<head>
<title>Embedded Styles</title>
<meta charset="utf-8">
```

```
<style>
body { background-color: #E6E6FA;
       color: #191970;
}
</style>
</head>
<body>
<h1>Embedded CSS</h1>
<p>This page uses embedded styles.</p>
</body>
</html>
```

Notice the way the style rules were coded, with each rule on its own line. This formatting is not required for the styles to work, but it makes the styles more readable and easier to maintain than one long row of text. The styles are in effect for the entire web page document because they were applied to the <body> tag using the body element selector.

## Hands-On Practice 3.2

Launch a text editor, and open the starter.html file from the chapter3 folder in the student files. Save your page as embedded.html, and test it in a browser. Your page should look similar to the one shown in Figure 3.9.

**Figure 3.9** The web page without any styles

Open the file in a text editor, and view the source code. Notice that the web page code uses the <header>, <nav>, <main>, <footer>, <h1>, <h2>, <p>, <ul>, and <li> elements. In this Hands-On Practice, you will code embedded styles to configure selected background and text colors. You will use the body element selector to configure the default background color (#E2FFFF) and default text color (#15495E) for the entire page. You will also use the h1 and h2 element selectors to configure different background and text colors for the heading areas. Edit the embedded.html file in a text editor, and add the following code below the `<title>` element in the head section of the web page:

```
<style>
body { background-color: #E2FFFF; color: #15495E; }
h1 { background-color: #237B7B; color: #E2FFFF; }
h2 { background-color: #B0E6E6; color: #237B7B; }
</style>
```

Save your file, and test it in a browser. Figure 3.10 displays the web page along with corresponding color swatches. A teal monochromatic color scheme was chosen. Notice how the repetition of a limited number of colors unifies the design of the web page. View the source code for your page, and review the CSS and HTML code. An example of this web page is in the student files at chapter3/3.2/index.html. Note that all the styles were located in a single place on the web page. Since embedded styles are coded in a specific location, they are easier to maintain over time than inline styles. Also, notice that you coded the styles for the h2 element selector only once (in the head section), and *both* of the `<h2>` elements applied the h2 style. This approach is more efficient than coding the same inline style on each `<h2>` element. However, it is uncommon for a website to have only one page. Repeating the CSS in the head section of each web page file is inefficient and difficult to maintain. In the next section, you'll use a more productive approach—configuring an external style sheet.

Figure 3.10 The web page after embedded styles are configured

FAQ **My CSS doesn't work; what can I do?**

Coding CSS is a detail-oriented process. There are several common errors that can cause the browser not to apply CSS correctly to a web page. With a careful review of your code and the following tips, you should get your CSS working:

- Verify that you are using the colon (:) and semicolon (;) symbols in the right spots— they are easy to confuse. The colon should separate the properties from their values, while the semicolon should be placed between each `property:value` configuration.

- Check that you are not using equal (=) signs instead of colons (:) between each property and its value.

- Verify that curly braces ({ and }) are properly placed around the style rules for each selector.

- Check the syntax of your selectors, the selectors' properties, and the property values for correct usage.

- If part of your CSS works and part doesn't, read through the CSS and determine the first rule that is not applied. Often, the error is in the rule above the rule that is not applied.

- Use a validation application to check your CSS code. The W3C has a free CSS code validator at http://jigsaw.w3.org/css-validator. The W3C's CSS validator can help you find syntax errors. See Section 3.11 for an overview of how to use this tool to validate your CSS.

 **Checkpoint 3.1**

1. List three reasons to use CSS on a web page.

2. When designing a page that uses colors other than the default colors for text and background, explain why it is a good reason to configure both the text color and the background color.

3. Describe one advantage to using embedded styles instead of inline styles.

# 3.5  Configuring Text with CSS

In Chapter 2, you discovered how to use HTML to configure some characteristics of text on web pages, including phrase elements such as the `<strong>` element. You have also already configured text color using the CSS color property. In this section, you will learn to use CSS to configure font typeface. Using CSS to configure text is more flexible (especially when using an external style sheet, as you will discover later in the chapter) than using HTML elements and is the method preferred by modern web developers.

## The `font-family` Property

The **font-family property** configures font typeface. A web browser displays text using the fonts that have been installed on the user's computer. When a font is specified that is not installed on your web visitor's computer, the default font is substituted. Times New Roman is the default font displayed by most web browsers. Figure 3.11 shows font family categories.

The Verdana, Tahoma, and Georgia font typefaces were specifically designed to display well on computer monitors. A common practice is to use a serif font (such as Georgia or Times New Roman) for headings and a sans-serif font (such as Verdana or Arial) for detailed text content. Not every computer has the same fonts installed. See http://www.ampsoft.net/webdesign-l/WindowsMacFonts.html for a list of web-safe fonts. Create a built-in backup plan by listing multiple fonts and categories for the value of the font-family property. The browser will attempt to use the fonts in the order listed. The following CSS configures the p element selector to display text in Arial (if installed), Helvetica (if installed), or the default installed sans-serif font:

```
p { font-family: Arial, Helvetica, sans-serif; }
```

| Font Family Category | Font Family Description | Font Typeface Examples |
|---|---|---|
| serif | Serif fonts have small embellishments on the end of letter strokes; often used for headings. | Times New Roman, Georgia, Palatino |
| sans-serif | Sans-serif fonts do not have serifs; often used for web page text. | Arial, **Tahoma**, Helvetica, Verdana |
| monospace | Fixed-width font; often used for code samples. | Courier New, Lucida Console |
| cursive | Hand-written style; use with caution; may be difficult to read on a web page. | *Lucida Handwriting*, *Brush Script*, Comic Sans MS |
| fantasy | Exaggerated style; use with caution; sometimes used for headings; may be difficult to read on a web page. | Jokerman, **Impact**, Papyrus |

Figure 3.11
Common fonts

## Hands-On Practice 3.3

Launch a text editor, and open the starter2.html file from the chapter3 folder in the student files.

Locate the style tags in the head section, and code embedded CSS to style the following:

1. Configure the body element selector to set global styles to use a sans-serif font typeface, such as Verdana or Arial. An example is

```
body { font-family: Verdana, Arial, sans-serif; }
```

2. Configure h2 and h3 element selectors to use a serif font typeface, such as Georgia or Times New Roman. You can configure more than one selector in a styles rule by placing a comma before each new selector. Notice that "Times New Roman" is enclosed within quotation marks because the font name is more than a single word. Code the following style rule:

```
h2, h3 { font-family: Georgia, "Times New Roman", serif; }
```

Save your page as index.html in a folder named kayak3. Launch a browser and test your page. It should look similar to the one shown in Figure 3.12. A sample solution is in the chapter3/3.3 folder.

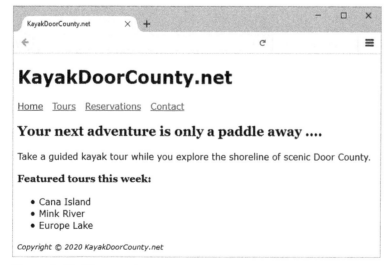

Figure 3.12  The new home page

**FAQ**   **I've heard about "embedding" fonts in order to use special fonts on a web page—what's that all about?**

For many years, web designers have been limited to a set of common fonts for text on web pages. CSS3 introduced @font-face, which can be used to "embed" other fonts within web pages although you actually provide the location of the font and the browser downloads it. For example, if you own the rights to freely distribute the font named MyAwesomeFont and it is stored in a file myawesomefont.woff in the same folder as your web page, the following CSS will make it available to your web page visitors:

```
@font-face { font-family: MyAwesomeFont;
             src: url(myawesomefont.woff) format("woff"); }
```

After you code the @font-face rule, you can apply that font to a selector in the usual way, such as in the following example that configures h1 elements:

```
h1 { font-family: MyAwesomeFont, Georgia, serif; }
```

Current browsers support @font-face but there can be copyright issues. When you purchase a font for use on your own computer you do not necessarily purchase the right to freely distribute it. Visit https://www.fontsquirrel.com to browse a selection of commercial-use free fonts available for download and use.

Google Web Fonts provides a collection of free hosted embeddable web fonts. Explore the fonts available at https://fonts.google.com. Once you choose a font, all you need to do is:

1. Copy and paste the link tag provided by Google in your web page document. (The link tag associates your web page with a CSS file that contains the appropriate @ font-face rule.)

2. Configure your CSS font-family property with the Google web font name.

See the Getting Started guide at for more information https://developers.google.com/fonts/docs/getting_started for more information. Use web fonts judiciously to conserve bandwidth and avoid applying multiple web fonts to a web page. It's a good idea to use just one web font on a web page along with your typical fonts. This can provide you a way to use an uncommon font typeface in page headings and/or navigation without the need to create graphics for these page areas.

## More CSS Text Properties

CSS provides you with lots of options for configuring the text on your web pages. In this section, you will explore the font-size, font-weight, font-style, line-height, text-align, text-decoration, text-indent, letter-spacing, word-spacing, text-shadow, and text-transform properties.

### The font-size Property

The **font-size property** sets the size of the font. Table 3.3 lists several commonly used categories of font-size values. As you review the table you'll see a wide variety of text and numeric values—there are almost too many choices available. See the notes in Table 3.3 for recommended use.

Table 3.3 Configuring font size

| Value Category | Values | Notes |
|---|---|---|
| Text Value | xx-small, x-small, small, medium (default), large, x-large, xx-large | Scales well when text is resized in browser; limited options for text size |
| Pixel Unit (px) | Numeric value with unit, such as 10 px | Pixel-perfect display depends on screen resolution; may not scale in every browser when text is resized |
| Point Unit (pt) | Numeric value with unit, such as 10 pt | Use to configure print version of web page (see Chapter 6); may not scale in every browser when text is resized |
| Em Unit (em) | Numeric value with unit, such as .75 em | Recommended by W3C; scales well when text is resized in browser; many options for text size |
| Percentage Value | Numeric value with percentage, such as 75% | Recommended by W3C; scales well when text is resized in browser; many options for text size |

The **em unit** is a relative font unit that has its roots in the print industry, dating back to the day when printers set type manually with blocks of characters. An em unit is the width of a square block of type (typically the uppercase M) for a particular font and type size. On web pages, an em unit corresponds to the width of the font and size used in the parent element (typically the body element). So, the size of an em unit is relative to the font typeface and default size. Percentage values work in a similar manner to em units. For example, `font-size: 100%` and `font-size: 1em` should render the same in a browser. To compare font sizes on your computer, launch a browser and view chapter3/fonts.html in the student files.

## The `font-weight` Property

The **font-weight property** configures the boldness of the text. Configuring the CSS rule `font-weight: bold;` has a similar effect as the `<strong>` or `<b>` HTML element.

## The `font-style` Property

The **font-style property** typically is used to configure text displayed in italics. Valid values for font-style are normal (the default), italic, and oblique. The CSS font-style: italic; has the same visual effect in the browser as an `<i>` or `<em>` HTML element.

## The `line-height` Property

The **line-height property** modifies the default height of a line of text and is often configured with a percentage value. For example, code `line-height: 200%;` to configure text to appear double spaced.

## The `text-align` Property

HTML elements are left-aligned by default; They begin at the left margin. The CSS **text-align property** configures the alignment of text and inline elements within block display elements such as headings, paragraphs, and divs. The values for the text-align property are left (default), right, and center. The following CSS code sample configures an h1 element to have centered text:

```
h1 { text-align: center; }
```

### The text-indent Property

The CSS **text-indent property** configures the indentation of the first line of text within an element. The value can be numeric (such as a px, pt, or em unit) or a percentage. The following CSS code sample configures the first line of all paragraphs to be indented:

```
p { text-indent: 5em; }
```

### The text-decoration Property

The purpose of the CSS **text-decoration property** is to modify the display of text. Commonly used values for the text-decoration property include none, underline, over-line, and line-through. Did you ever wonder why some hyperlinks are not underlined? Although hyperlinks are underlined by default, you can remove the underline with the text-decoration property. The following code sample removes the underline on a hyperlink:

```
a { text-decoration: none; }
```

### The text-transform Property

The **text-transform property** configures the capitalization of text. Valid values for text-transform are none (default), capitalize, uppercase, or lowercase. The following code sample causes all the text within an h3 element to be displayed in uppercase:

```
h3 { text-transform: uppercase; }
```

### The letter-spacing Property

The **letter-spacing property** configures the space between text characters. Valid values for letter-spacing are normal (default) and a numeric pixel or em unit. The following code sample configures extra spacing between characters within an h3 element:

```
h3 { letter-spacing: 3px; }
```

### The word-spacing Property

The **word-spacing property** configures the space between words. Valid values for word-spacing are normal (default) and a numeric pixel or em unit. The following code sample configures extra spacing between words within an h3 element:

```
h3 { word-spacing: 2em; }
```

## The white-space Property

The **white-space property** specifies the way that whitespace (such as a space character, or line feed within code) is displayed by the browser. The default browser behavior is to collapse adjacent whitespace to a single space character. Commonly used values for white-space are normal (default), nowrap (text will not wrap to the next line), and pre (preserves all whitespace in the browser display).

## The text-shadow Property

The **text-shadow property** adds depth and dimension to text displayed on web pages. Configure a text shadow by coding values for the shadow's horizontal offset, vertical offset, blur radius (optional), and color:

- **Horizontal offset.** Use a numeric pixel value. Positive value configures a shadow on the right. Negative value configures a shadow on the left.
- **Vertical offset.** Use a numeric pixel value. Positive value configures a shadow below. Negative value configures a shadow above.
- **Blur radius (optional).** Configure a numeric pixel value. If omitted, defaults to the value 0 which configures a sharp shadow. Higher values configure more blur.
- **Color value.** Configure a valid color value for the shadow.

The following code configures a dark gray shadow with 3px horizontal offset, 2px vertical offset, and 5px blur radius:

```
text-shadow: 3px 2px 5px #667788;
```

# Hands-On Practice 3.4

Now that you've got a collection of new CSS properties for font and text configuration, let's try them out. You will use the file from Hands-On Practice 3.2 (see the student files chapter3/3.2/index.html) as a starting point. Launch a text editor, and open the file. You will now code additional CSS styles to configure the text on the page.

## Set Default Font Properties for the Page

As you have already seen, CSS rules applied to the body selector apply to the entire page. Modify the CSS for the body selector to display text using a sans-serif font. The new font typeface style declaration shown in the following code will apply to the entire web page unless more specific style rules are applied to an element selector (such as h1 or p), a class, or an id (more on classes and ids later):

```
body { background-color: #E2FFFF;
       color: #15495E;
       font-family: Arial, Verdana, sans-serif;  }
```

Save your page as embedded1.html, and test it in a browser. Your page should look similar to the one shown in Figure 3.13. Notice that just a single line of CSS changed the font typeface of all the text on the page!

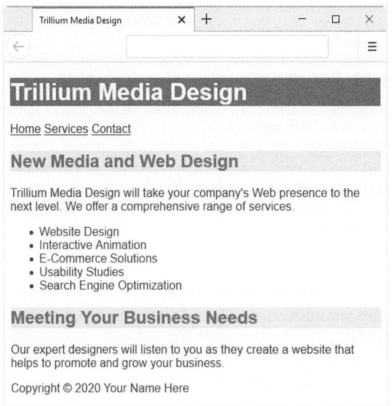

**Figure 3.13** CSS configures the font on the web page

## Configure the h1 Selector

Now you will configure the `line-height`, `font-family`, `text-indent`, and `text-shadow` CSS properties. Set the `line-height` property to 200%; this will add a bit of empty space above and below the heading text. (In Chapters 4 and 6, you will explore other CSS properties, such as the margin, border, and padding, that are more commonly used to configure space surrounding an element.) Next, modify the h1 selector to use a serif font. When a font name contains spaces, type quotes as indicated in the code that follows. While it is generally recognized that blocks of text using sans-serif fonts are easier to read, it is common to use a serif font to configure page or section headings. Indent the text 1em unit. Configure a black (#000000) text shadow with a 3 pixel vertical offset, 3 pixel horizontal offset, and 5 pixel blur radius.

```
h1 { background-color: #237B7B;
     color: #E2FFFF;
     font-family: Georgia, "Times New Roman", serif;
     line-height: 200%;
     text-indent: 1em;
     text-shadow: 3px 3px 5px #000000;   }
```

Save your page and test it in a browser.

## Configure the h2 Selector

Configure the CSS rule to use the same font typeface as the h1 selector and to display centered text.

```
h2 { background-color: #B0E6E6;
     color: #237B7B;
     font-family: Georgia, "Times New Roman", serif;
     text-align: center;   }
```

## Configure the Navigation Area

The navigation links would be more prominent if they were displayed in a larger and bolder font. Code a selector for the nav element that sets the font-size, font-weight, and word-spacing properties.

```
nav { font-weight: bold;
      font-size: 1.25em;
      word-spacing: 1em;}
```

## Configure the Paragraphs

Edit the HTML, and remove the line break tag that is after the first sentence of each paragraph; these line breaks look a bit awkward. Next, configure text in paragraphs to display just slightly smaller than the default text size. Use the `font-size` property set to .90em. Configure the first line of each paragraph to be indented. Use the `text-indent` property to configure a 3em indent.

```
p { font-size: .90em;
    text-indent: 3em;  }
```

## Configure the Unordered List

Configure the text displayed in the unordered list to be bold.

```
ul { font-weight: bold;  }
```

Save your page as index.html. Test it in a browser. Your page should look similar to the one shown in Figure 3.14. The student files contain a sample solution at chapter3/3.4/index.html. CSS is quite powerful—just a few lines of code significantly changed the appearance of the web page. You may be wondering if even more customization is possible. For example, what if you did not want all the paragraphs to display in exactly the same way? While you could add inline styles to the web page code, that is usually not the most efficient technique. The next section introduces the CSS class and id selectors, which are widely utilized to configure specific page elements.

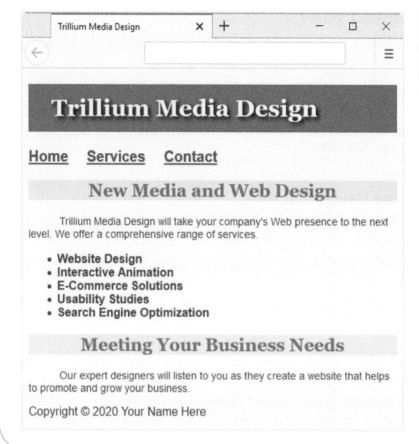

**Figure 3.14** CSS configures color and text properties on the web page

**FAQ   Is there a quick way to apply the same styles to more than one HTML tag or more than one class?**

Yes, you can apply the same style rules to multiple selectors (such as HTML elements, classes, or ids) by listing the selectors in front of the style rule. Place a comma between each selector. The following code sample shows the `font-size` of 2em being applied to both the paragraph and list item elements:

```
p, li { font-size: 2em; }
```

# 3.6  CSS Class, Id, and Descendant Selectors

## The Class Selector

Use a CSS **class selector** when you need to apply a CSS declaration to certain elements on a web page and not necessarily tie the style to a particular HTML element. See Figure 3.15, and notice that the last two items in the unordered list are displayed in a different color than the others; this is an example of using a class. A class name must begin with a letter and may contain numbers, hyphens, and underscores. Class names may not contain spaces. When setting a style for a class, configure the class name as the selector. Place a

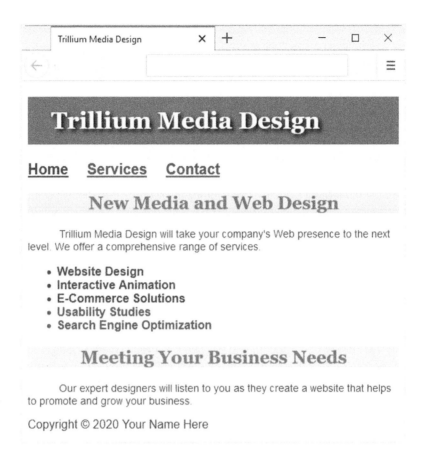

Figure 3.15
Using a class
selector

dot, or period (.), in front of the class name in the style sheet. The following code configures a class called `feature` in a style sheet with a foreground (text) color set to a medium red:

```
.feature { color: #C70000; }
```

The styles set in the new class can be applied to any element you wish. You do this by using the **class attribute**, such as `class="feature"`. Do not type the dot in front of the class value in the opening tag where the class is being applied. The following code will apply the `feature` class styles to two `<li>` elements:

```
<li class="feature">Usability Studies</li>
<li class="feature">Search Engine Optimization</li>
```

## The Id Selector

Use a CSS **id selector** to identify and apply a CSS rule uniquely to a *single* area on a web page. Unlike a class selector which can be applied multiple times on a web page, an id may only be applied once per web page. When setting a style for an id, place a hash mark (#) in front of the id name in the style sheet. An id name may contain letters, numbers, hyphens, and underscores. Id names may not contain spaces. The following code will configure an id called `feature` in a style sheet:

```
#feature { color: #333333; }
```

The styles set in the feature id can be applied to any element you wish by using the **id attribute,** `id="feature"`. Do not type the # in front of the id value in the opening tag. The following code will apply the `feature` id styles to a div tag:

```
<div id="feature">This sentence will be displayed using styles
configured in the feature id.</div>
```

Using CSS with an id selector is similar to using CSS with a class selector. Use an id selector to configure a single element on a web page. Use a class selector to configure one or more elements on a web page.

## The Descendant Selector

Use a CSS **descendant selector** when you want to specify an element within the context of its container (parent) element. Using descendant selectors can help you to reduce the number of different classes and ids but still allows you to configure CSS for specific areas on the web page. To configure a descendant selector, list the container selector (which can be an element selector, class, or id) followed by the specific selector you are styling. For example, to specify a green text color for paragraphs located *within* the main element, code the following style rule:

```
main p { color: #00ff00; }
```

## Hands-On Practice 3.5

In this Hands-On Practice, you will use the Trillium Media Design file from Hands-On Practice 3.4 (see the student files chapter3/3.4/index.html) as a starting point and modify the CSS and the HTML in the page to configure the navigation hyperlinks, content area, and page footer area. Launch a text editor, and open the index.html file.

### Configure the Navigation Hyperlinks

Navigation hyperlinks are often displayed on web pages without the default underline by configuring the text-decoration property and applying that property to a descendant selector that targets only the anchor tags in the navigation area. Configure embedded CSS before the closing style tag. Code a descendant selector that specifies the hyperlinks with the nav element and set the text-decoration property.

```
nav a { text-decoration: none; }
```

### Configure the Content Area

Trillium Media Design would like to draw attention to its new usability and search optimization services. Configure embedded CSS before the closing style tag. Create a class named `feature` that configures the text color to be a medium dark red (#C70000).

```
.feature { color: #C70000; }
```

Modify the last two items in the unordered list. Add a class attribute to each opening li tag that associates the list item with the `feature` class as follows:

```
<li class="feature">Usability Studies</li>
<li class="feature">Search Engine Optimization</li>
```

### Configure the Footer Area

Configure embedded CSS before the closing style tag. Code a selector for the footer element that sets the text color, font-size, and font-style properties.

```
footer { color: #333333;
         font-size: .75em;
         font-style: italic; }
```

Modify the HTML and code a yourfirstname@yourlastname.com e-mail hyperlink (refer to Chapter 2) within the footer element on a line below the copyright information.

Save your file and test it in a browser. Your page should look similar to the image shown in Figure 3.16. See chapter3/3.5/index.html in the student files for a sample solution. Notice how the footer element, class, and nav hyperlinks styles are applied. Although the hyperlinks in the navigation area do not display with an underline, the e-mail hyperlink in the footer area displays with the default underline.

Figure 3.16 The new home page

**FAQ    How do you choose class and id names?**

You can choose almost any name you wish for a CSS class or id. However, CSS class names are more flexible and easier to maintain over time if they are descriptive of the structure rather than of specific formatting. For example, a class name of largeBold would no longer be meaningful if the design were changed to display the area differently; however, a structural class name such as item, content, or subheading is meaningful regardless of how the area is configured. Here are more hints for class names:

- Use short but descriptive names.

- Always begin with a letter.

- Avoid spaces in class names.

- Feel free to use numerals, the dash character, and the underscore character in addition to letters.

Be wary of "classitis"—that is, creating a brand new class each time you need to configure text a bit differently. Decide ahead of time how you will configure page areas, code your classes, and apply them. The result will be a more cohesive and better organized web page.

## 3.7 Span Element

Recall from Chapter 2 that the div element configures a section or division on a web page with empty space above and below. The div element is useful when you need to format a section that is physically separated from the rest of the web page, referred to as a block display. In contrast, the **span element** defines a section on a web page that is *not* physically separated from other areas; this formatting is referred to as inline display. Use the `<span>` tag if you need to format an area that is contained within another, such as within a `<p>`, `<blockquote>`, `<li>`, or `<div>` tag.

## Hands-On Practice 3.6

You will experiment with the span element in this Hands-On Practice by configuring a new class to format the company name when it is displayed within the text on the page and using the span element to apply this class. Use the file from Hands-On Practice 3.5 (see the student files chapter3/3.5/index.html) as a starting point. Open the file in a text editor. Your web page will look similar to the one shown in Figure 3.17 after the changes are complete.

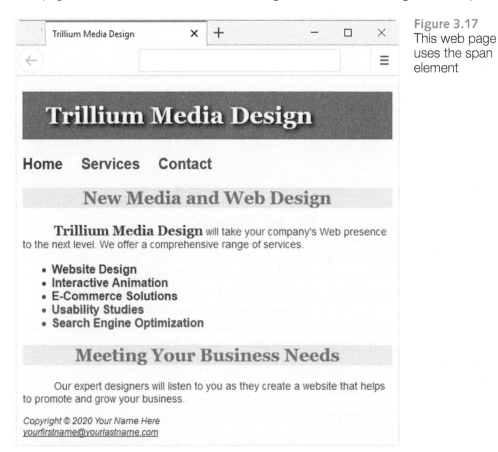

Figure 3.17
This web page uses the span element

### Configure the Company Name

View Figure 3.17, and notice that the company name, Trillium Media Design, is displayed in bold and serif font within the first paragraph. You will code both CSS and HTML to configure this formatting. First, create a new CSS rule above the closing style tag that configures a class called `company` in bold, serif font, and 1.25em in size. The code follows:

```
.company { font-weight: bold;
           font-family: Georgia, "Times New Roman", serif;
           font-size: 1.25em; }
```

Next, modify the beginning of the first paragraph of HTML to use the span element to apply the class as follows:

```
<p><span class="company">Trillium Media Design</span> will bring
```

Save your file, and test it in a browser. Your page should look similar to the one shown in Figure 3.17. A sample solution (chapter3/3.6/index.html) is in the student files. View the source code for your page, and review the CSS and HTML code. Note that all the styles were located in a single place on the web page. Since embedded styles are coded in a specific location, they are easier to maintain over time than inline styles. Also notice that you needed to code the styles for the `h2` element selector only once (in the head section), and *both* of the `<h2>` elements applied the `h2` style. This approach is more efficient than coding the same inline style on each `<h2>` element. However, it is uncommon for a website to have only one page. Repeating the CSS in the head section of each web page file is inefficient and difficult to maintain. In the next section, you will use a more efficient approach: configuring an external style sheet.

# 3.8  Using External Style Sheets

The flexibility and power of CSS are best utilized when the CSS is external to the web page document. An external style sheet is a text file with a .css file extension that contains CSS style rules. The external style sheet file is associated with a web page by using the link element. This approach provides a way for multiple web pages to be associated with the same external style sheet file. The external style sheet file does not contain any HTML tags; it contains only CSS style rules.

VideoNote
*External Style Sheets*

The advantage of external CSS is that styles are configured in a single file. This means that when styles need to be modified, only one file needs to be changed, instead of multiple web pages. On large sites, this approach can save a web developer much time and increase productivity. Let's get some practice with this useful technique.

## Link Element

The **link element** associates an external style sheet with a web page. It is placed in the head section of the page. The link element is a stand-alone, void tag. When coding in HTML5, two attributes are used with the link element: rel and href.

- The value of the **rel attribute** is `"stylesheet"`.
- The value of the **href attribute** is the name of the style sheet file.

Code the following in the head section of a web page to associate the document with the external style sheet named color.css:

```
<link rel="stylesheet" href="color.css">
```

## Hands-On Practice 3.7

Let's practice using external styles. First, you will create an external style sheet. Next, you will configure a web page to be associated with the external style sheet.

### Create an External Style Sheet

Launch a text editor, and type in the following style rules to set the background color of a page to blue and the text color to white. Save the file as color.css.

```
body { background-color: #0000FF;
       color: #FFFFFF; }
```

Figure 3.18 shows the external color.css style sheet displayed in Notepad. Notice that there is no HTML in this file. HTML tags are not coded within an external style sheet. Only CSS rules (selectors, properties, and values) are coded in an external style sheet.

**Figure 3.18** The external style sheet color.css.
Courtesy of Microsoft Corporation.

### Configure the Web Page

To create the web page shown in Figure 3.19, launch a text editor and open the template file located at chapter3/template.html in the student files. Modify the title element, add a link tag to the head section, and add a paragraph to the body section as indicated by the following code:

```
<!DOCTYPE html>
<html lang="en">
<head>
<title>External Styles</title>
<meta charset="utf-8">
<link rel="stylesheet" href="color.css">
</head>
<body>
 <p>This web page uses an external style sheet.</p>
</body>
</html>
```

**3.8** Using External Style Sheets **109**

Save your file as external.html. Launch a browser, and test your page. It should look similar to the page shown in Figure 3.19. You can compare your work with the solution in the student files (chapter3/3.7/external.html). The color.css style sheet can be associated with any number of web pages. If you ever need to change the style of formatting, you need to change only a single file (color.css) instead of multiple files (all of the web pages). As mentioned earlier, this technique can boost productivity on a large site.

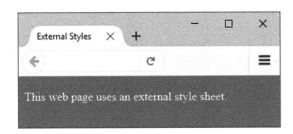

Figure 3.19 This page is associated with an external style sheet

The advantage of having only a single file to update is significant for both small and large websites. In the next Hands-On Practice, you will modify the Trillium home page to use an external style sheet.

## Hands-On Practice 3.8

In this Hands-On Practice, you will continue to gain experience using external style sheets as you create the external style sheet file named trillium.css, modify the Trillium home page to use external styles instead of embedded styles, and associate a second web page with the trillium.css style sheet.

Use the file from Hands-On Practice 3.6 (see the student files chapter3/3.6/index.html) as a starting point. Open the file in a browser. The display should be the same as the web page shown in Figure 3.17 from Hands-On Practice 3.6.

Now that you've seen what you're working with, let's begin. Launch a text editor, and save the file as index.html in a folder called trilliumext. You are ready to convert the embedded CSS to external CSS. Select the CSS rules (all the lines of code between, but not including, the opening and closing `<style>` tags). Use Edit > Copy, or press the Ctrl + C keys (Cmd + C keys on a Mac), to copy the CSS code to the clipboard. Now you will place the CSS in a new file. Launch a text editor and create a new file. Use Edit > Paste, or press the Ctrl + V keys (Cmd + V keys on a Mac), to paste the CSS style rules. Save the file as trillium.css. See Figure 3.20 for a screenshot of the new trillium.css file in Notepad. Notice that there are no HTML elements in trillium.css—not even the `<style>` element. The file contains CSS rules only.

```
📄 trillium.css - Notepad                           —    □    ×

File  Edit  Format  View  Help
body { background-color: #E2FFFF;                              ⌃
       color: #15495E;
       font-family: Arial, Verdana, sans-serif; }
h1 { background-color: #237B7B;
     color: #E2FFFF;
     line-height: 200%;
     font-family: Georgia, "Times New Roman", serif;
     text-indent: 1em;
     text-shadow: 3px 3px 5px #000000; }
h2 { background-color: #B0E6E6;
     color: #237B7B;
     font-family: Georgia, "Times New Roman", serif;
     text-align: center;  }
nav { font-weight: bold;
      font-size: 1.25em;
      word-spacing: 1em; }
nav a { text-decoration: none; }
p { font-size: .90em;
    text-indent: 3em; }
ul { font-weight: bold; }
.feature { color: #C70000; }
footer { color: #333333;
         font-size: .75em;
         font-style: italic; }
.company { font-weight: bold;
           font-family: Georgia, "Times New Roman", serif;
           font-size: 1.25em; }                               ⌄
```

**Figure 3.20**
The external
style sheet
named
trillium.css.
Courtesy of
Microsoft
Corporation.

Next, edit the index.html file in a text editor. Delete the CSS code you just copied. Delete the closing `</style>` tag. Replace the opening `<style>` tag with a link element to associate the style sheet named trillium.css. The **<link>** tag code is as follows:

```
<link href="trillium.css" rel="stylesheet">
```

Save the file, and test it in a browser. Your web page should look just like the one shown in Figure 3.17. Although it looks the same, the difference is in the code: The page now uses external, instead of embedded, CSS.

Now, for the fun part—you will associate a second page with the style sheet. The student files contain a services.html page for Trillium at chapter3/services.html. When you display this page in a browser, it should look similar to the one shown in Figure 3.21. Notice that although the structure of the page is similar to the home page, the styling of the text and colors is absent.

Copy the services.html file to your trilliumext folder. Launch a text editor to edit your services.html file. Code a `<link>` element to associate the services.html web page with the trillium.css external style sheet. Place the following code in the head section above the closing `</head>` tag:

```
<link href="trillium.css" rel="stylesheet">
```

Save your file, and test it in a browser. Your page should look similar to Figure 3.22—the CSS rules have been applied!

If you click the Home and Services hyperlinks, you can move back and forth between the index.html and services.html pages in the browser. The student files contain a sample solution in the chapter3/3.8 folder.

Figure 3.21 The services.html page is not associated with a style sheet

Figure 3.22 The services.html page has been associated with trillium.css

Notice that when using an external style sheet, if the use of color or fonts on the page ever needs to be changed, modifications are made only to the external style sheet. Think about how this approach can improve productivity on a site with many pages. Instead of modifying hundreds of pages to make a color or font change, only a single file—the CSS external style sheet—needs to be updated. Becoming comfortable with CSS will be important as you develop your skills and increase your technical expertise.

## Checkpoint 3.2

1. Describe a reason to use embedded styles. Explain where embedded styles are placed on a web page.

2. Describe a reason to use external styles. Explain where external styles are placed and how web pages indicate that they are using external styles.

3. Write the code to configure a web page to associate with an external style sheet called mystyles.css.

**FAQ    When designing a new web page or website, how do I begin to work with CSS?**

The following guidelines can be helpful when configuring a page using CSS:

- Review the design of the page. Check if common fonts are used. Define global properties (the default for the entire page) for characteristics such as fonts and colors attached to the body element selector.

- Identify typical elements used for organization in the page (such as <h1>, <h2>, and so on), and declare style rules for these elements if different from the default.

- Identify various page areas such as the header, navigation, footer, and so on. List any special configurations needed for these areas. You may decide to configure classes or ids in your CSS to configure these areas.

- Create one prototype page that contains most of the elements you plan to use and test. Revise your CSS as needed.

- Plan and test. These are important activities when designing a website.

# 3.9  Center HTML Elements with CSS

You learned how to center text on a web page earlier in this chapter—but what about centering the entire web page itself? A popular page layout design that is easy to accomplish with just a few lines of CSS is to center the entire contents of a web page within a browser viewport. The key is to configure a div element that contains, or "wraps," the entire page content. The HTML follows:

```
<body>
<div id="wrapper">
...  page content goes here  ...
</div>
</body>
```

Next, configure CSS style rules for this container. As will be discussed further in Chapter 6, the **margin** is the empty space surrounding an element. In the case of the body element, the margin is the empty space between the page content and the edges of the browser window. As you might expect, the **margin-left** and **margin-right properties** con-figure the space in the left and right margins, respectively. The margins can be set to 0, pixel units, em units, percentages, or auto. When margin-left and margin-right are both set to auto, the browser calculates the amount of space available and divides it evenly between the left and right margins. The **width property** configures the width of a block display element. The following CSS code sample sets the width of an id named wrapper to 960 pixels and centers it:

```
#wrapper { width: 960px;
          margin-left: auto;
          margin-right: auto; }
```

You'll practice this technique in the next Hands-On Practice.

## Hands-On Practice 3.9

In this Hands-On Practice, you will code CSS properties to configure a centered page layout, using the files from Hands-On Practice 3.8 as a starting point. Create a new folder called trilliumcenter. Locate the chapter3/3.8 folder in the student files. Copy the index.html, services.html, and trillium.css files to your trilliumcenter folder. Open the trillium.css file in a text editor. Create an id named wrapper. Add the margin-left, margin-right, and width style properties to the style rules as follows:

```
#wrapper { margin-left: auto;
           margin-right: auto;
           width: 80%; }
```

Save the file.

Open the index.html file in a text editor. Add the HTML code to configure a div element assigned to the id wrapper that "wraps," or contains, the code within the body section. Save the file. When you test your index.html file in a browser, it should look similar to the page shown in Figure 3.23. The student files contain a sample solution in the chapter3/3.9 folder.

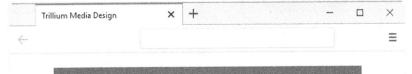

**Figure 3.23**
The page content is centered within the browser viewport

FAQ **Is there an easy way to add a comment for documentation purposes in CSS?**

Yes. An easy way to add a comment to CSS is to type "/*" before your comment and "*/" after your comment, as shown in the following example:

```
/* Configure Footer */
footer { font-size: .80em; font-style: italic; text-align: center; }
```

# 3.10 The "Cascade"

Figure 3.24 shows the "cascade" (**order of precedence**) that applies the styles in order from outermost (external styles) to innermost (inline styles). This set of rules allows the sitewide styles to be configured, but overridden when needed by more granular page-specific styles (such as embedded or inline styles).

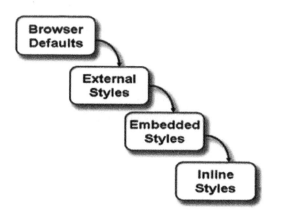

**Figure 3.24** The "cascade" of Cascading Style Sheets

External styles can apply to multiple pages. The order the styles are coded in the web page matters. When using both external and embedded styles, it is typical practice to code the link element (for external styles) before the style element (for embedded styles). So, when a web page contains both an association with an external style sheet and embedded styles, the external styles will be applied first, and then the embedded styles will be applied. This approach allows a web developer to override global external styles on selected pages.

If a web page also contains inline styles, any external and embedded styles are applied first as just described, and then the inline styles are applied. This approach allows a web developer to override page-wide styles for particular HTML tags or classes.

Note that an HTML tag or attribute will override styles. For example, a `<strong>` tag will override corresponding font-related styles configured for an element. If no attribute or style is applied to an element, the browser's default is applied. However, the appearance of the browser's default may vary by browser, and you might be disappointed with the result. Use CSS to specify the properties of your text and web page elements. Avoid depending on the browser's default.

In addition to the general cascade of CSS types described previously, the style rules themselves follow an order of precedence. Style rules applied to more local elements (such as a paragraph) take precedence over those applied to more global elements (such as a `<div>` that contains the paragraph).

Let's look at an example of the cascade. Consider the following CSS code:

```
.special { font-family: Arial, sans-serif; }
p { font-family: "Times New Roman", serif; }
```

The CSS has two style rules: a rule creating a class named `special` that configures text using the Arial (or generic sans-serif) font family, and a rule configuring all paragraphs to use the Times New Roman (or generic serif) font family. The HTML on the page contains a `<div>` with multiple elements, such as headings and paragraphs, as shown in the following code:

```
<div class="special">
<h2>Heading</h2>
<p>This is a paragraph. Notice how the paragraph is contained in the
div.</p>
</div>
```

Here is how the browser would render the code:

1. The text contained in the heading is displayed with Arial font because it is part of the `<div>` assigned to the `special` class. It inherits the properties from its parent (`<div>`) class. This is an example of **inheritance**, in which certain CSS properties are passed down to elements nested within a container element, such as a `<div>` or `<body>` element. Text-related properties (font-family, color, etc.) are generally inherited, but box-related properties (margin, padding, width, etc.) are not.

2. The text contained in the paragraph is displayed with Times New Roman font because the browser applies the styles associated with the most local element (the paragraph). Even though the paragraph is contained in (and is considered a child of) the `special` class, the local paragraph style rules takes precedence and are applied by the browser.

Don't worry if CSS and order of precedence seem a bit overwhelming at this point. CSS definitely becomes easier with practice. You will get a chance to practice with the "cascade" as you complete the next Hands-On Practice.

 ## Hands-On Practice 3.10

You will experiment with the "cascade" in this Hands-On Practice as you work with a web page that uses external, embedded, and inline styles.

1. Create a new folder named mycascade.
2. Launch a text editor. Open a new file. Save the file as site.css in the mycascade folder. You will create an external style sheet that sets the `background-color` of the web page to a shade of yellow (#FFFFCC) and the text color to black (#000000). The code follows:

```
body { background-color: #FFFFCC;
       color: #000000; }
```

Save and close the site.css file.

**3.** Open a new file in the text editor, and save it as mypage1.html in the mycascade folder. The web page will be associated with the external style sheet site.css, use embedded styles to set the global text color to blue, and use inline styles to configure the text color of the second paragraph. The file mypage1.html will contain two paragraphs of text. The code follows:

```
<!DOCTYPE html>
<html lang="en">
<head>
<title>The Cascade in Action</title>
<meta charset="utf-8">
<link rel="stylesheet" href="site.css">
<style>
  body { color: #0000FF; }
</style>
</head>
<body>
<p>This paragraph applies the external and embedded styles &mdash;
note how the blue text color that is configured in the embedded
styles takes precedence over the black text color configured in
the external stylesheet.</p>
<p style="color: #FF0000">Inline styles configure this paragraph
to have red text and take precedence over the embedded and
external styles.</p>
</body>
</html>
```

Save mypage1.html, and display it in a browser. Your page should look similar to the sample shown in Figure 3.25. The student files contain a sample solution at chapter3/3.10/mypage1.html.

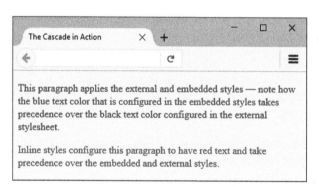

**Figure 3.25** Mixing external, embedded, and inline styles

Take a moment to examine the mypage1.html web page and compare it with its source code. The web page picked up the yellow background from the external style sheet. The embedded style configured the text to be the color blue, which overrides the black text color in the external style sheet. The first paragraph in the web page does not contain any inline styles, so it inherits the style rules in the external and embedded style sheets. The second paragraph contains an inline style of red text color; this setting overrides the corresponding external and embedded styles.

# 3.11  CSS Validation

VideoNote
*CSS Validation*

The W3C has a free Markup Validation Service (http://jigsaw.w3.org/css-validator) that will validate your CSS code and check it for syntax errors. **CSS validation** provides students with quick self-assessment—you can prove that your code uses correct syntax. In the working world, CSS validation serves as a quality assurance tool. Invalid code may cause browsers to render the pages more slowly than they would otherwise.

 ## Hands-On Practice 3.11

In this Hands-On Practice, you will use the W3C CSS Validation Service to validate an external CSS style sheet. This example uses the color.css file completed in Hands-On Practice 3.7 (student files chapter3/3.7/color.css). Locate color.css, and open it in a text editor. Now add an error to the color.css file by finding the body element selector style rule and deleting the first "r" in the `background-color` property. Add another error by removing the # from the `color` property value. Save the file.

Next, attempt to validate the color.css file. Visit the W3C CSS Validation Service page at http://jigsaw.w3.org/css-validator and select the "by file upload" tab. Click the Browse button and select the color.css file from your computer. Click the Check button. Your display should be similar to that shown in Figure 3.26. Notice that two errors were found. The selector is listed, followed by the reason an error was noted.

**Figure 3.26** The validation results indicate two errors. Screenshots of W3C. Courtesy of W3C (World Wide Web Consortium).

Notice that the first message in Figure 3.26 indicates that the "`backgound-color`" property does not exist. This is a clue to check the syntax of the property name. The second sentence in the message suggests a closely matching property name. Edit color.css and correct the first error. Test and revalidate your page. Your browser display should now look similar to the one shown in Figure 3.27 and should be reporting only one error.

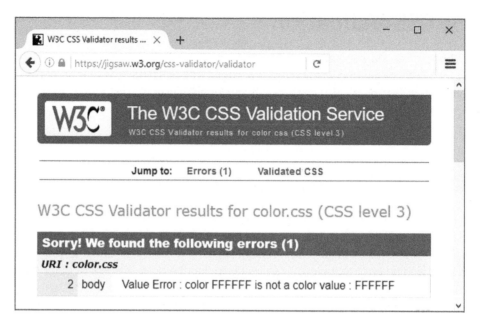

**Figure 3.27** The validation displays one error. Screenshots of W3C. Courtesy of W3C (World Wide Web Consortium).

The error reminds you that FFFFFF is not a color value; you are expected to already know that you need to add a "#" character to code a valid color value, as in #FFFFFF. Notice how any valid CSS rules are displayed below the error messages. Correct the color value, save the file, and test again.

Your results should look similar to those shown in Figure 3.28. There are no errors listed. The Valid CSS Information contains all the CSS style rules in color.css. This means your file passed the CSS validation test. Congratulations—your color.css file is valid CSS syntax! It is good practice to validate your CSS style rules. The CSS validator can help you to quickly identify code that needs to be corrected and indicate which style rules a browser is likely to consider valid. Validating CSS code is one of the many productivity techniques that web developers commonly use.

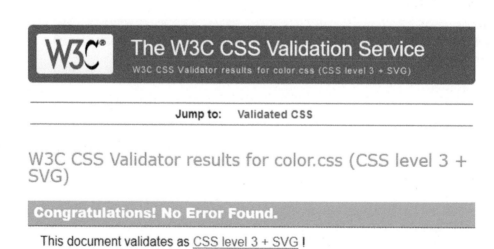

**Figure 3.28** The CSS is valid! Screenshots of W3C. Courtesy of W3C (World Wide Web Consortium).

# Chapter Summary

This chapter has introduced Cascading Style Sheet rules associated with color and text on web pages. There is much more that you can do with CSS, including positioning, hiding and showing page areas, formatting margins, and formatting borders. As you continue your study of web development with this textbook, you will learn about these additional uses. Visit this textbook's website at http://www.webdevfoundations.net for examples, information on the resources described in this chapter, and to view updated information.

## Key Terms

| | | |
|---|---|---|
| `<link>` | hexadecimal color values | RGB color |
| `<span>` | href attribute | rule |
| `<style>` | id attribute | selector |
| `background-color` property | id selector | span element |
| Cascading Style Sheets (CSS) | imported styles | `style` attribute |
| class attribute | inheritance | style element |
| class selector | inline styles | `text-align` property |
| `color` property | internal styles | `text-decoration` property |
| CSS validation | `letter-spacing` property | `text-indent` property |
| descendant selector | `line-height` property | `text-shadow` property |
| declaration | link element | `text-transform` property |
| em unit | `margin-left` property | `type` attribute |
| embedded styles | `margin-right` property | Web-Safe Color Palette |
| external styles | order of precedence | Web-Safe Colors |
| `font-family` property | pixels | `white-space` property |
| `font-size` property | point | `width` property |
| `font-style` property | property | `word-spacing` property |
| `font-weight` property | `rel` attribute | |

## Review Questions

### Multiple Choice

1. Which of the following is the declaration property used to set the font typeface for an area of a web page?
   a. face
   b. font-family
   c. font-face
   d. size

2. Which of the following is the CSS property used to set the background color of a web page?
   a. bgcolor
   b. background-color
   c. color
   d. none of the above

3. Which of the following describe two components of CSS rules?
   a. selectors and declarations
   b. properties and declarations
   c. selectors and attributes
   d. none of the above

4. Which of the following associates a web page with an external style sheet?
   a. `<style rel="external" href="style.css">`
   b. `<style src="style.css">`
   c. `<link rel="stylesheet" href="style.css">`
   d. `<link rel="stylesheet" src="style.css">`

5. Which type of CSS is coded in the body of the web page as an attribute of an HTML tag?

   a. embedded

   b. external

   c. inline

   d. imported

6. Which of the following do you configure to apply a style to only one area on a web page?

   a. group

   b. class

   c. id

   d. none of the above

7. Which of the following can be a CSS selector?

   a. an HTML element name

   b. a class name

   c. an id name

   d. all of the above

8. Where do you place the code to associate a web page with an external style sheet?

   a. in the external style sheet

   b. in the DOCTYPE of the web page document

   c. in the body section of the web page document

   d. in the head section of the web page document

9. Which of the following configures a background color of #00CED1 for a web page using CSS?

   a. `body { background-color: #00CED1; }`

   b. `document { background: #00CED1; }`

   c. `body { bgcolor: #00CED1;}`

   d. `document { bgcolor: #00CED1; }`

10. Which of the following uses CSS to configure a class called news with red text, large font, and Arial or a sans-serif font?

    a. `news { color: red;`
    `        font-size: large;`
    `        font-family: Arial,`
    `        sans-serif; }`

    b. `.news { color: red;`
    `        font-size: large;`
    `        font-family: Arial,`
    `        sans-serif; }`

    c. `.news { text: red;`
    `        font-size: large;`
    `        font-family: Arial,`
    `        sans-serif; }`

    d. `#news { text: red;`
    `        font-size: large;`
    `        font-family: Arial,`
    `        sans-serif;}`

11. Which of the following is true if a web page contains both a link to an external style sheet and embedded styles?

    a. Embedded styles will be applied first, and then the external styles will be applied.

    b. The inline styles will be used.

    c. External styles will be applied first, and then the embedded styles will be applied.

    d. The web page will not display.

## Fill in the Blank

12. The _____ element is useful for creating areas on a web page that are embedded within paragraphs or other block display elements.

13. The _____ CSS property can be used to center text within a block display element.

14. The _____ CSS property can be used to indent the first line of text.

15. The _____ CSS property can be used to configure bold text.

## Apply Your Knowledge

1. **Predict the Result.** Draw and write a brief description of the web page that will be created with the following HTML code:

```
<!DOCTYPE html>
<html lang="en">
<head>
<title>Trillium Media Design</title>
<meta charset="utf-8">
```

```
<style>
  body { background-color: #000066;
         color: #CCCCCC;
         font-family: Arial,sans-serif; }
  header { background-color: #FFFFFF;
           color: #000066; }
  footer { font-size: 80%;
           font-style: italic; }
</style>
</head>
<body>
<header><h1>Trillium Media Design</h1></header>
<nav>Home <a href="about.html">About</a> <a href="services.html">
Services</a>
</nav>
<p>Our professional staff takes pride in its working relationship
with our clients by offering personalized services that listen
to their needs, develop their target areas, and incorporate these
items into a website that works.</p>
<br><br>
<footer>
Copyright &copy; 2020 Trillium Media Design
</footer>
</body>
</html>
```

2. **Fill in the Missing Code.** The web page corresponding to the following code should be configured so that the background and text colors have good contrast. The header area should use Arial font. Consider the following code, in which some CSS properties and values, indicated by "_", and some HTML tags, indicated by <_>, are missing. Fill in the missing code.

```
<!DOCTYPE html>
<html lang="en">
<head>
<title>Trillium Media Design</title>
<meta charset="utf-8">
<style>
  body { background-color: #0066CC;
         color:  "_"; }
  header {  "_":  "_"  }
<_>
<_>
<body>
<header><h1>Trillium Media Design</h1></header>
   <p>Our professional staff takes pride in its working
relationship with our clients by offering personalized services
that listen to their needs, develop their target areas, and
incorporate these items into a website that works.</p>
</body>
</html>
```

3. **Find the Error.** Why won't the page corresponding to the following code display properly in a browser?

```
<!DOCTYPE html>
<html lang="en">
<head>
<title>Trillium Media Design</title>
<meta charset="utf-8">
<style>
  body { background-color: #000066;
         color: #CCCCCC;
         font-family: Arial,sans-serif;
         font-size: 1.2em; }
<style>
</head>
<body>
<header><h1>Trillium Media Design</h1></header>
   <main><p>Our professional staff takes pride in its working
relationship with our clients by offering personalized services
that listen to their needs, develop their target areas, and
incorporate these items into a website that works.</p></main>
</body>
</html>
```

# Hands-On Exercises

1. Write the HTML for a paragraph that uses inline styles to configure the background color of green and the text color of white.

2. Write the HTML and CSS code for an embedded style sheet that configures a background color of #eaeaea and a text color of #000033.

3. Write the CSS code for an external style sheet that configures the text to be brown, 1.2em in size, and in Arial, Verdana, or a sans-serif font.

4. Write the HTML and CSS code for an embedded style sheet that configures a class called new that is bold and italic.

5. Write the HTML and CSS code for an embedded style sheet that configures links without underlines; a background color of white; text color of black; is in Arial, Helvetica, or a sans-serif font; and has a class called new that is bold and italic.

6. Write the CSS code for an external style sheet that configures a page background color of #FFF8DC; has a text color of #000099; is in Arial, Helvetica, or a sans-serif font; and has an id called new that is bold and italic.

7. **Practice with External Style Sheets.** In this exercise, you will create two external style sheet files and a web page. You will experiment with linking the web page to the external style sheets and note how the display of the page is changed.

   a. Create an external style sheet (call it format1.css) to format as follows: document background color of white, document text color of #000099, and document font family of Arial, Helvetica, or sans-serif. Hyperlinks should have a background color of gray (#CCCCCC). Configure the h1 selector to use the Times New Roman font with red text color.

b. Create an external style sheet (call it format2.css) to format as follows: document background color of yellow and document text color of green. Hyperlinks should have a background color of white. Configure the h1 selector to use the Times New Roman font with white background color and green text color.

c. Create a web page about your favorite movie that displays the movie name in an `<h1>` tag, a description of the movie in a paragraph, and an unordered (bulleted) list of the main actors and actresses in the movie. The page should also have a hyperlink to a website about the movie. Place an e-mail link to yourself on the web page. This page should be associated with the format1.css file. Save the page as moviecss1.html. Be sure to test your page in more than one browser.

d. Modify the moviecss1.html page to link to the format2.css external style sheet instead of the format1.css file. Save the page as moviecss2.html and test it in a browser. Notice how different the page looks!

8. **Practice with the Cascade.**  In this exercise, you will create two web pages that link to the same external style sheet. After modifying the configuration in the external style sheet, you will test your pages again and find that they automatically pick up the new style configuration. Finally, you will add an inline style to one of the pages and find that it takes effect and overrides the external style.

a. Create a web page that includes an unordered list describing at least three CSS properties that can be used to format text. The text "CSS Properties" should be contained within `<h1>` tags. Write the HTML code so that one of the properties is configured to be a class called favorite. Place an e-mail link to yourself on the web page. The web page should be associated with the external style sheet called ex8.css. Save the page as properties.html.

b. Create an external style sheet (call it **ex8.css**) to format as follows: document background color of white; document text color of #000099; and document font family of Arial, Helvetica, or sans-serif. Hyperlinks should have a background color of gray (#CCCCCC). `<h1>` elements should use the Times New Roman font with black text color. The favorite class should use red italic text.

c. Launch a browser, and test your work. Display the properties.html page. It should use the formatting configured in ex8.css. Modify the web page or the CSS file until your page displays as requested.

d. Change the configuration of the external style sheet (ex8.css) to use a document background color of black, document text color of white, and `<h1>` text color of gray (#CCCCCC). Save the file. Launch a browser, and test the properties.html page. Notice how it picks up the new styles from the external style sheet.

e. Modify the properties.html file to use an inline style. The inline style should be applied to the `<h1>` tag and configure it to have red text. Save the properties.html page, and test in a browser. Notice how the `<h1>` text color specified in the style sheet is overridden by the inline style.

9. **Practice Validating CSS.**  Choose a CSS external style sheet file to validate; perhaps you have created one for your own website. Otherwise, use an external style sheet file that you worked with in this chapter. Use the W3C CSS validator at http://jigsaw.w3.org/css-validator. If your CSS does not immediately pass the validation test, modify it and test again. Repeat this process until the W3C validates your CSS code. Write a one- or two-paragraph summary about the validation process that answers the following questions: Was the CSS validator easy to use? Did anything surprise you? Did you encounter a number of errors or just a few? How easy was it to determine how to correct the CSS file? Would you recommend the validator to other students? Why or why not?

# Web Research

This chapter has introduced you to using CSS to configure web pages. A great place to learn about web technology is the Web itself. Use a search engine to find resources with either information about CSS or useful CSS tutorials. The following resources can help you get started:

- http://www.w3.org/Style/CSS
- https://developer.mozilla.org/en-US/docs/Web/CSS
- https://www.noupe.com/essentials/freebies-tools-templates/css-typography-contrast-techniques-tutorials-and-best-practices.html

Create a web page that provides a list of at least five CSS resources on the Web. For each CSS resource, provide the URL, website name, and a brief description. Configure text and background colors with good contrast. Place your name in the e-mail address at the bottom of the web page.

# Focus on Web Design

In this chapter, you have learned how to configure color and text with CSS. In this activity, you will design a color scheme, code an external CSS file for the color scheme, and code an example web page that applies the styles you configured. Use any of the following sites to help you get started with color and web design ideas:

### Psychology of Color

- https://www.infoplease.com/spot/colors1.html
- https://www.empower-yourself-with-color-psychology.com/meaning-of-colors.html
- https://www.designzzz.com/infographic-psychology-color-web-designers

### Color Scheme Generators

- https://meyerweb.com/eric/tools/color-blend
- http://www.colr.org
- https://color.adobe.com/create/color-wheel
- http://paletton.com

Complete the following tasks:

a. Design a color scheme. List three hexadecimal color values in addition to neutral colors such as white (#FFFFFF) or black (#000000) in your design.

b. Describe the process you went through as you selected the colors. Describe why you chose these colors. For what type of website would they be appropriate? List the URLs of any resources you used.

c. Create an external CSS file named color1.css that configures font properties, text color, and background color selections for the document, h1 element selector, p element selector, and footer class, using the colors you have chosen.

d. Create a web page named color1.html that shows examples of the CSS style rules.

# WEBSITE CASE STUDY

## Implementing CSS

Each of the case studies in this section continues throughout most of the text. This chapter implements CSS in the websites.

### JavaJam Coffee Bar

See Chapter 2 for an introduction to the JavaJam Coffee Bar Case Study. Figure 2.32 shows a site map for the JavaJam website. The Home page and Menu page were created in Chapter 2. You will develop a new version of the website that uses an external style sheet to configure text and color. Figure 2.33 depicts the wireframe page layout.

You have the following tasks:

1. Create a new folder for this JavaJam case study.

2. Create an external style sheet named javajam.css that configures the color and text for the JavaJam website.

3. Modify the Home page to utilize an external style sheet to configure colors and fonts. The new Home page and color swatches are shown in Figure 3.29.

Figure 3.29
New JavaJam
index.html

4. Modify the Menu page to be consistent with the new Home page.

5. Configure centered page layout.

## Hands-On Practice Case

**Task 1: The Website Folder.** Create a folder on your hard drive or portable storage device called javajamcss. Copy all the files from your Chapter 2 javajam folder into the javajamcss folder.

**Task 2: The External Style Sheet.** You will use a text editor to create an external style sheet named javajam.css. Code the CSS to configure the following:

1. Global styles for the document (use the body element selector) with background color #FCEBB6; text color #221811; and Tahoma, Arial, or any sans-serif font.

2. Styles for the header element selector that configure text color #8C3826, background color #D2B48C, and centered text.

3. Styles for the h1 element selector that configure 200% line height.

4. Styles for the h2 element selector that configure #8C3826 text color.

5. Styles for the nav element selector that configure centered, bold text. *Hint*: Use the CSS `text-align` and `font-weight` properties.

6. Styles for the footer element selector that configure background color #D2B48C, small font size (`.60em`), italics, and centered text.

Save the file as javajam.css in the javajamcss folder. Check your syntax with the CSS validator (http://jigsaw.w3.org/css-validator). Correct and retest if necessary.

**Task 3: The Home Page.** Launch a text editor, and open the index.html file. You will modify this file to apply styles from the javajam.css external style sheet as follows:

1. Add a `<link>` element to associate the web page with the javajam.css external style sheet file.

2. Configure the navigation area. Remove the `<b>` elements which are no longer needed because you have configured bold text with CSS.

3. Configure the page footer area. Remove the `<small>` and `<i>` elements—they are no longer needed since CSS is now used to configure the text.

Save the index.html file, and test it in a browser. Your page should look similar to the one shown in Figure 3.29 except that the background color and alignment of your page content is different. Don't worry—you'll center your page layout in Task 5 of this case study.

**Task 4: The Menu Page.** Launch a text editor, and open the menu.html file. You will modify this file in a similar manner as you modified the home page: Add the `<link>` element and configure the navigation and page footer areas. Save and test your new menu.html page. It should look similar to the one shown in Figure 3.30, except for the background and alignment.

**Task 5: Center Page Layout with CSS.** Modify javajam.css, index.html, and menu.html to configure page content that is centered with 80% width (refer to Hands-On Practice 3.9 if necessary):

1. Launch a text editor, and open the javajam.css file. Add a style rule for an id named `wrapper` with `width` set to 80%, #FEFAEB background color, `margin-right` set to auto, and `margin-left` set to auto.

2. Launch a text editor, and open the index.html file. Add the HTML code to configure a div element assigned to the id `wrapper` that "wraps," or contains, the code within the body section. Save and test your index.html page in a browser and you'll notice that the page content is now centered within the browser viewport as shown in Figure 3.29.

3. Launch a text editor, and open the menu.html file. Add the HTML code to configure a div element assigned to the id `wrapper` that "wraps," or contains, the code within the body section. Save and test your menu.html page in a browser and you'll notice that the page content is now centered within the browser viewport as shown in Figure 3.30.

Experiment with modifying the javajam.css file. Change the page background color, the font family, and so on. Test your pages in a browser. Isn't it amazing how a change in a single file can affect multiple files when external style sheets are used?

Figure 3.30
New menu.html page

## Fish Creek Animal Clinic

See Chapter 2 for an introduction to the Fish Creek Animal Clinic Case Study. Figure 2.36 shows a site map for the Fish Creek website. The Home page and Services page were created in Chapter 2. You will develop a new version that uses an external style sheet to configure text and color. Figure 2.37 depicts the wireframe page layout.

You have the following tasks:

1. Create a new folder for this Fish Creek case study.

2. Create an external style sheet named fishcreek.css that configures the color and text for the Fish Creek website.

3. Modify the Home page to utilize an external style sheet to configure colors and fonts. The new Home page and color swatches are shown in Figure 3.31.

4. Modify the Services page to be consistent with the new Home page.

5. Configure centered page layout.

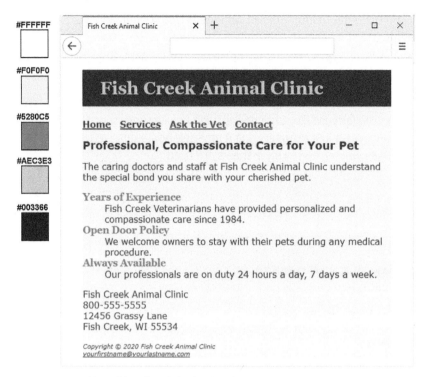

**Figure 3.31**  New Fish Creek index.html

# Hands-On Practice Case Study

**Task 1: The Website Folder.** Create a folder on your hard drive or portable storage device called fishcreekcss. Copy all the files from your Chapter 2 fishcreek folder into the fishcreekcss folder.

**Task 2: The External Style Sheet.** You will use a text editor to create an external style sheet named fishcreek.css. Code the CSS to configure the following:

1. Global styles for the document (use the body element selector) with background color #FFFFFF; text color #003366; and Verdana, Arial, or any sans-serif font.

2. Styles for the header element selector that configure background color #003366, text color #AEC3E3, and a serif font such as Georgia or Times New Roman.

3. Styles for the h1 element selector that configure 200% line height and set the text-indent property to 1em.

4. Styles for the h2 element selector that configure 1.2em font size.

5. Styles for the nav element selector that display text in bold.

6. Styles for the dt element selector that configure #5280C5 text color, size 1.1em font in bold, and a serif font such as Georgia or Times New Roman.

7. Styles for a class named `category` with bold font, text color #5380C5, and a serif font such as Georgia or Times New Roman.

8. Styles for the footer element selector with a small font size (.70em) and italic text.

Save the file as fishcreek.css in the fishcreekcss folder. Check your syntax with the CSS validator (http://jigsaw.w3.org/css-validator). Correct and retest if necessary.

**Task 3: The Home Page.** Launch a text editor, and open the index.html file. You will modify this file to apply styles from the fishcreek.css external style sheet as follows:

1. Add a `<link>` element to associate the web page with the fishcreek.css external style sheet file.

2. Configure the navigation area. Remove the `<b>` element from the navigation area, because the CSS will configure the bold font style.

3. Configure the content area. Remove the `<strong>` tags from within each dt element, because the CSS will configure the bold font style.

4. Configure the page footer area. Remove the `<small>` and `<i>` elements—they are no longer needed since CSS is now used to configure the text.

Save the index.html file, and test in a browser. Your page should look similar to the one shown in Figure 3.31, except that the background color and alignment of your page content will be different. Don't worry—you'll finish configuring your page layout in Task 5 of this case study.

**Task 4: The Services Page.** Launch a text editor, and open the services.html file. You will modify this file in a similar manner: Add the `<link>` element, configure the navigation area and page footer areas, configure the `category` classes (*Hint*: Use the `<span>` element to contain the name of each service offered), and remove the strong tags.) Save and test your new services.html page. It should look similar to the one shown in Figure 3.32 except for the alignment and background color.

**Task 5: Center Page Layout with CSS.** Modify fishcreek.css, index.html, and services.html to configure page content that is centered with 80% width with a light gray background color. Refer to Hands-On Practice 3.9 if necessary.

1. Launch a text editor, and open the fishcreek.css file. Add a style rule for an id named `wrapper` with `width` set to 90%, `margin-right` set to auto, `margin-left` set to auto, and background color set to #F0F0F0.

2. Launch a text editor, and open the index.html file. Add the HTML code to configure a div element assigned to the id `wrapper` that "wraps," or contains, the code within the body section. Save and test your index.html page in a browser and you'll notice that the page content is now centered within the browser viewport as shown in Figure 3.31.

3. Launch a text editor, and open the services.html file. Add the HTML code to configure a div element assigned to the id `wrapper` that "wraps," or contains, the code within the body section. Save and test your services.html page in a browser and you'll notice that the page content is now centered within the browser viewport as shown in Figure 3.32.

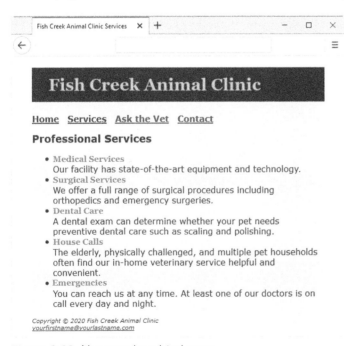

Figure 3.32  New services.html page

Experiment with modifying the fishcreek.css file. Change the page background color, the font family, and so on. Test your pages in a browser. Isn't it amazing how a change in a single file can affect multiple files when external style sheets are used?

# Pacific Trails Resort

See Chapter 2 for an introduction to the Pacific Trails Resort Case Study. Figure 2.40 shows a site map for the Pacific Trails Resort website. The Home page and Yurts page were created in Chapter 2. You will develop a new version of this website that uses an external style sheet to configure text and color. Figure 2.41 depicts the wireframe page layout.

You have the following tasks:

1. Create a new folder for this Pacific Trails case study.

2. Create an external style sheet named pacific.css that configures the color and text for the Pacific Trails website.

3. Modify the Home page to utilize an external style sheet to configure colors and fonts. The new Home page and color swatches are shown in Figure 3.33.

4. Modify the Yurts page to be consistent with the new Home page.

5. Configure centered page layout.

## Hands-On Practice Case Study

**Task 1: The Website Folder.**  Create a folder on your hard drive or portable storage device called pacificcss. Copy all the files from your Chapter 2 pacific folder into the pacificcss folder.

**Figure 3.33** New Pacific Trails index.html

**Task 2: The External Style Sheet.** You will use a text editor to create an external style sheet named pacific.css. Code the CSS to configure the following:

1. Global styles for the document (use the body element selector) with background color #FFFFFF, text color #666666, and Verdana, Arial, or any sans-serif font.

2. Styles for the header element selector that configure background color #002171, text color #FFFFFF, and Georgia or any serif font.

3. Styles for the h1 element selector that configure 200% line height.

4. Styles for the nav element selector that display text in bold and has a sky-blue background color (#BBDEFB).

5. Styles for the h2 element selector that configure medium-blue text color (#1976D2) and Georgia or any serif font.

6. Styles for the dt element selector that configure dark-blue text color (#002171) and bold font.

7. Styles for a class named resort that configure medium-blue text color (#1976D2) and 1.2em font size.

8. Styles for the footer element selector with a small font size (.70em) and italic, centered text.

Save the file as pacific.css in the pacificcss folder. Check your syntax with the CSS validator (http://jigsaw.w3.org/css-validator). Correct and retest if necessary.

**Task 3: The Home Page.** Launch a text editor, and open the index.html file. You will modify this file to apply styles from the pacific.css external style sheet as follows:

1. Add a <link> element to associate the web page with the pacific.css external style sheet file.

2. Configure the navigation area. Remove the <b> element from the navigation area, because the CSS will configure the bold font weight.

3. Find the company name ("Pacific Trails Resort") in the first paragraph below the h2. Configure a span that contains this text. Assign the span element to the resort class.

4. Look for the company name ("Pacific Trails Resort") directly above the street address. Configure a span that contains this text. Assign the span element to the resort class.

5. Configure the page footer area. Remove the <small> and <i> elements—they are no longer needed since CSS is now used to configure the text.

Save the index.html file, and test in a browser. Your page should look similar to the one shown in Figure 3.33 except that your page content will be left-aligned instead of indented from the margins. Don't worry—you'll configure your page layout in Task 5 of this case study.

**Task 4: The Yurts Page.** Launch a text editor, and open the yurts.html file. You will modify this file in a similar manner: Add the <link> element, configure the navigation area, and configure the page footer area. Delete the strong tags contained within each dt element. Save and test your new yurts.html page. It should look similar to the one shown in Figure 3.34 except for the alignment.

**Task 5: Center Page Layout with CSS.** Modify pacific.css, index.html, and yurts.html to configure page content that is centered with 80% width. Refer to Hands-On Practice 3.9 if necessary.

1. Launch a text editor, and open the pacific.css file. Add a style rule for an id named `wrapper` with `width` set to 80%, `margin-right` set to auto, and `margin-left` set to auto.

2. Launch a text editor, and open the index.html file. Add the HTML code to configure a div element assigned to the id `wrapper` that "wraps," or contains, the code within the body section. Save and test your index.html page in a browser and you'll notice that the page content is now centered within the browser viewport as shown in Figure 3.33.

3. Launch a text editor and open the yurts.html file. Add the HTML code to configure a div element assigned to the id `wrapper` that "wraps," or contains, the code within the body section. Save and test your yurts.html page in a browser and you'll notice that the page content is now centered within the browser viewport as shown in Figure 3.34.

Experiment with modifying the pacific.css file. Change the page background color, the font family, and so on. Test your pages in a browser. Isn't it amazing how a change in a single file can affect multiple files when external style sheets are used?

Figure 3.34 New yurts.html page

## Path of Light Yoga Studio

See Chapter 2 for an introduction to the Path of Light Yoga Studio Case Study. Figure 2.44 shows a site map for the Path of Light Yoga Studio website. The Home page and Classes page were created in Chapter 2. You will develop a new version of this website that uses an external style sheet to configure text and color. Figure 2.45 depicts the wireframe page layout.

You have the following tasks:

1. Create a new folder for this Path of Light Yoga Studio case study.

2. Create an external style sheet named yoga.css that configures the color and text for the Path of Light Yoga Studio website.

3. Modify the Home page to utilize an external style sheet to configure colors and fonts. The new Home page and color swatches are shown in Figure 3.35.

4. Modify the Classes page to be consistent with the new Home page.

5. Configure centered page layout.

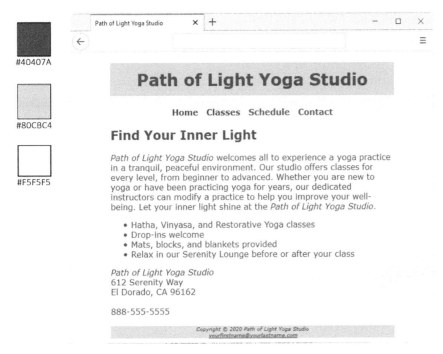

Figure 3.35 New Path of Light Yoga Studio index.html

## Hands-On Practice Case Study

**Task 1: The Website Folder.** Create a folder on your hard drive or portable storage device called yogacss. Copy all the files from your Chapter 2 yoga folder into the yogacss folder.

**Task 2: The External Style Sheet.** You will use a text editor to create an external style sheet named yoga.css. Code the CSS to configure the following:

1. Global styles for the document (use the body element selector) with background color #F5F5F5; text color #40407A and Verdana, Arial, or any sans-serif font.

2. Styles for the header element that configure background color #80CBC4 with centered text.

3. Styles for the h1 element selector that configure 200% line height.

4. Styles for the nav element selector that configure centered and bold font.

5. Styles for the anchor elements within the nav area to eliminate the default underline (Hint: use the nav a selector).

6. Styles for a class named studio that configures italic text.

7. Styles for the footer element selector with #80CBC4 background color, small font size (.60em), and italic, centered text.

Save the file as yoga.css in the yogacss folder. Check your syntax with the CSS validator (http://jigsaw.w3.org/css-validator). Correct and retest if necessary.

**Task 3: The Home Page.** Launch a text editor, and open the index.html file. You will modify this file to apply styles from the yoga.css external style sheet.

1. Add a `<link>` element to associate the web page with the yoga.css external style sheet file.

2. Configure the navigation area. Remove the `<b>` element from the navigation area, because the CSS will configure the bold font style.

3. Look in the main content area for the company name ("Path of Light Yoga Studio") and configure a span element to contain this text each time it appears. Assign each span element to the `studio` class.

4. Configure the page footer area. Remove the `<small>` and `<i>` elements—they are no longer needed since CSS is now used to configure the text.

Save the index.html file, and test in a browser. Your page should look similar to the one shown in Figure 3.35 except that your page content will be left-aligned instead of indented from the margins. Don't worry—you'll configure your page layout in Task 5 of this case study.

**Task 4: The Classes Page.** Launch a text editor, and open the classes.html file. You will modify this file in a similar manner: Add the `<link>` element, configure the navigation area, and configure the page footer area. Save and test your new classes.html page. It should look similar to the one shown in Figure 3.36 except for the alignment.

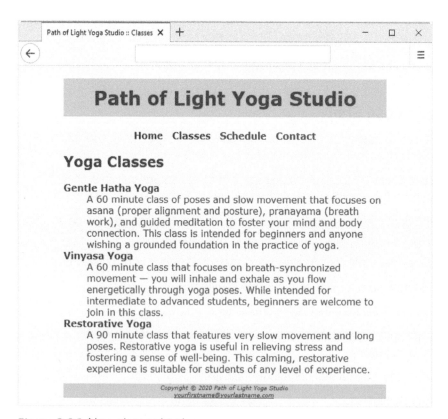

Figure 3.36 New classes.html page

**Task 5: Center Page Layout with CSS.** Modify yoga.css, index.html, and classes.html to configure page content that is centered with 80% width. Refer to Hands-On Practice 3.9 if necessary.

1. Launch a text editor, and open the yoga.css file. Add a style rule for an id named `wrapper` with `width` set to 80%, `margin-right` set to auto, and `margin-left` set to auto.

2. Launch a text editor, and open the index.html file. Add the HTML code to configure a div element assigned to the id `wrapper` that "wraps," or contains, the code within the body section. Save and test your index.html page in a browser and you'll notice that the page content is now centered within the browser viewport as shown in Figure 3.35.

3. Launch a text editor, and open the classes.html file. Add the HTML code to configure a div element assigned to the id `wrapper` that "wraps," or contains, the code within the body section. Save and test your classes.html page in a browser and you'll notice that the page content is now centered within the browser viewport as shown in Figure 3.36

Experiment with modifying the yoga.css file. Change the page background color, the font family, and so on. Test your pages in a browser. Notice how a change in a single file can affect multiple files when external style sheets are used.

# Visual Elements and Graphics

A key component of a compelling website is the use of interesting and appropriate graphics. This chapter introduces you to working with visual elements on web pages.

When you include images on your website, it is important to remember that not all users are able to view them. Some users may have vision problems and need assistive technology such as a screen reader application that reads the web page to them. In addition, search engines send out spiders and robots to walk the web and catalog pages for their indexes and databases; such programs do not access your images. Visitors using a mobile device may have images disabled. As a web developer, strive to create pages that are enhanced by graphical elements, but are usable without them.

# 4.1 Configuring Lines and Borders

Web designers often use visual elements such as lines and borders to separate or define areas on web pages. In this section, you'll explore two coding techniques to configure a line on a web page: the HTML horizontal rule element and the CSS `border` and `padding` properties.

## Horizontal Rule Element

A **horizontal rule element**, **`<hr>`**, visually separates areas of a page and configures a horizontal line across a web page. Since the horizontal rule element does not contain any text, it is coded as a void tag and not in a pair of opening and closing tags. The horizontal rule element has a new semantic meaning in HTML5, it can be used to indicate a thematic break or change in the content.

 ## Hands-On Practice 4.1

Open the web page found at chapter4/starter1.html in the student files in a text editor. Add an `<hr>` tag after the opening footer element.

Save your file as hr.html, and test it in a browser. The lower portion of your web page should look similar to the partial screenshot shown in Figure 4.1.

> ### Meeting Your Business Needs
>
> Our expert designers will listen to you as they create a website that helps to promote and grow your business.
>
> ―――――――――――――――――――――
>
> *Copyright © 2020 Your Name Here*
> *yourfirstname@yourlastname.com*

**Figure 4.1**  The `<hr>` tag configures a horizontal line

Compare your work with the solution in the student files (chapter4/4.1/hr.html). While a horizontal rule can be easily created using HTML, a more modern technique for configuring lines on web pages is to use CSS to configure a border.

## The border and padding Properties

As you may have noticed when you configured background colors for heading elements in Chapter 3, block display HTML elements form the shape of a rectangular box on a web page. This is an example of the CSS box model, which you will explore in detail in Chapter 6. For now, let's focus on two CSS properties that can be configured for the "box": the `border` and `padding` properties.

## The `border` Property

The **border property** configures the border, or boundary, around an element. By default, the border has a width set to 0 and does not display. You can set the `border-width`, `border-color`, and `border-style` with the border property. And there's more—you can even configure individual settings for the `top`, `right`, `bottom` and `left` borders using the `border-top`, `border-right`, `border-bottom`, and `border-left` properties.

## The `border-style` Property

The **`border-style` property** configures the type of line displayed in the border. The formatting options include `inset`, `outset`, `double`, `groove`, `ridge`, `solid`, `dashed`, and `dotted`. Be aware that these property values are not all uniformly applied by browsers. Figure 4.2 shows how a recent version of Firefox renders various border-style values.

| default | none |
|---|---|
| inset | outset |
| double | groove |
| ridge | solid |
| dashed | dotted |

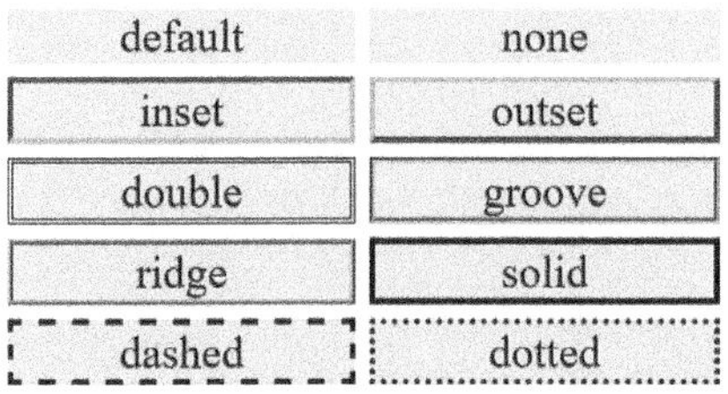

**Figure 4.2** Examples of the various border-style values rendered by Firefox

The CSS to configure the borders shown in Figure 4.2 uses a `border-width` of 4 pixels, the value indicated for the `border-style` property, and a `border-color` of `#000000`. For example, the style rule to configure the dashed border follows:

```
.dashedborder { border-width: 4px;
                border-style: dashed;
                border-color: #000000; }
```

A shorthand notation allows you to configure all the border properties in one style rule by listing the values of `border-width`, `border-style`, and `border-color`, as in the following example:

```
.dashedborder { border: 4px dashed #000000; }
```

## The `padding` Property

The **`padding` property** configures empty space between the content of the HTML element (usually text) and the border. By default, the padding is set to `0`. If you configure a background color for an element, the color is applied to both the padding and the content areas. The padding property can be configured with a variety of values, including pixels, em units, and percentages. You'll apply the `padding` and `border` properties in the next Hands-On Practice. You may want to refer to Table 4.1, which presents a description of the CSS properties introduced in this chapter, as you work through the Hands-On Practice exercises.

Table 4.1 New CSS properties introduced in this chapter

| Property | Description | Values |
|---|---|---|
| background | Configures multiple properties related to the background; can configure multiple background images | Valid values for one or more of the following properties related to a background: `background-attachment`, `background-clip`, `background-color`, `background-image`, `background-origin`, `background-position`, `background-repeat`, `background-size` |
| background-attachment | Configures whether the background image scrolls with the page or is fixed in place | `fixed`, `local`, `scroll` (default) |
| background-clip | Configures the background painting area. | `padding-box`, `border-box`, or `content-box` |
| background-image | Background image on an element | To display an image, use `url`(imagename.gif), `url`(imagename.jpg), or `url`(imagename.png). To disable image display, use `none` (default). |
| background-origin | Configures the background positioning area. | `padding-box`, `border-box`, or `content-box` |
| background-position | Position of the background image | Two percentage values or numeric pixel values. The first value configures the horizontal position, and the second configures the vertical position starting from the upper left corner of the container's box. Text values can also be used: `left`, `top`, `center`, `bottom`, and `right`. |
| background-repeat | Controls how the background image will repeat | Text values `repeat` (default), `repeat-y`, (vertical repeat), `repeat-x` (horizontal repeat), `no-repeat` (no repeat). `space` (repeat and adjust empty space to avoid clipping), and `round` (repeat and scale the image to avoid clipping). |
| background-size | Configures the size of the background image. | Two percentages, pixel values, `auto`, `contain`, or `cover`. The first value indicates width. The second value indicates height. If only one value is provided, the second value defaults to auto. The value `contain` causes the background image to be scaled (with aspect ratio intact) to horizontally fill the container. The value `cover` causes the background image to be scaled (with aspect ratio intact) to vertically fill the container. |
| border | Shorthand notation to configure the values for `border-width`, `border-style`, and `border-color` of an element | The values for `border-width`, `border-style`, and `border-color` separated by spaces—for example, `border: 1px solid #000000;` |
| border-bottom | Shorthand notation to configure the bottom border of an element | The values for `border-width`, `border-style`, and `border-color` separated by spaces—for example, `border-bottom: 1px solid #000000;` |
| border-bottom-left-radius | Configures rounded corners on the bottom left corner of a border. | One numeric value (px or em) or percentage that configures the radius of the corner. |
| border-bottom-right-radius | Configures rounded corners on the bottom right corner of a border. | One numeric value (px or em) or percentage that configures the radius of the corner. |
| border-color | The color of the border around an element | Any valid color value |
| border-left | Shorthand notation to configure the left border of an element | The values for `border-width`, `border-style`, and `border-color` separated by spaces—for example, `border-left: 1px solid #000000;` |

Table 4.1 (*Continued*)

| Property | Description | Values |
|---|---|---|
| `border-radius` | Configures rounded corners on an element. | One to four numeric values (px or em) or percentages that configure the radius of the corners. If a single value is provided, it configures all four corners. The corners are configured in order of top left, top right, bottom right, and bottom left. |
| `border-right` | Shorthand notation to configure the right border of an element | The values for `border-width`, `border-style`, and `border-color` separated by spaces—for example, `border-right: 1px solid #000000;` |
| `border-style` | The type of border around an element | `double`, `groove`, `inset`, `none` (the default), `outset`, `ridge`, `solid`, `dashed`, `dotted`, and `hidden` |
| `border-top` | Shorthand notation to configure the top border of an element | The values for `border-width`, `border-style`, and `border-color` separated by spaces—for example, `border-top: 1px solid #000000;` |
| `border-top-left-radius` | Configures a rounded top left corner. This CSS3 property is not supported in all browsers. | One numeric value (px or em) or percentage that configures the radius of the corner. |
| `border-top-right-radius` | Configures a rounded top right corner. | One numeric value (px or em) or percentage that configures the radius of the corner. |
| `border-width` | The width of a border around an element | A numeric pixel value (such as 1px) or the text values `thin`, `medium`, and `thick` |
| `box-shadow` | Configures a drop shadow on an element. | Two to four numerical values (px or em) to indicate horizontal offset, vertical offset, blur radius (optional), and spread distance (optional), and a valid color value. Use the inset keyword to configure an inner shadow. |
| `height` | The height of an element | A numeric pixel value or percentage |
| `linear-gradient` | Configures a linear blending of shades from one color to another. | Numerous syntax options for starting points of the gradient and color values. For example, the following configures a two-color linear gradient: `linear-gradient(#FFFFFF, #8FA5CE);` |
| `max-width` | Configures a maximum width for an element | A numeric pixel value or percentage |
| `min-width` | Configures a minimum width for an element | A numeric pixel value or percentage |
| `opacity` | Configures the transparency of an element. | Numeric values between 1 (fully opaque) and 0 (completely transparent). This property is inherited by all child elements. |
| `padding` | Shorthand notation to configure the amount of padding—the blank space between the element and its border | 1. A single numeric value (px or em) or percentage; configure padding on all sides of the element.<br>2. Two numeric values (px or em) or percentages; the first value configures the top and bottom padding, and the second value configures the left and right padding—for example, `padding: 2em 1em;`<br>3. Three numeric values (px or em) or percentages; the first value configures the top padding, the second value configures the left and right padding, the third value configures the bottom padding—for example, `padding: 5px 30px 10px;`<br>4. Four numeric values (px or em) or percentages; the values configure the padding in the following order: `padding-top, padding-right, padding-bottom, padding-left.` |

(*Continued*)

Table 4.1 (*Continued*)

| Property | Description | Values |
|---|---|---|
| padding-bottom | Blank space between an element and its bottom border | A numeric value (px or em) or percentage |
| padding-left | Blank space between an element and its left border | A numeric value (px or em) or percentage |
| padding-right | Blank space between an element and its right border | A numeric value (px or em) or percentage |
| padding-top | Blank space between an element and its top border | A numeric value (px or em) or percentage |
| radial-gradient | Configures a radial (circular) blending of shades from one color to another. | Numerous syntax options for starting points of the gradient and color values. For example, the following configures a two-color radial gradient:<br>`radial-gradient(#FFFFFF,#8FA5CE);` |

## Hands-On Practice 4.2

In this Hands-On Practice you will work with the `border` and `padding` properties. Launch a text editor, and open the web page found at chapter4/starter1.html in the student files. You will modify the CSS style rules for the h1 element selector, h2 element selector, and footer element selector. When you are finished, your page should look similar to the one shown in Figure 4.3.

Edit the CSS style rules as follows:

1. Edit the styles for the h1 element selector. Remove the styles for the text-indent and line-height properties. Add a declaration to configure 1em padding. The code follows:

   ```
   padding: 1em;
   ```

2. Add a style to the h2 element selector to configure a 2-pixel, dashed, bottom border in the color #237B7B. The code follows:

   ```
   border-bottom: 2px dashed #237B7B;
   ```

3. Add styles to the footer element selector to configure a thin, solid, top border in the color #B0E6E6 along with 10 pixels of top padding. Also configure the footer to have gray text. The new style declarations follow:

   ```
   border-top: thin solid #B0E6E6;
   padding-top: 10px;
   color: #333333;
   ```

Save your file as border.html.

Test your page in multiple browsers. Expect your page to look slightly different in various browsers. See Figure 4.3 for a screenshot of the page using Firefox. Figure 4.4 shows the page displayed in Microsoft Edge. The student files contain a sample solution (chapter4/4.2/border.html).

**Figure 4.3** CSS `border` and `padding` properties add visual interest to the page.

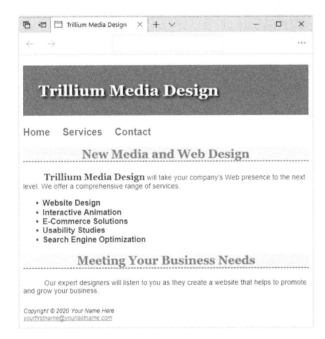

**Figure 4.4** Microsoft Edge renders the dashed border differently than Firefox.
Screenshots of Microsoft Edge. Copyright by Microsoft Corporation. Courtesy of Microsoft Corporation.

**FAQ**    **My web page looks different in some browsers. What can I do?**

Do not expect your web pages always to look the same in every browser and every browser version. Web pages that look slightly different in various browsers and on a variety of devices are a part of life in the world of web developers.

## Checkpoint 4.1

1. Is it reasonable to try to code a web page that looks exactly the same on every browser and every platform? Explain your answer.

2. Describe what is incorrect with the following CSS code, which causes a web page containing it not to display a border when rendered in a browser:

```
h2 { background-color: #FF0000
     border-top: thin solid #000000 }
```

3. True or False: CSS can be used to configure visual elements such as rectangular shapes and lines on web pages.

# 4.2 Graphics on the Web

Graphics can make web pages compelling and engaging. This section discusses features of graphic files commonly used on the Web: GIF, JPEG, PNG, and WebP.

## Graphic Interchange Format (GIF)

The **GIF** image format is best used for line drawings containing mostly solid tones and simple images such as clip art. The maximum number of colors in a GIF file is 256. GIF images have a .gif file extension. Figure 4.5 shows a logo image created in GIF format.

### Transparency

**Figure 4.5**
This logo is a GIF

The format GIF89A used by GIF images supports image **transparency**. In a graphics application, such as the open-source GIMP, one color (typically the background color) of the image can be set to be transparent. The background color (or background image) of the web page shows through the transparent area in the image. Figure 4.6 displays two GIF images on a blue textured background.

**Figure 4.6**
Comparison of transparent and nontransparent GIFs

### Animation

An **animated GIF** consists of multiple images or frames, each of which is slightly different. When the frames display on the screen in order, the image appears animated.

### Compression

**Lossless compression** is used when a GIF is saved. This means that nothing in the original image is lost and that the compressed image, when rendered by a browser, will contain the same pixels as the original.

## Optimization

To avoid slow-loading web pages, graphic files should be optimized for the Web. Photos taken with a digital camera are too large—in both their dimensions and their file size—to display well on a web page. **Image optimization** is the process of creating an image with the lowest file size that still renders a good-quality image—balancing image quality and file size. GIF images are typically optimized by using a graphics application to reduce the number of colors in the image.

## Interlacing

Browsers render, or display, web page documents in order, line by line, starting at the top of the document. They display standard images as the files are read in order from top to bottom. The top of a standard image begins to display after 50% of the image has been read by a browser. When a GIF graphic file is created, it can be configured as interlaced. An **interlaced image** progressively displays and seems to fade in as it downloads. The image first appears fuzzy but gradually becomes clearer and sharper, which can help to reduce the perceived load time of your web page.

# Joint Photographic Experts Group (JPEG)

The **JPEG** image format is best used for photographs. In contrast to a GIF image, a JPEG image can contain 16.7 million colors. However, JPEG images cannot be made transparent, and they cannot be animated. JPEG images have a .jpg or .jpeg file extension.

## Compression

JPEG images are saved using **lossy compression**. This means that some pixels in the original image are lost or removed from the compressed file. When a browser renders the compressed image, the display is similar to, but not exactly the same as, the original image.

## Optimization

There are trade-offs between the quality of the image and the amount of compression. An image with less compression will have higher quality and result in a larger file size. An image with more compression will have lower quality and result in a smaller file size. Graphics applications allow you to configure the compression quality and choose the image that best suits your needs.

When you take a photo with a digital camera, the file size is too large for optimal display on a web page. Figure 4.7 shows an optimized version of a digital photo with an original file size of 250KB. The image was optimized using a graphics application set to 80% quality, is now only 55KB, and displays well on a web page.

Figure 4.7 A JPEG saved at 80% quality (55KB file size) displays well on a web page

**Figure 4.8** JPEG saved at 20% quality (19KB file size)

Figure 4.8 was saved with 20% quality and is only 19KB, but its quality is unacceptable. The quality of the image degrades as the file size decreases. The square blockiness you see in Figure 4.8 is called **pixelation** and should be avoided.

Another technique used with web graphics is to display a small version of the image, called a **thumbnail image**. Often, the thumbnail is configured as an image hyperlink that displays the larger image when clicked. Figure 4.9 shows a thumbnail image.

### Progressive JPEG

When a JPEG file is created, it can be configured as progressive. A **progressive JPEG** is similar to an interlaced GIF in that the image progressively displays and seems to fade in as it downloads.

**Figure 4.9** This small thumbnail image is only 5KB

## Portable Network Graphic (PNG)

The **Portable Network Graphics (PNG)** image format (https://www.w3.org/TR/PNG/) was initially developed as a replacement for the GIF image format. PNG (pronounced "ping") graphics can support millions of colors, variable transparency levels, and interlacing. PNG images use **lossless compression**, so the image can be perfectly reconstructed after being compressed (to reduce file size) and decompressed for display. Animation is not supported by PNG images. PNG images are well-supported by modern browsers.

## WebP Image Format

The relatively new **WebP** (https://developers.google.com/speed/webp/) offers improved file compression over other types of images used on the Web. WebP (prounouced "weppy") graphics can support millions of colors, transparency, and animation. WebP images do not support interlacing. The WebP image format supports both lossy (like JPG) and lossless (like PNG) compression. In a Google comparison test, WebP images were 26% in smaller file size than comparable PNG images and 25–34% smaller in file size than comparable JPG images.

Initially, only the Chrome, Opera, and Android browsers displayed WebP images. At the time this was written, Firefox and Edge had recently added support for WebP. Check https://caniuse.com/#feat=webp for the current level of browser support. Since some browsers, such as Internet Explorer, do not support WebP, special consideration is needed for backward compatibility (see Chapter 7). In the next section, you'll begin coding the HTML img element to display GIF, JPEG, and PNG images on web pages. Table 4.2 summarizes the characteristics of GIF, JPEG, PNG, and WebP file formats.

**Table 4.2** Overview of common web graphic file formats

| Image Type | File Extension | Compression | Transparency | Animation | Colors | Progressive Display |
|---|---|---|---|---|---|---|
| GIF | .gif | Lossless | Yes | Yes | 256 | Interlacing |
| JPEG | .jpg or .jpeg | Lossy | No | No | Millions | Progressive |
| PNG | .png | Lossless | Yes | No | Millions | Interlacing |
| WebP | .webp | Lossy and Lossless | Yes | Yes | Millions | None |

## Popular Graphics Applications

A variety of graphics applications can be used to edit, optimize, and export images in GIF, JPEG, and PNG file formats such as:

- Adobe Photoshop (https://www.adobe.com/products/photoshop.html)
- GIMP (https://www.gimp.org)
- Sketch (https://www.sketchapp.com)

There are several options for converting a GIF, JPG, or PNG image to WebP format, including Google's command line encoder (https://developers.google.com/speed/webp/download), online converters (such as https://ezgif.com/jpg-to-webp and https://image.online-convert.com/convert-to-webp), a Photoshop plugin, and Sketch.

# 4.3 Img Element

The **img element** (often referred to as the image element) configures graphics on a web page. These graphics can be photographs, banners, company logos, navigation buttons, and so on; you are limited only by your creativity and imagination.

The img element is a void element and is not coded as a pair of opening and closing tags. The following code example configures an image named logo.gif, which is located in the same folder as the web page:

```
<img src="logo.gif" height="200" width="500" alt="My Company Name">
```

The **src attribute** specifies the file name of the image. The **alt attribute** provides a text replacement, typically a text description, of the image. The browser reserves the correct amount of space for your image if you use the `height` and `width` attributes with values either equal to or approximately the size of the image. Provide accurate values for the height and width of the image to retain the image's **aspect ratio** which is the proportional relationship between the width and height of an image. The image could be skewed or distorted by the browser if you provide inaccurate values for the image height and/or width. Table 4.3 lists `<img>` tag attributes and their values. Commonly used attributes are shown in bold.

Table 4.3 Attributes of the img element

| Attribute | Value |
| --- | --- |
| align | `right`, `left` (default), `top`, `middle`, `bottom`; obsolete—use the CSS float or position property instead (see Chapter 6) |
| **alt** | Text phrase that describes the image |
| **height** | Height of image in pixels |
| id | Text name—alphanumeric, beginning with a letter, no spaces; the value must be unique and not used for other id values on the same web page document |
| longdesc | URL of a resource that contains an accessible description of a complex image |
| **src** | The URL or file name of the image |
| srcset | HTML 5.1 attribute that supports the browser display of responsive images (see Chapter 7) |
| title | A text phrase containing advisory information about the image; typically more descriptive than the alt text |
| **width** | Width of image in pixels |

## Accessibility and Images

**Focus on Accessibility**

Use the `alt` attribute to provide accessibility. The `alt` attribute configures an alternative text description of the image. This alt text is used by the browser in two ways. The browser will display the alt text in the image area before the graphic is downloaded and displayed. Some browsers will also display the alt text as a tool tip whenever a visitor to the web page places the mouse cursor over the image area. Applications such as screen readers will read the text in the `alt` attribute out loud. A mobile browser may display the alt text instead of the image.

Standard browsers such as Firefox and Safari are not the only type of application or user agent that can access your website. Major search engines run programs called spiders or robots; these programs index and categorize websites. They cannot process text within images, but some process the value of the `alt` attributes in image tags.

The W3C recommends that alt text be no longer than 100 characters. Avoid using the file name or words like picture, image, and graphic as the value of the alt attribute. Instead, use a brief phrase that describes the image. If the purpose of an image, such as a logo, is to display text, then configure the text as the value of the alt attribute.

## Hands-On Practice 4.3

In this Hands-On Practice you will place a logo graphic and a photograph on a web page. Create a new folder called kayakch4. The images used in this Hands-On Practice are located in the student files chapter4/starters folder. Copy the kayakdc.gif and hero.jpg files into your kayakch4 folder. A starter version of the KayakDoorCounty.net Home page is ready for you in the student files. Copy the chapter4/starter2.html file into your kayakch4 folder. Rename the file as index.html. When you complete this Hands-On Practice, your page will look similar to the one shown in Figure 4.10—with two images. Launch a text editor and open the index.html file.

1. Delete the text contained between the h1 opening and closing tags. Code an img element for kayakdc.gif in this area. Remember to include the `src`, `alt`, `height`, and `width` attributes. Sample code follows:

```
<img src="kayakdc.gif"
alt="KayakDoorCounty.net"
width="500" height="60">
```

2. Code an img element to display the hero.jpg photo below the h2 element. The photo is 500 pixels wide and 350 pixels high. Configure appropriate alt text.

3. Save your page in the kayakch4 folder. Launch a browser and test your page. It should look similar to the one shown in Figure 4.10.

Figure 4.10 A web page
with images

*Note*: If the images did not display on your web page, verify that you have saved the files inside the kayakch4 folder and that you have spelled the file names correctly in the img elements. The student files contain a sample solution in the chapter4/4.3 folder. Isn't it interesting how images can add visual interest to a web page?

 FAQ    **What if I don't know the height and width of an image?**

Most graphics applications can display the height and width of an image. If you have a graphics application such as Adobe Photoshop, Adobe Fireworks, Microsoft Paint, or GIMP handy, launch the application and open the image. These applications include options that will display the properties of the image, such as height and width.

It's also easy to use Windows Explorer to determine the dimensions of the image. First, display the folder containing the image and verify that the "Details pane" view is selected. Next, select the image file to display the dimensions, file size, and other image information.

## Image Hyperlinks

Writing the code to make an image function as a hyperlink is very easy. To create an **image link** all you need to do is surround your `<img>` tag with anchor tags. For example, to place a link around an image called home.gif, use the following code:

```
<a href="index.html"><img src="home.gif" height="19" width="85"
alt="Home"></a>
```

A thumbnail image link is a small image configured as an image link with an href attribute value that points to another image file instead of to a web page. For example,

```
<a href="sunset.jpg"><img src="thumb.jpg" height="100" width="100"
alt="view a larger sunset"></a>
```

To see this in action, launch a browser and view chapter4/thumb.html in the student files.

## Hands-On Practice 4.4

You will add image links to the KayakDoorCounty.net Home page in this Hands-On Practice. You should already have the index.html, kayakdc.gif, and hero.jpg files in your kayakch4 folder. The new graphics used in this Hands-On Practice are located in the student files in the chapter4/starters folder. Copy the home.gif, tours.gif, reservations.gif, and contact.gif files into your kayakch4 folder. View Figure 4.11 to see how your page should look after you are done with this Hands-On Practice.

Figure 4.11 The new Home page navigation with image links

Let's get started. Launch a text editor and open index.html. Notice that the anchor tags are already coded—you'll just need to convert the text links to image links!

1. Whenever the main navigation consists of media, such as an image, some individuals may not be able to see the images (or may have images turned off in their browser). To provide navigation that is accessible to all, configure a set of plain text navigation links in the page footer area. Copy the `<nav>` element containing the navigation area to the lower portion of the page and paste it within the footer element, above the copyright line.

2. Locate the style tags in the head section and code the following style rules:

   a. Configure a green background color for an id named `bar`:

   ```
   #bar { background-color: #152420; }
   ```

   b. Some browsers display a border around image links by default. Prevent the border display by setting the border property to none for the img element selector:

   ```
   img { border: none; }
   ```

3. Now, focus on the top navigation area. Code `id="bar"` on the opening nav tag. Next, replace the text contained between each pair of anchor tags with an

img element. Use home.gif for the link to index.html, tours.gif for the link to tours.html, reservations.gif for the link to reservations.html, and contact.gif for the link to contact.html. Be careful not to leave any extra spaces between the img tag and the opening and closing anchor tags. A sample follows:

```
<a href="index.html"><img src="home.gif" alt="Home" width="90"
height="35"></a>
```

As you code the img tags be mindful of the width of each image: home.jpg (90 pixels), tours.jpg (90 pixels), reservations.jpg (190 pixels), and contact.jpg (130 pixels).

4. Save your page as index.html. Launch a browser and test your page. It should look similar to the one shown in Figure 4.11.

The student files contain a sample solution in the chapter4/4.4 folder.

## Accessibility and Image Hyperlinks

When using an image for main navigation, there are two methods to provide for accessibility:

1. Add a row of plain text navigation hyperlinks in the page footer. These won't be noticed by most people but could be helpful to a person using a screen reader to visit your web page.

2. Configure the `alt` attribute for each image to contain the exact text that displays in the image. For example, code `alt="Home"` in the `<img>` tag for the Home button.

**Focus on Accessibility**

FAQ   **What if my images don't display?**

The following are common reasons for an image to not display on a web page:

- Is your image *really* in the website folder? Use Windows Explorer or the Mac Finder to double check.

- Did you code the HTML and CSS correctly? Perform W3C CSS and HTML validation testing to find syntax errors that could prevent the image from displaying.

- Does your image have the exact file name that you have used in the CSS or HTML code? Attention to detail and consistency will be very helpful here.

FAQ   **How should I name my image files?**

Guidelines for naming image files:

- Use all lowercase letters.

- Do not use punctuation symbols and spaces.

- Do not change the file extensions (should be .gif, .jpg, .jpeg, or .png).

- Keep your file names short, but descriptive. Here are some examples:

  i1.gif is probably too short.

  myimagewithmydogonmybirthday.gif is too long.

  dogbday.gif may be just about right.

# 4.4 More Visual Elements

You'll explore configuring images with captions in this section. In the next Hands-On Practice you'll configure an image and a caption using a div element as a container. Next, you'll explore an approach to configure a image with a caption that implements the figure and figcaption elements.

## Hands-On Practice 4.5

In this Hands-On Practice you will configure an image with a caption on a web page. The photo used in this Hands-On Practice is located in the student files chapter4/starters folder. Save the myisland.jpg file in a folder named mycaption.

**Step 1:** Launch a text editor and open chapter4/template.html in the student files. Modify the title element. Add an img element to the body section to display the myisland.jpg image as follows:

```
<img src="myisland.jpg" alt="Tropical Island" height="480" width="640">
```

Save the file as index.html in the mycaption folder. Launch a browser to test your page. It should look similar to the page shown in Figure 4.12.

**Figure 4.12** The image is displayed on the web page

**Step 2:** Configure a figure caption and border for the image. To do so, launch a text editor and open the web page file. Add embedded CSS to the head section that configures an id named `figure` that is 640 pixels wide, has a border, has padding set to 5px, and has centered text using the Papyrus font typeface (or the default fantasy family font). The code follows:

```
<style>
#figure {  border: 1px solid #000000;
        font-family: Papyrus, fantasy;
        padding: 5px;
        text-align: center;
        width: 640px; }
</style>
```

Edit the body section to add a div to contain the image. Add the text "Tropical Island Getaway" below the image but within the div element. Assign the div to the id named `figure`. Save the file as index.html in the mycaption folder. Launch a browser to test your page. It should look similar to the page shown in Figure 4.13. The student files contains a sample solution in the chapter4/4.5 folder.

Figure 4.13 CSS configures the placement of the border and figure caption

## Figure and Figcaption Elements

The block display **figure element** comprises a unit of content that is self-contained, such as an image, along with one optional `figcaption` element.

The block display **figcaption element** provides a caption for a figure.

You might be wondering why these new HTML5 elements were created when the same design can be configured using a div element as a container. The reason is semantics. The div element is useful but very generic in nature. When the figure and figcaption elements are used, the structure of the content is well defined.

## Hands-On Practice 4.6

In this Hands-On Practice you will configure an area on a web page that contains an image with a caption by using the HTML5 figure and figcaption elements. The graphic used in this Hands-On Practice is located in the student files chapter4/starters folder. Save the myisland.jpg file in a folder named mycaption2.

**Step 1:** Launch a text editor and open chapter4/template.html in the student files. Modify the title element. Add an img element to the body section to display the myisland.jpg image as follows:

```
<img src="myisland.jpg" alt="Tropical Island" height="480"
width="640">
```

Save the file as index.html in the mycaption2 folder. Launch a browser to test your page. It should look similar to the page shown in Figure 4.12.

**Step 2:** Configure a figure caption and border for the image. Launch a text editor and open the web page file. Add embedded CSS to the head section that configures the figure element selector to be 640 pixels wide, with a border, and with padding set to 5px. Configure the figcaption element selector to have centered text using the Papyrus font typeface (or the default fantasy family font). The code follows:

```
<style>
figure { border: 1px solid #000000;
       padding: 5px; width: 640px; }
figcaption { font-family: Papyrus, fantasy;
           text-align: center; }
</style>
```

Edit the body section. Below the image, add a `figcaption` element that contains the following text: "Tropical Island Getaway." Configure a `figure` element that contains both the img and the figcaption. The code follows:

```
<figure>
   <img src="myisland.jpg" width="640" height="480" alt="Tropical
   Island">
   <figcaption> Tropical Island Getaway</figcaption>
</figure>
```

Save the file as index.html in the mycaption2 folder. Launch a browser to test your page. It should look similar to the page shown in Figure 4.14. The student files contains a sample solution in the chapter4/4.6 folder.

**Figure 4.14** The figure and figcaption elements were used in this web page

## Meter Element

The **meter element** displays a visual gauge of a numeric value within a known range, typically as part of a bar chart. The meter element is configured with several attributes, including `value` (the value displayed), `min` (the lowest value in the range), and `max` (the highest possible value in the range). The following code snippet (student files chapter4/meter.html) configures the display of a report that shows total visits and the number of visits by users for each browser:

```
<h1>Monthly Browser Report</h1>
<meter value="14417" min="0" max="14417">14417
</meter>14,417 Total Visits<br>
<meter value="7000" min="0" max="14417">7000</meter> 7,000 Chrome<br>
<meter value="3800" min="0" max="14417">3800</meter> 3,800 Edge<br>
<meter value="2062" min="0" max="14417">2062</meter> 2,062 Firefox<br>
<meter value="1043" min="0" max="14417">1043</meter> 1,043 Safari<br>
<meter value="312" min="0" max="14417">312</meter>   
312 Opera<br>
<meter value="200" min="0" max="14417">200</meter>    200
other<br>
```

**Figure 4.15** The `meter` element

As shown in Figure 4.15, the meter element provides a handy way to display a bar chart on a web page.

## Progress Element

The **progress element**, shown in Figure 4.16, displays a bar that depicts a numeric value within a specified range. The progress element is configured with the `value` (the value displayed) and `max` (highest possible value) attributes. Place information for nonsupporting browsers to display between the opening and closing progress tags. The following code snippet (student files chapter4/progress.html) shows 50% completion of a task:

```
<h1>Progress Report</h1>
<progress value="5" max="10">50%</progress>
Progress Toward Our Goal
```

**Figure 4.16** The `progress` element

# 4.5 Background Images

Back in Chapter 3, you learned how to configure background color with the CSS `background-color` property. For example, the following CSS code configures the background of a web page to be a soft yellow:

```
body { background-color: #FFFF99; }
```

## The `background-image` Property

Use the CSS **background-image property** to configure a background image. The following CSS code configures the HTML body selector with a background of the graphic texture1.png located in the same folder as the web page file:

```
body { background-image: url(texture1.png); }
```

### Using Both Background Color and a Background Image

VideoNote
*CSS Background Images*

You can configure both a background color and a background image. The background color (specified by the `background-color` property) will display first. Next, the image specified as the background will be displayed as it is loaded by the browser.

By coding both a background color and a background image, you provide your visitor with a more pleasing visual experience. If the background image does not load for some reason, the background color will still have the expected contrast with your text color. If the background image is smaller than the web browser window and the web page is configured with CSS not to automatically tile (repeat the image), the background color of the page will display in areas not covered by the background image. The CSS for a page with both a background color and a background image follows:

```
body { background-color: #99cccc;
       background-image: url(background.jpg); }
```

## Browser Display of a Background Image

You may think that a graphic created to be the background of a web page would always be about the size of the browser window viewport. However, the dimensions of the background image are often much smaller than the typical viewport. The shape of a background image is often either a thin rectangle or a small rectangular block. Unless otherwise specified in a style rule, browsers repeat, or tile, these images to cover the page's background, as shown in Figures 4.17 and 4.18. The images have small file sizes so that they download as quickly as possible.

Background Image

Web Page with Background Image

Figure 4.17  A long, thin background image tiles down the page

Background Image

Web Page with Background Image

Figure 4.18  A small rectangular background is repeated to fill the web page window

## The `background-repeat` Property

As just discussed, the default behavior of a browser is to repeat, or tile, background images to cover the entire element's background. This behavior also applies to other elements, such as backgrounds for headings, paragraphs, and so on. You can modify this tiling behavior with the CSS **background-repeat property**. Values for the `background-repeat` property are shown in Table 4.4.

Table 4.4 Values for the background-repeat property

| Value | Purpose |
|---|---|
| repeat | Default value. Repeats ("tiles") the image across and down to fill the background |
| repeat-y | Vertically repeats the image in the background |
| repeat-x | Horizontally repeats the image in the background |
| no-repeat | The image is not repeated |
| space | Repeats the image in the background without clipping (or cutting off) parts of the image by adjusting empty space around the repeated images. |
| round | Repeats the image in the background and scales (adjusts) the dimensions of the image to avoid clipping. |

Figure 4.19 provides examples of background images and the results of applying the `repeat-y`, `repeat-x`, and `no-repeat` values for the `background-repeat` property.

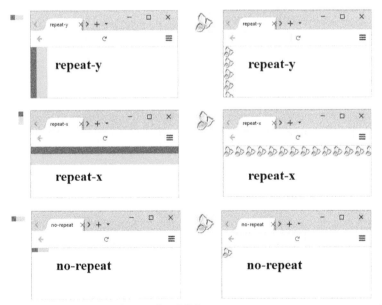

Figure 4.19 Examples of the CSS `background-repeat` property

## Hands-On Practice 4.7

Let's practice using a background image. In this exercise, you will use your files in the kayakch4 folder from Hands-On Practice 4.4 (also see the student files chapter4/4.4 folder) as a starting point. In this Hands-On Practice you will configure the main element selector with a background image that does not repeat. Obtain the heroback.jpg image from the student files chapter4/starters folder. Copy the image into your kayakch4 folder. When you have completed this exercise, your page should look similar to the one shown in Figure 4.20. Launch a text editor and open index.html.

1. Locate the style tags in the head section. Code a new style rule for the main element selector to configure the `background-image` and `background-repeat` properties. Set the background image to be heroback.jpg. Set the background not to repeat. The main element selector style rules follow:

```
main { background-image: url(heroback.jpg);
       background-repeat: no-repeat; }
```

Figure 4.20 The background image for the main element is configured with `background-repeat: no-repeat`

2. Remove the img element that displays the hero.jpg image from the body of the web page.

3. Save your page as index.html. Launch a browser, and test your page. You may notice that the text within the main element is displayed over the background image. In this case, the page would look more appealing if the paragraph did not extend across the background image. Open index.html in a text editor and code a line break tag before the word "explore".

4. Save and test your page again. It should look similar to the page shown in Figure 4.20 if you are using a browser other than Internet Explorer. The student files contain a sample solution in the chapter4/4.7 folder. Internet Explorer does not support default styles for the HTML5 main element. If you are concerned about the display of your page in Internet Explorer, you can nudge this browser to comply by adding the `display: block;` declaration (see Chapter 6) to the styles for the main element selector. An example solution is in the student files (chapter4/4.7/iefix.html).

**FAQ** **What if my images are in their own folder?**

It's a good idea to organize your website by placing all your images in a folder. Notice that the CircleSoft website whose file structure is shown in Figure 4.21 contains a folder called images, which contains GIF and JPEG files. To refer to these files in code, you also need to refer to the images folder. The following are some examples:

- The CSS code to configure the background.gif file from the images folder as the page background follows:

```
body { background-image:
     url(images/background.gif); }
```

- The HTML to display the logo.jpg file from the images folder follows:

```
<img src="images/logo.jpg"
alt="CircleSoft" width="588" height="120">
```

**Figure 4.21** A folder named "images" contains the graphic files

## The background-position Property

You can specify other locations for the background image besides the default top left location by using the CSS **background-position property**. Valid values for the background-position property include percentages; pixel values; or `left`, `top`, `center`, `bottom`, and `right`. The first value indicates horizontal position. The second value indicates vertical position. If only one value is provided, the second value defaults to center. In Figure 4.22, the small flower image has been placed in the background on the right side of the element by using the following style rule:

New Media and Web Design

```
h2 { background-image: url(flower.gif);
    background-position: right;
    background-repeat: no-repeat; }
```

**Figure 4.22** The flower background image was configured to display on the right side with CSS

## The background-attachment Property

Use the CSS **background-attachment property** to configure whether the background image remains fixed in place or scrolls along with the page in the browser viewport. Valid values for the `background-attachment` property include:

- `scroll` (default)

  The background image scrolls with the page in the browser viewport.

- `fixed`

  The background image does not scroll with the page in the browser viewport.

- `local`

  The background image scrolls with the element's content the browser viewport.

## The background-clip Property

The CSS **background-clip property** confines the display of the background image with the following values:

- `content-box` (clips the display to the area behind the content)
- `padding-box` (clips the display to the area behind the content and padding)
- `border-box` (default; clips the display to the area behind the content, padding, and border; similar to the padding-box property except that the image will display behind a border configured to be transparent)

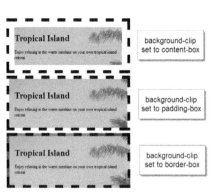

Figure 4.23 shows div elements configured with different values of the background-clip property. Note that the dashed border is intentionally large in these examples. The student files (chapter4/clip folder) contains an example page.

The CSS is shown as follows:

```
.test { background-clip: content-box;
        background-image: url(myislandback.jpg);
        border: 10px dashed #000;
        padding: 20px;
        width: 400px;  }
```

**Figure 4.23** The CSS `background-clip` property

## The background-origin Property

The CSS **background-origin property** positions the background image, using the following values:

- `content-box` (positions relative to the content area)
- `padding-box` (default; positions relative to the padding area)
- `border-box` (positions relative to the border area)

The `background-origin` property is supported by current versions of modern browsers. Figure 4.24 shows div elements configured with different values of the background-origin property. The sample page is located in the student files (chapter4/origin folder).

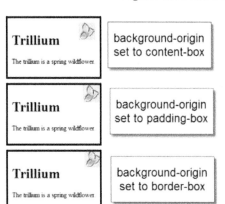

The CSS for the first div follows:

```
.test { background-image: url(trilliumsolo.jpg);
        background-origin: content-box;
        background-position: right top;
        background-repeat: no-repeat;
        border: 1px solid #000;
        padding: 20px; width: 200px;  }
```

You may have noticed that it's common to use several CSS properties when configuring background images. The properties typically work together. However, be aware that the `background-origin` property has no effect if the `background-attachment` property is set to the value "fixed".

**Figure 4.24** The CSS `background-origin` property

## The background-size Property

The CSS **background-size property** can be used to resize or scale the background image. Valid values for the background-size property include:

- a pair of percentage values (width, height)

  If only one percentage value is provided, the second value defaults to auto and is determined by the browser.

- a pair of pixel values (width, height)

  If only one numeric value is provided, the second value defaults to auto and is determined by the browser.

- cover

  The value cover will preserve the aspect ratio of the image as it scales the background image to the *smallest size* for which both the height and width of the image can completely cover the area.

- contain

  The value contain will preserve the aspect ratio of the image as it scales the background image to the *largest size* for which both the height and width of the image will fit within the area.

Figure 4.25 shows two div elements that are each configured with the same background image to display without repeating.

Figure 4.25 Configuring a background image.

The backgound-size property is not configured for the first div element's background image which only partially fills the space. The CSS for the second div configures the background-size to be 100% 100% so the browser scales and resizes the background image to fill the space. The sample page is located in the student files (chapter4/size/sedona.html). The CSS for the second div follows:

```
#test1 { background-image: url(sedonabackground.jpg);
         background-repeat: no-repeat;
         background-size: 100% 100%; }
```

Figure 4.26 demonstrates use of the cover and contain values to configure the display of a 500 × 500 background image within a 200 pixel wide area on a web page.

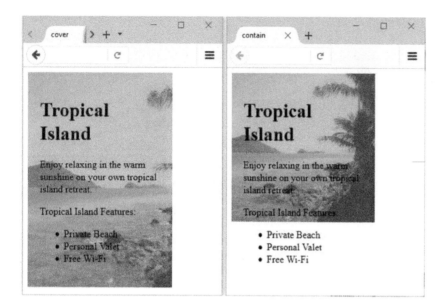

Figure 4.26 Examples of `background-size: cover;` and `background-size: contain`

The web page on the left uses `background-size: cover;` to scale and resize the image to completely cover the area while keeping the aspect ratio of the image intact. The web page on the right uses `background-size: contain;` to scale and resize the image so that both the height and width of the image will fit within the area. Review the sample pages in the student files (chapter4/size/cover.html and chapter4/size/contain.html).

## Multiple Background Images

Now that you are familiar with background images, let's explore applying multiple background images to a web page. Figure 4.27 shows a web page with two background images configured on the body selector: a large photograph of a coffee cup on a table that displays across the entire web page and a small coffee cup drawing that displays once in lower left corner.

Use the CSS **background property** to configure multiple background images. Each image declaration is separated by a comma. You can optionally add property values to indicate the image's position and whether the image repeats. The `background` property uses a shorthand notation—just list the values that are needed for relevant properties such as `background-position` and `background-repeat`.

Figure 4.27 The browser displays multiple background images.

To provide for progressive enhancement when using multiple background images, first configure a separate `background-image` property with a single image (rendered by browsers that do not support multiple background images) prior to the background property configured for multiple images (to be rendered by supporting browsers and ignored by nonsupporting browsers).

## Hands-On Practice 4.8

Let's practice configuring multiple background images. In this Hands-On Practice, you will configure the body element selector to display multiple background images on the web page. Create a new folder named coffee4. Copy all the files from the student files chapter4/coffeestarters folder into your coffee4 folder.

Launch a text editor and open coffee.html. Style declarations for browsers that do not support multiple backgrounds are already coded. Add style declarations to the body selector to configure the background property for multiple background images: configure coffee.gif to display on the bottom left without repeating, configure coffeepour.jpg to display without repeating as a fixed background. Also set the background-size property for multiple images by separating their background-size values by a comma: configure auto for coffee.gif and cover for coffeepour.jpg. The new code follows:

```
background: url(coffee.gif) no-repeat left bottom,
            url(coffeepour.jpg) no-repeat fixed;
background-size: auto, cover;
```

Save your file as index.html. Launch a browser and test your page in a modern browser. Your display should be similar to Figure 4.27. If the page is displayed in a browser that does not support multiple background images, only the large photograph will be displayed. The student files contain a sample solution in the chapter4/4.8 folder.

A **cinemagraph** is a type of animated GIF created by taking a video or series of photos with small changes (such as coffee pouring into a cup or hair waving in the wind), processing them in a graphics application such as Adobe Photoshop, and exporting the file as an animated GIF or PNG. Figure 4.28 shows a web page with three background images: a large coffee cup cinemagraph GIF, a solid color rectangle, and a small sketch of a coffee cup.

**Figure 4.28** Multiple background images.

## Hands-On Practice 4.9

In this Hands-On Practice, you will rework the example in Hands-on Practice 4.8 to display a cinemagraph as one of three background images on the web page. Use your files from Hands-On Practice 4.8 (see the chapter4/4.8 folder in the student files).

Launch a text editor and open index.html. You will modify the style rules for the body element selector. Configure the style rules to display the coffeepour.gif image instead of the coffeepour.jpg image. Edit the background property values to display a third image (coffeeback.gif) under the coffee.gif and above the coffeepour.gif. Configure coffeback.gif to repeat vertically down the browser viewport (the value repeat-y). Also configure the background-size property for each image: set cover for coffeepour.gif and auto for the other two images. The style rule for the body element selector follows:

```
body { font-size: 150%; font-family: Arial; color: #992435;
       background-image: url(coffeepour.gif); background-size: cover;
       background-repeat: no-repeat; background-attachment: fixed;
       background: url(coffee.gif) no-repeat left bottom,
              url(coffeeback.gif) repeat-y;
              url(coffeepour.gif) no-repeat fixed;
       background-size: auto, auto, cover; }
```

Save your file as coffepour.html. Launch a browser and test your page in a modern browser. Your display should be similar to Figure 4.28. You will see an animation of coffee pouring into the cup. If the page is displayed in a browser that does not support multiple background images, only the large pouring coffee image will be displayed. The student files contain a sample solution in the chapter4/4.9 folder.

## Checkpoint 4.2

1. Describe the CSS to configure a graphic named circle.jpg to display once in the background of all `<h1>` elements. Code the CSS.

2. Describe the CSS that configures a file named bg.gif to repeat vertically down the background of a web page. Code the CSS.

3. Explain how the browser will render the web page if you use CSS to configure both a background image and a background color.

# 4.6 More About Images

This section introduces several additional techniques used with images on web pages. Topics discussed include image maps, the favorites icon, image slicing, and CSS Sprites.

## Image Maps

An **image map** is an image that can be used as one or more hyperlinks. An image map will typically have multiple clickable or selectable areas that link to another web page or website. The selectable areas are called **hotspots**. Image maps can configure selectable areas in three shapes: rectangles, circles, and polygons. An image map requires the use of the image element, map element, and one or more area elements.

## Map Element

The **map element** is a container tag that indicates the beginning and ending of the image map description. The `name` attribute is coded to associate the `<map>` tag with its corresponding image. The `id` attribute must have the same value as the `name` attribute. To associate a map element with an image, configure the img element with the **usemap attribute** to indicate which `<map>` to use.

## Area Element

The **area element** defines the coordinates or edges of the clickable area. It is a void tag that uses the `href`, `alt`, `title`, `shape`, and `coords` attributes. The `href` attribute identifies the web page to display when the area is clicked. The `alt` attribute provides a text description for screen readers. Use the `title` attribute to specify text that some browsers may display as a tooltip when the mouse is placed over the area. The `coords` attribute indicates the coordinate position of the clickable area. Table 4.5 describes the type of coordinates needed for each shape attribute value.

Table 4.5 Shape coordinates

| Shape | Coordinates | Meaning |
|---|---|---|
| rect | "x1,y1, x2,y2" | The coordinates at point (x1,y1) represent the upper-left corner of the rectangle. The coordinates at point (x2,y2) represent the lower-right corner of the rectangle. |
| circle | "x,y,r" | The coordinates at point (x,y) indicate the center of the circle. The value of r is the radius of the circle, in pixels. |
| poly | "x1,y1, x2,y2, x3,y3", etc. | The values of each (x,y) pair represent the coordinates of a corner point of the polygon. |

## Exploring a Rectangular Image Map

We'll focus on a rectangular image map. For a rectangular image map, the value of the `shape` attribute is `rect`, and the coordinates indicate the pixel positions as follows:

- distance of the upper-left corner from the left edge of the image
- distance of the upper-left corner from the top of the image
- distance of the lower-right corner from the left edge of the image
- distance of the lower-right corner from the top of the image.

Figure 4.29 Sample image map

Figure 4.29 shows an image of a fishing boat. The dotted rectangle around the fishing boat indicates the location of the hotspot. The coordinates shown (24, 188) indicate that the top-left corner is 24 pixels from the left edge of the image and 188 pixels from the top of the image. The pair of coordinates in the lower-right corner (339, 283) indicates that this corner is 339 pixels from the left edge of the image and 283 pixels from the top of the image. This example is in the student files at chapter4/map.html. The HTML code to create this image map follows:

**Focus on
Accessibility**

```
<map name="boat" id="boat">
    <area href="http://www.fishingdoorcounty.com" shape="rect"
        coords="24, 188, 339, 283" alt="Door County Fishing Boat">
</map>
<img src="fishingboat.jpg" usemap="#boat" alt="Door County" width="416"
height="350">
```

Note the use of the `alt` attribute on the area element in the previous code sample. Configure a descriptive `alt` attribute for each area element associated with an image map to provide for accessibility.

Most web developers do not hand-code image maps. Web authoring tools, such as Adobe Dreamweaver, have features that help you to generate image maps. There are also free online image map generators available at:

- http://www.maschek.hu/imagemap/imgmap
- http://image-maps.com
- https://mobilefish.com/services/image_map/image_map.php

## The Favorites Icon

Ever wonder about the small icon you sometimes see in the address bar or tab of a browser? That's a favorites icon, usually referred to as a **favicon**, which is a square image (either 16 × 16 pixels or 32 × 32 pixels) associated with a web page. The favicon, shown in Figure 4.30, may display in the browser's address bar, tab, or the favorites and bookmarks lists.

**Figure 4.30** The favorites icon displays in the browser tab and address bar

## Configuring a Favorites Icon

While some versions of early browsers expected the file to be named favicon.ico and to reside in the root directory of the web server, a more modern approach is to associate the favicon.ico file with a web page by using the link element. Recall that in Chapter 3, you coded the <link> tag in the head section of a web page to associate an external style sheet file with a web page file. You can also use the <link> tag to associate a favorites icon with a web page. Three attributes are used to associate a web page with a favorites icon: rel, href, and type. The value of the rel attribute is icon. The value of the href attribute is the name of the image file. The value of the type attribute describes the MIME type of the image—which defaults to image/x-icon for .ico files. The HTML code to associate a favorites icon named favicon.ico to a web page follows:

```
<link rel="icon" href="favicon.ico" type="image/x-icon">
```

You may need to publish your files to the Web (see the FTP tutorial in the Appendix) in order for the favicon to display in Microsoft Edge and Internet Explorer. Other browsers, such as Firefox, display favicons more reliably and also support GIF, JPG, and PNG image formats. Be aware that if you use a .gif, .png, or .jpg as a favorites icon, then the MIME type should be image/ico. For example,

```
<link rel="icon" href="favicon.gif" type="image/ico">
```

## Hands-On Practice 4.10

Let's practice using a favorites icon. Obtain the favicon.ico file from the student files in the chapter4/starters folder. In this exercise, you will use your files in the kayakch4 folder from Hands-On Practice 4.7 (also see the student files chapter4/4.7 folder) as a starting point.

1. Launch a text editor, and open index.html. Add the following link tag to the head section of the web page:

   ```
   <link rel="icon" href="favicon.ico" type="image/x-icon">
   ```

2. Save your file. Launch the Firefox browser, and test your page. You should notice the small kayaker image in the Firefox browser tab as shown in Figure 4.31. The student files contain a sample solution in the chapter4/4.10 folder.

**Figure 4.31** The favorites icon displays in the Firefox browser tab

**FAQ   How can I create my own favorites icon?**

You can create your own favicon with a graphics application, such as GIMP, or with one of the following online tools:

- http://favicon.cc
- http://www.favicongenerator.com
- http://www.freefavicon.com
- http://www.xiconeditor.com

**FAQ   What about icons on mobile devices?**

Apple, Google Android, and Microsoft each specify the icon image usage guidelines and required syntax for their devices. Visit https://webdevfoundations.net/10e/chapter4.html for current links to these guidelines. You'll first need to create multiple versions of your icon file in a variety of sizes, such as `180x180` (iPhone), `192x192` (Android), and `167x167` (iPad Pro). The PNG file format is typically used for these icons. Then, configure a link element for each icon with the rel, href, and sizes attributes. The sizes attribute specifies the dimensions of the icon file. The following is an example of the HTML to specify icon files for a typical iPhone, iPad, and Android Device.

```
<link rel="apple-touch-icon" sizes="180x180" href="iPhoneIcon.png">
<link rel="apple-touch-icon" sizes="167x167" href="iPadIcon.png">
<link rel="icon" sizes="192x192" href="AndroidIcon.png">
```

## CSS Sprites

A modern technique to optimize the use of images on web pages is called CSS Sprites. A **sprite** is an image file that contains multiple small graphics that are configured as background images for various web page elements. The CSS `background-image`, `background-repeat`, and `background-position` properties are used to manipulate the placement of the image. Having just a single image saves download time, because the browser needs to make only one http request for the combined image instead of many requests for the individual smaller images. You'll work with CSS Sprites in Chapter 6.

# 4.7  Sources and Guidelines for Graphics

## Sources of Graphics

There are many ways to obtain graphics: You can create them using a graphics application, download them from a website which provides them for free, purchase and download them from a graphics website, purchase a graphics collection on a DVD, take digital photographs, scan photographs, scan drawings, or hire a graphic designer to create graphics for you. Adobe Photoshop and GIMP (https://www.gimp.org/) are popular graphics applications. Pixlr offers a free, easy-to-use, online photo editor at https://pixlr.com/x/. These applications usually include tutorials and sample images to help you get started.

Sometimes you might be tempted to right-click on an image on a web page and download it for use on your own website. Be aware that materials on a website are copyrighted (even if a copyright symbol or notice does not appear) and are not free to use unless the owner of the site permits it. So, contact the owner of an image and request permission for use of a graphic rather than just taking it.

**Focus on Ethics**

There are many websites that offer free and low-cost graphics. Choose a search engine and search for "free graphics"—you'll get more results than you have time to view. The following are a few sites that you may find helpful when looking for images:

- Free Images: https://www.freeimages.com
- Free Stock Photo Search Engine: http://www.everystockphoto.com
- Free Digital Photos: http://www.freedigitalphotos.net
- Pixabay: https://pixabay.com
- iStockphoto: https://www.istockphoto.com
- Adobe Stock: https://stock.adobe.com

## Guidelines for Using Images

Images enhance your web page by creating an engaging, interesting user experience. Images can also hurt your web page by slowing down its performance to a crawl and discouraging visitors. This section explores some guidelines for using images on web pages.

### Reuse Images

Once an image from your site is requested for a web page, it is stored in the cache on your visitor's hard drive. Subsequent requests for the image will use the file from the hard drive instead of another download. This approach results in faster page loads for all pages that use the image. It is recommended that you reuse common graphics such as logos and navigation buttons on multiple pages instead of creating different versions of these common graphics.

### Consider the Size vs. Quality Issue

You can choose among varying levels of image quality when using a graphics application to create or optimize an image. There is a correlation between the quality of the image and the size of the image file: The higher the quality, the larger the file size will be. Choose the smallest file that gives you appropriate quality. You may need to experiment until you get the right match.

### Consider Image Load Time

Be careful when using images on web pages—it takes time for them to load. Optimize the file size and the dimensions of images for efficient web page display.

### Use Appropriate Resolution

Most desktop and laptop web browsers display images at relatively low **resolution**—typically 96ppi (pixels per inch). Many digital cameras and scanners can create images with much higher resolution. Of course, higher resolution means larger file size. Even though the browser does not display the depth of resolution, more bandwidth is still used for the large file size. Be aware that some devices (such as tablets and smartphones) have high pixel density displays (such as over 400ppi) which can affect the rendering of an image. In Chapter 7, you'll be introduced to configuring flexible, responsive images for multiple devices.

### Specify Dimensions

Use accurate height and width attributes on image tags. This will allow the browser to allocate the appropriate space on the web page for the image and load the page faster. Do not try to resize the appearance of an image by modifying the settings of the height and width attributes. While this approach will work, your page will load more slowly, and your image quality may suffer. Instead, use a graphics application to create a smaller or larger version of the graphic when needed.

### Be Aware of Brightness and Contrast

**Gamma** refers to the brightness and contrast of the monitor display. Monitors used with Macintosh and Windows operating systems use a different default gamma setting (Macintosh uses 1.8; Windows uses 2.2). Images that have good contrast on a computer running Windows may look slightly washed out on a Macintosh. Images created on a Macintosh may look darker, with less contrast, when displayed on a computer with a Windows operating system. Be aware that even monitors on the same operating system may have slightly different gamma values than the default for the platform. A web developer cannot control gamma, but should be aware that images will look different on various platforms because of this issue.

## Accessibility and Visual Elements

**Focus on Accessibility**

Even though images help to create a compelling, interesting website, remember that not all your visitors will be able to view your images. The Web Accessibility Initiative's WCAG 2.1 includes a number of guidelines for web developers in the use of color and images:

- Don't rely on color alone. Some visitors may have color perception deficiencies. Use high contrast between background and text color. Tools that can verify appropriate contrast are described in Chapter 10.

- Provide a text equivalent for every nontext element. Use the `alt` attribute on your image tags.

  - If an image displays text, configure that text as the value of the `alt` attribute.

  - Use `alt=""` for an image that is purely decorative.

- If your site navigation uses image hyperlinks, provide simple text links at the bottom of the page.

Vinton Cerf, the co-inventor of TCP/IP and the former chairman of the Internet Society, said, "The Internet is for everyone." Follow web accessibility guidelines to ensure that this is true.

# Checkpoint 4.3

1. Search for a site that uses image hyperlinks to provide navigation. List the URL of the page. What colors are used on the image links? If the image links contain text, is there good contrast between the background color and the letters on the image links? Would the page be accessible to a visitor who is sight challenged? How have accessibility issues been addressed? Is the `alt` attribute used to describe the image link? Is there a row of text links in the footer section of the page? Answer these questions and discuss your findings.

2. When configuring an image map, describe the relationship between the image, map, and area tags.

3. True or False: You should save your images using the smallest file size possible.

# 4.8 CSS Visual Effects

This section introduces CSS properties that provide visual effects on web pages, including rounded corners, box shadows, text shadows, opacity effects, transparent color with RGBA, transparent color with HSLA, and gradients.

## CSS Rounded Corners

VideoNote
*Rounded Corners*
*with CSS*

As you've worked with borders and the box model, you may have begun to notice a lot of rectangles on your web pages! The **border-radius property** can be used to create rounded corners and soften up those rectangles.

Valid values for the `border-radius` property include one to four numeric values (using pixel or em units) or percentages that configure the radius of the corner. If a single value is provided, it configures all four corners. If four values are provided the corners are configured in order of top left, top right, bottom right, and bottom left. You can configure corners individually with the `border-bottom-left-radius`, `border-bottom-right-radius`, `border-top-left-radius`, and `border-top-right-radius` properties.

CSS declarations to set a border with rounded corners are shown in the next segment of code. If you would like a visible border to display, configure the border property. Then set the value of the `border-radius` property to a value below 20px for best results. For example:

```
border: 3px ridge #330000;
border-radius: 15px;
```

See Figure 4.32 (chapter4/box.html in the student files) for an example of this code in action. Keep in mind that another approach to getting a rounded look is to create a rounded rectangle background image with a graphics application.

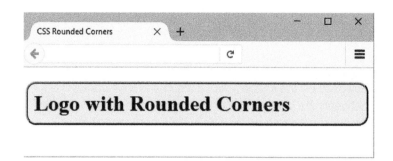

**Figure 4.32** Rounded corners were configured with CSS

## Hands-On Practice 4.11

You'll configure a logo header area that uses a background image and rounded borders in this Hands-On Practice.

1. Create a new folder called borderch4. Copy the following files in the chapter4/starters folder to your borderch4 folder: lighthouselogo.jpg and background.jpg. A starter file is ready for you in the student files. Save the chapter4/starter3.html file to your borderch4 folder. Launch a browser to display the starter3.html web page shown in Figure 4.33.

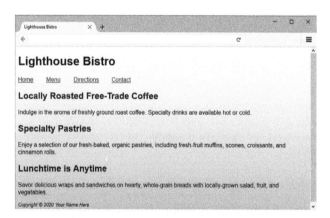

**Figure 4.33** The starter3.html file

2. Launch a text editor, and open the starter3.html file. Save the file as index.html. Edit the embedded CSS, and add the following style declarations to the h1 element selector that will configure the lighthouselogo.jpg image as a background image that does not repeat: height set to 100px, width set to 650px, font size set to 3em, 150px of left padding, 30px of top padding, and a solid dark-blue border (#000033) with a border radius of 15px. The style declarations are as follows:

```
h1 { background-image: url(lighthouselogo.jpg);
     background-repeat: no-repeat;
     height: 100px; width: 650px; font-size: 3em;
     padding-left: 150px; padding-top: 30px;
     border: 1px solid #000033;
     border-radius: 15px; }
```

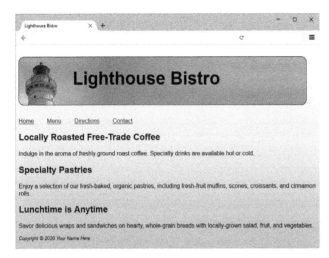

Figure 4.34 The web page with the logo area configured

3. Save the file. When you test your index.html file in a browser, it should look similar to the one shown in Figure 4.34 if you are using a browser that supports rounded corners. Otherwise the logo will have right-angle corners, but the web page will still be usable. The student files (chapter4/4.11.index.html) has a sugggested solution.

## The `box-shadow` Property

The CSS **box-shadow property** can be used to create a shadow effect on block-display elements such as div and paragraph elements. Configure a box shadow by coding values for the shadow's horizontal offset, vertical offset, blur radius (optional), spread distance (optional), and color:

- **Horizontal offset.** Use a numeric pixel value. Positive value configures a shadow on the right. Negative value configures a shadow on the left.
- **Vertical offset.** Use a numeric pixel value. Positive value configures a shadow below. Negative value configures a shadow above.
- **Blur radius (optional).** Configure a numeric pixel value. If omitted, defaults to the value 0 which configures a sharp shadow. Higher values configure more blur.
- **Spread distance (optional).** Configure a numeric pixel value. If omitted, defaults to the value 0. Positive values configure the shadow to expand. Negative values configure the shadow to contract.
- **Color value.** Configure a valid color value for the shadow.

Here's an example that configures a dark-gray drop shadow with 5px horizontal offset, 5px vertical offset, and a 5px blur radius:

```
box-shadow: 5px 5px 5px #828282;
```

**Inner Shadow Effect.** To configure an inner shadow, include the optional `inset` value. For example:

```
box-shadow: inset 5px 5px 5px #828282;
```

# Hands-On Practice 4.12

You'll configure a centered content area and apply the `box-shadow` and `text-shadow` properties in this Hands-On Practice. When complete, your web page will look similar to the one shown in Figure 4.35.

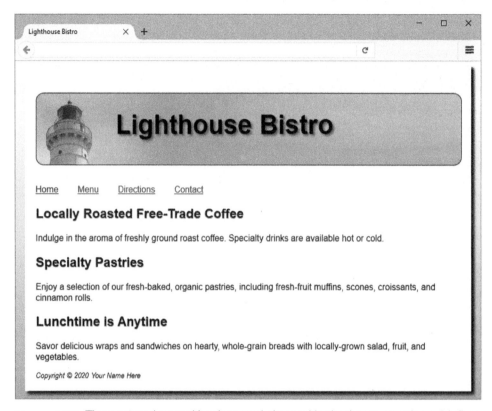

**Figure 4.35** The centered neutral background along with shadow properties add dimension

Create a new folder called shadowch4. Copy the lighthouselogo.jpg and the background.jpg files from the chapter4/starters folder to your shadowch4 folder. Launch a text editor, and open the chapter4/4.11/index.html file (shown in Figure 4.34). Save the file in your shadowch4 folder.

1. Configure the page content to be centered, with an 800-pixel width, a white background, and some padding.

   a. Edit the HTML. Configure a div element assigned to the id named `container` that wraps the code within the body section. Code the opening `<div>` tag on a new line after the opening body tag. Code a closing div tag on a new line before the closing body tag.

   b. Edit the embedded CSS to configure a new selector, an id named `container`. Configure a white background color and padding set to 1.25em. Recall from Chapter 3 the style declarations that will center the page content. Use the `width`, `min-width`, `max-width`, `margin-left`, and `margin-right` properties as follows:

```
#container { background-color: #FFFFFF;
             padding: 1.25em;
             width: 80%; min-width: 800px; max-width: 960px;
             margin-left: auto;
             margin-right: auto; }
```

2. Edit the embedded CSS to add the following style declarations to the `#container` selector to configure a box shadow:

```
box-shadow: 5px 5px 5px #1E1E1E;
```

3. Add the following style declaration to the h1 element selector to configure a dark-gray text shadow:

```
text-shadow: 3px 3px 3px #676767;
```

4. Add the following style declaration to the h2 element selector to configure a light-gray text shadow with no blur:

```
text-shadow: 1px 1px 0 #CCC;
```

5. Save the file. When you test your index.html file in a browser, it should look similar to the one shown in Figure 4.35. See the student files for a solution (chapter4/4.12/index.html).

## Hands-On Practice 4.13

In this Hands-On Practice you will practice your new skills as you configure a web page with centered content and apply CSS properties. When complete, your web page will look similar to the one shown in in Figure 4.36.

**Figure 4.36** CSS drastically changes the look of the web page

Create a new folder called kayakch4a. Copy the background.jpg, heroback2.jpg, and headerbackblue.jpg files from the chapter4/starters folder to your kayakch4 folder.

Launch a text editor and open the chapter4/starter2.html file. Save the file in your kayakch4a folder with the name index.html. Modify the file as follows:

1. Center the page content.

   a. Configure embedded CSS between the style tags and code a new selector, an id named `container` with style declarations for the `width`, `margin-left`, and `margin-right` properties as follows:

   ```
   #container { margin-left: auto;
                margin-right: auto;
                width: 80%; }
   ```

   b. Edit the HTML. Configure a div element assigned to the id `container` that "wraps" or contains the code within the body section. Code an opening div tag on a new line after the opening body tag. Assign the div to the id named `container`.

2. Configure embedded CSS.

   a. **The body element selector.**   Configure a declaration to display background.jpg as the background image.

   ```
   body { background-image: url(background.jpg);
   ```

   b. **The container id selector.**   Add declarations to configure a white background color, 650px minimum width, 1280px maximum width, and a box shadow with a 3px offset in the color #333.

   ```
   #container { margin-left: auto;
                margin-right: auto;
                width: 80%;
                background-color: #FFFFFF;
                min-width: 650px; max-width: 1280px;
                box-shadow: 3px 3px 3px #333;  }
   ```

   c. **The header element selector.**   Configure declarations to configure #000033 background color, #FF9 text color, a display of the headerbackblue.jpg image on the right without repeating, 80px height, 5px top padding, 2em left padding, and a text shadow in the color #FFF with a 1px offset.

   ```
   header { background-color: #000033; color:#FF9;
            background-image: url(headerbackblue.jpg);
            background-position: right;
            background-repeat: no-repeat;
            height: 80px;
            padding-top: 5px;
            padding-left: 2em;
            text-shadow: 1px 1px 1px #FFF; }
   ```

   d. **The nav element selector.**   Code declarations to configure bold, 1.5em size, and centered text with 1em word-spacing.

   ```
   nav { word-spacing: 1em;
         font-weight: bold;
         font-size: 1.5em;
         text-align: center; }
   ```

   e. **The nav a descendant selector.**   Code a declaration to eliminate the underline from hyperlinks.

   ```
   nav a { text-decoration: none; }
   ```

f. **The main element selector.**   Code declarations to configure heroback2.jpg as the background image and set `background-size: 100% 100%;` Also configure white text (use #FFF) and 2em of padding.

```
main { background-image: url(heroback2.jpg);
        background-size: 100% 100%;
        color: #FFF;
        padding: 2em; }
```

g. **The footer element selector.**   Configure declarations for italic, .80em size centered text with 0.5em of padding.

```
footer { font-style: italic; font-size: .80em;
        text-align: center; padding: 0.5em; }
```

3. Save the file. When you test your index.html file, it should look similar to the one shown in Figure 4.36. Compare your work with the solution in the student files (chapter4/4.13/index.html).

## The opacity Property

The CSS **opacity property** configures the transparency of an element. Opacity values range from 0 (which is completely transparent) to 1 (which is completely opaque and has no transparency). An important consideration when using the opacity property is that this property applies to both the text and the background. If you configure a semi-transparent opacity value for an element with the opacity property, both the background and the text displayed will be semi-transparent. See Figure 4.37 for an example of using the opacity property to configure a white background that is only 60% opaque. If you look very closely at Figure 4.37 or view the actual web page (student files chapter4/4.14/index.html), you'll see that both the white background and the black text in the h1 element are semi-transparent. The opacity property was applied to both the background color and to the text color.

Figure 4.37 The background of the h1 area is transparent

## Hands-On Practice 4.14

In this Hands-On Practice you'll work with the opacity property as you configure the web page shown in Figure 4.37.

1. Create a new folder called opacitych4. Copy fall.jpg file from the chapter4/starters folder to your opacitych4 folder. Launch a text editor and open the chapter4/template.html file. Save it in your opacitych4 folder with the name index.html. Change the page title to "Fall Nature Hikes".

2. Let's create the structure of the web page with a div that contains an h1 element. Add the following code to your web page in the body section:

```
<div id="content">
 <h1>Fall Nature Hikes</h1>
</div>
```

3. Now, add style tags to the head section, and configure the embedded CSS. You'll create an id named content to display the fall.jpg as a background image that does not repeat. The content id also has a width of 640 pixels, a height of 480 pixels, left and right auto margins (which will center the object in the browser viewport), and 20 pixels of top padding. The code is

```
#content { background-image: url(fall.jpg);
           background-repeat: no-repeat;
           margin-left: auto;
           margin-right: auto;
           width: 640px;
           height: 480px;
           padding-top: 20px; }
```

4. Now configure the h1 element selector to have a white background color with opacity set to 0.6, font size set to 4em, and 10 pixels of padding. Sample code is

```
h1 { background-color: #FFFFFF;
     opacity: 0.6;
     font-size: 4em;
     padding: 10px; }
```

5. Save the file. When you test your index.html file in a browser that supports opacity, it should look similar to the page shown in Figure 4.37. See the student files for a solution (chapter4/4.14/index.html).

## CSS RGBA Color

CSS3 supports syntax for the color property that configures transparent color, called **RGBA color**. Four values are required: red color, green color, blue color, and alpha (transparency). RGBA color does not use hexadecimal color values. Instead, decimal color values are configured; see the partial color chart in Figure 4.38 and the Web-Safe Color Palette in the Appendix for examples.

| | | | |
|---|---|---|---|
| #FFFFFF<br>rgb (255, 255, 255) | #FFFFCC<br>rgb(255, 255, 204) | #FFFF99<br>rgb(255,255,153) | #FFFF66<br>rgb(255,255,102) |
| #FFFF33<br>rgb(255,255,51) | #FFFF00<br>rgb(255,255,0) | #FFCCFF<br>rgb(255, 204, 255) | #FFCCCC<br>rgb(255,204,204) |
| #FFCC99<br>rgb(255,204,153) | #FFCC66<br>rgb(255,204,102) | #FFCC33<br>rgb(255,204,51) | #FFCC00<br>rgb(255,204,0) |
| #FF99FF<br>rgb(255,153,255) | #FF99CC<br>rgb(255,153,204) | #FF9999<br>rgb(255,153,153) | #FF9966<br>rgb(255,153,102) |

Figure 4.38 Hexadecimal and RGB decimal color values

The values for red, green, and blue must be decimal values from 0 to 255. The alpha value must be a number between 0 (transparent) and 1 (opaque). Figure 4.39 shows a web page with the text configured to be slightly transparent.

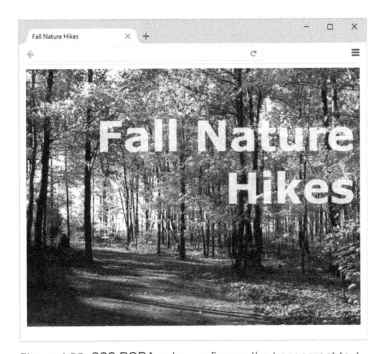

Figure 4.39 CSS RGBA color configures the transparent text

 FAQ  **How is using RGBA color different from using the `opacity` property?**

The `opacity` property applies to both the background and the text within an element. If you would like to specifically configure a semi-transparent background color, code the `background-color` property with RGBA color or HSLA color (described in the next section) values. If you would like to specifically configure semi-transparent text, code the `color` property with RGBA color or HSLA color values.

## Hands-On Practice 4.15

In this Hands-On Practice you'll configure transparent text as you code the web page shown in Figure 4.39.

1. Create a new folder called rgbach4. Copy fall.jpg file from the chapter4/starters folder to your rgbach4 folder. Launch a text editor, and open the file you created in the previous Hands-On Practice (also located in the student files chapter4/4.14/index.html). Save the file with the name rgba.html in your rgbach4 folder.

2. Delete the current style declarations for the h1 element selector. You will create new style rules for the h1 selector to configure 10 pixels of right padding and right-aligned sans-serif white text that is 70% opaque, with a font size of 5em. Since not all browsers support RBGA color, you'll configure the color property twice. The first instance will be the standard color value that is supported by all modern browsers; the second instance will configure the RGBA color. Older browsers will not understand the RGBA color and will ignore it. Newer browsers will "see" both of the color style declarations and will apply them in the order they are coded, so the result will be transparent color. The CSS code is

```
h1 { color: #FFFFFF;
     color: rgba(255, 255, 255, 0.7);
     font-family: Verdana, Helvetica, sans-serif;
     font-size: 5em;
     padding-right: 10px;
     text-align: right; }
```

3. Save the file. When you test your rgba.html file in a browser that supports RGBA color, it should look similar to the page shown in Figure 4.39. See the student files for a solution (chapter4/4.15/rgba.html).

## CSS HSLA Color

For many years web designers have configured RGB color using either hexadecimal or decimal values on web pages. Recall that RGB color is based on hardware—the red, green, and blue light that is emitted by computer monitors. CSS introduced a new color notation system called **HSLA color**, based on a color wheel model, which stands for hue, saturation, lightness, and alpha.

### Hue, Saturation, Lightness, and Alpha

When you work with HSLA color, think of a color wheel—a circle of color—with the color red at the top of the wheel as shown in Figure 4.40. Hue is the actual color which is represented by numeric values ranging from 0 to 360 (like the 360 degrees in a circle). For example, red is represented by both the values 0 and 360, green is represented by 120, and blue is represented by 240. Set hue to 0 when configuring black, gray, and white. Saturation configures the intensity of the color and is indicated by a percentage value (full color saturation = 100%, gray = 0%). Lightness determines the brightness or darkness of the color and is indicated by a percentage value (normal color = 50%, white = 100%, black = 0%). Alpha represents the transparency of the color and has a value from 0 (transparent) to 1 (opaque). Note that you can omit the alpha value and use the `hsl` keyword instead of the `hsla` keyword.

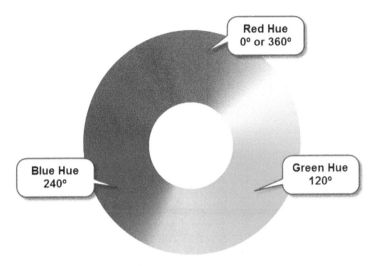

Figure 4.40 A color wheel

## HSLA Color Examples

Configure HSLA color as shown in Figure 4.41 with the following syntax:
hsla(hue value, saturation value, lightness value, alpha value);

- Red: `hsla(360, 100%, 50%, 1.0);`
- Green: `hsla(120, 100%, 50%, 1.0);`
- Blue: `hsla(240, 100%, 50%, 1.0);`
- Black: `hsla(0, 0%, 0%, 1.0);`
- Gray: `hsla(0, 0%, 50%, 1.0);`
- White: `hsla(0, 0%, 100%, 1.0);`

According to the W3C, an advantage to using HSLA color is that it is more intuitive to work with than the hardware-oriented RGB color. You can use a color wheel model to choose colors and generate the hue value from the degree placement on the circle. If you would like to use a tone of a color, which is a color with gray added, vary the saturation value. If you would like to use a shade or tint of a color, use the same hue value, but vary the lightness value to meet your needs. Figure 4.42 shows three shades of cyan blue configured using three different values for lightness: 25% (dark cyan blue), 50% (cyan blue), 75% (light cyan blue).

- Dark Cyan Blue:
  `hsla(210, 100%, 25%, 1.0);`
- Cyan Blue:
  `hsla(210, 100%, 50%, 1.0);`
- Light Cyan Blue:
  `hsla(210, 100%, 75%, 1.0);`

**Red**
hsla(360, 100%, 50%, 1.0);

**Green**
hsla(120, 100%, 50%, 1.0);

**Blue**
hsla(240, 100%, 50%, 1.0);

**Black**
hsla(0, 0%, 0%, 1.0);

**Gray**
hsla(0, 0%, 50%, 1.0);

**White**
hsla(0, 0%, 100%, 1.0);

Figure 4.41 HSLA color examples

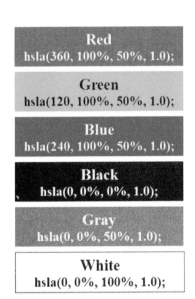

hsla(210, 100%, 25%, 1.0);

hsla(210, 100% 50%, 1.0);

hsla(210, 100%, 75%, 1.0);

Figure 4.42 Shades of cyan blue

# Hands-On Practice 4.16

In this Hands-On Practice you'll configure light yellow transparent text as you work with the web page shown in Figure 4.43.

Figure 4.43 HSLA color

1. Create a new folder called hslach4. Copy fall.jpg file from the chapter4/starters folder to your hslach4 folder. Launch a text editor and open the file you created in the previous Hands-On Practice (also located in the student files, chapter4/4.15/rgba.html). Save the file with the name hsla.html in your hslach4 folder.

2. Delete the style declarations for the h1 selector. You will create new style rules for the h1 selector to configure 20 pixels of padding and serif light yellow text with a 0.8 alpha value and a font size of 6em. Since not all browsers support HSLA color, you'll configure the color property twice. The first instance will be the standard color value that is supported by all modern browsers; the second instance will configure the HSLA color. Older browsers will not understand the HSLA color and will ignore it. Newer browsers will "see" both of the color style declarations and will apply them in the order they are coded, so the result will be transparent color. The CSS for the h1 selector is

```
h1 { color: #FFCCCC;
     color: hsla(60, 100%, 90%, 0.8);
     font-family: Georgia, "Times New Roman", serif;
     font-size: 6em;
     padding: 20px; }
```

3. Save the file. When you test your hsla.html file in a browser that supports HSLA color it should look similar to the page shown in Figure 4.43. See the student files for a solution (chapter4/4.16/hsla.html).

# CSS Gradients

CSS provides a method to configure color as a **gradient**, which is a smooth blending of shades from one color to another color. A CSS gradient background color is defined purely with CSS—no image file is needed! This provides flexibility for web designers, along with a savings in the bandwidth required to serve out gradient background image files.

Figure 4.35 displays a web page with a JPG gradient background image that was configured in a graphics application. The web page shown in Figure 4.44 (available at chapter4/gradient/index.html in the student files) does not use a JPG for the background; CSS gradient properties recreated the look of the linear gradient image.

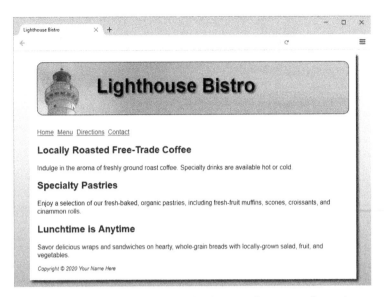

Figure 4.44  The gradient in the background was configured with CSS without an image file

## Linear Gradient Syntax

A **linear gradient** is a smooth blending of color in a single direction such as from top to bottom or from left to right. To configure a basic linear gradient, code the `linear-gradient` function as the value of the background-image property. Indicate the direction of the gradient by coding the keyword phrase "`to bottom`", "`to top`", "`to left`" or "`to right`". Next, list two or more color values to indicate the color stops. The basic format for a two-color linear gradient that blends from white to green follows:

```
background-image: linear-gradient(to bottom, #FFFFFF, #00FF00);
```

## Radial Gradient Syntax

A **radial gradient** is a smooth blending of color emanating outward from a single point. Code the `radial-gradient` function as the value of the background-image property to configure a radial gradient. List two or more color values to indicate the color stops. The first color will be displayed by default in the center of the element and gradually blend outward until the second color is displayed. The basic format for a two-color radial gradient that blends from white to blue follows:

```
background-image: radial-gradient(#FFFFFF, #0000FF);
```

## CSS Gradients and Progressive Enhancement

The term **progressive enhancement** is defined by web developer and HTML5 evangelist Christian Heilmann as "starting with a baseline of usable functionality, then increasing the richness of the user experience step by step by testing for support for enhancements before applying them." In other words, start with a web page that displays well in most browsers and then add newer design techniques, such as CSS gradients, in a way that enhances the display for visitors who are using browsers that support the new technique. It's useful to keep progressive enhancement in mind when using CSS gradients. Configure a "fallback" `background-color` property or `background-image` property which will be rendered by browsers that do not support CSS gradients. In Figure 4.44 the background color was configured to be same value as the ending gradient color.

## Hands-On Practice 4.17

You'll work with CSS gradient backgrounds in this Hands-On Practice. Create a new folder called gradientch4. Copy the chapter4/starter4.html file into your gradientch4 folder. Rename the file index.html. Launch a text editor and open the file.

1. First, you will configure a linear gradient. Code embedded CSS in the head section. Configure the body of the web page to display a fallback orchid background color of #DA70D6 and a linear gradient background that blends white to orchid from top to bottom without repeating:

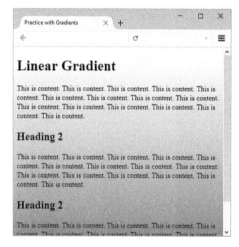

Figure 4.45  Linear gradient background

```
body { background-color: #DA70D6;
       background-image:
          linear-gradient(to
       bottom, #FFFFFF, #DA70D6);
       background-repeat: no-repeat;
}
```

2. Save your file and test it in a modern browser. The display should be similar to the results shown in Figure 4.45. The background gradient displays behind the page content, so scroll down the page to see the full gradient. Compare your work with the solution in the student files (chapter4/4.17/linear.html).

3. Next, you will configure a radial gradient. Edit the body section of the web page and code change the text within the h1 element to: Radial Gradient.

4. Edit the CSS and modify the value of the background-image property to configure a radial gradient linear gradient that blends white to orchid from center outward without repeating:

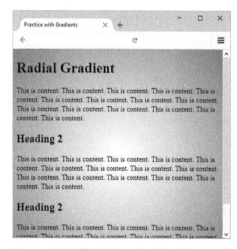

Figure 4.46  Radial gradient background

```
body { background-color: #DA70D6;
       background-image:
       radial-gradient(#FFFFFF,
       #DA70D6);
       background-repeat:
       no-repeat; }
```

5. Save your file and test in in a modern browser. The display should be similar to the results shown in Figure 4.46. Scroll down the page to see the full gradient. Compare your work with the solution in the student files (chapter4/4.17/radial.html).

## FAQ   Where can I find out more about CSS gradients?

Visit https://css-tricks.com/css3-gradients to delve deeper into CSS gradients. Experiment with generating CSS gradient code at http://www.colorzilla.com/gradient-editor, http://www.css3factory.com/linear-gradients, and http://www.westciv.com/tools/gradients.

# Chapter Summary

This chapter has introduced the use of visual elements and graphics on web pages. The number-one reason visitors leave web pages is long download times. When using images, be careful to optimize the images for the Web, reducing both the size of the file and the dimensions of the image, in order to minimize download time.

You explored new HTML5 elements and many CSS properties in this chapter. When using the new CSS properties and HTML5 elements, be mindful of the concepts of progressive enhancement and accessibility. Verify that the pages display in an acceptable manner even if new techniques are not supported by the browser. Provide text alternatives to images with the `alt` attribute.

Visit the textbook's website at https://www.webdevfoundations.net for examples, the links listed in this chapter, and updated information.

## Key Terms

| | | |
|---|---|---|
| `<figcaption>` | `border-width` property | lossy compression |
| `<figure>` | `box-shadow` property | `max-width` property |
| `<hr>` | cinemagraph | meter element |
| `<img>` | favicon | `min-width` property |
| `<meter>` | figcaption element | `opacity` property |
| `<progress>` | figure element | `padding` property |
| `alt` attribute | gamma | pixelation |
| animated GIF | GIF | PNG |
| area element | gradient | progress element |
| aspect ratio | `height` attribute | progressive enhancement |
| `background` property | hotspots | progressive JPEG |
| `background-attachment` property | HSLA color | radial gradient |
| `background-clip` property | horizontal rule element | RGBA color |
| `background-image` property | image element | resolution |
| `background-origin` property | image link | sprite |
| `background-position` property | image map | `src` attribute |
| `background-repeat` property | image optimization | `srcset` attribute |
| `background-size` property | image slicing | thumbnail image |
| `border` property | interlaced image | transparency |
| `border-color` property | JPEG | `usemap` attribute |
| `border-radius` property | linear gradient | WebP |
| `border-style` property | lossless compression | `width` attribute |

## Review Questions

### Multiple Choice

1. Which of the following graphic types can be made transparent?
   a. GIF
   b. JPG
   c. PNG
   d. GIF and PNG
   e. GIF and JPG

2. Which of the following configures empty space between the content of the HTML element (typically text) and the border?
   a. space property
   b. padding property
   c. margin property
   d. border property

**3.** Which of the following creates an image link to the index.html page when the home.gif graphic is clicked?

a. `<a href="index.html" src="home.gif" alt="Home"></a>`

b. `<a href="index.html"> <img src="home.gif" alt="Home"></a>`

c. `<img src="home.gif" href="index.html" alt="Home">`

d. `<a href="index.html"> <img href="home.gif" alt="Home"></a>`

**4.** What is the purpose of coding height and width attributes on an `<img>` tag?

a. They are required attributes and must always be included.

b. They help the browser render the page faster because it reserves the appropriate space for the image.

c. They help the browser display the image in its own window.

d. none of the above

**5.** Which attribute specifies text that is available to browsers and other user agents that do not support graphics?

a. `alt`

b. `text`

c. `src`

d. none of the above

**6.** What is the term used to describe a square icon that is associated with a web page and is displayed in the browser address bar or tab?

a. background

b. bookmark icon

c. favicon

d. logo

**7.** Which of the following graphic types is well-suited to photographs?

a. GIF

b. JPG

c. WebP

d. JPG and WebP

e. GIF and JPG

**8.** Which CSS property configures the background color?

a. bgcolor

b. background-color

c. color

d. none of the above

**9.** Which HTML tag configures a horizontal line on a web page?

a. `<line>`

b. `<br>`

c. `<hr>`

d. `<border>`

**10.** Which of the following configures a graphic to repeat vertically down the side of a web page?

a. `background-repeat: left;`

b. `background-repeat:repeat;`

c. `repeat: left;`

d. `background-repeat: repeat-y;`

## Fill in the Blank

**11.** A background image will automatically be repeated, or _____, by a web browser.

**12.** If your web page uses graphic links, include _____ at the bottom of the page to increase accessibility.

**13.** A(n) _____ image is a smaller version of a larger image that usually links to the larger image.

**14.** The _____ CSS property configures a drop-shadow effect on an HTML element.

**15.** The _____ element displays a visual gauge of a numeric value within a known range.

## Apply Your Knowledge

1. **Predict the Result.** Draw and write a brief description of the web page that will be created with the following HTML code:

```
<!DOCTYPE html>
<html lang="en">
<head>
<title>Predict the Result</title>
<meta charset="utf-8">
</head>
<body>
<header> <img src="logo.gif" alt="CircleSoft Design" height="100"
width="1000">
</header>
<nav> Home <a href="about.html">About</a>
<a href="services.html">Services</a>
</nav>
<main><p>Our professional staff takes pride in its working
relationship with our clients by offering personalized services
that take their needs into account, develop their target areas, and
incorporate these items into a website that works.</p>
</main>
</body>
</html>
```

2. **Fill in the Missing Code.** This web page contains an image link and should be configured so that the background and text colors have good contrast. The image used on this web page should link to a page called services.html. Some HTML attribute values, indicated by "_", are missing. Some CSS style rules, indicated by "_", are incomplete. The code follows:

```
<!DOCTYPE html>
<html lang="en">
<head>
<title>CircleSoft Design</title>
<meta charset="utf-8">
<style>
body {  "_":  "_";
       color:  "_";
}
</style>
</head>
<body>
  <div>
  <a href="_"><img src="logo.gif" alt="_"  height="100"
width="1000">
  <br>Enter CircleSoft Design</a>
</div>
</body>
</html>
```

3. **Find the Error.** This page displays an image called trillium.jpg. The image is 307 pixels wide by 200 pixels high. When this page is displayed, the image does not look right. Find the error. Describe any attributes that you would code in the `<img>` tag to provide accessibility. The code follows:

```
<!DOCTYPE html>
<html lang="en">
<head>
<title>Find the Error<title>
<meta charset="utf-8">
</head>
<body>
<img src="trillium.jpg" height="100" width="100">
</body>
</html>
```

## Hands-On Exercises

1. Write the HTML to place an image called primelogo.gif on a web page. The image is 100 pixels high by 650 pixels wide.

2. Write the HTML to create an image for the schaumburgthumb.jpg image. It is 100 pixels high by 150 pixels wide. The image should link to a larger image called schaumburg.jpg. There should be no border on the image.

3. Write the HTML to create a nav element that contains three images used as navigation links. Table 4.6 provides information about the images and their associated links.

Table 4.6

| Image Name | Link Page Name | Image Height | Image Width |
|---|---|---|---|
| homebtn.gif | index.html | 50 | 200 |
| productsbtn.gif | products.html | 50 | 200 |
| orderbtn.gif | order.html | 50 | 200 |

4. Experiment with page backgrounds. Locate the twocolor.gif file in the student files chapter4/starters folder. Design a web page that uses this file as a background image that repeats down the left side of the browser window. Save your file as bg1.html.

5. Experiment with page backgrounds. Locate the twocolor1.gif file in the student files chapter4/starters folder. Design a web page that uses this file as a background image that repeats across the top of the browser window. Save your file as bg2.html.

6. Visit one of your favorite websites. Note the colors used for background, text, headings, images, and so on. Write a paragraph that describes how the site uses color for these elements. Code a web page that uses colors in a similar manner. Save your file as color.html.

**7.** Practice with CSS.

   a. Write the CSS for an HTML selector footer with the following characteristics: a light-blue background color, Arial font, dark-blue text color, 10 pixels of padding, and a narrow, dashed border in a dark-blue color.

   b. Write the CSS for an id named `notice` that is configured to 80% width and centered.

   c. Write the CSS to configure a class that will produce a headline with a dotted line underneath it. Choose a color that you like for the text and dotted line.

   d. Write the CSS to configure an h1 element selector with drop-shadow text, a 50% transparent background color, and sans-serif font that is 4em in size.

   e. Write the CSS to configure an id named `feature` with small, red, Arial font; a white background; a width of 80%; and a drop shadow.

**8.** Design a new web page about you. Use CSS to configure a background color and text color for the page. Include the following on your web page:

   - Your name
   - A description of your favorite hobbies and activities
   - A photo of yourself (be sure to optimize the image for display on the Web)

   Save the page as yourlastname.html.

**9.** Design a web page that provides a list of resources for free stock photographs. The list should contain at least five different websites. Use your favorite graphic sites, the sites suggested in this chapter, or sites you have found on the Web. Save the page as freegraphics.html.

**10.** Visit the textbook's website at http://webdevfoundations.net/10e/chapter4.html and follow the link to the Adobe Photoshop tutorial. Follow the instructions to create a logo banner. Hand in the printouts described in the tutorial to your instructor.

## Web Research

**1.** Providing access to the Web for all people is an important issue. Visit the W3C's Web Accessibility Initiative and explore its WCAG 2.0 Quick Reference at https://www.w3.org/WAI/WCAG21/quickref/. View additional pages at the W3C's site as necessary. Explore the checkpoints that are related to the use of color and images on web pages. Create a web page that uses color, uses images, and includes the information that you discovered.

**2.** This chapter has introduced you to image formats used on the Web. Obtain the butterfly.jpg image found in the student files chapter4/starters folder. Use one of the resources listed below (or locate your own resource) to convert the image file to WebP format. Create an example web page that indicates the file size of the original image and the WebP image. Also code two img tags on the web page to configure the original image and the WebP image. Use a modern browser (such as Chrome, Firefox, or Edge) to display your web page. Note that if you display your page in a non-supporting browser, such as Internet Explorer, the WebP image will not display. Resources for image conversion are listed below:

- https://ezgif.com/jpg-to-webp
- https://image.online-convert.com/convert-to-webp
- https://developers.google.com/speed/webp/

## Focus on Web Design

Visit a website that interests you. Print the home page or one other pertinent page from the site. Write a one-page summary and reaction to the website you chose to visit. Address the following topics:

**a.** What is the purpose of the site?

**b.** Who is the intended audience?

**c.** Do you believe the site reaches its audience?

**d.** Was this site useful to you? Why or why not?

**e.** List the colors and/or graphics that are used on the home page of this website: background, backgrounds of page sections, text, logo, navigation buttons, and so on.

**f.** How does the use of color and graphics enhance the website?

# WEBSITE CASE STUDY
## Using Graphics & Visual Elements

Each of the case studies in this section continues throughout most of the text. In this chapter, we add images to the websites, create a new page, and modify existing pages.

## JavaJam Coffee Bar

See Chapter 2 for an introduction to the JavaJam Coffee Bar Case Study. Figure 2.32 shows a site map for the JavaJam website. The Home page and Menu page were created in earlier chapters. Using the existing website as a starting point, you will modify the design of the pages and create a new page, the Music page. You have five tasks in this case study:

1. Create a new folder for this JavaJam case study, and obtain the starter image files.

2. Modify the Home page to display the winding road image as shown in Figure 4.47 using the wireframe in Figure 4.48 as a guide.

3. Modify the Menu page to display the same background image as the Home page and to display an image, as shown in Figure 4.49.

4. Create a new Music page, as shown in Figure 4.50.

5. Modify the style rules in the javajam.css file as needed.

## Hands-On Practice Case

**Task 1: The Website Folder.** Create a folder on your hard drive or portable storage device called javajam4. Copy all the files from your Chapter 3 javajamcss folder into the javajam4 folder. Obtain the images used in this case study from the student files. Copy all the files from the chapter4/starters/javajam folder into your javajam4 folder.

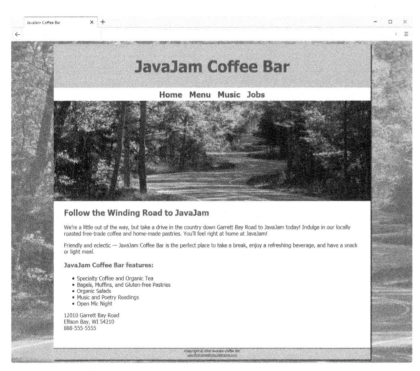

Figure 4.47  New JavaJam Home page

**Task 2: The Home Page.** Launch a text editor, and open the index.html file from your javajam4 folder. It is common for the Home page of a website to have a slightly different layout than the content pages. Modify the index.html file to look similar to the web page shown in Figure 4.47.

```
wrapper
┌─────────────────────────────┐
│ ┌─────────────────────────┐ │
│ │ header                  │ │
│ └─────────────────────────┘ │
│ ┌─────────────────────────┐ │
│ │ nav                     │ │
│ └─────────────────────────┘ │
│ ┌─────────────────────────┐ │
│ │ div with large image    │ │
│ └─────────────────────────┘ │
│ ┌─────────────────────────┐ │
│ │ main                    │ │
│ │ ┌─────────────────────┐ │ │
│ │ │ div with contact info│ │ │
│ │ └─────────────────────┘ │ │
│ └─────────────────────────┘ │
│ ┌─────────────────────────┐ │
│ │ footer                  │ │
│ └─────────────────────────┘ │
└─────────────────────────────┘
```

Figure 4.48  Home page wireframe

1. Configure a div element to display the hero.jpg image. Code an opening div tag assigned to the id named `homehero` after the closing nav tag. Next, code a closing div tag. As shown in the wireframe in Figure 4.48, this div is located between the nav element and the main element. There is no HTML or text content for this div. The purpose of this div is to display a large image (configured with CSS in Task 5).

2. Replace the "Relax at JavaJam" text contained within the h2 element with "Follow the Winding Road to JavaJam."

3. Add a paragraph with the following text below the h2 element and above the existing paragraph:

   "We're a little out of the way, but take a drive in the country down Garrett Bay Road to JavaJam today! Indulge in our locally roasted free-trade coffee and home-made pastries. You'll feel right at home at JavaJam!"

4. Configure the text "JavaJam Coffee Bar features:" within an h3 element below the second paragraph and above the unordered list.

Save and test your new index.html page. It will be similar to Figure 4.47, but you'll notice that a few final touches (including the background image and the winding road image) are missing; you'll configure these with CSS in Task 5.

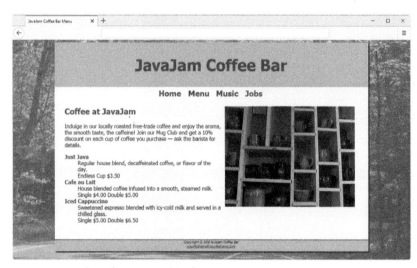

Figure 4.49  JavaJam menu.html

**Task 3: The Menu Page.** Launch a text editor, and open the menu.html page from your javajam4 folder. Modify the menu.html file to look similar to the web page shown in Figure 4.49.

1. Code an img element for the mugs.jpg image above the h2 element in the main content area. Be sure to include the `alt`, `height`, and `width` attributes. Also configure the image to appear to the right of the text content by coding the `align="right"` attribute on the `<img>` tag. Note: The W3C HTML validator will indicate that the align attribute is invalid. We'll ignore the error for this case study. In Chapter 6, you'll learn to use the CSS float property (instead of the align attribute) to configure this type of layout.

2. Add a paragraph with the following text below the h2 element:

"Indulge in our locally roasted free-trade coffee and enjoy the aroma, the smooth taste, the caffeine! Join our Mug Club and get a 10% discount on each cup of coffee you purchase — ask the barista for details." *Hint:* See Appendix B, "Special Characters," for the character code to display the em dash (—).

Save and test your new menu.html page. It will be similar to Figure 4.49, but missing a few final touches (see Task 5).

**Task 4: The Music Page.** Use the Menu page as the starting point for the Music page. Launch a text editor, and open the menu.html file in the javajam4 folder. Save the file as music.html. Modify the music.html file to look similar to the Music page, as shown in Figure 4.50:

Figure 4.50  JavaJam music.html

1. Change the page title to an appropriate phrase.
2. Delete the image and description list from the page.
3. Configure "Music at JavaJam" as the text within the h2 element.
4. Configure the following as the text within the paragraph element:

   "The first Friday night each month at JavaJam is a special night. Join us from 8 pm to 11 pm for some music you won't want to miss!"
5. The rest of the content in the page will consist of two areas describing music performances. The area describing each music performance consists of an h4 element, a div assigned to the class named `details`, and an image link.

January Music Performance:

- Configure an h4 element with the following text: January
- Code an opening div tag. Assign the div to the class named `details`.
- Configure the melaniethumb.jpg as an image link to melanie.jpg. Code appropriate attributes on the `<img>` tag.
- Configure the following text within the div after the image link:

  Melanie Morris entertains with her melodic folk style.

February Music Performance:

- Configure an h4 element with the following text: February
- Code an opening div tag. Assign the div to the class named `details`.

- Configure the gregthumb.jpg as an image link to greg.jpg. Code appropriate attributes on the `<img>` tag.
- Configure the following text within the div after the image:

  Tahoe Greg is back from his tour. New songs. New stories.

Save the music.html file. If you test your page in a browser, you'll notice that it looks different from Figure 4.50—you still need to configure style rules.

**Task 5: Configure the CSS.** Open javajam.css in a text editor. Edit the style rules as follows:

1. Modify the body element selector style rules. Configure fadedroad50.jpg as the background image that does not repeat. This background image will fill the entire browser viewport so set the background-attachment property to fixed and the background-size property to cover.

2. Modify the style rules for the `wrapper` id. Configure a minimum width of 900px (use `min-width`). Configure a maximum width of 1280px (use `max-width`). Use the `box-shadow` property to configure a drop-shadow effect.

3. Modify the header element selector style rules. Configure declarations to set top and bottom padding to 5px.

4. Modify the h1 element selector style rules. Remove the `line-height` declaration. Code a declaration to set font size to 3em.

5. Modify the nav element selector style rules. Configure declarations for 1.5em font size size,  5px of top padding, and 5px bottom padding.

6. Code a new style rule to prevent the hyperlinks in the nav area from displaying the default underline. Use `nav a { text-decoration: none; }`

7. Modify the footer element selector style rules. Configure declarations for 1em of padding and a solid 2px top border (use #8C3826 as the color).

8. Add a new style rule for the h4 element selector that configures a background color (#D2B48C), font size (1.2em), left padding (.5em), and bottom padding (.25em).

9. Configure style rules for the h3 and dt element selectors to set the text color to #8C3826.

10. Add a new style rule for the main element selector to configure 2em of padding on the left, right, and bottom. You may need to nudge Internet Explorer to display the page as intended by adding the `display: block;` declaration (see Chapter 6).

11. Add a new style rule for the class named `details` to add 20% left and right padding. This will configure empty space on either side of the music performance description and image on the music.html page.

12. Add a new style rule for the img element selector that configures 10px left padding and 10px right padding.

13. Add a new selector for an id named `homehero`. Code declarations to configure 300px height and to display the hero.jpg background image to fill the space (use `background-size: cover;`) without repeating.

Save the javajam.css file. Test your pages (index.html, menu.html, and music.html) in a browser. If your images do not appear or your image links do not work, examine your work carefully. Use Windows Explorer or Mac Finder to verify that the images are saved in your javajam4 folder. Examine the `src` attribute on the `<img>` tags to be sure you spelled the image names correctly. Examine your CSS to verify that you have spelled the image names correctly.

Another useful troubleshooting technique is to validate the HTML and CSS code. See Chapters 2 and 3 for Hands-On Practice exercises that describe how to use these validators.

## Fish Creek Animal Clinic

See Chapter 2 for an introduction to the Fish Creek Animal Clinic Case Study. Figure 2.36 shows a site map for Fish Creek. The Home page and Services page were created in earlier chapters. Using the existing website as a starting point, you will modify the design of the pages and create a new page, the Ask the Vet page. You have five tasks in this case study:

1. Create a new folder for this Fish Creek case study, and obtain the starter image files.

2. Modify the Home page to display a logo image and navigation image links as shown in Figure 4.51.

3. Modify the Services page to be consistent with the Home page.

4. Create a new Ask the Vet page, as shown in Figure 4.52.

5. Modify the style rules in the fishcreek.css file as needed.

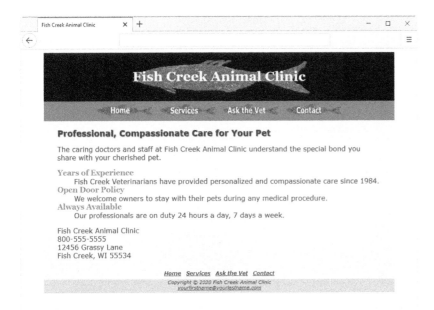

Figure 4.51  New Fish Creek Home page

## Hands-On Practice Case

**Task 1: The Website Folder.** Create a folder on your hard drive or portable storage device called fishcreek4. Copy all the files from your Chapter 3 fishcreekcss folder into the fishcreek4 folder. Obtain the images used in this case study from the student files. Copy all the files from the chapter4/starters/fishcreek folder into your fishcreek4 folder.

**Task 2: The Home Page.** Launch a text editor, and open the index.html file from your fishcreek4 folder. Modify the index.html file to look similar to the web page shown in Figure 4.51.

Update the navigation area.

- Since you will be replacing the top navigation with image links, it's a good idea to provide for accessibility by including a set of text navigation links in the footer section of the web page. Copy the nav element, and paste it inside the footer area above the copyright line.

- Refer to Figure 4.51, and replace the top navigation text hyperlinks with image links. The home.gif should link to index.html. The services.gif should link to services.html. The askthevet.gif should link to askvet.html. The contact.gif should link to contact.html. Use appropriate attributes on the `<img>` tag: `alt`, `height`, and `width`.

Save and test your new index.html page. It will be similar to Figure 4.51, but you'll notice that the header, footer, and navigation areas still need work; you'll configure these with CSS in Task 5.

**Task 3: The Services Page.** Launch a text editor, and open the services.html page from your fishcreek4 folder. Configure the navigation areas in a similar way as the home page. Save and test your new services.html page.

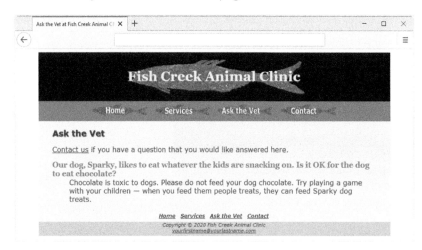

**Figure 4.52** Fish Creek askvet.html

**Task 4: The Ask the Vet Page.** Use the Services page as the starting point for the Ask the Vet page. Launch a text editor, and open the services.html file in the fishcreek4 folder. Save the file as askvet.html. Modify the askvet.html file to look similar to the Ask the Vet page, as shown in Figure 4.52:

1. Change the page title to an appropriate phrase.

2. Change the text in the `<h2>` to be "Ask the Vet".

3. Delete the unordered list from the page.

4. The page content consists of a paragraph of text followed by a description list that contains a question and an answer.

    a. Configure the text in the paragraph as follows:

    Contact us if you have a question that you would like answered here.

    b. The phrase "Contact us" should link to the contact.html page.

    c. The description list displays the question and answer. The `<dt>` element configures the question. The `<dd>` element configures the answer. The content of the description list follows:

    Question: Our dog, Sparky, likes to eat whatever the kids are snacking on. Is it OK for the dog to eat chocolate?"

Answer: Chocolate is toxic to dogs. Please do not feed your dog chocolate. Try playing a game with your children — when you feed them people treats, they can feed Sparky dog treats.

   d. *Hint:* See Appendix B, "Special Characters," for the character code to display the em dash (—).

Save the askvet.html file. If you test your page in a browser, you'll notice that it looks different from Figure 4.52—you still need to configure style rules.

**Task 5: Configure the CSS.**  Open fishcreek.css in in a text editor. Edit the style rules as follows:

1. Modify the style rules for the `wrapper` id. Configure a minimum width of 700px (use `min-width`).

2. Modify the style rules for the header element selector. Change the text color to `#F0F0F0`. Configure fishcreeklogo.gif as a background image that is centered and does not repeat. Configure 1em padding. Configure the text alignment to be centered (use `text-align:center`).

3. Remove the style rules for the h1 element selector.

4. Modify the style rules for the nav element selector. Add a new declaration to center the text. Also set the background color to `#5280C5` and padding to .5em.

5. Modify the styles for the h2 element selector to display text with a drop shadow (use `text-shadow: 1px 1px 1px #777`).

6. Modify the style rules for the footer element selector.  Configure centered text, bottom padding set to .5em, and set background color to `#AEC3E3`.

7. Add a new style rule for the main element selector. Set left and right padding to 2em.

8. Add a new style rule for the navigation in the footer area (use `footer nav` as the selector) to overrule the previous nav style rule and configure a `#F0F0F0` background color. Also set font size to 110% and bottom padding to .5em.

Save the fishcreek.css file. Test your pages (index.html, services.html, and askvet.html) in a browser. The Home page (index.html) should look similar to Figure 4.51. The new Ask the Vet page (askvet.html) should look similar to Figure 4.52. If your images do not appear or your image links do not work, examine your work carefully. Use Windows Explorer or Mac Finder to verify that the images are saved in your fishcreek4 folder. Examine the `src` attribute on the `<img>` tags to be sure you spelled the image names correctly. Examine your CSS to verify that you have spelled the image names correctly. Another useful troubleshooting technique is to validate the HTML and CSS code. See Chapters 2 and 3 for Hands-On Practice exercises that describe how to use these validators.

## Pacific Trails Resort

See Chapter 2 for an introduction to the Pacific Trails Case Study. Figure 2.40 shows a site map for Pacific Trails. The Home page and Yurts page were created in earlier chapters. Using the existing website as a starting point, you will modify the design of

wrapper

**Figure 4.53** New Pacific Trails wireframe

the pages to display a large image on each page, as indicated in the wireframe in Figure 4.53. You will also create a new page, the Activities page. You have five tasks in this case study:

1. Create a new folder for this Pacific Trails case study, and obtain the starter image files.

2. Modify the Home page to display a logo image and scenic photograph as shown in Figure 4.54.

3. Modify the Yurts page to be consistent with the Home page.

4. Create a new Activities page, as shown in Figure 4.55.

5. Modify the style rules in the pacific.css file as needed.

## Hands-On Practice Case

**Task 1: The Website Folder.** Create a folder on your hard drive or portable storage device called pacific4. Copy all the files from your Chapter 3 pacificcss folder into the pacific4 folder. Obtain the images used in this case study from the student files. Copy all the files from the chapter4/starters/pacific folder into your pacific4 folder.

**Task 2: The Home Page.** Launch a text editor, and open the index.html file from your pacific4 folder. Modify the index.html file to look similar to the web page shown in Figure 4.54. Configure a div element to display the coast.jpg image. Code an opening div tag assigned to the id named `homehero` after the closing nav tag. Next, code a closing div tag. As shown in the wireframe in Figure 4.53, this div is located between the nav element and the main element. There is no HTML or text content for this div. The purpose of this div is to display a large image (configured with CSS in Task 5).

Save and validate your new index.html page. It will not yet be similar to Figure 4.54; you'll configure CSS in Task 5.

**Figure 4.54** New Pacific Trails Resort Home page

**Task 3: The Yurts Page.** Launch a text editor, and open the yurts.html page from your pacific4 folder. Configure a div element to display the yurt.jpg image. Code an opening div tag assigned to the id named `yurthero` after the closing nav tag. Next, code a closing div tag. As shown in the wireframe in Figure 4.53, this div is located between the nav element and the main element. There is no HTML or text content for this div. The purpose of this div is to display a large image (configured with CSS in Task 5). Save and validate your new yurts.html page.

Figure 4.55  Pacific Trails Resort activities.html

**Task 4: The Activities Page.** Use the Yurts page as the starting point for the Activities page. Launch a text editor, and open the yurts.html file in the pacific4 folder. Save the file as activities.html. Modify the activities.html file to look similar to the Activities page, as shown in Figure 4.55:

1. Change the page title to an appropriate phrase.

2. Modify the div assigned to the id `yurthero`. Replace `yurthero` with `trailhero`.

3. Change the text in the `<h2>` to be "Activities at Pacific Trails".

4. Delete the description list from the page.

5. Configure the following text, using h3 tags for the headings and paragraph tags for the sentences:

**Hiking**

Pacific Trails Resort has 5 miles of hiking trails and is adjacent to a state park. Go it alone or join one of our guided hikes.

**Kayaking**

Ocean kayaks are available for guest use.

**Bird Watching**

While anytime is a good time for bird watching at Pacific Trails, we offer guided bird-watching trips at sunrise several times a week.

6. Configure a span element to contain the phrase "Pacific Trails Resort" in the first paragraph on the page. Assign the span to the class named `resort`.

Save the activities.html file. If you test your page in a browser, you'll notice that it looks different from Figure 4.55; you still need to configure style rules.

**Task 5: Configure the CSS.** Open pacific.css in in a text editor. Edit the style rules as follows:

1. Modify the body element selector style rules. Change the background color to light blue: #90C7E3. Add style declarations to display a linear gradient that blends from white (#FFFFFF) to light blue (#90C7E3) and does not repeat.

2. Modify the style rules for the `wrapper` id. Configure the background color to be #FFFFFF. Configure a minimum width of 960px (use `min-width`). Configure a maximum width of 2048px (use `max-width`). Use the `box-shadow` property to configure a drop-shadow effect.

3. Modify the style rules for the header element selector. Configure the sunset.jpg as a background image that displays on the right and does not repeat. Configure a 72-pixel height (the same height as the background image).

4. Modify the style rules for the h1 element selector. Remove the line-height declaration. Configure centered text and .5em top padding.

5. Modify the style rules for the nav element selector. Set top, right, and bottom padding to .5em. Remove the style rule for the background color. Configure centered text.

6. Modify the style rules for the footer element selector. Set padding to 1em.

7. Add a new style rule for the h3 element selector to configure the font to be Georgia or a generic serif.

8. Add a new style rule for the main element selector that configures 2em of left and right padding. You may need to nudge Internet Explorer to display the page as intended by adding the `display: block;` declaration (see Chapter 6).

9. Add a new selector for an id named `homehero`. Code declarations to configure 300px height and to display the coast.jpg background image to fill the space (use `background-size: 100% 100%;`) without repeating.

10. Add a new selector for an id named `yurthero`. Code declarations to configure 300px height and to display the yurt.jpg background image to fill the space (use `background-size: 100% 100%;`) without repeating.

11. Add a new selector for an id named `trailhero`. Code declarations to configure 300px height and to display the trail.jpg background image to fill the space (use `background-size: 100% 100%;`) without repeating.

12. Code a new style rule to prevent the hyperlinks in the nav area from displaying the default underline. Use `nav a { text-decoration: none; }`

Save the pacific.css file. Test your pages (index.html, yurts.html, and activities.html) in a browser. The Home page (index.html) should look similar to Figure 4.54. The new Activities page (activities.html) should look similar to Figure 4.55. If your images do not appear, examine your work carefully. Use Windows Explorer or Mac Finder to verify that the images are saved in your pacific4 folder. Examine your CSS to be sure you spelled the image names correctly. Another useful troubleshooting technique is to validate the HTML and CSS code. See Chapters 2 and 3 for Hands-On Practice exercises that describe how to use these validators.

## Path of Light Yoga Studio

See Chapter 2 for an introduction to the Path of Light Yoga Studio Case Study. Figure 2.44 shows a site map for Path of Light Yoga Studio. The Home page and Classes page were created in earlier chapters. Using the existing website as a starting point, you will modify the design of the pages and create a new page, the Schedule page. You have five tasks in this case study:

1. Create a new folder for this Path of Light Yoga Studio case study, and obtain the starter image files.
2. Modify the Home page to display as shown in Figure 4.56.
3. Modify the Classes page to display as shown in Figure 4.58.
4. Create a new Schedule page, as shown in Figure 4.59.
5. Modify the style rules in the yoga.css file as needed.

### Hands-On Practice Case

**Task 1: The Website Folder.** Create a folder on your hard drive or portable storage device called yoga4. Copy all the files from your Chapter 3 yogacss folder into the yoga4 folder. Obtain the images used in this case study from the student files. Copy all the files from the chapter4/starters/yoga folder into your yoga4 folder.

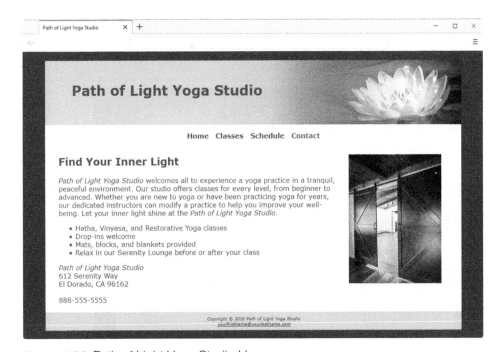

**Figure 4.56** Path of Light Yoga Studio Home page

**Task 2: The Home Page.** Launch a text editor, and open the index.html file from your yoga4 folder. Modify the index.html file to look similar to the web page shown in Figure 4.56.

Code an img element for the yogadoor.jpg photo above the h2 element in the main content area. Be sure to include the `alt`, `height`, and `width` attributes. Also configure the image to appear to the right of the text by coding the `align="right"` attribute on the

wrapper

```
┌─────────────────────────────┐
│  header                     │
├─────────────────────────────┤
│  nav                        │
├─────────────────────────────┤
│  main                       │
│  ┌───────────────────────┐  │
│  │ div with large image  │  │
│  └───────────────────────┘  │
│                             │
│                             │
├─────────────────────────────┤
│  footer                     │
└─────────────────────────────┘
```

**Figure 4.57** New Path of Light Yoga Studio wireframe

`<img>` tag. Note: The W3C HTML validator will indicate that the align attribute is invalid. We'll ignore the error for this case study. In Chapter 6, you'll learn to use the CSS float property (instead of the align attribute) to configure this type of layout.

Save and test your new index.html page. It will be similar to Figure 4.56 but you'll notice that a few final touches (including dark page background and lily image in the header) are missing; you'll configure these with CSS in Task 5.

**Task 3: The Classes Page.** It's common for the content pages of a website to have a slightly different structure than the home page. The wireframe shown in Figure 4.57 depicts the structure of the Classes and Schedule pages. Launch a text editor, and open the classes.html page from your yoga4 folder. Configure a div element to display the yogamat.jpg image. As shown in the wireframe in Figure 4.57, this div is located within the main element. Code an opening div tag after the opening main tag. Assign the div to an id named `hero`. Code an img element for the yogamat.jpg image. Be sure to include the alt, height, and width attributes. Next, code a closing div tag. Save and test your new classes.html page. If you test your page in a browser, you'll notice that it looks a bit different from Figure 4.58; you still need to configure style rules.

**Figure 4.58** Path of Light Yoga Studio Classes Page

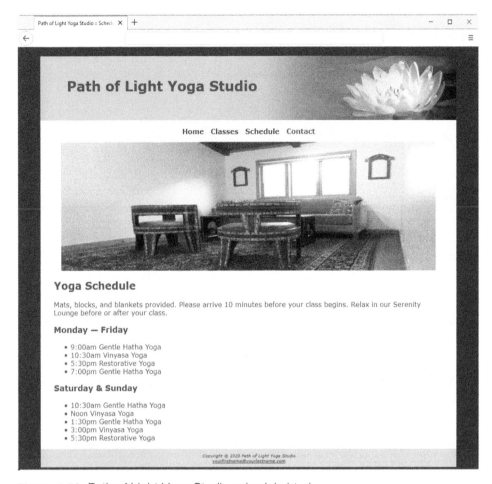

Figure 4.59 Path of Light Yoga Studio schedule.html

**Task 4: The Schedule Page.** Use the Classes page as the starting point for the Schedule page. Launch a text editor, and open the classes.html file in the yoga4 folder. Save the file as schedule.html. Modify your file to look similar to the Schedule page, as shown in Figure 4.59.

1. Change the title to an appropriate phrase.

2. Replace the h2 element text "Yoga Classes" with "Yoga Schedule".

3. Modify the img tag to display the yogalounge.jpg image. Configure appropriate alt text.

4. Delete the description list.

5. Configure content for the Schedule page.

   - Configure a paragraph element that contains the following text:

     Mats, blocks, and blankets provided. Please arrive 10 minutes before your class begins. Relax in our Serenity Lounge before or after your class.

   - Configure an h3 element with the following text:

     Monday — Friday

   - Configure an unordered list with the following text:

     9:00am Gentle Hatha Yoga

     10:30am Vinyasa Yoga

     5:30pm Restorative Yoga

     7:00pm Gentle Hatha Yoga

- Configure an h3 element with the following text:

  Saturday & Sunday

- Configure an unordered list with the following text:

  10:30am Gentle Hatha Yoga

  Noon Vinyasa Yoga

  1:30pm Gentle Hatha Yoga

  3:00pm Vinyasa Yoga

  5:30 pm Restorative Yoga

Save the schedule.html file. If you test your page in a browser, you'll notice that it looks different from Figure 4.59; you still need to configure style rules.

**Task 5: Configure the CSS.** Open yoga.css in in a text editor. Edit the style rules as follows:

1. Modify the style rules for the body element selector to configure a very dark background color (#3F2860).

2. Modify the style rules for the `#wrapper` id. Configure #F5F5F5 as the background color. Configure a minimum width of 1000px (use `min-width`) and a maximum width of 1280px (use `max-width`).

3. Modify the style rules for the header element selector. Remove the `text-align` declaration. Configure lilyheader.jpg as a background image that displays on the right without repeating. Set height to 150px.

4. Modify the style rules for the h1 element selector. Remove the `line-height` declaration. Configure 50px top padding and 2em left padding.

5. Modify the style rules for the nav element selector. Configure 1em padding.

6. Modify the style rules for the footer element selector. Configure 1em padding.

7. Configure styles for the main element selector. Set left and right padding to 2em. You may need to nudge Internet Explorer to display the page as intended by adding the `display: block;` declaration (see Chapter 6).

8. Configure styles for the img element selector. Set left and right padding to 1em.

9. Configure styles for an id selector named `hero`. Set `text-align` to center.

Save the yoga.css file. Test your pages (index.html, classes.html, and schedule.html) in a browser. Your pages should be similar to Figures 4.56, 4.58, and 4.59. If your images do not appear, examine your work carefully. Use Windows Explorer or Mac Finder to verify that the images are saved in your yoga folder. Examine the `src` attributes on the `<img>` tags to be sure you spelled the image names correctly. Examine your CSS to verify that you have spelled the image names correctly. Another useful troubleshooting technique is to validate the HTML and CSS code. See Chapters 2 and 3 for Hands-On Practice exercises that describe how to use these validators.

# 5

# Web Design

## Chapter Objectives    In this chapter, you will learn how to . . .

- Describe the most common types of website organization
- Describe the principles of visual design
- Design for your target audience
- Design clear, easy-to-use navigation
- Improve the readability of the text on your web pages
- Use graphics appropriately on web pages
- Apply the concept of universal design to web pages
- Describe web page layout design techniques
- Describe the concept of responsive web design
- Apply best practices of web design

As a website visitor, you have probably found that certain websites are appealing and easy to use while others seem awkward or just plain annoying. What separates the good from the bad? This chapter discusses recommended web design practices. The topics include site organization, navigation design, page layout design, text design, graphic design, choosing a color scheme, accessibility considerations, designing for the mobile web, and responsive web design concepts.

# 5.1 Design for Your Target Audience

Whatever your personal preferences, design your website to appeal to your **target audience**—the people who will use your site. Your intended target audience may be specific, such as children, teenagers, college students, young couples, or seniors, or you may intend your site to appeal to everyone. The purpose and goals of your visitors will vary—they may be casually seeking information, performing research for school or work, comparison shopping, job hunting, and so on. The design of a website should appeal to and meet the needs of the target audience.

Figure 5.1  The compelling graphic draws you in

For example, the web page shown in Figure 5.1 features compelling graphics and has a different look and feel from the web page displayed in Figure 5.2.

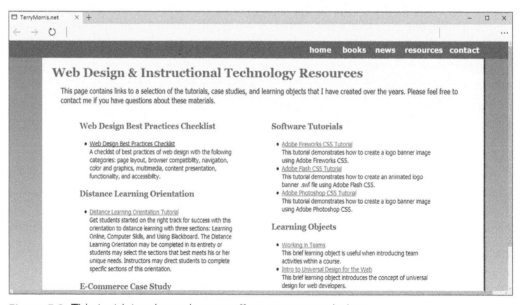

Figure 5.2  This text-intensive web page offers numerous choices

The first site engages you, draws you in, and invites exploration. The second site provides you with text-based information so that you can quickly get down to work. The layout, navigation, and even the use of color and text can work together to appeal to your target audience. Keep your target audience in mind as you explore the web design practices in this chapter.

# 5.2 Website Organization

How will visitors move around your site? How will they find what they need? This is largely determined by the website's organization or architecture. There are three common types of website organization:

- Hierarchical
- Linear
- Random (sometimes called Web organization)

A diagram of the organization of a website is called a **site map**. Creating the site map is one of the initial steps in developing a website (more on this in Chapter 10).

## Hierarchical Organization

Most websites use **hierarchical organization**. A site map for hierarchical organization, such as the one shown in Figure 5.3, is characterized by a clearly defined home page with links to major site sections. Web pages within sections are placed as needed. The home page and the first level of pages in a hierarchical site map typically indicate the hyperlinks on the main navigation bar of each web page.

It is important to be aware of the pitfalls of hierarchical organization. Figure 5.4 shows a site design that is too shallow—there are too many major site sections.

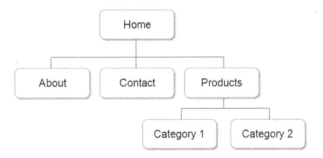

Figure 5.3 Hierarchical site organization

This site design needs to be organized into fewer, easily managed topics or units of information, a process called **chunking**. In the case of web page design, each unit

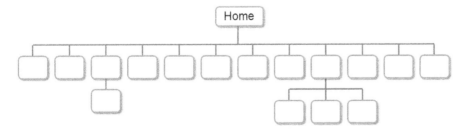

Figure 5.4 This site design uses a shallow hierarchy

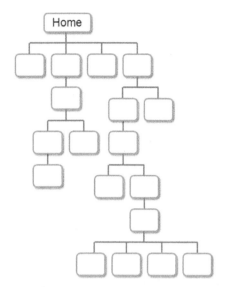

Figure 5.5 This site design uses a deep hierarchy

of information is a page. Nelson Cowan, a research psychologist at the University of Missouri, found that adults typically can keep about four items or chunks of items (such as the three parts of a phone number 888-555-5555) in their short-term memory (https://memory.psych.missouri.edu/cowan.html). Following this principle, be aware of the number of major navigation links and try to group them into visually separate sections on the page with each group having no more than about four links.

Another pitfall is designing a site that may be too deep. Figure 5.5 shows an example of this. A visitor who cannot get to the information they want will begin to feel frustrated and may leave your site. Organize your site so that your visitors can easily navigate from page to page within the site structure and locate the information they seek.

## Linear Organization

When the purpose of a site or series of pages on a site is to provide a tutorial, tour, or presentation that needs to be viewed sequentially, **linear organization**, as shown in Figure 5.6, is useful.

Figure 5.6 Linear site organization

In linear organization, the pages are viewed one after another. Some websites use hierarchical organization in general, but with linear organization in a few small areas.

## Random Organization

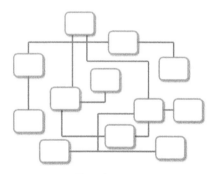

Figure 5.7 Random site organization

**Random organization** (sometimes called Web organization) offers no clear path through the site, as shown in Figure 5.7. There is often no clear home page and no discernable structure. Random organization is not as common as hierarchical or linear organization and is usually found only on artistic sites or sites that strive to be especially different and original. This type of organization is typically not used for commercial websites.

 FAQ  **What's a good way to build my site map?**

Sometimes it is difficult to begin creating a site map for a website. Some design teams meet in a room with a blank wall and a package of large Post-it® Notes. They write the titles of topics and subtopics needed in the site on the Post-it® Notes. They arrange the notes on the wall and discuss them until the site structure becomes clear and there is consensus within the group. If you are not working in a group, you can try this on your own and then discuss the organization of the website with a friend or fellow student.

# 5.3 Principles of Visual Design

There are four visual design principles that you can apply to the design of just about anything: repetition, contrast, proximity, and alignment. Whether you are designing a web page, a button, a logo, a DVD cover, a brochure, or a software interface, the design principles of repetition, contrast, proximity, and alignment will help to create the "look" (visual aesthetic), of your project and will determine whether your message is effectively communicated.

VideoNote
*Principles of Visual Design*

## Repetition: Repeat Visual Components Throughout the Design

When applying the principle of **repetition**, the web designer repeats one or more components throughout the page. The repeating aspect ties the work together. Figure 5.8 displays the home page for a bed and breakfast business. The page design demonstrates the use of repetition in a variety of design components, including color, shape, font, and images.

- The large photograph on the web page draws the viewer's attention. The smaller image repeats some of the same colors: terracotta, green, off-white, and grey. Colors that either occur in the photographs (off-white and grey) or that coordinate with the photographs (a dark red/rust) are repeated in other elements on the page. The rust color is used in the headings, navigation, e-mail address box, call to action button backgrounds, and horizontal line. The page background is off-white.

- The call-to-action "Book Now" and "Sign Up" buttons both have a rectangular shape and format with heading, content, and button.

- The use of only two font typefaces on the page also demonstrates repetition and helps to create a cohesive look.

Whether it is color, shape, font, or image, repetition helps to unify a design.

## Contrast: Add Visual Excitement and Draw Attention

To apply the principle of **contrast**, emphasize the differences between page elements in order to make the design interesting and direct attention. There should be good contrast between the background color and the text color on a web page. If there is too little contrast, the text will be difficult to read. Notice how the upper right navigation area in Figure 5.8 uses a dark text color that has good contrast with the light background color. The BOOK NOW call to action button has a dark background that both contrasts well with the light text and serves to make it stand out from the navigation. The area under the large photograph features a light background that has good contrast with the dark text. The dark text in the footer area contrasts well with the light background color.

**Figure 5.8** The design principles of repetition, contrast, proximity, and alignment are applied on this web page.

## Proximity: Group Related Items

When designers apply the principle of **proximity**, related items are placed physically close together. Unrelated items should have space separating them. In Figure 5.8, the horizontal navigation links are all placed in close proximity to each other. This creates a visual group on the page and makes the navigation easier to use. Proximity is used well on this page to group related elements such as each heading and its related paragraph and call to action button.

## Alignment: Align Elements to Create Visual Unity

Another principle that helps to create a cohesive web page is **alignment**. When applying this principle, the designer organizes the page so that each element placed has some alignment (vertical or horizontal) with another element on the page. The page shown in Figure 5.8 also applies this principle. Notice how the page components under the large photograph are vertically aligned in columns of equal height.

Repetition, contrast, proximity, and alignment are four visual design principles that can greatly improve your web page designs. If you apply these principles effectively, your web pages will look more professional and you will communicate your message more clearly. Keep these principles in mind as you design and build web pages.

# 5.4  Design to Provide Accessibility

**Focus on Accessibility**

In Chapter 1, you were introduced to the concept of universal design. Let's take a closer look in this section at how the concept of universal design can apply to web design.

## Who Benefits from Universal Design and Increased Accessibility?

Consider the following scenarios:

- Maria, a young woman in her twenties with physical challenges who cannot manipulate a mouse and who uses a keyboard with much effort: Accessible web pages designed to function without a mouse will help Maria to access content.

- Leotis, a college student who is deaf and wants to be a web developer: Captions for audio/video content and transcripts will provide Leotis access to content.

- Jim, a middle-aged man who has a dial-up Internet connection and is using the Web for personal enjoyment: Alternate text for images and transcripts for multimedia will provide Jim improved access to content.

- Nadine, a mature woman with age-related macular degeneration who has difficulty reading small print: Web pages that are designed so that text can be enlarged in the browser will make it easier for Nadine to read.

- Karen, a college student using a smartphone to access the Web: Accessible content organized with headings and lists will make it easier for Karen to surf the Web on a mobile device.

- Prakesh, a man in his thirties who is legally blind and needs access to the Web in order to do his job: Web pages that are designed to be accessible (which are organized with headings and lists, display descriptive text for hyperlinks, provide alternate text descriptions for images, and are usable without a mouse) will help Prakesh to access content.

All of these individuals benefit from web pages that are designed with accessibility in mind. A web page that is designed to be accessible is typically more usable for all—even a person who has no physical challenges and is using a broadband connection benefits from the improved presentation and organization of a well-designed web page.

## Accessible Design Can Benefit Search Engine Listing

Search engine programs (commonly referred to as bots or spiders) walk the Web and follow hyperlinks on websites. An accessible website with descriptive page titles that is well organized with headings, lists, descriptive text for hyperlinks, and alternate text for images is more visible to search engine robots and may result in a better ranking.

## Accessibility is the Right Thing to Do

The Internet and the World Wide Web are such a pervasive part of our culture that accessibility is mandated by law in the United States. Section 508 of the Rehabilitation Act requires electronic and information technology, including web pages, used by federal agencies to be accessible to people with disabilities. In 2017, an update to Section 508 Standards became official which requires meeting the requirements of WCAG 2.0 Level A & AA Success Criteria. The accessibility recommendations presented in this text are intended to satisfy the Section 508 standards and the **Web Content Accessibility Guidelines (WCAG)** recommended by the W3C's **Web Accessibility Initiative (WAI)**. The following four principles are essential to conformance with WCAG: **P**erceivable, **O**perable, **U**nderstandable, and **R**obust, referred to by the acronym **POUR**.

1. Content must be **Perceivable**. Perceivable content is easy to see or hear. Any graphic or multimedia content should be available in a text format, such as text descriptions for images, closed captions for videos, and transcripts for audio.

2. Interface components in the content must be **Operable**. Operable content has navigation forms, or other interactive features that can be used or operated with either a mouse or a keyboard. Multimedia content should be designed to avoid flashing, which may cause a seizure.

3. Content and controls must be **Understandable**. Understandable content is easy to read, organized in a consistent manner, and provides helpful error messages when appropriate.

4. Content should be **Robust** enough to work with current and future user agents, including assistive technologies. Robust content is written to follow W3C recommendations and should be compatible with multiple operating systems, browsers, and assistive technologies such as screen reader applications.

The W3C has approved a new version of WCAG, called WCAG 2.1, which extends the guidelines in WCAG 2.0. The WCAG 2.1 Quick Reference in the Appendix contains a brief list of guidelines for designing accessible web pages. You can access WAI's Web Content Accessibility Guidelines 2.1 (WCAG 2.1) at https://www.w3.org/WAI/standards-guidelines/wcag/. These guidelines are segmented into three levels of conformance: Level A, Level AA, and Level AAA. In addition to satisfying the Section 508 guidelines, the accessibility recommendations discussed in this textbook are also intended to fully satisfy the WCAG 2.1 Level AA (includes Level A) guidelines and partially satisfy the Level AAA guidelines. Visit https://www.w3.org/WAI/WCAG21/quickref for an interactive checklist of these guidelines. Developing accessible web pages is an important aspect of web design. The University of Toronto (http://achecker.ca/checker/index.php) provides a free accessibility validation service.

As you work through this book, you'll learn to include accessibility features as you create practice pages. You've already discovered the importance of the title tag, heading tags, descriptive text for hyperlinks, and alternate text for images in Chapters 2, 3, and 4. You're well on your way to creating accessible web pages!

# 5.5  Writing for the Web

Long-winded sentences and explanations are often found in academic textbooks and romance novels, but they really are not appropriate on a web page. Large blocks of text and long paragraphs are difficult to read on the Web. The following suggestions will help to increase the readability of your web pages.

## Organize Your Content

According to web usability expert Jakob Neilsen, people don't really read web pages; they scan them. Organize the text content on your pages to be quickly scanned. Be concise. Use headings, subheadings, brief paragraphs, and unordered lists to organize web page content so that it is easy to read and visitors can quickly find what they need. See Figure 5.9 for an example of organizing web page content with headings, subheadings, and brief paragraphs.

**Figure 5.9** The web page content is well organized with headings

## Choosing a Font

Use common font typefaces such as Arial, Verdana, Georgia, or Times New Roman. Remember that the web page visitor must have the font installed on his or her computer in order for that particular font to appear. Your page may look great with Gill Sans Ultra Bold Condensed, but if your visitor doesn't have the font, the browser's default font will be displayed. A list of "browser safe fonts" is available at http://www.ampsoft.net/webdesign-l/WindowsMacFonts.html.

Serif fonts, such as Times New Roman, were originally developed for printing text on paper, not for displaying text on a computer monitor. Sans-serif fonts such as Verdana and Tahoma were specifically designed for display on screens.

## Font Size

Be aware that fonts display smaller on a Mac than on a PC. Even within the PC platform, the default font size displayed by browsers may not be the same. Consider creating prototype pages of your font size settings to test on a variety of browsers and screen resolution settings.

## Font Weight

**Bold** or *emphasize* important text (use the `<strong>` element for bold and the `<em>` element to configure italics). However, be careful not to bold everything—that has the same effect as bolding nothing.

## Font Color Contrast

Written content is easier to read when there is sufficient contrast between text and background color. Visit https://webdevbasics.net/10e/chapter5.html for links to online tools that can help you verify that your page background color properly contrasts with your text and hyperlink colors.

## Line Length

Be aware of line length—use white space and multiple columns if possible. Christian Holst at the Baymard Institute (https://baymard.com/blog/line-length-readability) describes studies that recommend between 50 and 75 characters per line for readability.

## Alignment

A paragraph of centered text is more difficult to read than left-aligned text.

## Text in Hyperlinks

Hyperlink key words or descriptive phrases; do not hyperlink entire sentences. Avoid use of the words "Click here" in hyperlinks because users know what to do by now. Also, be aware that an increasing number of people are using touch screens so they'll be selecting or tapping rather than clicking.

## Reading Level

Match the reading level and style of writing to your target audience. Use vocabulary that they will be comfortable with. Juicy Studio offers a free online readability test at http://juicystudio.com/services/readability.php.

## Spelling and Grammar

Unfortunately, many websites contain misspelled words. Most web authoring tools such as Adobe Dreamweaver have built-in spell checkers; consider using this feature. Finally, be sure that you proofread and test your site thoroughly. It's very helpful if you can find web developer buddies—you check their sites and they check yours. It's always easier to see someone else's mistake than your own.

# 5.6 Use of Color

You may be wondering how to select colors to display on web pages. The right color scheme can attract and engage your website visitors while a garish color scheme can drive them away. This section introduces several methods for choosing a color scheme.

## Color Scheme Based on an Image

One of the easiest ways to select a color scheme for your website is to start with an existing graphic image, such as a logo or a photograph of nature. If the organization already has a logo, select colors from the logo for use as the basis of your color scheme. Another option is to use a photograph that captures the mood of the website—you can create a color scheme using colors found in the image.

Figure 5.10 shows a photograph along with two potential color schemes created by selecting colors from the image. If you are comfortable using a graphic application (such as Adobe Photoshop or GIMP), you can use the color picker tool within the application to determine the colors used in an image. There are also websites that will generate a color scheme based on a photograph, including

- https://www.degraeve.com/color-palette/index.php
- http://www.cssdrive.com/imagepalette

Even if you use an existing graphic as the basis for a color scheme, it's helpful to have a working knowledge of **color theory**, the study of color and its use in design. Let's explore color theory and the color wheel.

Figure 5.10 A color scheme selected from a photo

## Color Wheel

A **color wheel** (see Figure 5.11) is a circle of color depicting the primary colors (red, yellow, and blue), the secondary colors (orange, violet, and green), and the tertiary colors (yellow-orange, red-orange, red-violet, violet-blue, blue-green, and yellow-green). There is no need to restrict your choices to the web-safe color palette.

### Shades, Tints, and Tones

Modern monitors can display millions of colors. Feel free to choose a shade, tint, or tone of a color. Figure 5.12 shows four swatches: yellow, a shade of yellow, a tint of yellow, and a tone of yellow. A **shade** of a color is darker than the original color and is created by mixing the color with black. A **tint** of a color is lighter than the original color and is created by mixing color with white. A **tone** of a color has less saturation than the original color and is created by mixing the color with gray.

Next, let's explore the six commonly used types of color schemes: monochromatic, analogous, complementary, split complementary, triadic, and tetradic.

Figure 5.11 Color wheel

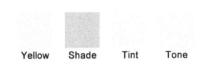

Yellow    Shade    Tint    Tone

Figure 5.12 Yellow with a shade, tint, and tone

# Color Scheme Based on the Color Wheel

## Monochromatic Color Scheme

Figure 5.13 shows a **monochromatic color scheme** which consists of shades, tints, or tones of the same color. You can determine these values yourself, or use an online tool provided by one of the following resources:

- https://meyerweb.com/eric/tools/color-blend
- http://www.colorsontheweb.com/Color-Tools/Color-Wizard (choose a color and view a variety of color schemes including monochromatic)
- http://paletton.com (choose a color and select monochromatic)

**Figure 5.13**  Monochromatic color scheme

## Analogous Color Scheme

**Figure 5.14**  Analogous color scheme

To create an **analogous color scheme**, select a main color and the two colors that are adjacent to it on the color wheel. Figure 5.14 displays an analogous color scheme with orange, red-orange, and yellow-orange. When you design a web page with an analogous color scheme, the main color is the most dominant on the web page. The adjacent colors are typically configured as accents.

## Complementary Color Scheme

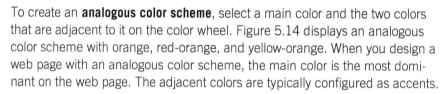

A **complementary color scheme** consists of two colors that are opposite each other on the color wheel. Figure 5.15 displays a complementary color scheme with yellow and violet. When you design a web page with a complementary color scheme, choose one color to be the main or dominant color. The other color is considered to be the **complement**. Configure the complement along with colors adjacent to the dominant color as accents.

**Figure 5.15** Complementary color scheme

## Split Complementary Color Scheme

A **split complementary color scheme** is comprised of a main color, the color opposite it on the color wheel (the complement), and two colors adjacent to the complement. Figure 5.16 shows a split complementary color scheme with yellow (main), violet (complementary), red-violet, and blue-violet.

**Figure 5.16**  Split complementary color scheme

## Triadic Color Scheme

Choose three colors that are equidistant on the color wheel to create a **triadic color scheme**. Figure 5.17 displays a triadic color scheme with blue-green (teal), yellow-orange, and red-violet.

**Figure 5.17**  Triadic color scheme

## Tetradic Color Scheme

Figure 5.18 shows a **tetradic color scheme**, which consists of four colors that are two complementary pairs. For example, the complementary pair yellow and violet along with the complementary pair yellow-green and red-violet make up a tetradic color scheme.

**Figure 5.18**  Tetradic color scheme

## Implementing a Color Scheme

When designing a web page with a color scheme, one color is typically dominant. The other colors are configured as accents such as colors for headings, subheadings, borders, list markers, and backgrounds. No matter what your color scheme, you will typically also use neutral colors such as white, off-white, gray, black, or brown. Ensure that the colors you choose for text and background have good contrast. Selecting the best color scheme for your website often takes some trial and error. Feel free to use tints, shades, or tones of the primary, secondary, and tertiary colors. There are so many colors to choose from! The following resources can help you choose a color scheme for your website:

- http://paletton.com
- http://www.colorsontheweb.com/Color-Tools/Color-Wizard
- https://color.adobe.com
- https://www.colorspire.com

## Accessibility and Color

While color can help you create a compelling web page, keep in mind that not all of your visitors will see or be able to distinguish between colors. Some visitors will use a screen reader and will not experience your colors, so your information must be clearly conveyed even if the colors cannot be viewed.

Focus on Accessibility

Your color choices can be crucial. For example, red text on a blue background, as shown in Figure 5.19, is usually difficult for everyone to read. Also avoid using a red and green color scheme or a brown and purple color scheme because individuals with color-deficient vision may have difficulty differentiating the colors. According to Color Blindness Awareness (http://www.colourblindawareness.org/), 1 in 12 men and 1 in 200 women experience some type color blindness. Visit https://www.toptal.com/designers/colorfilter to simulate how a person with a color deficiency experiences the colors on a web page. White, black, and shades of blue and yellow are easier for most people to discern.

Figure 5.19
Some color combinations are difficult to read

Choose background and text colors with a high amount of contrast. The WCAG 2.0 and 2.1 guidelines recommend a contrast ratio of 4.5:1 for standard text. If the text has a large font, the contrast ratio can be as low as 3:1. New to WCAG 2.1 are minimum requirements of 3:1 for non-text contrast such as user interface components and graphics. Jonathan Snook's Colour Contrast Check at https://snook.ca/technical/colour_contrast/colour.html can help you to verify the contrast level of your text and background colors. When choosing color, it's important to consider the preferences of your target audience. The next sections focus on this aspect of web design.

## Colors and Your Target Audience

Choose colors that will appeal to your target audience. Younger audiences, such as children and preteens, prefer bright, lively colors. The web page shown in Figure 5.20, features bright graphics, lots of color, and interactivity.

Figure 5.20 A web page intended to appeal to children

Individuals in their late teens and early twenties generally prefer dark background colors with occasional use of bright contrast, music, and dynamic navigation. Figure 5.21 shows a web page designed for this age group. Note how it has a completely different look and feel from the site designed for young children.

Figure 5.21 Many teens and young adults find dark sites appealing

If your goal is to appeal to everyone, follow the example of the popular Amazon.com and eBay.com websites in their use of color. These sites display a neutral white background with splashes of color to add interest and highlight page areas. Use of white as a background color was found to be quite popular by Jakob Nielsen and Marie Tahir in *Homepage Usability: 50 Websites Deconstructed*, a book that analyzed 50 top websites. According to this study, 84% of the sites used white as the background color, and 72% used black as the text color. This maximized the contrast between text and background—providing maximum ease of reading.

You'll also notice that websites targeting "everyone" often include compelling visual graphics. The web page shown in Figure 5.22 provides the text content on a white background for maximum contrast while engaging the visitor with a large graphic, called a **hero**, intended to grab attention and entice the visitor to want to explore the website.

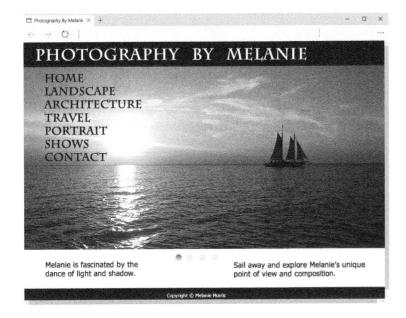

Figure 5.22 A compelling graphic along with white background for the content area

For an older target audience, light backgrounds, well-defined images, and large text are appropriate. The web page shown in Figure 5.23 is an example of a web page intended for the 55-and-older age group.

Figure 5.23 A site designed specifically for the 55-and-older age group

## Checkpoint 5.1

1. List the four basic principles of design. View the home page of your school and describe how each principle is applied.

2. Choose one best practice of writing for the Web. Locate a web page that demonstrates the use of your chosen best practice. Provide the URL of the web page and describe why you believe the web page exemplifies the best practice.

3. View the following three websites:

   - https://www.walmart.com

   - http://www.willyporter.com

   - https://www.sesamestreet.org/art-maker

Describe the target audience for each website. How do their designs differ? How are their designs similar? Do the sites meet the needs of their target audiences? Why or why not?

# 5.7 Use of Graphics and Multimedia

As shown in Figure 5.1, a compelling graphic can be an engaging element on a web page. However, avoid relying on images to convey meaning. Some individuals may not be able to see your images and multimedia—they may be accessing your site with a mobile device or using an assistive technology such as a screen reader to visit your page. You may need to include text descriptions of important concepts or key points that a graphic image or multimedia file conveys. In this section, you'll explore recommended techniques for the use of graphics and multimedia on web pages.

## File Size and Image Dimensions Matter

Keep both the file size and the dimensions of images as small as possible. Try to display only exactly what is needed to get your point across. Use a graphic application to crop an image or create a thumbnail image that links to a larger version of the image.

# Antialiased

Figure 5.24 Antialiased text

## Antialiased/Aliased Text in Media

**Antialiasing** introduces intermediate colors to smooth jagged edges in digital images. Graphic applications such as Adobe Photoshop and GIMP can be used to create antialiased text images. The graphic shown in Figure 5.24 was created using antialiasing. Figure 5.25 displays an image created without antialiasing; notice the jagged edges.

## A

Figure 5.25 This graphic was not antialiased: The letter "A" has a jagged look

## Use Only Necessary Multimedia

Use animation and multimedia only if it will add value to your site. Limit the use of animated items. Only use animation if it makes the page more effective. Consider limiting how long an animation plays.

In general, younger audiences find animation more appealing than older audiences. The web page shown in Figure 5.20 is intended for children and uses lots of animation. This would be too much animation for a website targeted to adult shoppers. However, a well-done navigation animation or an animation that describes a product or service could be appealing to almost any target group, as shown in Figure 5.26. You'll work with CSS properties to add animation and interactivity to web pages in Chapter 11.

## Provide Alternate Text

As discussed in Chapter 4, each image on your web page should be configured with alternate text. Alternate text may be displayed by mobile devices, displayed briefly when an image is slow to load, and displayed when a browser is configured to not show images. Alternate text is also read aloud when a person with a disability uses a screen reader to access your website.

To satisfy accessibility requirements, also provide alternate text equivalents for multimedia, such as video and audio. A text transcript of an audio recording can be useful not only to those with hearing challenges, but also to individuals who prefer to read when accessing new information.

Figure 5.26 The slideshow adds visual interest and interactivity

In addition, the text transcript may be accessed by a search engine and used when your site is categorized and indexed. Captions help to provide accessibility for video files. See Chapter 11 for more on accessibility and multimedia.

**Focus on Accessibility**

# 5.8 More Design Considerations

## Mobile Devices

According to a recent study by the PEW Internet and American Life Project (http://www.pewinternet.org), 20% of American adults depend on their smartphones for Internet access. A Statcounter report (http://gs.statcounter.com/platform-market-share/desktop-mobile-tablet) showed that mobile devices (49%) have more market share than desktops (47%), and tablets (4%). PEW also reported that the percentage of U.S. Internet users with a broadband connection (cable, DSL, and so on) at home or at work has decreased from a peak of 73% in 2016. As of 2018, 65% percent of adult Americans studied had access to broadband at home.

Apply the principle of **progressive enhancement**. Design your website so that it looks good when displayed in mobile devices and the browsers commonly used by your target audience; then add enhancements with CSS and/or HTML5 to take advantage of the capabilities of modern browsers. Always try to test your pages with the most popular versions of desktop browsers (on both PC and Mac operating systems) and popular mobile devices such as smartphones and tablets. Many web page components, including default text size and default margin size, are different among devices, operating systems, and browsers. Chapter 7 will introduce techniques for designing web pages that display well on both mobile devices and standard desktop computers.

**Perceived load time** is the amount of time a web page visitor is aware of waiting while your page is loading. Since visitors often leave a website if a page takes too long to load, it is important to shorten their perception of waiting. In addition to optimizing all images, another common technique for shortening perceived load time is to utilize image sprites (see Chapter 7), which combine multiple small images into a single file.

## Browsers

Unless you are designing for an intranet within an organization, expect your website to be visited using a wide variety of browsers. Just because your web page looks great in your favorite browser doesn't automatically mean that all browsers will render it well. A recent survey by Statcounter (http://gs.statcounter.com/browser-market-share) reports that about 71% of desktop website visitors use Chrome, 10% use Firefox, 6% use Internet Explorer, and 5% use Microsoft Edge. The market share of the top four mobile/tablet browsers was reported by Statcounter as: Chrome (56%), Safari (21%), Samsung Internet (7.4%), and UC Browser (7.3%).

## Screen Resolution

Your website visitors will use a variety of screen resolutions. A recent survey by Statcounter (http://gs.statcounter.com/screen-resolution-stats) reported the use of popular screen resolutions. The top four desktop screen resolutions were 1366 × 768 (with 28%), 1920 × 1080 (19%), 1440 × 900 (7%), and 2600 × 900 (5%). Mobile use will vary with the purpose of the website, but it is expected to grow as the use of smartphones and tablets increases. Be aware that some smartphones have low screen resolution, such as 360 × 640. The top four mobile screen resolutions were reported by Statcounter to be 360 × 640 (40%), 375 × 667 (9.41%), 414 × 736 (4.31%), and 720 × 1280 (3.87%). Popular tablet devices offer a higher screen resolution: Apple iPad Pro (2732 × 2048), Samsung Galaxy Tab S2 (2048 × 1536), and Kindle Fire HD (1200 × 1920). Visit https://www.browserstack.com/test-on-the-right-mobile-devices for a list of popular mobile devices. In Chapter 7, you'll explore CSS media queries, which is a technique for configuring a web page to display well on various screen resolutions.

## White Space

The term **white space** is borrowed from the publishing industry. Placing blank or white space (because paper is usually white) in areas around blocks of text increases the readability of the page. Placing white space around graphics helps them to stand out. Allow for some blank space between blocks of text and images. How much is adequate? It depends—experiment until the page is likely to look appealing to your target audience.

## Flat Web Design

**Flat web design** is a minimalistic design style with a focus on simplicity, blocks of color, empty space between design elements, hero images, and use of typography. Because the design is so minimalistic and uncluttered, web pages with flat design often feature vertical scrolling.

Flat web design initially avoided the use of 3D effects such as drop shadows and gradients. However, as time went along, **Flat Design 2.0** emerged which includes gradients, shadows,

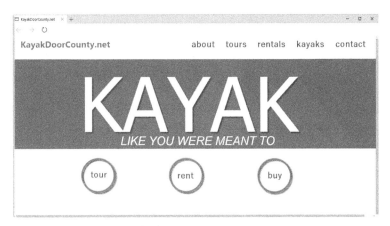

Figure 5.27  Flat web design

expanded color palettes, animation, and ghost buttons which are buttons with transparent backgrounds. The page shown in Figure 5.27 demonstrates a flat minimalistic design that emphasizes typography, has large blocks of color, and has quite a bit of empty space. Visit the following resources to explore the trend of flat web design:

- https://designmodo.com/flat-design-principles/

- https://flatuicolors.com/

- https://speckyboy.com/flat-web-design

- https://spyrestudios.com/flat-design-2-0/

- https://www.uxpin.com/studio/blog/the-7-minute-guide-to-flat-design-2-0

## Single Page Website

A **single page website** (sometimes called a **one page website**) is a website that contains one very long page (a single HTML file) with a clearly defined navigation area, usually at the top of the page. This navigation takes you to specific areas on the page. You can also scroll up and down to see the entire page. The first view of the page often displays a large attention-grabbing header element. Since the website is on one long page, there should be clearly separated sections for the information topics. Single page websites often feature large compelling images, so care must be taken to optimize them to prevent a slow-loading page. A single page website can be quick to create and may be a good choice for a portfolio website, a brochure website, or an initial website for a small business. You will explore creating a single page website in Chapter 6.

# 5.9  Navigation Design

## Ease of Navigation

Sometimes web developers are so close to their sites that they can't see the forest for the trees. A new visitor will wander onto the site and not know what to click or how to find the information he or she seeks. Clearly labeled navigation on each page is helpful. For maximum usability, the navigation should be in the same location on each page.

Figure 5.28 Horizontal text-based navigation

## Navigation Bars

Clear **navigation bars**, either graphic or text based, make it obvious to website users where they are and where they can go next. It's quite common for site-wide navigation to be located either in a horizontal navigation bar placed under the logo (see Figure 5.28) or in a vertical navigation bar on the left side of the page (see Figure 5.29). Less common is a vertical navigation bar on the right side of the page because this area can be cut off at lower screen resolutions.

Figure 5.29 Visitors can follow the "breadcrumbs" to replace their steps

## Breadcrumb Navigation

A **breadcrumb trail** indicates the path of web pages a visitor has viewed during the current session. Figure 5.29 shows a page with a vertical navigation area in addition to the breadcrumb trail navigation above the main content area that indicates the pages the visitor has viewed during this visit: Home > Tours > Half-Day Tours > Europe Lake Tour. Visitors can easily retrace their steps or jump back to a previously viewed page. This page demonstrates that a website may use more than one type of navigation.

## Using Graphics for Navigation

Sometimes graphics are used instead of text to provide navigation, as in the pink navigation buttons on the web page shown in Figure 5.20. The "text" for the navigation is actually stored in image files. Be aware that using graphics for navigation is an outdated design technique—the more modern approach is to configure text navigation with CSS background images. A website with text navigation is more accessible and more easily indexed by search engines. Even when image hyperlinks instead of text hyperlinks provide the main navigation for the site, you can use two techniques that provide for accessibility:

- Configure each image with an alternate text description.
- Configure text hyperlinks in the footer section.

## Skip Repetitive Navigation

Provide a method to skip repetitive navigation links. It is easy for visitors without vision and mobility challenges to scan a web page and quickly focus on the page content. However, long, repetitive navigation bars quickly become tedious to access when utilizing a screen reader or a keyboard to visit a web page. Consider adding a "Skip navigation" or "**Skip to content**" hyperlink before your main navigation bar that links to a named fragment (see Chapter 6) at the beginning of the content section of your page. Figure 5.30 presents another way to implement the skip navigation feature. Although not immediately visible in the browser, visitors using a screen reader or a keyboard to tab through the page will immediately encounter the "Skip to content" hyperlink near the top of the web page at https:// webdevbasics.net.

**Focus on Accessibility**

## Dynamic Navigation

In your experiences visiting websites you've probably encountered navigation menus that display additional options when your mouse cursor moves over an item. This is dynamic navigation, which provides a way to offer many choices to visitors while at the same time avoid overwhelming them. Instead of showing all the navigation links all the time, menu items are dynamically displayed (typically using a combination of HTML and CSS) as appropriate. The additional items are made available when a related top-level menu item has focus or is selected. In Figure 5.31, "Tours" has been selected, causing the vertical menu to appear.

Figure 5.30 Press the tab key to access the "Skip to content" link for this web page

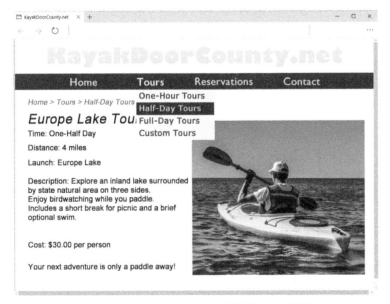

Figure 5.31 Dynamic navigation with HTML and CSS

## Site Map

Even with clear and consistent navigation, visitors sometimes may lose their way on large websites. A site map page, also referred to as a site index, provides an outline of the organization of the website with hyperlinks to each major page. This can help visitors find another route to get to the information they seek, as shown Figure 5.32.

**Figure 5.32**  This large site offers a site search and a site index to visitors

## Site Search Feature

Note the search feature on the right side of the web page in Figure 5.31. This **site search** feature helps visitors to find information that is not apparent from the navigation or the site map.

# 5.10  Page Layout Design

## Wireframes and Page Layout

A **wireframe** is a sketch or diagram of a web page that shows the structure (but not the detailed design) of basic page elements such as the header, navigation, content area, and footer. Wireframes are used as part of the design process to experiment with various **page layouts**, develop the structure and navigation of the site, and provide a basis for communication among project members. Note that the exact content (text, images, logo, and navigation) does not need to be placed in the wireframe diagram—the wireframe depicts the overall structure of the page.

Figures 5.33, 5.34, and 5.35 show wireframe diagrams of three possible page designs with horizontal navigation. The wireframe in Figure 5.33 is adequate and may be appropriate for when the emphasis is on text information content, but it's not very engaging.

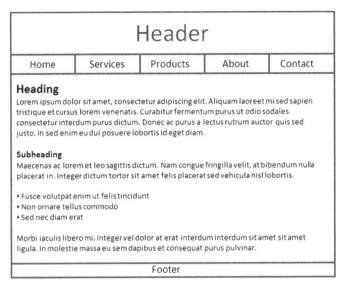

Figure 5.33  An adequate page layout

Figure 5.34 shows a diagram of a web page containing similar content formatted in three columns of varying widths with a header area, navigation area, content area (with headings, subheadings, paragraphs, and unordered list), and a footer area.

The wireframe in Figure 5.35 is formatted in three columns with a header area, top navigation area, large hero image, content area (with headings, subheadings, paragraphs, and unordered list), and a footer area. Notice how the use of columns and images in Figures 5.34 and 5.35 increase the appeal of the page.

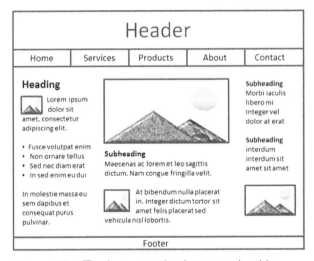

Figure 5.34  The image and columns make this page layout more interesting

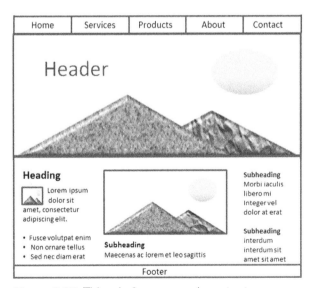

Figure 5.35  This wireframe page layout a top navigation area and a hero image

The wirefame in Figure 5.36 displays a webpage with a header, vertical navigation area, content area (with headings, subheadings, images, paragraphs, and unordered list), and a footer area.

Often the page layout for the home page is different from the page layout used for the content pages. Even in this situation, a consistent logo header, navigation, and color scheme will produce a more cohesive website. You'll learn to use Cascading Style Sheets (CSS) along with HTML to configure color, text, and layout as you work through this book. In the next section you will explore two commonly used layout design techniques: fixed layout and fluid layout.

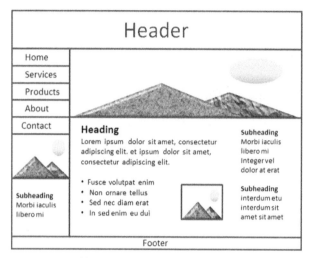

Figure 5.36 Wireframe with vertical navigation

## Page Layout Design Techniques

Now that you have been introduced to wireframes as a way to sketch page layout, let's explore two commonly used design techniques to implement those wireframes: fixed layout and fluid layout.

### Fixed Layout

The **fixed layout** technique is sometimes referred to as a solid or "ice" design. The web page content has a fixed width and may hug the left margin as shown in Figure 5.37.

Figure 5.37 This page is configured with a fixed layout design

Notice the empty space in the right side of the browser viewport in Figure 5.37. To avoid this unbalanced look, a popular method to create a fixed layout design is to configure the content with a specific width in pixels (such as 960px) and center it in the browser viewport as shown in Figure 5.38. As the browser is resized, it will expand or contract the left and right margin areas to center the content in the viewport.

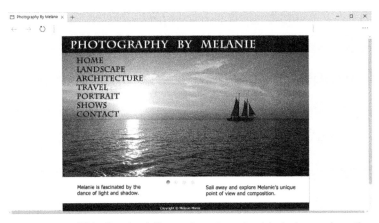

**Figure 5.38** This fixed-width centered content is balanced on the page by left and right margins

## Fluid Layout

The **fluid layout** technique, sometimes referred to as a "liquid" layout, results in a fluid web page with content typically configured with percentage values for widths—often taking up 100% of the browser viewport. The content will flow to fill whatever size browser window is used to display it, as shown in Figure 5.39. One disadvantage of liquid layout is that when displayed in maximized browser viewports using high screen resolutions the lines of text may be quite wide and become difficult to scan and read.

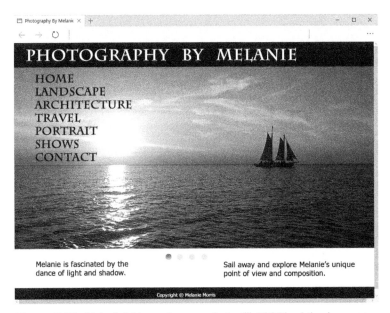

**Figure 5.39** This fluid layout expands to fill 100% of the browser viewport

Figure 5.40 shows an adaptation of liquid layout that utilizes a 100% width for the navigation area along with an 80% width for the centered page content. Compare this to Figure 5.39. The centered content area grows and shrinks as the browser viewport is resized. Readability can be ensured by using CSS to configure a maximum width value for this area.

Figure 5.40 This
fluid layout also
has a maximum
width value
configured for
the centered
content area

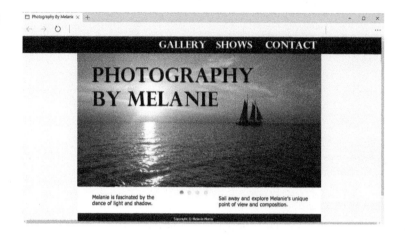

Websites designed using fixed and fluid layout techniques can be found throughout the Web. Fixed-width layouts provide the web developer with the most control over the page configuration but can result in pages with large empty areas when viewed at higher screen resolutions. Fluid designs may become less readable when viewed at high screen resolutions due to the page stretching to fill a wider area than originally intended by the developer. Configuring a maximum width on text content areas can alleviate the text readability issues. Even when using an overall fluid layout, portions of the design can be configured with a fixed width (such as the two columns of text at the bottom of the content in Figures 5.39 and 5.40). Whether employing a fixed or fluid layout, web pages with centered content are typically pleasing to view on a variety of desktop screen resolutions.

## 5.11 Design for the Mobile Web

Coding techniques to configure responsive web page layouts that display differently on desktop browsers and mobile devices will be introduced in Chapter 7. Figures 5.41 and 5.42 show the same website but look different. Figure 5.41 depicts the desktop browser display. Figure 5.42 shows the display in a small mobile device. Let's explore some design considerations for mobile display.

Figure 5.41
Desktop
browser display.

# Mobile Web Design Considerations

Mobile web users are typically on-the-go, need information quickly, and may be easily distracted. A web page that is optimized for mobile access should try to serve these needs. Take a moment to review Figures 5.41 and 5.42 and observe how the design of the mobile website addresses the following design considerations:

Figure 5.42 Mobile display.

- **Small screen size.** The size of the header area is reduced to accommodate a small screen display. It's also common to configure nonessential content, such as sidebar content to not display on a mobile device.

- **Low bandwidth (slow connection speed).** Note that a smaller image is displayed on the mobile version of the web page.

- **Font, color, and media issues.** Common font typefaces are utilized. There is also good contrast between text and background color.

- **Awkward controls, limited processor, and limited memory.** The mobile website uses a single-column page layout that facilitates keyboard tabbing and will be easy to control by touch. The page is mostly text, which will be quickly rendered by a mobile browser.

- **Functionality.** A single-column layout is utilized with navigation areas that can be easily selected with a fingertip. The W3C recommends a target size of at least 44 × 22 pixels for controls requiring tapping such a navigation hyperlink.

Let's build on this base of design considerations and expand them.

## Optimize Layout for Mobile Use

A single-column page layout (Figure 5.43) with a small header, key navigation links, content, and page footer works well for a mobile device display. Mobile screen resolutions vary greatly (for example, 320 × 480, 360 × 640, 375 × 667, 640 × 690, and 720 × 1280). W3C recommendations include the following:

- Limit scrolling to one direction.

- Use heading elements.

- Use lists to organize information (such as unordered lists, ordered lists, and description lists).

- Avoid using tables (see Chapter 8) because they typically force both horizontal and vertical scrolling on mobile devices.

- Provide labels for form controls (see Chapter 9).

- Avoid using pixel units in style sheets.

- Avoid absolute positioning in style sheets.

- Hide content that is not essential for mobile use.

Figure 5.43 Wireframe for a typical single-column page layout.

## Optimize Navigation for Mobile Use

Easy-to-use navigation is crucial on a mobile device. The W3C recommends the following:

- Provide minimal navigation near the top of the page.

- Provide consistent navigation.

- Avoid hyperlinks that open files in new windows or pop-up windows.
- Try to balance both the number of hyperlinks on a page and the number of levels of links needed to access information.

## Optimize Graphics for Mobile Use

Graphics can help to engage visitors, but be aware of the following W3C recommendations for mobile use:

- Avoid displaying images that are wider than the screen width (assume a 320-pixel screen width on a smartphone display).
- Configure alternate small, optimized background images.
- Some mobile browsers will downsize all images, so images with text can be difficult to read.
- Avoid the use of large graphic images.
- Specify the size of images.
- Provide alternate text for graphics and other nontext elements.

## Optimize Text for Mobile Use

It can be difficult to read text on a small mobile device. The following W3C recommendations will aid your mobile visitors:

- Configure good contrast between text and background colors.
- Use common font typefaces.
- Configure font size with em units or percentages.
- Use a short, descriptive page title.

The W3C has published Mobile Web Best Practices 1.0, a list of 60 mobile web design best practices, at https://www.w3.org/TR/mobile-bp. Flipcards that summarize the Mobile Web Best Practices 1.0 document are available at https://www.w3.org/2007/02/mwbp_flip_cards.html.

## Mobile Design Quick Checklist

- Be aware of the small screen size and bandwidth issues.
- Configure nonessential content, such as sidebar content, to not display.
- Consider replacing desktop background images with graphics optimized for small screen display.
- Provide descriptive alternate text for images.
- Use a single-column layout for mobile display.
- Choose colors to maximize contrast.

# 5.12 Responsive Web Design

**Responsive web design** is a term coined by noted web developer Ethan Marcotte (http://alistapart.com/article/responsive-web-design) to describe progressively enhancing a web page for different viewing contexts (such as smartphones and tablets) through the use of coding techniques, including fluid layouts, flexible images, and media queries. In Chapter 7, you'll configure flexible images and responsive page layouts with a variety of CSS coding techniques including CSS Flexible Box Layout, CSS Grid Layout, and CSS **media queries**, which is a technique for configuring a web page to display well at various screen resolutions.

Visit the Media Queries website (https://mediaqueri.es) to view a gallery of sites that demonstrate this method for responsive web design. The screen captures in the Media Queries gallery show web pages at the following screen widths: 320px (smartphone display), 768px (tablet portrait display), 1024px (netbook display and landscape tablet display), and 1600px (large desktop display).

You might be surprised to discover that Figures 5.44, 5.45, and 5.46 are actually the same web page .html file that is configured with CSS to display differently, depending on the viewport size detected by media queries. Figure 5.44 shows the standard desktop browser display.

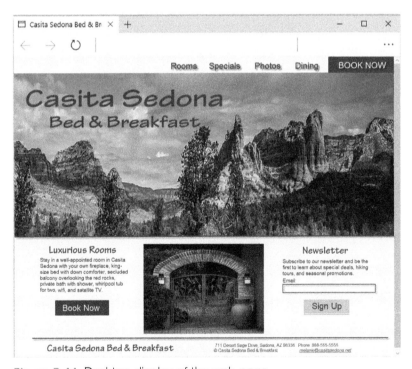

Figure 5.44 Desktop display of the web page

Figure 5.45 demonstrates how the page would render on a tablet using portrait orientation. Figure 5.46 shows the web page displayed on a mobile device such as a smartphone—note the smaller images and prominent phone number.

**Figure 5.45** Portrait orientation tablet display of the web page

**Figure 5.46** Smartphone display of the web page

# 5.13  Web Design Best Practices Checklist

Table 5.1 contains a checklist of recommended web design practices. Use this as a guide to help you create easy-to-read, usable, and accessible web pages.

Table 5.1  Web design best practices checklist Note: Web Design Best Practices Checklist is copyrighted by Terry Ann Morris, Ed.D. (https://terrymorris.net/bestpractices). Used with permission.

### Page Layout

| | | |
|---|---|---|
| ❏ | 1. | Appealing to target audience |
| ❏ | 2. | Consistent site header/logo |
| ❏ | 3. | Consistent navigation area |
| ❏ | 4. | Informative page title that includes the company/organization/site name |
| ❏ | 5. | Page footer area includes copyright, last update, contact e-mail address |
| ❏ | 6. | Good use of basic design principles: repetition, contrast, proximity, and alignment |
| ❏ | 7. | Balance of text/graphics/white space on page |
| ❏ | 8. | Good contrast between text and background |
| ❏ | 9. | Home page downloads within 10 seconds on mobile device |
| ❏ | 10. | Viewport meta tag is used to enhance display on smartphones (see Chapter 7) |
| ❏ | 11. | Media queries configure responsive page layout for smartphone and tablet display (see Chapter 7) |

### Browser Compatibility

| | | |
|---|---|---|
| ❏ | 1. | Displays on current versions of Microsoft Edge |
| ❏ | 2. | Displays on current versions of Firefox |
| ❏ | 3. | Displays on current versions of Google Chrome |
| ❏ | 4. | Displays on current versions of Safari |
| ❏ | 5. | Displays on current versions of Internet Explorer |
| ❏ | 6. | Displays on mobile devices (including tablets and smartphones) |

Table 5.1 (*Continued*)

## Navigation

| | | |
|---|---|---|
| ❏ | 1. | Main navigation links are clearly and consistently labeled |
| ❏ | 2. | Navigation is easy to use for target audience |
| ❏ | 3. | If main navigation uses images, clear text links are in the footer section of the page |
| ❏ | 4. | Navigation is structured in an unordered list |
| ❏ | 5. | Navigation aids (such as site map, skip to content link, and/or breadcrumbs) are used |
| ❏ | 6. | All navigation hyperlinks work |

## Color and Graphics

| | | |
|---|---|---|
| ❏ | 1. | Color scheme is limited to a maximum of three or four colors plus neutrals |
| ❏ | 2. | Color is used consistently |
| ❏ | 3. | Background and text colors have sufficient contrast |
| ❏ | 4. | Color is not used alone to convey meaning |
| ❏ | 5. | Use of color and graphics enhances rather than detracts from the site |
| ❏ | 6. | Graphics are optimized and do not slow download significantly |
| ❏ | 7. | Each graphic used serves a clear purpose |
| ❏ | 8. | Img elements use the alt attribute to configure alternate text replacement |
| ❏ | 9. | Animated images do not distract from the site |

## Multimedia (see Chapter 11)

| | | |
|---|---|---|
| ❏ | 1. | Each audio or video file used serves a clear purpose |
| ❏ | 2. | The audio or video files used enhance rather than distract from the site |
| ❏ | 3. | Captions or transcripts are provided for each audio or video file used |
| ❏ | 4. | The file size is indicated for audio or video file downloads |
| ❏ | 5. | If needed, hyperlinks to downloads for media plug-ins are provided |
| ❏ | 6. | Animation enhances rather than distracts from the site content |

## Content Presentation

| | | |
|---|---|---|
| ❏ | 1. | Common fonts such as Arial, Verdana, Georgia, or Times New Roman are used |
| ❏ | 2. | Writing techniques for the Web are used: headings, bullet points, brief paragraphs, and so on |
| ❏ | 3. | Fonts, font sizes, and font colors are consistently used |
| ❏ | 4. | If web fonts are configured, no more than one font typeface is used. |
| ❏ | 5. | Content provides meaningful, useful information |
| ❏ | 6. | Content is organized in a consistent manner |
| ❏ | 7. | Information is easy to find (minimal clicks) |
| ❏ | 8. | Timeliness: The date of the last revision and/or copyright date is accurate |
| ❏ | 9. | Content does not include outdated material |
| ❏ | 10. | Content is free of typographical and grammatical errors |
| ❏ | 11. | Avoids the use of "Click here" when writing text for hyperlinks |
| ❏ | 12. | Hyperlinks use a consistent set of colors to indicate visited/nonvisited status |
| ❏ | 13. | Alternate text equivalent to content is provided for graphics and media |

(*Continued*)

Table 5.1  (*Continued*)

| Functionality | | |
|---|---|---|
| ❏ | 1. | All internal hyperlinks work |
| ❏ | 2. | All external hyperlinks work |
| ❏ | 3. | All forms (see Chapter 9) function as expected |
| ❏ | 4. | No JavaScript (see Chapters 11 and 14) errors are generated by the pages |

| Accessibility | | |
|---|---|---|
| ❏ | 1. | When the main navigation consists of images and/or multimedia, the page footer area contains text hyperlinks |
| ❏ | 2. | Navigation is structured in an unordered list |
| ❏ | 3. | Navigation aids, such as site map, skip navigation link, or breadcrumbs are used |
| ❏ | 4. | Color is not used alone to convey meaning |
| ❏ | 5. | Text color has sufficient contrast with background color |
| ❏ | 6. | Img element use the alt attribute to configure alternate text replacement |
| ❏ | 7. | If graphics are used to convey meaning, the alternate text equivalent is provided |
| ❏ | 8. | If media is used to convey meaning, the alternate text equivalent is provided |
| ❏ | 9. | Captions or transcripts are provided for each audio or video file used |
| ❏ | 10. | Attributes designed to improve accessibility, such as alt and title, are used where *appropriate* |
| ❏ | 11. | Use the id and headers attributes to improve the accessibility of table data (see Chapter 8) |
| ❏ | 12. | If the site uses frames, frame titles are configured and meaningful content is placed in the no-frames area |
| ❏ | 13. | To assist screen readers, the spoken language of the page is indicated with the HTML element's *lang* attribute |

 **Checkpoint 5.2**

1. View the home page of your school. Use the Web Design Best Practices Checklist (Table 5.1) to evaluate the page. Describe the results.

2. View your favorite website or a URL provided by your instructor. Maximize and resize the browser window. Decide whether the site uses fixed or fluid design. Adjust the screen resolution on your monitor to a different resolution than you normally use. Does the website look similar or very different? Offer two recommendations for improving the design of the site.

3. List three best practices used when placing graphics on web pages. View the home page of your school. Describe the use of web graphic design best practices on this page.

# Chapter Summary

This chapter introduced recommended web design practices. The choices you make in the use of page layout, color, graphics, text, and media depend on your particular target audience. Developing an accessible website should be the goal of every web developer. Visit the textbook website at https://www.webdevfoundations.net for examples, the links listed in this chapter, and updated information.

## Key Terms

alignment
analogous color scheme
antialiasing
breadcrumb trail
chunking
color theory
color wheel
complement
complementary color scheme
contrast
fixed layout
flat web design
fluid layout
hero
hierarchical organization
horizontal scrolling

linear organization
load time
media queries
monochromatic color scheme
navigation bars
page layouts
perceived load time
POUR
progressive enhancement
proximity
random organization
repetition
responsive web design
screen resolutions
shade
single page website

site map
site search
skip to content
split complementary color scheme
target audience
tetradic color scheme
tint
tone
triadic color scheme
WAI (Web Accessibility Initiative)
Web Content Accessibility
    Guidelines 2.1 (WCAG 2.1)
white space
wireframe

## Review Questions

### Multiple Choice

1. Which of the following is a sketch or blueprint of a web page that shows the structure (but not the detailed design) of basic page elements?
   a. drawing
   b. HTML code
   c. site map
   d. wireframe

2. Which of the following is not a web design recommended practice?
   a. Design your site to be easy to navigate.
   b. Colorful pages appeal to everyone.
   c. Design your pages to load quickly.
   d. Limit the use of animated items.

3. Which of the following are the three most common methods for organizing websites?
   a. horizontal, vertical, and diagonal
   b. hierarchical, linear, and random
   c. accessible, readable, and maintainable
   d. contrast, repetition, and proximity

4. Which of the following are the four principles of the Web Content Accessibility Guidelines?
   a. repetition, contrast, proximity, and alignment
   b. perceivable, operable, understandable, and robust
   c. accessible, readable, maintainable, and reliable
   d. hierarchical, linear, random, and sequential

5. Which of the following would a consistent website design *not* have?

   a. a similar navigation area on each content page

   b. the same fonts on each content page

   c. a different background color on each page

   d. the same logo

6. Which of the following are influenced by the intended or target audience of a site?

   a. the amount of color used on the site

   b. the font size and styles used on the site

   c. the overall look and feel of the site

   d. all of the above

7. Which of the following recommended design practices apply to a website that uses images for its main site navigation?

   a. Provide alternative text for the images.

   b. Place text links at the bottom of the page.

   c. Both a and b.

   d. No special considerations are needed.

8. Which of the following is known as white space?

   a. the empty screen area around blocks of text and images

   b. the background color of white used for a page

   c. configuring the color of the text to be white

   d. none of the above

9. Which of the following should you do when creating text hyperlinks?

   a. Create the entire sentence as a hyperlink.

   b. Include the words "Click here" in your text.

   c. Use a key phrase as a hyperlink.

   d. none of the above

10. Which of the following is a color scheme that consists of two colors that are opposite each other on the color wheel?

    a. analogous

    b. complementary

    c. split complementary

    d. contrasting

## Fill in the Blank

11. The most common structure used for commercial websites is _____ organization.

12. All browsers and browser versions _____ display web pages in exactly the same way.

13. The _____ is a group whose mission is to create guidelines and standards for web accessibility.

## Short Answer

14. Describe an issue to consider when designing for the mobile Web.

15. Describe one of the four principles of WCAG.

## Hands-On Exercises

1. **Web Design Evaluation.** As you read this chapter, you explored web page design, including navigation design techniques and the design principles of repetition, contrast, proximity, and alignment. In this exercise, you'll review and evaluate the design of a website. Your instructor may provide you with the URL of a website to evaluate. If not, choose a website to evaluate from the following list of URLs:

   https://www.telework.gov

   https://www.dcmm.org

   https://www.sedonalibrary.org

   https://bostonglobe.com

   https://www.alistapart.com

Visit the website you are evaluating. Write a paper that includes the following information:

a. URL of the website

b. Name of the website

c. Target audience

d. Screenshot of the home page

e. Indicate the type(s) of navigation evident.

f. Describe how the design principles of contrast, repetition, alignment, and contrast are applied. Be specific.

g. Complete the Web Design Best Practices Checklist (see Table 5.1).

h. Recommend one improvement for the website.

2. Practice creating site maps for the following situations.

a. Doug Kowalski is a freelance photographer who specializes in nature photography. He often gets contract work shooting photos for textbooks and journals. Doug would like a website that showcases his talents and provides publishers with an easy way to contact him. He would like a home page, a few pages with samples of his nature photographs, and a contact page. Create a site map based on this scenario.

b. Mary Ruarez owns a business, named Just Throw Me, which sells handcrafted specialty pillows. She currently sells at craft fairs and local gift shops, but would like to expand her business to the Web. She would like a website with a home page, a page that describes her products, a page for each of her seven pillow styles, and an order page. She has been advised that because she is collecting information from individuals, a page describing her privacy policy would be a good idea. Create a site map based on this scenario.

c. Prakesh Khan owns a dog-grooming business named A Dog's Life. He would like a website that includes a home page, a page about grooming services, a page with a map to his shop, a contact page, and a section that explains how to select a good pet. The content for the part of the website on selecting a pet will be a step-by-step presentation. Create a site map based on this scenario.

3. Practice creating wireframe page layouts for the following situations. Use the style for page layout composition shown in Figures 5.33 – 5.36 where places for logo, navigation, text, and images are indicated. Do not worry about exact wording or exact images.

a. Create sample wireframe page layouts for Doug Kowalski's photography business, described in 2(a). Create a wireframe layout for the home page. Create another wireframe page layout for the content pages.

b. Create sample wireframe page layouts for the Just Throw Me website described in 2(b). Create a wireframe layout for the home page. Create another wireframe page layout for the content pages.

c. Create sample wireframe page layouts for the A Dog's Life website described in 2(c). Create a wireframe layout for the home page and the regular content pages. Create another wireframe page layout for the presentation pages.

4. Choose two sites that are similar in nature or have a similar target audience, such as the following:

   - Amazon.com (https://www.amazon.com) and Barnes & Noble (http://www.bn.com)
   - Kohl's (https://www.kohls.com) and JCPenney (http://www.jcpenney.com)
   - CNN (https://www.cnn.com) and MSNBC (http://www.msnbc.com)

   Describe how the two sites you chose to review exhibit the design principles of repetition, contrast, proximity, and alignment.

5. Choose two sites that are similar in nature or have a similar target audience, such as the following:

   - Crate & Barrel (https://www.crateandbarrel.com)
     Pottery Barn (https://www.potterybarn.com)
   - Harper College (https://goforward.harpercollege.edu)
     College of Lake County (http://www.clcillinois.edu)
   - Chicago Bears (https://www.chicagobears.com)
     Green Bay Packers (https://www.packers.com)

   Describe how the two sites you chose to review exhibit web design best practices. How would you improve these sites? Recommend three improvements for each site.

6. How would you design a home page for the following businesses using a single page website design? Create a wireframe page layout for the home page.

   a. See 2(a) for the description of Doug Kowalski's photography business.

   b. See 2(b) for the description of Just Throw Me.

   c. See 2(c) for the description of A Dog's Life.

7. How would you design a home page for the following businesses using a responsive layout design? Create two wireframe page layouts for the home page: a wireframe for mobile devices and a wireframe for desktop browsers.

   a. See 2(a) for the description of Doug Kowalski's photography business.

   b. See 2(b) for the description of Just Throw Me.

   c. See 2(c) for the description of A Dog's Life.

8. Visit the Media Queries website at https://mediaqueri.es to view a gallery of sites that demonstrate responsive web design. Choose one of the example responsive websites to explore. Write a one-page paper that includes the following:

   - URL of the website
   - Name of the website
   - Three screenshots of the website (desktop display, tablet display, and smartphone display)
   - Describe the similarities and differences between the three screenshots.
   - Describe two ways in which the display has been modified for smartphones.
   - Does the website meet the needs of its target audience in all three display modes? Why or why not? Justify your answer.

## Web Research

This chapter introduced techniques that are useful when writing for the Web. Explore this topic further. Visit the resources listed below to get started.

- Writing for the Web: https://www.useit.com/papers/webwriting
- 9 Simple Tips for Writing Persuasive Web Content:
  https://www.enchantingmarketing.com/writing-for-the-web-vs-print/
- Web Writing that Works!: http://www.webwritingthatworks.com/CGuideJOBAID.htm
- A List Apart: 10 Tips on Writing the Living Web:
  http://www.alistapart.com/articles/writeliving

If these resources are no longer available, search the Web for information on "writing for the Web." Read one or more articles. Select five techniques that you would like to share with others. Write a one-page summary of your findings. Include the URLs of your resources.

## Focus on Web Design

Visit any of the websites referenced in this chapter that interest you. Write a one-page summary and reaction to the website you chose to visit. Address the following topics:

- What is the purpose of the site?
- Who is the intended audience?
- Do you think the site reaches the intended audience?
- Does the website display well on a mobile device?
- List three examples of how this website uses recommended web design guidelines.
- How could this site be improved?

In this activity you will design a color scheme, code an external CSS file for the color scheme, and code an example web page that applies the styles you configured. First, choose a topic for your web page. Explore the resources below to find out about the psychology of color:

- http://www.infoplease.com/spot/colors1.html
- https://precisionintermedia.com/color
- http://www.webpagefx.com/blog/web-design/psychology-of-color-infographic/

Complete the following tasks:

a. Design a color scheme. List three hexadecimal color values in addition to neutrals such as white (#FFFFFF), black, #000000, gray (#EAEAEA or #CCCCCC), and dark brown (#471717) in your design.

b. Describe the process you went through as you selected the colors. Describe why you chose these colors and why they would be appropriate for your website topic. List the URLs of any resources you used.

c. Create an external CSS file named colors.css that configures font properties, text color, and background color selections for the document, h1 element selector, p element selector, and footer class using the colors you have chosen.

d. Create a web page named color1.html that shows examples of the colors configured in the CSS style rules.

# WEBSITE CASE STUDY

## Web Design Best Practices

Each of the following case studies continues throughout most of this textbook. In this chapter, you are asked to analyze the design of the websites.

## JavaJam Coffee Bar

See Chapter 2 for an introduction to the JavaJam Coffee Bar case study. Figure 2.32 shows a site map for the JavaJam website. Three pages for this site were created in earlier chapters. In this case study, you will review the site for recommended web design practices.

### Hands-On Practice Case

1. Examine the site map in Figure 2.32. What type of site organization is used for the JavaJam website? Is it the most appropriate organization for the site? Why or why not?

2. Review the recommended web design practices from this chapter. Use the Web Design Best Practices Checklist (Table 5.1) to evaluate the JavaJam site that you created in earlier chapters. Cite three design practices that have been well implemented. Cite three design practices that could be implemented in a better way. How else would you improve the website?

## Fish Creek Animal Clinic

See Chapter 2 for an introduction to the Fish Creek Animal Clinic case study. Figure 2.36 shows a site map for the Fish Creek website. Three pages for the site were created in earlier chapters. In this case study, you will review the site for recommended web design practices.

### Hands-On Practice Case

1. Examine the site map in Figure 2.36. What type of site organization is used for the Fish Creek website? Is it the most appropriate organization for the site? Why or why not?

2. Review the recommended web design practices from this chapter. Use the Web Design Best Practices Checklist (Table 5.1) to evaluate the Fish Creek site that you created in earlier chapters. Cite three design practices that have been well implemented. Cite three design practices that could be implemented in a better way. How else would you improve the website?

## Pacific Trails Resort

See Chapter 2 for an introduction to the Pacific Trails Resort case study. Figure 2.40 shows a site map for the Pacific Trails Resort website. Three pages for the site were created in earlier chapters. During this case study, you will review the site for recommended web design practices.

## Hands-On Practice Case

1. Examine the site map in Figure 2.40. What type of site organization is used for the Pacific Trails Resort website? Is it the most appropriate organization for the site? Why or why not?

2. Review the recommended web design practices from this chapter. Use the Web Design Best Practices Checklist (Table 5.1) to evaluate the Pacific Trails Resort site that you created in earlier chapters. Cite three design practices that have been well implemented. Cite three design practices that could be implemented in a better way. How else would you improve the website?

# Path of Light Yoga Studio

See Chapter 2 for an introduction to the Path of Light Yoga Studio case study. Figure 2.44 shows a site map for the Path of Light Yoga Studio website. Three pages for the site were created in earlier chapters. During this case study, you will review the site for recommended web design practices.

## Hands-On Practice Case

1. Examine the site map in Figure 2.44. What type of site organization is used for the Path of Light Yoga Studio website? Is it the most appropriate organization for the site? Why or why not?

2. Review the recommended web design practices from this chapter. Use the Web Design Best Practices Checklist (Table 5.1) to evaluate the Path of Light Yoga Studio site you created in earlier chapters. Cite three design practices that have been well implemented. Cite three design practices that could be implemented in a better way. How else would you improve the website?

# Web Project

The purpose of this Web Project case study is to design a website using recommended design practices. Your website might be about a favorite hobby or subject, your family, a church or club you belong to, a company a friend owns, or the company you work for. Your website will contain a home page and at least six (but no more than ten) content pages. Complete the following documents: Topic Approval, Site Map, and Page Layout Design. You will not develop web pages at this point; you will complete that task in later chapters.

## Hands-On Practice Case

1. **Web Project Topic Approval.** The topic of your website must be approved by your instructor. Provide the following information:

   - What is the purpose of the website?
     List the reasons you are creating the website.
   - What do you want the website to accomplish?
     List the goals you have for the website.
   - Describe what needs to happen for you to consider your website a success.
   - Who is your target audience?
     Describe your target audience by age, gender, socioeconomic characteristics, and so on.

- What opportunity or issue is your website addressing?

  For example, your website might address the opportunity to provide information about a topic to others or create an initial web presence for a company.

- What type of content might be included in your website?

  Describe the type of text, graphics, and media you will need for the website. While you should write the text content yourself, you may use outside sources for royalty-free images and multimedia. Review copyright considerations (see Chapter 1).

- List the URLs for at least two related or similar websites found on the Web.

2. **Web Project Site Map.**  Use the drawing feature of a word processing program, a graphics application, or a paper and pencil to create a site map of your website that shows the hierarchy of pages and relationships between pages.

3. **Web Project Page Layout Design.**  Use the drawing feature of a word processing program, a graphics application, or paper and pencil to create wireframe page layouts for the home page and content pages of your site. Unless otherwise directed by your instructor, use the style for page layout composition shown in Figures 5.33–5.36. Indicate where the logo, navigation, text, and images will be located. Do not worry about exact wording or exact images.

# 6

# Page Layout

## Chapter Objectives    In this chapter, you will learn how to . . .

- Describe and apply the CSS Box Model
- Configure width and height with CSS
- Configure margins with CSS
- Configure float with CSS
- Configure positioning with CSS
- Create two-column page layouts using CSS
- Configure navigation in unordered lists and style with CSS

- Add interactivity to hyperlinks with CSS pseudo-classes
- Configure a hyperlink to a named fragment internal to a web page
- Configure images with CSS sprites
- Configure an interactive image gallery
- Configure CSS for printing
- Configure a single page website with parallax scrolling

**You've already configured the centered page layout with CSS.** We'll add to your toolbox of CSS page layout techniques in this chapter, starting with the box model. You'll explore floating and positioning elements with CSS. You'll be introduced to using CSS to add interactivity to hyperlinks with pseudo-classes and use CSS to style navigation in unordered lists. You will configure a single-page website using hyperlinks to named fragments. You will build many page layout skills in this chapter.

# 6.1  Width and Height with CSS

There are many ways to configure width and height with CSS. You've already used the width and height properties to configure elements on web pages. This section takes a closer look at the width, min-width, max-width, and height properties. Table 6.1 lists commonly used width and height units and their purpose.

**Table 6.1**   Unit Types and Purpose

| Unit | Purpose |
| --- | --- |
| px | px Configures a fixed number of pixels as the value |
| em | Configures a value relative to the font size |
| % | Configures a percentage value of the parent element |
| vh | Configures a value relative to 1% of the viewport height |
| vw | Configures a value relative to 1% of the viewport width |

**Figure 6.1**  The web page is set to 80% width.

## The `width` Property

The **width property** configures the width of an element's content in the browser viewport with either a numeric value unit (such as `100px` or `20em`), percentage (such as `80%`, as shown in Figure 6.1) of the parent element, or viewport width value (such as 50vw, which is 50% of the viewport width). The actual width of an element displayed in the browser viewport includes the width of the element's content, padding, border, and margin—it is not the same as the value of the width property, which only configures the width of the element's *content*.

## The `min-width` Property

The **min-width property** sets the minimum width of an element's content in the browser viewport. This minimum width value can prevent content from jumping around when a browser is resized. Scrollbars appear if the browser viewport is resized below the minimum width (see Figures 6.2 and 6.3).

**Figure 6.2**  As the browser is resized, the "Coffee House" and navigation text wrap.

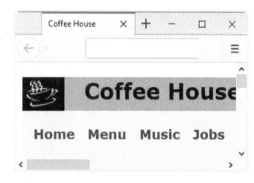

**Figure 6.3**  The min-width property avoids display issues.

## The `max-width` Property

The **`max-width` property** sets the maximum width of an element's content in the browser viewport. This maximum width value can reduce the possibility of text stretching across large expanses of the screen by a high-resolution monitor.

## The `height` Property

The **`height` property** configures the height of an element's content in the browser viewport with either a numeric value unit (such as `900px`), percentage (such as `60%`) of the parent element, or viewport height value (such as 50vw), which is 50% of the viewport height. Figure 6.4 shows a web page with an h1 area without a `height` or `line-height` property configured. Notice how part of the background image is truncated and is hidden from view. In Figure 6.5, the h1 area is configured with the `height` property. Notice the improved display of the background image.

Figure 6.4 The background image is truncated.

Figure 6.5 The height property value corresponds to the height of the background image.

## Hands-On Practice 6.1

You'll work with the height and width properties in this Hands-On Practice.

Create a new folder called coffeech6. Copy the coffeelogo.jpg file from the student files chapter6/starters folder into your coffeech6 folder. Copy the chapter6/starter.html file into your coffeech6 folder. Launch a text editor and open the file.

1. Edit the embedded CSS to configure the document to take up 80% of the browser window but with a minimum width of 750px. Add the following style rules to the body element selector:

   ```
   width: 80%; min-width: 750px;
   ```

2. Add style declarations to the h1 element selector to configure height as 150px (the height of the background image) and line height as 220%.

   ```
   height: 150px; line-height: 220%;
   ```

Save your file as index.html. Launch a browser and test your page. Your web page should look similar to Figure 6.1. A sample solution is in the chapter6/6.1 folder.

# 6.2 The Box Model

Each element in a document is considered to be a rectangular box. As shown in Figure 6.6, this box consists of a content area surrounded by padding, a border, and margins. This is known as the **box model**.

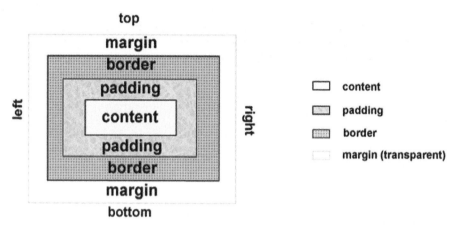

Figure 6.6 The CSS box model

## Content

The content area can consist of a combination of text and web page elements such as images, paragraphs, headings, lists, and so on. The **visible width** of the element on a web page is the total of the content width, the padding width, and the border width. However, the **width property** only configures the actual width of the content; it does not include any padding, border, or margin.

## Padding

The **padding** area is between the content and the border. The default padding value is zero. When the background of an element is configured, the background is applied to both the padding and the content areas. Use the `padding` property to configure an element's padding (refer to Chapter 4).

## Border

The **border** area is between the padding and the margin. The default border has a value of 0 and does not display. Use the `border` property to configure an element's border (refer to Chapter 4).

## Margin

The **margin** determines the empty space between the element and any adjacent elements. The solid line in Figure 6.6 that contains the margin area does not display on a web page.

### The margin Property

Use the **margin property** to configure margins on all sides of an element. The margin is always transparent—the background color of the web page or parent element shows in this area. Browsers have default margin values set for the web page document and for certain elements such as paragraphs, headings, forms, and so on. Use the margin property to override the default browser values.

To configure the size of the margin, use a numeric value (px or em) or a percentage. To eliminate the margin, configure it to 0 (with no unit). Use the value auto to indicate that the browser should calculate the margin. In Chapters 3 and 4, you used margin-left: auto; and margin-right: auto; to configure a centered page layout. Table 6.2 shows CSS properties that configure margins.

Table 6.2  Configuring margins with CSS

| Property | Description and Common Values |
| --- | --- |
| margin | Shorthand notation to configure the margin surrounding an element |
| | A numeric value (px or em) or percentage; for example, margin: 10px; |
| | The value auto causes the browser to automatically calculate the margin for the element |
| | Two numeric values (px or em) or percentages: The first value configures the top margin and bottom margin, and the second value configures the left margin and right margin; for example, margin: 20% 10%; |
| | Three numeric values (px or em) or percentages: The first value configures the top margin, the second value configures the left margin and right margin, and the third value configures the bottom margin; for example, margin: 10% 20% 5px; |
| | Four numeric values (px or em) or percentages; the values configure the margin in the following order: margin-top, margin-right, margin-bottom, and margin-left; for example, margin: 10% 30px 20% 5%; |
| margin-bottom | Bottom margin; a numeric value (px or em), percentage, or auto |
| margin-left | Left margin; a numeric value (px or em), percentage, or auto |
| margin-right | Right margin; a numeric value (px or em), percentage, or auto |
| margin-top | Top margin; a numeric value (px or em), percentage, or auto |

## The Box Model in Action

The web page shown in Figure 6.7 (chapter6/box.html in the student files) depicts the box model in action with an h1 and a div element.

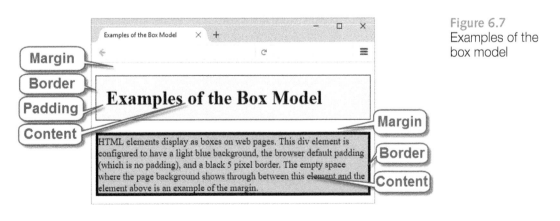

Figure 6.7
Examples of the box model

- The h1 element is configured to have a light-blue background, 20 pixels of padding (the space between the content and the border), and a black, 1 pixel border.

- The empty space where the white web page background shows through is the margin. When two vertical margins meet (such as between the h1 element and the div element), the browser collapses the margin size to be the larger of the two margin values instead of applying both margins.

- The div element has a medium-blue background; the browser default padding (which is no padding); and a black, 5 pixel border.

You will get more practice using the box model in this chapter. Feel free to experiment with the box model and the chapter6/box.html file.

## 6.3 Normal Flow

Browsers render your web page code line by line in the order it appears in the .html document. This processing is called normal flow. **Normal flow** displays the elements on the page in the order they appear in the web page source code.

Figures 6.8 and 6.9 each display two div elements that contain text content. Let's take a closer look. Figure 6.8 shows a screenshot of two div elements placed one after another on a web page. In Figure 6.9, the boxes are nested inside each other. In both cases, the browser used normal flow (the default) and displayed the elements in the order that they appeared in the source code. As you've worked through the exercises in the previous chapters, you created web pages that the browser has rendered using normal flow.

You'll practice this a bit more in the next Hands-On Practice. Then, later in the chapter, you'll experiment with CSS positioning and float to configure the flow, or placement, of elements on a web page.

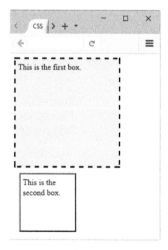

**Figure 6.8** Two div elements

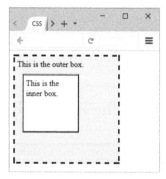

**Figure 6.9** Nested div elements

# Hands-On Practice 6.2

You will explore the box model and normal flow in this Hands-On Practice as you work with the web pages shown in Figure 6.8 and Figure 6.9.

## Practice with Normal Flow

Launch a text editor and open chapter6/starter1.html in the student files. Save the file with the name box1.html. Edit the body of the web page and add the following code to configure two div elements:

```
<div class="div1">
This is the first box.
</div>
<div class="div2">
This is the second box.
</div>
```

Now let's add embedded CSS in the head section to configure the "boxes." Add a new style rule for a class named `div1` to configure a light-blue background, dashed border, width of 200 pixels, height of 200 pixels, and 5 pixels of padding. The code is

```
.div1 { width: 200px;
        height: 200px;
        background-color: #D1ECFF;
        border: 3px dashed #000000;
        padding: 5px; }
```

Create a style rule for a class named `div2` to configure a width and height of 100 pixels, white background color, ridged border, 10 pixel margin, and 5 pixels of padding. The code is

```
.div2 { width: 100px;
        height: 100px;
        background-color: #FFFFFF;
        border: 3px ridge #000000;
        margin: 10px;
        padding: 5px; }
```

Save the file. Launch a browser and test your page. It should look similar to the one shown in Figure 6.8. The student files contain a sample solution (see chapter6/6.2/box1.html).

## Practice with Normal Flow and Nested Elements

Launch a text editor and open your box1.html file. Save the file as box2.html.

Edit the code. Delete the content from the body section of the web page. Add the following code to configure two div elements—one nested inside the other.

```
<div class="div1">
This is the outer box.
  <div class="div2">
  This is the inner box.
  </div>
</div>
```

Save the file. Launch a browser and test your page. It should look similar to the one shown in Figure 6.9. Notice how the browser renders the nested div elements: The second box is nested inside the first box because it is coded inside the first div element in the web page source code. This is an example of normal flow. The student files contain a sample solution (see chapter6/6.2/box2.html). The examples in this Hands-On Practice happened to use two div elements. However, the box model applies to block display HTML elements in general, not just to div elements. You will get more practice using the box model in this chapter.

## 6.4 CSS Float

Elements that seem to float on the right or left side of either the browser window or another element are often configured using the **float property**. The browser renders these elements using normal flow and then shifts them to either the right or left as far as possible within their container (usually either the browser viewport or a div element).

- Use `float: right;` to float the element on the right side of the container.

- Use `float: left;` to float the element on the left side of the container.

- Specify a width for a floated element unless the element already has an implicit width, such as an img element.

- Other elements and web page content will flow around the floated element.

**Figure 6.10** The image is configured to float

Figure 6.10 shows a web page with an image configured with `float: right;` to float on the right side of the browser viewport (see chapter6/float.html in the student files). When floating an image, the margin property is useful to configure empty space between the image and text on the page.

View Figure 6.10 and notice how the image stays on the right side of the browser viewport. An id called `yls` was created that applies the `float`, `margin`, and `border` properties. The attribute `id="yls"` was placed on the image tag. The CSS is

```
h1 { background-color: #A8C682;
     padding: 5px;
     color: #000000; }
p { font-family: Arial, sans-serif; }
#yls { float: right;
       margin: 0 0 5px 5px;
       border: 1px solid #000000; }
```

The HTML source code is

```
<h1>Wildflowers</h1>
<img id="yls" src="yls.jpg" alt="Yellow Lady Slipper" height="100"
width="100">
    <p>The heading and paragraph follow normal flow. The Yellow Lady
    Slipper pictured on the right is a wildflower. It grows in wooded
    areas and blooms in June each year. The Yellow Lady Slipper is a
    member of the orchid family.</p>
```

## Hands-On Practice 6.3

In this Hands-On Practice, you'll use the CSS float property as you configure the web page shown in Figure 6.11.

**Figure 6.11** The CSS float property left-aligns the image

Create a folder named ch6float. Copy the starteryls.html and yls.jpg files from the chapter6 folder in the student files into your ch6float folder. Launch a text editor and open starteryls.html. Notice the order of the images and paragraphs. Note that there is no CSS configuration for floating the images. Display starteryls.html in a browser. The browser renders the page using normal flow and displays the HTML elements in the order they are coded.

Let's add CSS to float the image. Save the file as index.html in your ch6float folder. Open the file in a text editor and modify the code as follows:

**1.** Add a style rule for a class name `float` that configures float, margin, and border properties.

```
.float { float: left;
        margin-right: 10px;
        border: 3px ridge #000000; }
```

**2.** Assign the image element to the class named `float` (use `class="float"`).

Save the file. Launch a browser and test your page. It should look similar to the web page shown in Figure 6.11. The student files (chapter6/6.3/index.html) contain a sample solution.

### The Floated Element and Normal Flow

Take a moment to examine your file in a browser (see Figure 6.11) and consider how the browser rendered the page. The div element is configured with a light background color to demonstrate how floated elements are rendered outside of normal flow. Observe that the image and the first paragraph are contained within the div element. The h2 element follows the div. If all the elements were rendered using normal flow, the area with the light background color would contain both child elements of the div: the image and the first paragraph. In addition, the h2 element would be placed on its own line under the div element.

However, once the image is placed vertically on the page, it is floated outside of normal flow—that's why the light background color only appears behind the first paragraph and why the h2 element's text begins immediately after the first paragraph and appears next to the floated image. In the following sections, you'll explore properties that can "clear" this float and improve the display.

# 6.5 CSS Clearing a Float

## The `clear` Property

The **clear property** is often used to terminate, or clear, a float. You can set the value of the clear property to `left`, `right`, or `both`, depending on the type of float you need to clear.

Review Figure 6.11 and the code sample (see chapter6/6.3/index.html in the student files). Notice that although the div element contains both an image and the first paragraph, the light background color of the div only displays behind the screen area occupied by the first paragraph—it stops a bit earlier than expected. Clearing the float will help take care of this display issue.

### Clear a Float with a Line Break

A common technique to clear a float within a container element is to add a line break element configured with the `clear` property. See chapter6/clear1.html in the student files for an example. Observe that a CSS class is configured to clear the left float:

```
.clearleft { clear: left; }
```

Also, a line break tag assigned to the `clearleft` class is coded before the closing `div` tag. The code for the div element is

```
<div>
<img class="float" src="yls.jpg" alt="Yellow Lady Slipper"
height="100" width="100">
<p>The Yellow Lady Slipper grows in wooded areas and blooms in June
each year. The flower is a member of the orchid family.</p>
<br class="clearleft">
</div>
```

Figure 6.12 displays a screen shot of this page. Review Figure 6.11 and note two changes: the light background color of the div element extends farther down the page and the h2 element's text begins on its own line under the image.

### Another Technique to Clear a Float

If you are not concerned about the light background color display, another option is to omit the line break tag and, instead, apply the `clearleft` class to the h2 element, which is the first block display element after the div. This does not change the display of the light background color, but it does force the h2 element's text to begin on its own line, as shown in Figure 6.13 (see chapter6/clear2.html in the student files).

Figure 6.12 The clear property is applied to a line break tag

Figure 6.13 The clear property is applied to the h2 element

## The overflow Property

The **overflow property** is often used to clear a float, although its intended purpose is to configure how content should display if it is too large for the area allocated. See Table 6.3 for a list of commonly used values for the overflow property.

Table 6.3 The overflow property

| Value | Purpose |
| --- | --- |
| visible | Default value; the content is displayed, and if it's too large, the content will overflow and extend outside the area allocated to it |
| hidden | The content is clipped to fit the area allocated to the element in the browser viewport |
| auto | The content fills the area allocated to it and, if needed, scrollbars are displayed to allow access to the remaining content |
| scroll | The content is rendered in the area allocated to it and scrollbars are displayed |

## Clear a Float

Review Figure 6.11 and the code sample (chapter6/6.3/index.html in the student files). Observe the div element, which contains the floated image and first paragraph on the page. Notice that although the div element contains both an image and the first paragraph, the light background color of the div element does not extend as far as expected; it is only visible in the area occupied by the first paragraph. You can use the `overflow` property assigned to the container element to resolve this display issue and clear the float. In this case, we'll apply the `overflow` and `width` properties to the div selector. The CSS to configure the div in this manner is

```
div { background-color: #F3F1BF;
      overflow: auto;
      width: 100%; }
```

This will clear the float. The web page will display as shown in Figure 6.14 (see chapter6/overflow.html in the student files).

Figure 6.14 The overflow property is applied to the div selector

Figure 6.15 The browser displays scrollbars

Notice that using the `overflow` property (see Figure 6.14) and applying the `clear` property to a line break tag (see Figure 6.12) result in a similar web page display. You may be wondering about which CSS property (`clear` or `overflow`) is the best one to use when you need to clear a float.

Although the `clear` property is widely used, in this example, it is more efficient to apply the `overflow` property to the container element (for example, a div element). This will clear the float, avoid adding an extra line break tag, and ensure that the container element expands to enclose the entire floated element. You'll get more practice with the `float`, `clear`, and `overflow` properties as you continue working through this textbook. Floating elements is a key technique for designing multicolumn page layouts with CSS.

## Configure Scrollbars

The web page in Figure 6.15 demonstrates the use of `overflow: auto;` to automatically display scrollbars if the content exceeds the space allocated to it. In this case, the div that contains the paragraph and the floated image was configured with a width of 300px and a height of 100px.

See the example web page (chapter6/scroll.html in the student files). The CSS for the div is shown below:

```
div { background-color: #F3F1BF;
      overflow: scroll;
      width: 300px;
      height: 100px; }
```

# Checkpoint 6.1

**1.** List the components of the box model from innermost to outermost.

**2.** Describe the purpose of the CSS float property.

**3.** Which two CSS properties can be used to clear a float?

# 6.6  CSS Box Sizing

When you view an element on a web page it's intuitive to expect that the width of an element on a page includes the size of the element's padding and border. However, this isn't the default behavior of browsers. Recall from the box model introduction in Section 6.2 that the `width` property by default only includes the actual width of the content itself within the element and does not also include the width of any padding or border that may exist for the element. The purpose of the `box-sizing` property is to alleviate this issue. The **box-sizing property** causes the browser calculation of the width or height to include the content's actual width or height in addition to the width or height of any padding and border that may exist.

Valid `box-sizing` property values include `content-box` (the default) and `border-box`. Use the CSS `box-sizing: border-box;` declaration to configure the browser to also include the values of the border and padding when calculating the width and height properties of an element.

Figures 6.16 and 6.17 show web pages (boxsizing1.html and boxsizing2.html in the student files chapter6 folder) that each have floated elements configured with 30% width, 150px height, 20px padding, and 10px margin. The page in Figure 6.16 uses default box-sizing. The page in Figure 6.17 uses box-sizing set to `border-box`. The size of the elements and the placement of the elements on the pages differ. You may notice at first glance that the elements look larger in Figure 6.16. The larger display is because the browser sets the content to 30% width before adding the 20 pixels of padding on each side. The elements are smaller in Figure 6.17. The smaller display is because the browser applies the 30% width to the combination of the padding and the content.

Let's take a closer look at the placement of the three floated elements on the pages. Figure 6.16 does not display all three elements side-by-side. This web page uses default `box-sizing` so the browser assigned the 30% width to each element's content only and then added 20 pixels of padding to each side of each element. Due to these calculations, the browser determined there was not enough room in the browser viewport to display all three elements next to each other and the browser dropped the third floated element to the next line. The web page in Figure 6.17 is coded with `box-sizing` set to `border-box` which configures the three floated elements to be displayed side-by-side because the browser assigned the 30% width to the combined content and padding areas (including 20 pixels of padding on each side).

It is common practice for web developers to apply border-box box-sizing when they plan to use floated elements or multicolumn layouts. It's also common practice to apply `box-sizing` by configuring

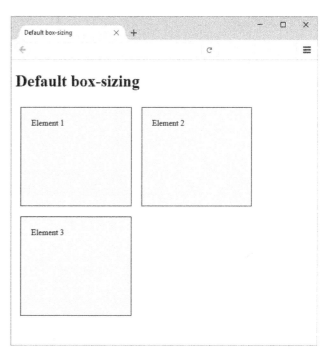

**Figure 6.16**  Default box-sizing

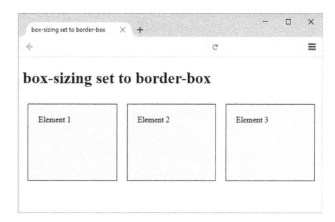

**Figure 6.17**  box-sizing set to border-box

the **\*** **universal selector**, which will target all HTML elements. The CSS style rule to apply border-box box-sizing to all elements with the universal selector is

```
* { box-sizing: border-box; }
```

Feel free to experiment with the box-sizing property and the example files (chapter6/boxsizing1.html and chapter6/boxsizing2.html in the student files).

# 6.7  CSS Two-Column Layout

## Your First Two-Column Layout

A common design for a web page is a two-column layout. This is accomplished with CSS by configuring one of the columns to float on the web page. Coding HTML is a skill and skills are best learned by practice. The next Hands-On Practice guides you as you convert a single-column page layout (Figure 6.18) into your first two-column layout (Figure 6.19).

Figure 6.18  Single-column layout.

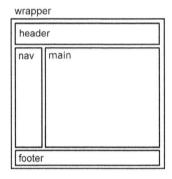

Figure 6.19  Two-column layout.

## Hands-On Practice 6.4

A. **Review single-column layout.** Launch a text editor, and open the singlecol.html file from the chapter6 folder in the student files. Take a moment to look over the code. Notice the structure of the HTML tags correspond to wireframe in Figure 6.18.

```
<body>
<div id="wrapper">

  <header> </header>

  <nav> </nav>

  <main> </main>

  <footer> </footer>

</div>
</body>
```

Save the file as index.html. When you display index.html in a browser, your display should be similar to Figure 6.20.

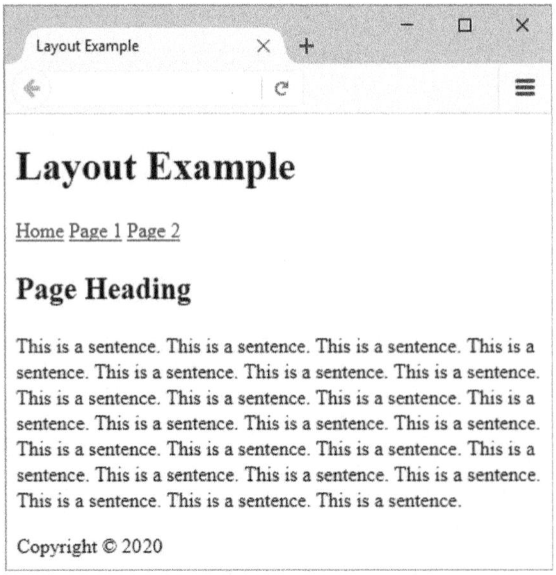

Figure 6.20  Web page with single-column layout.

B. **Configure a two-column layout.** Launch a text editor and open the index.html file. You will edit the HTML and CSS to configure a two-column layout as shown in Figure 6.19 wireframe.

1. **Edit the HTML.** The single-column navigation is horizontal but the two-column navigation will be displayed in a vertical orientation. Later in this chapter, you'll learn how to configure navigation hyperlinks within an unordered list but for now, a quick adjustment is to code a line break tag after each of the first two hyperlinks in the nav area.

2. **Configure the float with CSS.** Locate the style tags in the head section of the document and code the following style rule as embedded CSS to configure a nav element with a width of 90px that floats to the left.

```
nav { float: left;
      width: 90px; }
```

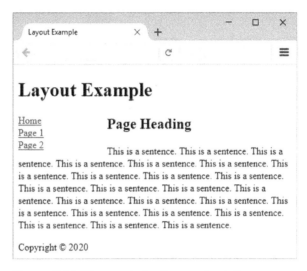

Figure 6.21 The nav is floating on the left

Save the file and test it in the Firefox or Chrome browser. Your display will be similar to Figure 6.21. Notice that the content in the main area wraps around the floated nav element.

3. **Configure two columns with CSS.** You just configured the nav element to float on the left. The main element will be in the right-side column and will be configured with a left margin (the same side as the float). To get a two-column look, the value of the margin should be greater than the width of the floated element. Open the index.html file in a text editor and code the following style rule to configure a 100px left margin for the main element.

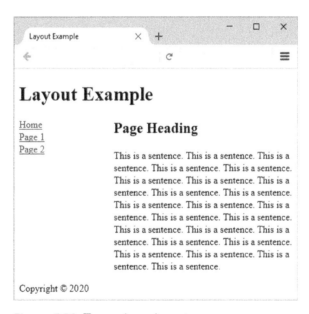

Figure 6.22 Two-column layout

```
main { margin-left: 100px; }
```

Save the file and test it in the Firefox or Chrome browser. Your display will be similar to Figure 6.22 with a two-column layout.

Figure 6.23 Final two-column layout

4. **Enhance the page with CSS.** Code the following style rules as embedded CSS to create a more appealing web page. When you have completed this step, your page should be similar to Figure 6.23.

a. **The body element selector.** Configure a dark background color.

```
body { background-color:
#000066; }
```

b. **The wrapper id selector.** Configure 80% width, centered on the page, and a light (#EAEAEA) background color. This background color will display behind child elements (such as the nav element) that do not have a background color configured.

```
#wrapper { width: 80%;
          margin-left: auto;
          margin-right: auto;
          background-color: #EAEAEA; }
```

c. **The header element selector.** Configure #CCCCFF background color.

```
header { background-color: #CCCCFF; }
```

d. **The h1 element selector.** Configure 0 margin and 10px of padding.

```
h1 { margin: 0;
     padding: 10px; }
```

e. **The nav element selector.** Edit the style rule and add a declaration for 10 pixels of padding.

```
nav { float: left;
      width: 90px;
      padding: 10px;  }
```

f. **The main element selector.** Edit the style rule and add a declaration for 10 pixels of padding and #FFFFFF background color.

```
main { margin-left: 100px;
       padding: 10px;
       background-color: #FFFFFF;  }
```

g. **The footer element selector.** Configure centered, italic text, and a #CCCCFF background color. Also configure the footer to clear all floats.

```
footer { text-align: center;
         font-style: italic;
         background-color: #CCCCFF;
         clear: both; }
```

Save your file and test it in the Firefox or Chrome browser. Your display should be similar to Figure 6.23. You can compare your work to the sample in the student files (chapter6/6.4/index.html). Internet Explorer does not support the HTML5 main element. You will need to nudge Internet Explorer to comply by adding the `display: block;` declaration (introduced later in this chapter) to the styles for the main element selector. An example solution is in the student files (chapter6/6.4/iefix.html).

# Two-Column Layout Example

The web page you coded in Hands-On Practice 6.4 is just one example of a two-column layout design. Let's explore coding the two-column layout with a footer in the right column as shown in Figure 6.24 wireframe. The HTML template for the page layout is

```
<div id="wrapper">
  <header>
  </header>
  <nav>
  </nav>
  <main>
  </main>
  <footer>
  </footer>
</div>
```

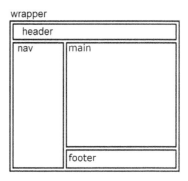

**Figure 6.24** Alternate wireframe

The key CSS configures a floating nav element, a main element with a left margin, and a footer with a left margin.

```
nav { float: left; width: 150px; }
main { margin-left: 165px; }
footer { margin-left: 165px; }
```

The web page shown in Figure 6.25 implements this layout. An example is in the student files, chapter6/layout/twocol.html.

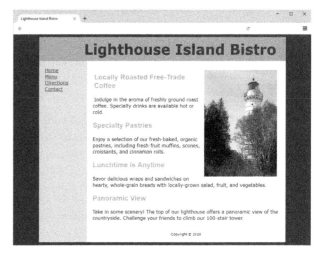

**Figure 6.25** Page with alternate layout

 FAQ **Does the order of the floated and non-floated elements matter?**

A key to coding successful layouts with float is in the HTML—code the element that needs to float BEFORE its companion elements. The browser will shift the floated element over to the side of the browser viewport and display the elements that follow alongside the floated element.

 FAQ **Do I have to use a wrapper?**

No, you are not required to use a wrapper or container for a web page layout. However, it does make it easier to get the two-column look because the background color of the wrapper div will display behind any of its child elements that do not have their own background color configured. This technique also provides you with the option of configuring a different background color or background image for the page using the body element selector.

### Not Yet Ready for Prime Time

There is one more aspect of the two-column layout web page design to consider before it is ready for "prime time." The navigation area is a list of hyperlinks. In order to more closely semantically describe the navigation area, the hyperlinks should be configured in an unordered list. In the next section, you'll learn techniques to configure horizontal and vertical navigation hyperlinks in unordered lists.

# 6.8 Hyperlinks in an Unordered List

One of the advantages of using CSS for page layout involves the use of semantically correct code. Writing semantically correct code means choosing the markup tag that most accurately reflects the purpose of the content. Using the various levels of heading tags for content headings and subheadings or placing paragraphs of text within paragraph tags (rather than using line breaks) are examples of writing semantically correct code. This type of coding is a step in the direction of supporting the Semantic Web. Leading Web developers such as Eric Meyer, Mark Newhouse, Jeffrey Zeldman, and others have promoted the idea of using unordered lists to configure navigation menus. After all, a navigation menu is a list of hyperlinks.

**Focus on
Accessibility**

Configuring navigation with a list also helps to provide accessibility. Screen reader applications offer easy keyboard access and verbal cues for information organized in lists, such as the number of items in the list.

### Configure List Markers with CSS

Recall that the default display for an unordered list is to show a disc marker (often referred to as a bullet) in front of each list item. The default display for an ordered list is to show a decimal number in front of each list item. When you configure navigation hyperlinks in an unordered list, you may not always want to see those **list markers**. It's easy to configure them with CSS. Use the `list-style-type` **property** to configure the marker for an unordered or ordered list. See Table 6.4 for common property values.

Table 6.4  CSS properties for ordered and unordered list markers

| Property | Description | Value | List Marker Display |
|---|---|---|---|
| `list-style-type` | Configures the style of the list marker | `none` | No list markers display |
| | | `disc` | Circle |
| | | `circle` | Open circle |
| | | `square` | Square |
| | | `decimal` | Decimal numbers |
| | | `upper-alpha` | Uppercase letters |
| | | `lower-alpha` | Lowercase letters |
| | | `lower-roman` | Lowercase Roman numerals |
| `list-style-image` | Image replacement for the list marker | The `url` keyword with parentheses surrounding the file name or path for the image | Image displays in front of each list item |
| `list-style-position` | Configures placement of the list marker | `inside` | Markers are indented; text wraps under the markers |
| | | `outside` (default) | Markers have default placement |

Figure 6.26 shows an unordered list configured with square markers using the following CSS:

```
ul { list-style-type: square; }
```

Figure 6.27 shows an ordered list configured with uppercase letter markers using the following CSS:

```
ol { list-style-type: upper-alpha; }
```

- Website Design
- Interactive Animation
- E-Commerce Solutions
- Usability Studies
- Search Engine Optimization

A. Website Design
B. Interactive Animation
C. E-Commerce Solutions
D. Usability Studies
E. Search Engine Optimization

Website Design
Interactive Animation
E-Commerce Solutions
Usability Studies
Search Engine Optimization

**Figure 6.26** The unordered list markers are square

**Figure 6.27** The ordered list markers use uppercase letters

**Figure 6.28** The list markers are replaced with an image

### Configure an Image as a List Marker

Use the **list-style-image property** to configure an image as the marker in an unordered or ordered list. In Figure 6.28, an image named trillium.gif was configured to replace the list markers using the following CSS:

```
ul {list-style-image: url(trillium.gif); }
```

## Vertical Navigation with an Unordered List

Figure 6.29 shows the navigation area of a web page (see chapter6/layout/twocolnav.html in the student files) that uses an unordered list to organize the navigation links. The HTML is

```
<ul>
<li><a href="index.html">Home</a></li>
<li><a href="menu.html">Menu</a></li>
<li><a href="directions.html">Directions</a></li>
<li><a href="contact.html">Contact</a></li>
</ul>
```

- Home
- Menu
- Directions
- Contact

**Figure 6.29** Navigation in an unordered list

### Configure with CSS

OK, so now that we're semantically correct, how about improving the visual aesthetic? Let's use CSS to eliminate the list marker. We also need to make sure that our special styles only apply to the unordered list in the navigation area (within the `nav` element), so we'll use a descendant selector. The CSS to configure the list in Figure 6.30 is

```
nav ul { list-style-type: none; }
```

Home
Menu
Directions
Contact

**Figure 6.30** The list markers have been eliminated with CSS

### Remove the Underline with CSS

The **text-decoration property** modifies the display of text in the browser. This property is most often used to eliminate the underline from the navigation hyperlinks with `text-decoration: none;`.

The CSS to configure the list in Figure 6.31 (see chapter6/layout/twocolnav2.html in the student files) that eliminates the underline on the hyperlinks in the navigation area (within the `nav` element) is

```
nav a { text-decoration: none; }
```

Home
Menu
Directions
Contact

**Figure 6.31** The CSS text-decoration property has been applied

## The `display` Property

The CSS **display property** configures how the browser renders, or displays, an element on a web page. There is a default display value setting for each element, such as block display for a div element and inline display for a span element. It's even possible to hide the display of an element. See Table 6.5 for a list of commonly used values.

Table 6.5 The display property

| Value | Purpose |
|---|---|
| none | The element will not display |
| inline | The element will display as an inline element in the same line as the surrounding text and/or elements |
| inline-block | The element will display as an inline display element adjacent to other inline display elements but also can be configured with properties of block display elements including width and height. |
| block | The element will display as a block element with a margin above and below |
| flex | The element will display as a block-level flex container (see Chapter 7). |
| grid | The element will display as a block-level grid container (see Chapter 7). |

## Horizontal Navigation with an Unordered List

You may be wondering how to use an unordered list for a horizontal navigation menu. The answer is CSS! List items are block display elements. They need to be configured as inline display elements to display in a single line. To create a horizontal navigation menu, use the CSS display property to set the li elements to inline display or inline-block display.

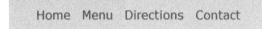

Home   Menu   Directions   Contact

Figure 6.32 Navigation in an unordered lisxt

Figure 6.32 shows the navigation area of a web page (see chapter6/layout/horizontal.html in the student files) with a horizontal navigation area organized in an unordered list. The HTML is

```
<nav>
<ul>
    <li><a href="index.html">Home</a></li>
    <li><a href="menu.html">Menu</a></li>
    <li><a href="directions.html">Directions</a></li>
    <li><a href="contact.html">Contact</a></li>
</ul>
</nav>
```

### Configure with CSS

The following CSS was applied in this example:

- To eliminate the list marker, apply `list-style-type: none;` to the ul element selector:

  ```
  nav ul { list-style-type: none; }
  ```

- To render the list items horizontally instead of vertically, apply `display: inline;` to the li element selector:

  ```
  nav li { display: inline; }
  ```

- To eliminate the underline from the hyperlinks, apply `text-decoration: none;` to the a element selector. Also, to add some space between the hyperlinks, apply `padding-right: 10px;` to the a element selector:

```
nav a { text-decoration: none; padding-right: 10px; }
```

# 6.9 CSS Interactivity with Pseudo-Classes

Have you ever visited a website and found that the text hyperlinks changed color when you moved the mouse pointer over them? Often, this is accomplished using a CSS **pseudo-class**, which can be used to apply a special effect to a selector. The five pseudo-classes that can be applied to the anchor element are shown in Table 6.6.

VideoNote
Interactivity with CSS pseudo-classes

Table 6.6 Commonly used CSS pseudo-classes

| Pseudo-Class | When Applied |
|---|---|
| `:link` | Default state for a hyperlink that has not been clicked (visited) |
| `:visited` | Default state for a visited hyperlink |
| `:focus` | Triggered when the hyperlink has keyboard focus |
| `:hover` | Triggered when the mouse pointer moves over the hyperlink |
| `:active` | Triggered when the hyperlink is actually clicked |

Notice the order in which the pseudo-classes are listed in Table 6.6. Anchor element pseudo-classes *must be coded in this order* (although it's OK to omit one or more of those listed). If you code the pseudo-classes in a different order, the styles will not be reliably applied. It's common practice to configure the `:hover`, `:focus`, and `:active` pseudo-classes with the same styles.

To apply a pseudo-class, write it after the selector. The following code sample will configure text hyperlinks to be red initially. The sample also uses the `:hover` pseudo-class to configure the hyperlinks to change their appearance when the visitor places the mouse pointer over them so that the underline disappears and the color changes.

```
a:link { color: #ff0000; }
a:hover { text-decoration: none;
          color: #000066; }
```

Figure 6.33 shows part of a web page that uses a similar technique. Note the position of the mouse pointer over the Print This Page hyperlink. The text color has changed and has no underline.

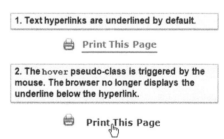

Figure 6.33 Using the `hover` pseudo-class

# Hands-On Practice 6.5

You will use pseudo-classes to create interactive hyperlinks in this Hands-On Practice. Create a folder named ch6hover. Copy the lighthouse.jpg and lightlogo.jpg, files from the chapter6/starters folder in the student files into your ch6hover folder. Copy the starter2.html file from the chapter6 folder into your ch6hover folder. Display the web page in a browser. It should look similar to Figure 6.34. Notice that the navigation area needs to be configured.

Launch a text editor and open starter2.html. Save the file as index.html in your ch6hover folder.

**Figure 6.34** The navigation area needs to be styled in this two-column page layout

1. Review the code for this page, which uses a two-column layout. Examine the nav element and modify the code to configure the navigation in an unordered list.

```
<ul>
    <li><a href="index.html">Home</a></li>
    <li><a href="menu.html">Menu</a></li>
    <li><a href="directions.html">Directions</a></li>
    <li><a href="contact.html">Contact</a></li>
</ul>
```

Let's add CSS to the embedded styles to configure the unordered list elements in the nav element. Eliminate the list marker, set the left margin to 0, and set the padding to 10 pixels.

```
nav ul { list-style-type: none;
         margin-left: 0;
         padding: 10px; }
```

2. Next, configure basic interactivity with pseudo-classes.
   • Configure the anchor tags in the nav element to have 10 pixels of padding, use bold font, and display no underline.

```
nav a { text-decoration: none;
        padding: 10px;
        font-weight: bold; }
```

   • Use pseudo-classes to configure anchor tags in the nav element to display white (#FFFFFF) text for unvisited hyperlinks, light-gray (#EAEAEA) text for visited hyperlinks, and dark-blue (#000066) text when the mouse pointer hovers over hyperlinks:

```
nav a:link { color: #FFFFFF; }
nav a:visited { color: #EAEAEA; }
nav a:hover { color: #000066; }
```

Save your page and test in a browser. Move your mouse pointer over the navigation area and notice the change in the text color. Your page should look similar to Figure 6.35 (see chapter6/6.5/index.html in the student files).

Figure 6.35  CSS pseudo-classes add interactivity to the navigation

## CSS Button

In addition to configuring an interactive text hyperlink, another use of CSS and pseudo-classes is to configure a hyperlink that looks like a button. This coding technique saves on the bandwidth used by button image files. Figure 6.36 shows a web page with a "button" configured with CSS instead of with an image. The following CSS was applied in this example:

A `button` class selector was configured with 60px border radius, 1em padding, #FFFFFF text color, #E38690 background color, Arial or sans-serif font family, 2em size bold font, centered text, and no text decoration. The CSS follows

Figure 6.36  CSS button

```
.button { border-radius: 60px;
          padding: 1em;
          color: #FFFFFF;
          background-color: #E38690;
          font-family: Arial, sans-serif;
          font-size: 2em;
          font-weight: bold;
          text-align: center;
          text-decoration: none; }
```

To provide for interactivity, the `:link`, `:visited`, and `:hover` pseudo-classes for the `button` class were configured. The CSS follows

```
.button:link    { color : #FFFFFF; }
.button:visited { color : #CCCCCC; }
.button:hover   { color : #965251;
                  background-color: #F7DEE1; }
```

You can find a sample page that demonstrates a button with these styles in the student files (chapter6/button.html).

## Hands-On Practice 6.6

You've had some experience with a two-column layout, organizing navigation links in an unordered list, and configuring CSS pseudo-classes. Let's reinforce these skills with a Hands-On Practice. You'll create a new version of the Lighthouse Island Bistro home page with a header spanning two columns, content in the left column, vertical navigation in the right column, and a footer below the two columns. See Figure 6.37 for a wireframe. You will configure the CSS in an external style sheet. Create a folder named ch6practice. Copy the lighthouse.jpg and lightlogo.jpg files from the chapter6/starters folder in the student files into your ch6practice folder. Copy the starter3.html file from the chapter6 folder into your ch6practice folder.

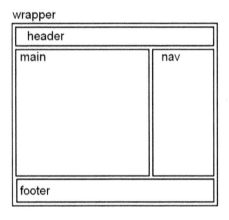

**Figure 6.37** Wireframe for a two-column layout with navigation in the right-side column.

1. Launch a text editor and open starter3.html. Save the file as index.html. Add a link element to the head section of the web page that associates this file with an external style sheet named lighthouse.css. A code sample follows.

```
<link href="lighthouse.css" rel="stylesheet">
```

2. Save the index.html file. Launch a text editor and create a new file named lighthouse.css in your ch6practice folder. Configure the CSS for the wireframe sections as follows:

- The universal selector: set the box-sizing property to border-box.

```
* { box-sizing: border-box; }
```

- The body element selector: very-dark-blue background (#00005D) and Verdana, Arial, or the default sans-serif font typeface

```
body { background-color: #00005D;
       font-family: Verdana, Arial, sans-serif; }
```

- The wrapper id: centered, width set to 80% of the browser viewport, minimum width of 960px, maximum width of 1200px, display text in a dark-blue color (#000066), and display a medium-blue (#B3C7E6) background color (*this color will display behind the nav area*)

```
#wrapper { margin: 0 auto;
           width: 80%;
           min-width: 960px; max-width: 1200px;
           background-color: #B3C7E6;
           color: #000066; }
```

- The header element selector: slate-blue (#869DC7) background color; very-dark-blue (#00005D) text color; 150% font size; top, right, and bottom padding of 10px; 155 pixels of left padding; and the lightlogo.jpg background image

```
header { background-color: #869DC7;
        color: #00005D;
        font-size: 150%;
        padding: 10px 10px 10px 155px;
        background-repeat: no-repeat;
        background-image: url(lightlogo.jpg); }
```

- The nav element selector: float on the right, width set to 200px, display bold text, letter spacing of 0.1 em

```
nav { float: right;
     width: 200px;
     font-weight: bold;
     letter-spacing: 0.1em; }
```

- The main element selector: white background color (#FFFFFF), black text color (#000000), 10 pixels of padding on the top and bottom, 20 pixels of padding on the left and right, display set to block (to prevent an Internet Explorer display issue), and overflow set to auto

```
main { background-color: #FFFFFF;
      color: #000000;
      padding: 10px 20px;
      overflow: auto; }
      display: block; }
```

- The footer element selector: 70% font size, centered text, 10 pixels of padding, slate-blue background color (#869DC7), and clear set to both

```
footer { font-size: 70%;
        text-align: center;
        padding: 10px;
        background-color: #869DC7;
        clear: both;}
```

Save the file and display it in a browser. Your display should be similar to Figure 6.38.

Figure 6.38 Home page with major sections configured using CSS

3. Continue editing the lighthouse.css file to style the h2 element selector and floating image. Configure the h2 element selector with slate-blue text color (#869DC7) and Arial or sans-serif font typeface. Configure the `floatright` id to float on the right side with 10 pixels of margin.

```
h2 { color: #869DC7;
    font-family: Arial, sans-serif; }
#floatright { float: right;
            margin: 10px; }
```

**4.** Continue editing the lighthouse.css file and configure the navigation bar.

- The ul element selector: Eliminate the list markers. Set a zero margin and zero padding.

```
nav ul { list-style-type: none; margin: 0; padding: 0; }
```

- The a element selector: no underline, 20 pixels of padding, medium-blue background color (#B3C7E6), and 1 pixel solid white bottom border Use `display: block;` to allow the web page visitor to click anywhere on the anchor "button" to activate the hyperlink.

```
nav a { text-decoration: none;
        padding: 20px;
        display: block;
        background-color: #B3C7E6;
        border-bottom: 1px solid #FFFFFF; }
```

Configure the `:link`, `:visited`, and `:hover` pseudo-classes as follows:

```
nav a:link { color: #FFF; }
nav a:visited { color: #EAEAEA; }
nav a:hover { color: #869DC7;
              background-color: #EAEAEA; }
```

**5.** It's common practice for the header area of a website to link to the home page—even though your don't see the underline for the hyperlink. The header text "Lighthouse Island Bistro" is coded as a hyperlink. Continue editing your lighthouse.css file to configure any hyperlinks in the header to have no underline. Also configure the `:link`, `:visited`, and `:hover` pseudo-classes for anchor elements in the header.

```
header a { text-decoration: none; }
header a:link { color: #00005D; }
header a:visited { color: #00005D; }
header a:hover { color: #FFFFFF; }.
```

Save your files. Open your index.html file in a browser. Move your mouse pointer over the navigation area and notice the interactivity, as shown in Figure 6.39 (see chapter6/6.6/index.html in the student files).

Figure 6.39 CSS pseudo-classes add interactivity to the page

**FAQ**  **In Hands-On Practice 6.6 why did we set the display property to block for the main element selector?**

Although all modern browsers support the newer HTML5 elements such as main, header, nav, and footer as valid block display elements, Internet Explorer does not. Sometimes this causes a web page to render poorly in Internet Explorer. If your layout depends on an element being treated as block display, add CSS to force Internet Explorer (and any other older browsers) to comply. For example, code the following CSS to force block display for the header, nav, main, and footer elements:

```
header, nav, main, footer { display: block; }
```

## 6.10  CSS Sprites

When browsers display web pages, they must make a separate http request for every file used by the page, including .css files and image files such as .gif, .jpg, and .png files. Each http request takes time and resources. As mentioned in Chapter 4, a **sprite** is an image file that contains multiple small graphics. Using CSS to configure the small graphics combined in the sprite as background images for various web page elements is called **CSS sprites**, a technique made popular by David Shea (http://www.alistapart.com/articles/sprites).

The CSS sprites technique uses the CSS `background-image`, `background-repeat`, and `background-position` properties to manipulate the placement of the background image. The single graphics file saves download time because the browser only needs to make one http request for the combined image instead of many requests for the individual smaller images. Figure 6.40 shows a sprite with two lighthouse images on a transparent background. These images are configured as background images for the navigation hyperlinks with CSS as shown in Figure 6.41. You'll see this in action as you complete the next Hands-On Practice.

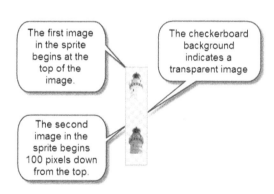

Figure 6.40  The sprite consists of two images in a single graphics file

Figure 6.41  Sprites in action

## Hands-On Practice 6.7

You will work with CSS sprites in this Hands-On Practice as you create the web page shown in Figure 6.41. Create a new folder named ch6sprites. Use your files from Hands-On Practice 6.6 or in the chapter6/6.6 folder. Copy all the files into your ch6sprites folder. Copy the sprites.gif file from the chapte6/starters folder into your ch6sprites folder. The sprites.gif, shown in Figure 6.40, contains two lighthouse images. The first lighthouse image starts at the top of the graphics file. The second lighthouse image begins 100 pixels down from the top of the graphics file. We'll use the value 100 when we configure the display of the second image.

Launch a text editor and open lighthouse.css. You will edit the styles to configure background images for the navigation hyperlinks.

1. Configure the background image for navigation hyperlinks. Add the following styles to the `nav a` selector to set the background image to the sprites.gif with no repeat. The value `right` in the `background-position` property configures the lighthouse image to display at the right of the navigation element. The value 0 in the `background-position` property configures the display at offset 0 from the top (at the very top) so the first lighthouse image displays.

   ```
   nav a { text-decoration: none;
           display: block;
           padding: 20px;
           background-color: #B3C7E6;
           border-bottom: 1px solid #FFFFFF;
           background-image: url(sprites.gif);
           background-repeat: no-repeat;
           background-position: right 0; }
   ```

2. Configure the second lighthouse image to display when the mouse pointer passes over the hyperlink. Add the following styles to the `nav a:hover` selector to display the second lighthouse image. The value `right` in the `background-position` property configures the lighthouse image to display at the right of the navigation element. The value `-100px` in the `background-position` property configures the display at an offset of 100 pixels down from the top so the second lighthouse image appears.

   ```
   nav a:hover { background-color: #EAEAEA;
                 color: #869dc7;
                 background-position: right -100px;  }
   ```

Save the file and test it in a browser. Your page should look similar to Figure 6.41. Move your mouse pointer over the navigation hyperlinks to see the background images change. Compare your work with the sample found in the student files (chapter6/6.7/index.html).

## FAQ    How can I create my own sprite graphics file?

Most web developers use a graphics application such as Adobe Photoshop, Adobe Fireworks, or GIMP to edit images and save them in a single graphics file for use as a sprite. Or, you could use a web-based sprite generator such as the ones listed below:

- CSS Sprites Generator: https://www.toptal.com/developers/css/sprite-generator
- CSS Sprite Generator: http://spritegen.website-performance.org
- Instant Sprite: https://instantsprite.com/

# 6.11 CSS for Printing

Even though the "paperless society" has been talked about for decades, the fact is that many people still love paper, and you can expect your web pages to be printed. CSS offers you some control over what gets printed and how the printouts are configured. This is easy to do using external style sheets. Create one external style sheet with the configurations for browser display and a second external style sheet with the special printing configurations. Associate both of the external style sheets to the web page using two link elements. Configure a **media attribute** on each link element. Table 6.7 describes commonly used values of the media attribute.

Table 6.7  The media Attribute

| Value | Purpose |
| --- | --- |
| screen | The default value; indicates the style sheet that configures typical browser viewport display on a color computer screen |
| print | Indicates the style sheet that configures the printed formatting |

Modern browsers will use the correct style sheet depending on whether they are rendering a screen display or preparing to print a document. Use media="screen" to configure the link element for your browser display. Use media="print" to configure the link element for your printout. Sample HTML follows:

```
<link rel="stylesheet" href="lighthouse.css" media="screen">
<link rel="stylesheet" href="lighthouseprint.css" media="print">
```

## Print Styling Best Practices

You might be wondering how a print style sheet should differ from the CSS used to display the web page in a browser. Let's explore some commonly used techniques for styling printed web pages.

- **Hide Nonessential Content.**   It's common practice to prevent banner ads, navigation, or other extraneous areas from appearing on the printout. Use the display: none; style declaration to hide content that is not needed on a printout of the web page.

- **Configure Font Size and Color for Printing.**   Another common practice is to configure the font sizes on the print style sheet to use pt units. This will better control the text on the printout. You might also consider configuring the text color to black (#000000) if you envision the need for visitors to print your pages often. The default setting on most browsers prevent background colors and background images from printing, but you can also prevent background image and background color display in your print style sheet.

- **Control Page Breaks.**   Use the CSS page-break-before or page-break-after properties to control page breaks when printing the web page. Well-supported values for these properties are always (the page break will always occur as designated), avoid (if possible, the page break will not occur before or after, as designated), and auto (default). For example, to configure a page break at a specific point in the document (in this case, right before an element assigned to the class named `newpage`), configure the CSS as shown below:

```
.newpage { page-break-before: always; }
```

## Hands-On Practice 6.8

In this Hands-On Practice, you'll rework the Lighthouse Island Bistro page from Hands-On Practice 6.7 to be configured for optimal screen display and printing. Create a new folder named ch6print. Copy the files from either your ch6sprites folder or the student files chapter6/6.7 folder into the ch6print folder.

1. Edit the index.html file and add a link tag in the head section that associates the web page with the lightprint.css file for printing (use `media="print"`). Save the index.html file.

2. Launch a text editor and open lighthouse.css. Since you want to keep most of the styles for printing, you will start by creating a new version of the external style sheet. Save lighthouse.css with the name of lightprint.css in the ch6print folder. You will modify three areas on this style sheet: the header selector, the main selector, and the nav selector.

   • Modify the header styles to print using black text in 20 point font size:

   ```
   header { color: #000000; font-size: 20pt; }
   ```

   • Modify the main element area to print using a serif typeface in a 12 point font size:

   ```
   main { font-family: "Times New Roman", serif; font-size: 12pt; }
   ```

   • Modify the navigation area to not display:

   ```
   nav { display: none; }
   ```

   Save your file.

3. Test your work. Display your index.html file in a browser. Select Print from the menu. Your display should look similar to the page shown in Figure 6.42. The header and content font sizes have been configured. The navigation does not display. The student files contain a sample solution in the chapter6/6.8 folder.

Figure 6.42 The print preview display of the web page.

# 6.12  Positioning with CSS

You've seen how normal flow causes the browser to render the elements in the order that they appear in the HTML source code. You have also experienced how floating elements can move and shift as the browser viewport is resized. When using CSS for page layout there are situations when you may want more control over the position of an element. The **position property** configures the type of positioning used when the browser renders an element. Table 6.8 lists position property values and their purpose.

Table 6.8  The position Property

| Value | Purpose |
|---|---|
| static | Default value; the element is rendered in normal flow |
| fixed | Configures the location of an element within the browser viewport; the element does not move when the page is scrolled |
| relative | Configures the location of an element relative to where it would otherwise render in normal flow |
| absolute | Precisely configures the location of an element outside of normal flow |
| sticky | Combines features of relative and fixed positioning. Not supported in Internet Explorer. |

## Static Positioning

**Static positioning** is the default and causes the browser to render an element in normal flow. As you've worked through the exercises in this book, you have created web pages that the browser rendered using normal flow.

## Fixed Positioning

Use **fixed positioning** to cause an element to be removed from normal flow and to remain stationary, or "fixed in place," when the web page is scrolled in the browser viewport. Figure 6.43 shows a web page (see chapter6/fixed.html in the student files) with a navigation area configured with fixed position. The navigation stays in place even though the user has scrolled down the page. The CSS follows:

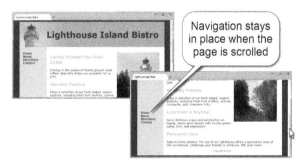

```
nav { position: fixed; }
```

Figure 6.43  The navigation is configured with fixed positioning

## Relative Positioning

Use **relative positioning** to change the location of an element slightly, relative to where it would otherwise appear in normal flow. However, the area in normal flow is still reserved for the element and other elements will flow around that reserved space. Configure relative positioning with the position: relative; property along with one or more of the following offset properties: left, right, top, bottom. Table 6.9 lists the offset properties.

Table 6.9 The Position Offset Properties

| Property | Value | Purpose |
|---|---|---|
| left | Numeric value or percentage | The position of the element offset from the left side of the container element |
| right | Numeric value or percentage | The position of the element offset from the right side of the container element |
| top | Numeric value or percentage | The position of the element offset from the top of the container element |
| bottom | Numeric value or percentage | The position of the element offset from the bottom of the container element |

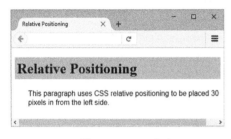

Figure 6.44 The paragraph is configured using relative positioning

Figure 6.44 shows a web page (chapter6/relative.html in the student files) that uses relative positioning along with the **left property** to configure the placement of an element in relation to the normal flow. In this case, the container element is the body of the web page. The result is that the content of the element is rendered as being offset or shifted by 30 pixels from the left where it would normally be placed at the browser's left margin. Notice also how the background-color and padding properties configure the h1 element. The CSS is

```
p { position: relative;
    left: 30px;
    font-family: Arial, sans-serif; }
h1 { background-color: #cccccc;
    padding: 5px;
    color: #000000; }
```

The HTML source code follows:

```
<h1>Relative Positioning</h1>
<p>This paragraph uses CSS relative positioning to be placed 30 pixels
in from the left side.</p>
```

## Sticky Positioning

**Sticky positioning** combines features of relative and fixed positioning. With sticky positioning, the element initially displays relative to where it would be rendered in normal flow (which may even be its final sticky position, depending on where the element is located within the source code and other CSS that may be applied). If the element is not initially rendered at its final sticky position, as soon as the browser scrolls the element to the specified position the element gets "stuck," remains there as a fixed position element, and no longer moves when the page is scrolled. If an element is initially rendered at its sticky position, it will will remain there when the browser scrolls. Explore an example in the student files (chapter6/layout/sticky.html) of using sticky positioning to force a navigation bar to move up to the top of the page when scrolled. The positioning CSS follows:

```
nav  { position: sticky;
        top: 0; }
```

## Absolute Positioning

Use **absolute positioning** to precisely specify the location of an element outside of normal flow in relation to its first parent non-static element. If there is no non-static parent element, the absolute position is specified in relation to the body of the web page. Configure absolute positioning with the `position: absolute;` property along with one or more of the offset properties (`left`, `right`, `top`, `bottom`) listed in Table 6.9.

Figure 6.45 depicts a web page that configures an element with absolute positioning to display the content 200 pixels in from the left margin and 100 pixels down from the top of the web page document. An example is in the student files, (chapter6/absolute.html).

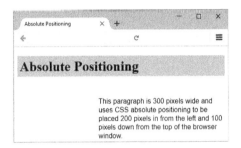

Figure 6.45 The paragraph is configured with absolute positioning

The CSS is

```
p {  position: absolute;
     left: 200px;
     top: 100px;
     font-family: Arial, sans-serif;
     width: 300px; }
```

The HTML source code is

```
<h1>Absolute Positioning</h1>
    <p>This paragraph is 300 pixels wide and uses CSS absolute
    positioning to be placed 200 pixels in from the left and 100 pixels
    down from the top of the browser window.</p>
```

## Practice with Positioning

Recall that the CSS `:hover` pseudo-class provides a way to configure styles to display when the web page visitor moves the mouse over an element. You'll use this basic interactivity along with CSS positioning and display properties to configure an interactive image gallery with CSS and HTML. Figure 6.46 shows the interactive image gallery in action (see chapter6/6.9/gallery.html in the student files). When you place the mouse over a thumbnail image, the larger version of the image is displayed along with a caption. If you click on the thumbnail, the larger version of the image displays in its own browser window.

Figure 6.46 An interactive image gallery with CSS

# Hands-On Practice 6.9

In this Hands-On Practice, you will create the interactive image gallery web page shown in Figure 6.46. Copy the following images located in the student files chapter6/starters folder into a folder named gallery2: photo1.jpg, photo2.jpg, photo3.jpg, photo4.jpg, photo1thumb.jpg, photo2thumb.jpg, photo3thumb.jpg, and photo4thumb.jpg.

Launch a text editor and modify the chapter6/template.html file to configure a web page as indicated:

1. Configure the text, Image Gallery, within an h1 element, and within the title element.

2. Code a div assigned to the id named `gallery`. This div will contain the thumbnail images, which will be configured within an unordered list.

3. Configure an unordered list within the div. Code four li elements, one for each thumbnail image. The thumbnail images will function as image links with a `:hover` pseudo-class that causes the larger image to display on the page. We'll make this all happen by configuring an anchor element containing both the thumbnail image and a span element that comprises the larger image along with descriptive text. An example of the first li element is

```
<li><a href="photo1.jpg"><img src="photo1thumb.jpg" width="100"
   height="75" alt="Golden Gate Bridge">
   <span><img src="photo1.jpg" width="250" height="150"
   alt="Golden Gate Bridge"><br>Golden Gate Bridge</span></a>
</li>
```

4. Configure all four li elements in a similar manner. Substitute the actual name of each image file for the href and src values in the code. Write your own descriptive text for each image. Use photo2.jpg and photo2thumb.jpg in the second li element. Use photo3.jpg and photo3thumb.jpg in the third li element. Use photo4.jpg and photo4thumb.jpg for the fourth li element. Save the file as index.html in the gallery2 folder. Display your page in a browser. You'll see an unordered list with the thumbnail images, the larger images, and the descriptive text. Figure 6.47 shows a partial screen capture.

5. Now, let's add embedded CSS. Open your index.html file in a text editor and code a style element in the head section. The `gallery` id will use relative positioning instead of the default static positioning. This does not change the location of the gallery but sets the stage to use absolute positioning on the span element in relation to its container (`#gallery`) instead of in relation to the entire web page document. This won't matter too much for our very

Figure 6.47 The web page display before CSS

basic example, but it would be very helpful if the gallery were part of a more complex web page. Configure embedded CSS as follows:

a. Set the `gallery` id to use relative positioning.

```
#gallery { position: relative; }
```

b. The unordered list in the gallery should have a width of 250 pixels and no list marker.

```
#gallery ul { width: 250px; list-style-type: none; }
```

c. Configure the list item elements in the gallery with inline display, left float, and 10 pixels of padding.

```
#gallery li { display: inline; float: left; padding: 10px; }
```

d. The images in the gallery should not display a border.

```
#gallery img { border-style: none; }
```

e. Configure anchor elements in the gallery to have no underline, #333 text color, and italic text.

```
#gallery a { text-decoration: none; color: #333;
             font-style: italic; }
```

f. Configure span elements in the gallery not to display initially.

```
#gallery span { display: none; }
```

g. Configure the span elements in the gallery to display *only* when the web visitor hovers the mouse over the thumbnail image link. Set the location of the span to use absolute positioning. Locate the span 10 pixels down from the top and 300 pixels in from the left. Center the text within the span:

```
#gallery a:hover span { display: block; position: absolute;
         top: 10px; left: 300px; text-align: center; }
```

Save your page and display it in a browser. Your interactive image gallery should work well in modern browsers. Compare your work to Figure 6.46 and the sample in the student files (chapter6/6.9/gallery.html).

# 6.13 Fixed Position Navigation Bar

You've probably seen web pages that feature a header area or navigation bar that is fixed in place across the top of the browser window. This popular page layout technique is easy to accomplish with CSS positioning and the CSS z-index property.

## The `z-index` property

CSS positioning allows us to configure the vertical and horizontal placement of an element. The **z-index property** provides a way to configure a third dimension—to configure the stacking of positioned elements on a web page. In order for z-index to apply, the element must be positioned with either absolute, relative, fixed, or sticky positioning. The default z-index for a positioned element is 0. To configure a different z-index use an integer value. Elements with higher z-index values will stack on top of elements with lower z-index values. Given two or more elements placed in overlapping space on a web page, the positioned element with the highest z-index value will stack on the top and display over the other element(s).

# Hands-On Practice 6.10

In this Hands-On Practice, you will configure a fixed navigation area across the top of a web page that remains in place when the page is vertically scrolled in a browser. Create a new folder named ch6z. Copy the following files from the chapter6/layout folder into the ch6z folder: lightlogo.jpg, lighthouse.jpg, and horizontal.html.

1. **Open the horizontal.html file in a browser.** The top of the page should consist of a horizontal navigation bar below the header area. You will modify the layout of this page so that it looks like Figure 6.48—with a fixed top navigation bar above the header area. When you scroll the page in the browser, the fixed navigation area remains in place as the rest of the page moves. Rename the file index.html.

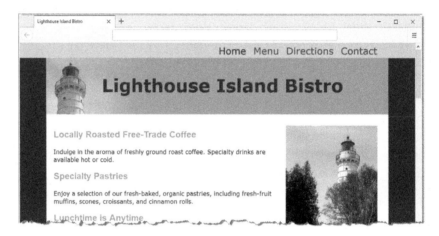

Figure 6.48 The web page has a fixed top navigation bar.

2. Launch a text editor and open the file. You will edit the embedded CSS as follows.

   • The nav element selector. Configure a new style rule that sets fixed position beginning at the top left of the page, 40px height, 40em minimum width, 100% width, #B3C7E6 background color, and z-index set to a high value, such as 9999.

   ```
   nav { position: fixed; top: 0; left: 0;
       height: 40px; width: 100%; min-width: 40em;
       background-color: #B3C7E6;
       z-index: 9999; }
   ```

   • **The nav ul element selector.** Edit the style rule. Configure new style declarations for right-aligned text, 5px margin, and 10% right padding.

   ```
   nav ul { list-style-type: none;
         font-size: 1.5em;
         text-align: right;
         margin: 5px;
         padding-right: 10%; }
   ```

- **The header element selector.** Edit the style rule. To allow room for the navigation bar at the top of the page, add a declaration for a 40px top margin.

```
header { background-color: #869DC7; color: #00005D;
         font-size: 150%; padding: 10px 10px 10px 155px;
         background-image: url(lightlogo.jpg);
         background-repeat: no-repeat; height: 130px;
         margin-top: 40px; }
```

3. Edit the HTML. The current page content is too short to showcase the fixed navigation bar. You will need to edit the content of the page to make it longer. Since this is a practice page, a quick way to get length is to copy and paste the h2 and paragraph code three or four times on the page within the main element.

   Save the file and test in a browser. Your page should be similar to Figure 6.48. Scroll down the page and your display should be similar to Figure 6.49. The navigation bar is fixed in place even though the rest of the place scrolls up and down. A sample solution is in the Student Files chapter6/6.10 folder.

Figure 6.49 The navigation bar stays in place while the content is scrolled.

4. You just configured a fixed navigation bar using `position: fixed`. Next, explore what happens when you use the position property set to `sticky`.

   Open your index.html file in a text editor. Edit the nav element style rule and change the position property value from fixed to sticky. Save your file as sticky1.html.

   When you display sticky1.html in a browser, the nav area is shown below the header area (which is where it appears in the source code). As you scroll the page down and the nav area shifts to the top of the browser viewport, the nav area gets "stuck" and remains there while you continue to scroll down. If you scroll up, the nav area will eventually revert to its initial position below the header. This is an interesting effect. An example is in the student files (chapter6/6.10/sticky1.html).

What if you wanted the nav to always be fixed in place at the top of the browser viewport and you wanted to use position: sticky? In this case, you would need to edit the HTML and move the nav element above the header element. An example is in the student files (chapter6/6.10/sticky2.html).

# 6.14  Single Page Website

Recall from Chapter 5 that a single page website consists of one very long page (a single HTML file) with a clearly defined navigation area, typically at the top of the page. The navigation takes you to specific areas on the page because each hyperlink points to a specific element on the page indicated by a fragment identifier.

## Fragment Identifiers

VideoNote
*Linking to a Named Fragment*

Browsers begin the display of a web page at the top of the document. However, there are times when you need to provide the capability to link to a specific portion of a web page instead of the top. You can accomplish this by coding a hyperlink to a **fragment identifier** (sometimes called a named fragment or fragment id), which is simply an HTML element assigned to an id attribute.

There are two components to your coding when using fragment identifiers:

1. The tag that identifies the **named fragment** of a web page: The tag must be asigned to an id. For example, `<div id="content">`

2. The anchor tag that links to the named fragment on a web page.

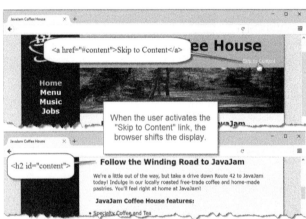
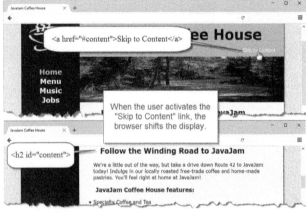

Figure 6.50  The "Skip to Content" link in action

Linking to a named fragment is often used on long web pages, such as a single page website. Lists of frequently asked questions (FAQs) also often use fragment identifiers to jump to a specific part of the page and display the answer to a question. Another use of a fragment identifier is a "Back to top" hyperlink that a visitor could select to cause the browser to quickly scroll the page back to the top of the page. Fragment identifiers can help to provide for accessibility. Web pages may have a fragment identifier to indicate the beginning of the actual page content. When the visitor clicks on a "Skip to content" hyperlink, the browser links to the fragment identifier and shifts focus to the content area of the page. This "Skip to content" or "Skip navigation" link provides a way for screen reader users to skip repetitive navigation links (see Figure 6.50).

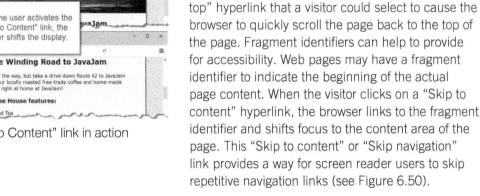

**Focus on Accessibility**

This is accomplished in two steps:

1. **Establish the Target.** Create the "Skip to content" fragment identifier by configuring an element that begins the page content with an id, for example,
   `<div id="content">`

2. **Reference the Target.** At the point of the page where you want to place a hyperlink to the content, code an anchor element. Use the `href` attribute and place a # symbol (called a hash mark) before the name of the fragment identifier. The code for a hyperlink to the named fragment "content" is

   `<a href="#content">Skip to Content></a>`

The hash mark indicates that the browser should search for an id on the same page. If you forget to type the hash mark, the browser will not look on the same web page; it will look for an external file.

There may be times when you need to link to a named fragment on another web page. To accomplish this, place a "#" followed by the fragment identifier id value after the file name in the anchor tag. For example, to link to a specific area, such as the Contact Info, configured with id="contact" in the index.html file from any other page on the same website, you could use the following HTML:

```
<a href="index.html#contact">Contact Info</a>
```

In the next Hands-On Practice, you'll use fragment identifiers to configure the navigation on a single page website.

## Hands-On Practice 6.11

In this Hands-On Practice you'll configure a single page website that with a fixed top navigation bar, fixed bottom footer, and four sections: home, tours, rentals, and contact. Each of these sections will function as a "page" in the single page website, as shown in Figure 6.51. Notice the fixed navigation is at the top of the browser viewport and the fixed footer is at the bottom of the browser viewport. The screen captures shown in Figure 6.51 are all using a single HTML file—a single page website.

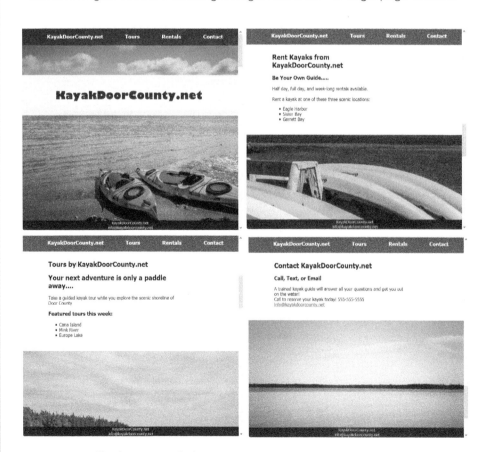

Figure 6.51 Single page website

Create a new folder called ch6spw. Copy the starter4.html file from the chapter6 folder in the student files into your ch6spw folder. Copy the following files from the chapter6/starters folder into your ch6spw folder: kayaksdc.gif, beached.jpg, kayaks.jpg, rentals.jpg, and lonekayak.jpg.

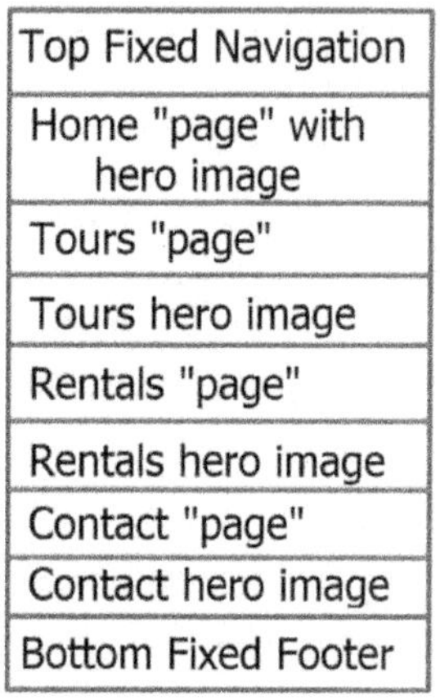

| Top Fixed Navigation |
| --- |
| Home "page" with hero image |
| Tours "page" |
| Tours hero image |
| Rentals "page" |
| Rentals hero image |
| Contact "page" |
| Contact hero image |
| Bottom Fixed Footer |

**Figure 6.52** Wireframe for single page website

1. The wireframe in Figure 6.52 shows the structural areas of the web page and the organization of the HTML. Observe the top fixed navigation area, Home "page" text content and hero image, Tours "page" text content, Tours hero image, Rentals "page" text content, Rentals hero image, Contact "page" text content, Contact hero image, and footer.

   Launch a text editor and open your starter4.html file. Scroll down to the HTML and notice that there are comments indicating Home Page, Tours Page, Rentals Page, and Contact Page. Notice that each page area begins with a section element. Configure a named fragment for each area.

   - Assign the Home Page section to the named fragment home by coding id="home" on the opening section tag.

   - Assign the Tours Page section to the named fragment home by coding id="tours" on the opening section tag

   - Assign the Rentals Page section to the named fragment home by coding id="rentals" on the opening section tag.

   - Assign the Contact Page section to the named fragment home by coding id="contact" on the opening section tag

2. Continue editing the file and configure the navigation area. Locate the nav element below the opening body tag. Code an ordered list to configure the navigation links within the nav element.

   - The text "KayakDoorCounty.net" will hyperlink to #home

   - The text "Tours" will hyperlink to #tours

   - The text "Rentals" will hyperlink to #rentals

   - The text "Contact" will hyperlink to #contact

   The HTML is shown below:

```
<nav>
 <ul>
   <li><a href="#home">KayakDoorCounty.net</a></li></p>
   <li><a href="#tours">Tours</a></li></p>
   <li><a href="#rentals">Rentals</a></li></p>
   <li><a href="#contact">Contact</a></li></p>
 </ul>
</nav>
```

Save your file as index.html and display it in a browser. Your display should be similar to the first browser screen shot in Figure 6.51. Click the navigation hyperlinks view the other page sections. Scroll down and up the single page website to view all the information and view the photographs. You can compare your work to chapter6/6.11/index.html in the student files. If you'd prefer that the footer does not always appear in the browser viewport, you can edit the CSS and remove the position and bottom style declarations (chapter6.11/index2.html in the student files).

## Parallax Scrolling

You may have noticed single page websites in which the background images scrolled at a different speed than the text content – this is a technique called **parallax scrolling**. There are many ways to accomplish this effect, some requiring the use of JavaScript or advanced CSS techniques. A very easy way to get the look of parallax scrolling on a single page website is to use the background-attachment property, which configures whether the background remains fixed in place or scrolls along with the page in the browser viewport.

## Hands-On Practice 6.12

In this Hands-On Practice you'll apply a parallax scrolling effect on your single page website from Hands-On Practice 6.11. Create a new folder named ch6plx. Copy all the files from either your ch6spw folder or the chapter6/6.11 folder in the student files.

Launch a text editor and open the index.html file. Locate the CSS in the head section and view the styles for the hero images. Each hero image is already configured with a minimum height (`min-height` property), centered position (`background-position: center;`), no repeats (`background-repeat: no-repeat;`), and to scale (`background-size: cover;`). There is one more CSS property that needs to be in place to obtain the parallax scrolling effect: `background-attachment`. Recall from Chapter 4 that setting the `background-attachment` property to the value `fixed` will prevent the background image from scrolling with the page.

Edit the CSS in the head section and add a `background-attachment: fixed;` style declaration to the style rules for the `hero`, `tourshero`, `rentalshero`, and `contacthero` class selectors.

Save your file as index.html and display it in a browser. Your display should be similar to the first browser screen shot in Figure 6.53.

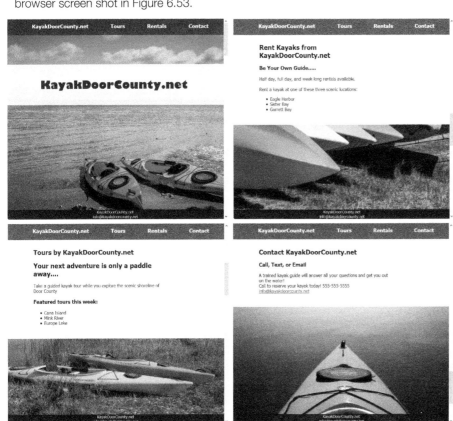

Figure 6.53 Using the background-attachment property

Click the navigation hyperlinks to view the other page sections. Notice Figures 6.51 and 6.53 are similar, but that the kayak photographs in Figure 6.53 are positioned slightly differently, due to the background-attachment property. Setting the background-attachment property to fixed creates a more noticeable difference when you begin to scroll the page. While the text sections move smoothly up and down as the page is scrolled, the background images appear and disappear as though the text is a window shade that's being rolled up or down – that's a very subtle parallax scrolling effect. You can compare your work to chapter6/6.12/index.html in the student files.

 **FAQ**   **Sometimes it takes me a while to find my CSS errors. Can you share some CSS debugging tips?**

Using CSS for page layout requires some patience. It takes a while to get used to it. Fixing problems in code is called **debugging**. This term dates back to the early days of programming when an insect (a bug) lodged inside the computer and caused a malfunction. Debugging CSS can be frustrating and requires patience. One of the biggest issues is that even modern browsers implement CSS in slightly different ways. Browser support changes with each new browser version. Testing is crucial. Expect your pages to look slightly different in various browsers. The following are helpful techniques to use when your CSS isn't behaving properly:

## Verify Correct HTML Syntax

Invalid HTML code can cause issues with CSS. Use the W3C Markup Validation Service at http://validator.w3.org to verify the correct HTML syntax.

## Verify Correct CSS Syntax

Sometimes a CSS style does not apply because of a syntax error. Use the W3C CSS Validation Service at https://jigsaw.w3.org/css-validator to verify your CSS syntax. Carefully check your code. Many times, the error is in the line *above* the style that is not correctly applied.

## Configure Temporary Background Colors

Sometimes your code is valid but the page is not rendered in the way that you would expect. If you temporarily assign distinctive background colors such as red or yellow and test again, it should be easier to see where the boxes are ending up.

## Configure Temporary Borders

Similar to the temporary background colors, you could temporarily configure an element with a 3 pixel red solid border. This will really jump out at you and help you recognize the issue quickly.

## Use Comments to Find the Unexpected Cascade

Style rules and HTML attributes configured farther down the page can override earlier style rules. If your styles are misbehaving, try "commenting out" (see below) some styles and test with a smaller group of statements. Then add the styles back in one by one to see where or when the breakdown occurs. Work patiently and test the entire style sheet in this manner.

Browsers ignore code and text that is contained between comment markers. A CSS comment begins with /* and ends with */. The comment below is an example of documentation that explains the purpose of a style rule.

```
/* Set Page Margins to Zero */
body { margin: 0; }
```

Comments can span multiple lines. The following comment begins on the line above the style declaration for the new class and ends on the line below the style declaration for the new class. This causes the browser to skip the new class when applying the style sheet. This technique can be useful for testing when you are experimenting with a number of properties and may need to temporarily disable a style rule.

```
/* temporarily commented out during testing
.new { font-weight: bold; }
*/
```

A common mistake when using comments is to type the beginning /* without subsequently typing */ to end the comment. As a result, *everything* after the /* is treated as a comment by the browser.

## Checkpoint 6.2

**1.** State an advantage of using CSS to style for print.

**2.** State an advantage of using CSS sprites in a website.

**3.** Describe a technique to keep an HTML element, such as a nav element, displayed at the top of the browser viewport even while the browser is scrolled.

# Chapter Summary

This chapter introduced CSS page layout techniques. Techniques for positioning elements, floating elements, and configuring two-column page layouts were demonstrated. You also worked with a single page website that used parallax scrolling. The topic of page layout is very deep and you have much to explore. Visit the resources cited in the chapter to continue learning about this technology.

Visit the textbook website at https://www.webdevfoundations.net for examples, the links listed in this chapter, and updated information.

## Key Terms

| | | |
|---|---|---|
| `:active` | fragment identifier | `position` property |
| `:focus` | `left` property | pseudo-class |
| `:hover` | list markers | relative positioning |
| `:link` | `list-style-image` property | `right` property |
| `:visited` | `list-style-type` property | single page website |
| absolute positioning | margin | sprite |
| `background-attachment` property | `margin` property | static positioning |
| border | media attribute | sticky positioning |
| `bottom` property | normal flow | `text-decoration` property |
| box model | `overflow` property | `top` property |
| `box-sizing` property | padding | universal selector |
| `clear` property | `padding` property | visible width |
| `display` property | `page-break-after` property | `width` property |
| fixed positioning | `page-break-before` property | `z-index` property |
| `float` property | parallax scrolling | |

## Review Questions

### Multiple Choice

1. Which of the following, from outermost to innermost, are components of the box model?
   a. margin, border, padding, content
   b. content, padding, border, margin
   c. content, margin, padding, border
   d. margin, padding, border, content

2. Which of the following can be used to change the location of an element slightly in relation to where it would otherwise appear on the page?
   a. relative positioning
   b. the float property
   c. absolute positioning
   d. this cannot be done with CSS

3. Which of the following properties can be used to clear a float?
   a. float or clear
   b. clear or overflow
   c. position or clear
   d. overflow or float

4. Which of the following configures a class called side to float to the left?
   a. `.side { left: float; }`
   b. `.side { float: left; }`
   c. `.side { float-left: 200px; }`
   d. `.side { position: left; }`

**5.** Which of the following is the rendering flow used by a browser by default?

a. regular flow

b. normal display

c. browser flow

d. normal flow

**6.** Which of the following is an example of using a descendant selector to configure the anchor tags within the nav element?

a. `nav. a`

b. `a nav`

c. `nav a`

d. `a#nav`

**7.** Which property and value are used to configure an unordered list item with a square list marker?

a. `list-bullet: none;`

b. `list-style-type: square;`

c. `list-style-image: square;`

d. `list-marker: square;`

**8.** Which of the following causes an element to display as a block of content with white space above and below?

a. `display: none;`

b. `block: display;`

c. `display: block;`

d. `display: inline;`

**9.** Which of the following pseudo-classes is the default state for a hyperlink that has been clicked?

a. `:hover`

b. `:link`

c. `:onclick`

d. `:visited`

**10.** Which of the following is the attribute used to indicate whether the style sheet is for printing or screen display?

a. rel

b. media

c. type

d. content

## Fill in the Blank

**11.** Use a(n) _____ to define a fragment identifier on a page.

**12.** If an element is configured with `float: right;`, the other content on the page will appear to its _____.

**13.** The _____ is always transparent.

**14.** The _____ pseudo-class can be used to modify the display of a hyperlink when a mouse pointer passes over it.

**15.** The _____ property configures the stacking of positioned elements on a web page.

# Apply Your Knowledge

**1. Predict the Result.** Draw and write a brief description of the web page that will be created with the following HTML code:

```
<!DOCTYPE html>
<html lang="en">
<head>
<title>CircleSoft Web Design</title>
<meta charset="utf-8">
<style>
  h1 { border-bottom: 1px groove #333333;
       color: #006600;
       background-color: #cccccc }
  #goal { position: absolute;
          left: 200px;
          top: 75px;
          font-family: Arial, sans-serif;
          width: 300px; }
  nav a { font-weight: bold; }
</style>
```

```
</head>
<body>
<h1>CircleSoft Web Design</h1>
<div id="goal">
<p>Our professional staff takes pride in its working relationship
with our clients by offering personalized services that listen
to their needs, develop their target areas, and incorporate these
items into a website that works.</p>
</div>
<nav>
<ul>
   <li>Home</li>
   <li><a href="about.html">About</a></li>
   <li><a href="services.html">Services</a></li>
</ul>
</nav>
</body>
</html>
```

2. **Fill in the Missing Code.** This web page should be configured as a two-column page layout with a right column (containing the navigation area) that is 150 pixels wide. The right column should have a 1 pixel border. The margin in the left-column main content area needs to allow for space that will be used by the right column. Some CSS selectors, properties, and values, indicated by "_", are missing. Fill in the missing code.

```
<!DOCTYPE html>
<html lang="en">
<head>
<title>Trillium Media Design</title>
<meta charset="utf-8">
<style>
nav {  "_": "_";
      width: "_";
      background-color: #cccccc;
      border:  "_"; }
header { background-color: #cccccc;
        color: #663333;
        font-size: 4em;
        border-bottom: 1px solid #333333; }
main { margin-right:  "_"; }
footer { font-size: x-small;
         text-align: center;
         clear:  "_"; }
 "_"  a { color: #000066;
        text-decoration: none; }
ul {list-style-type:  "_"; }
</style>
</head>
<body>
<nav>
```

```
<ul>
  <li><a href="index.html">Home</a></li>
  <li><a href="products.html">Products</a></li>
  <li><a href="services.html">Services</a></li>
  <li><a href="about.html">About</a></li>
</ul>
</nav>
<main>
<header>
<h1>Trillium Media Design</h1>
</header>
<p>Our professional staff takes pride in its working relationship
with our clients by offering personalized services that listen
to their needs, develop their target areas, and incorporate these
items into a website that works.</p>
</main>
<footer>
Copyright &copy; 2020 Trillium Media Design<br>
Last Updated on 06/03/20
</footer>
</body>
</html>
```

3. **Find the Error.** When this page is displayed in a browser, the heading information obscures the floating image and paragraph text. Correct the errors and describe the process that you followed.

```
<!DOCTYPE html>
<html lang="en">
<head>
<title>CSS Float</title>
<meta charset="utf-8">
<style>
body { width: 500px; }
h1 { background-color: #eeeeee;
     padding: 5px;
     color: #666633;
     position: absolute;
     left: 200px;
     top: 20px; }
p { font-family: Arial, sans-serif;
    position; absolute;
    left: 100px;
    top: 100px; }
#yls { float: right;
       margin: 0 0 5px 5px;
       border: solid; }
</style>
</head>
<body>
```

```
<h1>Floating an Image</h1>
<img id="yls" src="yls.jpg" alt="Yellow Lady Slipper" height="100"
width="100">
<p>The Yellow Lady Slipper pictured on the right is a wildflower.
It grows in wooded areas and blooms in June each year. The Yellow
Lady Slipper is a member of the orchid family.</p>
</body>
</html>
```

## Hands-On Exercises

1. Write the CSS for an id with the following attributes: float to the left of the page, light tan background, Verdana or sans-serif large font, and 20 pixels of padding.

2. Write the CSS to configure a class that will produce a headline with a dotted line underneath it. Choose a color that you like for the text and dotted line.

3. Write the CSS for an id that will be absolutely positioned on a page 20 pixels from the top and 40 pixels from the right. This area should have a light gray background and a solid border.

4. Write the CSS for a class that is relatively positioned. This class should appear 15 pixels in from the left. Configure the class to have a light green background.

5. Write the CSS for an id with the following characteristics: fixed position at the top of the browser viewport, light gray background color, bold font weight, and 10 pixels of padding.

6. Write the CSS to configure an image file named myimage.gif as the list marker in an unordered list.

7. Write the CSS to configure an unordered list to display a square list marker.

8. Write the HTML to create a fragment identifier at the beginning of a web page designated by "top".

9. Write the HTML to create a hyperlink to the named fragment designated by "top".

10. Write the HTML to associate a web page with an external style sheet named myprint.css to configure a printout.

11. Write the CSS to configure a graphic named mysprite.gif to display as a background image on the left side of a hyperlink. Note that mysprite.gif contains two different images. Configure the image that is located 67 pixels from the top of the mysprite.gif graphic to display.

12. Configure a web page with a list of hyperlinks to your favorite sites. Use an unordered list without any list markers to organize the hyperlinks. Refer to Chapter 5 for color scheme resources. Choose a background color for the web page and a background color for the following states: unvisited hyperlink, hyperlink with a mouse pointer passing over it, and visited hyperlink. Use embedded CSS to configure the background and text colors. Also use CSS to configure the hyperlink's underline to not display when the mouse pointer is passing over it. Save the file as mylinks.html.

13. Use the mylinks.html file you created in 8 as a starting point. Modify the web page to use external rather than embedded CSS. Save the CSS file as links.css.

14. Create a single page website about a favorite location—it could be somewhere you have gone on vacation or somewhere you would like to visit. Use the coding techniques in Hands-On Practice 6.11 and 6.12 as a guide. Make a list of things to do (activities) at this location. Make a list of things to see or famous places (sights) to visit at this location. The single page website should include three "pages"—Home, Activities,

and Sights. Either use your own vacation photos or select relevant royalty-free photos from the Web (refer to Chapter 4). Use one photo for each "page". If you use photos from the Web, be sure to provide appropriate credit in the footer area. Include your name in an e-mail address in the page footer area. Save the file as location.html.

## Web Research

This chapter introduced using CSS to configure web page layout. Use the resources listed in the textbook as a starting point. You can also use a search engine to search for CSS resources. Create a web page that provides a list of at least five CSS resources on the Web. For each CSS resource, provide the URL (configured as a hyperlink), the name of the website, a brief description, and a rating that indicates how helpful it is to beginning web developers.

## Focus on Web Design

There is still much for you to learn about CSS. A great place to learn about web technology is on the Web itself. Use a search engine to search for CSS page layout tutorials. Choose a tutorial that is easy to read. Select a section that discusses a CSS technique that was not covered in this chapter. Create a web page that uses this new technique. Consider how the suggested page layout follows (or does not follow) principles of design such as contrast, repetition, alignment, and proximity (see Chapter 5). The web page should provide the URL of your tutorial (configured as a hyperlink), the name of the website, a description of the new technique you discovered, and a discussion of how the technique follows (or does not follow) principles of design.

# WEBSITE CASE STUDY

## Implementing a CSS Two-Column Page Layout

Each of the following case studies continues throughout most of the textbook. This chapter implements a CSS two-column page layout in the websites.

### JavaJam Coffee Bar

See Chapter 2 for an introduction to the JavaJam Coffee Bar case study. Figure 2.32 shows a site map for the JavaJam. In this case study, you will implement a new two-column CSS page layout for JavaJam. Figure 6.54 shows a wireframe for a two-column page layout with wrapper, header, navigation, main content, hero image, and footer areas.

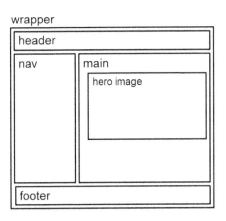

Figure 6.54 Wireframe for a two-column page layout for the JavaJam website

You will modify the external style sheet and the Home, Menu, and Music pages. Use the Chapter 4 JavaJam website as a starting point for this case study. You have five tasks in this case study:

1. Create a new folder for this JavaJam case study.

2. Modify the style rules in the javajam.css file to configure a two-column page layout, as shown in Figure 6.54.

3. Modify the Home page to implement the two-column page layout, as shown in Figure 6.55.

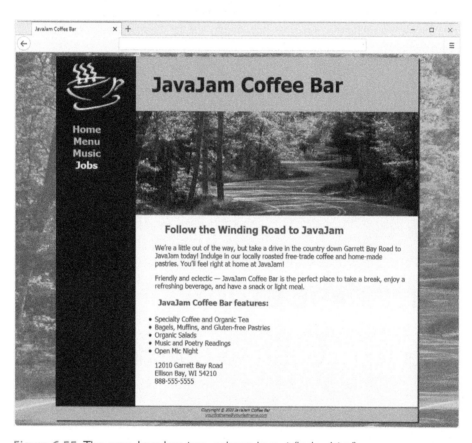

Figure 6.55  The new JavaJam two-column layout (index.html)

4. Modify the Menu page (Figure 6.56) to be consistent with the Home page.

5. Modify the Music page (Figure 6.57) to be consistent with the Home page.

## Hands-On Practice Case

**Task 1: The Website Folder.**  Create a folder called javajam6. Copy all of the files from your Chapter 4 javajam4 folder into the javajam6 folder. Copy all of the files from the chapter6/starters/javajam folder. You will modify the javajam.css file and each web page file (index.html, menu.html, and music.html) to implement the two-column page layout shown in Figure 6.54. See the new JavaJam Home page, as shown in Figure 6.55.

**Task 2: Configure the CSS.**  Open javajam.css in a text editor. Edit the style rules as follows:

1. Configure the universal selector with a `box-sizing: border-box` style declaration.

   ```
   * { box-sizing: border-box; }
   ```

2. Configure styles for the hero image on each page.

   a. Configure styles for the id selector named `homehero`. Set background-size to 100% 100%.

   b. Configure an id selector named `heromugs`. Configure the styles similar to the homehero id. Set the background image to heromugs.jpg.

   c. Configure an id selector named `heroguitar`. Configure the styles similar to the homehero id. Set the background image to heroguitar.jpg.

3. Edit the style rules for the main selector. Change left padding to 0. Change right padding to 0. Also configure a 200px left margin, 0 top padding, and #FEF6C2 background color. To allow for the main element to contain floated elements, set overflow to auto.

4. Since the main content area no longer has any left or right padding, configure descendant selectors to configure style rules for the following elements within the main element: h2, h3, h4, p, div, ul, dl. Set left padding to 3em and right padding to 2em.

5. Configure the left-column navigation area. Add style declarations to the nav element selector to configure an area that floats to the left and is 200 pixels wide.

6. Configure the `:link`, `:visited`, and `:hover` pseudo-classes for the navigation hyperlinks. Use the following text colors: #FEF6C2 (unvisited hyperlinks), #D2B48C (visited hyperlinks), and #CC9933 (hyperlinks with `:hover`). For example,
   `nav a:link { color: #FEF6C2; }`

7. You will organize the navigation hyperlinks within an unordered list in later tasks. The navigation area in Figure 6.55 does not show list markers. Code a `nav ul` descendant selector to configure unordered lists in the navigation area to display without list markers and with 0 left padding.

8. Modify the `wrapper` id. Configure a dark background color (#231814) which will display behind the column with the navigation area. Also set padding to 0.

9. Modify the header element selector style rules. Remove the declaration for text-align. Set the background image to coffeelogo.jpg. Configure this image to not repeat. Set left padding to 240px. Change the text color to #231814.

10. Modify the h4 element selector style rules. View the Music page shown in Figure 6.57 and notice that the `<h4>` tags are styled differently, with all uppercase text (use `text-transform`), a bottom border, and 0 bottom padding. Also configure a style declaration to clear floats on the left.

11. Refer to the Music page shown in Figure 6.57 and notice how the images float on the left side of the paragraph description. Configure a new class named `floatleft` that floats to the left with 2em of right and bottom padding.

12. Modify the style rules for the `details` class and add the `overflow: auto;` style declaration.

13. Configure a style rule for a class named `onethird`. Set left float and 33% width.

14. Configure hyperlinks in the header area. Use descendant selectors to configure hyperlinks within the header element with no underline, dark brown (#231814) text color for the `:link` and `:visited` pseudo-classes, and rust (#FEF6C2) text color for the `:hover` pseudo-class.

   Save the javajam.css file.

**Task 3: The Home Page.** Open index.html in a text editor. Edit the code as follows:

1. Configure the "JavaJam Coffee Bart" text in the header area to be a hyperlink to the Home page (index.html).

2. Configure the left-column navigation area, which is contained within the nav element. Remove any ` ` characters that may be present. Code an unordered list to organize the navigation hyperlinks. Each hyperlink should be contained within `<li>` tags.

3. Move the div assigned to the id homehero inside the main element as indicated in the Figure 6.54 wireframe.

Save the index.html file. It should look similar to the web page shown in Figure 6.55. Remember that validating your HTML and CSS can help you find syntax errors. Test and correct this page before you continue.

**Task 4: The Menu Page.** Open menu.html in a text editor.

1. Configure the header area and the left-column navigation area hyperlinks in the same manner as the home page.

2. Remove the img tag for the mugs.jpg image. Configure a div element assigned to the `heromugs` id between the opening main tag and the opening h2 tag.

3. Observe Figure 6.56 and note that the menu information is formatted in three columns. Remove the tags that configure the description list from the page. Also remove the strong tags coded within the description list. Notice the text content is a series of menu item names and descriptions. Configure each menu item name within an h3 element. Configure each menu item description within a paragraph element. Code a section element to contain each menu item name and menu item description pair. Assign each section element to the CSS class named `onethird`.

Save your new menu.html page and test it in a browser. It should look similar to the web page shown in Figure 6.56. Use the CSS and HTML validators to help you find syntax errors. Edit the page and add line break tags so that each price is on its own line. Save and test again.

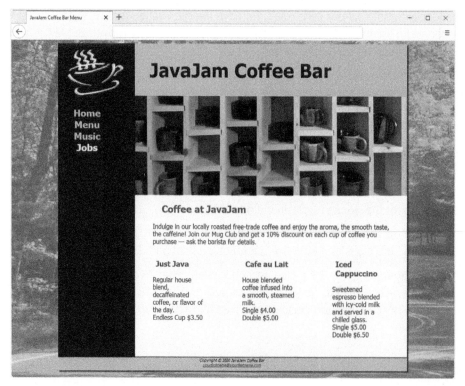

Figure 6.56 The new JavaJam Menu page

**Task 5: The Music Page.** Open music.html in a text editor.

1. Configure the header area and the left-column navigation area hyperlinks in the same manner as the home page.

2. Configure a div element assigned to the `heroguitar` id between the opening main tag and the opening h2 tag.

3. Configure the thumbnail images to float to the left. Add `class="floatleft"` to the img tag for each thumbnail image.

Save your new music.html page and test it in a browser. It should look similar to the web page shown in Figure 6.57. Use the CSS and HTML validators to help you find syntax errors.

Figure 6.57  The new JavaJam Music Page

In this case study, you changed the page layout of the JavaJam website. Notice that with just a few changes in the CSS and HTML code, you configured a two-column page layout.

## Fish Creek Animal Clinic

See Chapter 2 for an introduction to the Fish Creek Animal Clinic case study. Figure 2.36 shows a site map for Fish Creek. In this case study, you will implement a redesign with a new two-column CSS page layout. Figure 6.58 displays a wireframe for a two-column page layout with wrapper, header, navigation, main content, and footer areas.

**wrapper**

| header |
| nav | main |
| | footer |

Figure 6.58  Wireframe for a two-column page layout for the Fish Creek website

You will modify the external style sheet and the Home, Services, and Ask the Vet pages. Use the Chapter 4 Fish Creek website as a starting point for this case study. You have five tasks in this case study:

1. Create a new folder for this Fish Creek case study.

2. Modify the style rules in the fishcreek.css file to configure a two-column page layout, as shown in Figure 6.58.

3. Modify the Home page to implement the two-column page layout, as shown in Figure 6.59.

4. Modify the Services page (Figure 6.60) to be consistent with the Home page.

5. Modify the Ask the Vet page (Figure 6.61) to be consistent with the Home page.

## Hands-On Practice Case

**Task 1: The Website Folder.**  Create a folder called fishcreek6. Copy all of the files from your Chapter 4 fishcreek4 folder into the fishcreek6 folder. Copy all the files from the chapter6/starters/fishcreek folder. You will modify the fishcreek.css file and each web page file (index.html, services.html, and askvet.html) to implement the two-column page layout, as shown in Figure 6.58. See the new Fish Creek home page, as shown in Figure 6.59.

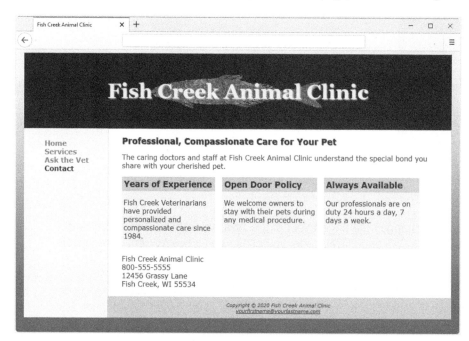

Figure 6.59  The new Fish Creek two-column home page (index.html)

**Task 2: Configure the CSS**.  Open fishcreek.css in a text editor. Edit the style rules as follows:

1. Configure the universal selector with a `box-sizing: border-box` style declaration.

   `* { box-sizing: border-box; }`

2. Modify the styles for the body element selector. Set the background color to #5280C5. Configure gradientblue.jpg as a background image.

3. Configure the header element selector. Change the background color to dark-blue (#000066). Change the background image to bigfish.gif.

4. Code an h1 element selector. Configure style declarations for 3em font-size, 0.2em padding, and gray text shadow (#CCCCCC).

5. Configure the left column area. Configure new style declarations for the nav element selector to configure an area that floats to the left and is 180 pixels wide. Remove the style declarations for text alignment and background color.

6. You will organize the navigation hyperlinks within an unordered list in later tasks. The navigation area in Figure 6.59 does not show list markers. Code a `nav ul` descendant selector to configure unordered lists in the navigation area to display without list markers.

7. Configure the navigation anchor tags to display no underline.

8. Configure the `:link`, `:visited`, and `:hover` pseudo-classes for the navigation hyperlinks. Use the following text colors: #000066 (unvisited hyperlinks), #5280C5 (visited hyperlinks), and #3262A3 (hyperlinks with `:hover`). For example,
   `nav a:link { color: #000066; }`

9. Configure the right column area. Add style declarations for the main element selector to configure an area with a 180 pixel left margin, a white background color, and a 1 pixel solid medium blue (#AEC3E3) border. Set overflow to auto (prevents display issues for floated elements within the main element). Set display to block (prevents an Internet Explorer display issue).

10. Remove the `footer nav` descendant selector and style declarations.

11. Configure the footer area. Remove the style declaration for bottom padding. Add style declarations to set 1em of padding and a 180px left margin.

12. Configure styles for a class named `address`. Set the clear property to left.

13. Configure styles for a class named `floatright`. Set float to right, 1em left padding, and 1em right padding.

14. Configure a section element selector. Code style declarations that set left float, 30% width, 1em right margin, 1em bottom margin, 0 padding, #EAEAEA background color, and minimum height set to 200px.

15. Configure headings within the section element. Add a new style rule for the `section h3` descendant selector that sets .25em padding, 0 top margin, 0 bottom margin, 110% font size, and #AEC3E3 background color.

16. Configure paragraphs within the section element. Add a new style rule for the `section p` descendant selector that sets top padding to 0, left padding to .25em, right padding to .25em, and bottom padding to .25em.

17. Configure hyperlinks in the header area. Use descendant selectors to configure hyperlinks within the header element with no underline, light (#F0F0F0) text color for the `:link` and `:visited` pseudo-classes, and light blue (#AEC3E3) text color for the `:hover` pseudo-class.

Save the fishcreek.css file.

**Task 3: Modify the Home Page.** Open index.html in a text editor and modify the code as follows:

1. Configure the "Fish Creek Animal Clinic" text in the header area to be a hyperlink to the Home page (index.html).

2. Rework the navigation area. Remove any ` ` characters that may be present. Replace the fish image links with text links. Then, code an unordered list to organize the navigation hyperlinks. Each hyperlink should be contained within `<li>` tags.

3. Assign the div that contains the address to a class named `address`.

4. Remove the nav element and navigation hyperlinks from the footer area.

5. Observe Figure 6.59 and note that information is formatted in three columns. Remove the tags that configure the description list from the page. Notice the text content is a series of brief headings and sentences. Configure each heading within an h3 element. Configure each sentence within a paragraph element. Code a section element to contain each heading and paragraph pair.

Save the index.html file. It should look similar to the web page shown in Figure 6.59. Remember that validating your HTML and CSS can help you find syntax errors. Test and correct this page before you continue.

**Task 4: Modify the Services Page.** Open services.html in a text editor.

1. Configure the header area, navigation area, navigation hyperlinks, and footer area in the same manner as the home page.

2. Observe Figure 6.60 and note that the page content is no longer displayed in an unordered list. Remove the tags that configure the unordered list from the page. Also remove the span and line break tags. Notice the text content is a series of brief headings and sentences. Configure each heading within an h3 element. Configure each sentence within a paragraph element. Code a section element to contain each h3 and paragraph pair.

Save your new services.html page and test it in a browser. Use the CSS and HTML validators to help you find syntax errors.

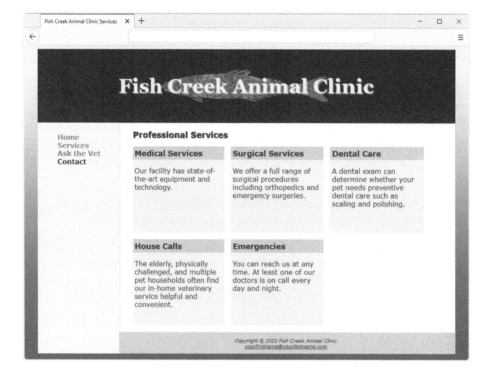

**Figure 6.60** Fish Creek services.html

**Task 5: Modify the Ask the Vet Page.** Open askvet.html in a text editor.

1. Configure the header area, navigation area, navigation hyperlinks, and footer area in the same manner as the home page.

2. View Figure 6.61 and notice that there is a new dog photo on the page. Add an img tag above the h2 tag to display dog.gif. Configure the height, width, and alt attributes. Assign this element to a class called `floatright`.

Save your new askvet.html page and test it in a browser. Use the CSS and HTML validators to help you find syntax errors.

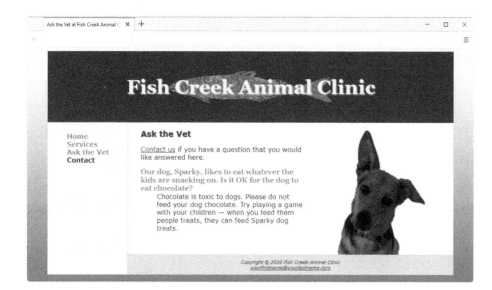

**Figure 6.61** Fish Creek askvet.html page

In this case study, you changed the page layout of the Fish Creek website. Notice that with just a few changes in the CSS and HTML code, you configured a two-column page layout with a completely new visual aesthetic.

## Pacific Trails Resort

See Chapter 2 for an introduction to the Pacific Trails Resort case study. Figure 2.40 shows a site map for Pacific Trails. The pages were created in earlier chapters. In this case study, you will implement a new two-column CSS page layout. Figure 6.62 displays a wireframe for a two-column page layout with wrapper, header, nav, main content, hero image, and footer areas.

You will modify the external style sheet and the Home, Yurts, and Activities pages. Use the Chapter 4 Pacific Trails website as a starting point for this case study. You have five tasks in this case study:

1. Create a new folder for the Pacific Trails case study.

2. Modify the style rules in the pacific.css file to configure a two-column page layout, as shown in Figure 6.62.

3. Modify the Home page to implement the two-column page layout, as shown in Figure 6.63.

4. Modify the Yurts page to be consistent with the Home page.
5. Modify the Activities page to be consistent with the Home page.

## Hands-On Practice Case

**Task 1: The Website Folder.** Create a folder called pacific6. Copy all of the files from your Chapter 4 pacific4 folder into the pacific6 folder. You will modify the pacific.css file and each web page file (index.html, yurts.html, and activities.html) to implement the two-column page layout, as shown in Figure 6.62. See the new Pacific Trails home page, as shown in Figure 6.63.

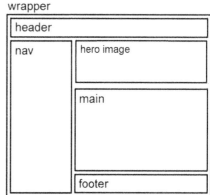

**Figure 6.62** Wireframe for a two-column page layout for the Pacific Trails website

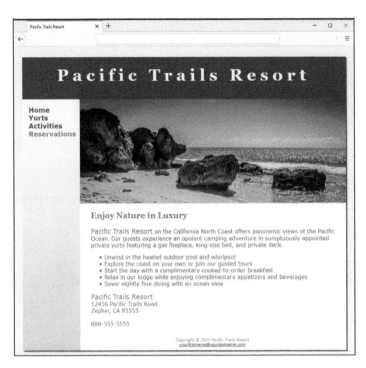

**Figure 6.63** The new Pacific Trails two-column home page
(index.html)

**Task 2: Configure the CSS.** Open pacific.css in a text editor. Edit the style rules as follows:

1. Configure the universal selector with a `box-sizing: border-box` style declaration.

   `* { box-sizing: border-box; }`

2. Modify the `wrapper` id. Copy the linear gradient from the style rules for the body element selector. The wrapper background will display behind the navigation area.

3. Configure the body element selector. Change the background color to #EAEAEA. Remove the background-image and background-repeat style declarations.

4. Configure the header area. Remove the styles associated with the background image. Change the height to 120px.

5. Configure the h1 element selector. Add styles for 3em size font and 0.25em letter spacing.

6. Configure the left-column navigation area. Modify the styles for the nav element selector. Remove the text-align declaration. The nav area will inherit the background color of the `wrapper` id. Add style declarations to configure this area to float to the left with a width of 160 pixels. Also set padding to 0 and font size to 1.2em.

7. Configure the `:link`, `:visited`, and `:hover` pseudo-classes for the navigation hyperlinks. Use the following text colors: #5C7FA3 (unvisited hyperlinks), #344873 (visited hyperlinks), and #A52A2A (hyperlinks with `:hover`). For example,

   `nav a:link { color: #5C7FA3; }`

8. You will organize the navigation hyperlinks within an unordered list in later tasks. The navigation area in Figure 6.59 does not show list markers. Code a `nav ul` descendant selector to configure unordered lists in the navigation area to display without list markers. Also configure the unordered list to have 1em left padding.

9. Configure the nav element to have a fixed position.

10. Configure the right-column main content area. Modify the styles for the main element selector. Add style declarations to configure a white (#FFFFFF) background and 170 pixels of left margin. Set overflow to auto (prevents display issues for floated elements within the main element).

11. Configure each hero image area (`#homehero`, `#yurthero`, and `#trailhero`) with a 170 pixel left margin.

12. Configure the footer area. Add style declarations to set a white (#FFFFFF) background color and a 170px left margin.

13. Configure the section element selector. Add a new style rule for the section element with left float, 33% width, 2em left padding, and 2em right padding.

14. Configure hyperlinks in the header area. Use descendant selectors to configure hyperlinks within the header element with no underline, white (#FFFFFF) text color for the `:link` and `:visited` pseudo-classes, and light blue (#90C7E3) text color for the `:hover` pseudo-class.

Save the pacific.css file.

**Task 3: Modify the Home Page.** Open index.html in a text editor. Configure the left-column navigation area, which is contained within the nav element. Remove any ` ` characters that may be present. Code an unordered list to organize the navigation hyperlinks. Each hyperlink should be contained within `<li>` tags. Configure the "Pacific Trails Resort" text in the header area to be a hyperlink to the Home page (index.html).

Save the index.html file and test it in a browser. Your page should look similar to Figure 6.63. Remember that validating your HTML and CSS can help you find syntax errors. Test and correct this page before you continue.

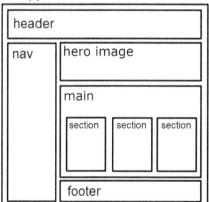

Figure 6.64 Wireframe for Pacific Trails content pages

**Task 4: Modify the Yurts Page.** Open yurts.html in a text editor. Modify the page in the same manner as the home page. Examine the wireframe in Figure 6.64 and notice that there are three sections within the main element. Remove the tags that configure the description list from the page. Notice the text content is a series of questions and answers. Configure each question within an h3 element. Configure each answer within a paragraph element. Code a section element to contain each question and answer pair. Save your new yurts.html page and test it in a browser. Your page should be similar to Figure 6.65. Use the CSS and HTML validators to help you find syntax errors.

**Figure 6.65** Pacific Trails yurts.html page

**Task 5: Modify the Activities Page.** Open activities.html in a text editor. Modify the page in the same manner as the home page. Examine the wireframe in Figure 6.64 and notice that there are three sections within the main element. Code a section element to contain each pair of h3 and p elements. Save your new activities.html page and test it in a browser. It should be similar to the overall page layout shown in Figure 6.65. Use the CSS and HTML validators to help you find syntax errors.

In this case study, you changed the page layout of the Pacific Trails Resort website. Notice that with just a few changes in the CSS and HTML code, you configured a two-column page layout.

## Path of Light Yoga Studio

See Chapter 2 for an introduction to the Path of Light Yoga Studio case study. Figure 2.44 shows a site map for the Path of Light Yoga Studio. In this case study, you will implement a new two-column CSS page layout for the Path of Light Yoga Studio. Figure 6.66 displays a wireframe for a two-column page layout with a wrapper, header, navigation, main content, and footer area.

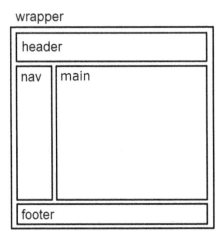

**Figure 6.66** Wireframe for a two-column page layout for the Path of Light Yoga Studio website

You will modify the external style sheet and the Home, Classes, and Schedule pages. Use the Chapter 4 Path of Light Yoga Studio website as a starting point for this case study. You have five tasks in this case study:

1. Create a new folder for the Path of Light Yoga Studio case study.

2. Modify the style rules in the yoga.css file to configure a two-column page layout, as shown in Figure 6.66.

3. Modify the Home page (Figure 6.67) to implement the two-column page layout.

4. Modify the Classes page (Figure 6.69) to implement the two-column content page layout, as shown in Figure 6.68.

5. Modify the Schedule page (Figure 6.70) to be consistent with the Classes page.

## Hands-On Practice Case

**Task 1: The Website Folder.** Create a folder called yoga6. Copy all of the files from your Chapter 4 yoga4 folder into the yoga6 folder. Copy the yogadoor2.jpg file from the chapter6/starters/yoga folder into your yoga6 folder. You will modify the yoga.css file and each web page file (index.html, classes.html, and schedule.html) to implement the two-column page layout shown in Figure 6.66. See the new Path of Light Yoga Studio home page in Figure 6.67.

Figure 6.67  The new Path of Light Yoga Studio two-column home page (index.html)

**Task 2: Configure the CSS.** Open yoga.css in a text editor. Edit the style rules as follows:

1. Configure the universal selector with a `box-sizing: border-box` style declaration.

   `* { box-sizing: border-box; }`

2. Edit the styles for the `wrapper` id. Change min-width to 1200px. Change max-width to 1480px.

3. Configure the left-column navigation area. Modify the styles for the nav element selector. Remove the text-align declaration. The nav area will inherit the background color of the `wrapper` id. Add style declarations to configure this area to float to the left with a width of 160 pixels.

4. Configure the navigation hyperlinks to look like buttons. We'll set up the CSS in this step.

   a. Edit the styles for the `nav a` selector. Configure new styles to use block display, centered text, a 3 pixel gray (#CCCCCC) outset border, 1em padding, and a 1em bottom margin.

   b. Configure the `:link`, `:visited`, and `:hover` pseudo-classes for the navigation hyperlinks. Use the following text colors: #3F2860 (unvisited hyperlinks), #497777 (visited hyperlinks), and #A26100 (hover). Also configure a 3 pixel inset #333333 border for hyperlinks in the hover state.

   ```
   nav a:link { color: #3F2860; }
   nav a:visited { color: #497777; }
   nav a:hover { color: #A26100; border: 3px inset #333333; }
   ```

5. You will organize the navigation hyperlinks within an unordered list in later tasks. The navigation area in Figure 6.65 does not show list markers. Code a `nav ul` descendant selector to configure unordered lists in the navigation area to display without list markers. Also configure the unordered list to have no left padding.

6. Edit the styles for the main element selector. Add new style declarations to configure a 170 pixel left margin and 1em top padding.

7. Remove the img element selector and style declarations.

8. Configure a new class named `floatleft` that floats to the left with right margin set to 4em and bottom margin set to 1em.

9. Edit the styles for the `#hero` selector. Remove the text-align style declaration. Configure 1em top and bottom padding.

10. Configure styles for a new class named `clear` with a `clear: both;` style declaration.

11. Configure a style rule for a class named `onehalf`. Set left float, 50% width, 2em left padding, and 2em right padding.

12. Configure a style rule for a class named `onethird`. Set left float, 33% width, 2em left padding, and 2em right padding.

13. Configure hyperlinks in the header area. Use descendant selectors to configure hyperlinks within the header element with no underline, purple (#40407A) text color for the `:link` and `:visited` pseudo-classes, and white (#FFFFFF) text color for the `:hover` pseudo-class.

Save the yoga.css file.

**Task 3: Modify the Home Page**. Open index.html in a text editor and modify the code as follows:

1. Configure the "Path of Light Yoga Studio" text in the header area to be a hyperlink to the Home page (index.html).

2. Rework the navigation area. Remove any ` ` characters that may be present. Configure an unordered list to organize the navigation hyperlinks. Each hyperlink should be contained within `<li>` tags.

3. Edit the img tag. Remove the `align="right"` attribute. Assign the img tag to the class named `floatleft`. Change the value of the src attribute to yogadoor2.jpg.

4. Edit the div element that contains the address information. Assign the div to the class named `clear`.

Save the index.html file. It should look similar to the web page shown in Figure 6.67. Remember that validating your HTML and CSS can help you find syntax errors. Test and correct this page before you continue.

**Task 4: Modify the Classes Page.** Open classes.html in a text editor and modify the code as follows.

1. Configure the header area and navigation hyperlinks in the same manner as the home page.

2. Move the div assigned to the `id="hero"` below the description list; just above the closing tag for the main element.

3. Examine the wireframe in Figure 6.68 and notice that there are three sections within the main element. Remove the tags that configure the description list from the page. Also remove the strong tags. Notice the text content is a series of yoga class titles and yoga class descriptions. Configure each yoga class title within an h3 element. Configure each yoga class description within a paragraph element. Code a section element to contain each yoga class title and yoga class description pair. Assign each section to the CSS class named `onethird`.

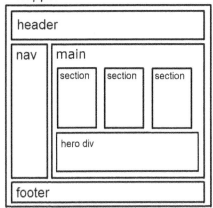

Figure 6.68 Path of Light Yoga Studio content page layout

Save your new classes.html page and test it in a browser. It should look similar to Figure 6.69. Use the CSS and HTML validators to help you find syntax errors.

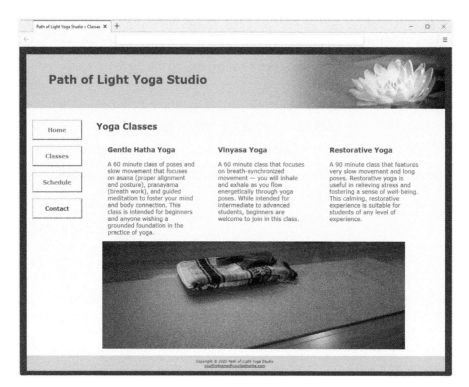

**Figure 6.69** The new Path of Light Yoga Studio two-column Classes page

**Task 5: Modify the Schedule Page.** Open schedule.html in a text editor and modify the code as follows.

1. Configure the header area and navigation hyperlinks in the same manner as the home page.

2. Move the div assigned to the id="hero" below the second unordered list; just above the closing tag for the main element.

3. View the wireframe in Figure 6.68 and notice that there are three sections within the main element. This web page is a little different, It will have only two sections. Use Figure 6.69 as a guide. Code a section element to contain each pair of h3 and ul elements. Assign each section element to the CSS class named onehalf.

Save your new schedule.html page and test it in a browser. It should be similar to Figure 6.70. Use the CSS and HTML validators to help you find syntax errors.

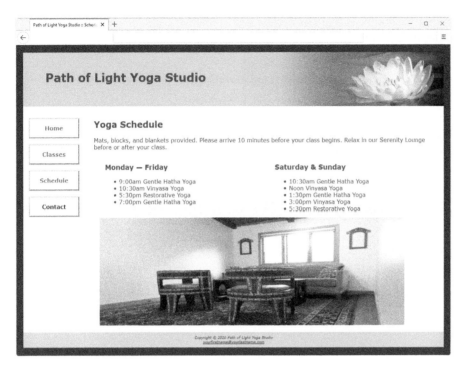

**Figure 6.70** The new Path of Light Yoga Studio Schedule page.

In this case study, you changed the page layout of the Path of Light Yoga Studio website. Notice that with just a few changes in the CSS and HTML code, you configured a two-column page layout.

## Web Project

See Chapter 5 for an introduction to the Web Project case study. As you completed the Chapter 5 Web Project case study activities, you completed a Web Project Topic Approval, Web Project Site Map, and Web Project Page Layout Design. In this case study, you will use your design documents as a guide as you develop the pages for your Web Project using CSS in an external style sheet for both formatting and page layout.

### Hands-On Practice Case

1. Create a folder called project. All of your project files and graphics will be organized in this folder and in subfolders as needed.

2. Refer to your Site Map to view the pages that you need to create. Jot down a list of the file names. Add these to the Site Map.

3. Refer to the Page Layout Design. Make a list of the common fonts and colors used on the pages. These may become the CSS you configure for the body element. Note where typical elements used for organization (such as headings, lists, paragraphs, and so on) may be used. You may want to configure CSS for these elements. Identify various page areas such as header, navigation, footer, and so on, and list any special formatting needed for these areas. These will also be configured in your CSS. Create an external style sheet, called project.css, which contains these configurations.

4. Using your design documents as a guide, code a representative page for your site. Use CSS to format text, color, and layout. Apply classes and ids where appropriate. Associate the web page to the external style sheet.

   Save and test the page. Modify both the web page and the project.css file as needed. Test and modify them until you have achieved the look you want.

5. Using the completed page as a template wherever possible, code the rest of the pages on your site. Test and modify them as needed.

6. Experiment with modifying the project.css file. Change the page background color, the font family, and so on. Test your pages in a browser. Notice how a change in a single file can affect multiple files when external style sheets are used.

# 7

# Responsive Page Layout

## Chapter Objectives    In this chapter, you will learn how to . . .

- Describe the purpose of CSS Flexible Box Layout
- Configure a Flexbox Container and Flexbox Items
- Create a web page that applies CSS Flexible Box Layout
- Describe the purpose of CSS Grid Layout
- Configure a Grid Container
- Configure grid rows, grid columns, and grid gaps, and grid areas
- Create responsive page layouts with CSS Grid Layout
- Configure web pages for mobile display using the viewport meta tag
- Apply responsive web design techniques with CSS media queries
- Apply responsive image techniques including the new HTML5 picture element

Now that you've had some experience in coding HTML and CSS you're ready to delve into designing web pages with responsive layouts that display well on both desktop and mobile browsers. you will explore new coding techniques, including CSS Flexible Box Layout, CSS Grid Layout, CSS media queries, CSS feature queries, and responsive images.

# 7.1  CSS Flexible Box Layout

Since the early days of the Web, designers have striven to configure multicolumn web pages. Back in the 1990s, it was common to use HTML tables to configure a two- or three-column page layout. As browsers offered increased support for CSS, web developers discovered CSS float property techniques like the one you used in Chapter 6 to create the look of multicolumn pages. You will find many pages on the Web configured using CSS float techniques.

However, the quest for more robust and responsive multicolumn layout methods has continued. There are two new CSS layout systems that have recently gained widespread browser support: CSS Flexible Box Layout and CSS Grid Layout. This section introduces CSS Flexible Box Layout.

The purpose of **CSS Flexible Box Layout** (called **flexbox**) is to provide a flexible layout— elements contained within a flex container can be configured in *one* dimension (either horizontally or vertically) in a flexible manner with flexible sizing. In addition to changing the horizontal or vertical organization of elements, flexbox can also be used to change the order of display of the elements. Due to its flexibility, flexbox is well suited for responsive web design.

CSS Flexible Box Layout Module (https://www.w3.org/TR/css-flexbox-1/) has reached W3C Candidate Recommendation status and is well supported by recent versions of popular browsers.

## Configure a Flexible Container

Flexbox is typically used to configure a specific area of a web page rather than the entire page layout. To configure an area on a web page that uses flexbox layout, you need to indicate the **flex container**, which is the element that will contain the flexible area.

## The `display` Property

Use the CSS **display property** to configure a flex container. The value `flex` indicates a flexible block container. The value `inline-flex` indicates a flexible inline-display container.

For example, to configure an id named `gallery` as a flex container, code the following CSS:

```
#gallery { display: flex; }
```

Each child element of the flex container is a **flex item**. In the following HTML, each img tag is considered a flex item within the div element assigned to the `gallery` id.

```
<div id="gallery">
  <img src="bird1.jpg" width="200" height="150" alt="Red Crested Cardinal">
  <img src="bird2.jpg" width="200" height="150" alt="Rose-Breasted Grosbeak">
  <img src="bird3.jpg" width="200" height="150" alt="Gyrfalcon">
  <img src="bird4.jpg" width="200" height="150" alt="Rock Wren">
  <img src="bird5.jpg" width="200" height="150" alt="Coopers Hawk">
  <img src="bird6.jpg" width="200" height="150" alt="Immature Bald Eagle">
</div>
```

Figure 7.1 shows a page that uses flexbox to display an image gallery. By default, the flex area will have a horizontal flow direction and be configured as one horizontal row. If the content does not fit in the browser area, the browser may either try to reduce the size of some of the objects or display a scroll bar as shown in Figure 7.1. To try this out, launch a browser to display the example in the student files (chapter7/flex1.html).

Even though there are six images within the flexible area, the items in the flex area will not automatically wrap to another line if the browser window is not large enough to display them all. Next, let's explore a property that will correct this issue.

Figure 7.1  A flex area with default properties.

## The `flex-wrap` Property

The **flex-wrap property** configures whether flex items are displayed on multiple lines. Values for this property include `nowrap`, `wrap`, and `wrap-reverse`. The default value is `nowrap`, which configures single-line display for horizontal flow flex containers and a single-column display for vertical flow flex containers. The value `wrap` will allow flex items to display on multiple lines for horizontal flow flex containers and to display on multiple columns for vertical flow flex containers. The `wrap-reverse` value provides for wrapping and displays the flex items in reverse order.

The flex items in Figure 7.2 (student files chapter7/flex2.html) wrap to the next line. The following CSS configures the flex container:

Figure 7.2  Flex Items wrap to the next line.

```
#gallery { display: flex;
           flex-wrap: wrap; }
```

## The `flex-direction` Property

Configure the flow direction of the flex items with the **flex-direction property**. The value `row` is the default and configures a horizontal flow direction, `column` configures a vertical flow direction, `row-reverse` configures a horizontal flow with the flex items in reverse order, and `column-reverse` configures a vertical flow with the flex items in reverse order.

# 7.2 More About Flex Containers

## Flow Direction

Flex containers can be configured with either horizontal flow or vertical flow. Figure 7.3 shows a diagram of a flex container configured with horizontal flow direction. The **main size** is the width of the flex container content area. The **main axis** is the direction of the flow (in this case horizontal). The **main start** indicates the beginning of the flex area. The **main end** indicates the end of the flex area. The **cross axis** is the direction of the wrap (if any exists).

Figure 7.4 shows a diagram of a flex container configured with vertical flow direction. The **main size** is the height of the flex container content. The **main axis** is the direction of the flow (in this case vertical). The **main start** indicates the beginning of the flex area. The **main end** indicates the end of the flex area. The **cross axis** is the direction of the wrap (if any exists).

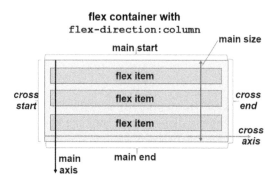

Figure 7.3 Horizontal flow direction

Figure 7.4 Vertical flow direction

## The `justify-content` Property

Use the **`justify-content` property** to configure how the browser should display extra space along the main axis in the flex container. Values for this property are shown in Table 7.1.

Table 7.1 Values for the justify-content Property of a Flex Area

| Value | Purpose |
| --- | --- |
| flex-start | Default. Flex items begin at main start |
| flex-end | Flex items begin at main end |
| center | Flex items display centered in the flex container with equal empty space before the first flex item and after the last flex item |
| space-between | Flex items are evenly distributed in the flex container. The first flex item begins at main start. The last flex item is placed at main end |
| space-around | Flex items are evenly distributed in the flex container with space before the first flex item and after the last flex item |

As you examine Figure 7.5, which displays a series of flex containers with horizontal flow, observe how each value of the `justify-content` property configures both the placement of the flex items and the space between the flex items. The student files (chapter7/flexj.html) contain the sample code.

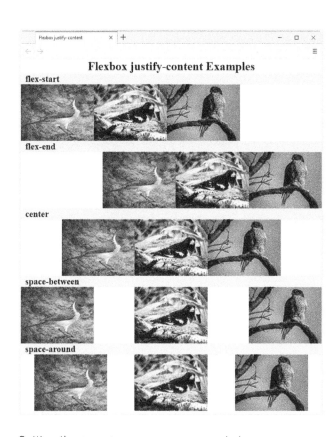

Figure 7.5 The justify-content property

Setting the `justify-content` property to `space-between` or `space-around` causes the browser to automatically calculate and display empty space between the flex items.

## The `align-items` Property

The **align-items property** configures the way the browser displays extra space along the *cross-axis* of the container. Values include `flex-start`, `flex-end`, `center`, `base-line`, and `stretch`. The `align-items` property can be used along with the `justify-content` property to vertically and horizontally center content. For example, to configure a 400px high header element with a vertically and horizontally centered flex item (chapter7/flex3.html in the student files), code the following CSS:

```
header { height: 400px;
         display: flex;
         justify-content: center;
         align-items: center; }
```

## The `flex-flow` Property

The **flex-flow property** is a shorthand property that configures both the flex-direction and the flex-wrap. To configure an id named `demo` as a flexible container with a horizontal flow that wraps, code the following CSS:

```
#demo { display: flex; flex-flow: row wrap; }
```

At this point, you've been introduced to some of the many different ways that a flex container can be configured to display flex items. Don't be concerned if it seems a bit overwhelming at first. It is a new approach to page layout and you will begin to feel more comfortable after you use it in the hands-on practice exercises.

## Flexbox Image Gallery

# Hands-On Practice 7.1

You'll configure an image gallery with flexbox properties in this Hands-On Practice. Create a new folder called ch7flex1. Copy the starter1.html file from the chapter7 folder in the student files into your ch7flex1 folder. Copy the following files from the chapter7/starters folder into your ch7flex1 folder: bird1.jpg, bird2.jpg, bird3.jpg, bird4.jpg, bird5.jpg, and bird6.jpg.

1. Launch a text editor and open the starter1.html file. Add the following HTML below the opening main tag to create a div assigned to the `gallery` id that contains six images.

```
<div id="gallery">
  <img src="bird1.jpg" width="200" height="150" alt="Red Crested
  Cardinal">
  <img src="bird2.jpg" width="200" height="150" alt="Rose-Breasted
  Grosbeak">
  <img src="bird3.jpg" width="200" height="150" alt="Gyrfalcon">
  <img src="bird4.jpg" width="200" height="150" alt="Rock Wren">
  <img src="bird5.jpg" width="200" height="150" alt="Coopers Hawk">
  <img src="bird6.jpg" width="200" height="150" alt="Immature Bald
  Eagle">
</div>
```

The div is the flex container. Each img element is a flex item in the flex container. Save the file with the name index.html.

2. Edit the index.html file and configure CSS between the style tags in the head section. Configure an id named `gallery`. Set the `display` property to `flex`, `flex-direction` property to `row`, `flex-wrap` to `wrap`, and `justify-content` to `space-around`. The code follows:

```
#gallery { display: flex;
          flex-direction: row;
          flex-wrap: wrap;
          justify-content: space-around: }
```

Save the file and test it in a browser. Your page should look similar to Figure 7.6. Observe that while the browser configured empty space between the flex items on each row (the main axis), there is no empty space in the vertical (cross axis) area between each row element.

3. Next, you'll configure the flex items to have a margin, which

**Figure 7.6** The first version of the gallery

will force some empty space between the rows. Recall that a flex item is a child element of the flex container. In our page, each img element is a flex item. Edit the index.html file and code CSS above the closing style tag for the img selector that sets a 1em margin and a box-shadow.

```
img { margin: 1em;
      box-shadow: 10px 10px #777; }
```

Save the file and test in a browser. As you resize your browser smaller and larger, your page should be similar to Figures 7.7, 7.8, and 7.9. A sample solution is in the student files chapter7/7.1 folder.

Figure 7.7 Two rows of flex items

Figure 7.8 Each row now has two items

Figure 7.9 As the browser is resized, more items fit on the first row

Notice that the display is flexible and responsive to browser size, although the flex items are not necessarily displayed in a grid – that's what CSS Grid Layout can do and you'll explore that later in the chapter. In the next section, you'll delve more into configuring flexible sizes for flex items.

# 7.3 Configure Flex Items

By default, all elements contained within a flex container are flexible in size and are allocated the same amount of display area in the flex container. Use the **flex property** to customize the size of each flex item and indicate whether it can grow (flex grow factor) or shrink (flex shrink factor) depending on the size of the browser viewport. The flex property can be set to the keyword `none`, the keyword `initial`, or a list of up to three values that configure the `flex-grow`, `flex-shrink`, and `flex-basis` properties. Table 7.2 describes these properties.

Table 7.2 The flex Properties

| Flex Properties | Description | | |
|---|---|---|---|
| `flex-grow` | A positive number that determines the growth of the flex item relative to the other items in the flex container. Default value is 0. | | |
| `flex-shrink` | A positive number that determines how much the flex item will shrink relative to the other items in the flex container. Default value is 1. | | |
| `flex-basis` | Configures the initial dimension along the main axis of the flex item. | | |
| | **Value** | **Purpose** | |
| | `content` | Indicates the width of the item's content. | |
| | `auto` | Default value, a specified width or if there is no specified width, the width of the item's content. | |
| | Positive numeric value | A value indicating the width of the item in units or percentage. | |

It's not always necessary to list all three values when configuring the flex property. Table 7.3 describes some common situations encountered when configuring a flex item (also see https://www.w3.org/TR/css-flexbox-1/#flexibility).

Table 7.3 Flex Item Examples

| Flex Item Situation | Shorthand Notation | Equivalent |
|---|---|---|
| **Fully Flexible Item**<br>*free space evenly distributed* | `flex: auto;` | `flex: 1 1 auto;` |
| **Fully Inflexible Item** | `flex: none;` | `flex: 0 0 auto;` |
| **Partially Inflexible Item**<br>*shrinks to minimum size if needed* | `flex: initial` | `flex: 0 1 auto;` |
| **Proportional Flexible Item**<br>*The item takes up the specified proportion of free space in the container.* | `flex: positive number;`<br>For example:<br>`flex: 3;` | `flex: 3 1 0;` |

## Proportional Flexible Item

Let's focus on the last row of Table 7.3. One of the most powerful ways to use the flex property is to configure proportional flexible items. Setting one numeric value for the flex property sets the flex grow factor. If you configure an element with `flex: 2`; it will take up twice as much space within the container element as the others. Since the values work in proportion to the whole, you may find it helpful to use flex values that add up to 10. Examine the three-column page layout in Figure 7.10 and notice how the nav, main, and aside elements are organized in a row within another element that will serve as a flex container. The CSS to configure the proportion of the flexible area allocated to each column could be as follows:

```
nav   { flex: 1; }
main  { flex: 7; }
aside { flex: 2; }
```

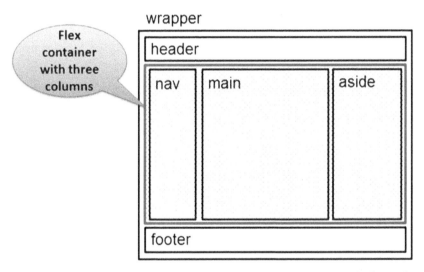

Figure 7.10 Three-column page layout with the flex container indicated

## The `order` Property

Use the **order property** to display the flex items in a different order than they are coded. The order property accepts numeric values. The default value is 0.

Be aware that the W3C cautions that web designers should use the order property only for visual reordering. The change in order should not change the meaning or intent of the content because accessibility software such as screen readers will render the content in the order it was coded.

**Focus on Accessibility**

In the next section, you'll get to practice configuring a flex container and flex items.

## Practice with Flexbox

## Hands-On Practice 7.2

In this Hands-On Practice, you'll begin with a web page using the float layout technique from Chapter 6 and apply flexbox properties to configure a three-column layout similar to Figure 7.10.

Create a new folder called ch7flex2. Copy the starter2.html file from the chapter7 folder in the student files into your ch7flex2 folder. Copy the lighthouse.jpg and light.gif files from the chapter7/starters folder into your ch7flex2 folder.

1. Open the starter2.html file in a browser. It should look similar to Figure 7.11. Launch a text editor and open the starter2.html file. Observe the HTML and notice that there is a div named `content` that contains the nav, aside, and main elements in that order.

Figure 7.11 The web page before flexbox is configured

2. Your goal is to configure the layout of the `content` div with flexbox. Configure CSS with a flex container assigned to the id named `content`. The nav, main, and aside elements are children of the div and are the flex items. You'll configure them with different color backgrounds to emphasize the three columns. To prevent the nav element from growing in size, set the nav element's flex value to `none`. Set the main element's flex value to 6 and the aside element's flex value to 4. Add the following CSS below the opening style tag to configure the flex container and flex items:

```
#content { display: flex; }
nav      { flex: none;
           background-color: #B3C7E6; }
main     { flex: 6;
           min-width: 20em;
            background-color: #FFFFFF; }
aside    { flex: 4;
           background-color: #EAEAEA; }
```

Save the file with the name index.html and test in a browser. Your page should be similar to Figure 7.12. Notice that there are three columns but that the aside (area with lighthouse image) displays to the left of the main content text area because that is the order of the HTML. If this is what the owners of Lighthouse Bistro want, that's great. However, if they would prefer the main content text to display between the nav area and the aside area, you'll need to use the `order` property to change the order of the display of the flexbox items.

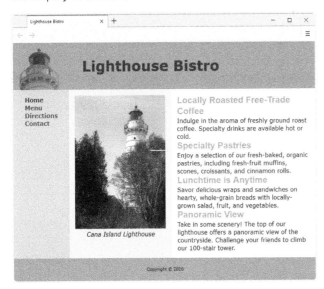

Figure 7.12  Flexbox properties have been applied

3. Launch a text editor and open the index.html file. You will add CSS to configure the order of the left to right display of the flex items nav, main, and aside. You'll use the `order` property and assign values for each flex item. The CSS follows:

```
nav    { order: 1;  }
main   { order: 2;  }
aside  { order: 3;  }
```

Figure 7.13  The flexbox order property has been applied

Save the file and test in a browser. Your page should be similar to Figure 7.13. A sample solution is in the student files chapter7/7.2 folder.

**FAQ    What happens to the old CSS float property when Flexbox layout is applied?**

Browsers applying the flexbox layout system ignore the float property when it is applied to a flex item. However, any floats that are applied to content within a flex item are still rendered by the browser.

You've just been introduced to flexbox, but there is more to explore. Check out these resources:

- https://css-tricks.com/snippets/css/a-guide-to-flexbox/
- https://developer.mozilla.org/en-US/docs/Web/CSS/CSS_Flexible_Box_Layout

# 7.4  CSS Grid Layout

You have used both the CSS float property and CSS Flexible Box Layout (flexbox) to create multicolumn web pages. There is another new emerging layout system: CSS Grid Layout. The purpose of **CSS Grid Layout** is to configure a two-dimensional grid-based layout. The grid can be created as either fixed-size or flexible and contains one or more grid items that can be individually defined as fixed-size or flexible. Unlike flexbox which is intended for one-dimensional page layout, CSS Grid Layout is optimized for two-dimensional page layout.

CSS Grid Layout (https://www.w3.org/TR/css-grid-1/) has reached W3C Candidate Recommendation status and is well-supported by recent versions of popular browsers. Browsers that do not support grid layout ignore the style rules associated with grid properties.

## Configure a Grid Container

To configure an area on a web page that uses CSS Grid Layout, you need to define the **grid container**, which is the element that will contain the grid area.

## The `display` Property

Use the CSS **display property** to configure a grid container. The value `grid` indicates a block container. The value `inline-grid` indicates an inline-display container. For example, to configure an id named `gallery` as a grid container, code the following CSS:

```
#gallery { display: grid; }
```

## Designing a Grid

A **grid** is comprised of horizontal and vertical **grid lines** that delineate **grid rows** and **grid columns** (generically referred to as **grid tracks**). A **grid cell** (which is a **grid item**) is the intersection of a grid row and a grid column. A **grid area** is a rectangle that can contains one or more grid items. A **grid gap** is optional and indicates an empty area or gutter between items in the grid container.

A first step is to visualize the grid, usually by sketching out the layout. Figure 7.14 shows a wireframe for a grid that shows grid lines, three columns, and two rows. A grid of this type could be used to display an image gallery.

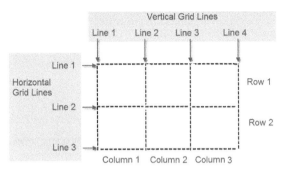

Figure 7.14 A grid with three columns and two rows

Each child element of the grid container is a **grid item**. In the following HTML, each img element within the `gallery` div is considered to be a grid item.

```
<div id="gallery">
  <img src="bird1.jpg" width="200" height="150" alt="Red Crested
  Cardinal">
  <img src="bird2.jpg" width="200" height="150" alt="Rose-Breasted
  Grosbeak">
  <img src="bird3.jpg" width="200" height="150" alt="Gyrfalcon">
  <img src="bird4.jpg" width="200" height="150" alt="Rock Wren">
  <img src="bird5.jpg" width="200" height="150" alt="Coopers Hawk">
  <img src="bird6.jpg" width="200" height="150" alt="Immature Bald
  Eagle">
</div>
```

## Configure Grid Columns and Grid Rows

A basic method to configure grid rows and columns is to use the **grid-template-columns property** and the **grid-template-rows property** to tell the browser how to reserve space for the columns and rows in the grid. These properties accept a variety of values which will be introduced in the next section. In this example, we'll use pixel units.

In our image gallery example, we'll configure the `grid-template-columns` property to display three columns with a fixed width in two rows with a fixed height. The CSS to configure the grid follows:

```
#gallery { display: grid;
      grid-template-columns: 220px 220px 220px;
      grid-template-rows: 170px 170px; }
```

The code above explicitly creates a grid with three columns and two rows. Figure 7.15 shows a display of this grid in the browser (see the student files chapter7/grid1.html).

Observe that this very basic grid is fixed—it does not change when you resize the browser window. Grid layout becomes powerful when it is flexible, and the grid can change dimensions based on the browser viewport.

Figure 7.15 A Basic Grid

The empty space between the grid items in Figure 7.15 is configured by setting the size of the rows and columns to be larger than the size of the images in the image gallery. For this basic image gallery grid, another method to configure empty space could be to set padding and/or margin for the img element selector. Another method is to configure grid gap or gutter between items, which will be introduced in the next section along with techniques to configure a flexible grid.

# 7.5 Grid Columns, Rows, and Gap

You've used the `grid-template-columns` and `grid-template-rows` properties with pixel unit values to inform the browser to reserve space for each row and column in a grid. Table 7.4 lists other commonly used values for these properties. Visit https://www.w3.org/TR/css-grid-1/#propdef-grid-template-columns for a complete list of values.

**Table 7.4** Commonly Used Values to Configure Columns and Rows

| Value | Description |
|---|---|
| numeric length unit | Configures a fixed size with a length unit such as px or em<br>Example: `220px` |
| numeric percentage | Configures a percentage size; Example: 20% |
| numeric `fr` unit | Configures a **fractional unit** (denoted by `fr`) that directs the browser to allocate a fractional part of the remaining space. The value 1fr indicates one part of the remaining space in a grid container. |
| `auto` | Configures a size to hold the maximum content |
| `minmax` (min, max) | Configures a size range greater or equal to min value and less than or equal to max value. The max can be set to a fractional unit |
| `repeat` (repetition amount, format value) | Repeats the column or row the number of times specified by the repetition amount numeric value or keyword and uses the format value to configure the column or row. The `auto-fill` keyword indicates to repeat but stop before an overflow<br>Example: `repeat(autofill, 250px)` |

## Grid Gap

The **`grid-gap` property** informs the browser to provide empty space or gutters between grid tracks. At the time this was written, the W3C was in the process of changing the syntax to configure this feature and it was recommended to code both the old and new properties. Table 7.5 lists the old (currently supported) and new property names.

**Table 7.5** Changing Syntax for Grid Gap

| Property | Description |
|---|---|
| Old: `grid-column-gap` | Value: Numeric length or percentage |
| New: `column-gap` | Defines a gap between columns |
| Old: `grid-row-gap` | Value: Numeric length or percentage |
| New: `row-gap` | Defines a gap between rows |
| Old: `grid-gap` | Value: `row-gap` value `column-gap` value |
| New: `gap` | Shorthand property. Providing just one value sets both the `row-gap` and the `column-gap` |

## The order Property

Use the **order property** to display the grid items in a different order than they are coded. The order property accepts a numeric value. The default value is 0. Be aware that the W3C cautions that web designers should use the order property only for visual reordering. The change in order should not change the meaning or intent of the content because accessibility software such as screen readers will render the content in the order it was coded.

## Hands-On Practice 7.3

You'll explore two more ways to configure the image gallery grid displayed in Figure 7.15 in this Hands-On Practice. Create a new folder called ch7grid1. Copy the starter3.html file from the chapter7 folder in the student files into your ch7grid1 folder. Copy the following files from the chapter7/starters folder into your ch7grid1 folder: bird1.jpg, bird2.jpg, bird3.jpg, bird4.jpg, bird5.jpg, and bird6.jpg.

1. Launch a text editor and open the starter3.html file. Review the HTML and note that it contains a div assigned to the `gallery` id with six img elements for your image gallery. The div is the grid container. Each img element is a grid item since it is a child element of the div. Save the file with the name index.html.

2. Edit the index.html file and configure CSS between the style tags in the head section. Configure an id named `gallery`. Set the `display` property to `grid`. To divide the available browser space into three columns of 200 pixels each, set the `grid-template-columns` property to `repeat(3, 200px)`. To cause the browser to automatically generate rows as needed, set the `grid-template-rows` property to `auto`. Configure the base size of the gutters between row and column tracks by setting the `grid-gap` (and `gap`) properties to 2em. The CSS code follows:

```
#gallery { display: grid;
           grid-template-columns: repeat(3, 200px);
           grid-template-rows: auto;
           grid-gap: 2em; gap: 2em; }
```

Save the file and test it in a browser. Your page should look similar to Figure 7.15 (student files chapter7/7.3/a.html).

3. Configure the image gallery grid to be responsive and automatically change the number of columns and rows displayed as the browser viewport is resized. Use the `auto-fill` keyword in the `repeat()` function to direct the browser to fill the viewport with as many columns as it can without overflowing. Edit the index.html file and change `repeat(3, 200px)` to `repeat(auto-fill, 200px)`.

Figure 7.16 The grid stretches as you widen the browser

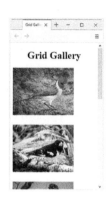

**4.** Save the file and test it in a browser. Your page will look like Figure 7.15 when the browser viewport is just large enough to display three images in a row. As you widen the browser viewport, more columns will display in a single row, similar to Figure 7.16. As you narrow the browser viewport, the number of columns will decrease as shown in Figure 7.17. A sample solution is in the student files (chapter7/7.3/index.html).

Figure 7.17
Responsive Grid

# 7.6 Two-Column Grid Page Layout

VideoNote
*CSS Grid Layout*

Figure 7.18 shows a sample grid wireframe for a two-column page layout with grid lines, rows, and columns indicated. The browser will use the content to automatically determine the column width and row height unless you otherwise configure it. As you can see in the wireframe, this layout requires some specific column widths and row heights, so we'll need to code CSS to configure grid columns and rows.

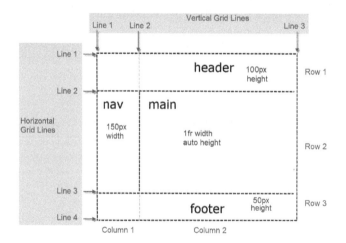

Figure 7.18 Two-column CSS Grid Layout

## Configure Grid Columns and Rows

Using the wireframe as a guide, configure the `grid-template-columns` and `grid-template-rows` properties. Recall that values include pixel units, percentages, keywords such as `auto`, and fractional units. A new unit, `fr`, denotes a fractional unit and directs the browser to allocate portions of the remaining space. Use `1fr` to allocate all remaining space.

The grid wireframe shown in Figure 7.18 contains two columns and three rows.

- The header is 100px in height, takes up the first row, and spans two columns.
- The nav is 150px wide and is located in the first column of the second row.
- The main content is located in the second column of the second row and needs to be large enough to hold whatever content is provided. The width of the main content is `1fr` and occupies all available space left after the nav element is rendered with a 150px width. The height of the main content is the `auto` value and will expand to contain whatever content is present.
- The footer takes up the third row, is 50px in height, and spans three columns.

Now you're ready to configure the grid for an id named `wrapper`. Set the display property to grid. Use the `grid-template-columns` property to set the first column to 150px and the second column to `1fr`. Use the `grid-template-rows` property to set the first row to 100px, the second row to `auto`, and the third row to 50px. The CSS follows:

```
#wrapper { display: grid;
           grid-template-columns: 150px 1fr;
           grid-template-rows: 100px auto 50px; }
```

## Configure Grid Items

Once you have declared the grid and coded a template for the columns and rows you need to indicate what elements should be placed in each grid item and grid area. There are a variety of techniques than can be used to configure grid items. One method uses the grid-row and grid-column properties. The **grid-row property** configures the area in rows that is reserved for the item in the grid. The **grid-column property** configures the area in columns that is reserved for the item in the grid. A variety of values are accepted by these properties, such as grid line numbers and grid line names. For a complete list of values, visit https://www.w3.org/TR/css-grid-1/#typedef-grid-row-start-grid-line.

## Grid Line Numbers

In this example we will assign the `grid-row` and `grid-column` properties for each grid item with a starting grid line number and an ending grid line number separated by a / character. View Figure 7.18 and observe that the header area begins at vertical grid line 1 and ends at vertical grid line 3 in the first row (the grid track between horizontal grid line 1 and horizontal grid line 2). The CSS to configure the header is:

```
header { grid-row: 1 / 2;
         grid-column: 1 / 3; }
```

Each grid item shown in Figure 7.18 is configured in a similar manner. Configure the navigation, main, and footer elements with the following CSS:

```
nav    { grid-row: 2 / 3; grid-column: 1 / 2; }
main   { grid-row: 2 / 3; grid-column: 2 / 3; }
footer { grid-row: 3 / 4; grid-column: 1 / 3; }
```

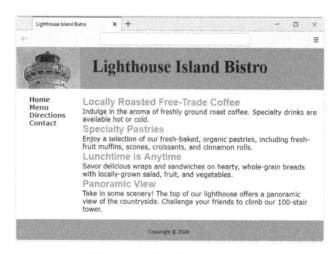

**Figure 7.19** Web page with CSS Grid Layout

Figure 7.19 shows a web page that uses this grid layout. You will create this page in the next Hands-On Practice.

### Configure a Grid Page Layout with Grid Line Numbers

To create a grid page layout using grid line numbers, configure the following:

1. Use the display property to declare the grid container. Each child element of the grid container will be an item in the grid. If needed, use the grid-template-columns and grid-template-rows properties to specify the row and column dimensions. Recall that the browser will use the content to automatically determine the column width and row height unless you otherwise configure it.

2. Using your wireframe sketch as a guide, carefully determine the vertical grid lines and horizontal grid lines. Use the grid-rows and grid-column properties to indicate the vertical and horizontal grid lines for each grid item in the grid.

## Hands-On Practice 7.4

In this Hands-On Practice you'll configure the grid shown in Figure 7.18 to create the layout for the web page shown in Figure 7.20, which was configured using float methods from Chapter 6 and is not yet using grid layout. Create a new folder called ch7grid2. Copy the starter4.html file from the chapter7 folder in the student files into your ch7grid2 folder. Copy light2.jpg file from the chapter7/starters folder into your ch7grid2 folder.

**Figure 7.20** The web page without grid layout

1. Open your starter4.html file in a browser and the display should be similar to Figure 7.20 – this is the display before any code for grid layout is added.

2. Launch a text editor and open the starter4.html file. Save the file as index.html. You will edit the CSS in the head section. Our grid layout will follow the two-column grid wireframe in Figure 7.18. Use the horizontal grid lines to indicate the rows. Use the vertical grid lines to indicate the columns. Add style rules in the header section to configure an id named `wrapper` as a grid container with a two-column, three-row grid layout. The CSS follows

```
#wrapper { display: grid;
           grid-template-columns: 150px 1fr;
           grid-template-rows: 100px auto 50px; }
```

3. Next, use the wireframe in Figure 7.18 as a guide to configure the HTML element selectors and their starting and ending grid lines. Use the horizontal grid line numbers to configure the `grid-row` property. Use the vertical grid line numbers to configure the `grid-column` property. The CSS follows:

```
header { grid-row: 1 / 2; grid-column: 1 / 3; }
nav    { grid-row: 2 / 3; grid-column: 1 / 2; }
main   { grid-row: 2 / 3; grid-column: 2 / 3; }
footer { grid-row: 3 / 4; grid-column: 1 / 3; }
```

Save your file. Launch a browser that supports grid layout and test your page. Your page should look similar to Figure 7.19. A sample solution is in the student files chapter7/7.4 folder.

As you completed this Hands-On Practice you may have noticed that it is a bit tedious to determine and code all those vertical and horizontal grid line numbers. Perhaps you wondered if there is another method to configure a grid with CSS. The next section introduces you to a method to configure a grid template without all those line numbers!

# 7.7 Layout with Grid Areas

Recall that a grid area is a rectangle that can contain one or more grid items. The rectangle is bounded by grid lines. In our previous examples, you have configured grid areas by indicating grid line numbers. CSS Grid Layout provides a way to name the grid areas which eliminates keeping track of all those grid line numbers! Let's take a closer look.

## The grid-area Property

The **grid-area property** (https://www.w3.org/TR/css-grid-1/ #propdef-grid-area) can be used to associate a grid item with a named area of the grid. The wireframe in Figure 7.21 specifies the layout for the web page shown in Figure 7.22. Note the four grid areas in Figure 7.21: header, nav, main, and footer. Use the grid-area property to associate a CSS selector (either an HTML element selector,

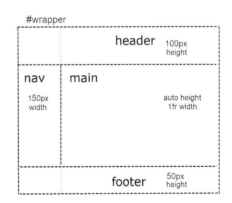

Figure 7.21 A grid wireframe

**Figure 7.22** Web page configured with grid template areas

class selector or id selector) with each of these named grid areas. We will use HTML element selectors in this example. To associate the HTML elements header, nav, main, and footer with uniquely named grid areas, code the following CSS:

```
header    { grid-area: header; }
nav       { grid-area: nav; }
main      { grid-area: main; }
footer    { grid-area: footer; }
```

## The `grid-template-areas` Property

Use the **grid-template-areas property** (https://www.w3.org/TR/css-grid-1/ #grid-template-areas-property) to visually indicate the placement of the named grid areas on the grid. The value is a series of strings that contain named grid areas. Each string is a row on the grid. The number of named grid areas in the string indicates the number of columns in the row. If a column in a row should be skipped, use the period "." symbol. Each row must indicate the same number of columns.

To configure the grid in Figure 7.21, start out by declaring the grid and assigning the `grid-template-columns` and `grid-template-rows` properties. Then, use the `grid-template-areas` property to write the named grid area values row by row within quotation marks. The first row is the header named area which takes up two columns. The second row contains the nav area in the first column and the main area in the second column. The third row contains the footer area across two columns. The CSS follows:

```
#wrapper { display: grid;
           grid-template-columns: 150px 1fr;
           grid-template-rows: 100px auto 50px;
           grid-template-areas:
                            "header  header"
                            "nav     main"
                            "footer  footer"; }
```

It's possible to have empty areas within a grid layout, as shown in the wireframe in Figure 7.23. The third row indicated the footer area in the second column and nothing in the first column. This a situation where the "." symbol comes in handy. The following

CSS will configure the `grid-template-areas` property for the wireframe shown in Figure 7.23:

```
#wrapper { display: grid;
           grid-template-columns: 150px 1fr;
           grid-template-rows: 100px auto 50px;
           grid-template-areas:
               "header header"
               "nav    main"
               ".  footer" ; }
```

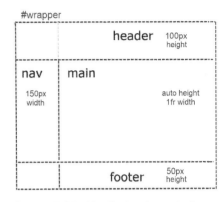

**Figure 7.23** The first column in the third row is empty

## Hands-On Practice 7.5

You will work with grid template areas in this Hands-On Practice. Create a new folder called ch7grid3. Copy the starter5.html file from the chapter7 folder in the student files into your ch7grid3 folder. Copy the following files from the chapter7/starters folder into your ch7grid3 folder: header.jpg and scenery.jpg. You will configure a three-column grid layout based on the wireframe in Figure 7.24 for the web page displayed in Figure 7.25.

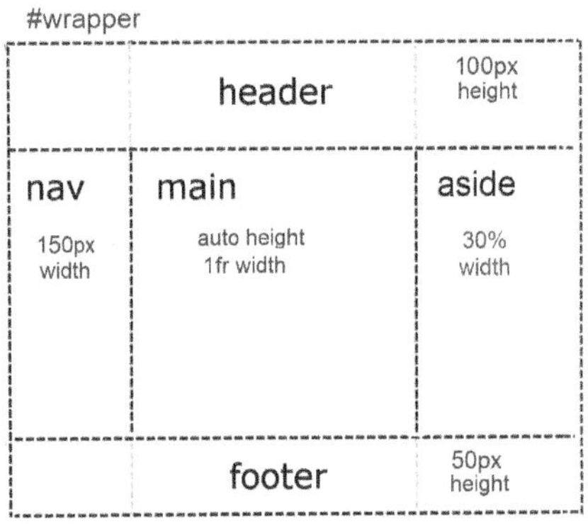

**Figure 7.24** Three column grid layout

**Figure 7.25** The web page configured with grid layout

Launch a text editor and open the starter5.html file. Save the file with the name index.html. You will edit the CSS in the head section: use the `grid-area` property to associate HTML elements with named grid areas, declare the grid, use the `grid-template-columns` and `grid-template-rows` properties to indicate the row and column dimensions, and use the `grid-template-areas` property to describe the layout of the grid.

**1.** With the Figure 7.24 wireframe in mind, add style rules in the header section to associate the HTML elements with the named grid areas (header, nav, main, aside, and footer) using the `grid-area` property. The CSS follows:

```
header { grid-area: header; }
nav    { grid-area: nav; }
main   { grid-area: main; }
aside  { grid-area: aside; }
footer { grid-area: footer; }
```

2. Configure a grid layout for the Figure 7.24 wireframe. Add style rules in the header section to configure an id named `wrapper` as a grid container with a three-column, three-row grid layout. Specify three columns (width set to 150px, 1fr, and 30%) with the grid-template-columns property. Specify three rows (height set to 100px, auto, and 50px) with the `grid-template-rows` property. Also configure the `grid-template-areas` property with the placement of the header, nav, main, aisde, and footer grid areas indicated. The CSS follows:

```
#wrapper { display: grid;
          grid-template-columns: 150px 1fr 30%;
          grid-template-rows: 100px auto 50px;
          grid-template-areas:
                  "header    header    header"
                  "nav       main      aside"
                  "footer    footer    footer"  ;  }
```

Save the file. Launch a browser that supports grid layout and test your page. Your page should look similar to Figure 7.25. A sample solution is in the student files (chapter7/7.5/index.html).

## The `grid-template` Property

The **grid-template property** (https://www.w3.org/TR/css-grid-1/#propdef-grid-template) is a shorthand property that combines the grid-template-areas, grid-template-rows, and grid- template-columns properties. The value of this property begins with a series of strings for each row followed by the height of each row. The string for each row is the named grid areas for that row enclosed in quotation marks. The width of the columns is indicated on a final row that begins with a `"/"` symbol.

To create the grid for the wireframe in Figure 7.24 (corresponding web page in Figure 7.25), the following steps are involved:

1. Configure each named grid area with the `grid-area` property.

2. Identify the `#wrapper` selector as the grid container.

3. Configure the `grid-template` property based on the Figure 7.24 wireframe. The first row is the header area which takes up three columns and is 100px in height. The second row contains the nav area in the first column, main area in the second column, and the aside area in the third column. Configure the height of this row as `auto` to use up all available space. The third row contains the footer area across three columns and is 50 pixels high. Note that the named areas that comprise each row are contained within quotation marks. The last row begins with a `"/"` symbol followed by the actual values for the column widths (in this case 150px, 1fr, and 30%).

The CSS follows:

```
header { grid-area: header; }
nav    { grid-area: nav; }
main   { grid-area: main; }
aside  { grid-area: aside; }
footer { grid-area: footer; }
```

```
#wrapper { display: grid;
          grid-template:
                 "header     header    header"    100px
                 "nav        main      aside"     auto
                 "footer     footer    footer"    50px
                 / 150px    1fr   30%;   }
```

A sample page with this coding technique is in the student files (chapter7/7.5/grid3.html). This shorthand technique provides a convenient way to indicate not only the locations of the named grid areas but also the dimensions of the columns and rows in one property. There are many different methods available for configuring a CSS grid layout system. The rest of this chapter configures grid page layout with the grid-template property and named grid areas.

 ## Checkpoint 7.1

1. Which CSS property is used to identify a CSS selector as a grid or flexbox container?

2. The CSS justify-content property used in flexbox layout is quite versatile. Choose three values and describe their purpose.

3. Which CSS property can be used to indicate the location and dimensions of named grid areas?

# 7.8 Progressive Enhancement with Grid

A design strategy for using grid layout is to first configure the web page layout so it displays well in nonsupporting browsers, next use a new technique called a CSS feature query to check for grid support, and then configure the grid layout to be used by supporting browsers.

## CSS Feature Query

A **feature query** is a conditional that can be used to test for support of a CSS property, and if support is found, apply the specified style rules. Feature queries are part of the CSS Conditional Rules Module which was in Candidate Recommendation status at the time this was written (https://www.w3.org/TR/css3-conditional/#at-supports). If a browser does not support feature queries, it simply ignores the code.

A feature query is coded using the **@supports() rule**. You code the property and value you are checking for within the parentheses. For example, to check for grid layout support, code the following CSS:

```
@supports ( display: grid) {
}
```

All the style rules needed for grid layout are coded between the "{" opening brace and the "}" ending brace. You'll get some experience with this in the next Hands-On Practice.

## Hands-On Practice 7.6

You'll use a feature query to progressively enhance an existing web page with grid layout in this Hands-On Practice. Create a new folder called ch7grid4. Copy the starter6.html file from the chapter7 folder in the student files into your ch7grid4 folder. Copy the lighthouse.jpg and light2.jpg files from the chapter7/starters folder into your ch7grid4 folder.

1. Open your starter6.html file in a browser and the display should be similar to Figure 7.26, which is the display before any code for grid layout is added. This is a three-column layout with the nav, main, and aside elements floating next to each other.

**Figure 7.26** The web page displayed in a browser

2. Next, launch a text editor and open the starter6.html file. Our grid layout will follow the wireframe in Figure 7.27. Notice that there are three rows and three columns. The header takes up the entire first row. The nav, main, and aside elements are in the second row. The footer takes up the entire third row. Observe Figure 7.27 and note the heights and widths indicated. You will add an @supports rule to the CSS before the ending style tag to check for grid support. You will place code to configure a three-column grid layout. The CSS follows:

| | | |
|---|---|---|
| | header | 100px height |
| nav | main | aside |
| 150px width | auto height 1fr width | 300 px width |
| | footer | 50px height |

**Figure 7.27** Grid Layout

```
@supports (display: grid) {
     #wrapper { display: grid;
          grid-template:
               "header    header    header"    100px
               "nav       main      aside"     auto
               "footer    footer    footer"    50px
               / 150px  1fr      300px ;       }
     header { grid-area: header; }
     nav     { grid-area: nav; }
     main    { grid-area: main; }
     aside   { grid-area: aside; }
     footer  { grid-area: footer; }
}
```

Save your file and test it in a browser that supports grid layout. Your page should look similar to Figure 7.28. Notice that the page looks a bit odd with the main content area text taking up only part of the middle area.

Figure 7.28  Grid layout

3. Open your file in a text editor and notice that the main element selector has 50% width set—this is causing the awkward display in Figure 7.28. You need to rework this when grid layout is implemented. It's easy to do this by adding a style rule to the @supports feature query that resets the width. Add the following style rule to the styles within the @supports feature query:

```
main { width: 100%; }
```

Save your file. Launch a browser that supports grid layout and test your page. It should look similar to Figure 7.26. Be mindful that sometimes when you work with this technique you might also need to reset margins or padding – it depends on the specific web page and CSS that was originally coded. Note that we didn't need to write any new styles resetting the float property because CSS grid layout ignores the float property.

To recap, we applied the principle of progressive enhancement. We began with a web page that was configured with old-fashioned three-column layout using the float property. Next, we configured grid layout within a feature query (which nonsupporting browsers will ignore). Then we looked for any styles that were causing a display issue (the `width` property for the main element in this case) and coded new styles within the feature query to correct the display. The result is a web page that looks good on both supporting and nonsupporting browsers. A sample solution is in the student files chapter7/7.6 folder.

FAQ    **What happens to the old CSS float property when Grid layout is applied?**

Browsers applying the grid layout system ignore the float property when it is applied to a grid item. However, any floats that are applied to content within a grid item are still rendered by the browser.

You've just been introduced to grid layout, but there is more to explore. Check out these resources:

• https://css-tricks.com/snippets/css/complete-guide-grid/

• https://developer.mozilla.org/en-US/docs/Web/CSS/CSS_Grid_Layout

# 7.9  Centering with Flexbox and Grid

In Chapter 3, you were introduced to the technique of horizontally centering a block display element with CSS by setting its margin property to the value `auto`. However, until flexbox and grid layout, it has been difficult to vertically center an element within a browser viewport. Figures 7.29 shows a web page with text that is centered both vertically and horizontally. Locate the page in the student files (chapter7/center.html) and display it in a browser. As you resize the browser viewport, the text remains both vertically and horizontally centered.

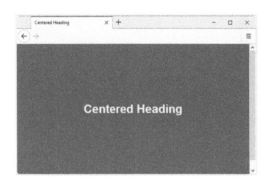

**Figure 7.29**  Centered text

To accomplish this layout, configure the container element with the following CSS:

- `display: flex;`
- `min-height: 100vh;` (This indicates 100% of the viewport height.)
- `justify-content: center;`
- `align-items: center;`
- *Optional:* `flex-wrap: wrap;` (This will allow multiple centered flex items.)

## Hands-On Practice 7.7

You'll explore creating web pages with both horizontally and vertically centered content in this Hands-On Practice. Create a new folder called ch7center. Copy the template.html file from the chapter7 folder in the student files into your ch7center folder. Copy the lake.jpg file from the chapter7/starters folder into your ch7center folder.

**1.** Launch a text editor and open your template.html file. Change the title of the web page to "Centered Heading". Edit the HTML and configure a header element, h1 element, and main element between the opening and closing body tags. The code follows:

```
<header>
  <h1>Centered Heading</h1>
</header>
<main>
  Additional page content and navigation go here
</main>
```

2. Continue editing the file and configure the CSS. Code opening and closing style tags in the head section. Next, code style rules within the style tags. Configure the body element selector with zero margin. Configure the header element selector as a flex container with `justify-content` set to `center`, `align-items` set to `center`, minimum height `100vh`, and #227093 background color. Configure the h1 element selector with white, Arial font. The code follows:

```
<style>
   body { margin: 0; }
   header { display: flex; min-height: 100vh;
            justify-content: center; align-items: center;
            background color: #227093; }
   h1 { color: #FFFFFF; font-family: Arial, sans-serif; }
</style>
```

Save your file as index.html and display it in a browser. Your display should be similar to Figure 7.29. Resize the browser window and see how the h1 text remains centered in the viewport. Scroll down the page to see the text within the main element. You can compare your work to chapter7/center.html in the student files.

3. Next, add a background image that covers the entire browser viewport. Open index.html in a text editor and add styles for the header element selector that will configure the lake.jpg background image with 100% size that does not repeat. Remove the style rule for the background color. The code follows:

```
header { display: flex; min-height: 100vh;
         justify-content: center; align-items: center;
         background-color: #227093;
         background-image: url(lake.jpg);
         background-size: 100% 100%;
         background-repeat: no-repeat; }
```

Save your file and display it in a browser. Your display should be similar to Figure 7.30. As you resize the browser window, notice how the h1 text remains centered and the background image changes in size. Scroll down the page to see the text within the main element. You can compare your work to chapter7/7.7/index.html in the student files.

Figure 7.30 Centered text with background image

4. There is another way to accomplish this layout when grid or flex layout is being used. Setting the margin property to `auto` causes the browser to both vertically and horizontally center an item. You will demonstrate this handy behavior as you rework the CSS.

   a. Open index.html in a text editor. Remove the `justify-content` and `align-items` style rules. Add a style rule for the h1 element selector that sets margin to `auto`. Save your file and display it in a browser. Your display should still be similar to Figure 7.30. You can compare your work to the sample in the student files (chapter7/7.7/flex.html).

   b. Open index.html in a text editor. Change the value of the display property from `flex` to `grid`. Save your file and display it in a browser. Your display should still be similar to Figure 7.30. You can compare your work to chapter7/7.7/grid.html in the student files.

You explored several layout techniques in this Hands-On Practice. The new flexbox and grid layout systems offer a wide variety of page layout options for web developers.

# 7.10  Viewport Meta Tag

There are multiple uses for meta tags. You've used the meta tag since Chapter 2 to configure the character encoding on a web page. Now, we'll explore the new **viewport meta tag**, which was created as an Apple extension that helps with displays on mobile devices such as iPhones and Android smartphones by setting the width and scale of the viewport. Figure 7.31 displays a screen shot of a web page displayed on an Android smartphone without the viewport meta tag. Examine Figure 7.31 and notice that the mobile device zoomed out to display the entire web page on the tiny screen. The text on the web page is difficult to read.

**Figure 7.31**  Mobile display of a typical desktop web page without the viewport meta tag

Figure 7.32 The viewport meta tag
helps with mobile displays

Figure 7.32 shows the same web page after the viewport meta tag was added to the head section of the document. The code is shown below:

```
<meta name="viewport"
content="width=device-width, initial-scale=1.0">
```

Code the viewport meta tag with the HTML `name="viewport"` and `content` attributes. The value of the HTML `content` attribute can be one or more **directives** (also referred to as properties by Apple), such as the `device-width` directive and directives that control zooming and scale. Table 7.6 lists viewport meta tag directives and their values.

Now that you've scaled the page to be readable, what about styling it for optimal mobile use? That's where CSS comes into play. You'll explore CSS Media Queries in the next section.

Table 7.6 Viewport meta tag directives

| Directive | Values | Purpose |
|---|---|---|
| width | Numeric value or `device-width` which indicates actual width of the device screen | The width of the viewport in pixels |
| height | Numeric value or `device-height` which indicates actual height of the device screen | The height of the viewport in pixels |
| initial-scale | Numeric multiplier; Set to 1 for 100% initial scale | Initial scale of the viewport |
| minimum-scale | Numeric multiplier; Mobile Safari default is 0.25 | Minimum scale of the viewport |
| maximum-scale | Numeric multiplier; Mobile Safari default is 1.6 | Maximum scale of the viewport |
| user-scalable | `yes` allows scaling, `no` disables scaling | Determines whether a user can zoom in or out |

# 7.11 CSS Media Queries

Recall from Chapter 5 that the term **responsive web design** refers to progressively enhancing a web page for different viewing contexts (such as smartphones and tablets) through the use of coding techniques including fluid layouts, flexible images, and media queries.

For examples of the power of responsive web design techniques, review Figures 5.44, 5.45, and 5.46, which are actually the same .html web page file that was configured with CSS to display differently, depending on the viewport size detected by media queries. Also visit the Media Queries website at https://mediaqueri.es to view a gallery of sites that demonstrate responsive web design. The screen captures in the gallery show web pages displayed with the following browser viewport widths: 320px (smartphone display), 768px (tablet portrait display), 1024px (netbook display and tablet landscape display), and 1600px (large desktop display).

## What's a Media Query?

According to the W3C (https://www.w3.org/TR/css3-mediaqueries) a **media query** is made up of a media type (such as screen) and a logical expression that determines the capability of the device that the browser is running on, such as screen resolution and orientation (portrait or landscape). When the media query evaluates as true, the media query directs browsers to CSS you have coded and configured specifically for those capabilities. Media queries are supported by current versions of popular browsers.

## Media Query Example Using a Link Element

Figure 7.33 shows the same web page as Figure 7.31, but it looks quite different because of a link element that includes a media query and is associated with a style sheet configured for optimal mobile display on a popular smartphone. The HTML is shown below:

```
<link href="lighthousemobile.css" rel="stylesheet"
               media="(max-width: 480px)">
```

The code sample above will direct browsers to an external stylesheet that has been configured for optimal display on the most popular smartphones. Commonly used media types and keywords are listed in Table 7.7.

**Figure 7.33** CSS media queries help to configure the page for mobile display

Table 7.7 Media types

| Media Type | Value Purpose |
| --- | --- |
| all | All devices (default) |
| screen | Computer screen display of web page |
| speech | Devides that "read out" a web page such as screenreaders |
| print | Printout of web page |

In the link element shown above, the `max-width` **media feature** is set to 480px. While there are many different screen sizes for smartphones these days, a maximum width of 480px will target the display size of many popular models. A maximum width of 768px will target many modern large smartphones and small tablets. A media query may test for both minimum and maximum values. For example,

```
<link href="lighthousetablet.css" rel="stylesheet"
      media="(min-width: 768px) and (max-width: 1024px)">
```

## Media Query Example Using an `@media` Rule

A second method of using media queries is to code them directly in your CSS using an **@media rule**. Begin by coding `@media` followed by the media type and logical expression. Then enclose the desired CSS selector(s) and declaration(s) within a pair of braces. The sample code below configures a different background image specifically for mobile devices with small screens. Table 7.8 lists commonly used media query features.

```
@media (max-width: 480px) {
  header { background-image: url(mobile.gif);
  }
}
```

Table 7.8 Commonly used media features

| Media Feature | Values | Criteria |
|---|---|---|
| max-device-height | Numeric value | The height of the screen size of the output device in pixels is smaller than or equal to the value |
| max-device-width | Numeric value | The width of the screen size of the output device in pixels is smaller than or equal to the value |
| min-device-height | Numeric value | The height of the screen size of the output device in pixels is greater than or equal to the value |
| min-device-width | Numeric value | The width of the screen size of the output device in pixels is greater than or equal to the value |
| max-height | Numeric value | The height of the viewport in pixels is smaller than or equal to the value; (reevaluated when screen is resized) |
| min-height | Numeric value | The height of the viewport in pixels is greater than or equal to the value; (reevaluated when screen is resized) |
| max-width | Numeric value | The width of the viewport in pixels is smaller than or equal to the value; (reevaluated when screen is resized) |
| min-width | Numeric value | The width of the viewport in pixels is greater than or equal to the value; (reevaluated when screen is resized) |
| orientation | Portrait or landscape | The orientation of the device |

## Mobile First

Many web developers follow a responsive design layout strategy called Mobile First, a term coined by Luke Wroblewski almost a decade ago.

The Mobile First Process:

1. Configure a single-column page layout optimized for small, narrow screens, Test with a small browser viewport if needed.

2. Resize the browser viewport to be larger until the design "breaks" and needs to be reworked for a pleasing display—this is the point where you may need to code a media query.

3. Continue resizing the browser viewport to be larger until the design breaks and code additional media queries.

# 7.12 Responsive Layout with Media Queries

 ### Hands-On Practice 7.8

You'll practice a Mobile First strategy for responsive design in this Hands-On Practice. First, you will configure a page layout that works well in smartphones (test with a small browser window). Then you'll resize the browser viewport to be larger until the design "breaks" and code media queries and additional CSS as appropriate using traditional float layout techniques (as introduced in Chapter 6). Figure 7.34 shows wireframes for three different layouts.

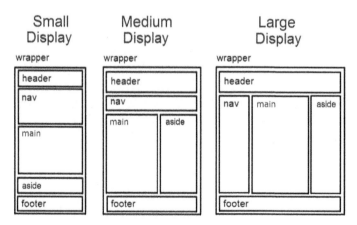

Figure 7.34  Three wireframe layouts

Create a new folder called ch7resp. Copy the starter7.html file from the chapter7 folder in the student files into your ch7resp folder. Copy the lighthouse.jpg and light.gif files from the chapter7/starters folder into your ch7resp folder.

1. Launch a text editor and open your starter7.html file. View the HTML and notice that a div assigned to the `wrapper` id has child elements of header, nav, main, aside, and footer as shown.

```
<div id="wrapper">
  <header> . . . </header>
  <nav> . . . </nav>
  <main> . . . </main>
  <aside> . . . </aside>
  <footer> . . . </footer>
</div>
```

Observe the CSS and note the `wrapper` id's child elements (header, nav, main, aside, and footer) do not have the float property associated with them. Browsers render this page using normal flow with each element displayed under the preceding element, similar to the Small Display wireframe in Figure 7.33. Notice also that there are no minimum widths assigned. This layout will work well on a small display such as a smartphone. Save the file with the name index.html.

2. Display your index.html file in a desktop browser. If your browser viewport is a typical size, it will look a bit awkward and similar to Figure 7.35. Don't worry though, we intend this layout to be displayed on narrow mobile screens—so resize your browser to be narrower until your display is similar to Figure 7.36, which simulates the mobile display.

Figure 7.35 Normal flow full width block elements

3. There is one more item needed for a more pleasing and usable display on an actual mobile device: the viewport meta tag. Launch a text editor and open index.html. Add a viewport meta tag in the head section of the document below the meta tag. The HTML follows:

```
<meta name="viewport"
content="width=device-width,
initial-scale=1.0">
```

Figure 7.36 Smartphone display simulation

Save your file. If you display it in a desktop browser, it will look the same. See the student files (chapter7/7.8/step3.html) for an example. Figure 7.37 shows a smartphone display of the page.

4.  In the past, web developers would try to target specific devices (such as smartphone and tablet). However, the modern process is to determine the condition for the media query by widening the browser until the display begins to "break" or look awkward. Display your index.html file in a browser—first narrow it and then gradually widen it. The point where it starts to seem awkward is around 600px wide, so that's what we'll code for our media query.

    You'll configure the layout to follow the Medium Display wireframe in Figure 7.34. Observe the layout: horizontal header, horizontal navigation, adjacent main and aside elements, and horizontal footer.

    Launch a text editor and open index.html. Code a CSS media query after the other style rules to change the display when the `min-width` of the viewport is at least 600px. Add style rules within the media query that will create a horizontal navigation area with `inline-block` display, width, padding, centered text, and no border; configure the main element selector with a left float and a width of 55%, set a 55% left margin for the aside element selector, and configure the footer element selector to clear floats. The CSS follows:

**Figure 7.37**
Smartphone display

```
@media (min-width: 600px) {
 nav li { display: inline-block;
          width: 7em;
          padding: 0.5em;
          border: none; }
 nav ul    { text-align: center; }
 main      { float: left;
             width: 55%; }
 aside     { margin-left: 55%; }
 footer    { clear: both; }
 }
```

Save the file and launch it in a browser. You should be able to resize your browser viewport and obtain a display similar to Figure 7.38. An example is in the Student Files (chapter7/7.8/step4.html).

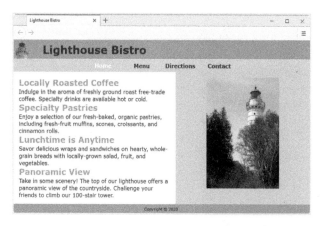

**Figure 7.38** Implementing the Medium Display wireframe

**5.** Repeat the process to determine the condition for the next breakpoint. When displayed in a browser, the web page seems to be a bit awkward around 1024px, so that's what you'll code for in the next media query. Configure the layout to follow the Large Display wireframe in Figure 7.34. Observe the layout: horizontal header; adjacent nav, main and aside elements; and horizontal footer.

Launch a text editor and open index.html. Code a CSS media query after the other style rules to change the display when the `min-width` of the viewport is at least 1024px. Add style rules within the media query that will set left float for the nav element, a centered `wrapper` id with 80% width and 1200px maximum width, and a #000066 background color for the body element selector. The CSS follows:

```
@media (min-width: 1024px){
 nav li { display: block; }
 nav ul { text-align: left; }
 nav { float: left; }
 #wrapper { width: 80%; margin: auto; max-width: 1200px; }
 body { background-color: #000066; }
}
```

Save the file and test it in a browser. You should be able to resize your browser viewport and obtain a display similar to Figure 7.39. A sample solution is in the student files (chapter7/7.8/index.html). In this Hands-On Practice, you applied media queries to a web page and configured float layout. Since float layout will be in use for quite some time, it's good to be familiar with it. In the next Hands-On Practice, you will follow a more modern approach which is applying media queries and configuring grid layout.

**Figure 7.39** Implementing the Large Display wireframe on a desktop browser

**FAQ    What values should I use in my media queries?**

There is no single correct way to configure a media query. When web developers first began writing media queries, there were very few mobile devices and they could be targeted with pixel-perfect precision. While this is no longer the case, web developers often use the `max-width` and/or `min-width` features to determine the size of the view-port being used. Here is a typical media query to target a smartphone display which checks for a maximum width value of 480 pixels:

```
@media (max-width: 480px) {
}
```

A list of media query breakpoints for common devices is available at https://responsivedesign.is/develop/browser-feature-support/media-queries-for-common-device-breakpoints/. However, today, there are a huge number of different mobile devices with various screen resolutions, so a modern approach is to focus on the responsive display of your content and then configure media queries as needed for your content to reflow on a variety of screen sizes. You will need to test your responsive web pages to find the best choices for your specific content. Check for long line lengths or too much empty space on the page—that's probably a signal that a new media query is needed.

Most of the examples in this chapter use pixel values for media query conditions, but some web developers prefer to use em unit values. The first media query in Hands-On Practice 7.8 could have been written to check for `min-width` of 40em:

```
@media (min-width: 40em) {
}
```

An example file with em unit media queries is in the student files (chapter7/7.8/emunit.html).

**FAQ    Where can I find more information about media queries?**

Visit the following resources for more information about media queries:

- https://developers.google.com/web/fundamentals/design-and-ux/responsive/
- https://www.smashingmagazine.com/2018/02/media-queries-responsive-design-2018/
- https://css-tricks.com/snippets/css/media-queries-for-standard-devices/

**FAQ    Can you suggest any other helpful tools for testing responsive web pages?**

Google Chrome Dev Tools can be helpful when testing responsive web pages. Visit these resources to get started:

- https://developers.google.com/web/tools/chrome-devtools/device-mode/
- https://developers.google.com/web/tools/chrome-devtools/device-mode/#responsive

# 7.13 Responsive Grid Layout with Media Queries

 Hands-On Practice 7.9

You'll practice a Mobile First strategy for responsive design using grid layout and media queries in this Hands-On Practice. First, you will configure a page layout that works well in smartphones (test with a small browser window). Then you'll resize the browser viewport to be larger until the design "breaks" and code media queries and additional CSS as appropriate using grid layout for the page and flexbox layout for the navigation area. Figure 7.40 shows wireframes for three different layouts.

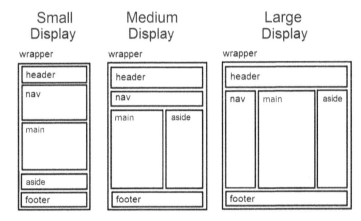

Figure 7.40  Three wireframe layouts

Create a new folder called ch7resp2. Copy the starter7.html file from the chapter7 folder in the student files into your ch7resp2 folder. Copy the lighthouse.jpg and light.gif files from the chapter7/starters folder into your ch7resp2 folder.

1. Launch a text editor and open your starter7.html file. View the HTML and notice that a div assigned to the `wrapper` id has child elements of header, nav, main, aside, and footer as shown. The `wrapper` id will be the grid container. The header, nav, main, aside, and footer elements are the grid items.

```
<div id="wrapper">
  <header> … </header>
  <nav> … </nav>
  <main> … </main>
  <aside> … </aside>
  <footer> … </footer>
</div>
```

Observe the CSS and note that while there are styles that set the visual look of the elements, the CSS does not include any styles for layout. Browsers render this page using normal flow with each element displayed under the preceding element, similar to the Small Display wireframe in Figure 7.40. Notice also that there are no minimum widths assigned. This layout will work well on a small display such as a smartphone. Save the file with the name index.html.

2. Display your index.html file in a desktop browser. If your browser viewport is a typical size, it will look a bit awkward and similar to Figure 7.41. Don't worry though, we intend this layout to be displayed on narrow mobile screens—so resize your browser to be narrower until your display is similar to Figure 7.42, which simulates the mobile display.

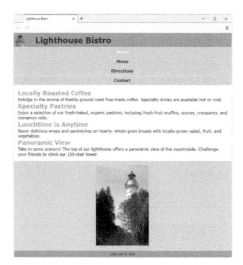

Figure 7.41 The web page initial display

Figure 7.42
Smartphone
display simulation

3. There is one more item needed for a more pleasing and usable display on an actual mobile device: the viewport meta tag. Launch a text editor and open index.html. Add a viewport meta tag in the head section of the document below the meta tag. The HTML follows:

```
<meta name="viewport"
content="width=device-width,
initial-scale=1.0">
```

Save your file. If you display it in a desktop browser, it will look the same. Figure 7.37 shows a display of how a smartphone would render this page. An example is in the student files (chapter7/7.9/step3.html).

4. Since the initial display of the web page is rendered well in normal flow, you will only need to configure grid layout when the media queries are triggered. You will determine the condition for the media query by widening the browser until the display begins to "break" or look awkward. Display your index.html file in a browser—first narrow it and then gradually widen it. The point where it starts to seem awkward is around 600px wide, so that's what we'll code for our first media query and grid layout.

You'll configure the layout to follow the Medium Display wireframe in Figure 7.40. Observe the layout: horizontal header, horizontal navigation, adjacent main and aside elements, and horizontal footer.

Launch a text editor and open index.html. Since the browser display seems a bit awkward around 600px wide, code a media query below the existing CSS that checks for 600px `min-width`. You will add style rules within the media query. Figure 7.43 shows a grid layout wireframe that corresponds to the Medium Display shown in Figure 7.39.

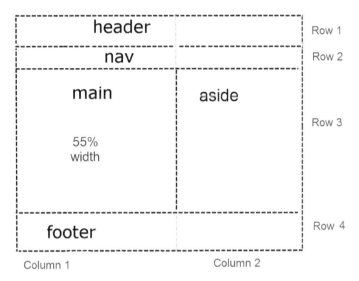

**Figure 7.43** Grid layout for Medium Display

Figure 7.44 depicts the browser rendering of the page. Notice that the navigation area is now horizontal instead of vertical. You will use flexbox layout to configure this. Configure the `nav ul` element selector to be a flexbox container and set the `flex-direction` to `row`, `flex-wrap` to `nowrap`, and `justify-content` to `space-around`. Also code CSS to eliminate the bottom border on the li elements in the navigation area.

**Figure 7.44** Implementing the Medium Display wireframe in grid layout

Next, assign grid areas for header, nav, aside, main, and footer to HTML element selectors. Configure a grid assigned to the `wrapper` id. Use the `grid-template` property to describe a grid that contains grid areas header, nav, main, aside, and footer. Use the grid layout in Figure 7.43 as a guide. Set the first column in the grid to 55% width. The CSS follows:

```
@media (min-width: 600px) {
    nav ul { display: flex;
             flex-flow: row nowrap;
             justify-content: space-around; }
    nav ul li { border-bottom: none; }
    header { grid-area: header; }
    nav     { grid-area: nav; }
    main    { grid-area: main; }
    aside   {grid-area: aside; }
    footer  { grid-area: footer; }
    #wrapper { display: grid;
             grid-template:
                "header header"
                "nav    nav"
                "main   aside"
                "footer footer"
                / 55%  }

}
```

Save your file and test it in a browser. It should look similar to Figure 7.44. An example is in the student files (chapter 7/7.9/step4.html).

5.  Repeat the process to determine the condition for the next breakpoint. When displayed in a browser, the web page seems to be a bit awkward around 1024px, so that's what you'll code for in the next media query. Configure the layout to follow the Large Display wireframe in Figure 7.40. Observe the layout—horizontal header; adjacent nav, main and aside elements; and horizontal footer. Figure 7.45 shows a grid layout wireframe for the Large Display.

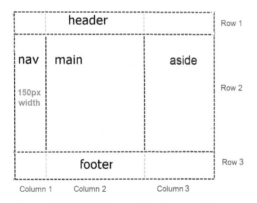

**Figure 7.45**  Grid layout for Large Display

Figure 7.46 depicts the browser rendering of the page. Notice the changes in the page: a dark blue background showing on either side of the centered web page and a vertical navigation area.

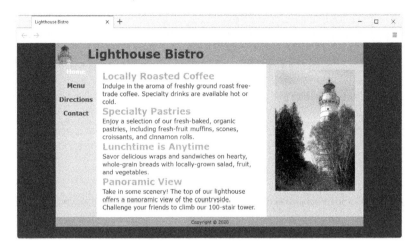

**Figure 7.46** Implementing the Large Display wireframe with grid layout on a desktop browser

Launch a text editor and open index.html. Code a CSS media query after the other style rules to change the display when the `max-width` of the viewport is at least 1024px. Add style rules within the media query that will set a dark blue background color for the body element selector, center the `wrapper` id, and configure the `nav ul` element selector as a flexbox container with `flex-direction` set to `column` and `flex-wrap` set to `nowrap`.

Next, assign grid areas for header, nav, aside, main, and footer to HTML element selectors. Configure a grid assigned to the `wrapper` id. Use the `grid-template` property to describe a grid that contains grid areas header, nav, main, aside, and footer. Use the grid layout in Figure 7.45 as a guide. Set the first column in the grid to 55% width. The CSS follows:

```
@media (min-width: 1024px) {
        body { background-color: #000066; }
        nav ul { display: flex;
                flex-direction: column;
                flex-wrap: nowrap; }
        header { grid-area: header; }
        nav    { grid-area: nav; }
        main   { grid-area: main; }
        aside  { grid-area: aside; }
        footer { grid-area: footer; }
        #wrapper { width: 80%;
                margin: auto; max-width: 1200px;
                display: grid;
                grid-template:
                        "header    header    header"
                        "nav       main      aside"
                        "footer    footer    footer"
                        / 150px; }
    }
```

Save the file and test it in a browser. You should be able to resize your browser viewport and obtain a display similar to Figure 7.46. A sample solution is in the student files (chapter7/7.9/index.html).

# 7.14  Responsive Images

In his book, *Responsive Web Design*, Ethan Marcotte described a **flexible image** as a fluid image that will not break the page layout as the browser viewport is resized. Flexible images (often referred to as responsive images), along with fluid layouts and media queries, are the components of responsive web design. You will be introduced to several different coding techniques to configure a responsive image in this section.

## Flexible Images with CSS

The most widely supported technique to configure an image as flexible requires a change to the HTML and additional CSS to style the flexible image.

1. Edit the img elements in the HTML. Remove the height and width attributes.

2. Configure the `max-width: 100%;` style declaration in the CSS. If the width of the image is less than the width of the container element, the image will display with its actual dimensions. If the width of the image is greater than the width of the container element, the image will be resized by the browser to fit in the container (instead of hanging out over the margin).

3. To keep the dimensions of the image in proportion and maintain the aspect ratio of the image, Bruce Lawson suggests to also set the `height: auto;` style declaration in the CSS (see https://brucelawson.co.uk/2012/responsive-web-design-preserving-images-aspect-ratio).

Background images can also be configured for a more fluid display at various viewport sizes. Although it's common to code a height property when configuring a background image with CSS, the result is a somewhat non-responsive background image. Explore configuring other CSS properties for the container such as font-size, line-height, and padding in percentage values. The background-size: cover; property can also be useful. You'll typically see a more pleasing display of the background image in various-sized viewports. Another option is to configure different image files to use for backgrounds and use media queries to determine which background image is displayed. A disadvantage to this option is that multiple files are downloaded although only one file is displayed. You'll apply flexible image techniques in the next Hands-On Practice.

## Hands-On Practice 7.10

In this Hands-On Practice you'll work with a web page that demonstrates responsive web design. Figure 7.47 depicts the single-column smartphone display and shows the effects of media queries which are configured to display a two-column page when the viewport width is at least 38em (a tablet display) and display a three-column page when the viewport width is at least 65em. You will edit the CSS to configure flexible images.

Desktop Browser          Tablet
Display Width

Smartphone
Display Width

**Figure 7.47** The web page demonstrates responsive web design techniques

Create a folder named flexible7. Copy the starter8.html file from the chapter7 folder into the flexible7 folder and rename it index.html. Copy the following images from the student files chapter7/starters folder into the flexible7 folder: header.jpg and pools.jpg. Launch a browser and view index.html as shown in Figure 7.48. View the code in a text editor and notice that the img tag's `height` and `width` attributes have already been removed from the HTML. View the CSS and notice that the web page uses a responsive grid layout. Edit the embedded CSS.

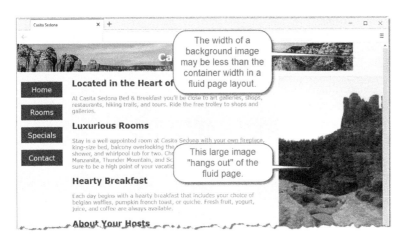

**Figure 7.48** The web page before the images are configured to be flexible

1. Locate the header element selector. Add the `background-size: cover;` declaration to cause the browser to scale the background image to fill the container. The CSS follows:

```
header { background-image: url(header.jpg);
         background-repeat: no-repeat;
         background-size: cover; }
```

2. Add a style rule for the img element selector that sets maximum width to 100% and height to the value auto. The CSS follows:

```
img { max-width: 100%;
      height: auto; }
```

3. Save the index.html file. Test your index.html file in a desktop browser. As you resize the browser window, you'll see your page respond and look similar to the screen captures in Figure 7.47. The web page demonstrates responsive web design with the following techniques: fluid layout, media queries, and flexible images. A suggested solution is in the student files chapter7/7.10 folder.

You just applied basic techniques for configuring flexible, fluid images. These techniques should work well on popular browsers. Next, you'll explore two new HTML5.1 responsive image techniques which offer even more options when designing web pages with responsive images.

## Picture Element

New to HTML5.1 (http://www.w3.org/TR/html51), the purpose of the **picture element** is to provide a method for a browser to display different images depending on specific criteria indicated by the web developer. The picture element is supported by current versions of modern browsers. The picture element begins with the `<picture>` tag and ends with the `</picture>` tag. The picture element is a container element that is coded along with source elements and a fallback img element to provide multiple image files that can be chosen for display by the browser.

## Source Element

The **source element** is a self-contained, or void, tag that is used together with a container element. The picture element is one of several elements (see the video and audio elements in Chapter 11) that can contain one or more source elements. When used with a picture element, multiple source elements are typically configured to specify different images. Code the source elements between the opening and closing picture tags. Table 7.9 lists attributes of the source element when coded within a picture element container.

Table 7.9 Attributes of the source element

| Attribute | Value |
|---|---|
| srcset | Required. Provides image choices for the browser in a comma-separated list. Each item can contain the image URL (required), optional maximum viewport dimension, and optional pixel density for high resolution devices. |
| media | Optional. Media query to specify conditions for browser display. |
| sizes | Optional. Numeric or percentage value to specify the dimensions of the image display. May be further configured with a media query. |
| Value | Optional. MIME type of the resource |

There are many potential ways to configure responsive images with the picture and source elements. We will focus on a basic technique that uses the media attribute to specify conditions for display.

## Hands-On Practice 7.11

In this Hands-On Practice you will configure responsive images with the picture, source, and img elements as you create the page shown in Figure 7.49.

Figure 7.49 Responsive image with the picture element

Create a new folder named ch7picture. Copy the large.jpg, medium.jpg, small.jpg, large.webp, medium.wepb, small.webp, and fallback. jpg files from the chapter7/starters folder into your ch7picture folder. Launch a text editor and open the template file located at chapter7/template.html in the student files. Save the file as index.html in your ch7picture folder. Modify the file to configure a web page as indicated:

1. Configure the text, Picture Element, within an h1 element and within the title element.

2. Code the following in the body of the web page:

```
<picture>
    <source media="(min-width: 1200px)" srcset="large.jpg">
    <source media="(min-width: 800px)" srcset="medium.jpg">
    <source media="(min-width: 320px)" srcset="small.jpg">
    <img src="fallback.jpg" alt="waterwheel">
</picture>
```

Save your file and test your page in a current version of Firefox or Chrome. Notice how a different image is displayed depending on the width of the browser viewport. If the viewport's minimum width is 1200px or greater, the large.jpg image is shown. If the viewport's minimum width is 800px or greater but less than 1200px, the medium.jpg image is displayed. If the viewport's minimum width is 320px greater but less than 800px, the small.jpg image is shown. If none of these criteria are met, the fallback.jpg image should be displayed. As you test, try resizing and refreshing the browser display. You may need to resize the browser, close it, and launch it again to test for display of the different images. Browsers that do not support the new picture element will process the img tag and display the fallback.jpg image. A suggested solution is in the student files chapter7/7.11 folder.

Next, you will configure the web page to also provide WebP images for supporting browsers. Recall from Chapter 4 that the WebP image format is a relatively new image format which can provide improved image compression.

Launch a text editor and open index.html. Locate the picture element. Immediately below the opening picture tag, add three additional source elements for the WebP images. Edit the source element for each .jpg image and assign the type attribute to the value "image/jpeg" to indicate the MIME type for .jpg files. The HTML code is shown below.

```
<picture>
    <source media="(min-width: 1200px)"
    srcset="large.webp" type="image/webp">
    <source media="(min-width: 800px)"
    srcset="medium.webp" type="image/webp">
    <source media="(min-width: 320px)"
    .srcset="small.webp" type="image/webp">
    <source media="(min-width: 1200px)"
    srcset="large.jpg" type="image/jpeg">
    <source media="(min-width: 800px)"
    srcset="medium.jpg" type="image/jpeg">
    <source media="(min-width: 320px)"
    srcset="small.jpg" type="image/jpeg">
    <img src="fallback.jpg" alt="waterwheel">
</picture>
```

Save your file with the name index2.html. When you display your page in a modern browser, the browser will display the first image file that it supports. Modern browsers, such as Chrome, will display a WebP image of the appropriate size. Browsers with picture element support without WebP image support, will display the jpg images of the appropriate size. Other browsers will display the fallback image. Compare your work to the solution in the in the student files (chapter7/7.11/index2.html).

This Hands-On Practice provided a very basic example of responsive images with the picture element. The picture and element responsive image technique is intended to eliminate multiple image downloads that can occur with CSS flexible image techniques. The browser downloads only the image it chose to display based on the criteria provided.

## Responsive Img Element Attributes

New to HTML5.1 (http://www.w3.org/TR/html51), the new `srcset` and `sizes` attributes have been created for the img element. Current versions of modern browsers support these new attributes.

### The `sizes` Attribute

The purpose of the img element's **sizes attribute** is to inform the browser as it processes the srcset attribute about how much of the viewport should be used to display the image. The default value of the sizes attribute is `100vw`, which indicates 100% of the viewport width is available to display the image. The value of the sizes attribute can be a percentage of the viewport width or a specific pixel width (such as 400px). The sizes attribute can also contain one or more media queries along with the width for each condition.

### The `srcset` Attribute

The purpose of the img element's **srcset attribute** is to provide a method for a browser to display different images depending on specific criteria indicated by the web developer. The value of the srcset attribute provides image choices for the browser in a comma-separated list. Each list item can contain the image URL (required), optional maximum viewport dimension, and optional pixel density for high resolution devices.

There are many potential ways to configure responsive images with the img element, sizes, attribute, and srcset attribute. We will focus on a basic technique that uses the browser viewport dimension to specify conditions for display.

 ## Hands-On Practice 7.12

In this Hands-On Practice you will configure responsive images with the picture, source, and img elements as you create the page shown in Figure 7.50.

Create a new folder named ch7image. Copy the large.jpg, medium.jpg, small.jpg, and fallback.jpg files from the chapter7/starters folder into your ch7image folder. Launch a text editor and open the template file located at chapter7/template.html in the student

Figure 7.50 Responsive image with the image element's srcset attribute

files. Save the file as index.html in your ch7image folder. Modify the file to configure a web page as indicated:

1. Configure the text, Img Element, within an h1 element and within the title element.

2. Code the following in the body of the web page:

```
<img src="fallback.jpg"
  sizes="100vw"
  srcset="large.jpg 1200w, medium.jpg 800w, small.jpg 320w"
  alt="waterwheel">
```

Save your file and test your page in a current version of Firefox or Chrome. Notice how a different image is displayed depending on the width of the browser viewport. If the viewport's minimum width is 1200px or greater, the large.jpg image is shown. If the viewport's minimum width is 800px or greater but less than 1200px, the medium.jpg image is displayed. If the viewport's minimum width is 320px greater but less than 800px, the small.jpg image is shown. If none of these criteria are met, the fallback.jpg image should be displayed. As you test, try resizing and refreshing the browser display. You may need to resize the browser, close it, and launch it again to test for display of the different images. Browsers that do not support the image element's new sizes and srcset attributes will ignore these attributes and display the fallback.jpg image. A suggested solution is in the student files chapter7/7.12 folder.

This Hands-On Practice provided a very basic example of responsive images with the img element and new sizes and srcset attributes which (like the picture element responsive image technique) is intended to eliminate multiple image downloads that can occur with CSS flexible image techniques. The browser downloads only the image it chose to display based on the criteria provided.

## Explore Responsive Images

There is so much to learn about responsive image techniques! Visit the following resources to explore the topic of responsive images:

- http://responsiveimages.org
- https://developer.mozilla.org/en-US/docs/Learn/HTML/Multimedia_and_embedding/Responsive_images
- http://blog.cloudfour.com/responsive-images-101-part-5-sizes

# Checkpoint 7.2

1. What is meant by the phrase "Mobile First"?
2. Are there certain values that must be used in CSS media queries? Why or why not?
3. Describe coding techniques that will configure an image with a flexible display.

Figure 7.51 Testing a web page with the Opera Mobile Emulator. © Opera Software 1995–2019.

Figure 7.52 Approximating the mobile display with a desktop browser

# 7.15  Testing Mobile Display

The best way to test the mobile display of a web page is to publish it to the Web and access it from mobile devices. (See the Appendix for an introduction to publishing a website with FTP.) However, not everyone has access to multiple mobile devices. Several options for emulating a mobile display are listed below:

- **Opera Mobile Emulator** (shown in Figure 7.51) Windows, Mac, and Linux download; Supports media queries https://dev.opera.com/articles/opera-mobile-emulator/
- **Google Chrome Dev Tools** Runs in Chrome; Supports media queries https://developers.google.com/web/tools/chrome-devtools/device-mode/
- **iPhone Emulator** Runs in a browser window; Supports media queries http://www.testiphone.com

## Testing with a Desktop Browser

If you don't have a smartphone and/or are unable to publish your files to the Web-no worries-as you've seen in this chapter (also see Figure 7.52) you can approximate the mobile display of your web page using a desktop browser. Verify the placement of your media queries.

- If you have coded media queries within your CSS, display your page in a desktop browser and then reduce the width and height of the viewport until it approximates a mobile screen size.
- If you have coded media queries within a link tag, edit the web page and temporarily modify the link tag to point to your mobile CSS style sheet. Then, display your page in a desktop browser and reduce the width and height of the viewport until it approximates a mobile screen size.

## Browser Viewport Size

It can be helpful to know the size of your browser viewport as you are testing a responsive web page. The following tools can help you determine your browser viewport size:

- **Chris Pederick's Web Developer Extension**

  Available for Firefox and Chrome

  http://chrispederick.com/work/web-developer

  *Select Resize > Display Window Size*

- **Viewport Dimensions Extension**

  Available for Chrome at https://github.com/CSWilson/Viewport-Dimensions

## Responsive Testing Tools

Another option for testing your responsive web pages is to use one of the following online tools that provide instant views of your web page in a variety of screen sizes and devices:

- Mobile-Friendly Test https://search.google.com/test/mobile-friendly
- Sizzy https://sizzy.co
- Am I Responsive http://ami.responsivedesign.is
- Screenfly http://quirktools.com/screenfly

It's fun to view your responsive website on these browser tools. The true test, however, is to view your web pages on a variety of physical mobile devices. Figure 7.53 shows a web page displayed on a smartphone.

## For Serious Developers Only

If you are a software developer or information systems major, you may want to explore the SDKs (Software Developer Kits) for the iOS and Android platforms. Each SDK includes a mobile device emulator. Visit http://developer.android.com/sdk/index.html for information about the Android Studio SDK.

Figure 7.53 Testing the web page with a smartphone

 FAQ    **I would like to put a phone number on a web page so that a visitor with a mobile phone can tap on it and place a call. How do you do that?**

It's very easy to configure a telephone hyperlink or SMS (short message service) text message hyperlink for use by smartphones.

According to RFC 3966, you can configure a telephone hyperlink by using a telephone scheme: Begin the `href` value with `tel:` followed by the phone number. For example, to configure a telephone hyperlink on a web page for use by mobile browsers, code as follows:

```
<a href="tel:888-555-5555">Call 888-555-5555</a>
```

RFC 5724 indicates that an SMS scheme hyperlink intended to send a text message can be configured by beginning the `href` value with `sms:` followed by the phone number, as shown in the following code:

```
<a href="sms:888-555-5555">Text 888-555-5555</a>
```

Not all mobile browsers and devices support telephone and text hyperlinks, but expect increased use of this technology in the future. You'll get a chance to practice using the `tel:` scheme in Chapter 7 case study.

# Chapter Summary

This chapter introduced you to modern layout techniques which configure responsive web pages that display well on desktop browsers and mobile devices. Visit the textbook website at https://www.webdevfoundations. net for examples, the links listed in this chapter, and updated information.

## Key Terms

<picture>
<source>
@media rule
@supports rule
directive
feature query
flex container
flex item
flex property
flex-direction property
flex-wrap property
flexbox
flexible image
fractional unit

grid
grid area
grid column
grid container
grid item
grid line
grid row
grid track
grid-area property
grid-column property
grid-row property
grid-template property
grid-template-areas
    property

grid-template-columns
    property
grid-template-rows property
justify-content property
media feature
media query
order property
picture element
responsive web design
sizes attribute
source element
srcset attribute
type attribute
viewport meta tag

## Review Questions

### Multiple Choice

1. Which meta tag is used to configure display for mobile devices?

   a. viewport

   b. handheld

   c. mobile

   d. screen

2. Which of the following properties configures proportional flexible items?

   a. flex

   b. flex-wrap

   c. align-items

   d. justify

3. Which of the following is a container element used to configure responsive images?

   a. display

   b. flex

   c. picture

   d. link

4. Which of the following values would you assign to the display property to configure a flexbox container?

   a. grid

   b. flex

   c. flexbox

   d. block

5. Which of the following is optimized for responsive two-dimensional page layout?

   a. CSS absolute positioning

   b. CSS Display Layout

   c. CSS Grid Layout

   d. CSS Flexible Box Layout

6. Which of the following is a conditional that can be used to test for support of a CSS property?

   a. feature query

   b. support query

   c. media query

   d. property query

7. Which of the following properties configures whether flex items are displayed on multiple lines?

    a. `flex-direction`

    b. `flex-wrap`

    C. `flex-template`

    d. `flex-basis`

8. Which of the following properties identifies a CSS selector as a grid container?

    a. grid

    b. directive

    c. display

    d. grid-template

9. Which of the following properties associates a grid item (HTML element) with a named area of the grid?

    a. grid-name

    b. grid-item

    c. grid-area

    d. grid

10. Which of the following properties configures empty space between grid tracks?

    a. align

    b. grid-gap

    c. gutter

    d. grid-template

## Fill in the Blank

1. The _____ property is a shorthand property that combines the grid-template-areas, grid-template-rows, and grid-template-columns properties.

2. _____ determine the capability of the mobile device, such as browser viewport dimensions and resolution.

3. When using flexbox to vertically and horizontally center text within an element, set both the _____ and _____ properties to the value center.

4. The _____ property is a shorthand property that configures both the flex-direction and the flex-wrap.

5. The purpose of the _____ attribute is to provide a method for a browser to display different images depending on specific criteria.

## Apply Your Knowledge

1. **Predict the Result.** Carefully examine the code below for a responsive web page. Consider how the web page will display in a browser with a narrow viewport (less than 600 pixels). Sketch a wireframe of the page and label it "Mobile." Consider how the web page will display in a typical desktop browser viewport. Sketch a wireframe of the page. Label it "Desktop."

```
<!DOCTYPE html>
<html lang="en">
<head>
<title>Predict the Result</title>
<meta charset="utf-8">
<style>
body   { background-color: #EAEAEA;
         color: #636363;
         font-family: Verdana, Arial, sans-serif; }
```

```
#wrapper { background-color: #D5EDB3; }
header    { color: #FFFFFF;
            text-shadow: 3px 3px 3px #333;
            padding: 1em;    }
#content { background-color: #FFFFFF; }
nav      { width: 150px; padding: 1em; }
main     { padding: 1em 2em; }
aside    { padding: 1em;    }
@media (min-width: 600px) {
          #content { display: flex;
                     flex-wrap: nowrap;    }
}
</style>
</head>
<body>
<div id="wrapper">
  <header>
    <h1>Trillium Media Design</h1>
  </header>
  <div id="content">
    <nav>
      <ul>
        <li><a href="index.html">Home</a></li>
        <li><a href="products.html">Products</a></li>
        <li><a href="services.html">Services</a></li>
        <li><a href="clients.html">Clients</a></li>
        <li><a href="contact.html">Contact</a></li>
      </ul>
    </nav>
    <main>
      <p>Our professional staff takes pride in its working
      relationship with our clients by offering personalized
      services that listen to their needs, develop their target
      areas, and incorporate these items into a website that works.
      </p>
    </main>
    <aside>
      <p>Get monthly updates and free offers. Contact <a
      href="mailto:me@trilliummediadesign.com">Trillium</a>
      to sign up for our newsletter.</p>
    </aside>
  </div>
</div>
</body>
</html>
```

2. **Fill in the Missing Code.** This responsive web page should be configured so that
the appearance of the main navigation changes depending on whether the page is
displayed on a mobile device or on a typical desktop browser. When displayed on a
viewport that is less than 600 pixels, the navigation should display above the main
content with each navigation link on its own line. When displayed on a typical browser
viewport, the navigation should display to the left of the main content using CSS grid
layout. CSS properties and values, indicated by "_" (underscore), are missing.

```
<!DOCTYPE html>
<html lang="en">
<head>
<title>Predict the Result</title>
<meta charset="utf-8">
<style>
body       { background-color: #EAEAEA; color: #636363; }
#wrapper   { background-color: #D5EDB3; height: 100vh; }
header     { color: #FFFFFF; text-align: center;
               text-shadow: 3px 3px 3px #333;    }
nav ul     { display: flex; flex-wrap: _____ ;
               list-style-type: none; padding-left: 0;    }
nav ul li  { width: 100%; padding: .5em; text-align: center;
               border-bottom: 1px solid #636363; }
nav ul li a { display: block; text-decoration: none; }
main       { padding: 1em 2em; }
@media     ( min-width: 600px ) {
           header     { grid-area: header; }
           nav        {_____    : nav; }
           main       { grid-area: main; }
           #wrapper { display:_____;
                   grid-template:
                   "_____ header" 100px
                   "nav       main"
                   / 150px    1fr ; }
}
</style>
</head>
<body>
<div id="wrapper">
  <header> <h1>Trillium Media Design</h1> </header>
  <nav>
    <ul>
      <li><a href="index.html">Home</a></li>
      <li><a href="products.html">Products</a></li>
      <li><a href="services.html">Services</a></li>
      <li><a href="clients.html">Clients</a></li>
      <li><a href="contact.html">Contact</a></li>
    </ul>
  </nav>
```

```
    <main>
        <p>Our professional staff takes pride in its working
        relationship with our clients by offering personalized
        services that listen to their needs, develop their target
        areas, and incorporate these items into a website that works.
        </p>
    </main>
</div>
</body>
</html>
```

3. **Find the Error.** The page below is intended for the navigation area to display on the right side of the browser window. What needs to be changed to make this happen?

```
<!DOCTYPE html>
<html lang="en">
<head>
<title>Find the Error</title>
<meta charset="utf-8">
<style>
body     {   background-color: #d5edb3; color: #636363; }
header   { grid-area: header; }
nav      { grid-area: nov; }
nav ul   { list-style-type: none; }
nav ul a { text-decoration: none; }
main     { grid-area: main;
             padding: 1em 2em; background-color: #FFFFFF; }
#wrapper { display: grid;
                 grid-template:
                     "header header"
                     "nav main"
                     / 1fr 120px;    }
</style>
</head>
<body>
<div id="wrapper">
  <header>
    <h1>Trillium Media Design</h1>
  </header>
  <nav>
    <ul>
      <li><a href="index.html">Home</a></li>
      <li><a href="services.html">Services</a></li>
      <li><a href="contact.html">Contact</a></li>
    </ul>
  </nav>
```

```
    <main>
      <p>Our professional staff takes pride in its working
      relationship with our clients by offering personalized
      services that listen to their needs, develop their target
      areas, and incorporate these items into a website that works.
      </p>
    </main>
  </div>
  </body>
  </html>
```

## Hands-On Exercises

1. Write the CSS to configure the nav element selector as a flex container with rows that wrap.

2. Write the CSS for a feature query that checks for support of CSS grid layout.

3. Write the CSS to configure a grid for an id named container that has two columns and two rows. The first row is 100 pixels high. The first grid item in the second row takes up 75% of the width. It may be helpful to draw a wireframe of the grid layout before you write the code.

4. Write the @media rule to target a typical smartphone device and configure the nav element selector with width set to auto.

5. Create a web page that displays eight of your favorite photos (or eight photos supplied by your instructor). Also include a header and footer area on the page. The page layout should implement flexbox layout to configure a responsive display. Include your name in an e-mail address in the page footer area.

6. Create a web page that displays eight of your favorite photos (or eight photos supplied by your instructor). Also include a header and footer area on the page. The page layout should implement grid layout to configure a responsive display. Include your name in an e-mail address in the page footer area.

7. Draw a wireframe for the home page of your school's website. Write the CSS to configure a grid layout for the wireframe.

## Web Research

The next development in CSS Grid Layout will be CSS Grid Layout Module Level 2 (https://www.w3.org/TR/css-grid-2/) which includes the introduction of subgrids. Use the resources listed below as a starting point to research the purpose of a subgrid. Write a one-page, double-spaced summary that describes the purpose of a subgrid, an example of code for a subgrid, and the current level of browser support.

- https://www.smashingmagazine.com/2018/07/css-grid-2/
- https://css-tricks.com/why-we-need-css-subgrid/
- https://www.w3.org/blog/CSS/2018/08/04/subgrid-spec-completed/
- https://rachelandrew.co.uk/archives/2018/04/27/grid-level-2-and-subgrid/
- https://www.w3.org/TR/css-grid-2/#subgrid

## Focus on Web Design

Now that you've had some practice creating responsive web pages, it's a good idea to explore resources on the web about responsive web design best practices. Use the following URLs as a starting point as you research this topic. Write a one-page, double-spaced summary that describes four recommended practices of responsive web design.

- https://www.smashingmagazine.com/2018/02/media-queries-responsive-design-2018/
- https://www.uxpin.com/studio/blog/best-practices-examples-of-excellent-responsive-design/
- https://www.impactbnd.com/blog/responsive-design-best-practices
- https://crossbrowsertesting.com/blog/development/future-responsive-design-2019/
- https://fireart.studio/blog/how-to-design-responsive-website-best-practices/

# WEBSITE CASE STUDY

## Modern, Responsive Layout

Each of the following case studies continues throughout most of the text. This chapter configures the website with a modern, responsive layout.

## JavaJam Coffee Bar Case Study

In this chapter's case study, you will use the existing JavaJam Coffee Bar (Chapter 6) website as a starting point to create a new version with a responsive layout that implements media queries. You'll practice a Mobile First strategy for responsive design. First, you will configure a page layout that works well in smartphones (test with a small browser window). Then you'll resize the browser viewport to be larger until the design "breaks" and code media queries and additional CSS as needed. Figure 7.54 shows wireframes for three different layouts. The Home page displays will be similar to Figure 7.55.

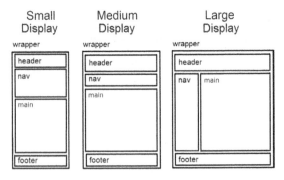

Figure 7.54 JavaJam Coffee Bar wireframes

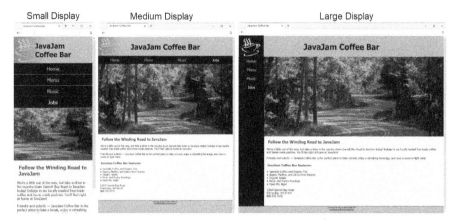

Small Display    Medium Display    Large Display

**Figure 7.55** The Home page

You have four tasks in this case study:

1. Create a new folder for the JavaJam Coffee Bar website.

2. Configure the HTML and CSS needed for pleasing display of a single-column (smartphone) display.

3. Configure the HTML and CSS needed for pleasing display of the web pages on medium sized mobile devices.

4. Configure the CSS needed for a pleasing display of the web pages on large mobile devices and desktops.

**Task 1:** Create a folder called javajam7 to contain your JavaJam Coffee Bar website files. Copy the files from the Chapter 6 Case Study javajam6 folder into the javajam7 folder. Copy the files from the chapter7/starters/javajam folder into the javajam7 folder.

**Task 2: Configure a Small Single-Column Layout.** First, you will edit the CSS. Then you will edit the Home page and test each page in a browser.

**Configure the CSS.** Launch a text editor and open the javajam.css style sheet. Edit the styles to achieve a layout that displays well on small devices using normal flow (no floats) with full-width block elements.

1. Edit the styles for the body element selector. Remove all declarations for the background image. Set margin to 0 and background color to #D2B48C.

2. Edit the styles for the `wrapper` id selector. Remove all declarations associated with width, margin, and box-shadow.

3. Edit the styles for the header element selector. Change the background image to cup.jpg. Set left padding to 105px and height to 128px.

4. Edit the styles for the h1 element selector. Set the font size to 2em.

5. Edit the styles for the nav element selector. Remove the declarations that configure float, width, font-weight, and padding.

6. Edit the styles for the `nav ul` selector. Configure this selector as a flex container with `flex-direction` set to column. Set 0 margin, 0 padding, and 1.25em font size.

7. Code styles for the `nav li` selector. Set .5em top and bottom padding, 1em left and right padding, 100% width, and a 1px solid bottom border.

8. Remove the style declarations for the `onethird` class selector and `floatleft` class selector.

9. Edit the styles for the main element selector. Remove the declarations that configure margin and overflow.

10. Edit the styles for the hero images. Set the background image for the `homehero` id selector to road.jpg. Set the background image for the `heroguitar` id selector to guitar.jpg. Set the background image for the `heromugs` id selector to threemugs.jpg.

11. Edit the styles for the h3, h3, h4, p, div, and dl element selectors within the main element. Change the left and right padding to 1em.

12. Code styles for the `main ul` selector. Set left padding to 2em;

13. Configure styles for the telephone number to display a hyperlink when on the small display and display plain text otherwise.
    a. Code a style rule for the `mobile` id selector. Set display to `inline`.
    b. Code a style rule for the `desktop` id selector. Set display to `none`.

Save your javajam.css file. Use the CSS validator (http://jigsaw.w3.org/css-validator) to check your syntax. Correct and retest if necessary.

**Configure the HTML.** Modify the pages as indicated.

1. Launch a text editor and open index.html. Save the file when you have completed the following edits.
   a. The home page displays a phone number in the contact information area. Wouldn't it be handy if a person using a smartphone could click on the phone number to call the resort? You can make that happen by using tel: in a hyperlink. Configure a hyperlink assigned to an id named `mobile` that contains the phone number as shown:

   ```
   <a id="mobile" href="tel:888-555-5555">888-555-5555</a>
   ```

   However, a telephone link could confuse those visiting the site with a desktop browser. Code another phone number directly after the hyperlink. Code a span element assigned to an id named `desktop` around the phone number as shown:

   ```
   <span id="desktop">888-555-5555</span>
   ```

   b. Code a viewport meta tag in the head section that configures the width to the device-width and sets the initial-scale to 1.0.

2. Add a viewport meta tag to the menu.html and music.html files in the same manner as the Home page. Save your files.

**Test the web pages.** Display your index.html file in a browser. This layout is intended for narrow mobile screens. Resize your browser to be narrower until your display is similar to the Small Display shown in Figure 7.55, which simulates mobile display. Test the menu.html and music.html files in a similar manner.

**Task 3: Configure a Medium Layout.** Edit the CSS and the content pages to configure a more pleasing display on a wider viewport, setting 600px as the breakpoint for the first media query. When you test your web pages and trigger the media query, the layout in the Medium Display wireframe in Figure 7.54 will be implemented and your pages should look similar to the Medium Display in Figures 7.55, 7.56, and 7.57.

**Configure the CSS.** Launch a text editor and open the javajam.css style sheet. Place your cursor below the existing styles. Code a media query that is triggered when the minimum width is 600px or greater. Code the following styles within the media query.

1. Code styles for the header element selector. Configure centered text and 0 left padding.

2. Code styles for the h1 element selector. Set font size to 3em.

3. Code styles for the `nav ul` selector. Configure the flex container with rows that do not wrap. Also set `justify-content` to `space-around`.

4. Code styles for the `nav li` selector. Set the bottom border to `none`.

5. Code styles for the hero images. Configure the `homehero` id selector with 50vh height and the hero.jpg background image. Configure `heromugs` id selector with the heromugs.jpg background image. Configure the `heroguitar` id selector with the heroguitar.jpg background image.

6. Code styles for the `flow` id selector. Configure a flex container. The flex direction is `row`.

7. Code styles for the phone number. Configure the `mobile` id selector with display set to `none`. Configure the `desktop` id selector with display set to `inline`.

8. Code styles for the `details` class selector. Configure a flex container. The flex direction is `row`.

9. Code styles for the h4 element selector. Set left and right margin to 10%.

Save your javajam.css file. Use the CSS validator (http://jigsaw.w3.org/css-validator) to check your syntax. Correct and retest if necessary.

**Edit the HTML.** You need to rework the content area on the Menu and Music pages

1. Launch a text editor and open menu.html. Locate the section elements and remove the `class="onethird"` code from each. Code a div assigned to an id named `flow` that contains all section elements. Save the file.

2. Launch a text editor and open music.html. Locate the img tags and remove the `class="floatleft"` code. Each img is followed by some descriptive text. Enclose each group of descriptive text within a paragraph element. Save the file.

**Test the web pages**. Display your menu.html file in a browser. You should be able to resize your browser viewport and obtain a display similar to the Medium Display in Figure 7.56. Test the index.html and music.html files in a similar manner.

Figure 7.56 The Menu page

**Task 4: Configure a Large Layout.** Edit the CSS to configure a second media query with a 1024px breakpoint that will configure a grid layout with two columns. When you test your web pages and trigger the media query, the layout in the Large Display wireframe in Figure 7.54 will be implemented and your pages should look similar to the Large Display in Figures 7.55, 7.56, and 7.57.

Figure 7.57  The Music page

**Configure the CSS.** Launch a text editor and open the javajam.css style sheet. Place your cursor below the existing styles. Configure a media query that is triggered when the minimum width is 1024px or greater. Within the media query, configure a feature query to check for support of grid layout. Code the following styles within the feature query.

1. Configure the grid areas.
   a. Code styles for the header element selector: set grid-area to header.
   b. Code styles for the nav element selector: set grid-area to nav.
   c. Code styles for the main element selector: set grid-area to main.
   d. Code styles for the footer element selector: set grid-area to footer.

2. Configure the wrapper id selector as a grid container. Use the grid-template property to describe the grid layout shown for large display in Figure 7.54. Use 200px for the width of the navigation area. The CSS follows:

```
#wrapper { display: grid;
        grid-template:
            "header header"
            "nav    main"
            "footer   footer"
            / 200px; }
```

3. Configure the navigation area. Code styles for the nav ul selector to set the value column for flex-direction.

4. Configure the header area. Code styles for the header selector to set coffeelogo.jpg as the background image.

Save your javajam.css file. Use the CSS validator (http://jigsaw.w3.org/css-validator) to check your syntax. Correct and retest if necessary.

**Test the web pages**. Display your index.html file in a modern browser. You should be able to resize your browser viewport and obtain a display similar to the Large Display in Figure 7.55. Browsers that do not support grid layout will render the pages similar to the Medium Display in Figure 7.55. Test the Menu and Music pages in a similar manner.

You have accomplished a great deal as you completed this case study. The design is now responsive, utilizes CSS Flexbox and CSS Grid layout, and displays well on devices with various size viewports. JavaJam Coffee Bar is responsive and mobile!

## Fish Creek Animal Clinic Case Study

In this chapter's case study, you will use the existing Fish Creek Animal Clinic (Chapter 6) website as a starting point to create a new version with a responsive layout that implements media queries. You'll practice a Mobile First strategy for responsive design. First, you will configure a page layout that works well in smartphones (test with a small browser window). Then you'll resize the browser viewport to be larger until the design "breaks" and code media queries and additional CSS as needed. Figure 7.58 shows wireframes for three different layouts. The Home page displays will be similar to Figure 7.59.

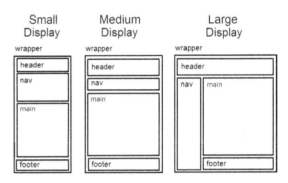

**Figure 7.58** Fish Creek Animal Clinic wireframes

**Figure 7.59** The Home page

You have four tasks in this case study:

1. Create a new folder for the Fish Creek Animal Clinic website.
2. Configure the HTML and CSS needed for pleasing display of a single-column (smartphone) display.
3. Configure the HTML and CSS needed for pleasing display of the web pages on medium sized mobile devices.
4. Configure the CSS needed for a pleasing display of the web pages on large mobile devices and desktops.

**Task 1:** Create a folder called fishcreek7 to contain your Fish Creek Animal Clinic website files. Copy the files from the Chapter 6 Case Study fishcreek6 folder into the fishcreek7 folder. Copy the lilfish.gif file from the chapter7/starters/fishcreek folder to the fishcreek7 folder.

**Task 2: Configure a Small Single-Column Layout**. First, you will edit the CSS. Then you will edit the Home page and test each page in a browser.

**Configure the CSS.** Launch a text editor and open the fishcreek.css style sheet. Edit the styles to achieve a layout that displays well on small devices using normal flow (no floats) with full-width block elements.

1. Edit the styles for the body element selector. Remove the declaration for the background image. Set margin to 0.

2. Edit the styles for the `wrapper` id selector. Remove all declarations associated with width and margin.

3. Edit the styles for the header element selector. Change the background image to lilfish.gif.

4. Edit the styles for the h1 element selector. Change the font size to 2em.

5. Edit the styles for the nav element selector. Remove the declarations that configure float, width, font-weight, and padding. Set centered text.

6. Edit the styles for the `nav ul` selector. Configure this selector as a flex container with `flex-direction` set to column. Set 0 margin, 0 padding, and 1.5em font size.

7. Code styles for the `nav li` selector. Set .5em top and bottom padding, 100% width, and a 1px solid bottom border.

8. Edit the styles for the main element selector. Remove the declaration that configures the left margin.

9. Remove the style declarations for the `floatright` class selector.

10. Edit the styles for the section element selector. Remove the declarations that configures float, width, and height.

11. Edit the styles for the footer element selector. Remove the declaration that configures the left margin.

12. Configure styles for the telephone number to display a hyperlink when on the small display and display plain text otherwise.
    a. Code a style rule for the `mobile` id selector. Set display to `inline`.
    b. Code a style rule for the `desktop` id selector. Set display to `none`.

Save your fishcreek.css file. Use the CSS validator (http://jigsaw.w3.org/css-validator) to check your syntax. Correct and retest if necessary.

**Configure the HTML.** Modify the pages as indicated.

1. Launch a text editor and open index.html. Save the file when you have completed the following edits.
   a. The home page displays a phone number in the contact information area. Wouldn't it be handy if a person using a smartphone could click on the phone number to call the resort? You can make that happen by using tel: in a hyperlink. Configure a hyperlink assigned to an id named `mobile` that contains the phone number as shown:

   ```
   <a id="mobile" href="tel:800-555-5555">800-555-5555</a>
   ```

But wait a minute, a telephone link could confuse those visiting the site with a desktop browser. Code another phone number directly after the hyperlink. Code a span element assigned to an id named `desktop` around the phone number as shown:

```
<span id="desktop">800-555-5555</span>
```

b. Code a viewport meta tag in the head section that configures the width to the device-width and sets the initial-scale to 1.0.

2. Add a viewport meta tag to the services.html page in the same manner as the Home page. Save your file.

3. Add a viewport meta tag to the askvet.html page in the same manner as the Home page. Move the img tag after the description list. Remove the `floatright` class from the img tag. Save your file.

**Test the web pages.** Display your index.html file in a browser. This layout is intended for narrow mobile screens. Resize your browser to be narrower until your display is similar to the Small Display shown in Figure 7.58, which simulates mobile display. Test the services.html and askvet.html files in a similar manner.

**Task 3: Configure a Medium Layout.** Edit the CSS and the web pages to configure a more pleasing display on a wider viewport, setting 600px as the breakpoint for the first media query. When you test your web pages and trigger the media query, the layout in the Medium Display wireframe in Figure 7.58 will be implemented and your pages should look similar to the Medium Display in Figures 7.59, 7.60, and 7.61.

Figure 7.60 The Services page

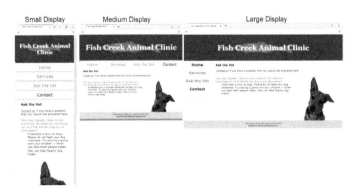

Figure 7.61 The Ask the Vet page

**Configure the CSS.** Launch a text editor and open the fishcreek.css style sheet. Place your cursor below the existing styles. Configure a media query that is triggered when the minimum width is 600px or greater. Code the following styles within the media query.

1. Code styles for the header element selector. Configure bigfish.gif as the background image.

2. Code styles for the h1 element selector. Set font size to 3em.

3. Code styles for the `nav ul` selector. Configure the flex container with rows that do not wrap.

   Also set `justify-content` to `space-around`.

4. Code styles for the `nav li` selector. Set the bottom border to `none`.

5. Code styles for the `flow` id selector. Configure a flex container. The flex direction is `row`. Allow the content to wrap.

6. Code styles for the section element selector. Set minimum width to 30%. Set the `flex` property to 1. Setting the flex property to the value 1 will allocate equal areas for each section flex item.

7. The description list on the Ask the Vet page will be part of a flex layout. Code styles for the dl selector to set `flex` to 2.

8. The img element on the Ask the Vet page will be part of a flex layout. Code styles for the img selector to set `flex` to 1.

9. Code styles for the `mobile` id selector. Set display to `none`.

10. Code styles for the `desktop` id selector. Set display to `inline`.

Save your fishcreek.css file. Use the CSS validator (http://jigsaw.w3.org/css-validator) to check your syntax. Correct and retest if necessary.

**Configure the HTML.** You need to rework the content area on the web pages

1. Launch a text editor and open index.html. Locate the section elements. Code a div assigned to an id named `flow` that contains all section elements. Save the file.

2. Launch a text editor and open services.html. Locate the section elements. Code a div that is assigned to an id named `flow` that contains all the section elements. Save the file.

3. Launch a text editor and open askvet.html. Code a div that is assigned to an id named `flow` that contains the dl and img elements. Save the file.

**Test the web pages.** Display your index.html file in a browser. You should be able to resize your browser viewport and obtain a display similar to the Medium Display in Figure 7.58. Test the services.html and askvet.html files in a similar manner.

**Task 4: Configure a Large Layout.** Edit the CSS to configure a second media query with a 1024px breakpoint that will configure a grid layout with two columns. When you test your web pages and trigger the media query, the layout in the Large Display wireframe in Figure 7.58 will be implemented and your pages should look similar to the Large Display in Figures 7.59, 7.60, and 7.61.

**Configure the CSS.** Launch a text editor and open the fishcreek.css style sheet. Place your cursor below the existing styles. Configure a media query that is triggered when the minimum width is 1024px or greater. Within the media query, configure a feature query to check for support of grid layout. Code the following styles within the feature query.

1. Configure the grid areas.
   a. Code styles for the header element selector: set `grid-area` to header.
   b. Code styles for the nav element selector: set `grid-area` to nav.
   c. Code styles for the main element selector: set `grid-area` to main.
   d. Code styles for the footer element selector: set `grid area` to footer.

2. Configure the `wrapper` id selector as a grid container. Use the `grid-template` property to describe the grid layout shown for large display in Figure 7.58. Use 180px for the width of the navigation area. The CSS follows:

```
#wrapper { display: grid;
        grid-template:
                "header header"
                "nav    main"
                " nav   footer"
                / 180px   ; }
```

3. Configure the navigation area. Code styles for the `nav ul` selector to set the `flex-direction` to `column`. Also configure 1.25em bold font.

Save your fishcreek.css file. Use the CSS validator (http://jigsaw.w3.org/css-validator) to check your syntax. Correct and retest if necessary.

**Test the web pages.** Display your index.html file in a modern browser. You should be able to resize your browser viewport and obtain a display similar to the Large Display in Figure 7.58. Browsers that do not support grid layout will render the pages similar to the Medium Display in Figure 7.58. Test the Services and Ask the Vet pages in a similar manne.

You have accomplished a great deal as you completed this case study. The design is now responsive, utilizes CSS Flexbox and CSS Grid layout, and displays well on devices with various size viewports. Fish Creek Animal Clinic is responsive and mobile!

## Pacific Trails Resort Case Study

In this chapter's case study, you will use the existing Pacific Trails Resort (Chapter 6) website as a starting point to create a new responsive version of the website that utilizes media queries. The new design has full width header element, a full width nav element, and an 80% width centered div that contains the main element and footer element. You'll practice a Mobile First strategy for responsive design. First, you will configure a page layout that works well in smartphones (test with a small browser window). Then you'll resize the browser viewport to be larger until the design "breaks" and code media queries and additional CSS as needed. Figure 7.62 shows wireframes for three different layouts. The Home page displays will be similar to Figure 7.63.

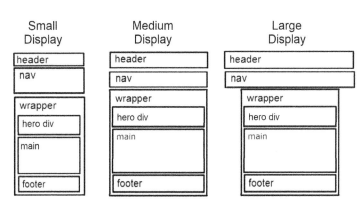

Figure 7.62 Pacific Trails Resort wireframes

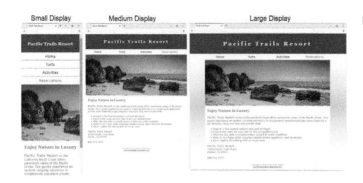

**Figure 7.63** The Home page

You have four tasks in this case study:

1. Create a new folder for the Pacific Trails Resort website.

2. Configure the HTML and CSS needed for pleasing display of a single-column (smartphone) display.

3. Configure the HTML and CSS needed for pleasing display of the web pages on medium sized mobile devices.

4. Configure the CSS needed for a pleasing display of the web pages on large mobile devices and desktops.

**Task 1:** Create a folder called pacific7 to contain your Pacific Trails Resort website files. Copy the files from the Chapter 6 Case Study pacific6 folder into the pacific7 folder.

**Task 2: Configure a Small Single-Column Layout.** First, you will edit the CSS. Then you will edit each web page and test in a browser.

**Configure the CSS.** Launch a text editor and open the pacific.css style sheet. Edit the styles to achieve a layout that displays well on small devices using normal flow (no floats) with full-width block elements.

1. Edit the styles for the body element selector. Set margin to 0. Change the background color to #90C7E3.

2. Edit the styles for the `wrapper` id selector. Remove the declarations for the background image, width, margin, and box-shadow.

3. Edit the styles for the header element selector. Remove the declaration for height. Set 1em padding.

4. Edit the styles for the h1 element selector. Set 1.5em font size. Remove the declarations for letter spacing and padding.

5. Edit the styles for the nav element selector. Remove the declarations that configure float, position, width, font-weight, and padding. Set centered text and white background color.

6. Edit the styles for the `nav ul` selector. Configure this selector as a flex container with `flex-direction` set to column. Set 0 margin and 0 left padding.

7. Code styles for the `nav li` selector. Set .5em top and bottom padding, 1em left and right padding, 100% width, and a 1px solid bottom border.

8. Edit the styles for the main element selector. Remove the style declarations for background color, margin, and overflow. Set 0 top and bottom padding. Set 1em left and right padding.

9. Edit styles for the section element selector. Remove the declarations for float and width. Set left and right padding to .5em.

10. Edit the styles for the `homehero`, `yurthero`, and `trailhero` id selectors. Remove margin-left declaration from each style rule. Set background-size property to 200% 100%, to cause the browser to display cropped versions of the images which will be more pleasing on a small viewport.

11. Edit the styles for the footer element selector. Remove the margin-left declaration.

12. Configure styles for the telephone number to display a hyperlink when on the small display and display plain text otherwise.
    a. Code a style rule for the `mobile` id selector. Set display to `inline`.
    b. Code a style rule for the `desktop` id selector. Set display to `none`.

Save your pacific.css file. Use the CSS validator (http://jigsaw.w3.org/css-validator) to check your syntax. Correct and retest if necessary.

**Configure the HTML.** Modify the pages as indicated.

1. Launch a text editor and open index.html. Complete the following edits and save the file.
   a. Using the wireframe in Figure 7.62 as a guide, move the opening div tag assigned to the `wrapper` id below the closing nav tag.
   b. The home page displays a phone number in the contact information area. Wouldn't it be handy if a person using a smartphone could click on the phone number to call the resort? You can make that happen by using tel: in a hyperlink. Configure a hyperlink assigned to an id named `mobile` that contains the phone number as shown:

   ```
   <a id="mobile" href="tel:888-555-5555">888-555-5555</a>
   ```

   But wait a minute, a telephone link could confuse those visiting the site with a desktop browser. Code another phone number directly after the hyperlink. Code a span element assigned to an id named `desktop` around the phone number as shown:

   ```
   <span id="desktop">888-555-5555</span>
   ```

   c. Code a viewport meta tag in the head section that configures the width to the device-width and sets the initial-scale to 1.0.

2. Launch a text editor and open yurts.html. Using the wireframe in Figure 7.62 as a guide, move the opening div tag assigned to the `wrapper` id below the closing nav tag. Add a viewport meta tag to head section in the same manner as the Home page. Save the file.

3. Launch a text editor and open activities.html. Using the wireframe in Figure 7.62 as a guide, move the opening div tag assigned to the `wrapper` id below the closing nav tag. Add a viewport meta tag to head section in the same manner as the Home page. Save the file.

**Test the web pages.** Display your index.html file in a browser. This layout is intended for narrow mobile screens. Resize your browser to be narrower until your display is similar to the Small Display shown in Figure 7.63, which simulates mobile display. Test the yurts.html and activities.html files in a similar manner.

**Task 3: Configure a Medium Layout.** Edit the CSS and web pages to configure a more pleasing display on a wider viewport, setting 600px as the breakpoint for the first media query. You will configure flexbox layout for two areas: the main navigation and the columns of information on the content pages. When you test your web pages and trigger the media query, the layout in the Medium Display wireframe in Figure 7.62 will be implemented and your pages should look similar to the Medium Display in Figures 7.63, 7.64, and 7.65.

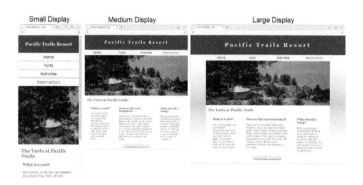

Figure 7.64　The Yurts page

Figure 7.65　The Activities page

**Configure the CSS.** Launch a text editor and open the pacific.css style sheet. Place your cursor below the existing styles. Configure a media query that is triggered when the minimum width is 600px or greater. Code the following styles within the media query.

1. Code styles for the h1 element selector. Set font-size to 2em and letter-spacing to .25em.

2. Code styles for the `nav ul` selector. Configure a flex container. The flex direction is row without wrapping. Set `justify-content` to `space-around`. Configure 2em padding on the right.

3. Code styles for the `nav li` selector. Set width to 12em. Set the bottom border to `none`.

4. Code styles for the section element selector. Set 2em left and right padding.

5. Code styles for the `flow` id selector. Configure a flex container. The flex direction is `row`.

6. Code styles for the `mobile` id selector. Set display to `none`.

7. Code styles for the `desktop` id selector. Set display to `inline`.

8. Code styles for the `homehero`, `yurthero`, and `trailhero` id selectors. Set background-size to 100% 100%.

Save your pacific.css file. Use the CSS validator (http://jigsaw.w3.org/css-validator) to check your syntax. Correct and retest if necessary.

**Configure the HTML.** You need to rework the content area on the Yurts and Activities pages.

1. Launch a text editor and open yurts.html. Code a div assigned to an id named `flow` that contains all section elements. Save the file.

2. Launch a text editor and open activities.html. Code a div assigned to an id named `flow` that contains all section elements. Save the file.

**Test the web pages.** Display your index.html file in a browser. You should be able to resize your browser viewport and obtain a display similar to the Medium Display in Figure 7.63. Test the yurts.html and activities.html files in a similar manner.

**Task 4: Configure a Large Layout.** Edit the CSS to configure a second media query with a 1024px breakpoint. When you test your web pages and trigger the media query, the layout in the Large Display wireframe in Figure 7.62 will be implemented and your pages should look similar to the Large Display in Figures 7.63, 7.64, and 7.65.

**Configure the CSS.** Launch a text editor and open the pacific.css style sheet. Place your cursor below the existing styles. Configure a media query that is triggered when the minimum width is 1024px or greater. Code the following styles within the media query.

1. Code styles for the body element selector. Configure a linear gradient as the background image that displays the color white for 20% of the viewport height, transitions to light blue, and transitions back to white. The CSS for the linear gradient follows:

   ```
   linear-gradient(to bottom, #FFFFFF 20%, #90C7E3 60%, #FFFFFF 100%);
   ```

2. Code styles for the `nav ul` selector. Set 10% right and left padding.

3. Code styles for the `#wrapper` id selector. Set the area to be horizontally centered (hint: `margin: auto;`) with 80% width.

Save your pacific.css file. Use the CSS validator (http://jigsaw.w3.org/css-validator) to check your syntax. Correct and retest if necessary.

**Test the web pages.** Display your index.html file in a browser. You should be able to resize your browser viewport and obtain a display similar to the Large Display in Figure 7.62. Test the yurts.html and activities.html files in a similar manner

You have accomplished a great deal as you completed this case study. The design is now responsive, utilizes CSS Flexbox, and displays well on devices with various size viewports. Pacific Trails Resort is responsive and mobile!

## Path of Light Yoga Studio Case Study

In this chapter's case study, you will use the existing Path of Light Yoga Studio (Chapter 6) website as a starting point to create a new responsive version of the website that utilizes media queries. The new design has a full width nav element, full width header element, and an 80% width centered div that contains the main element and footer element. The header area for the home page will be larger than the header area for the content pages. You'll practice a Mobile First strategy for responsive design. First, you will configure a page layout that works well in smartphones (test with a small browser window). Then you'll resize the browser viewport to be larger until the design "breaks" and code media queries and additional CSS as appropriate using flexbox layout for the navigation area. Figure 7.66 shows wireframes for three different layouts. The Home page displays will be similar to Figure 7.67.

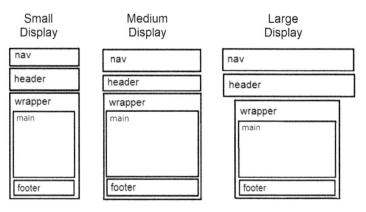

Figure 7.66  Path of Light Yoga Studio wireframes

Figure 7.67  The Home Page

You have four tasks in this case study:

1. Create a new folder for the Path of Light Yoga Studio website.

2. Configure the HTML and CSS needed for pleasing display of a single-column (smartphone) display.

3. Configure the HTML and CSS needed for pleasing display of the web pages on medium sized mobile devices.

4. Configure the CSS needed for a pleasing display of the web pages on large mobile devices and desktops.

**Task 1:** Create a folder called yoga7 to contain your Path of Light Yoga Studio website files. Copy the files from the Chapter 6 Case Study yoga6 folder into the yoga7 folder. Copy the sunrise.jpg file from the chapter7/starters/yoga folder.

**Task 2: Configure a Small Single-Column Layout.** First, you will edit the CSS. Then you will edit each web page and test in a browser.

**Configure the CSS.** Launch a text editor and open the yoga.css style sheet. Edit the styles to achieve a layout that displays well on small devices using normal flow (no floats) with full-width block elements.

1. Edit the styles for the body element selector. Set margin to 0.

2. Edit the styles for the `wrapper` id selector. Remove all declarations associated with width and margin. Configure 2em padding.

3. Edit the styles for the header element selector. Change the background image to sunrise.jpg. Change the background color to #40407A. Remove the background-position, background-repeat, and height declarations. Set background-size to 100% 100%, text color to white, font size to 90%, top margin to 50px, and minimum height to 200px.

4. Edit the styles for hyperlinks in the header area. Change the text color to #FFF for both unvisited and visited hyperlinks. Set the `header a:hover` selector's text color to #EDF5F5.

5. Code styles for a `home` class selector and a `content` class selector. Both selectors will start with the same property values. Set the height to 20vh (20% of the viewport height), top padding to 2em, left padding to 10%.

6. Edit the styles for the nav element selector. Remove the styles that configure float and bold text. Set width to 100%, and padding-top to 0.5em. The navigation will be fixed at the top of the viewport. Set position to fixed, top to 0 and left to 0. Also set right-aligned text, white background color, 0 margin, 0 right padding, and 9999 z-index.

7. Edit the styles for the `nav ul` selector. Remove the declaration for left padding. Configure this selector as a flex container which has rows that wrap. Set 0 margin, 1.2em font size.

8. Code styles for the `nav li` selector. Set 40% width, 0 top and bottom padding, 1em left and right padding, and inline display.

9. Edit the styles for the `nav a` selector. Remove the style declarations for text alignment, border, padding, and margin.

10. Edit the styles for `nav a:hover` selector. Remove the declaration that sets the border.

11. Remove the style declarations for the main element selector, h1 element selector, `onethird` class selector, `onehalf` class selector, `clear` class selector, `floatleft` class selector and `hero` id selector.

12. The hero images will be treated differently in this new version of the website. The home page will not display the hero image. The content pages will only display hero images on medium and larger viewports.
    a. Code styles for the `mathero` id selector. Set the background image to yogamat.jpg with no repeats. Configure 300px height. Set background-size to cover. Set display to `none`.
    b. Code styles for the `loungehero` id selector. Set the background image to yogalounge.jpg with no repeats. Configure 300px height. Set background-size to cover. Set display to `none`.

13. Code styles for the section element selector. Set left and right padding to .5em.

14. Edit the styles for the footer element selector. Remove the styles for background color, and padding.

**15.** Configure styles for the telephone number to display a hyperlink when on the small display and display plain text otherwise.

  a. Code a style rule for the `mobile` id selector. Set display to `inline`.

  b. Code a style rule for the `desktop` id selector. Set display to `none`.

Save your yoga.css file. Use the CSS validator (http://jigsaw.w3.org/css-validator) to check your syntax. Correct and retest if necessary.

**Configure the HTML.** Modify areas on the pages as indicated.

**1.** Launch a text editor and open index.html. Complete the following edits and save the file.

  a. Using the wireframe in Figure 7.66 as a guide, move the opening div tag assigned to the `wrapper` id above the opening main tag. Remove the img tag. Assign the header element to the class named `home`.

  b. The home page displays a phone number in the contact information area. Wouldn't it be handy if a person using a smartphone could click on the phone number to call the resort? You can make that happen by using tel: in a hyperlink. Configure a hyperlink assigned to an id named `mobile` that contains the phone number as shown:

```
<a id="mobile" href="tel:888-555-5555">888-555-5555</a>
```

  But wait a minute, a telephone link could confuse those visiting the site with a desktop browser. Code another phone number directly after the hyperlink. Code a span element assigned to an id named `desktop` around the phone number as shown:

```
<span id="desktop">888-555-5555</span>
```

  c. Code a viewport meta tag in the head section that configures the width to the device-width and sets the initial-scale to 1.0.

**2.** Launch a text editor and open classes.html. Code a viewport meta tag in the head section in the same manner as the Home page. Use the wireframe in Figure 7.66 as a guide, and move the opening div tag assigned to the `wrapper` id above the opening main tag. Assign the header element to the class named `content`. Locate the div assigned to the `hero` id. Replace the value `hero` with `mathero`. Remove the img tag. Save the file.

**3.** Launch a text editor and open schedule.html. Code a viewport meta tag in the head section in the same manner as the Home page. Use the wireframe in Figure 7.66 as a guide and move the opening div tag assigned to the `wrapper` id above the opening main tag. Assign the header element to the class named `content`. Locate the div assigned to the `hero` id. Replace the value `hero` with `loungehero`. Remove the img tag. Save the file.

**Test the web pages.** Display your index.html file in a browser. This layout is intended for narrow mobile screens. Resize your browser to be narrower until your display is similar to the Small Display shown in Figure 7.66, which simulates mobile display. Test the classes.html and schedule.html files in a similar manner.

**Task 3: Configure a Medium Layout.** Edit the CSS and web pages to configure a more pleasing display on a wider viewport, setting 600px as the breakpoint for the first media query.

You will configure flexbox layout for two areas: the main navigation and the columns of information on the content pages. When you test your web pages and trigger the media query, the layout in the Medium Display wireframe in Figure 7.66 will be implemented and your pages should look similar to the Medium Display in Figures 7.67, 7.68, and 7.69.

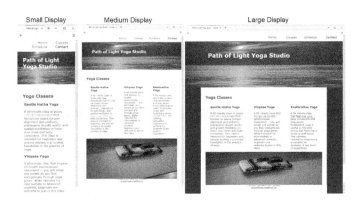

Figure 7.68 The Classes page

Figure 7.69 The Schedule page

**Configure the CSS.** Launch a text editor and open the yoga.css style sheet. Place your cursor below the existing styles. Configure a media query that is triggered when the minimum width is 600px or greater. Code the following styles within the media query.

1. Code styles for the `nav ul` selector. Configure the flex container with rows that do not wrap. Also set `justify- content` to `flex-end`.

2. Code styles for the `nav li` selector. Set width to 7em.

3. Code styles for the section element selector. Set 2em left and right padding.

4. The hero images will display on medium and large displays. Code styles for the `mathero` and `loungehero` id selectors. Set display to `block` with 1em bottom padding.

5. Code styles for the `flow` id selector. Configure a flex container. The flex direction is `row`.

6. Code styles for the `mobile` id selector. Set display to `none`.

7. Code styles for the `desktop` id selector. Set display to `inline`.

Save your yoga.css file. Use the CSS validator (http://jigsaw.w3.org/css-validator) to check your syntax. Correct and retest if necessary.

**Configure the HTML.** You need to rework the content area on the Classes and Schedule pages.

1. Launch a text editor and open classes.html. Locate the section elements and remove the class="onethird" code from each. Code a div assigned to an id named `flow` that contains all section elements. Save the file.

2. Launch a text editor and open schedule.html. Locate the section elements and remove the class="onehalf" code from each. Code a div assigned to an id named `flow` that contains both section elements. Save the file.

**Test the web pages**. Display your index.html file in a browser. You should be able to resize your browser viewport and obtain a display similar to the Medium Display in Figure 7.66. Text the classes.html and schedule.html files in a similar manner.

**Task 4: Configure a Large Layout.** Edit the CSS and web pages to configure a second media query with a 1024px breakpoint. When you test your web pages and trigger the media query, the layout in the Large Display wireframe in Figure 7.66 will be implemented and your pages should look similar to the Large Display in Figures 7.67, 7.68, and 7.69.

**Configure the CSS**. Launch a text editor and open the yoga.css style sheet. Place your cursor below the existing styles. Configure a media query that is triggered when the minimum width is 1024px or greater. Code the following styles within the media query.

1. Code styles for the header element selector. Set font size to 120%.

2. Configure styles for the `home` class selector. Set the height to 50% of the viewport height (50vh), 5em top padding, and 8em left padding.

3. Code styles for the `content` class selector. Set the height to 30% of the viewport height (30vh), 1em top padding and 8em left padding.

4. Code styles for the `wrapper` id selector. Set the area to be horizontally centered (hint: margin: auto;) with 80% width.

Save your yoga.css file. Use the CSS validator (http://jigsaw.w3.org/css-validator) to check your syntax. Correct and retest if necessary.

**Test the web pages.** Display your index.html file in a browser. You should be able to resize your browser viewport and obtain a display similar to the Large Display in Figure 7.67. Test the schedule.html and classes.html files in a similar manner

You have accomplished a great deal as you completed this case study. The design is now responsive, utilizes CSS Flexbox, and displays well on devices with various size viewports. Path of Light Yoga Studio is responsive and mobile!

# Tables

**In this chapter** you'll become familiar with coding HTML tables to organize information on a web page.

# 8.1  Table Overview

**VideoNote**
**Configure a Table**

The purpose of a table is to organize information. In the past, before CSS was well supported by browsers, tables were also used to format web page layouts. An HTML table is composed of rows and columns, like a spreadsheet. Each individual table `cell` is at the intersection of a specific row and column.

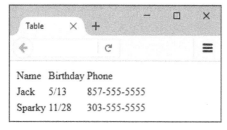

**Figure 8.1** Table with three rows and three columns

- Each table begins with a `<table>` tag and ends with a `</table>` tag.
- Each table row begins with a `<tr>` tag and ends with a `</tr>` tag.
- Each cell (table data) begins with a `<td>` tag and ends with a `</td>` tag.
- Table cells can contain text, graphics, and other HTML elements.

Figure 8.1 shows a sample table with three rows and three columns. The sample HTML for this table is

```
<table>
  <tr>
    <td>Name</td>
    <td>Birthday</td>
    <td>Phone</td>
  </tr>
  <tr>
    <td>Jack</td>
    <td>5/13</td>
    <td>857-555-5555</td>
  </tr>
  <tr>
    <td>Sparky</td>
    <td>11/28</td>
    <td>303-555-5555</td>
  </tr>
</table>
```

Notice how the table is coded row by row. Also, each row is coded cell by cell. This attention to detail is crucial for the successful use of tables. An example can be found in the student files (chapter8/table1.html).

## Table Element

A **table element** is a block display element that contains tabular information. The table begins with a **`<table>`** tag and ends with a **`</table>`** tag. See Table 8.1 for common attributes of the table element. Notice that most of the attributes listed in Table 8.1 are obsolete in HTML5 and should be avoided. Although these attributes are obsolete in HTML5, as you work with the Web you'll see many web pages coded with earlier versions of HTML and it is useful to be aware of even obsolete attributes. Modern web developers prefer to configure the style of tables with CSS properties instead of with HTML attributes.

Table 8.1 Table element attributes

| Attribute | Value | Purpose |
|---|---|---|
| align | left (default), right, center | Horizontal alignment of the table (obsolete in HTML5) |
| bgcolor | Valid color value | Background color of the table (obsolete in HTML5) |
| border | (default; indicates no visible border)<br>Integer value (1-100) indicating pixel width of border | Describes the table border (obsolete in HTML5) |
| cellpadding | Numeric value | Specifies the number of pixels of padding between the content of a table cell and its border (obsolete in HTML5) |
| cellspacing | Numeric value | Specifies the number of pixels of space between the borders of each cell in a table (obsolete in HTML5) |
| summary | Text description | Provides accessibility with a text description that gives an overview of and the context for the information in the table (obsolete in HTML5) |
| title | Text description | A brief text description that provides an overview of the table; may be displayed by some browsers as a tooltip |
| width | Numeric value or percentage | Specifies the width of the table (obsolete in HTML5) |

## The Border Attribute

In earlier versions of HTML (such as HTML4 and XHTML), the purpose of the border attribute was to indicate the presence and the width of a visible table border. The border attribute is obsolete in HTML5. Configure CSS to style the border of a table. The following CSS configures a border around a table and around each table cell:

```
table, td, th { border: 1px solid #000; }
```

## Table Captions

The **caption element** is often used with a table to describe its contents. The caption begins with a **<caption>** tag and ends with a </caption> tag. The text contained within the caption element displays on the web page above the table, although you'll see later in the chapter that you can configure the placement with CSS. The table shown in Figure 8.2 uses the caption element to set the table caption to "Bird Sightings". Notice that the caption element is coded on the line immediately after the opening <table> tag. An example can be found in the student files (chapter8/table2.html). The HTML for the table is

Figure 8.2 The caption for this table is "Bird Sightings"

```
<table>
<caption>Bird Sightings</caption>
   <tr>
   <td>Name</td>
   <td>Date</td>
  </tr>
  <tr>
   <td>Bobolink</td>
   <td>5/25/20</td>
  </tr>
  <tr>
   <td>Upland Sandpiper</td>
   <td>6/03/20</td>
  </tr>
</table>
```

# 8.2  Table Rows, Cells, and Headers

## Table Row Element

The **table row element** configures a row within a table on a web page. The table row begins with a **`<tr>`** tag and ends with a `</tr>` tag. Table 8.2 shows obsolete attributes of the table row element. Web pages coded with older versions of HTML may use these obsolete attributes. Modern web developers configure alignment and background color with CSS instead of with HTML.

Table 8.2  Obsolete attributes of the table row element

| Attribute | Value | Purpose |
|---|---|---|
| align | left (default), right, center | Horizontal alignment of the table (obsolete in HTML5) |
| bgcolor | Valid color value | Background color of the table (obsolete in HTML5) |

## Table Data Element

The **table data element** configures a cell within a row in a table on a web page. The table cell begins with a **`<td>`** tag and ends with a `</td>` tag. See Table 8.3 for attributes of the table data cell element. Some attributes are obsolete and should be avoided. You'll explore configuring table styles with CSS later in the chapter.

Table 8.3  Attributes of the table data and table header cell elements

| Attribute | Value | Purpose |
|---|---|---|
| align | left (default), right, center | Horizontal alignment of the table (obsolete in HTML5) |
| bgcolor | Valid color value | Background color of the table (obsolete in HTML5) |
| colspan | Numeric value | The number of columns spanned by a cell |
| headers | The id value(s) of a column or row header cell | Associates the table data cells with table header cells; may be accessed by screen readers |
| height | Numeric value or percentage | Height of the cell (obsolete in HTML5) |
| rowspan | Numeric value | The number of rows spanned by a cell |
| scope | row, col | The scope of the table header cell contents (row or column); may be accessed by screen readers |
| valign | top, middle (default), bottom | The vertical alignment of the contents of the cell (obsolete in HTML5) |
| width | Numeric value or percentage | Width of the cell (obsolete in HTML5) |

## Table Header Element

The **table header element** is similar to a table data element and configures a cell within a row in a table on a web page. Its purpose is to configure column and row headings. Text displayed within a table header element is centered and bold. The table header element begins with a **`<th>`** tag and ends with a `</th>` tag. See Table 8.3 for common attributes of the table header element. Figure 8.3 shows a table with column headings configured

| Name | Birthday | Phone |
|---|---|---|
| Jack | 5/13 | 857-555-5555 |
| Sparky | 11/28 | 303-555-5555 |

Figure 8.3  Using `<th>` tags to indicate column headings

by `<th>` tags. The HTML for the table shown in Figure 8.3 is as follows (also see chapter8/table3.html in the student files). Notice that the first row uses `<th>` instead of `<td>` tags.

```
<table>
  <tr>
    <th>Name</th>
    <th>Birthday</th>
    <th>Phone</th>
  </tr>
  <tr>
    <td>Jack</td>
    <td>5/13</td>
    <td>857-555-5555</td>
  </tr>
  <tr>
    <td>Sparky</td>
    <td>11/28</td>
    <td>303-555-5555</td>
  </tr>
</table>
```

## Hands-On Practice 8.1

In this Hands-On Practice, you will create a web page similar to Figure 8.4 that describes two schools you have attended. Use the caption "School History Table." The table has three rows and three columns. The first row will have table header elements with the headings School Attended, Years, and Degree Awarded. You will complete the second and third rows with your own information within table data elements.

To get started, launch a text editor and open chapter8/template.html in the student files. Save the file as mytable.html. Modify the title element. Use table, table row, table header, table data, and caption elements to configure a table similar to Figure 8.4.

Figure 8.4 School History Table

| School Attended | Years | Degree Awarded |
|---|---|---|
| Schaumburg High School | 2015—2019 | High School Diploma |
| Harper College | 2019—2020 | Web Developer Certificate |

School History Table

Hints:
- The table has three rows and three columns.
- Use the table header element for the cells in the first row.
- Configure the table and cell borders with embedded CSS in the head section of the web page:

```
<style>
table, td, th  { border: 1px solid #000; }
</style>
```

Save your file and display it in a browser. A sample solution is found in the student files (chapter8/8.1/index.html).

# 8.3 Span Rows and Columns

You can alter the gridlike look of a table by applying the colspan and rowspan attributes to table data or table header elements. As you get into more complex table configurations like these, be sure to sketch the table on paper before you start typing the HTML.

## The Colspan Attribute

| This spans two columns ||
|----------|----------|
| Column 1 | Column 2 |

**Figure 8.5** Table with a row that spans two columns

The **colspan attribute** specifies the number of columns that a cell will occupy. Figure 8.5 shows a table cell that spans two columns.

The HTML for the table is

```
<table>
  <tr>
    <td colspan="2">This spans two columns</td>
  </tr>
  <tr>
    <td>Column 1</td>
    <td>Column 2</td>
  </tr>
</table>
```

## The Rowspan Attribute

| This spans two rows | Row 1 Column 2 |
|---------------------|----------------|
|                     | Row 2 Column 2 |

**Figure 8.6** Table with a column that spans two rows

The **rowspan attribute** specifies the number of rows that a cell will occupy. An example of a table cell that spans two rows is shown in Figure 8.6.

The HTML for the table is

```
<table>
  <tr>
    <td rowspan="2">This spans two rows</td>
    <td>Row 1 Column 2</td>
  </tr>
  <tr>
    <td>Row 2 Column 2</td>
  </tr>
</table>
```

An example of the tables in Figures 8.5 and 8.6 can be found in the student files (chapter8/table4.html).

# Hands-On Practice 8.2

You will practice with the `rowspan` attribute in this Hands-On Practice. To create the web page shown in Figure 8.7, launch a text editor and open chapter8/template.html in the student files. Save the file as myrowspan.html. Modify the title element. Use table, table row, table head, and table data elements to configure the table.

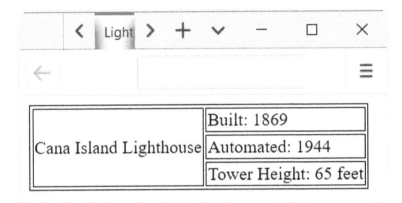

Figure 8.7 Practice with the `rowspan` attribute

1. Code the opening `<table>` tag

2. Begin the first row with a `<tr>` tag.

3. The table data cell with "Cana Island Lighthouse" spans three rows. Code a table data element. Use the `rowspan="3"` attribute.

4. Code a table data element that contains the text "Built: 1869".

5. End the first row with a `</tr>` tag.

6. Begin the second row with a `<tr>` tag. This row will only have one table data element because the cell in the first column is already reserved for "Cana Island Lighthouse".

7. Code a table data element that contains the text "Automated: 1944".

8. End the second row with a `</tr>` tag.

9. Begin the third row with a `<tr>` tag. This row will only have one table data element because the cell in the first column is already reserved for "Cana Island Lighthouse".

10. Code a table data element that contains the text "Tower Height: 65 feet".

11. End the third row with a `</tr>` tag.

12. Code the closing `</table>` tag.

13. Configure the table and cell borders with embedded CSS in the head section of the web page:

```
<style>
table, td, th { border: 1px solid #000; }
</style>
```

Save the file and view it in a browser. A sample solution is found in the student files (chapter8/8.2/index.html). Notice how the "Cana Island Lighthouse" text is vertically aligned in the middle of the cell, which is the default vertical alignment. You can modify the vertical alignment using CSS—see section "8.5 Style a Table with CSS" later in this chapter.

# 8.4 Configure an Accessible Table

**Focus on Accessibility**

Tables can be useful to organize information on a web page, but what if you couldn't see the table and were relying on assistive technology like a screen reader to read the table to you? You'd hear the contents of the table just the way it is coded—row by row, cell by cell. This might be difficult to understand. This section discusses coding techniques to improve the accessibility of tables.

For a simple informational data table like the one shown in Figure 8.8, the W3C Web Accessibility Initiative (WAI) Web Content Accessibility Guidelines 2.0 (WCAG 2.0) recommend the following:

- Use table header elements (`<th>` tags) to indicate column or row headings.
- Use the caption element to provide a text title or caption for the table.

## Bird Sightings

| Name | Date |
|------|------|
| Bobolink | 5/25/20 |
| Upland Sandpiper | 6/03/20 |

**Figure 8.8** This simple data table uses `<th>` tags and the caption element to provide accessibility

An example web page is in the student files (chapter8/table5.html). The HTML is

```
<table>
<caption>Bird Sightings</caption>
  <tr>
    <th>Name</th>
    <th>Date</th>
  </tr>
  <tr>
    <td>Bobolink</td>
    <td>5/25/20</td>
  </tr>
  <tr>
    <td>Upland Sandpiper</td>
    <td>6/03/20</td>
  </tr>
</table>
```

However, for more complex tables, the W3C recommends specifically associating the table data cell values with their corresponding headers. The technique that is recommended uses the id attribute (usually in a `<th>` tag) to identify a specific header cell and the **headers attribute** in a `<td>` tag. The code to configure the table in Figure 8.8 using headers and ids is as follows (also see chapter8/table6.html in the student files):

```
<table>
<caption>Bird Sightings</caption>
  <tr>
    <th id="name">Name</th>
    <th id="date">Date</th>
  </tr>
  <tr>
    <td headers="name">Bobolink</td>
    <td headers="date">5/25/20</td>
  </tr>
```

```
  <tr>
    <td headers="name">Upland Sandpiper</td>
    <td headers="date">6/03/20</td>
  </tr>
</table>
```

**Focus on Accessibility**

**FAQ**   **What about the scope attribute?**

The **scope attribute** specifies the association of table cells and table row or column headers.

It is used to indicate whether a table cell is a header for a column (scope="col") or row (scope="row"). An example of the code for the table in Figure 8.8 that uses this attribute is as follows (also see chapter8/table7.html in the student files):

```
<table>
<caption>Bird Sightings</caption>
    <tr>
        <th scope="col">Name</th>
        <th scope="col">Date</th>
    </tr>
    <tr>
        <td>Bobolink</td>
        <td>5/25/20</td>
    </tr>
    <tr>
        <td>Upland Sandpiper</td>
        <td>6/03/20</td>
    </tr>
</table>
```

As you reviewed the code sample in the previous page, you may have noticed that using the scope attribute to provide accessibility requires less coding than implementing the headers and id attributes. However, because of inconsistent screen reader support of the scope attribute, the WCAG recommendations for coding techniques encourage the use of headers and id attributes rather than the scope attribute.

## Checkpoint 8.1

**1.** What is the purpose of using a table on a web page?

**2.** How is the text contained within a th element displayed by the browser?

**3.** Describe one coding technique that increases the accessibility of an HTML table.

# 8.5 Style a Table with CSS

Before CSS was well supported by browsers, it was common practice to configure the visual aesthetic of a table with HTML attributes. The modern approach is to use CSS to style a table. In this section, you'll explore using CSS to style the border, padding, alignment, width, height, vertical alignment, and background of table elements. Table 8.4 lists corresponding CSS properties with the HTML attributes used to style tables.

Table 8.4 CSS properties used to style tables

| HTML Attribute | CSS Property |
|---|---|
| align | To align a table, configure the width and margin properties for the table selector. For example, to center a table with a width of 75% of the container element, use<br><br>`table { width: 75%;`<br>`         margin: auto; }`<br><br>To align items within table cells, use `text-align` |
| width | width |
| height | height |
| cellpadding | padding |
| cellspacing | **border-spacing**; a numeric value (px or em) or percentage. If you set a value to 0, omit the unit. One numeric value with unit (px or em) configures both horizontal and vertical spacing. Two numeric values with unit (px or em): The first value configures the horizontal spacing and the second value configures the vertical spacing.<br><br>**border-collapse** configures the border area. The values are separate (default) and collapse. Use border-collapse: collapse; to remove extra space between table and table cell borders. |
| bgcolor | background-color |
| valign | **vertical-align** specifies the vertical placement of content. The values are numeric pixel or percentage, baseline (default), sub (subscript), super (superscript), top, text-top, middle, bottom, and text-bottom |
| border | border, border-style, border-spacing |
| none | background-image |
| none | **caption-side** specifies the placement of the caption. Values are top (default) and bottom |

## Hands-On Practice 8.3

In this Hands-On Practice, you will code CSS style rules to configure an informational table on a web page. Create a folder named ch8table. Copy the starter.html file from the chapter8 folder to your ch8table folder. We'll use embedded styles for ease of editing and testing your page. Open the starter.html file in a browser. The display should look similar to the one shown in Figure 8.9.

Lighthouse Island Bistro Specialty Coffee Menu

| Specialty Coffee | Description | Price |
|---|---|---|
| Lite Latte | Indulge in a shot of espresso with steamed, skim milk. | $3.50 |
| Mocha Latte | Choose dark or mile chocolate with steamed milk. | $4.00 |
| MCP Latte | A lucious mocha latte with caramel and pecan syrup. | $4.50 |

Figure 8.9 This table is configured with HTML

Launch a text editor and open starter.html from your ch8table folder. Locate the style tags in the head section. You will code embedded CSS in this Hands-On Practice. Place your cursor on the blank line between the style tags.

1. Configure the table element selector to be centered, have a dark blue, 5 pixel border, and have a width of 600px.

```
table { margin: auto;
        border: 5px solid #000066;
        width: 600px; }
```

Save the file as menu.html. Open your page in a browser. Notice that there is a border surrounding the entire table but not surrounding each table cell.

2. Configure the td and th element selectors with a border, padding, and Arial or the default sans-serif font typeface.

```
td, th { border: 1px solid #000066;
         padding: 0.5em;
         font-family: Arial, sans-serif; }
```

Save the file and open your page in a browser. Each table cell should now be outlined with a border and should display text in a sans-serif font.

3. Notice the empty space between the borders of the table cells. This empty space can be eliminated with the **border-spacing property**. Add a `border-spacing: 0;` declaration to the table element selector. Save the file and open your page in a browser to see the result.

4. Configure the caption to be displayed with Verdana or the default sans-serif font typeface, bold font weight, 1.2em font size, and 0.5em of bottom padding. Configure a style rule as follows:

```
caption { font-family: Verdana, sans-serif;
          font-weight: bold;
          font-size: 1.2em;
          padding-bottom: 0.5em; }
```

5. Let's experiment and configure background colors for the rows instead of cell borders. Modify the style rule for the td and th element selectors, remove the border declaration, and set `border-style` to none. The new style rule for the cells is

```
td, th { padding: 0.5em;
         border-style: none;
         font-family: Arial, sans-serif; }
```

6. Create a new class called `altrow` that sets a background color.
   `.altrow { background-color: #EAEAEA; }`

7. Modify the `<tr>` tags in the HTML. Assign the second and fourth `<tr>` tags to the `altrow` class. Save the file and open your page in a browser. The table area should look similar to the one shown in Figure 8.10.

**Lighthouse Island Bistro Specialty Coffee Menu**

| Specialty Coffee | Description | Price |
|---|---|---|
| Lite Latte | Indulge in a shot of espresso with steamed, skim milk. | $3.50 |
| Mocha Latte | Choose dark or mile chocolate with steamed milk. | $4.00 |
| MCP Latte | A lucious mocha latte with caramel and pecan syrup. | $4.50 |

Figure 8.10  Rows are configured with alternating background colors

Notice how the background color of the alternate rows adds subtle interest to the web page. In this Hands-On Practice, you configured the display of an HTML table using CSS. Compare your work with the sample in the student files (chapter8/8.3/index.html).

# 8.6  CSS Structural Pseudo-Classes

In the previous section, you configured CSS and applied a class to every other table row to configure alternating background colors, often referred to as "zebra striping." You may have found this to be a bit inconvenient and wondered if there was a more efficient method. Well, there is! CSS **structural pseudo-class selectors** allow you to select and apply styles to elements based on their position in the structure of the document, such as every other row. Table 8.5 lists common CSS structural pseudo-class selectors and their purpose.

Table 8.5  Common CSS structural pseudo-classes

| Pseudo-class | Purpose |
|---|---|
| `:first-of-type` | Applies to the first element of the specified type |
| `:first-child` | Applies to the first child of an element |
| `:last-of-type` | Applies to the last element of the specified type |
| `:last-child` | Applies to the last child of an element |
| `:nth-of-type(n)` | Applies to the "nth" element of the specified type<br>Values: a number, odd, or even |

To apply a pseudo-class, write it after the selector. The following code sample will configure the first item in an unordered list to display with red text.

```
li:first-of-type { color: #FF0000; }
```

## Hands-On Practice 8.4

In this Hands-On Practice, you will rework the table you configured in Hands-On Practice 8.3 to use structural pseudo-class selectors to configure color.

1. Launch a text editor and open menu.html in your ch8table folder (it can also be found as chapter8/8.3/index.html in the student files). Save the file as menu2.html.

2. View the source code and notice that the second and fourth tr elements are assigned to the `altrow` class. You won't need this class assignment when using CSS structural pseudo-class selectors. Delete `class="altrow"` from the tr elements.

3. Examine the embedded CSS and locate the `altrow` class. Change the selector to use a structural pseudo-class that will apply the style to the even-numbered table rows. Replace `.altrow` with `tr:nth-of-type(even)` as shown in the following CSS declaration:

```
tr:nth-of-type(even) { background-color: #eaeaea; }
```

4. Save the file and open your page in a browser. The table area should look similar to the one shown in Figure 8.10 if you are using a modern browser that supports structural pseudo-classes.

5. Let's configure the first row to have a dark blue background (#006) and light gray text (#EAEAEA) with the `:first-of-type` structural pseudo-class. Add the following to the embedded CSS:

```
tr:first-of-type { background-color: #006;
                   color: #EAEAEA; }
```

**6.** Save the file and open your page in a browser. The table area should look similar to the one shown in Figure 8.11 if you are using a modern browser that supports CSS structural pseudo-classes. A sample solution is available in the student files (chapter8/8.4/index.html).

**Lighthouse Island Bistro Specialty Coffee Menu**

| Specialty Coffee | Description | Price |
|---|---|---|
| Lite Latte | Indulge in a shot of espresso with steamed, skim milk. | $3.50 |
| Mocha Latte | Choose dark or mile chocolate with steamed milk. | $4.00 |
| MCP Latte | A lucious mocha latte with caramel and pecan syrup. | $4.50 |

Figure 8.11  CSS pseudo-class selectors style the table rows

## 8.7  Configure Table Sections

There are a lot of configuration options for coding tables. Table rows can be put together into three types of groups: table head with **<thead>**, table body with **<tbody>**, and table footer with **<tfoot>**.

Figure 8.12  CSS configures the thead, tbody, and tfoot element selectors

These groups can be useful when you need to configure the areas in the table in different ways, using either attributes or CSS. The `<tbody>` tag is required if you configure a `<thead>` or `<tfoot>` area, although you can omit either the table head or table footer if you like.

The following code sample (see chapter8/tfoot.html in the student files) configures the table shown in Figure 8.12 and demonstrates the use of CSS to configure a table head, table body, and table footer with different styles.

The CSS styles a centered 200-pixel-wide table with a caption that is rendered in large, bold font; a table head section with a light-gray (#EAEAEA) background color; a table body section styled with slightly smaller text (.90em) using Arial or sans-serif font; table body td element selectors set to display with some left padding and a dashed bottom border; and a table footer section that has centered, bold text and a light-gray background color (#eaeaea). The CSS code is

```
table { width: 200px;
        margin: auto; }
caption { font-size: 2em;
          font-weight: bold; }
thead { background-color: #EAEAEA; }
tbody { font-family: Arial, sans-serif;
        font-size: .90em; }
tbody td { border-bottom: 1px #000033 dashed;
           padding-left: 25px; }
tfoot { background-color: #EAEAEA;
        font-weight: bold;
        text-align: center; }
```

The HTML for the table is

```
<table>
<caption>Time Sheet</caption>
   <thead>
      <tr>
         <th id="day">Day</th>
         <th id="hours">Hours</th>
      </tr>
   </thead>
   <tbody>
      <tr>
         <td headers="day">Monday</td>
         <td headers="hours">4</td>
      </tr>
      <tr>
         <td headers="day">Tuesday</td>
         <td headers="hours">3</td>
      </tr>
      <tr>
         <td headers="day">Wednesday</td>
         <td headers="hours">5</td>
      </tr>
      <tr>
         <td headers="day">Thursday</td>
         <td headers="hours">3</td>
      </tr>
      <tr>
         <td headers="day">Friday</td>
         <td headers="hours">3</td>
      </tr>
   </tbody>
   <tfoot>
      <tr>
         <td headers="day">Total</td>
         <td headers="hours">18</td>
      </tr>
   </tfoot>
</table>
```

This example demonstrates the power of CSS in styling documents. The `<td>` tags within each table row group element selector (thead, tbody, and tfoot) inherited the font styles configured for their parent group element selector. Notice how a descendant selector configures the padding and border only for `<td>` tags that are contained within (actually, "children of") the `<tbody>` element. Sample code is located in the student files (chapter8/tfoot.html). Take a few moments to explore the web page code and open the page in a browser.

## Checkpoint 8.2

1. Describe a reason to configure a table with CSS properties instead of HTML attributes.

2. List three elements that are used to group table rows.

# Chapter Summary

This chapter introduces both the HTML techniques used to code tables to organize information and the CSS properties that configure the display of tables on web pages. Visit the textbook website at http://www.webdevfoundations.net for examples, the links listed in this chapter, and updated information.

## Key Terms

<caption>
<table>
<tbody>
<td>
<tfoot>
<th>
<thead>
<tr>
:first-child
:first-of-type
:last-child

:last-of-type
:nth of type
align attribute
border attribute
border-collapse property
border-spacing property
caption element
caption-side property
cell
cellpadding attribute
cellspacing attribute

colspan attribute
headers attribute
rowspan attribute
scope attribute
structural pseudo-class selectors
summary attribute
table element
table data element
table header element
table row element
vertical-align property

## Review Questions

### Multiple Choice

1. Which HTML tag pair is used to specify table headings?
   a. <td> </td>
   b. <th> </th>
   C. <head> </head>
   d. <tr> </tr>

2. Which CSS property specifies the background color of a table?
   a. background
   b. bgcolor
   C. background-color
   d. table-color

3. Which HTML tag pair is used to group rows in the footer of a table?
   a. <footer> </footer>
   b. <tr> </tr>
   C. <tfoot> </tfoot>
   d. <td> </td>

4. Which of the following describes the appearance of text within a th element?
   a. the text is centered
   b. the text is displayed one size larger
   c. the text has bold font weight
   d. the text has bold font weight and is centered

5. Which HTML attribute associates a table data cell with a table header cell?
   a. head
   b. align
   C. headers
   d. th

6. Which CSS property eliminates the space between the borders on table cells?
   a. border-style
   b. border-spacing
   C. padding
   d. cellspacing

7. Which HTML tag pair is used to begin and end a table row?
   a. <td> </td>
   b. <tbody> </tbody>
   C. <table> </table>
   d. <tr> </tr>

8. Which of the following is the intended use of tables on web pages?
   a. configuring the layout of an entire page
   b. organizing information
   c. forming hyperlinks
   d. configuring a resume

9. Which CSS property specifies the distance between the cell text and the cell border?

   a. `border-style`

   b. `padding`

   c. `border-spacing`

   d. `cellpadding`

10. Which CSS pseudo-class applies to the first element of a specified type?

    a. `:first-of-type`

    b. `:first-type`

    c. `:first-child`

    d. `:first`

## Fill in the Blank

11. The CSS _____ property can be used to configure the color and width of a table border.

12. The _____ CSS property specifies the vertical alignment of the contents of a cell in a table.

13. Use the _____ attribute to configure a table cell to occupy more than one row in the table.

14. _____ is an attribute of the td element that associates the table data cell with a table header cell.

15. Use the _____ element to provide a brief description of a table that displays on the web page.

## Apply Your Knowledge

1. **Predict the Result.** Draw and write a brief description of the web page that will be created with the following HTML code:

```
<!DOCTYPE html>
<html lang="en">
<head>
<title>Predict the Result</title>
<meta charset="utf-8">
</head>
<body>
<table>
    <tr>
        <th>Year</th>
        <th>School</th>
        <th>Major</th>
    </tr>
    <tr>
        <td>2014-2018</td>
        <td>Schaumburg High School</td>
        <td>College Prep</td>
    </tr>
    <tr>
        <td>2018-2020</td>
        <td>Harper College</td>
        <td>Web Development Associates Degree</td>
    </tr>
</table>
</body>
</html>
```

2. **Fill in the Missing Code.** This web page should have a table with a background color of #cccccc and a border. Some CSS properties and values, indicated by "\_", are missing. Fill in the missing code.

```
<!DOCTYPE html>
<html lang="en">
<head>
<title>CircleSoft Web Design</title>
<meta charset="utf-8">
<style>
table {  "_":"_";
        "_":"_"; }
</style>
</head>
<body>
<h1>CircleSoft Web Design</h1>
<table>
<caption>Contact Information</caption>
   <tr>
      <th>Name</th>
      <th>Phone</th>
   </tr>
   <tr>
      <td>Mike Circle</td>
      <td>920-555-5555</td>
   </tr>
</table>
</body>
</html>
```

3. **Find the Error.** Why doesn't the table information display in the order it was coded?

```
<!DOCTYPE html>
<html lang="en">
<head>
<title>CircleSoft Web Design</title>
<meta charset="utf-8">
</head>
<body>
<h1>CircleSoft Web Design</h1>
<table>
<caption>Contact Information</caption>
<tr>
   <th>Name</th>
   <th>Phone</th>
</tr>
<tr>
   <tr>Mike Circle</td>
   <td>920-555-5555</td>
</tr>
</table>
</body>
</html>
```

## Hands-On Exercises

1. Write the HTML for a two-column table that contains the names of your friends and their birthdays. The first row of the table should span two columns and contain the following heading: Birthday List. Include at least two people in your table.

2. Write the HTML for a three-column table to describe the courses you are taking this semester. The columns should contain the course number, course name, and instructor name. The first row of the table should use th tags and contain descriptive headings for the columns. Use the table row grouping tags `<thead>` and `<tbody>` in your table.

3. Write the HTML for a table with three rows, two columns, and no border. The cell in the first column of each row will contain the name of one of your favorite movies. The corresponding cell in the second column of each row will contain a description of the movie. Configure alternating rows to use the background color #CCCCCC.

4. Use CSS to configure a table that has a border around both the entire table and the table cells. Write the HTML to create a table with three rows and two columns. The cell in the first column of each row will contain the name of one of your favorite movies. The corresponding cell in the second column of each row will contain a description of the movie.

5. Modify the table you created in Hands-On Exercise 1 to be centered on the page, use a background color of #CCCC99, and display text in Arial or the browser default sans-serif font. Configure this table using CSS instead of obsolete HTML attributes. Place an e-mail link to yourself on the web page. Save the file as mytable.html.

6. Create a web page about your favorite sports team with a two-column table that lists the positions and starting players. Use embedded CSS to style the table border, background color, and center the table on the web page. Place an e-mail link to yourself on the web page. Save the file as sport8.html.

7. Create a web page about your favorite movie that uses a two-column table containing details about the movie. Use CSS to style the table border and background color. Include the following in the table:
   - Title of the movie
   - Director or producer
   - Leading actor
   - Leading actress
   - Rating (G, PG, PG-13, R, NC-17, NR)
   - A brief description of the movie
   - An absolute link to a review about the movie

   Place an e-mail link to yourself on the web page. Save the page as movie8.html.

8. Create a web page about your favorite music album that uses a four-column table. The column headings should be as follows:
   - **Group:** Place the name of the group and the names of its principal members in this column.
   - **Tracks:** List the title of each music track or song.
   - **Year:** List the year the album was recorded.
   - **Links:** Place at least two absolute links to sites about the group in this column.

   Include an e-mail link to yourself on the web page. Save the page as band8.html.

**9.** Create a web page about your favorite recipe. Organize the ingredients and directions in a single table. Use two columns for the ingredients. Use a row that spans two columns to contain the instructions for creating your culinary delight. Place an e-mail link to yourself on the web page. Save the page as recipe8.html.

## Web Research

Search the Web and find a web page configured with one or more HTML tables. Print the browser view of the page. Print out the source code of the web page. On the printout, highlight or circle the tags related to tables. On a separate sheet of paper, create some HTML notes by listing the tags and attributes related to tables found on your sample page, along with a brief description of their purpose. Hand in the browser view of the page, source code printout, and your HTML notes page to your instructor.

## Focus on Web Design

Good artists view and analyze many paintings. Good writers read and evaluate many books. Similarly, good web designers view and scrutinize many web pages. Search the Web and find two web pages, one that is appealing to you and one that is unappealing to you. Print out each page. Create a web page that answers the following questions for each of your examples:

a. What is the URL of the website?

b. Does this page use tables? If so, for what purpose (page layout, organization of information, or another reason)?

c. Does this page use CSS? If so, for what purpose (page layout, text and color configuration, or another reason)?

d. Is this page appealing or unappealing? List three reasons for your answer.

e. If this page is unappealing, what would you do to improve it?

# WEBSITE CASE STUDY

## Using Tables

Each of the following case studies continues throughout most of the textbook. This chapter incorporates an HTML table in the case study websites.

### JavaJam Coffee Bar

See Chapter 2 for an introduction to the JavaJam Coffee Bar case study. Figure 2.32 shows a site map for JavaJam. Use the Chapter 7 JavaJam website as a starting point for this case study. In this case study, you will modify the Menu page (menu.html) to display information in an HTML table. You will use CSS to style the table. You have three tasks in this case study:

1. Create a new folder for this JavaJam case study.

2. Modify the style sheet (javajam.css) to configure style rules for the new table.

3. Modify the Menu page to use a table to display information as shown in Figure 8.13.

Figure 8.13 Menu page with a table

## Hands-On Practice Case Study

**Task 1: The Website Folder.** Create a folder called javajam8. Copy all the files from your Chapter 7 javajam7 folder into the javajam8 folder.

**Task 2: Configure the CSS.** Modify the external style sheet (javajam.css). Open javajam.css in a text editor. Review Figure 8.13 and note the menu descriptions, which are coded in an HTML table. Add style rules above the media queries in the javajam.css external style sheet to configure a table that is centered, takes up 90% the width of its container, and is configured with 0 `border-spacing`. Configure td and th selectors with 10 pixels of padding. Also configure a background color of #D2B48E in alternate rows (use a class or the `:nth-of-type` pseudo-class to configure odd table rows). Save the javajam.css file.

**Task 3: Modify the Menu Page.** Open menu.html in a text editor. Each menu item consists of a title (within h3 tags) and a description (within p tags). You will format this information with a table that has three rows and two columns. Use th and td elements where appropriate. Delete the h3, p, and section tags that surround each menu item. Save your page and test it in a browser. If the page does not display as you intended, review your work, validate the CSS, validate the HTML, modify as needed, and test again.

## Fish Creek Animal Clinic

See Chapter 2 for an introduction to the Fish Creek Animal Clinic case study. Figure 2.36 shows a site map for Fish Creek. Use the Chapter 7 Fish Creek website as a starting point for this case study. You will modify the Services page (services.html) to display information in an HTML table. You will use CSS to style the table. You have three tasks in this case study:

1. Create a new folder for this Fish Creek case study.

2. Modify the style sheet (fishcreek.css) to configure style rules for the new table.

3. Modify the Services page to use a table to display information as shown in Figure 8.14.

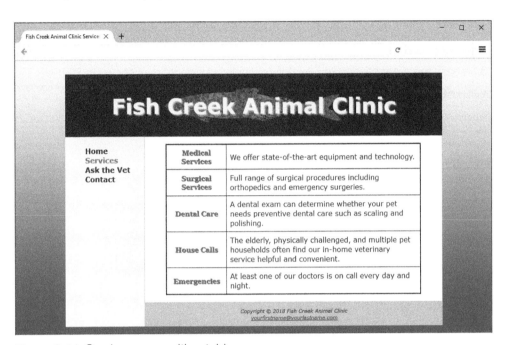

Figure 8.14  Services page with a table

## Hands-On Practice Case Study

**Task 1: The Website Folder.** Create a folder called fishcreek8. Copy all the files from your Chapter 7 fishcreek7 folder into the fishcreek8 folder.

**Task 2: Configure the CSS.** Modify the external style sheet (fishcreek.css). Open fishcreek.css in a text editor. Review Figure 8.14 and note the services descriptions, which are coded in an HTML table. Add style rules above the media queries in the fishcreek.css external style sheet as indicated:

1. Configure a table that has a 1em margin and a dark blue, 2 pixel border.

2. Configure the borders in the table to collapse (use `border-collapse: collapse;`).

3. Configure td and th element selectors with 0.5em of padding and a dark blue 1 pixel border.

Save the fishcreek.css file.

**Task 3: Modify the Services Page.** Open services.html in a text editor. Each service item consists of a title (within h3 tags) and a description (within p tags). You will format this information with a table that has five rows and two columns. Use th and td elements where appropriate. Delete the h3, p, and section tags that surround each service item. Save your page and test it in a browser. If the page does not display as you intended, review your work, validate the CSS, validate the HTML, modify as needed, and test again.

## Pacific Trails Resort

See Chapter 2 for an introduction to the Pacific Trails Resort case study. Figure 2.40 shows a site map for Pacific Trails. Use the Chapter 7 Pacific Trails website as a starting point for this case study. You will modify the Yurts page (yurts.html) to display additional information in an HTML table. You will use CSS to style the table. You have three tasks in this case study:

1. Create a new folder for this Pacific Trails case study.

2. Modify the style sheet (pacific.css) to configure style rules for the new table.

3. Modify the Yurts page to use a table to display information as shown in Figure 8.15.

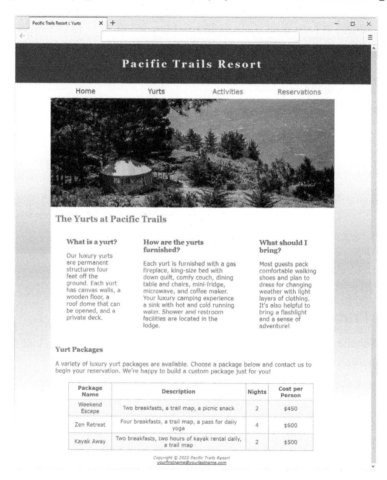

**Figure 8.15** Yurts page with a table

## Hands-On Practice Case Study

**Task 1: The Website Folder.** Create a folder called pacific8. Copy all the files from your Chapter 7 pacific7 folder into the pacific8 folder.

**Task 2: Configure the CSS.** Modify the external style sheet (pacific.css). Open pacific.css in a text editor. Add styles above the media queries to configure the table on the Yurts page as shown in Figure 8.15.

1. Configure the table. Code a new style rule for the table element selector that configures a centered table with a 1 pixel blue border (#3399CC) and 90% width.

Also configure the borders in the table to collapse (use `border-collapse: collapse;`).

2. Configure the table cells. Code a new style rule for the td and th element selectors that configure 5 pixels of padding and a 1 pixel blue border (#3399CC).

3. Center the td content. Code a new style rule for the td element selector that centers text (use `text-align: center;`).

4. Configure the `text` class. Notice that the content in the table data cells that contain the text description is not centered. Code a new style rule for a class named `text` that will override the td style rule and left-align the text (use `text-align: left;`).

5. Configure alternate-row background color. The table looks more appealing if the rows have alternate background colors, but it is still readable without them. Apply the `:nth-of-type` CSS pseudo-class to configure the even table rows with a light-blue background color (#DFEDF8).

6. Save the pacific.css file.

**Task 3: Modify the Yurts Page.**  Open yurts.html in a text editor.

1. Configure an h3 element with the following text: "Yurt Packages" above the closing main tag.

2. Below the new h3 element, configure a paragraph with the following text:

   A variety of luxury yurt packages are available. Choose a package below and contact us to begin your reservation. We're happy to build a custom package just for you!

3. You are ready to configure the table. Code a table below the paragraph with four rows and four columns. Use the table, th, and td elements. Assign the td elements that contain the detailed descriptions to the class named `text`. The content for the table is as follows.

| Package Name | Description | Nights | Cost per Person |
|---|---|---|---|
| Weekend Escape | Two breakfasts, a trail map, a picnic snack | 2 | $450 |
| Zen Retreat | Four breakfasts, a trail map, a pass for daily yoga | 4 | $600 |
| Kayak Away | Two breakfasts, two hours of kayak rental daily, a trail map | 2 | $500 |

Save your page and test it in a browser. If the page does not display as you intended, review your work, validate the CSS, validate the HTML, modify as needed, and test again.

## Path of Light Yoga Studio

See Chapter 2 for an introduction to the Path of Light Yoga Studio case study. Figure 2.44 shows a site map for Path of Light Yoga Studio. Use the Chapter 7 Path of Light Yoga Studio website as a starting point for this case study. You will modify the Schedule page (schedule.html) to display the class schedule in an HTML table. You will use CSS to style the table. You have three tasks in this case study:

1. Create a new folder for this Path of Light Yoga Studio case study.

2. Modify the style sheet (yoga.css) to configure style rules for the new table.

3. Modify the Schedule page to use a table to display information as shown in Figure 8.16.

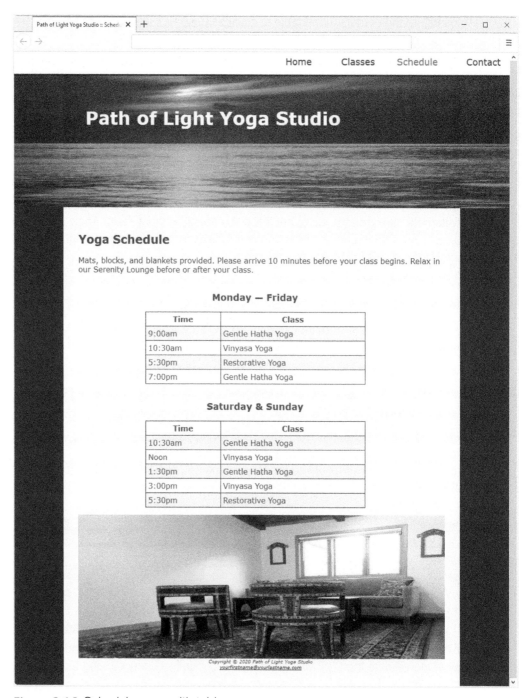

**Figure 8.16** Schedule page with tables

## Hands-On Practice Case Study

**Task 1: The Website Folder.** Create a folder called yoga8. Copy all the files from your Chapter 7 yoga7 folder into the yoga8 folder.

**Task 2: Configure the CSS.** Modify the external style sheet (yoga.css). Open yoga.css in a text editor. Review Figure 8.16 and note the class schedule information, which is coded in two HTML tables. Add style rules above the media queries in the yoga.css external style sheet to configure the following:

1. A centered table with 60% width, a 1 pixel purple (#3F2860) border, collapsed borders (use `border-collapse: collapse;`), and a 1em bottom margin.

2. A style for the td and th element selectors that configures 5 pixels of padding and a 1 pixel purple border (#3F2860).

3. Configure alternate-row background color. The table looks more appealing if the rows have alternate background colors, but it is still readable without them. Apply the :nth-of-type CSS pseudo-class to configure the even table rows with a #DBE8E9 background color.

4. A caption element selector with a 1em margin, bold text, and 120% font size.

Save the yoga.css file.

**Task 3: Modify the Schedule Page.** Open schedule.html in a text editor. You will rework the page to use two tables to display the schedule information instead of the section, h3, and unordered list tags. Remove the tags for the section elements, h3 elements, ul elements, li elements, and the div assigned to the `flow` id. Use a caption element within each table. Note that the table rows have two columns. Configure "Time" and "Class" table headings within each table. Refer to Figure 8.16.

Save your page and test it in a browser. If the page does not display as you intended, review your work, validate the CSS, validate the HTML, modify as needed, and test again.

# Web Project

See Chapters 5 and 6 for an introduction to the Web Project case study. You will modify the design of one of the pages to display information in an HTML table. Use CSS to style the table.

## Hands-On Practice Case Study

1. Choose one of your project web pages to modify. Sketch a design of the table you plan to create. Decide on borders, background color, padding, alignment, and so on.

2. Modify your project's external CSS file (project.css) to configure the table (and table cells) as needed.

3. Update your chosen web page and add the HTML code for a table.

Save and test the page. Modify both the web page and the project.css file as needed. Test and modify until you have achieved the look you want.

# Forms

## Chapter Objectives   In this chapter, you will learn how to . . .

- Describe common uses of forms on web pages

- Create forms on web pages using the form, input, textarea, and select elements

- Create forms that provide additional accessibility features using the accesskey and tabindex attributes

- Associate form controls and groups using the label, fieldset, and legend elements

- Create custom image buttons and use the button element

- Use the CSS float property to style a form

- Use CSS Grid Layout to style a form

- Configure form controls new to HTML5, including the e-mail address, URL, datalist, range, spinner, calendar, and color controls

- Describe the features and common uses of server-side processing

- Invoke server-side processing to handle form data

- Find free server-side processing resources on the Web

**Forms are used for many purposes all over the Web.** They are used by search engines to accept keywords and by online stores to process e-commerce shopping carts. Websites use forms to help with a variety of functions, including accepting visitor feedback, encouraging visitors to send a news story to a friend or colleague, collecting e-mail addresses for a newsletter, and accepting order information. This chapter introduces a very powerful tool for web developers—forms that accept information from web page visitors.

# 9.1 Overview of Forms

Every time you use a search engine, place an order, or join an online mailing list, you use a **form**. A form is an HTML element that contains and organizes objects called **form controls**, including text boxes, check boxes, and buttons, that can accept information from website visitors.

For example, you may have used Google's search form (https://www.google.com) many times but never thought about how it works. The form is quite simple; it contains just three form controls: the text box that accepts the keywords used in the search and two search buttons. The "Google Search" button submits the form and invokes a process to search the Google databases and display a results page. The whimsical "I'm Feeling Lucky" button submits the form and displays the top page for your keywords.

Figure 9.1 shows a form that is used to enter shipping information. This form contains text boxes to accept information such as name and address. Select lists (sometimes called drop-down boxes) are used to capture information with a limited number of correct values, such as state and country information.

Figure 9.1 This form accepts shipping information

When a visitor clicks the continue button, the form information is submitted and the ordering process continues.

Whether a form is used to search for web pages or to order a publication, the form alone cannot do all of the processing. The form needs to invoke a program or script on the web server in order to search a database or record an order. There are usually two components of a form:

1. The HTML form itself, which is the web page user interface

2. The server-side processing, which works with the form data and sends e-mail, writes to a text file, updates a database, or performs some other type of processing on the server

## Form Element

Now that you have a basic understanding of what forms do, let's focus on the HTML code to create a form. The **form element** contains a form on a web page. The **<form>** tag specifies the beginning of a form area. The closing `</form>` tag specifies the end of a form area. There can be multiple forms on a web page, but they cannot be nested inside one another. The form element can be configured with attributes that specify which server-side program or file will process the form, how the form information will be sent to the server, and the name of the form. These attributes are listed in Table 9.1.

Table 9.1 Attributes of the form element

| Attribute | Value | Purpose |
|---|---|---|
| action | URL or file name/path of server-side processing script | Required; indicates where to send the form information when the form is submitted; mailto:e-mailaddress will launch the visitor's default e-mail application to send the form information |
| autocomplete | on<br>off | Default value; browser will use autocomplete to fill form fields<br>Browser will not use autocomplete to fill form fields |
| id | Alphanumeric, no spaces; the value must be unique and not used for other id values on the same web page document | Optional; provides a unique identifier for the form |
| method | get<br>post | Default value; the value of get causes the form data to be appended to the URL and sent to the web server<br>The post method is more private and transmits the form data in the body of the HTTP response; this method is preferred by the W3C; the post method must be used if enctype is set to mutlipart/form-data |
| name | Alphanumeric, no spaces, begins with a letter; choose a form name value that is descriptive but short (for example, OrderForm is better than Form1 or WidgetsRUsOrderForm) | Optional; names the form so that it can be easily accessed by client-side scripting languages to edit and verify the form information before the server-side processing is invoked |
| enctype | application/x-www-form-urlencoded (default)<br>multipart/form-data (required when uploading a file)<br>text-plain (spaces are converted to "+") | Indicates how the data on the form should be encoded when sent to the server. The attribute is required when the form will upload one or more files. |

For example, to configure a form with the name attribute set to the value "order", using the post method and invoking a script called demo.php on your web server, the code is

```
<form name="order" method="post" id="order" action="demo.php">

. . . form controls go here . . .

</form>
```

## Form Controls

The purpose of a form is to gather information from a web page visitor. Form controls are the objects that accept the information. Types of form controls include text boxes, scrolling text boxes, select lists, radio buttons, check boxes, and buttons. HTML5 offers new form controls, including those that are customized for e-mail addresses, URLs, dates, times, numbers, and even date selection. HTML elements that configure form controls will be introduced in the following sections.

# 9.2 Input Element Form Controls

The **input element** is a stand-alone, or void, tag that is used to configure several different types of form controls. The input element is not coded as a pair of opening and closing tags. Use the type attribute to specify the type of form control that the browser should display.

## Sample Text Box

E-mail:

**Figure 9.2** The `<input>` tag with `type="text"` configures this form element

## Text Box

The **`<input>`** tag with `type="text"` configures a **text box** form control. The text box form control accepts text or numeric information such as names, e-mail addresses, phone numbers, and other text. Common input element attributes for text boxes are listed in Table 9.2. A text box is shown in Figure 9.2.

The code for the text box is shown below:

```
E-mail: <input type="text" name="email" id="email">
```

**Table 9.2** Common text box attributes

| Attribute | Value | Purpose |
|---|---|---|
| type | text | Configures a text box |
| name | Alphanumeric, no spaces, begins with a letter | Names the form element so that it can be easily accessed by client-side scripting languages or by server-side processing; the name should be unique |
| id | Alphanumeric, no spaces, begins with a letter | Provides a unique identifier for the form element |
| size | Numeric value | Configures the width of the text box as displayed by the browser; if size is omitted, the browser displays the text box with its own default size |
| maxlength | Numeric value | Configures the maximum length of data accepted by the text box |
| value | Text or numeric characters | Assigns an initial value to the text box that is displayed by the browser; accepts information typed in the text box; this value can be accessed by client-side scripting languages and by server-side processing |
| disabled | | A boolean attribute that is coded without any value; if present, the form control is disabled |
| readonly | | A boolean attribute that is coded without any value; if present, the form control is for display; cannot be edited |
| autocomplete | on, off, token, value | Supporting browsers will use autocompletion to fill in the form control; See https://www.w3.org/TR/html51/sec-forms.html#autofilling-form-controls-the-autocomplete-attribute |
| autofocus | | A boolean attribute that is coded without any value; if present, the browser places cursor in the form control and sets the focus |
| list | Datalist element id value | Associates the form control with a datalist element |
| placeholder | Text or numeric characters | Brief information intended to assist the user |
| required | | A boolean attribute that is coded without any value; if present, the browser verifies entry of information before submitting the form |
| accesskey | Keyboard character | Configures a hot key for the form control |
| tabindex | Numeric value | Configures the tab order of the form control |

You may have noticed that there is no value indicated for the disabled, readonly, autofocus, and required attributes in Table 9.2. These attributes are boolean attributes. A boolean attribute is not coded with a value. If a **boolean attribute** is present, the browser behavior is triggered. The **`required` attribute** is a boolean attribute that will cause supporting browsers to perform form validation. Browsers that support the required attribute will automatically verify that information has been entered in the text box and display an error message when the condition is not met. In the code sample below, the required attribute is coded without a value:

```
E-mail: <input type="text" name="email"
id="email" required>
```

Figure 9.3 shows an error message automatically generated by Firefox that is displayed after the user clicked the form's submit button without entering information in the required text box. Browsers that do not support the required attribute will ignore the attribute.

**Figure 9.3** The browser displayed an error message

 FAQ   **Why use both the name and id attributes on form controls?**

The **name attribute** names the form element so that it can be easily accessed by client-side scripting languages such as JavaScript and by server-side processing languages such as PHP. The value given to a name attribute for a form element should be unique for that form. The id attribute is included for use with CSS and access by client-side scripting languages such as JavaScript. The value of the id attribute should be unique to the entire web page document that contains the form. Typically, the values assigned to the name and id attributes on a particular form element are the same.

## Submit Button

The **submit button** form control is used to submit the form. When clicked, it triggers the action method on the form element and causes the browser to send the form data (the name and value pairs for each form control) to the web server. The web server will invoke the server-side processing program or script listed on the form's action property.

The input element with type="submit" configures a submit button. For example,

```
<input type="submit">
```

## Reset Button

The **reset button** form control is used to reset the form fields to their initial values. A reset button does not submit the form.

The input element with type="reset" configures a reset button. For example,

```
<input type="reset">
```

A form with a text box, a submit button, and a reset button is shown in Figure 9.4.

**Figure 9.4** This form contains a text box, a submit button, and a reset button

Common attributes for submit buttons and reset buttons are listed in Table 9.3.

**Table 9.3** Common attributes for submit and reset buttons

| Attribute | Value | Purpose |
|---|---|---|
| `type` | `submit` | Configures a submit button |
| | `reset` | Configures a reset button |
| `name` | Alphanumeric, no spaces, begins with a letter | Names the form element so that it can be easily accessed by client-side scripting languages (such as JavaScript) or by server-side processing; the name should be unique |
| `id` | Alphanumeric, no spaces, begins with a letter | Provides a unique identifier for the form element |
| `value` | Text or numeric characters | Configures the text displayed on the button; a submit button displays the text "Submit Query" by default; a reset button displays "Reset" by default |
| `accesskey` | Keyboard character | Configures a hot key for the form control |
| `tabindex` | Numeric value | Configures the tab order of the form control |

## Hands-On Practice 9.1

You will code a form in this Hands-On Practice. To get started, launch a text editor and open chapter9/template.html in the student files. Save the file as form1.html. You will create a web page with a form similar to the example in Figure 9.5.

**Figure 9.5** The text on the submit button says "Sign Me Up!"

1. Modify the title element to display the text "Form Example".

2. Configure an h1 element with the text "Join Our Newsletter".

   You are ready to configure the form area. A form begins with the form element. Insert a blank line under the heading you just added and type in a `<form>` tag as follows:

   ```
   <form method="get">
   ```

   In your first form, we are using the minimal HTML needed to create the form; we'll begin working with the `action` attribute later in the chapter.

3. To create the form control for the visitor's e-mail address to be entered, type the following code on a blank line below the form element:

```
E-mail: <input type="text" name="email" id="email"><br><br>
```

This places the text "E-mail:" in front of the text box used to enter the visitor's e-mail address. The input element has a `type` attribute with the value of `text` that causes the browser to display a text box. The `name` attribute assigns the name `e-mail` to the information entered into the text box (the `value`) and could be used by server-side processing. The `id` attribute uniquely identifies the element on the page. The `<br>` elements configure line breaks.

4. Now you are ready to add the submit button to the form on the next line. Add a value attribute set to "Sign Me Up!":

```
<input type="submit" value="Sign Me Up!">
```

This causes the browser to display a button with "Sign Me Up!" instead of the default value of "Submit Query".

5. Add a blank space after the submit button and code a reset button:

```
<input type="reset">
```

6. Next, code the closing form tag:

```
</form>
```

Save form1.html and test your web page in a browser. It should look similar to the page shown in Figure 9.5.

You can compare your work with the solution found in the student files (chapter9/9.1/ form.html). Try entering some information into your form. Try clicking the submit button. Don't worry if the form redisplays but nothing seems to happen when you click the button—you haven't configured this form to work with any server-side processing. Connecting forms to server-side processing is demonstrated later in this chapter. The next sections will introduce you to more form controls.

## Check Box

The **check box** form control allows the user to select one or more of a group of predetermined items. The input element with `type="checkbox"` configures a check box. Common check box attributes are listed in Table 9.4.

Figure 9.6 shows an example with several check boxes. Note that more than one check box can be selected by the user. The HTML is

```
Choose the browsers you use: <br>
<input type="checkbox" name="GO" id="GO" value="yes">
Google Chrome<br>
<input type="checkbox" name="Firefox" id="Firefox"
value="yes"> Firefox<br>
<input type="checkbox" name="Edge" id="Edge"
value="yes"> Microsoft Edge<br>
```

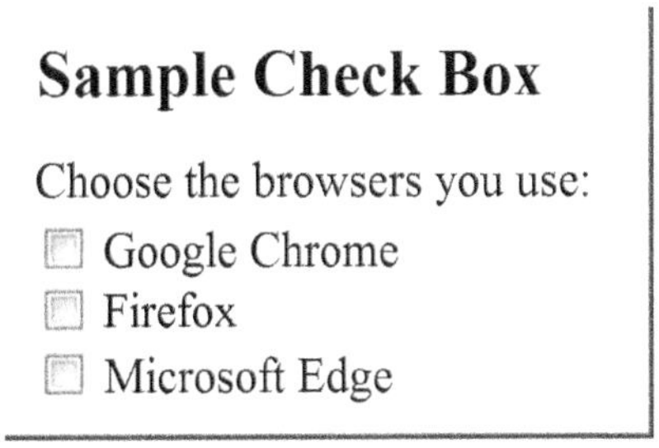

**Sample Check Box**

Choose the browsers you use:
- ☐ Google Chrome
- ☐ Firefox
- ☐ Microsoft Edge

Figure 9.6 Sample check box

Table 9.4 Common check box attributes

| Attribute | Value | Purpose |
|---|---|---|
| type | checkbox | Configures a check box |
| name | Alphanumeric, no spaces, begins with a letter | Names the form element so that it can be easily accessed by client-side scripting languages (such as JavaScript) or by server-side processing; the name should be unique |
| id | Alphanumeric, no spaces, begins with a letter | Provides a unique identifier for the form element |
| checked | | A boolean attribute that is coded without any value; if present, the browsers displays the check box as checked |
| value | Text or numeric characters | Assigns a value to the check box that is triggered when the check box is checked; this value can be accessed by client-side and server-side processing |
| disabled | | A boolean attribute that is coded without any value; if present, form control is disabled |
| readonly | | A boolean attribute that is coded without any value; if present, form control is for display; cannot be edited |
| autofocus | | A boolean attribute that is coded without any value; if present, browser places cursor in the form control and sets the focus |
| required | | A boolean attribute that is coded without any value; if present, browser verifies entry of information before submitting the form |
| accesskey | Keyboard character | Configures a hot key for the form control |
| tabindex | Numeric value | Configures the tab order of the form control |

## Sample Radio Button

Select your favorite browser:
- ◉ Google Chrome
- ◉ Firefox
- ◉ Microsoft Edge

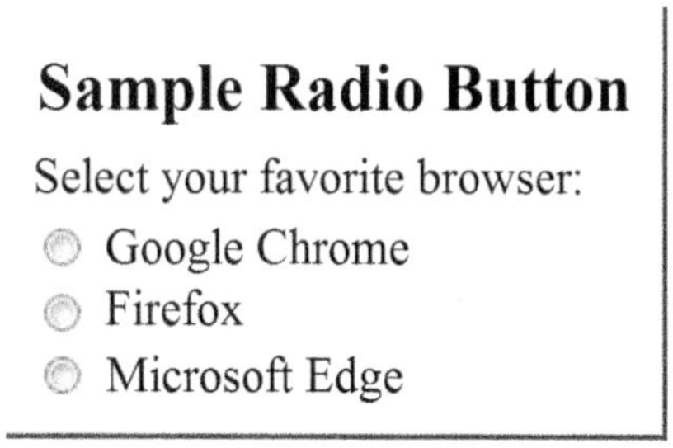

Figure 9.7 Use radio buttons when only one choice is an appropriate response

## Radio Button

The **radio button** form control allows the user to select exactly one (and only one) choice from a group of predetermined items. Each radio button in a group is given the same name attribute and a unique value attribute. Because the name attribute is the same, the elements are identified as part of a group by the browsers and only one may be selected.

The input element with type="radio" configures a radio button. Figure 9.7 shows an example with a radio button group. Note that only one radio button can be selected at a time by the user. Common radio button attributes are listed in Table 9.5. The HTML is

```
Select your favorite browser:<br>
<input type="radio" name="favbrowser" id="favGO" value="GO"> Google
Chrome<br>
<input type="radio" name="favbrowser" id="favFirefox" value="Firefox">
Firefox<br>
<input type="radio" name="favbrowser" id="favEdge" value="Edge">
Microsoft Edge<br>
```

Notice that all the name attributes have the same value: favbrowser. Radio buttons with the same name attribute are treated as a group by the browser. Each radio button in the same group can be uniquely identified by its value attribute. Common radio button attributes are listed in Table 9.5.

Table 9.5 Common radio button attributes

| Attribute | Value | Purpose |
|---|---|---|
| type | radio | Configures a radio button |
| name | Alphanumeric, no spaces, begins with a letter | Names the form element so that it can be easily accessed by client-side scripting languages or by server-side processing |
| id | Alphanumeric, no spaces, begins with a letter | Provides a unique identifier for the form element |
| checked | | A boolean attribute that is coded without any value; if present, the browsers displays the radio button as selected |
| value | Text or numeric characters | Assigns a value to the radio button that is triggered when the radio button is selected; this should be a unique value for each radio button in a group |
| disabled | | A boolean attribute that is coded without any value; if present, form control is disabled |
| readonly | | A boolean attribute that is coded without any value; if present, form control is for display; cannot be edited |
| autofocus | | A boolean attribute that is coded without any value; if present, browser places cursor in the form control and sets the focus |
| required | | A boolean attribute that is coded without any value; if present, browser verifies entry of information before submitting the form |
| accesskey | Keyboard character | Configures a hot key for the form control |
| tabindex | Numeric value | Configures the tab order of the form control |

## Hidden Input Control

The **hidden input control** stores text or numeric information, but it is not visible in the browser viewport. Hidden controls can be accessed by both client-side scripting and server-side processing.

The input element with `type="hidden"` configures a hidden input control. Common attributes for hidden input controls are listed in Table 9.6. The HTML to create a hidden input control with the `name` attribute set to "sendto" and the `value` attribute set to an e-mail address is

```
<input type="hidden" name="sendto" id="sendto" value="order@site.com">
```

Table 9.6 Common hidden input control attributes

| Attribute | Value | Purpose |
|---|---|---|
| type | hidden | Configures a hidden element |
| name | Alphanumeric, no spaces, begins with a letter | Names the form element so that it can be easily accessed by client-side scripting languages or by server-side processing; the name should be unique |
| id | Alphanumeric, no spaces, begins with a letter | Provides a unique identifier for the form element |
| value | Text or numeric characters | Assigns a value to the hidden control; this value can be accessed by client-side scripting languages and server-side processing |
| disabled | | A boolean attribute that is coded without any value; if present, form control is disabled |

## File Upload Control

The **file upload control** form control provides for files to be uploaded.

The input element with `type="file"` configures a file upload control. The form control display varies depending on the browser and operating system being used. The user is able to choose one or more files to upload. Common attributes for the file upload control are listed in Table 9.7. Note that `enctype="mutlipart/form-data"` must be coded on the form element when the form contains a file upload control. The HTML to create a form control that accepts a typical photograph file is

```
Profile Photo:
<input type="file" name="photo" id="photo" accept="images/*"
```

Table 9.7 Common file upload form control attributes

| Attribute | Value | Purpose |
|---|---|---|
| type | input | Configure a file upload control |
| name | Alphanumeric, no spaces, begins with a letter | Names the form element so that it can be easily accessed by client-side scripting languages or by server-side processing; the name should be unique |
| id | Alphanumeric, no spaces, begins with a letter | Provides a unique identifier for the form element |
| accept | A comma delineated list of file extensions and/or MIME types | Indicates which file types are acceptable for upload. For example, the value `"image/*"` accepts any file with an image MIME type; See https://www.w3.org/TR/html-media-capture/ |
| capture | user | File is captured from the inward-facing camera/microphone |
|  | environment | File is captured from the outward-facing camera/microphone |
| multiple |  | A boolean attribute that is coded without any value; if present, more than one file can be uploaded |

## Password Box

The **password box** form control is similar to the text box, but it is used to accept information that must be hidden as it is entered, such as a password.

### Sample Password Box

Password: ●●●●●●●

Figure 9.8 The characters secret9 were typed, but the browser does not display them. (Note: Your browser may use a different symbol, such as a stylized circle, to hide the characters.)

The input element with `type="password"` configures a password box. When the user types information in a password box, asterisks (or another symbol, depending on the browser) are displayed instead of the characters that have been typed, as shown in Figure 9.8. This hides the information from someone looking over the shoulder of the person typing. The actual characters typed are sent to the server and the information is not really secret or hidden. See Chapter 12 for a discussion of encryption and security.

A password box is a specialized text box. See Table 9.2 for a list of text box attributes.

The HTML is

```
Password: <input type="password" name="pword" id="pword">
```

# 9.3 Scrolling Text Box

## Textarea Element

The **scrolling text box** form control accepts free-form comments, questions, or descriptions. The **textarea element** configures a scrolling text box. The **<textarea>** tag denotes the beginning of the scrolling text box. The closing </textarea> tag denotes the end of the scrolling text box. Text contained between the tags will display in the scrolling text box area. A sample scrolling text box is shown in Figure 9.9.

**Figure 9.9** Scrolling text box

Common attributes for scrolling text boxes are listed in Table 9.8. The HTML is

```
Comments:<br>
<textarea name="comments" id="comments" cols="40" rows="2"> Enter your
comments here</textarea>
```

**Table 9.8** Common scrolling text box attributes

| Attribute | Value | Purpose |
|---|---|---|
| name | Alphanumeric, no spaces, begins with a letter | Names the form element so that it can be easily accessed by client-side scripting languages or by server-side processing; the name should be unique |
| id | Alphanumeric, no spaces, begins with a letter | Provides a unique identifier for the form element |
| cols | Numeric value | Required; configures the width in character columns of the scrolling text box; if cols is omitted, the browser displays the scrolling text box with its own default width |
| rows | Numeric value | Required; configures the height in rows of the scrolling text box; if rows is omitted, the browser displays the scrolling text box with its own default height |
| maxlength | Numeric value | Configures the maximum length of data accepted by the text box |
| disabled | | A boolean attribute that is coded without any value; if present, form control is disabled |
| readonly | | A boolean attribute that is coded without any value; if present, form control is for display; cannot be edited |
| autofocus | | A boolean attribute that is coded without any value; if present, browser places cursor in the form control and sets the focus |
| placeholder | Text or numeric characters | Brief information intended to assist the user |
| required | | A boolean attribute that is coded without any value; if present, browser verifies entry of information before submitting the form |
| wrap | hard or soft (default) | Configures line breaks within the information entered |
| accesskey | Keyboard character | Configures a hot key for the form control |
| tabindex | Numeric value | Configures the tab order of the form control |

# Hands-On Practice 9.2

In this Hands-On Practice, you will create a contact form (see Figure 9.10) with the following form controls: a First Name text box, a Last Name text box, an E-mail text box, and a Comments scrolling text box. You'll use the form you created in Hands-On Practice 9.1 (see Figure 9.5) as a starting point. Launch a text editor and open chapter9/9.1/form.html in the student files. Save the file as form2.html.

**Figure 9.10** A typical contact form

1. Modify the title element to display the text "Contact Form".

2. Configure the h1 element with the text "Contact Us".

3. A form control for the e-mail address is already coded. Refer to Figure 9.10 and note that you'll need to add text box form controls for the first name and last name above the e-mail form control. Add the following code on new lines below the opening form tag to accept the name of your web page visitor:

```
First Name: <input type="text" name="fname" id="fname"><br><br>
Last Name: <input type="text" name="lname" id="lname"><br><br>
```

4. Now you are ready to add the scrolling text box form control to the form using a `<textarea>` tag on a new line below the e-mail form control. The code is

```
Comments:<br>
<textarea name="comments" id="comments"></textarea><br><br>
```

5. Save your file and display your web page in a browser to view the default display of a scrolling text box. Note that this default display will differ by browser.

6. Let's configure the `rows` and `cols` attributes for the scrolling text box form control. Modify the `<textarea>` tag and set `rows="4"` and `cols="40"` as follows:

```
Comments:<br>
<textarea name="comments" id="comments" rows="4"
cols="40"></textarea><br><br>
```

7. Next, modify the text displayed on the submit button. Set the value attribute to "Contact". Save form2.html and test your web page in a browser. It should look similar to the page shown in Figure 9.10.

You can compare your work with the solution found in the student files (chapter9/9.2/form.html). Try entering some information into your form. Try clicking the submit button. Don't worry if the form redisplays but nothing seems to happen when you click the button—you haven't configured this form to work with any server-side processing. Connecting forms to server-side processing is demonstrated later in this chapter.

 **FAQ   How can I send form information in an e-mail?**

Forms usually need to invoke some type of server-side processing to perform functions such as sending e-mail, writing to text files, updating databases, and so on. Another option is to set up a form to send information using the e-mail program configured to work with the web page visitor's browser. In what is sometimes called using a mailto: URL, the `<form>` tag is coded to use your e-mail address in the action attribute:

```
<form method="post" action="mailto:me@webdevfoundations.net">
```

When a form is used in this manner, the web visitor will see a warning message. The warning message presents a nonprofessional image and is not the best way to inspire trust and confidence in your website or business.

Be aware that a person using a computer may choose to not use the default e-mail application. In this case, filling out a form that uses mailto: URL is a waste of their time. Even if the person using the computer also uses the default e-mail application, perhaps he or she may not want to divulge this particular e-mail address. Perhaps they have another e-mail address that is used for forms and newsletters, and do not want to waste time filling out your form. In either case, the result is an unhappy website visitor. So, while using mailto: URL is easy, it does not always create the most usable web form for your visitors. What's a web developer to do? Use server-side processing (see Hands-On Practice 9.5 ) to handle form data instead of mailto: URL.

# 9.4  Select List

The **select list** form control shown in Figures 9.11 and 9.12 is also known by several other names, including select box, drop-down list, drop-down box, and option box. A select list is configured with one select element and multiple option elements.

## Select Element

The **select element** contains and configures the select list form control. The **<select>** tag denotes the beginning of the select list. The closing </select> tag denotes the end of the select list. Attributes configure the number of options to display and whether more than one option item may be selected. Common attributes for select elements are listed in Table 9.9.

Table 9.9  Common select element attributes

| Attribute | Value | Purpose |
|---|---|---|
| name | Alphanumeric, no spaces, begins with a letter | Names the form element so that it can be easily accessed by client-side scripting languages or by server-side processing; the name should be unique |
| id | Alphanumeric, no spaces, begins with a letter | Provides a unique identifier for the form element |
| size | Numeric value | Configures the number of choices the browser will display; if set to 1, the element functions as a drop-down list (see Figure 9.12); scroll bars are automatically added by the browser if the number of options exceeds the space allowed |
| multiple | | A boolean attribute that is coded without any value; if present, configures a select list to accept more than one choice; by default, only one choice can be made from a select list |
| disabled | | A boolean attribute that is coded without any value; if present, form control is disabled |
| tabindex | Numeric value | Configures the tab order of the form control |

## Option Element

The **option element** contains and configures an option item displayed in the select list form control. The **<option>** tag denotes the beginning of the option item. The closing </option> tag denotes the end of the option item. Attributes configure the value of the option and whether they are preselected. Common attributes for option elements are listed in Table 9.10.

Table 9.10  Common option element attributes

| Attribute | Value | Purpose |
|---|---|---|
| value | Text or numeric characters | Assigns a value to the option; this value can be accessed by client-side and server-side processing |
| selected | | A boolean attribute that is coded without any value; if present, configures an option to be initially selected when displayed by a browser |
| disabled | | A boolean attribute that is coded without any value; if present, form control is disabled |

The HTML for the select list in Figure 9.11 is

```
<select size="1" name="favbrowser" id="favbrowser">
  <option>Select your favorite browser</option>
  <option value="Edge">Edge</option>
  <option value="Firefox">Firefox</option>
  <option value="Chrome">Chrome</option>
</select>
```

The HTML for the select list in Figure 9.12 is

```
<select size="4" name="jumpmenu" id="jumpmenu">
   <option value="index.html">Home</option>
   <option value="products.html">Products</option>
   <option value="services.html">Services</option>
   <option value="about.html">About</option>
   <option value="contact.html">Contact</option>
</select>
```

## Select List: One Initial Visible Item

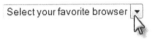

Figure 9.11  A select list with size set to 1 functions as a drop-down box when the arrow is clicked

## Select List: Four Items Visible

Figure 9.12  Because there are more than four choices, the browser displays a scroll bar

**FAQ    How does the menu in Figure 9.12 display the selected page?**

Well, it doesn't work, yet. It needs JavaScript (see Chapter 14) to check for the selected item and direct the browser to display the new document. Because it requires JavaScript to work, this type of menu would not be a good choice for your main navigation, but it might be useful for a secondary navigation area.

## Checkpoint 9.1

1. You are designing a website for a client who sells items in a retail store. They want to create a customer list for e-mail marketing purposes. Your client sells to consumers and needs a form that accepts a customer's name and e-mail address. Would you recommend using two input boxes (one for the name and one for the e-mail) or three input boxes (one each for the first name, last name, and e-mail address)? Explain your answer.

2. A question on a survey asks participants to indicate their favorite browsers. Most people will select more than one response. What type of form control would you use to configure this question on the web page? Explain your answer.

3. True or False? In a radio button group, the `value` attribute is used by the browser to process the separate radio buttons as a group.

# 9.5 Image Buttons and the Button Element

As you have worked with forms in this chapter, you may have noticed that the standard submit button (see Figure 9.10) is a little plain. You can make the form control that visitors select to submit the form a bit more compelling and visually interesting in two ways:

1. Configure an image with the input element.

2. Create a custom image that is configured with the button element.

## Image Button

**Figure 9.13** The web page visitor will select the image button to submit the form

Figure 9.13 shows an image used in place of the standard submit button. This is called an **image button**. When an image button is clicked or tapped, the form is submitted. The image button is coded using the `<input>` tag along with `type="image"` and a `src` attribute with the value of the name of the image file. For example, to use the image called login.gif as an image button, the HTML code is

```
<input type="image" src="login.gif" alt="Login
Button">
```

## Button Element

Another way to add more interest to a form is to use the **button element**, which can be used to configure not only images but also blocks of text as the selectable area that can submit or reset a form. Any web page content that is between the **<button>** and `</button>` tags is configured to be part of the button. Common attributes for button elements are listed in Table 9.11.

**Figure 9.14** The button element configured as a submit button

Figure 9.14 shows a form that has an image (signup.gif) configured as a submit button using the button element.

**Table 9.11** Common button element attributes

| Common Attributes | Values | Purpose |
|---|---|---|
| type | submit | Functions as a submit button |
| | reset | Functions as a reset button |
| | button | Functions as a button |
| name | Alphanumeric, no spaces, begins with a letter | Names the form element so that it can be easily accessed by client-side scripting languages or by server-side processing; the name should be unique |
| id | Alphanumeric, no spaces, begins with a letter | Provides a unique identifier for the form element |
| alt | Brief text description of the image | Provides accessibility to visitors who are unable to view the image |
| value | Text or numeric characters | A value given to a form element that is passed to the form handler |

The following HTML code creates the button shown in Figure 9.14:

```
<button type="submit">
<img src="signup.gif" width="80" height="28" alt="Sign up for free
newsletter"><br>Sign up for free newsletter
</button>
```

As you visit web pages and view their source code, you will find that the button element is not used as often as the standard submit button or the image button.

# 9.6 Accessibility and Forms

In this section, you'll explore techniques to increase the accessibility of form controls, including the label element, fieldset element, legend element, tabindex attribute, and accesskey attribute, which make it easier for individuals with vision and mobility challenges to use your form pages. The use of label, fieldset, and legend elements may increase the readability and usability of the web form for all visitors.

**Focus on Accessibility**

## Label Element

The **label element** is a container tag that associates a text description with a form control. This is helpful to visually challenged individuals who are using assistive technology such as a screen reader to match up the text descriptions on forms with their corresponding form controls. The label element also benefits individuals who have difficulty with fine motor control. Clicking anywhere on either a form control or its associated text label will set the cursor focus to the form control. The **<label>** tag specifies the beginning of the label. The closing </label> tag specifies the end of the label.

**Focus on Accessibility**

There are two different methods to associate a label with a form control.

1. The first method places the label element as a container around both the text description and the HTML form element. Notice that both the text label and the form control must be adjacent elements. The code is

   ```
   <label>E-mail: <input type="text" name="email" id="email"></label>
   ```

2. The second method uses the `for` attribute to associate the label with a particular HTML form element. This is more flexible and is does not require the text label and the form control to be adjacent. The code is

   ```
   <label for="email">E-mail: </label>
   <input type="text" name="email" id="email">
   ```

Notice that the value of the **for attribute** on the label element is the same as the value of the `id` attribute on the input element. This creates the association between the text label and the form control. The input element uses both the `name` and `id` attributes for different purposes. The `name` attribute can be used by client-side scripting and server-side processing. The `id` attribute creates an identifier that can be used by the label element, anchor element, and CSS selectors. The label element does not display on the web page—it works behind the scenes to provide for accessibility.

## Hands-On Practice 9.3

In this Hands-On Practice, you will add the label element to the text box and scrolling text area form controls on the form you created in Hands-On Practice 9.2 (see Figure 9.10) as a starting point. Launch a text editor and open chapter9/9.2/form.html in the student files. Save the file as form3.html.

**1.** Locate the text box for the first name. Add a label element to wrap around the input tag as follows:

```
<label>First Name: <input type="text" name="fname"
id="fname"></label>
```

**2.** In a similar manner, add a label element for the last name and the e-mail form controls.

**3.** Configure a label element to contain the text "Comments". Associate the label with the scrolling text box form control. The sample code is

```
<label for="comments">Comments:</label><br>
<textarea name="comments" id="comments" rows="4"
cols="40"></textarea>
```

Save form3.html and test your web page in a browser. It should look similar to the page shown in Figure 9.10—the label elements do not change the way that the page displays, but a web visitor with physical challenges should find the form easier to use.

You can compare your work with the solution found in the student files (chapter9/9.3/form.html). Try entering some information into your form. Try clicking the submit button. Don't worry if the form redisplays but nothing seems to happen when you click the button—you haven't configured this form to work with any server-side processing. Connecting forms to server-side processing is demonstrated later in this chapter.

## Fieldset and Legend Elements

A technique that can be used to create a more visually pleasing form is to group elements of a similar purpose together using the **fieldset element**, which will cause the browser to render a visual cue, such as an outline or a border, around form elements grouped together within the fieldset. The **<fieldset>** tag denotes the beginning of the grouping. The closing </fieldset> tag denotes the end of the grouping.

The **legend element** provides a text description for the fieldset grouping. The **<legend>** tag denotes the beginning of the text description. New to HTML5.2 is that the description can also include heading tags. The closing </legend> tag denotes the end of the text description. The HTML to create the grouping shown in Figure 9.15 is

```
<fieldset>
<legend>Billing Address</legend>
<label>Street: <input type="text" name="street" id="street"
       size="54"></label><br><br>
<label>City: <input type="text" name="city" id="city"></label>
<label>State: <input type="text" name="state" id="state" maxlength="2"
       size="5"></label>
<label>Zip: <input type="text" name="zip" id="zip" maxlength="5"
       size="5"></label>
</fieldset>
```

## Fieldset and Legend

┌─ Billing Address ─────────────────────────────────────────┐
│ Street:                                                    │
│                                                            │
│ City:                    State:        Zip:                │
└────────────────────────────────────────────────────────────┘

Figure 9.15  Form controls that are all related to a mailing address

The grouping and visual effect of the fieldset element creates an organized and appealing web page containing a form. Using the fieldset and legend elements to group form controls enhances accessibility by organizing the controls both visually and semantically. The fieldset and legend elements can be accessed by screen readers and are useful tools for configuring groups of radio buttons and check boxes on web pages.

**Focus on Accessibility**

## Hands-On Practice 9.4

In this Hands-On Practice, you will modify the contact form (form3.html) you worked with in Hands-On Practice 9.3 to use the fieldset and legend elements (see Figure 9.16).

Launch a text editor and open chapter9/9.3/form.html in the student files. Save the file as form4.html. Perform the following edits:

**1.** Add an opening `<fieldset>` tag after the opening `<form>` tag.

**2.** Immediately after the opening `<fieldset>` tag, code a legend element that contains the following text: "Customer Information".

Figure 9.16  The fieldset, legend, and label elements

3. Code the closing `</fieldset>` tag before the label element for the Comments scrolling text box.

4. Save your file and test your web page in a browser. It should look similar to the one shown in Figure 9.16. You can compare your work with the solution found in the student files (chapter9/9.4/form4.html). You may notice that when you activate the submit button, the form redisplays. This is because there is no action property in the form element. You'll work with setting the action property in Section 9.8.

5. How about a quick preview of styling a form with CSS? Figures 9.16 and 9.17 show the same form elements, but the form in Figure 9.17 is styled with CSS, which gives it the same functionality with increased visual appeal.

Figure 9.17 The fieldset, legend, and label elements are configured with CSS

Open form4.html in a text editor and add embedded styles to the head section as indicated below:

```
fieldset { width: 320px;
    border: 2px ridge #FF0000;
    padding: 10px;
    margin-bottom: 10px; }
legend { font-family: Georgia, "Times New Roman", serif;
        font-weight: bold; }
label { font-family: Arial, sans-serif; }
```

Save your file as form5.html and test your web page in a browser. It should look similar to the one shown in Figure 9.17. You can compare your work with the solution found in the student files (chapter9/9.4/form5.html).

## The Tabindex Attribute

**Focus on Accessibility**

Some of your website visitors may have difficulty using a mouse and will access your form with a keyboard. The Tab key can be used to move from one form control to another. The default action for the Tab key within a form is to move to the next form control in the order in which the form controls are coded in the web page document. This is usually appropriate. However, if the tab order needs to be changed for a form, use the **tabindex attribute** on each form control.

For each form tag (`<input>`, `<select>`, and `<textarea>`), code a `tabindex` attribute with a numeric value, beginning with 1, 2, 3, and so on in numerical order. The HTML code to configure the customer e-mail text box as the initial position of the cursor is

```
<input type="text" name="Email" id="Email" tabindex="1">
```

If you configure a form control with `tabindex="0"`, it will be visited after all of the other form controls that are assigned a `tabindex` attribute. If you happen to assign two form controls the same tabindex value, the one that is coded first in the HTML will be visited first.

You can configure the `tabindex` attribute for anchor tags in a similar manner. The default action for the Tab key and anchor tags is to move from hyperlink to hyperlink in the order they are coded on the page. Use the `tabindex` attribute if you need to modify this behavior.

## The Accesskey Attribute

**Focus on Accessibility**

Another technique that can make your form keyboard-friendly is the use of the **accesskey attribute** on form controls. You can also configure the `accesskey` attribute on an anchor tag. Assigning the `accesskey` attribute a value of one of the characters (a letter or number) on the keyboard will create a hot key that your website visitor can press to move the cursor immediately to a form control or hyperlink.

The method used to access this hot key varies depending on the operating system. Windows users will press the Alt key and the character key. Mac users will press the Ctrl key and the character key. For example, if the form shown in Figure 9.10 had the customer e-mail text coded with `accesskey="E"`, the web page visitor using Windows could press the Alt and E keys to move the cursor immediately to the e-mail text box. The HTML code for this is

```
<input type="text" name="email" id="email" accesskey="E">
```

Note that you cannot rely on the browser to indicate that a character is an access key, also called a hot key. You will have to manually code information about the hot key. A visual cue may be helpful, such as displaying the hot key in bold or by placing a message such as (Alt+E) after a form control or hyperlink that uses a hot key. When choosing accesskey values, avoid combinations that are already used by the operating system (such as Alt+F to display the File menu). Testing hot keys is crucial.

## Checkpoint 9.2

1. Describe the purpose of the fieldset and legend elements.

2. Describe the purpose of the `accesskey` attribute and how it supports accessibility.

3. When designing a form, should you use the standard submit button, an image button, or a button tag? Are these different in the way in which they provide for accessibility? Explain your answer.

# 9.7  Style a Form with CSS

The form in Figure 9.10 (from Hands-On Practice 9.2) looks a little "messy" and you might be wondering how that can be improved. In the time before CSS was well supported by browsers, web designers always used a table to configure the design of form elements, typically placing the text labels and form field elements in separate table data cells. However, the table approach is outdated, does not provide support for accessibility, and can be difficult to maintain over time. The modern approach is to style the form with CSS.

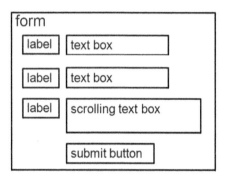

**Figure 9.18** Wireframe for a form

When styling a form with CSS, the box model is used to create a series of boxes, as shown in Figure 9.18. The outermost box defines the form area. Other boxes indicate label elements and form controls. CSS is used to configure these components.

## Form with CSS Float

## Hands-On Practice 9.5

You will style a form in this Hands-On Practice. To get started, launch a text editor and open the starter.html file in the chapter9 folder in the student files. Save the file with the name contactus.html. When you have completed the Hands-On Practice, your form will be similar to Figure 9.19.

**Figure 9.19** This form is configured with CSS

The HTML for the form is shown below for your reference:

```
<form>
  <label for="myName">Name:</label>
  <input type="text" name="myName" id="myName">
  <label for="myEmail">E-mail:</label>
  <input type="text" name="myEmail" id="myEmail">
  <label for="myComments">Comments:</label>
  <textarea name="myComments" id="myComments" rows="2" cols="20">
  </textarea>
  <input type="submit" value="Submit">
</form>
```

Configure embedded CSS within the style element as follows:

1. **The form element selector**. Configure with a #EAEAEA background color, Arial or sans serif font, 350px width, and 10 pixels of padding:

   ```
   form { background-color: #EAEAEA;
          font-family: Arial, sans-serif;
          width: 350px; padding: 10px; }
   ```

2. **The label element selector.** Configure to float to the left, clear left floats, and use block display. Also set width to 100px, 10 pixels of right padding, a 10px top margin, and right-aligned text:

   ```
   label { float: left; clear: left; display: block;
           width: 100px; padding-right: 10px;
           margin-top: 10px; text-align: right; }
   ```

3. **The input element selector.** Configure with block display and a 10px top margin.

   ```
   input { display: block; margin-top: 10px; }
   ```

4. **The textarea element selector.** Configure with block display and a 10px top margin.

   ```
   textarea { display: block; margin-top: 10px; }
   ```

5. **The submit button.** The submit button needs to display under the other form controls, with a 110 pixel margin on the left. You could configure a new id or class and then edit the HTML but there is a more efficient method. You will configure an attribute selector, which allows you to select using both the element name and the attribute value as the criteria. In this case, we need to style input tags that have a `type` attribute with the value `submit` in a different manner than the other input tags, so we'll configure an attribute selector for that purpose. The CSS follows:

   ```
   input[type="submit"] { margin-left: 110px; }
   ```

Save your file and test your page in a browser. It should look similar to Figure 9.19. You can compare your work with the sample in the student files (chapter9/9.5).

## Form with CSS Grid Layout

CSS Grid Layout offers another method to configure the layout of a form. Figure 9.18 shows a wireframe of a typical form.

When you work with grid layout, it is helpful to create a sketch of the grid, shown in Figure 9.20. Notice how the actual element names were placed within the grid. This will help us when we code the CSS to configure the placement of the elements in the grid columns and rows. Notice that, except for the submit button, we can allow the browser to autofill the grid with the labels and form controls.

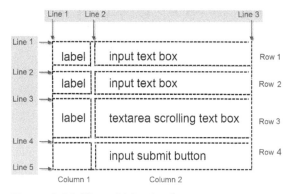

Figure 9.20 The grid for the form

 ## Hands-On Practice 9.6

In this Hands-On Practice you will use form you created in Hands-On Practice 9.5 and code a CSS feature query to configure grid layout in supporting browsers. Browsers that do not support grid layout will display the form as originally styled with CSS. Browsers that support grid will follow the grid layout styles. To get started, launch a text editor and open your Hands-on Practice 9.5 file (chapter9/9.5/contactus.html in the student files). Save the file with the name contact2.html. When you have completed, your form will be similar to the example in Figure 9.21.

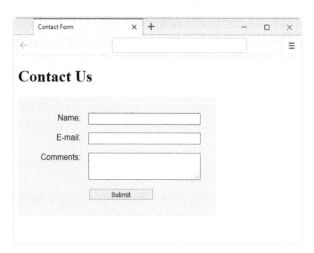

Figure 9.21 The form is styled with CSS grid layout

The HTML for the form is shown below for your reference:

```
<form>
  <label for="myName">Name:</label>
  <input type="text" name="myName" id="myName">
  <label for="myEmail">E-mail:</label>
  <input type="text" name="myEmail" id="myEmail">
  <label for="myComments">Comments:</label>
  <textarea name="myComments" id="myComments" rows="2" cols="20">
  </textarea>
  <input type="submit" value="Submit">
</form>
```

1. Locate the closing style tag. You will code CSS above the closing style tag and below the existing CSS in the file. Configure a feature query that will test for grid layout support:

```
@supports ( display: grid) {
  }
```

2. Configure the following CSS within the feature query to configure the form using grid layout.

   a. **The form element selector.** Configure declarations to set the display property to grid with auto rows and two columns (6em and 1fr). Also set 1em grid gap, #EAEAEA background color, Arial or sans serif font, 60% width, 20em minimum width, and 2em padding:

```
form { display: grid;
       grid-template-rows: auto;
       grid-template-columns: 6em 1fr;
       grid-gap: 1em; gap: 1em;
       background-color: #EAEAEA;
       font-family: Arial, sans-serif;
       width: 60%; min-width: 20em;
       padding: 1.5em; }
```

   b. **The submit button.** Review the grid sketch in Figure 10.19 and notice how the elements in the grid are placed one right after another to fill the grid except for the submit button, which is in the second column of the grid. Use an attribute selector to target the submit button and explicitly place it in the second column of the grid. Also set the width to 10em. Also set the left margin to 0. The CSS follows:

```
input[type="submit"] { grid-column: 2 / 3;
                       width: 10em; margin-left: 0; }
```

Save your file and test your page in a browser. It should look similar to Figure 9.21. You can compare your work with the sample in the student files (chapter9/9.6).

This section provided you with methods to style a form with CSS. As you've coded and displayed the forms in this chapter, you may have noticed that when you click the submit button, the form just redisplays—the form doesn't do anything. This is because there is no action attribute in the `<form>` tag. The next section focuses on the second component of using forms on web pages—server-side processing.

# 9.8 Server-Side Processing

Your web browser requests web pages and their related files from a web server. The web server locates the files and sends them to your web browser. Then the web browser renders the returned files and displays the requested web pages.

Sometimes a website needs more functionality than static web pages, possibly a site search, order form, e-mail list, database display, or other type of interactive, dynamic processing. This is when server-side processing is needed. Early web servers used a protocol called **Common Gateway Interface (CGI)** to provide this functionality. CGI is a protocol, or standard method, for a web server to pass a web page user's request (which is typically initiated through the use of a form) to an application program and to accept information to send to the user. The web server typically passes the form information to a small application program that is run by the operating system and that processes the data, usually sending back a confirmation web page or message. Perl and C are popular programming languages for CGI applications.

**Server-side scripting** is a technology by which a server-side script is run on a web server to dynamically generate web pages. Examples of server-side scripting technologies include PHP, Ruby on Rails, Microsoft Active Server Pages, Adobe ColdFusion, Oracle JavaServer Pages, and Microsoft .NET. Server-side scripting differs from CGI in that it uses **direct execution**: The script is run either by the web server itself or by an extension module to the web server.

A web page invokes server-side processing by either an attribute on a form or by a hyperlink (the URL of the script is used). Any form data that exists is passed to the script. The script completes its processing and may generate a confirmation or response web page with the requested information. When invoking a server-side script, the web developer and the server-side programmer must communicate about the form `method` **attribute** (`get` or `post`), form `action` **attribute** (the URL of the server-side script), and any special form element control(s) expected by the server-side script.

The `method` attribute is used on the form tag to indicate the way in which the name and value pairs should be passed to the server. The method attribute value of `get` causes the form data to be appended to the URL, which is easily visible and not secure. The method attribute value of `post` does not pass the form information in the URL; it passes it in the entity body of the HTTP request, which makes it more private. The W3C recommends the `method="post"` method.

The `action` attribute is used on the `<form>` tag to invoke a server-side script. The `name` attribute and the `value` attribute associated with each form control are passed to the server-side script. The `name` attribute may be used as a variable name in the server-side processing. In the next Hands-On Practice, you will invoke a server-side script from a form.

VideoNote
*Connect a Form to Server-Side Processing*

# Hands-On Practice 9.7

In this Hands-On Practice, you will configure a form to invoke a server-side script. Please note that your computer must be connected to the Internet when you test your work. When using a server-side script, you will need to obtain some information, or documentation, from the person or organization providing the script. You will need to know the location of the script, whether it requires any specific names for the form controls, and whether it requires any hidden form elements.

A server-side script has been created at the author's website (https://webdevbasics.net) for students to use for this exercise. The documentation for the server-side script is listed below:

- Script URL: https://webdevbasics.net/scripts/demo.php
- Form method: `post`
- Script purpose: This script will accept form input and display the form control names and values in a web page. This is a sample script for student assignments. It demonstrates that server-side processing has been invoked. A script used by an actual website would perform a function such as sending an e-mail message or updating a database.

Notice that the script's URL begins with https:// instead of http://. Coding https://in the action value will cause the browser to use HTTPS, which stands for Hypertext Transfer Protocol Secure. HTTPS combines HTTP with a security and encryption protocol called Secure Sockets Layer (SSL) – see Chapter 12 for a brief introduction to SSL. Using HTTPS provides a more secure transaction because the browser encrypts the information entered in the form before sending it to the server.

Now you will add the configuration required to use the demo.php server-side processing with a form. Launch a text editor and open your file from Hands-On Practice 9.6 (found in the student files chapter9/9.6 folder). Modify the `<form>` tag by adding an `action` attribute with a value of "`https://webdevbasics.net/scripts/demo.php`" and a `method` attribute with a value of "`post`". The HTML code for the revised `<form>` tag is

```
<form method="post"
      action="https://webdevbasics.net/scripts/demo.php">
```

Save your file as contact.html and test your web page in a browser. Your screen should look similar to Figure 9.21. Compare your work with the solution in the student files (chapter9/9.7/contact.html).

Now you are ready to test your form. You must be connected to the Internet to test your form successfully. Enter information in the form controls and click the submit button. You should see a confirmation page similar to the one shown in Figure 9.22.

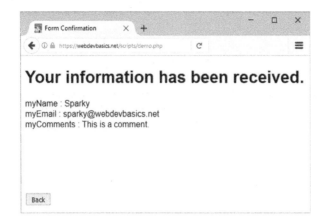

Figure 9.22 The server-side script has created this
web page in response to the form

The demo.php script creates a web page that displays a message and the form information that you entered. Where did this confirmation page originate? This confirmation page was created by the server-side script on the `action` attribute in the form
element. Sometimes students wonder what code is used in the demo.php file. Writing
scripts for server-side processing is beyond the scope of this textbook. However, if
you are curious, visit https://webdevfoundations.net/10e/chapter9.html to see the
source code for this script.

 **FAQ** **What do I do if nothing happened when I tested my form?**

Try these troubleshooting hints:

- Verify that your computer is connected to the Internet.
- Verify the spelling of the script location in the `action` attribute.
- Attention to detail is crucial!

## Privacy and Forms

You've just learned how to collect information from your website visitors. Do you think that
your visitors may want to know how you plan to use the information that you collect? The
guidelines that you develop to protect the privacy of your visitors' information is called
a **privacy policy**. Websites either indicate this policy on the form page itself or create a
separate page that describes the privacy policy (and other company policies).

If you browse popular sites such as Amazon.com or eBay.com, you'll find links to their privacy policies (sometimes called a privacy notice) in the page footer area. The privacy policy
of the Better Business Bureau can be found at https://www.bbb.org/privacy-policy. Include
a privacy notice on your site to inform your visitors how you plan to use the information that
they share with you. The Better Business Bureau offers a sample privacy policy template
at https://www.bbb.org/greater-san-francisco/for-businesses/understanding-privacy-policy/
sample-privacy-policy-template.

## Server-Side Processing Resources

### Sources of Free Remote-Hosted Form Processing

If your web host provider does not support server-side processing, free remotely hosted scripts may be an option. The script is not hosted on your server so you don't need to worry about installing it or whether your web host provider will support it. The disadvantage is that there may be is some advertising displayed. The following are a few sites that offer this service:

- FormBuddy.com: http://formbuddy.com

- FormMail: https://www.formmail.com

- Formspree: https://formspree.io

### Sources of Free Server-Side Scripts

To use free scripts, you need to have access to a web server that supports the language used by the script. Contact your web host provider to determine what is suppoted. Be aware that many free web host providers do not support server-side processing (you get what you pay for!). Visit http://scriptarchive.com and http://php.resourceindex.com for free scripts and related resources.

### Exploring Server-Side Processing Technologies

Many types of technologies can be used for server-side scripting, form processing, and information sharing:

- PHP: http://www.php.net

- Oracle JavaServer Pages Technology:
  http://www.oracle.com/technetwork/java/javaee/jsp

- Adobe ColdFusion and Web Applications:
  http://www.adobe.com/products/coldfusion

- Ruby on Rails: http://www.rubyonrails.org

- Microsoft .NET: http://www.microsoft.com/net

Any of these technologies could be a good choice for future study. Web developers often learn the client side first (HTML, CSS, and JavaScript) and then progress to learning a server-side scripting or programming language.

 **Checkpoint 9.3**

1. Describe server-side processing.

2. Why is communication needed between the developer of a server-side script and the web page designer?

# 9.9 HTML5 Form Controls

HTML5 introduced a variety of new form controls for web developers that provide increased usability with built-in browser edits and validation. Recent versions of popular browsers support the these form controls. Browsers that do not support the new input types will display the form controls as text boxes and ignore unsupported attributes or elements. In this section, you'll explore the HTML5 e-mail address, URL, telephone number, search field, datalist, slider, spinner, calendar, and color form controls.

## E-mail Address Input

The **e-mail address input** form control is similar to the text box. Its purpose is to accept information that must be in e-mail format, such as "DrMorris2010@gmail.com". The input element with `type="email"` configures an e-mail address input form control. Only browsers that support the HTML5 `email` attribute value will verify the format of the information. Other browsers will treat this form control as a text box. Attributes supported by the e-mail address input form control are listed in Table 9.2.

Figure 9.23 (see chapter9/email.html in the student files) shows an error message displayed by Firefox when text other than an e-mail address is entered. Note that the browser does not verify that the e-mail address actually exists, just that the text entered is in the correct format. The HTML is

```
<label for="myEmail">E-mail:</label>
<input type="email" name="myEmail" id="myEmail">
```

## URL Input

The **URL input** form control is similar to the text box. It is intended to accept any valid type of URL or URI, such as "https://webdevfoundations.net". The input element with `type="url"` configures a URL input form control. Only browsers that support the HTML5 `url` attribute value will verify the format of the information. Other browsers render this form control as a text box. Attributes supported by the URL input form control are listed in Table 9.2.

Figure 9.24 (see chapter9/url.html in the student files) shows an error message displayed by Firefox when text other than a URL is entered. Note that the browser does not verify that the URL actually exists, just that the text entered is in the correct format. The HTML is

```
<label for="myWebsite">Suggest a Website:</label>
<input type="url" name="myWebsite" id="myWebsite">
```

Figure 9.23 The browser displays an error message

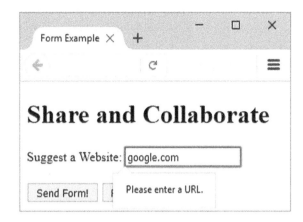

Figure 9.24 The browser displays an error message

## Telephone Number Input

The **telephone number input** form control is similar to the text box. Its purpose is to accept a telephone number. The input element with `type="tel"` configures a telephone number input form control. An example is in the student files (chapter9/tel.html). Attributes supported by the telephone number input form control are listed in Table 9.2. Browsers that do not support `type="tel"` will render this form control as a text box. The HTML is

```
<label for="mobile">Mobile Number:</label>
<input type="tel" name="mobile" id="mobile">
```

## Search Field Input

The **search field** is similar to the text box and is used to accept a search term. The input element with `type="search"` configures a search field input form control. An example is in the student files (chapter9/search.html). Attributes supported by the search field control are listed in Table 9.2. Browsers that do not support `type="search"` will render this form control as a text box. The HTML is

```
<label for="keyword">Search:</label>
<input type="search" name="keyword" id="keyword">
```

## Datalist Form Control

Figure 9.25 shows the **datalist form control** in action. Notice how a selection of choices is offered to the user along with a text box for entry. The datalist form control offers a convenient way to offer choices yet provide for flexibility on a form. The datalist is configured using three elements: an input element, the datalist element, and one or more option elements. Only browsers that support the HTML5 datalist element will display and process the datalist items. Other browsers ignore the datalist element and render the form control as a text box.

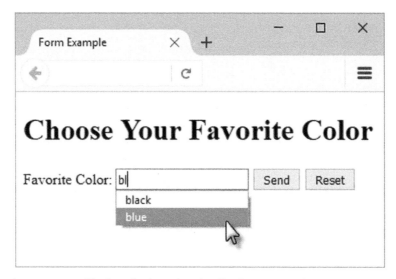

Figure 9.25 Firefox displays the datalist form control

The source code for the datalist is available in the student files (chapter9/list.html). The HTML is

```
<label for="color">Favorite Color:</label>
<input type="text" name="color" id="color" list="colors">
  <datalist id="colors">
    <option value="red"    label="red">
    <option value="green"  label="green">
    <option value="blue"   label="blue">
    <option value="yellow" label="yellow">
    <option value="pink"   label="pink">
    <option value="black"  label="black">
</datalist>
```

Notice that the value of the **list attribute** on the input element is the same as the value of the id attribute on the datalist element. This creates the association between the text box and the datalist form control. One or more option elements can be used to offer pre-defined choices to your web page visitor. The option element's label attribute configures the text displayed in each list entry. The option element's value attribute configures the text sent to server-side processing when the form is submitted. The web page visitor can choose an option from the list (see Figure 9.25) or type directly in the text box, as shown in Figure 9.26.

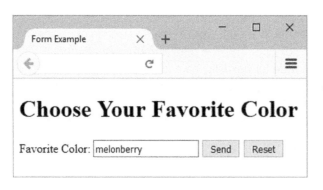

Figure 9.26 The user can choose to type any value into the text box

## Slider Form Control

The **slider form control** provides a visual, interactive user interface that accepts numerical information. The input element with type="range" configures a slider control in which a number within a specified range is chosen. The default range is from 1 to 100. Only browsers that support the HTML5 range attribute value will display the interactive slider control, shown in Figure 9.27 (see chapter9/range.html in the student files). Note the position of the slider in Figure 9.27; this resulted in the value 80 being chosen. The nondisplay of the value to the user may be a disadvantage of the slider control. Nonsupporting browsers render this form control as a text box.

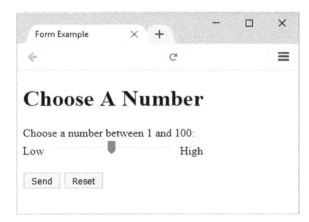

**Figure 9.27** The Firefox browser displays the range form control.

The slider control accepts attributes listed in Tables 9.2 and 9.12. The min, max, and step attributes are new. Use the **min attribute** to configure the minimum range value. Use the **max attribute** to configure the maximum range value. The slider controls sets numeric values in increments, or steps, of 1. Use the **step attribute** to configure a value for the incremental steps between values to be other than 1.

The HTML for the slider control rendered in Figure 9.27 is

```
<label for="myChoice">Choose a number between 1 and 100:</label><br>
Low <input type="range" name="myChoice" id="myChoice" min="1"
max="100"> High
```

**Table 9.12** Additional attributes for slider, spinner, and date/time form controls

| Attribute | Value | Purpose |
|-----------|-------|---------|
| max | Maximum numeric value | HTML5 attribute for range, number, and date/time input controls; specifies a maximum value |
| min | Minimum numeric value | HTML5 attribute for range, number, and date/time input controls; specifies a minimum value |
| step | Incremental numeric step value | HTML5 attribute for range, number, and date/time input controls; specifies a value for incremental steps |

## Spinner Form Control

The **spinner form control** displays an interface that accepts numerical information and provides feedback to the user. The input element with `type="number"` configures a spinner control in which the user can either type a number into the text box or select a number from a specified range. Only browsers that support the HTML5 `number` attribute value will display the interactive spinner control, shown in Figure 9.28 (see chapter9/spinner.html in the student files). Other browsers render this form control as a text box. You should expect increased support in the future.

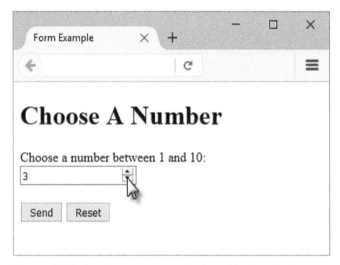

**Figure 9.28** A spinner control displayed in the Firefox browser

The spinner control accepts attributes listed in Tables 9.2 and 9.12. Use the `min` attribute to configure the minimum value. Use the `max` attribute to configure the maximum value. The spinner control sets numeric values in increments, or steps, of 1. Use the `step` attribute to configure a value for the incremental step between values to be other than 1. The HTML for the spinner control displayed in Figure 9.28 is

```
<label for="myChoice">Choose a number between 1 and 10:</label>
<input type="number" name="myChoice" id="myChoice" min="1" max="10">
```

## Date and Time Form Control

HTML5 provides a variety of **date and time form controls** to accept date- and time-related information. Use the input element and configure the type attribute to specify a date or time control. Table 9.13 lists the date and time form controls.

Table 9.13 Date and time form controls

| Type Attribute Value | Purpose | Format |
|---|---|---|
| date | A date | YYYY-MM-DD<br>Example:<br>January 2, 2020 is represented by "2020-01-02" |
| datetime | A date and time with time zone information; note that the time zone is indicated by the offset from UTC time | YYYY-MM-DDTHH:MM:SS-##:##Z<br>Example:<br>January 2, 2020, at exactly 9:58 a.m. Chicago time (CST) is represented by "2020-01-02T09:58:00-06:00Z" |
| datetime-local | A date and time without time zone information | YYYY-MM-DDTHH:MM:SS<br>Example:<br>January 2, 2020, at exactly 9:58 a.m. is represented by "2020-01-02T09:58:00" |
| time | A time without time zone information | HH:MM:SS<br>Example:<br>1:34 p.m. is represented by "13:34:00" |
| month | A year and month | YYYY-MM<br>Example:<br>January 2020 is represented by "2020-01" |
| week | A year and week | YYYY-W##, where ## represents the week in the year<br>Example:<br>The third week in 2020 is represented by "2020-W03" |

The form in Figure 9.29 (see chapter9/date.html in the student files) uses the input element with `type="date"` to configure a calendar date-picker control with which the user can select a date. The HTML is

```
<label for="myDate">Choose a Date</label>
<input type="date" name="myDate" id="myDate">
```

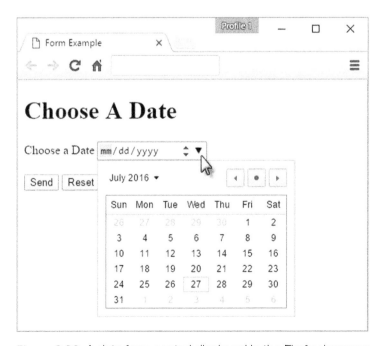

Figure 9.29 A date form control displayed in the Firefox browser

The date and time controls accept attributes listed in Tables 9.2 and 9.13. Only browsers that support the HTML5 date form control will display a calendar interface for date and time controls. Other browsers currently render the date and time form controls as a text box, but you should expect increased support in the future.

## Color-well Form Control

The **color-well form control** displays an interface that offers a color-picker interface to the user. The input element with `type="color"` configures a control with which the user can choose a color. Only browsers that support the HTML5 `color` attribute value will display a color-picker interface, shown in Figure 9.30 (see chapter9/color.html in the student files). Other browsers render this form control as a text box.

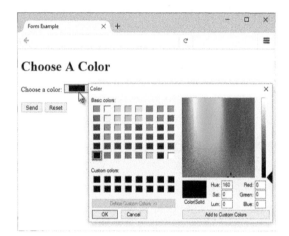

Figure 9.30 The Firefox browser supports the color-well form control

The HTML for the color-well form control rendered in Figure 9.30 is

```
<label for="myColor">Choose a color:</label>
<input type="color" name="myColor" id="myColor">
```

In the next Hands-On Practice, you'll get some experience with the new HTML5 form controls.

 ## Hands-On Practice 9.8

In this Hands-On Practice, you will code HTML5 form controls as you configure a form that accepts a name, e-mail address, rating value, and comments from a website visitor. Figure 9.31 displays the form in the Firefox browser, which supports the HTML5 features used in the Hands-On Practice.

Figure 9.31 The form displayed in the Firefox browser

To get started, launch a text editor and open your file from Hands-On Practice 9.7, found in the student files chapter9/9.7 folder. Save the file as comment.html. You will modify the file to create a web page similar to Figure 9.31.

1. Modify the title element to display the text "Comment Form". Configure the text contained within the h1 element to be "Send Us Your Comments". Add a paragraph to indicate "Required fields are marked with an asterisk *."

2. Modify labels and the form controls.

   a. Configure the name, e-mail, and comment information to be required. Use an asterisk to inform your web page visitor about the required fields.

   b. Code `type="email"` instead of `type="input"` for the e-mail address.

   c. Use the `placeholder` attribute (refer to Table 9.2) to provide hints to the user in the name and e-mail form controls.

3. Add a slider control (use `type="range"`) to generate a value from 1 to 10 for the rating.

   The HTML for the form follows:

```
<form method="post"
action="https://webdevbasics.net/scripts/demo.php">
  <label for="myName">*Name:</label>
  <input type="text" name="myName" id="myName"
         required placeholder="your first and last name">
  <label for="myEmail">*E-mail:</label>
  <input type="email" name="myEmail" id="myEmail"
         required placeholder="you@yourdomain.com">
  <label for="myRating">Rating (1 - 10):</label>
  <input type="range" name="myRating" id="myRating" min="1" max="10">
  <label for="myComments">*Comments:</label>
  <textarea name="myComments" id="myComments" rows="2" cols="20"
            required></textarea>
  <input id="mySubmit" type="submit" value="Submit">
</form>
```

4. Save comment.html and test your web page in a browser. If you use a browser that supports the HTML5 features used in the form, your page should look similar to Figure 9.31.

5. Try submitting the form without entering any information. Figure 9.32 shows the result when using Firefox. Note the error message which indicates that the name field is required. Compare your work with the solution in the student files (chapter9/9.8/comment.html).

Figure 9.32 The Firefox browser displays an error message

## Progressive Enhancement

Use HTML5 form elements with the concept of progressive enhancement in mind. Nonsupporting browsers will display text boxes in place of form elements that are not recognized. Supporting browsers will display and process the new form controls. This is progressive enhancement in action: Everyone sees a usable form and visitors who are using modern browsers benefit from the enhanced features.

# Chapter Summary

This chapter introduced the use of forms on web pages. You learned how to configure form controls, provide for accessibility, and configure a form to access server-side processing. Visit the textbook website at https://www.webdevfoundations.net for examples, the links listed in this chapter, and updated information.

## Key Terms

<button>
<fieldset>
<form>
<input>
<label>
<legend>
<option>
<select>
<textarea>
accept attribute
accesskey attribute
action attribute
autofocus attribute
boolean attribute
button element
capture attribute
check box
color-well form control
Common Gateway Interface (CGI)
datalist form control
date and time form controls

direct execution
e-mail address input
fieldset element
file upload control
for attribute
form
form controls
form element
hidden input control
image button
input element
label element
legend element
list attribute
max attribute
method attribute
min attribute
multiple attribute
name attribute
option element
password box

placeholder attribute
privacy policy
radio button
required attribute
reset button
scrolling text box
search field
select element
select list
server-side scripting
slider form control
spinner form control
step attribute
submit button
tabindex attribute
telephone number input
text box
textarea element
URL input
value attribute

## Review Questions

### Multiple Choice

1. You would like to conduct a survey and ask your web page visitors to vote for their favorite search engine. Which of the following form controls is best to use for this purpose?
   a. check box
   b. radio button
   c. text box
   d. scrolling text box

2. You would like to conduct a survey and ask your web page visitors to indicate the web browsers that they use. Which of the following form controls is best to use for this purpose?
   a. check box
   b. radio button
   c. text box
   d. scrolling text box

3. Which attribute of the form element is used to specify the name and location of the script that will process the form field values?
   a. action
   b. process
   c. method
   d. id

4. Choose the HTML tag that would configure a text box with the name "city" and a width of 40 characters.
   a. `<input type="text" id="city" width="40">`
   b. `<input type="text" name="city" size="40">`
   c. `<input type="text" name="city" space="40">`
   d. `<input type="text" width="40">`

451

5. Which of the following form controls would be appropriate for an area that your visitors can use to type in their e-mail address?
   a. select list
   b. text box
   c. scrolling text box
   d. label

6. Which of the following form controls would be appropriate for an area that your visitors can use to type in comments about your website?
   a. text box
   b. select list
   c. radio button
   d. scrolling text box

7. Forms contain various types of _____, such as text boxes and buttons, which accept information from a web page visitor.
   a. hidden elements
   b. labels
   c. form controls
   d. legends

8. Which HTML tag would configure a scrolling text box with the name "comments", 2 rows, and 30 characters?
   a. `<textarea name="comments" width="30" rows="2"></textarea>`
   b. `<input type="textarea" size="30" name="comments" rows="2">`
   c. `<textarea name="comments" rows="2" cols="30"></textarea>`
   d. `<input type="comments" rows="2" name="comments" cols="30">`

9. You would like to accept a number that's in a range from 1 to 25. The user needs visual verification of the number they selected. Which of the following form controls is best to use for this purpose?
   a. spinner
   b. check box

c. radio button
d. slider

10. Choose the HTML that would associate a label displaying the text "E-mail:" with the e-mail text box.
    a. `E-mail <input type="textbox" name="email" id="email">`
    b. `<label>E-mail: </label><input type="text" name="email" id="email">`
    c. `<label for="email">E-mail: </label> <input type="text" name="email" id="emailaddress">`
    d. `<label for="email">E-mail: </label> <input type="text" name="email" id="email">`

11. What will happen when a browser encounters a form control that it does not support?
    a. The computer will shut down.
    b. The browser will crash.
    c. The browser will display an error message.
    d. The browser will display an input text box.

## Fill in the Blank

12. To limit the number of characters that a text box will accept, use the _____ attribute.

13. To group a number of form controls visually on the page, use the _____ element.

14. To cause a number of radio buttons to be treated as a single group, the value of the _____ attribute must be identical.

## Short Answer

15. Describe at least three form controls that could be used to allow a visitor to your web page to select a color.

## Apply Your Knowledge

1. **Predict the Result.** Draw and write a brief description of the web page that will be created with the following HTML code:

```
<!DOCTYPE html>
<html lang="en">
<head>
<title>Predict the Result</title>
<meta charset="utf-8">
</head>
```

```
<body>
<h1>Contact Us</h1>
<form action="myscript.php">
<fieldset><legend>Complete the form and a consultant will contact
you.</legend>
E-mail: <input type="text" name="email" id="email" size="40">
<br>Please indicate which services you are interested in:<br>
<select name="inquiry" id="inquiry" size="1">
   <option value="development">Web Development</option>
   <option value="redesign">Web Redesign</option>
   <option value="maintain">Web Maintenance</option>
   <option value="into">General Information</option>
</select>
<br>
<input type="submit">
</fieldset>
</form>
<nav><a href="index.html">Home</a>
<a href="services.html">Services</a>
<a href="contact.html">Contact</a></nav>
</body>
</html>
```

2. **Fill in the Missing Code.** This web page configures a survey form to collect information on the favorite search engine used by web page visitors. The form action should submit the form to the server-side script, called survey.php. Some HTML tags and their attributes, indicated by **<_>**, are missing. Some HTML attribute values, indicated by **"_"**, are missing.

```
<!DOCTYPE html>
<html lang="en">
<head>
<title>Fill in the Missing Code</title>
<meta charset="utf-8">
</head>
<body>
<h1>Vote for your favorite Search Engine</h1>
<form method="_" action="_">
  <input type="radio" name="_" id="Ysurvey" value="Yahoo">
Yahoo!<br>
  <input type="radio" name="survey" id="Gsurvey" value="Google">
  Google<br>
  <input type="radio" name="_" id="Bsurvey" value="Bing"> Bing<br>
   <_>
</form>
</body>
</html>
```

3. **Find the Error.** Find the coding errors in the following subscription form:

```
<!DOCTYPE html>
<html lang="en">
<head>
<title>Find the Error</title>
<meta charset="utf-8">
</head>
<body>
<p>Subscribe to our monthly newsletter and receive free coupons!</p>
<form action="get" method="newsletter.php">
  <lable>E-mail: <input type="textbox" name="email" id="email"
  char="40"></lable>
  <br>
  <input button="submit"> <input type="rest">
</form>
</body>
</html>
```

## Hands-On Exercises

1. Write the HTML code to create the following:
   a. A text box named user that will be used to accept the user name of web page visitors. The text box should allow a maximum of 30 characters to be entered.
   b. A group of radio buttons that website visitors can check to vote for their favorite month of the year.
   c. A select list that asks website visitors to select their favorite social networking site
   d. A fieldset and legend with the text "Shipping Address" around the following form controls:
      AddressLine1, AddressLine2, City, State, ZIP
   e. An image called signup.gif as an image button on a form
   f. A hidden input control with the name userid
   g. A password box form control with the name pword
   h. A form tag to invoke server-side processing using https://webdevbasics.net/scripts/demo.php and the post method

2. Write the HTML to create a form that accepts requests for a brochure to be sent in the mail. Sketch out the form on paper before you begin.

3. Create a web page with a form that accepts feedback from website visitors. Use input `type="email"` along with the `required` attribute to configure the browser to verify the data entered. Also configure the browser to require user comments with a maximum length of 1600 characters accepted. Place your name and e-mail address at the bottom of the page. *Hint:* Sketch out the form on paper before you begin.

4. Create a web page with a form that accepts a website visitor's name, e-mail, and birthdate. Use input `type="date"` to configure a calendar date-picker control. Place your name and e-mail address at the bottom of the page. *Hint:* Sketch out the form on paper before you begin.

5. Write a web page that contains a music survey form similar to the example shown in Figure 9.33.

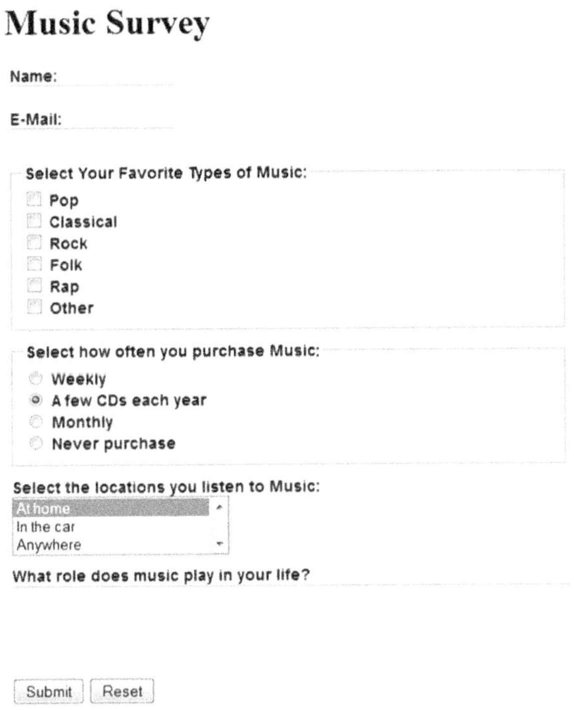

## Music Survey

Name: _____

E-Mail: _____

**Select Your Favorite Types of Music:**
- ☐ Pop
- ☐ Classical
- ☐ Rock
- ☐ Folk
- ☐ Rap
- ☐ Other

**Select how often you purchase Music:**
- ○ Weekly
- ◉ A few CDs each year
- ○ Monthly
- ○ Never purchase

Select the locations you listen to Music:

| At home |
|---------|
| In the car |
| Anywhere |

What role does music play in your life?

Submit    Reset

Figure 9.33
Sample music
survey form

Include the following form controls:

- Text box for name
- E-mail address input form control for the e-mail address
- A scrolling text box that is 60 characters wide and 3 rows high
- A radio button group with at least three choices
- A check box group with at least three choices
- A select box that initially shows three items but contains at least four items
- A submit button
- A reset button
- Use the fieldset and legend elements as shown in Figure 9.33 to configure the display of form areas with radio buttons and checkboxes.

Use a CSS to configure the display of your form. Place your name and e-mail address at the bottom of the page.

## Web Research

1. This chapter mentioned a number of sources of free remotely hosted scripts, including FormBuddy.com (http://formbuddy.com) and FormMail (https://www.formmail.com). Visit these sites or use a search engine to find other resources for free remotely hosted scripts. Register (if necessary) and examine the website to see exactly what is offered. Most sites that provide remotely hosted scripts have a demo you can view or try. If you

have time (or your instructor asks you to), follow the directions and access a remotely hosted script from one of your web pages. Now that you've at least been through a demo of the product or tried it yourself (even better!), it's time to write your review.

Create a web page that lists the two resource sites you chose and provides a comparison of what they offer. List the following for each website:

- Ease of registration
- Number of scripts or services offered
- Types of scripts or services offered
- Site banner or advertisement
- Ease of use
- Your recommendation

Provide links to the resource sites you reviewed and place your name and e-mail address at the bottom of the page.

2. Search the Web for a web page that uses an HTML form. Print the browser view of the page. Print out the source code of the web page. Using the printout, highlight or circle the tags related to forms. On a separate sheet of paper, create some HTML notes by listing the tags and attributes related to the forms found on your sample page along with a brief description of their purpose.

3. Choose one server-side technology mentioned in this chapter such as PHP, JSP, or Ruby on Rails. Use the resources listed in the chapter as a starting point, but also search the Web for additional resources on the server-side technology you have chosen. Create a web page that lists at least five useful resources along with information about each that provides the name of the site, the URL, a brief description of what is offered, and a recommended page (such as a tutorial, free script, and so on). Place your name in an e-mail link on the web page.

## Focus on Web Design

The design of a form, such as the justification of the labels, the use of background colors, and even the order of the form elements can either increase or decrease the usability of a form. Visit some of the following resources to explore form design:

- Designing Efficient Web Forms: https://www.smashingmagazine.com/2017/06/designing-efficient-web-forms/
- Form Design Best Practices: https://blog.hubspot.com/marketing/form-design
- Best Practices for Mobile Form Design: https://www.smashingmagazine.com/2018/08/best-practices-for-mobile-form-design/

Feel free to search on your own and locate additional resources. Create a web page that lists the URLs of at least two useful resources along with a brief description of the information you found most interesting or valuable. Design a form on the web page that applies what you've just learned in your exploration of form design. Place your name in an e-mail link on the web page.

# WEBSITE CASE STUDY

## Adding a Form

Each of the following case studies continues throughout most of the textbook. This chapter adds a page containing a form that invokes server-side processing to the websites.

### JavaJam Coffee Bar

See Chapter 2 for an introduction to the JavaJam Coffee Bar case study. Figure 2.32 shows a site map for the JavaJam site. Use the Chapter 8 JavaJam website as a starting point for this case study. You will create the new Jobs page that contains a form. You have three tasks in this case study:

1. Create a new folder for this JavaJam case study.

2. Modify the style sheet (javajam.css) to configure style rules for the new form.

3. Create the new Jobs page shown in Figure 9.34.

Figure 9.34  JavaJam Jobs page

### Hands-On Practice Case Study

**Task 1: The Website Folder.**  Create a folder called javajam9. Copy all of the files from your Chapter 8 javajam8 folder into the javajam9 folder. Copy the herojobs.jpg and coffeecup.jpg files from the chapter9/starters folder in the student files.

**Task 2: Configure the CSS.** Modify the external style sheet (javajam.css). Review Figure 9.34 and the grid layout sketch in Figure 9.35. Notice how the text labels for the form controls are on the left side of the content area. Notice the empty space between each form control. When displaying on a narrow viewport, the display will be more pleasing if there is only one column, as shown in Figure 9.36. Open javajam.css in a text editor. Configure the CSS as follows:

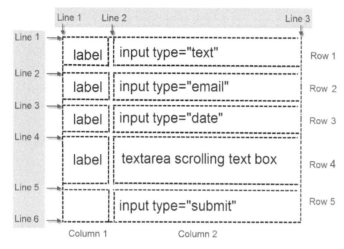

Figure 9.35  The grid layout sketch of the form

1. Format the hero image. Code a selector above the media queries for an id named `herojobs` with 300px height. Set the background image to coffeecup.jpg. The background image will not repeat. Also configure background-size: 100% 100%.

2. Configure the single column display for narrow viewports using flexbox. Add the following CSS above the media queries to configure the form element selector as a flex container with one column, 1em left padding, and 80% width. Also set a .5em bottom margin on the input and textarea element selectors.

```
form { display: flex;
       flex-direction: column;
       padding-left: 1em; width: 80%; }
input, textarea { margin-bottom: .5em; }
```

3. Configure the two-column display with grid layout and format a larger hero image. Add CSS to the first media query to accomplish this.
   a. Configure a form element selector. Set 40% width, grid display with 1em grid gap, and two columns (6em width and 1 fr width).
   b. Configure an attribute selector for the submit button. Use the `grid-column` property to place this in the second column. Set width to 9em.
   c. Configure a selector for an id named `herojobs`. Set the background image to herojobs.jpg.

Save the javajam.css file.

Figure 9.36  Single-column form in a narrow viewport

**Task 3: Create the Jobs Page.**  Use the Menu page as the starting point for the Jobs page. Launch a text editor and open menu.html. Save the file as jobs.html. Modify your jobs.html file to look similar to the Jobs page (shown in Figure 9.34) as follows:

1. Change the page title to an appropriate phrase.

2. The Jobs page will contain an h2, a paragraph, and a form in the main element. Assign the first div to an id named `herojobs`.

3. Edit the text within the h2 element to say "Jobs at JavaJam". Replace the text in the paragraph with the following: "Want to work at JavaJam? Fill out the form below to start your application. All information is required."

4. Delete the remaining menu-related content from the page: the table and the div assigned to the `flow` id.

5. Prepare to code the HTML for the form area. Begin with a form element that uses the post method and the action attribute to invoke server-side processing. Unless directed otherwise by your instructor, configure the action attribute to send the form data to https://webdevbasics.net/scripts/javajam8.php.

6. Configure the form control for the Name information. Create a label element that contains the text "Name:". Create a text box named myName. Configure the browser to require entry in the text box. Use the `for` attribute to associate the label element with the form control.

7. Configure the form control for the E-mail information. Create a label element that contains the text "E-mail:". Create e-mail address input form control named myEmail. Configure the browser to require entry in the text box. Use the `for` attribute to associate the label element with the form control.

8. Configure the form control for the date available to start work. Create a label element that contains the text "Start Date:" Create a calendar date-picker form control named myStart. Configure the browser to require the user to enter or select this information. Use the for attribute to associate the label element with the form control.

9. Configure the Experience area on the form. Create a label element that contains the text "Experience:". Create a textarea element named myExperience with `rows` set to 2 and `cols` set to 20. Configure the browser to require entry in the textarea. Use the `for` attribute to associate the label element with the form control.

10. Configure the submit button. Code an input element with `type="submit"` and `value="Apply Now"`. Assign the input element to an id named `mySubmit`.

11. Code an ending `</form>` tag on a blank line after the submit button.

Save your file and test your web page in a browser. It should look similar to the page shown in Figure 9.34. If you resize the browser viewport to be narrower, the display should be similar to Figure 9.36. If you are connected to the Internet, enter all the information and submit the form. This will send your form information to the server-side script configured in the form tag. A confirmation page that lists the form information and their corresponding names will be displayed.

Next, submit the form with missing information or only a partial e-mail address. Depending on the browser's level of HTML5 support, the browser may perform form validation and display an error message. Figure 9.37 shows the Jobs page rendered in the Firefox browser with an incorrectly formatted e-mail address.

**Figure 9.37** The Jobs page shows an error message

## Fish Creek Animal Clinic

See Chapter 2 for an introduction to the Fish Creek Animal Clinic case study. Figure 2.36 shows a site map for Fish Creek. Use the Chapter 8 Fish Creek website as a starting point for this case study. You will create the new Contact page that contains a form. You have three tasks in this case study:

1. Create a new folder for this Fish Creek case study.

2. Modify the fishcreek.css style sheet to configure style rules for the new form.

3. Create the new Contact page shown in Figure 9.38.

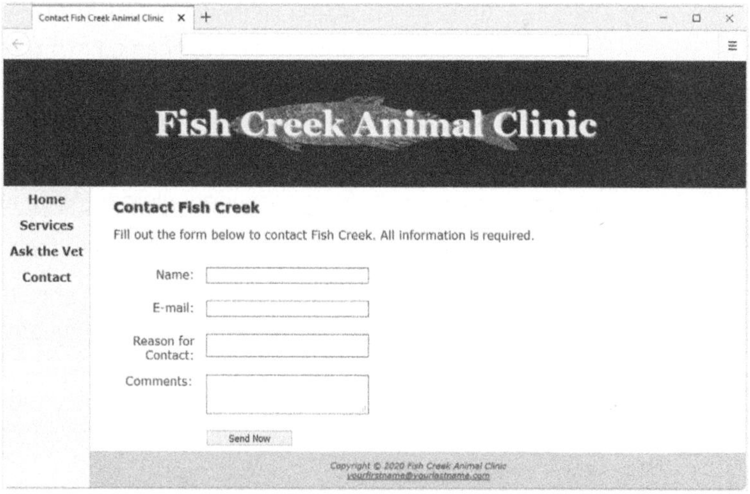

**Figure 9.38** Fish Creek Contact page

## Hands-On Practice Case Study

**Task 1: The Website Folder.** Create a folder called fishcreek9. Copy all of the files from your Chapter 8 fishcreek8 folder into the fishcreek9 folder.

**Task 2: Configure the CSS.** Modify the external style sheet (fischcreek.css). Open fishcreek.css in a text editor. Review Figure 9.38 and the grid layout sketch in Figure 9.39. Notice how the text labels for the form controls are on the left side of the content area but contain right-aligned text. Notice the empty vertical space between each form control. When displaying on a narrow viewport, the display will be more pleasing if there is only one column, as shown in Figure 9.40. Configure CSS as follows:

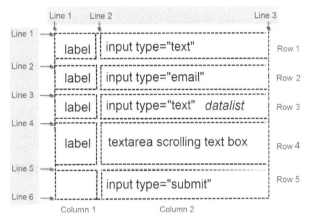

Figure 9.39 The grid layout sketch of the form

1. Configure the single column display for narrow viewports using flexbox. Add the following CSS above the media queries to configure the form element selector as a flex container with one column, 1em left padding, and 80% width. Also set a .5em bottom margin on the input and textarea element selectors.

```
form { display: flex;
       flex-direction: column;
       padding-left: 1em; width: 80%; }
input, textarea { margin-bottom: .5em; }
```

2. Configure the two-column display with grid layout. Add CSS to the first media query.

    a. Configure a form element selector. Set 40% width, grid display with 1em grid gap, and two columns (6em width and 1 fr width).

    b. Configure an attribute selector for the submit button. Place this in the second column using the `grid-column` property. Set width to 9em.

    c. Configure a label element selector with right alignment.

Save the fishcreek.css file.

Figure 9.40 Single-column form in a narrow viewport

**Task 3: Create the Contact Page.** Use the Ask the Vet page as the starting point for the Contact page. Launch a text editor and open askvet.html. Save the file as contact.html. Modify your contact.html file to look similar to the Contact page (shown in Figure 9.36) as follows:

1. Change the page title to an appropriate phrase.

2. Delete the description list, img element, and div assigned to the id `flow`.

3. Replace the text within the h2 element with following: "Contact Fish Creek".

4. Replace the text in the paragraph with the following:

    Fill out the form below to contact Fish Creek. All information is required.

5. Prepare to code the HTML for the form area. Begin with a form element that uses the post method and the action attribute to invoke server-side processing. Unless directed otherwise by your instructor, configure the action attribute to send the form data to https://webdevbasics.net/scripts/fishcreek.php.

6. Configure the form control for the Name information. Create a label element that contains the text "Name:". Create a text box named myName. Use the `for` attribute to associate the label element with the form control. Configure the browser to require entry in the text box.

7. Configure the form control for the E-mail information. Create a label element that contains the text "E-mail:". Create e-mail address input form control named myEmail. Use the `for` attribute to associate the label element with the form control. Configure the browser to require entry in the text box.

8. Configure the form control to accept the reason for contacting Fish Creek. Create a label element that contains the text "Reason for Contact:". Create a text box named myReason. Use the for attribute to associate the label element with the textbox. Configure the browser to require entry in the text box. Associate the text box with a datalist named reasons. Configure datalist and option elements to display the following reasons: New Patient, Appointment, House Call, Information, Ask the Vet.

9. Configure the Comments area on the form. Create a label element that contains the text "Comments:". Create a textarea element named myComments with `rows` set to 2 and `cols` set to 20. Use the `for` attribute to associate the label element with the form control. Configure the browser to require entry in the textarea.

10. Configure the submit button on the form. Configure "Send Now" to display on the button. Assign the input element to the id named `mySubmit`.

11. Code an ending `</form>` tag on a blank line after the submit button.

Save your file and test your web page in a browser. It should look similar to the page shown in Figure 9.38. If you resize the browser viewport to be narrower, the display should be similar to Figure 9.40. If you are connected to the Internet, submit the form. This will send your form information to the server-side script configured in the form tag. A confirmation page that lists the form information and their corresponding names will be displayed.

Next, save your file and display your web page in a browser. Submit the form with missing information or only a partial e-mail address. Depending on the browser's level of HTML5 support, the browser may perform form validation and display an error message. Figure 9.41 shows the Contact page rendered in the Firefox browser with missing required information.

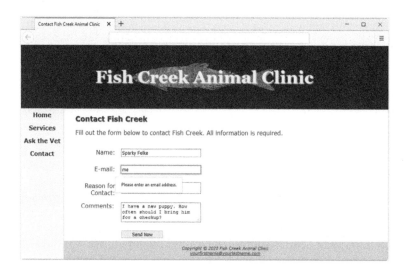

**Figure 9.41** The Contact page shows an error message

# Pacific Trails Resort

See Chapter 2 for an introduction to the Pacific Trails Resort case study. Figure 2.40 shows a site map for Pacific Trails. Use the Chapter 8 Pacific Trails website as a starting point for this case study. You will create the new Reservations page that contains a form. You have three tasks in this case study:

1. Create a new folder for this Pacific Trails case study.

2. Modify the style sheet (pacific.css) to configure style rules for the new form.

3. Create the new Reservations page shown in Figure 9.42.

## Hands-On Practice Case Study

**Task 1: The Website Folder.** Create a folder called pacific9. Copy all of the files from your Chapter 8 pacific8 folder into the pacific9 folder. Copy the ocean.jpg file from the student files chapter9/starters folder.

**Task 2: Configure the CSS.** Modify the external style sheet (pacific.css). Open pacific.css in a text editor. Review Figure 9.42 and the grid layout sketch in Figure 9.43. Notice how the text labels for the form controls are on the left side of the content area. Notice the empty vertical space between each form control. When displaying on a narrow viewport, the display will be more pleasing if there is only one column, as shown in Figure 9.44. Configure CSS as indicated below:

1. Configure the single column display for narrow viewports using flexbox. Add the following CSS above the media queries.

   a. Configure the form element selector as a flex container with one column, 1em left padding, and 80% width.

   ```
   form { display: flex;
          flex-direction: column;
          padding-left: 1em; width: 80%; }
   ```

   b. Set a .5em bottom margin on the input and textarea element selectors.

   c. Configure an id named `reshero` to with 300px height, ocean.jpg background image, background-size 200% 100%, and no background image repeat.

**Figure 9.42** Pacific Trails Reservations page

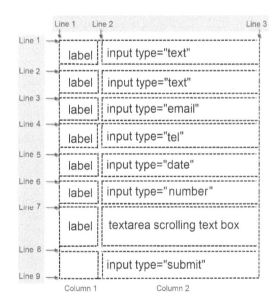

**Figure 9.43** The grid layout sketch of the form

2.  Configure the two-column display with grid layout. Add CSS to the first media query.

   a. Configure a form element selector. Set 60% width, grid display with 1em grid gap, and two columns (10em width and 1 fr width).

   b. Configure an attribute selector for the submit button. Place this in the second column with the `grid-column` property. Set width to 9em.

   c. Configure the `reshero` id with background size: 100% 100%.

Save the pacific.css file.

**Task 3: Create the Reservations Page.**   Use the Home page as the starting point for the Reservations page. Launch a text editor and open index.html. Save the file as reservations.html. Modify your reservations.html file to look similar to the Reservations page (shown in Figure 9.42) as follows:

1.  Change the page title to an appropriate phrase.

2.  Locate the div ssigned to the `homehero` id. Replace homehero with reshero.

3.  Delete all HTML tags and content within the main element except for the h2 element and text.

4.  Replace the text contained within the `<h2>` tags with: "Reservations at Pacific Trails".

5.  Configure an h3 element on a line under the h2 with the following text: "Contact Us".

6.   Configure a paragraph with the following text: Required fields are marked with an asterisk*.

7.  Prepare to code the HTML for the form area. Begin with a form element that uses the post method and the action attribute to invoke server-side processing. Unless directed otherwise by your instructor, configure the action attribute to send the form data to https://webdevbasics.net/scripts/pacific.php.

8.  Configure the form control for the First Name information. Create a label element that contains the text "*First Name:". Create a text box named myFName. Use the `for` attribute to associate the label element with the form control. Configure the browser to require entry in the text box.

9.  Configure the form control for the Last Name information. Create a label element that contains the text "*Last Name:". Create a text box named myLName. Use the `for` attribute to associate the label element with the form control. Configure the browser to require entry in the text box.

10. Configure the form control for the E-mail information. Create a label element that contains the text "*E-mail:". Create e-mail address input form control named myEmail. Use the `for` attribute to associate the label element with the form control. Configure the browser to require entry in the text box.

11. Configure the form control for the Phone information. Create a label element that contains the text "Phone:". Create a text box named myPhone. Use the `for` attribute to associate the label element with the form control. Configure the browser to require entry in the text box.

Figure 9.44  Single-column form in a narrow viewport

12. Configure the form control for the reservation arrival date. Create a label element that contains the text "Arrival Date:" Create a calendar date-picker form control named myDate. Use the for attribute to associate the label element with the form control.

13. Configure the form control for the number of nights. Create a label element that contains the text "Nights:" Create a spinner input form control (use type="number") named myNights. Use the for attribute to associate the label element with the form control. Configure the spinner form control to process a value between 1 and 14 to indicate the number of nights for the length of stay. Use the min and max attributes to configure the range of values.

14. Configure the Comments area on the form. Create a label element that contains the text *"Comments:". Create a textarea element named myComments with `rows` set to 2 and `cols` set to 20. Use the `for` attribute to associate the label element with the form control. Configure the browser to require entry in the textarea.

15. Configure the submit button on the form. Configure "Submit" to display on the button. Assign the input element to the id named `mySubmit`.

16. Code an ending `</form>` tag on a blank line after the submit button.

Save your file and test your web page in a browser. It should look similar to the page shown in Figure 9.42. If you resize the browser viewport to be narrower, the display should be similar to Figure 9.44. If you are connected to the Internet, submit the form. This will send your form information to the server-side script configured in the form tag. A confirmation page that lists the form information and their corresponding names will be displayed.

Next, submit the form with missing information or only a partial e-mail address. Depending on the browser's level of HTML5 support, the browser may perform form validation and display an error message. Figure 9.45 shows part of the Reservations page rendered with an incorrectly formatted e-mail address.

Figure 9.45 The Reservations page shows an error message

## Path of Light Yoga Studio

See Chapter 2 for an introduction to the Path of Light Yoga Studio case study. Figure 2.44 shows a site map for Path of Light Yoga Studio. Use the Chapter 8 Path of Light Yoga Studio website as a starting point for this case study. You will create the new Contact page that uses a form. You have three tasks in this case study:

1. Create a new folder for this Path of Light Yoga Studio case study.

2. Modify the style sheet (yoga.css) to configure style rules for the new form.

3. Create the Contact page shown in Figure 9.42.

**Figure 9.46** Path of Light Yoga Studio Contact page

## Hands-On Practice Case Study

**Task 1: The Website Folder.** Create a folder called yoga9. Copy all of the files from your Chapter 8 yoga8 folder into the yoga9 folder.

**Task 2: Configure the CSS.** Modify the external style sheet. Open yoga.css in a text editor. Review Figure 9.46 and the grid layout sketch in Figure 9.47. Notice how the text labels for the form controls are on the left side of the content area but contain right-aligned text. Notice the empty vertical space between each form control. When displaying on a narrow viewport, the display will be more pleasing if

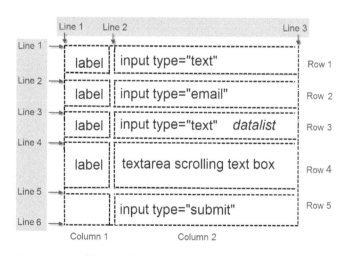

**Figure 9.47** The grid layout sketch of the form

there is only one column, as shown in Figure 9.48. Configure CSS as indicated below:

1. Configure the single column display for narrow viewports using flexbox. Add the following CSS above the media queries to configure the form element selector as a flex container with one column, 1em left padding, and 80% width. Also set a .5em bottom margin on the input and textarea element selectors.

2. Configure the two-column display with grid layout. Add CSS to the first media query.

   a. Configure a form element selector. Set 60% width, grid display with 1em grid gap, and two columns (12em width and 1 fr width).

   b. Configure an attribute selector for the submit button. Use the grid-column property to place this in the second column. Set width to 9em.

   c. Configure a label element selector with right alignment.

Save the yoga.css file.

**Task 3: Create the Contact Page.** Use the Classes page as the starting point for the Contact page. Launch a text editor and open classes.html. Save the file as contact.html. Modify your contact.html file to look similar to the Contact page (shown in Figure 9.42) as follows:

Figure 9.48 Single-column form in a narrow viewport

1. Change the page title to an appropriate phrase.

2. The Contact page will display a form in the main element. Delete all HTML and content within the main element except for the h2 element and its text.

3. Change the text in the h2 element to "Contact Path of Light Yoga Studio".

4. Configure a paragraph that contains the following:

   Fill out the form below to contact Path of Light Yoga Studio. All information is required.

5. Prepare to code the HTML for the form area. Begin with a form element that uses the post method and the action attribute to invoke server-side processing. Unless directed otherwise by your instructor, configure the action attribute to send the form data to https://webdevbasics.net/scripts/yoga.php.

6. Configure the form control for the Name information. Create a label element that contains the text "Name:". Create a text box named myName. Use the `for` attribute to associate the label element with the form control. Configure the browser to require entry in the text box.

7. Configure the form control for the E-mail information. Create a label element that contains the text "E-mail:". Create a text box named myEmail. Use the `for` attribute to associate the label element with the form control. Configure the browser to require entry in the text box.

8. Configure the form control to collect information about how the visitor heard about the yoga studio. Create a label element that contains the text "How did you hear about us?". Create a text box named myRefer. Use the for attribute to associate the label element with the textbox. Configure the browser to require entry in the text box. Associate the text box with a datalist named referral. Configure datalist and option elements to display the following referral types: Google, Bing, Facebook, Friend, Radio Ad.

9. Configure the Comments area on the form. Create a label element that contains the text "Comments:". Create a textarea element named myComments with `rows` set to 2 and `cols` set to 20. Use the `for` attribute to associate the label element with the form control. Configure the browser to require entry in the text box.

**10.** Configure the submit button on the form. Configure "Send Now" to display on the button. Assign the input element to the id named `mySubmit`.

**11.** Code an ending `</form>` tag on a blank line after the submit button.

Save your file and test your web page in a browser. It should look similar to the page shown in Figure 9.46. If you resize the browser viewport to be narrower, the display should be similar to Figure 9.48. If you are connected to the Internet, submit the form. This will send your form information to the server-side script configured in the form tag. A confirmation page that lists the form information and their corresponding names will be displayed.

Next, submit the form with missing information or only a partial e-mail address. Depending on the browser's level of HTML5 support, the browser may perform form validation and display an error message. Figure 9.49 shows the Contact page rendered in the Firefox browser with missing required information.

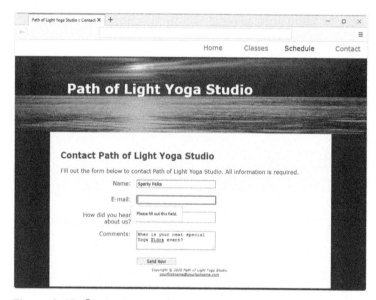

**Figure 9.49** Contact page shows an error message

# Web Project

See Chapters 5 and 6 for an introduction to the Web Project case study. You will either add a form to an existing page in your website or create a new page that contains a form. Use CSS to style the form.

## Hands-On Practice Case Study

**1.** Choose one of your project web pages to contain the form. Sketch a design of the form you plan to create.

**2.** Modify your project's external CSS file (project.css) to configure the form areas as needed.

**3.** Update your chosen web page and add the HTML code for the form.

**4.** The form element should use the post method and action attributes to invoke server-side processing. Unless directed otherwise by your instructor, configure the action attribute to send the form data to https://webdevbasics.net/scripts/demo.php.

Save and test the page. If you are connected to the Internet, submit the form. This will send your form information to the server-side script configured in the form element. A confirmation page that lists the form information and their corresponding names will be displayed.

# 10

# Web Development

## Chapter Objectives    In this chapter, you will learn how to . . .

- Describe the skills, functions, and job roles needed to develop a successful web project

- Utilize the stages in the standard System Development Life Cycle

- Identify other common system development methodologies

- Apply the System Development Life Cycle to the development of web projects

- Identify opportunities and determine goals during the Conceptualization phase

- Determine information topics and site requirements during the Analysis phase

- Create the site map, page layout, prototype, and documentation as part of the Design phase

- Complete the web pages and associated files during the Production phase

- Verify the functionality of the website and use a test plan during the Testing phase

- Obtain client approval and launch a website

- Modify and enhance the website during the Maintenance phase

- Compare the goals of the website to the results as part of the Evaluation phase

- Describe best practices for website file organization

- Find the right web hosting provider for your website

- Choose a domain name for your website

This chapter discusses the skills needed for successful large-scale project development and introduces you to common web development methods, choosing a domain name, and options for hosting a website.

# 10.1 Successful Large-Scale Project Development

Large-scale projects are not completed by only one or two individuals. They are created by a group of people working together as a team. The job roles of project manager, information architect, marketing representative, copywriter, editor, content manager, graphic designer, database administrator, network administrator, and web developer/designer are usually needed for large projects. In smaller companies or organizations, each person can wear many hats and juggle his or her job roles. For a smaller-scale project, one of the web developers may double as the project manager, web designer, graphic designer, database administrator, and/or information architect. It is important to realize that each project is unique; each has its own needs and requirements. Choosing the right people to work on a web project team can make it or break it.

## Project Job Roles

### Project Manager

The **project manager** oversees the website development process and coordinates team activities. The project manager creates the project plan and schedule. This individual is accountable for reaching project milestones and producing results. Excellent organizational, managerial, and communication skills are required.

### Information Architect

The **information architect** clarifies the mission and goals of the site; assists in determining the functionality of the site; and is instrumental in defining the site organization, navigation, and labeling. Web developers and/or the project manager sometimes take on this role.

### User Experience Designer

User experience (UX) is the user's interaction with a product, application, or website. A **user experience designer**, referred to as a **UX designer**, focuses on the user's interaction with the website. The UX designer may be involved with prototypes, conduct usability testing, and in some cases may work with information architecture. In a small project the project manager, web developer, or web designer may also take on the role of a UX designer.

### Marketing Representative

The **marketing representative** handles the organization's marketing plan and goals. He or she works with the web designers to create a **web presence**, or a look and feel, that aligns with the marketing goals of the organization. The marketing representative also helps to coordinate the website with other media used for marketing, such as print, radio, and television marketing.

### Copywriter and Editor

The **copywriter** prepares and evaluates copy. When material from existing brochures, newsletters, and white papers will be used on the website, it must be repurposed or reworked for the web media. An **editor** may work with the copywriter to check the text for correct grammar and consistency.

### Content Manager

The **content manager** participates in the strategic and creative development and enhancement of the website. He or she oversees changes in content. The skill set of a successful content manager includes editing, copywriting, marketing, technology, and communications. The person in this dynamic job role must be able to facilitate change.

### Graphic Designer

The **graphic designer** determines the appropriate use of color and graphics on the site, designs wireframes and page layouts, creates logos and graphic images, and optimizes images for display on the Web.

### Database Administrator

A **database administrator** is needed if the site accesses information stored in databases. Database administrators create databases, create procedures to maintain databases (including backup and recovery), and control access to databases.

### Network Administrator

The **network administrator** configures and maintains the **web server**, installs and maintains system hardware and software, and controls access security.

### Web Developer/Web Designer

The job titles of web developer and web designer are often used interchangeably, but typically a web developer has more of a coding and scripting focus and a web designer has more of a design and graphics focus. The **web designer** writes HTML and CSS code and may fulfill some graphic designer job duties, such as determining the appropriate use of color, designing wireframes and page layouts, creating logos and graphics, and optimizing images for display on the Web. The **web developer**, sometimes referred to as a **front-end web developer**, writes HTML, CSS, and client-side scripting such as JavaScript. Some web developers, often referred to as **back-end web developers**, may specialize in writing server-side scripting with database access. Typically, there are multiple web designers and web developers assigned to a large project, each with his or her area of expertise.

## Project Staffing Criteria

Whether the project is large or small, finding the right people to work on it is crucial. When selecting staff for a project, consider each individual's work experience, portfolio, formal education, and industry certifications.

Another option for staffing a web project (or developing an entire website) is to outsource the project—that is, hire another company to do the work for you. Sometimes portions of a project are outsourced, such as graphics creation, multimedia animation, or server-side scripting. When this option is chosen, communication between the project manager and the external organization is crucial. The outsourcing team needs to be aware of the project goals and deadlines.

Large or small, developed in-house or outsourced, the success of a website project depends on planning and communication. Formal project development methodology is used to coordinate and facilitate the planning and communication needed for a successful web project.

# 10.2 The Development Process

Large corporate and commercial websites don't just happen. They are carefully built, usually by following a project development methodology. A methodology is a step-by-step plan that encompasses the life cycle of a project from start to finish. It comprises a series of phases,

Figure 10.1 The
System Development
Life Cycle (SDLC)

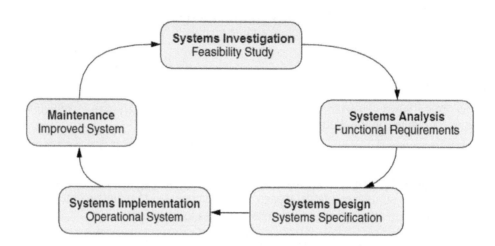

Figure 10.1 The
System Development
Life Cycle (SDLC)

each having specific activities and deliverables. Most modern methodologies have their roots in the **System Development Life Cycle (SDLC)**, a process that has been used for several decades to build large-scale information systems. The SDLC comprises a set of phases, sometimes called steps or stages. Each phase is usually completed before beginning the activities in the next phase. The basic phases of the standard SDLC (see Figure 10.1) are systems investigation, systems analysis, systems design, systems implementation, and maintenance.

Websites are often developed using a variation of the SDLC that is modified to apply to web projects. Large companies and web design firms usually create their own special methodology for use on projects. The Website Development Cycle is a guide to successful web project management. Depending on the scope and complexity of a particular project, some steps can be completed in a single meeting; other steps can take weeks or months.

The Website Development Cycle, shown in Figure 10.2, usually consists of the following steps: Conceptualization, Analysis, Design, Production, Testing, Launch, Maintenance, and Evaluation.

Figure 10.2 The Website
Development Cycle

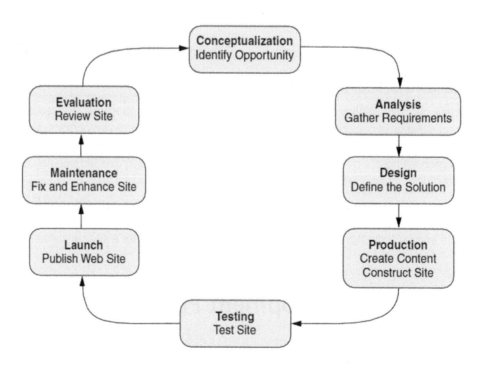

**FAQ    What about other development methodologies?**

The development methodology presented in this chapter is a version of the traditional SDLC modified for website development. Other development methods include the following:

- **Prototyping.** A small working model is created and shown to the client. It is continually revised by the developer until it is usable for the intended purpose. This method can easily be included in the Website Development Cycle during the Design phase.

- **Spiral System Development.** This is excellent for very-large-scale or phased projects where it is important to reduce risk. Small portions of the project are completed one after another in a spiral system of development.

- **Joint Application Development (JAD).** This type of development focuses on group meetings and collaboration between the users and developers of a website or system. It is generally used only with in-house development.

- **Agile Software Development.** This development methodology is viewed as innovative in that it stresses responsiveness based on generating and sharing knowledge within a development team and with the client. The philosophy emphasizes code over documentation and results in the project being developed in many small, iterative steps.

- **Organization-Specific Development Methodologies.** Large companies and web development firms often create their own version or interpretation of a site development methodology to be used for projects.

An important aspect of website development is that you are never finished—your site needs to be kept fresh and up-to-date, there will be errors or omissions that need to be corrected, and new components and pages will be needed. The first step is to decide why the website is needed in the first place.

## Conceptualization

What opportunity or issue is the site addressing? What is the motivation for the site? Perhaps your client owns a retail store and wishes to sell products over the Internet. Perhaps your client's competitor just launched a website and your client needs to create one just to keep up. Perhaps you have a great idea that will be the next eBay!

Because the focus of your work is to make the site usable and appealing to your target audience, you must determine the site's intended audience. It is crucial to be aware of who your audience is and what their preferences are.

Another task during **conceptualization** is to determine the site's long-term and short-term goals or mission. Perhaps a short-term goal is simply to publish a home page. Perhaps a long-term goal is for 20% of a company's product sales to be made on the website or you may simply want a certain number of website visitors each month. Whatever they are, it is better if the objectives are measurable. Decide how you will measure the success (or failure) of your website.

Determining the purpose and goals of a site is usually done with the cooperation of the client, project manager, and information architect. In a formal project environment, a document that details the results of this step is created and then approved by the client before development can proceed.

## Analysis

The Analysis phase involves meetings and interviews with key client personnel. **Analysis** is usually completed by the project manager, information architect or other analyst, and the client's marketing representative and related personnel. The network administrator and database administrator may be interviewed depending on the scope of the project. Common tasks completed during the Analysis phase are as follows:

- **Determine Information Topics.** Organize the information to be presented on the site into categories and create a hierarchy. These **information topics** will be used later as a starting point for developing the site navigation.

- **Determine Functionality Requirements.** State what the site will do, not how it will do it. For example, state that "the site will accept credit card orders from customers," not "the site will perform order processing using PHP to look up each price and sales tax information in MySQL databases and use real-time credit card verification supplied by somewebsite.com." Note the difference in the level of detail in these **functionality requirements**.

- **Determine Environmental Requirements.** What **environmental requirements**, such as hardware, operating system, memory capacity, screen resolution, and bandwidth, will your site visitors use? What type of hardware and software requirements will the web server need?

- **Determine Content Requirements.** Does content already exist in another format (for example, brochures, catalogs, white papers)? Determine who is responsible for creating and repurposing the content for the site. Does the client company or marketing department have any **content requirements** that must be met? For example, is there a specific visual aesthetic or corporate branding component that must be present on the site?

- **Compare the Old Approach to the New Approach.** Perhaps you are not creating a new website, but modifying an existing one. What benefits or added value will the new version provide?

- **Review Your Competitors' Sites.** A careful review of your competitors' web presence will help you design a site that will stand out from the crowd and be more appealing to your shared customer base. Note the good and bad components of these sites.

- **Estimate Costs.** Create an estimate of the costs and time involved to create the site. A formal project plan is often created or modified at this point. Often, an application such as Microsoft Project is used to estimate costs and plan project schedules.

- **Do a Cost/Benefit Analysis.** Create a document that compares the costs and benefits of the site. Measurable benefits are the most useful and most appealing to clients. In a formal project environment, a document that details the results of this **cost/benefit analysis** must be approved by the client before the team can proceed.

## Design

Once everyone knows what is needed, it is time to determine how it can be accomplished. The Design phase involves meetings and interviews with key client personnel. **Design** tasks are usually completed by the project manager, information architect or other analyst, graphic designer(s), senior web developer(s), and the client's marketing representative and related personnel. Common tasks during the Design phase include the following:

- **Choose a Site Organization.** As discussed in Chapter 5, common website organizational forms are hierarchical, linear, and random. Determine which is best for the project site and create a site map.

- **Design the Prototype.** As a starting point, sketch out the design on paper. Sometimes it's useful to sketch within an empty browser frame (see sketch.doc in the student files chapter10 folder). Often, a graphics application is used to create sample web page mock-ups, or wireframes. These can be shown to clients as a prototype, or working model, of the system for approval. They can also be shown to focus groups for usability testing.

- **Design a Page Layout.** Determine the visual aesthetic and layout with wireframes and sample page mock-ups. Items such as the site color scheme, the size of logo graphics, button graphics, and text should be determined. Using the page layout design and site map, create sample layouts for the home page and content pages. Use a graphic application to create mock-ups of these pages to get a good idea of how the site will function. If you use a web authoring tool at this early stage, you run the risk of your manager or client thinking that you already have the site half done and insisting on early delivery.

- **Document Each Page.** While this may seem unnecessary, lack of content is a frequent cause of website project delays. Prepare a content sheet for each page, such as the one shown in Figure 10.3 (see chapter10/contentsheet.doc in the student files), which describes the functionality of the document, text and graphic content requirements, source of content, and approver of content.

**Content Documentation**

**Page Title:**
**File Name:**
**Purpose of Page**

**Suggested Graphic Elements**

**Other Special Features**

**Information Needs**

**Information Sources**

**Content Providers**
*List name, e-mail, and phone number of each content provider*

**File Format of Content**
**Date Required:**
**Date Provided:**

**Content Approval** _____

Figure 10.3
Sample content sheet

The site map and page design prototypes are usually approved by the client before the team can progress to the Production phase.

## Production

During **production**, all the previous work comes together (hopefully) in a usable and effective website. During the Production phase, the web designers and web developers are on the critical path—their work must be completed as scheduled or the project will be late. The other project members are consulted, as needed, for clarification and approval. Common tasks of the Production phase include the following:

- **Choose a Web Authoring Tool.** The use of a web authoring tool, such as Adobe Dreamweaver, can greatly increase productivity. Specific productivity aids include designer notes, page templates, task management, and web page check-in and check-out to avoid overlapping page updates. The use of an authoring tool will serve to standardize the HTML used in the project pages. Any standards related to indentation, comments, and so on should be determined at this time.

- **Organize Your Site Files.** Consider placing images and media in their own folder. (see Section 10.3 File Organization). Also, place server-side scripts in a separate folder. Determine naming conventions for web pages, images, and media.

- **Develop and Individually Test Components.** During this task, the graphic designers and web developers create and individually test their contributions to the site. As the images, web pages, and server-side scripting are developed, they are individually tested. This is called **unit testing**. On some projects, a senior web developer or the project manager will review the components for quality and standards compliance.

Once all components have been created and unit tested, it's time to put them together and begin the Testing phase.

## Testing

The components should be published to a test web server. This test web server should have the same operating system and web server software that the production (actual) web server will be using. Some common site **testing** considerations follow:

- **Test on Different Browsers and Browser Versions.** It is very important to test your pages on commonly used browsers and versions of those browsers.

- **Test with Different Screen Resolutions.** Although, as a web developer, you may use a very high screen resolution, not everyone uses 2560×1440 screen resolution. The most commonly used screen resolutions at the time of this writing are 1366×768, 1920×1080, and 1024×768. Be sure to test your web pages on various resolutions—you might be surprised at the results.

- **Test Using Different Bandwidths.** If you live and work in a metropolitan area, everyone you know may have broadband access to the Internet. However, many people still use dial-up connections to access the Web. It is important to test your site on both slow and fast connections. Images that look great over your school's T3 line may load very slowly over a mobile hotspot.

- **Test from Another Location.** Be sure to test your website using a computer other than the one the website was developed on, in order to simulate the web page visitor's experience more closely.

- **Test Using Mobile Devices.** Mobile use of the Web is increasing all the time—test your site on one or more of the currently popular smartphones. Visit https://www.browserstack.com/test-on-the-right-mobile-devices for a list of popular mobile devices. See Chapter 7 for an overview of mobile web testing tools.

- **Test, Test, Test.** There is no such thing as too much testing. Humans make mistakes. It is much better for you and your team to find the errors than for your client to point them out to you when they review the website.

Does this sound like a lot to keep track of? It is. That's why it's a good idea to create a **test plan**, which is a document that describes what will be tested on each page of a website. A sample test plan for a web page, shown in Figure 10.4 (see chapter10/testplan.xls in the student files), can help you organize your testing as you check your document in different browsers and screen resolutions. The document validation section covers content, links, and any forms or scripting that are required for the page. Search engine optimization meta tags are discussed in Chapter 13. However, at this point, you should be able to verify that the page title is descriptive and includes the company or organization's name. Testing your page using different bandwidths is important because web pages that take too long to download are often abandoned.

**Figure 10.4**
Sample test plan

**Web Page Document Test Plan**

| File Name: | | | | | | | | | | Date: | |
| Page Title: | | | | | | | | | | Tester: | |

**Browser Compatibility**

| | 1366x768 | 1920x1080 | 1440x900 | Other | PC | Mac | Linux | Images Disabled | CSS Disabled | Other | Notes |
|---|---|---|---|---|---|---|---|---|---|---|---|
| Internet Explorer (Version #) | | | | | | | | | | | |
| Microsoft Edge (Version #) | | | | | | | | | | | |
| Firefox (Version #) | | | | | | | | | | | |
| Safari (Version #) | | | | | | | | | | | |
| Opera (Version #) | | | | | | | | | | | |
| Chrome (Version #) | | | | | | | | | | | |
| JAWS Screen Reader | | | | | | | | | | | |
| Tablet (Device Name) | | | | | | | | | | | |
| Smartphone 1 (Device Name) | | | | | | | | | | | |
| Smartphone 2 (Device Name) | | | | | | | | | | | |

**Document Validation**

| | Pass | Fail | Notes |
|---|---|---|---|
| HTML Validation | | | |
| CSS Validation | | | |
| Check Spelling | | | |
| Check for Required Content | | | |
| Check for Required Graphics | | | |
| Check alt Attributes | | | |
| Test Hyperlinks | | | |
| Accessibility Testing | | | |
| Form Processing | | | |
| Scripting/Dynamic Effects | | | |
| Usability Testing | | | |
| Other | | | |

**Search Engine Optimization**

| | Notes |
|---|---|
| Meta tag (description) | |
| Keywords in page title | |
| Keywords in headings | |
| Keywords in content | |
| Other | |

**Download Time Check**

| | Time | Notes |
|---|---|---|
| 56.6Kbps | | |
| 128Kbps | | |
| 512Kbps | | |
| T1/DS1 (1.544Mbps) | | |
| Other | | |

**Notes**

## Automated Testing Tools and Validators

The web authoring tool you use for your project will provide some built-in site reporting and testing features. Web authoring applications such as Adobe Dreamweaver provide functions such as spell-check, link checks, and load time calculations. Each application has unique features. Dreamweaver's reporting includes link checking, accessibility, and code validation. There are other **automated testing** tools and **validators** available. The W3C Markup Validation Service (https://validator.w3.org) can be used to validate both HTML and XHTML. Test CSS for proper syntax using the W3C CSS Validation Service (https://jigsaw.w3.org/css-validator). Analyze the download speed of your page using the Web Page Analyzer (http://www.websiteoptimization.com/services/analyze). Google's Mobile-Friendly automated test at https://search.google.com/test/mobile-friendly checks for common issues on mobile devices. The automated tool at https://web.dev/measure reviews your website according to performance, accessibility, best practices, and search engine optimization criteria.

## Accessibility Testing

**Focus on Accessibility**

**Accessible** web pages can be used by all individuals, including those with visual, hearing, mobility, and cognitive challenges. As you've worked through this book, accessibility has been an integral part of your web page design and coding rather than an afterthought. You've configured headings and subheadings, navigation within unordered lists, images with alternate text, and associations between text and form controls. These techniques all increase the accessibility of a web page.

### Web Accessibility Standards

**Section 508 of the Rehabilitation Act.**    Section 508 (https://www.section508.gov/) requires electronic and information technology, including web pages, that are used by U.S. federal agencies to be accessible to people with disabilities. The U.S. Access Board released a revision of Section 508 requirements (referred to as the Section 508 Refresh) in January 2017. The Section 508 refresh updates Section 508 requirements to harmonize with WCAG 2.0 Success Criteria.

### Web Content Accessibility Guidelines (WCAG 2.1).

The most recent version of WCAG is WCAG 2.1 (https://www.w3.org/TR/WCAG21/), which extends WCAG 2.0 and introduces additional success criteria including accessibility. WCAG considers an accessible web page to be perceivable, operable, and understandable for people with a wide range of abilities. The page should be robust enough to work with a variety of browsers and other user agents, such as assistive technologies (for example, screen readers) and mobile devices. The guiding principles of WCAG are known as POUR:

1. Content must be **P**erceivable.

2. Interface components in the content must be **O**perable.

3. Content and controls must be **U**nderstandable.

4. Content should be **R**obust enough to work with current and future user agents, including assistive technologies.

Prove your compliance with accessibility standards by performing **accessibility testing** on your site. A complete list of WCAG 2.1 Success Criteria is provided at https://www.w3.org/WAI/WCAG21/quickref/. As a starting point, go through the Easy Checks listed at https://www.w3.org/WAI/eval/preliminary. There are a variety of automated accessibility checkers available. WebAIM Wave (http://wave.webaim.org) and ATRC AChecker (https://www.achecker.ca/checker) are two popular free online accessibility evaluation tools. The Web Developer Extension is a browser toolbar that can be used to assess accessibility of a web page (https://chrispederick.com/work/web-developer). The ARC Toolkit (https://www.paciellogroup.com/toolkit) is an extension for Chrome that checks for WCAG 2.1 compliance.

It's important not to rely completely on automated tests—you'll want to review the pages yourself. For example, while an automated test can check for the presence of an alt attribute, it takes a human to critically think and decide whether the text of the alt attribute is an appropriate description for a person who cannot view the image.

## Usability Testing

**Usability** is the measure of the quality of a user's experience when interacting with a website. It's about making a website that is easy, efficient, and pleasant for your visitors. Usability.gov (https://www.usability.gov/what-and-why/usability-evaluation.html) describes factors that affect the user's experience:

- Intuitive Design. How easy is it for a new visitor to understand the organization of the site? Is the navigation intuitive for a new user?

- Ease of Learning. How easy is it to learn to use the website? Does a new visitor consider it easy to learn to perform basic tasks on the website or is he or she frustrated?

- Efficiency of Use. How do experienced users perceive the website? Once they are comfortable, are they able to complete tasks efficiently and quickly or are they frustrated?

- Memorability. When a visitor returns to a website, does he or she remember enough to use it productively or is the visitor back at the beginning of the learning curve (and frustrated)?

- Error Frequency and Severity. Do website visitors make errors when navigating or filling in forms on the website? Are they serious errors? Is it easy to recover from errors or are visitors frustrated?

- Subjective Satisfaction. Do users like using the website? Are they satisfied? Why or why not?

Testing how actual web page visitors use a website is called **usability testing**. It can be conducted at any phase of a website's development and is often performed more than once. A usability test is conducted by asking users to complete tasks on a website, such as placing an order, looking up the phone number of a company, or finding a product. The exact tasks will vary depending on the website being tested. The users are monitored while they try to perform these tasks. They are asked to think out loud about their doubts and hesitations. The results are recorded and discussed with the web design team. Often, changes are made to the navigation and page layouts based on these tests. Perform the small-scale usability test in Hands-On Exercise 5 at the end of this chapter to become more familiar with this technique.

If usability testing is done early in the development phase of a website, it may use the paper page layouts and site map. If the development team is struggling with a design issue, sometimes a usability test can help to determine which design idea is the better choice. When usability is done during a later phase, such as the Testing phase, the actual website is tested. This can lead to confirmation that the site is easy to use and well designed, to last minute changes in the website, or to a plan for website enhancements in the near future.

## Launch

Your client—whether another company or another department in your organization—needs to review and approve the test website before the files are published to the live site. Sometimes this approval takes place at a face-to-face meeting. Other times, the test URL is given to the client and the client e-mails approval or requested changes.

Once the test website has been approved, it is published to your live production website (this is called a **launch**). If you think you are finished, think again! It is crucial to test all site components after publishing to make sure the site functions properly in its new environment. Marketing and promotional activities for the website (see Chapter 13) usually take place at this time.

## Maintenance

A website is never finished. There are always errors or omissions that were overlooked during the development process. Clients usually find many new uses for a website once they have one and request modifications, additions, and new sections (this is called site **maintenance**). At this point, the project team identifies the new opportunity or enhancement and begins another loop through the development process.

Other types of updates needed may be relatively small—perhaps a link is broken, a word is misspelled, or a graphic needs to be changed. These small changes are usually made as soon as they are noticed. The question of who makes the changes and who approves them is often a matter of company policy. If you are a freelance web developer, the situation is more straightforward—you will make the changes and your client will approve them.

## Evaluation

Remember the goals set for the website in the Conceptualization phase? During the **evaluation** phase, it's time to review them and determine whether your website meets them. If not, consider how you can enhance the site and begin another loop through the development process.

 **Checkpoint 10.1**

**1.** Describe the role of the project manager.

**2.** Explain why many different roles are needed on a large-scale web project.

**3.** List three different techniques used to test a website. Describe each technique in one or two sentences.

# 10.3 File Organization

An unorganized website often contains a long list of files, which can become difficult to maintain over time. It's common practice to create a separate folder for images on a website. It's also a good idea to organize your web pages into folders by purpose or subject. This section introduces you to coding relative hyperlinks for a website with multiple folders.

As discussed in Chapter 2, a relative hyperlink is used to link to web pages within your site. You've been coding relative links to display web pages that are all inside the same folder. Let's consider a website for a bed and breakfast that features rooms and events. The folder and file listing is shown in Figure 10.5. The main folder for this website is called casita, and the web developer has created separate subfolders—named images, rooms, and events—to organize the site.

 casita
index.html
contact.html
casita.css

 images
logo.gif
scenery.jpg

 rooms
canyon.html
javelina.html

 events
weekend.html
festival.html

**Figure 10.5** The web page files are organized in folders.

## Relative Hyperlink Examples

Recall that when linking to a file located in the same folder or directory, the value of the `href` attribute is the name of the file. For example, to link from the home page (index.html) to the contact.html page, code the anchor element as follows:

```
<a href="contact.html">Contact</a>
```

When linking to a file that is inside a folder within the current directory, use both the folder name and the file name in the relative link. For example, to link from the home page (index.html) to the canyon.html page (located in the rooms folder), code the anchor element as follows:

```
<a href="rooms/canyon.html">Canyon</a>
```

As shown in Figure 10.5, the canyon.html page is located in the rooms subfolder of the casita folder. The home page for the site (index.html) is located in the casita folder. When linking to a file that is up one directory level from the current page, use the ". ./" notation. To link to the home page for the site from the canyon.html page, code the anchor element as follows:

```
<a href="../index.html">Home</a>
```

When linking to a file that is in a folder on the same level as the current folder, the href value will use the ". ./" notation to indicate moving up one level; then specify the desired folder. For example, to link to the weekend.html page in the events folder from the canyon.html page in the rooms folder, code the anchor element as follows:

```
<a href="../events/weekend.html">Weekend Events</a>
```

Don't worry if the use of ". ./" notation and linking to files in different folders seems new and different. You can explore the example of the bed and breakfast website located in the student files (see chapter10/CasitaExample) to become more familiar with coding references to files in different folders.

## Hands-On Practice 10.1

This Hands-On Practice provides an opportunity to practice coding hyperlinks to files in different folders. The website you'll be working with has pages in prototype form—the navigation and layout of the pages are configured, but the specific content has not yet been added. You'll focus on the navigation area in this Hands-On Practice. Figure 10.6 shows a partial screen shot of the bed and breakfast's home page with a navigation area on the left side of the page.

Examine Figure 10.7 and notice the new juniper.html file listed within the rooms folder. You will create a new web page (Juniper Room) named juniper.html and save it in the rooms folder. Then,

Figure 10.6 The navigation area.

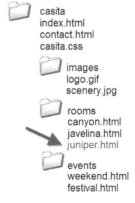

Figure 10.7 New juniper.html file is in the rooms folder.

you will update the navigation area on each existing web page to link to the new Juniper Room page.

1. Copy the CasitaExample folder (chapter10/CasitaExample) from the student files. Rename the folder casita.

2. Display the index.html file in a browser and click through the navigation links. View the source code of the pages and notice how the `href` values of the anchor tags are configured to link to and from files within different folders.

3. Launch a text editor and open the canyon.html file. You'll use this file as a starting point for your new Juniper Room page. Save the file as juniper.html in the rooms folder.

   a. Edit the page title and h2 text: change "Canyon" to "Juniper".

   b. Add a new li element in the navigation area that contains a hyperlink to the juniper.html file.

   ```
   <li><a href="juniper.html">Juniper Room
   </a></li>
   ```

   Place this hyperlink between the Javelina Room and Weekend Events navigation hyperlinks as shown in Figure 10.8. Save the file.

**Figure 10.8** The new navigation area.

4. Use the coding for the Canyon and Javelina hyperlinks as a guide as you add the Juniper Room link to the navigation area on each of the following pages:
   index.html
   contact.html
   rooms/canyon.html
   rooms/javelina.html
   events/weekend.html
   events/festival.html

Save all the .html files and test your pages in a browser. The navigation hyperlink to the new Juniper Room page should work from every other page. The hyperlinks on the new Juniper Room page should function well and open other pages as expected. A solution is in the student files (chapter10/10.1 folder).

VideoNote
**Choosing a Domain Name**

# 10.4 Domain Name Overview

A crucial part of establishing an effective web presence is choosing a **domain name**; it serves to locate your website on the Internet. If your business or organization is new, then it's often convenient to select a domain name while you are deciding on a company name. If your organization is well established, choose a domain name that relates to your existing business presence. Although many domain names have already been purchased, there are still a lot of available options.

## Choosing a Domain Name

- **Describe Your Business.** Although there is a long-standing trend to use "fun" words as domain names (for example, yahoo.com, google.com, bing.com, woofoo. com, and so on), think carefully before doing so. Domain names for traditional businesses and organizations are the foundation of the organization's web presence and should include the business name or purpose.

- **Be Brief, If Possible.** While most people find new websites with search engines, some of your website visitors will type your domain name in a browser. A shorter domain name is preferable to a longer one—it's easier for your visitors to remember.

- **Avoid Hyphens (-).** Using the hyphen character (commonly called a dash) in a domain name makes it difficult to pronounce the name. Also, someone typing your domain name may forget the dash and end up at a competitor's site! If you can, avoid the use of dashes in a domain name.

- **There's More Than .com.** While the .com top-level domain name (TLD) is still the most popular for commercial and personal websites, consider also registering your domain name with other TLDs, such as .biz, .net, .us, .mobi, and so on. Commercial businesses should avoid the .org TLD, which is the first choice for nonprofit organizations. You don't have to create a website for each domain name that you register. You can arrange with your domain name registrar, for example, Register.com (https://www.register.com), for the extra domain names to point visitors to the domain name where your website is located. This is called **domain name redirection**.

- **Brainstorm Potential Keywords.** Think about words that a potential visitor might type into a search engine when looking for your type of business or organization. This is the starting point for your list of **keywords**. If possible, work one or more keywords into your domain name (but still keep it as short as possible).

- **Avoid Trademarked Words or Phrases.** The U.S. Patent and Trademark Office (USPTO) defines a **trademark** as a word, phrase, symbol, or design, or a combination of words, phrases, symbols, or designs, that identifies and distinguishes the source of the goods of one party from those of others. A starting point in researching trademarks is the USPTO Trademark Electronic Search System (TESS); visit http://tess2.uspto.gov. See https://www.uspto.gov for more information about trademarks.

- **Know the Territory.** Explore the way your potential domain name and keywords are already used on the Web. It's a good idea to type your potential domain names (and related words) into a search engine to see what may already exist.

- **Verify Availability.** Check with one of the many **domain name registrars** to determine whether your domain name choices are available. A few of the many sites that offer domain name registration services are listed below:

  - Register.com: https://www.register.com

  - Network Solutions: https://www.networksolutions.com

  - GoDaddy.com: https://www.godaddy.com

Each of these sites offers a search feature that provides you with a way to determine whether a potential domain name is available, and if it is owned, who owns it. Often the domain name is already taken. If that's the case, the sites listed previously will provide you with alternate suggestions that may be appropriate. Don't give up; a domain name is out there waiting for your business.

## Registering a Domain Name

Once you've found your perfect domain name, don't waste any time in registering it. The cost to register a domain name varies, but it is quite reasonable. There are numerous opportunities for discounts with multiyear packages or bundled web hosting services. It's perfectly okay to register a domain name even if you are not ready to publish your website immediately. There are many companies that provide domain name registration services, as listed previously. When you register a domain name, your contact information (your name, phone number, mailing address, and e-mail address) will be entered into the WHOIS database and is available to anyone unless you choose the option for private registration. While there is usually a small annual fee for **private registration**, it shields your personal information from unwanted spam and curiosity seekers.

Obtaining a domain name is just one part of establishing a web presence. You also need to host your website somewhere. The next section introduces you to the factors involved in choosing a web host.

# 10.5 Web Hosting

Where is the appropriate place for your web project to "live"? Choosing the most appropriate web hosting provider for your business or client could be one of the most important decisions you make. A good web hosting service will provide a robust, reliable home for your website. A poor web hosting service will be a source of problems and complaints. Which would you prefer?

## Web Hosting Providers

A **web hosting provider** is an organization that offers storage for your website files along with the service of making them available on the Internet. Your domain name, such as webdevfoundations.net, is associated with an IP address that points to your website on the web server at the web hosting provider. It is common for web hosting providers to charge a setup fee in addition to the monthly hosting fee.

Hosting fees vary widely. The cheapest hosting company is not necessarily the one to use. Never consider using a free web hosting provider for a business website. These free sites are great for kids, college students, and hobbyists, but they are unprofessional. The last thing you or your client wants is to be perceived as unprofessional or not serious about the business at hand. As you consider different web hosting providers, try contacting their support phone numbers and e-mail addresses to determine just how responsive they really are. Word of mouth, web searches, and online directories such as Hosting Review (https://www.hosting-review.com) are all resources in your quest for the perfect web hosting provider.

### Types of Web Hosting

- **Virtual Hosting**, or shared hosting, is a popular choice for small websites. The web hosting provider's physical web server is divided into a number of virtual domains and multiple websites are set up on the same computer. You have the authority to update files in your own website space, while the web hosting provider maintains the web server computer and Internet connectivity.

- **Dedicated Hosting** is the rental and exclusive use of a computer and connection to the Internet that is housed on the web hosting company's premises. A dedicated server is usually needed for a website that could have a considerable amount of traffic, such as tens of millions of hits a day. The server can usually be configured and operated remotely from the client's company, or you can pay the web hosting provider to administer it for you.

- **Co-Located Hosting** uses a computer that your organization has purchased and configured. Your web server is housed and connected to the Internet at the web host's physical location, but your organization typically administers this computer.

## 10.6 Choosing a Virtual Host

A number of factors to consider when choosing a web host have been discussed, including bandwidth, disk storage space, technical support, and the availability of e-commerce packages. For a handy list of these factors and others to consider in your quest for a virtual web host, review the web host checklist shown in Table 10.1.

 FAQ   **Why do I care about knowing which operating system my web hosting provider uses?**

Knowing the operating system used by your web hosting provider is important because it can help you with troubleshooting your website. Often, students' websites work great on their own PC (usually with a Windows-based operating system) but fall apart (with broken links and images that do not load) after being published on a free web server that uses a different operating system.

Some operating systems, such as Windows, treat uppercase and lowercase letters in exactly the same way. Other operating systems, such as UNIX and Linux, consider uppercase and lowercase letters to be different. This is called being **case-sensitive**. For example, when a web server running on a Windows operating system receives a request generated by an anchor tag coded as `<a href="Index.html">Home</a>`, it will return a file named with any combination of uppercase or lowercase letters. File names such as Index.html, index.html, and INDEX.HTML can all be used. However, when the request generated by the same anchor tag is received by a web server running on a UNIX system (which is case-sensitive), the file would only be found if it were really saved as Index.html. If the file were named index.html, a 404 Not Found error would result. This is a good reason to be consistent when naming files; consider always using lowercase letters for file names.

Table 10.1 Web host checklist

| | | |
|---|---|---|
| Operating System | ❑ UNIX<br>❑ Linux<br>❑ Windows | Some web hosts offer a choice of these platforms. If you need to integrate your website with your business systems, choose the same operating system for both. |
| Web Server | ❑ Apache<br>❑ IIS | These two web server applications are the most popular. Apache usually runs on a UNIX or Linux operating system. Internet Information Services (IIS) is bundled with selected versions of Microsoft Windows. |
| Bandwidth | ❑ _____ GB per month<br>❑ _____ Charge for overage | Some web hosts carefully monitor your data transfer bandwidth and charge you for overages. While unlimited bandwidth is great, it is not always available. A typical low-traffic website may transfer between 100 and 500MB per month. A medium-traffic site should be okay with about 20GB of data transfer bandwidth per month. |
| Technical Support | ❑ E-mail<br>❑ Chat<br>❑ Forum<br>❑ Phone | Review the description of technical support on the web host's site. Is it available 24 hours a day, 7 days a week? E-mail or phone a question to test it. If the organization is not responsive to you as a prospective customer, be leery about the availability of its technical support later. |
| Service Agreement | ❑ Uptime guarantee<br>❑ Automatic monitoring | A web host that offers a **Service Level Agreement (SLA)** with an uptime guarantee shows that they value service and reliability. The use of automatic monitoring will inform the web host technical support staff when a server is not functioning. |
| Disk Space | ❑ _____ GB | Many virtual hosts routinely offer several gigabytes of disk storage space. If you have a small site that is not graphics-intensive, you may never even use 100MB of disk storage space. |
| E-mail | ❑ _____ Mailboxes | Most virtual hosts offer multiple e-mail boxes per site. These can be used to filter messages (customer service, technical support, general inquiries, and so on). |
| Uploading Files | ❑ FTP Access<br>❑ Web-based File Manager | A web host that offers FTP access will allow you the most flexibility. Others only allow updates through a web-based file manager application. Some web hosts offer both options. |
| Canned Scripts | ❑ Form processing | Many web hosts supply canned, pre-written scripts to process form information. |
| Scripting Support | ❑ PHP<br>❑ .NET<br>❑ _____ Other | If you plan to use server-side scripting on your site, determine which, if any, scripting is supported by your web host. |
| Database Support | ❑ MySQL<br>❑ SQL Server | If you plan to access a database with your scripting, determine which, if any, database is supported by your web host. |
| E-Commerce Packages | ❑ _____ | If you plan to enter into ecommerce (see Chapter 12), it may be easier if your web host offers a shopping cart package. Check to see if one is available. |
| SSL | ❑ $_____ setup fee<br>❑ $_____ per month | Determine if your web host offers SSL (see Chapter 12). You may want to use https in the future to prevent security issues. |
| Scalability | ❑ Scripting<br>❑ Database<br>❑ E-commerce | You probably will choose a basic (low-end) plan for your first website. Note the scalability of your web host: Are there other available plans with scripting, database, e-commerce packages, and additional bandwidth or disk space as your site grows? |
| Backups | ❑ Daily<br>❑ Periodic<br>❑ No backups | Most web hosts will back up your files regularly. Check to see how often the backups are made and if they are accessible to you. Be sure to make your own site backups as well. |
| Site Statistics | ❑ Raw log file<br>❑ Log reports<br>❑ No log access | The web server log contains useful information about your visitors, how they find your site, and what pages they visit. Check to see if the log is available to you. Some web hosts provide reports about the log. See Chapter 13 for more information on web server logs. |
| Domain Name | ❑ Required to register with host<br>❑ OK to register on your own | Some web hosts offer a package that includes registering your domain name. However, you will retain control of your domain name account if you register it yourself. |
| Price | ❑ $_____ setup fee<br>❑ $_____ per month | Price is last in this list for a reason. Do not choose a web host based on price alone—the old adage "you get what you pay for" is definitely true here. It is not unusual to pay a one-time setup fee and then a periodic fee—monthly, quarterly, or annually. |

# Checkpoint 10.2

1. Describe the type of web host that would meet the needs of a small company for its initial web presence.

2. What is the difference between a dedicated web server and a co-located web server?

3. Explain why price is not the most important consideration when choosing a web host.

# Chapter Summary

This chapter introduced the System Development Life Cycle and its application to web development projects. The job roles related to website development were discussed. The chapter also included an introduction to choosing a domain name and a website host provider. Visit the textbook website at https://www.webdevfoundations.net for examples, the links listed in this chapter, and updated information.

## Key Terms

accessibility testing
accessible
analysis
automated testing
back-end web developer
case-sensitive
co-located hosting
conceptualization
content manager
content requirements
copywriter
cost-benefit analysis
database administrator
dedicated hosting
design
domain name
domain name redirection

domain name registrars
editor
environmental requirements
evaluation
front-end web developer
functionality requirements
graphic designer
information architect
information topics
keywords
launch
maintenance
marketing representative
network administrator
private registration
production
project manager

Service Level Agreement (SLA)
System Development Life Cycle (SDLC)
test plan
testing
trademark
unit testing
user experience designer
usability
usability testing
UX designer
validators
virtual hosting
web designer
web developer
web hosting provider
web presence
web server

## Review Questions

### Multiple Choice

1. In which phase is a prototype of the website often created?
   a. Design phase
   b. Conceptualization phase
   c. Production phase
   d. Analysis phase

2. Which of the following are included in the role of an information architect?
   a. being instrumental in defining the site organization, navigation, and labeling
   b. attending all meetings and collecting all information
   c. managing the project
   d. none of the above

3. What is the purpose of private registration for a domain name?
   a. It protects the privacy of your website.
   b. It is the cheapest form of domain name registration.
   c. It protects the privacy of your contact information.
   d. none of the above

4. Which methodology is often used by web project teams?
   a. the SDLC
   b. a derivative of the SDLC that is similar to the one discussed in this chapter
   c. a methodology that is decided as the project is built
   d. no development methodology is necessary

5. Which of the following should be included when testing a website?
   a. checking all of the hyperlinks within the site
   b. viewing the site in a variety of web browsers
   c. viewing the site in a variety of screen resolutions
   d. all of the above

6. What do team members do during the Analysis phase of a website project?
   a. determine what the site will do—not how it will be done
   b. determine the information topics of the site
   c. determine the content requirements of the site
   d. all of the above

7. Which of the following occurs during the Production phase?
   a. A web authoring tool is often used.
   b. The graphics, web pages, and other components are created.
   c. The web pages are individually tested.
   d. all of the above

8. Which of the following occurs during the Evaluation phase?
   a. The goals for the site are reviewed.
   b. The web designers are evaluated.
   c. The competition is evaluated.
   d. none of the above

9. Which of the following is true about domain names?
   a. It is recommended to register multiple domain names that are redirected to your website.
   b. It is recommended to use long, descriptive domain names.
   c. It is recommended to use hyphens in domain names.
   d. There is no reason to check for trademarks when you are choosing a domain name.

10. Which web hosting option is appropriate for the initial web presence of an organization?
    a. dedicated hosting
    b. free web hosting
    c. virtual hosting
    d. co-located hosting

## Fill in the Blank

11. _____ can be described as testing how actual web page visitors use a website.

12. The _____ determines the appropriate use of graphics on the site and creates and edits graphics.

13. The _____ operating system(s) treat uppercase and lowercase letters differently.

## Short Answer

14. Why should the websites of competitors be reviewed when designing a website?

15. Why should you try to contact the technical support staff of a web hosting provider before you become one of its customers?

# Hands-On Exercises

1. Skip this exercise if you have completed Hands-On Practice 2.15 in Chapter 2. In this exercise, you will validate a web page. Choose one of the web pages that you have created. Launch a browser and visit the W3C Markup Validation Service (https://validator.w3.org). Click on the Validate by File Upload tab. Click the Browse button, select a file from your computer, and click the Check button to upload the file to the W3C site. Your page will be analyzed and a Results page will be generated that shows a report of violations of the doctype that is used by your web page. The error messages display the offending code along with the line number, column number, and a description of the error. Don't worry if your web page does not pass the validation the first time. Many well-known websites have pages that do not validate—even Yahoo! (https://www.yahoo.com) had validation errors at the time this was written. Modify your web page document and revalidate it until you see a message that states. "Document checking completed. No errors or warnings to show".

   You can also validate pages directly from the Web. Try validating the W3C's home page (https://www.w3.org), Yahoo! (https://www.yahoo.com), and your school's home page. Visit the W3C Markup Validation Service (https://validator.w3.org) and notice the

Validate by URI area. Enter the URL of the web page you would like to validate in the Address text box. Click the Check button and view the results. Experiment with the character encoding and doctype options. The W3C's page should pass the validation. Don't worry if the other pages do not validate. Validation is not required for web pages. However, web pages that pass the validation should display well in most browsers. (*Note:* If you have published pages to the web, try validating one of them instead of your school's home page.)

2. Run an automated accessibility test on the home page of your school's website. Use both the WebAIM Wave (http://wave.webaim.org) and ATRC AChecker (https://www.achecker.ca/checker) automated tests. Describe the differences in the way these tools report the results of the test. Did both tests find similar errors? Write a one-page report that describes the results of the tests. Include your recommendations for improving the website.

3. The Web Page Analyzer (http://www.websiteoptimization.com/services/analyze) calculates download times for a web page and associated assets, along with providing suggestions for improvement. Visit this site and test your school's home page (or a page assigned by your instructor). After the test is run, a web page speed report will display file sizes and include suggestions for improvement. Print out the browser view of this results page and write a one-page report that describes the results of the test and your own recommendations for improvement.

4. The Dr. Watson site (http://watson.addy.com) offers free web page validation. Visit this site and test your school's home page (or a page assigned by your instructor). After the test is run, a report is displayed with categories such as server response, estimated download speed, syntax and style analysis, spell-check, link verification, images, search engine compatibility (see Chapter 13), site link popularity (see Chapter 13), and source code. Print out the browser view of this results page and write a one-page report that describes the results of the test and your own recommendations for improvement.

5. Perform a small-scale usability test with a group of other students. Decide who will be the typical users, the tester, and the observer. You will perform a usability test on your school's website.

   • The typical users are the test subjects.
   • The tester oversees the usability test and emphasizes that the users are not being tested; the website is being tested.
   • The observer takes notes on the user's reactions and comments.

   **Step 1** The tester welcomes the users and introduces them to the website that they will be testing.

   **Step 2** For each of the following scenarios, the tester introduces the scenario and questions the users as they work through the task. The tester should ask the users to indicate when they are in doubt, confused, or frustrated. The observer takes notes.

   • Scenario 1: Find the phone number of the contact person for the web development program at your school.

   • Scenario 2: Determine when to register for the next semester.

   • Scenario 3: Find the requirements for earning a degree or certificate in web development or a related area.

   **Step 3** The tester and the observer organize the results and write a brief report. If this were a usability test for a website that you were developing, the development team would meet to review the results and discuss the necessary improvements to the site.

**Step 4** Hand in a report with your group's usability test results. Complete the report using a word processor. Write no more than one page about each scenario. Write one page of recommendations for improving your school's website.

*Note:* For more information on usability testing, see https://www.usability.gov/how-to-and-tools/methods/running-usability-tests.html and Keith Instone's classic presentation at http://instone.org/files/KEI-Howtotest-19990721.pdf. Another good resource is Steven Krug's book, *Don't Make Me Think*.

6. See the description of usability testing in Hands-On Exercise 5. In a small group, perform usability tests on two similar websites, such as the following:

   - Barnes and Noble (https://www.bn.com) and Powell's Books (https://powells.com)
   - AccuWeather.com (https://accuweather.com) and Weather Underground (https://www.wunderground.com)
   - Runner's World (https://www.runnersworld.com) and Cool Running (https://www.coolrunning.com)

   Select and list three scenarios to test. Decide who will be the users, the tester, and the observer. Follow the steps listed in Hands-On Exercise 5.

7. Pretend that you are on a job interview. Choose a role on a web project team that interests you. In three or four sentences, describe why you would be an excellent addition to a web development team in that role.

## Web Research

1. This chapter discussed options for hosting websites. In this research exercise, you will search for web hosting providers and report on three that meet the following criteria:

   - Support PHP and MySQL.
   - Offer e-commerce capabilities.
   - Provide at least 1GB disk space.

   Use your favorite search engine to find web hosting providers or visit web host directories such as Hosting Review (https://www.hosting-review.com) and HostIndex.com (http://www.hostindex.com). The web server survey results provided by Netcraft (http://uptime.netcraft.com/perf/reports/Hosters) may also be useful. Create a web page that presents your findings. Include links to your three web hosting providers. Your web page should include a table of information such as the setup fees, monthly fees, domain name registration costs, amount of disk space, type of e-commerce package, and cost of e-commerce package. Use color and graphics appropriately on your web page. Place your name and e-mail address at the bottom of your web page.

2. This chapter discussed the different job functions that are needed to develop large websites. Choose a job role that interests you. Search for information about available jobs in your geographical area. Search for technology jobs with your favorite search engine or visit a job site such as Monster.com (https://www.monster.com), Dice (https://www.dice.com), Indeed (https://www.indeed.com), or CareerBuilder.com (http://www.careerbuilder.com) and search for your desired location and job type. Find three possible job positions that interest you and report on them. Create a web page that includes a brief description of the job role you have chosen, a description of the three available positions, a description of the types of experience and/or educational background required for the positions, and the salary range (if available). Use color and graphics appropriately on your web page. Place your name and e-mail address at the bottom of your web page.

## Focus on Web Design

The U.S. Department of Health and Human Services provides a collection of researched-based usability guidelines at https://webstandards.hhs.gov/guidelines/. The website suggests guidelines for a variety of topics organized into chapters, including navigation, text appearance, scrolling and paging, writing content, usability testing, and accessibility. Choose one chapter topic that interests you. Read the chapter. Note four guidelines that you find intriguing or useful. In a one-page report, describe why you chose the chapter topic and the four guidelines you noted.

# WEBSITE CASE STUDY

## Testing Phase

This case study continues throughout the rest of the text. In this chapter, you will test the Web Project case study.

## Web Project

See Chapter 5 for an introduction to the Web Project. In this chapter, you will develop a test plan for the project. You will review the documents created in the previous chapters' Web Project and create a test plan.

### Hands-On Practice Case Study

**Part 1: Review the Design Documents and Completed Web Pages.** Review the Topic Approval, Site Map, and Page Layout Design documents that you created in the Chapter 5 Web Project. Review the web pages that you have created and/or modified in the Chapter 6 through Chapter 9 Web Project activities.

**Part 2: Prepare a Test Plan.** See Figure 10.4 for a sample test plan document (chapter10/testplan.pdf in the student files). Create a test plan document for your website, including CSS validation, HTML validation, and accessibility testing.

**Part 3: Test Your Website.** Implement your test plan and test each page that you have developed for your Web Project. Record the results. Create a list of suggested improvements.

**Part 4: Perform Usability Testing.** Describe three scenarios that typical visitors to your site may encounter. Using Hands-On Exercise 5 as a guide, conduct a usability test for these scenarios. Write a one-page report about your findings. What improvements would you suggest for the website?

# Web Multimedia and Interactivity

**Chapter Objectives**     In this chapter, you will learn how to . . .

- Describe the purpose of media containers and codecs
- Describe the types of multimedia files used on the Web
- Configure hyperlinks to multimedia files
- Configure audio and video on a web page
- Create an interactive drop down navigation menu with CSS
- Configure the CSS transform, transition, animation properties
- Create an interactive image gallery menu with CSS

- Configure an interactive widget with the details and summary elements
- Describe features and common uses of JavaScript
- Describe the purpose of HTML5 APIs such as geolocation, web storage, manifest, service workers, and canvas
- Describe features and common uses of Ajax
- Describe features and common uses of jQuery

**Video and sounds on your web pages** can make them more interesting and informative. In this chapter, you'll work with multimedia and interactive elements on web pages.

You began to work with **interactivity** in Chapter 6 when you used CSS pseudo-classes to respond to mouse movements over hyperlinks. You'll expand your CSS skill set as you configure an interactive image gallery, an interactive drop down navigation menu, and explore CSS transition, transform, and animation properties. Adding the right touch of interactivity to a web page can make it engaging and compelling for your visitors.

In addition to CSS, other technologies commonly used to add interactivity to web pages include JavaScript, Ajax, jQuery, and HTML APIs. Each of these topics is explored more fully in other books; each technology could be the sole subject of an entire book or college course. As you read this chapter and try the examples, concentrate on learning the features and capabilities of each technology, rather than trying to master the details.

# 11.1  Containers and Codecs

When working with native HTML5 audio and video, it's useful to be aware of the **container** (which is designated by the file extension) and the **codec** (which is the algorithm used to compress the media). There is no single codec that is supported by popular browsers. See https://caniuse.com for current information about browser support for HTML5 video and codecs.

Explore Table 11.1 and Table 11.2, which list common media file extensions and a description with codec information (if applicable for HTML5). Note that there is not always a one-to-one correspondence between file extensions and codecs. In some cases, multiple codecs may use the same file extension as their container.

Table 11.1  Common audio file types

| File Extension | Description |
| --- | --- |
| .aiif, .aif | Audio Interchange; popular audio file format on the Mac platform; also supported on the PC platform |
| .au | Sun UNIX Found File; older type of sound file that generally has poorer sound quality than the newer audio file formats |
| .m4a, .aac | MPEG-4 Audio; audio-only MPEG-4 format that uses the Advanced Audio Coding (AAC) codec |
| .mid | Musical Instrument Digital Interface (MIDI); contains instructions to recreate a musical sound rather than a digital recording of the sound itself; a limited number of types of sounds can be reproduced |
| .mp3 | MPEG-1 Audio Layer-3; popular for music files because of the MP3 codec, which supports two channels and advanced compression |
| .ogg | Open-source audio file format (see https://www.vorbis.com), Vorbis codec; Opus codec |
| .wav | Wave; Waveform Audio File format for uncompressed sound files; a standard on the PC platform |

Table 11.2  Common video file types

| File Extension | Description |
|---|---|
| .3gp | 3GPP Multimedia; H.264 codec; A standard for delivery of multimedia over 3G; also supported on some 2G and 4G phones |
| .av1, .mp4 | Newer open-source, royalty-free AV1 video codec; Alliance for Open Media (https://aomedia.org); |
| .avi | Audio Video Interleaved; Microsoft's original video format for the PC platform |
| .m4v, .mp4 | MPEG-4 (MP4) codec; H.264 codec |
| .mov | Developed by Apple and originally indicated a video with a MPEG-4 codec used in Apple's Quicktime application |
| .mov, .mp4, .hevc | Newer High-efficiency Video Coding HEVC codec (also called H.265 codec); Apple has begun using the .mov file extension HEVC video |
| .mpg | Developed under the sponsorship of the Moving Picture Experts Group (MPEG) (https://mpeg.chiariglione.org); MPEG-2 codec |
| .ogv, .ogg | Open-source video file format (https://www.theora.org); Theora codec |
| .webm | Open media file format (https://www.webmproject.org); VP9 and VP9 video codecs; Vorbis and Opus audio codecs |

# 11.2  Getting Started with Audio and Video

As you read this chapter, you'll explore several ways to provide audio and video for your website visitors, including a hyperlink, the audio element, and the video element. We'll get started with the easiest method, which is coding a hyperlink.

## Provide a Hyperlink

The easiest way to give your website visitors access to an audio or a video file is to create a simple hyperlink to the file. For example, the code to hyperlink to a sound file named WDFpodcast.mp3 is

```
<a href="WDFpodcast.mp3">Podcast Episode 1</a> (MP3)
```

When your website visitor clicks on the hyperlink, the plug-in for MP3 files that is installed on the computer typically will display embedded in a new browser window or tab. Your web page visitor can then use the plug-in to play the sound. If your website visitor right-clicks on the hyperlink, the media file can be downloaded and saved.

## Hands-On Practice 11.1

In this Hands-On Practice, you will create a web page similar to Figure 11.1 that contains an h1 tag and a hyperlink to an MP3 file. The web page will also provide a hyperlink to a text transcript of that file to provide for accessibility. It's useful to your web page visitors to also indicate the type of file (such as an MP3) and, optionally, the size of the file to be accessed.

**Figure 11.1** The default MP3 player will launch in the browser when the visitor clicks on Podcast Episode 1

Copy the podcast.mp3 and podcast.txt files from the chapter11/starters folder in the student files and save them to a folder named podcast. Launch a text editor and open chapter11/template.html in the student files. Edit the web page with the heading "Web Design Podcast", a hyperlink to the MP3 file, and a hyperlink to the text transcript. Save your web page as podcast2.html and display it in a browser. Test your web page in different browsers, using different versions. When you click on the MP3 hyperlink, an audio player (whichever player or plug-in is configured for the browser) will launch to play the file. When you click on the hyperlink for the text transcript, the text will display in the browser. Compare your work to chapter11/11.1/index.html in the student files.

## Working with Multimedia on the Web

### More About Audio Files

**Focus on Ethics**

There are a number of ways that you can obtain audio files. You can record your own sounds, download sounds or music from a free site, record music from a CD, or purchase a DVD of sounds. There are some ethical issues related to using sounds and music created by others. You may only publish sounds or music that you have created yourself or for which you have obtained the rights (sometimes called a license) to publish. When you purchase a CD or DVD, you have not purchased the rights for publishing to the Web. Contact the owner of the copyright to request permission to use the music. There are many sources of audio files on the Web, including websites that sell subscriptions for the use of royalty-free music.

The Windows and Mac operating systems contain audio recording utilities. Audacity is a free cross-platform digital audio editor (available at http://sourceforge.net/projects/audacity for both Windows and Mac).

### More About Video Files

**Focus on Ethics**

Just as with audio files, there are a number of ways that you can obtain video files, including recording your own, downloading videos, purchasing a DVD that contains videos, or searching for video files on the Web. Be aware that there are ethical issues related to using videos that you did not create yourself. You must obtain the rights or license to publish videos created by other individuals before publishing them on your website.

Many digital cameras and smartphones have the capability to take still photographs as well as short MP4 movies. This can be an easy way to create short video clips. Digital video cameras and webcams record digital videos. Once you have created your video, software such as Adobe Premiere Pro, Adobe Spark, and Nero Video can be used to edit and configure your video masterpiece. Many digital cameras and smartphones provide the ability record to videos and immediately upload them to YouTube to share with the world. You'll work with a YouTube video in Chapter 13.

### Multimedia and Accessibility Issues

Provide alternate content for the media files you use on your website in transcript, caption, or printable PDF format. Provide a text transcript for audio files such as podcasts. Often, you can use the podcast script as the basis of the text transcript file that you create as a PDF and upload to your website. Provide captions for video files. When you upload a video to YouTube (https://www.youtube.com), captions can be automatically generated (although you'll probably want to make some corrections). You can also create a transcript or text captions for an existing YouTube video (see https://support.google.com/youtube/topic/3014331).

**Focus on Accessibility**

# 11.3  Audio and Video Elements

The HTML5 audio and video elements enable browsers to natively play media files. When working with HTML5 audio and video, you need to be aware of the container (which is designated by the file extension) and the codec (which is the algorithm used to compress the media). Refer to Table 11.1 and Table 11.2, which list common media file extensions, the container file type, and a description with codec information (if applicable for HTML5). Let's get started using the audio element.

## Audio Element

The **audio element** supports native play of audio files in the browser. The audio element begins with the **`<audio>`** tag and ends with the `</audio>` tag. Table 11.3 lists the attributes of the audio element.

You'll need to supply multiple versions of the audio file because of the browser support of different codecs. Plan to supply audio files in at least two different containers, including OGG and MP3. It is typical to omit the `src` and `type` attributes from the audio tag and, instead, configure multiple versions of the audio file with the source element.

**Table 11.3** Audio element attributes

| Attribute | Value | Usage |
|-----------|-------|-------|
| `src` | File name | Optional; audio file name |
| `type` | MIME type | Optional; the MIME type of the audio file, such as audio/mpeg or audio/ogg |
| `autoplay` | `autoplay` | Optional; indicates whether audio should start playing automatically; use with caution |
| `controls` | `controls` | Optional; indicates whether controls should be displayed; recommended |
| `loop` | `loop` | Optional; indicates whether audio should be played over and over |
| `preload` | `none, metadata, auto` | Optional; values: `none` (no preload), `metadata` (only download media file metadata), and `auto` (download the media file) |
| `title` | Text description | Optional; specifies a brief text description that may be displayed by browsers or assistive technologies |

## Source Element

When used with an audio element, the **source element** specifies a media file and a MIME type. The `src` attribute identifies the file name of the media file. The `type` attribute indicates the MIME type of the file. Code `type="audio/mpeg"` for an MP3 file. Code `type="audio/ogg"` for audio files using the Vorbis codec. Configure a source element for each version of the audio file. Place the source element before the closing audio tag.

## Audio on a Web Page

The following code sample configures the web page shown in Figure 11.2 (see chapter11/audio.html in the student files) to display a controller for an audio file:

```
<audio controls="controls">
    <source src="soundloop.mp3" type="audio/mpeg">
    <source src="soundloop.ogg" type="audio/ogg">
    <a href="soundloop.mp3">Download the Audio File</a> (MP3)
</audio>
```

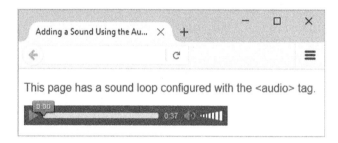

Figure 11.2 The Firefox browser supports the HTML5 audio element.

Current versions of popular browsers support the audio element. The controls displayed by each browser are different.

Review the previous code and note the hyperlink placed between the second source element and the closing audio tag. Any HTML elements or text placed in this area is rendered by browsers that do not support the audio element. This is referred to as fallback content; if the audio element is not supported, the MP3 version of the file is made available for download.

## Hands-On Practice 11.2

In this Hands-On Practice, you will launch a text editor and create a web page (see Figure 11.3) that displays an audio control to play a podcast.

Copy the podcast.mp3, podcast.ogg, and podcast.txt files from the chapter11/starters folder in the student files and save them to a folder named audio5. Use the chapter11/template.html file as a starting point and create a web page with the heading "Web Design Podcast", an audio control (use the audio element and two source elements), and a hyperlink to the podcast.txt transcript file.

Figure 11.3 Using the audio element to provide access to a podcast

Configure a hyperlink to the MP3 file as the fallback content. The code for the audio element is

```
<audio controls="controls">
    <source src="podcast.mp3" type="audio/mpeg">
    <source src="podcast.ogg" type="audio/ogg">
    <a href="podcast.mp3">Download the Podcast</a> (MP3)
</audio>
```

Save your web page as index.html in the audio5 folder and display it in a browser. Test your web page in different browsers, using different versions. When you click on the hyperlink for the text transcript, the text will display in the browser. Compare your work to chapter11/11.2/index.html in the student files.

 **FAQ    How can I convert an audio file to the Ogg Vorbis codec?**

The open-source Audacity application supports Ogg Vorbis. See https://sourceforge.net/projects/audacity for download information. If you're looking for a free Web-based converter, you can upload and share an audio file at the Internet Archive (https://www.archive.org) and an OGG format file will automatically be generated.

## Video Element

The HTML5 **video element** supports native play of video files in the browser. The video element begins with the **`<video>`** tag and ends with the `</video>` tag. Table 11.4 lists the attributes of the video element.

Table 11.4 Video element attributes

| Attribute | Value | Usage |
|---|---|---|
| src | File name | Optional; video file name |
| type | MIME type | Optional; the MIME type of the video file, such as video/mp4 or video/ogg |
| autoplay | autoplay | Optional; indicates whether video should start playing automatically; use with caution |
| controls | controls | Optional; indicates whether controls should be displayed; recommended |
| height | number | Optional; video height in pixels |
| loop | loop | Optional; indicates whether video should be played over and over |
| poster | File name | Optional; specifies an image to display when downloading and if the browser cannot play the video |
| preload | none, metadata, auto | Optional; values: none (no preload), metadata (only download media file metadata), and auto (download the media file) |
| title | Text description | Optional; specifies a brief text description that may be displayed by browsers or assistive technologies |
| width | Number | Optional; video width in pixels |

You'll need to supply multiple versions of the video file because of the browser support of different codecs. Plan to supply video files in at least two different containers, including MP4 and OGG (or OGV). It is typical to omit the `src` and `type` attributes from the video tag and, instead, configure multiple versions of the audio file with the source element.

## Source Element

When used with a video element, the source element is specifies a media file and a MIME type. The `src` attribute identifies the file name of the media file. The `type` attribute indicates the MIME type of the file. Code `type="video/mp4"` for video files using the MP4 codec. Code `type="video/ogg"` for video files using the Theora codec. Configure a source element for each version of the video file. Place the source elements before the closing video tag.

## Video on a Web Page

The following code configures the web page shown in Figure 11.4 (chapter11/sparky2.html in the student files) with the native HTML5 browser controls to display and play a video:

```
<video controls="controls" poster="sparky.jpg" width="160"
height="150">
   <source src="sparky.m4v" type="video/mp4">
   <source src="sparky.ogv" type="video/ogg">
   <a href="sparky.mov">Sparky the Dog</a> (.mov)
</video>
```

**Figure 11.4** The Firefox browser. Screenshots of Mozilla Firefox. Courtesy of Mozilla Foundation.

Current versions of popular browsers support the HTML5 video element. The controls displayed by each browser are different. Review the code just given and note the anchor element placed between the second source element and the closing video tag. Any HTML elements or text placed in this area is rendered by browsers that do not support the HTML5 video element. This is referred to as fallback content. In this case, a hyperlink to a .mov version of the file is supplied for the user to download.

In the past, another fallback option was to configure an embed element to play a Flash (.swf) version of the video. Adobe Flash multimedia content was once quite popular. Although the Flash Player is installed in many desktop web browsers, users of mobile devices cannot view Flash content. The lack of mobile support contributed to the decrease in the use of Flash on web pages and Adobe has announced that it is planning to end-of-life Flash. The Adobe Flash Player will no longer be updated and distributed by the end of 2020.

# Hands-On Practice 11.3

VideoNote
**HTML5 Video**

In this Hands-On Practice, you will launch a text editor and create the web page in Figure 11.5, which displays a video control to play a movie.

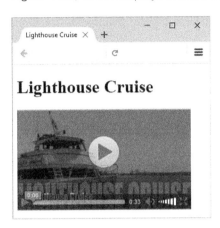

**Figure 11.5** HTML5 video element

Copy the lighthouse.m4v, lighthouse.ogv, lighthouse.mov, and lighthouse.jpg files from the chapter11/starters folder in the student files and save them to a folder named video. Open chapter11/template.html in a text editor and configure a web page with the heading "Lighthouse Cruise" and a video control (use the video element and two source elements). Configure a hyperlink to a video file (lighthouse.mov) as fallback content. Configure the lighthouse.jpg file as a poster image, which will display if the browser supports the video element, but it cannot play any of the video files. The code for the video element is

```
<video controls="controls" poster="lighthouse.jpg" width="320"
height="240">
    <source src="lighthouse.m4v" type="video/mp4">
    <source src="lighthouse.ogv" type="video/ogg">
    <a href="lighthouse.mov">Lighthouse Cruise</a> (.mov)
</video>
```

Save your web page as index.html in the video folder and display it in a browser. Test your web page in different browsers. Compare your work to Figure 11.5 and chapter11/11.3/index.html in the student files.

## FAQ    How can I convert a video file to the new codecs?

Online-Convert offers free conversion to WebM (https://video.online-convert.com/convert-to-webm) and to Ogg Theora (https://video.online-convert.com/convert-to-ogg). The free, open-source MiroVideoConverter (http://www.mirovideoconverter.com) can convert most video files to MP4, WebM, or OGG formats.

# 11.4 Multimedia Files and Copyright Law

**Focus on Ethics**

It is very easy to copy and download an image, audio, or video file from a website. It may be very tempting to place someone else's file in one of your own projects, but that may not be ethical or lawful. Only publish web pages, images, and other media that you have personally created or have obtained the rights or license to use. If another individual has created an image, sound, video, or document that you think would be useful on your own website, ask permission to use the material instead of simply taking it. All work (web pages, images, sounds, videos, and so on) is **copyrighted**, even if there is no copyright symbol and date on the material.

Be aware that there are times when students and educators can use portions of another's work and not be in violation of copyright law. This is called **fair use**. Fair use is the use of a copyrighted work for purposes such as criticism, reporting, teaching, scholarship, or research. The criteria used to determine fair use are as follows:

- The use must be educational rather than commercial.
- The nature of the work copied should be factual rather than creative.
- The amount copied must be as small a portion of the work as possible.
- The copy does not impede the marketability of the original work.

Visit the U.S. Copyright Office (https://copyright.gov) and Copyright Website (http://www.copyrightwebsite.com) for some additional information about copyright issues.

Some individuals may want to retain ownership of their work, but make it easy for others to use or adapt it. Creative Commons (https://creativecommons.org) provides a free service that allows authors and artists to register a type of copyright license called a **Creative Commons license**. There are several licenses to choose from, depending on the rights you wish to grant as the author. The Creative Commons license informs others exactly what they can and cannot do with the creative work.

## Checkpoint 11.1

1. Describe the HTML needed to display a video on a web page, including what happens if the browser or device does not support the video file.

2. Describe the purpose of the poster attribute on the video element.

3. Students can use anything they find on the Web for school assignments. Do you agree with this statement? Justify your answer.

# 11.5 CSS and Interactivity

## CSS Drop Down Menu

Recall from Chapter 6 that the CSS `:hover` pseudo-class provides a way to configure styles to display when the web page visitor moves the mouse over an element. You'll use this basic interactivity, along with CSS positioning and display properties, to configure an interactive navigation menu with CSS and HTML in the next Hands-On Practice.

## Hands-On Practice 11.4

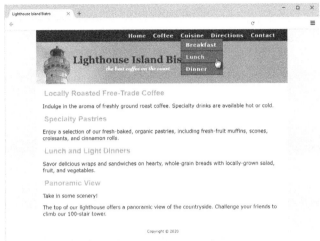

**Figure 11.6** An interactive navigation menu with CSS

In this Hands-On Practice you will configure a drop down menu that displays when a visitor hovers over the Cuisine navigation hyperlink as shown in Figure 11.6. The main menu has hyperlinks for Home, Coffee, Cuisine, Directions, and Contact. As shown in the site map (Figure 11.7) the Cuisine page has three subpages: Breakfast, Lunch, and Dinner. Create a folder named mybistro. Copy the files from the chapter11/

bistro folder in the student files into your mybistro folder. You will modify the CSS and edit each page to configure a Cuisine submenu that provides hyperlinks to three pages (Breakfast, Lunch, and Dinner).

**Figure 11.7** Site map

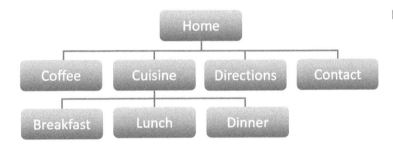

**Task 1: Configure the HTML.** Launch a text editor and open the index.html file. Modify the nav area to contain a new unordered list with hyperlinks to the Breakfast, Lunch, and Dinner pages. Configure a new ul element that is contained *within* the Cuisine li element. The new ul element will contain an li element for each meal. The HTML follows with the new code displayed in blue.

```
<nav>
<ul>
  <li><a href="index.html">Home</a></li>
  <li><a href="coffee.html">Coffee</a></li>
  <li><a href="cuisine.html">Cuisine</a>
    <ul>
      <li><a href="breakfast.html">Breakfast</a></li>
      <li><a href="lunch.html">Lunch</a></li>
      <li><a href="dinner.html">Dinner</a></li>
    </ul>
  </li>
  <li><a href="directions.html">Directions</a></li>
  <li><a href="contact.html">Contact</a></li>
</ul>
</nav>
```

Save the file and display it in a browser. Don't worry if the navigation area seems a bit garbled—you'll configure the submenu CSS in Step 2. Next, edit each page (coffee.html, cuisine.html, breakfast.html, lunch.html, dinner.html, directions.html and contact.html) and edit the nav area as you did in the index.html file.

**Task 2: Configure the CSS.** Launch a text editor and open the bistro.css file.

**a.** The submenu will be configured with absolute positioning. Recall from Chapter 7 that absolute positioning precisely specifies the location of an element outside of normal flow in relation to its first parent non-static element. The nav element's position is static by default so add the following declaration to the styles for the nav element selector:

```
position: relative;
```

**b.** The submenu that displays the hyperlinks for the Breakfast, Lunch, and Dinner pages is configured using a new ul element that is contained within the existing ul element in the nav area. Configure a descendant `nav ul ul` selector and code style declarations to use absolute positioning, #5564A0 background color, 0 padding, left text alignment and display set to none. The CSS follows:

```
nav ul ul { position: absolute;
            background-color: #5564A0;
            padding: 0;
            text-align: left;
            display: none; }
```

**c.** To style each li element within the submenu, use a descendant `nav ul ul li` selector and configure the li elements in the submenu with a border, block display, 8em width, 1em left padding, and 0 left margin. The CSS follows:

```
nav ul ul li { border: 1px solid #00005D;
               display: block;
               width: 8em;
               padding-left: 1em;
               margin-left: 0; }
```

**d.** Configure the submenu ul to display when the `:hover` is triggered for the li elements in the nav area. The CSS follows:

```
nav li:hover ul { display: block; }
```

Test your pages in a browser. The drop down menu should look similar to Figure 11.6. You can compare your work to the sample in the student files (chapter11/11.4/horizontal). An example of a web page with a vertical fly-out menu is available in the student files (chapter11/11.4/vertical).

## The `transform` Property

CSS transforms (https://www.w3.org/TR/css-transforms-1/) allow you to change the display of an element and provide functions to rotate, scale, skew, and reposition an element. Both two-dimensional (2D) and three-dimensional (3D) transforms are possible.

Table 11.5 lists commonly used 2D transform property function values and their purpose. See https://www.w3.org/TR/css3-transforms/#transform-property for a complete list. We'll focus on the rotate and scale transforms in this section.

Table 11.5 Transform Functions and Purpose

| Transform Function | Purpose |
|---|---|
| rotate (*degree*) | Rotates the element by the angle |
| scale (*number, number*) | Scales or resizes the element along the X and Y axis (X,Y) |
| scaleX (*number*) | Scales or resizes the element along the X axis |
| scaleY (*number*) | Scales or resizes the element along the Y axis |
| skewX (*number*) | Distorts the display of the element along the X axis |
| skewY (*number*) | Distorts the display of the element along the Y axis |
| translate (*number, number*) | Repositions the element along the X and Y axis (X,Y) |
| translateX (*number*) | Repositions the element along the X axis |
| translateY (*number*) | Repositions the element along the Y axis |

## Rotate Transform

The **rotate() transform** function takes a value in degrees (like an angle in geometry). Rotate to the right with a positive value. Rotate to the left with a negative value. The rotation is around the origin, which, by default, is the middle of the element. The web page in Figure 11.8 demonstrates the use of the transform property to slightly rotate the figure.

Figure 11.8 The transform property in action

## Scale Transform

The **scale() transform** function resizes an element in three different ways: along the X-axis, along the Y-axis, and along both the X- and Y-axes. Specify the amount of resizing using a number without units. For example, scale(1) does not change the element's size, scale(2) indicates the element should render two times as large, scale(3) indicates the element should render three times as large, and scale(0) indicates the element should not display.

## Hands-On Practice 11.5

In this Hands-On Practice you will configure the rotation and scale transforms shown in Figure 11.8. Create a new folder named transform. Copy the lighthouse.jpg and light.gif images from the chapter11/starters folder in the student files to your transform folder. Launch a text editor and open the starter.html file in the chapter11 folder. Save the file as index.html in your transform folder. Launch the file in a browser and it will look similar to Figure 11.9.

**Figure 11.9** Before the transform property

Open index.html in a text editor and view the embedded CSS.

1. Locate the figure element selector. You will add new style declarations to the figure element selector that will configure a three-degree rotation transform. The CSS follows:

```
figure { margin: auto; background-color: #FFF;
         padding: 8px; border: 1px solid #CCC;
         box-shadow: 5px 5px 5px #828282; width: 265px;
         transform: rotate(3deg); }
```

2. Locate the #offer selector. This configures the "Special Offer" div displayed above the page footer. You will add a style declaration to the #offer selector that configures the browser to display the element two times larger. The CSS follows:

```
#offer { background-color: #EAEAEA;
         width: 10em;
         margin: 2em auto 0 auto;
         text-align: center;
         transform: scale(2); }
```

Save the file and display it in a browser. You should see the figure displayed on a slight angle and the "Special Offer" text displayed in large text. Compare your work to Figure 11.8 and the sample in the student files (chapter11/11.5/index.html).

## Explore Transforms

This section provided an overview of the rotate and scale transforms. Visit http://www.westciv.com/tools/transforms/index.html to generate the CSS for rotate, scale, translate, and skew transforms. Find out more about transforms at http://www.css3files.com/transform and https://developer.mozilla.org/en/CSS/Using_CSS_transforms.

## The transition Property

CSS **transitions** provide for changes in property values to display in a smoother manner over a specified time. You can apply a transition to a variety of CSS properties including color, background-color, border, font-size, font-weight, margin, padding, opacity, and text-shadow. A full list of applicable properties is available at https://developer.mozilla.org/en-US/docs/Web/CSS/CSS_animated_properties. When you configure a transition for a property, you need to configure values for the transition-property, transition-duration, `transition-timing-function`, and `transition-delay` properties. These can be combined in a single **transition property**. Table 11.6 lists the transition properties and their purpose. Table 11.7 lists commonly used transition-timing-function values and their purpose.

Table 11.6 CSS transition properties

| Property | Description |
|---|---|
| `transition-property` | Indicates the CSS property to which the transition applies |
| `transition-duration` | Indicates the length of time to apply the transition; default value 0 configures an immediate transition; a numeric value specifies time (usually in seconds) |
| `transition-timing-function` | Configures changes in the speed of the transition by describing how intermediate property values are calculated; common values include `ease` (default), `linear, ease-in, ease-out, ease-in-out` |
| `transition-delay` | Indicates the beginning of the transition; default value 0 configures no delay; a numeric value specifies time (usually in seconds) |
| `transition` | Shorthand property; list the value for `transition-property, transition-duration, transition-timing-function,` and `transition-delay` separated by spaces; default values can be omitted, but the first time unit applies to `transition-duration` |

Table 11.7 Commonly used transition-timing-function values

| Value | Purpose |
|---|---|
| `ease` | Default; transition effect begins slowly, speeds up, and ends slowly |
| `linear` | Transition effect has a constant speed |
| `ease-in` | Transition effect begins slowly and speeds up to a constant speed |
| `ease-out` | Transition effect begins at a constant speed and slows down |
| `ease-in-out` | Transition effect is slightly slower; Begins slowly, speeds up, and slows down |

# Hands-On Practice 11.6

Recall that the CSS `:hover` pseudo-class provides a way to configure styles to display when the web page visitor moves the mouse over an element. The change in display happens somewhat abruptly. Web designers can use a CSS transition to create a more gradual change to the hover state. You'll try this out in this Hands-On Practice when you configure a transition for the navigation hyperlinks on a web page.

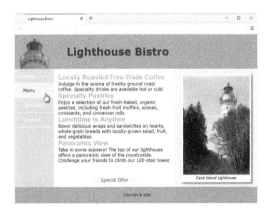

Figure 11.10 The transition in action

Create a new folder named transition. Copy the lighthouse.jpg and light.gif images from the chapter11/starters folder in the student files to your transition folder. Launch a text editor and open the starter.html file in the chapter11 folder. Save the file as index.html in your transition folder. Open index.html in a browser and it will look similar to Figure 11.9. Place your mouse over one of the navigation hyperlinks and notice that the background color and text color change immediately.

Open index.html in a text editor and view the embedded CSS. Locate the `nav a:hover` selector and notice that the color and background-color properties are configured. You will add new style declarations to the `nav a` selector to cause a more gradual change in the background color when the user places the mouse over the hyperlink. The CSS follows:

```
nav a { text-decoration: none; display: block; padding: 1em 2em;
        transition: background-color 2s linear; }
```

Save the file and display it in a browser. Place your mouse over one of the navigation hyperlinks and notice that while the text color changes immediately, the background color changes in a more gradual manner—the transition is working! Compare your work to Figure 11.10 and the student files (chapter11/11.6/index.html).

### Explore Transitions

If you'd like more control over the transition than what is provided by the values listed in Table 11.8, explore using the cubic-bezier value for the transition-timing-function. A Bezier curve is a mathematically defined curve often used in graphic applications to describe motion. Explore the following resources:

- http://www.the-art-of-web.com/css/timing-function
- http://roblaplaca.com/blog/2011/03/11/understanding-css-cubic-bezier
- http://cubic-bezier.com

 ## Hands-On Practice 11.7

In this Hands-On Practice you will use CSS `positioning`, `opacity`, and `transition` properties to configure an interactive image gallery with CSS and HTML. This is a slightly different version of the image gallery than the web page you created in Hands-On Practice 6.9.

Figure 11.11 shows the initial display of the gallery (see the student files chapter11/11.7/index.html) with a semi-opaque placeholder image. When you place the mouse over

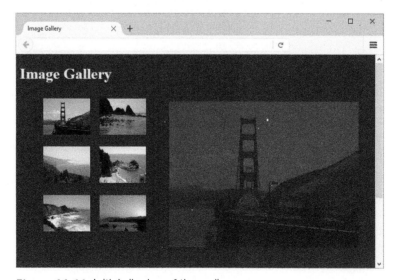

Figure 11.11 Initial display of the gallery

a thumbnail image, the larger version of that image is gradually displayed along with a caption (see Figure 11.12). If you click the thumbnail, the image will display in its own browser window.

Create a new folder called gallery2. Copy all the images from the chapter11/starters/ gallery folder in the student files to the new gallery2 folder.

Launch a text editor and modify the chapter11/template.html file to configure a web page as indicated:

1. Configure the text, "Image Gallery", within an h1 element and within the title element.

2. Code a div element assigned to the id named `gallery`. This div will contain a placeholder figure element and an unordered list that contains the thumbnail images.

3. Configure a figure element within the div. The figure element will contain a place-holder img element that displays photo1.jpg.

Figure 11.12 The new photo gradually displays

4. Configure an unordered list within the div. Code six li elements, one for each thumbnail image. The thumbnail images will function as image links with a `:hover` pseudo-class that causes the larger image to display on the page. We'll make this all happen by configuring an anchor element containing both the thumbnail image and a span element that comprises the larger image along with descriptive text. An example of the first li element is

```
<li><a href="photo1.jpg"><img src="photo1thumb.jpg" width="100"
  height="75" alt="Golden Gate Bridge">
  <span><img src="photo1.jpg" width="400" height="300"
  alt="Golden Gate Bridge"><br>Golden Gate Bridge</span></a>
</li>
```

5. Configure all six li elements in a similar manner. Substitute the actual name of each image file for the href and src values in the code. Write your own descriptive text for each image. Use photo2.jpg and photo2thumb.jpg in the second li element. Use photo3.jpg and photo3thumb.jpg in the third li element, and so on for all six images. Save the file as index.html in the gallery2 folder. Display your page in a browser. You'll see the placeholder image followed by an unordered list with the thumbnail images, the larger images, and the descriptive text.

**6.** Now, let's add CSS. Open your file in a text editor and code a style element in the head section. Configure embedded CSS as follows:

a. Configure the body element selector with a dark background color (#333333) and a light gray text color (#eaeaea).

b. Configure the `gallery` id selector. Set `position` to `relative`. This does not change the location of the gallery but sets the stage to use absolute positioning on the span element relative to its container (`#gallery`) instead of relative to the entire web page document.

c. Configure the figure element selector. Set `position` to `absolute`, `left` to 280px, `text-align` to center, and `opacity` to .25. This will cause the figure to initially be semi-opaque.

d. Configure the unordered list within the `#gallery` with a width of 300 pixels and no list marker.

e. Configure the list item elements within the `#gallery` with inline display, left float, and 10 pixels of padding.

f. Configure the img elements within the `#gallery` to not display a border.

g. Configure anchor elements within the `#gallery` with no underline, #eaeaea text color, and italic text.

h. Configure span elements within the `#gallery`. Set `position` to `absolute`, `left` to `-1000px` (which causes them not to display initially in the browser viewport), and `opacity` to 0. Also configure a three second `ease-in-out` transition.

```
#gallery span { position: absolute; left: -1000px; opacity: 0;
               transition: opacity 3s ease-in-out; }
```

i. Configure the span elements within the `#gallery` to display when the web visitor hovers the mouse over the thumbnail image link. Set `position` to `absolute`, `top` to 16px, `left` to 320px, centered text, and `opacity` to 1.

```
#gallery a:hover span { position: absolute; top: 16px; left: 320px;
                       text-align: center; opacity: 1; }
```

Save your file in the gallery2 folder and display it in a browser. Compare your work to Figure 11.11, Figure 11.12, and the student files (chapter11/11.7/index.html).

See the following resources for more examples:

- CSS Transitions 101:
  https://www.webdesignerdepot.com/2010/01/css-transitions-101
- Using CSS Transitions:
  https://developer.mozilla.org/en-US/docs/Web/Guide/CSS/Using_CSS_transitions

## CSS Animations

CSS animations (https://www.w3.org/TR/css-animations-1/) provide a way to animate the values of CSS properties over time. There are two steps to configuring a CSS animation:

- define the animation using the `@keyframes` rule
- apply the animation using the CSS `animation` property

## Define an Animation with @keyframes Rule

When working with animation, a **keyframe** is a point of change. The purpose of the **@keyframes rule** is to define an animation – naming the animation and grouping the keyframes. At least two keyframes are required, a `from` keyframe (the starting state) and a `to` keyframe (the ending state). The timing duration for a series of keyframes can be indicated by percentages; such as 0% for the first keyframe, 25% for the second keyframe, 50% for the third keyframe, and 100% for the last keyframe. These indicate how far into the animation duration the keyframe should be triggered. One or more CSS properties are listed within each keyframe block. The @keyframes rule below configures the name of the animation to be the value `test` and causes the scale of an element to change from 50% to 200% while changing the color from blue to red.

```
@keyframes test {
        from { transform: scale(0.5);
              background-color: blue; }
        to   { transform: scale(2);
               background-color: red; }
}
```

## Apply the Animation

Next, apply the animation by indicating the name of the animation and how long the animation should last. Use the CSS **animation property**, which is a shorthand property that typically accepts values for the `animation-name` and `animation-duration` properties.

To apply the animation named `test` for five seconds to a class called `myAnimate` (which also configures a horizontally centered blue square with a border), code the following CSS:

```
.myAnimate { width: 100px; height; 100px;
        background-color: blue; border: 3px solid #000;
        margin: auto;
        animation: test 5s; }
```

The student files (chapter11/animate1.html) has an example of this animation in action. When you display the page in a browser you will see the animation and notice that the square returns to its original state when the animation completes. You can change this by setting the `animation-fill-mode` property to the value `forwards`, as demonstrated in the student files (chapter11/animate2.html). Table 11.8 lists animation properties and their purpose.

Table 11.8    Animation Properties

| Property | Description |
|---|---|
| animation | Shorthand property; minimum requirements are the value for `animation-name` and `animation-duration` separated by spaces |
| animation-name | Indicates the associated `@keyframes` rule for the animation |
| animation-duration | Length of animation; default value `0s` configures no animation; a numeric value specifies length of animation in seconds or milliseconds |
| animation-delay | Delay before beginning animation; default value `0s` configures an immediate animation; a numeric value specifies delay time in seconds or milliseconds |
| animation-timing-function | Configures changes in the speed of the animation by describing how intermediate property values are calculated; common values include `ease` (default), `linear`, `ease-in`, `ease-out`, `ease-in-out` (see Table 11.7) |
| animation-iteration-count | Configures the number of times to repeat the animation; default value is 1; values include a positive number or keyword `infinite` |
| animation-direction | Configures if animation should play forward, backwards or alternating; values include `normal` (default), `reverse`, `alternate`, `alternate-reverse` |
| animation-play-state | Indicates if animation is playing or paused; values are `running` (default) and `paused` |
| animation-fill-mode | Configures what CSS properties apply when the animation is not running; values are `none` (default), `forwards` (last keyframe), `backwards` (first keyframe), `both` (apply styles for both forwards and backwards) |

## Hands-On Practice 11.8

In this Hands-On Practice you will configure a CSS animation that slides the h1 text "Lighthouse Bistro" in from the right while it increases in size. Create a new folder named animate. Copy the lighthouse.jpg and light.gif images from the chapter11/starters folder in the student files to your animate folder. Copy the starter.html file from the chapter11 folder into your animate folder.

Launch a text editor and open the starter.html file. View the CSS and notice that there is a media query – this is a responsive web page. We will configure the animation to play only when the viewport is at least 768 pixels wide and the media query is triggered. Save the file as index.html in your animate folder. Launch the file in a browser and it will look similar to Figure 11.9. Resize the browser and notice how the page changes along with the browser viewport.

Open index.html in a text editor and view the embedded CSS.

1. Place your cursor under the opening style tag and add a blank line. You will define the animation and code a `@keyframes` rule with the name of `slideme`. The first keyframe will have margin-left set to 100% and width set to 300%. The last keyframe sets 300% font-size, 0% left margin, and 100% width. The CSS follows:

```
@keyframes slideme {
      from { margin-left: 100%;
             width: 300%;    }
        to { font-size: 300%;
             margin-left: 0%;
             width: 100%;    }
}
```

2. Locate the media query. We will add code within the media query to apply the animation. Configure a style rule for an h1 element selector that sets `animation-name` to the value `slideme` and the `animation-duration` to five seconds. The CSS follows.

```
h1 {    animation-duration: 5s;
        animation-name: slideme; }
```

3. The animation slides text into the page, which can cause the page to become wider than the browser window and trigger a horizontal scroll bar. To prevent this, configure the container of the h1 (which is the header element) with the overflow property set to hidden. Locate the header element selector within the media query and add the `overflow: hidden` style declaration. Also set the height of the header to 160px. The CSS follows.

```
header { padding-left: 10em;
         overflow: hidden;
         height: 160px;    }
```

Save your file and display it in a browser. Since this is a responsive web page, if the browser viewport is narrow, the animation will not occur. If the browser viewport is at least 768 pixels wide and the media query is triggered, you should see the heading text slide in from the right, grow larger, and then suddenly reduce in size. The size reduction occurs because the element returns to its initial state by default after an animation. You can compare your work to chapter11/11.8/step3.html in the student files.

4. To freeze the animation at the ending frame, locate the h1 element selector within the media query and set the `animation-fill-mode` to `forwards` as indicated below:

```
h1 {    animation-duration: 5s;
        animation-name: slideme;
        animation-fill-mode: forwards; }
```

Save your file and display it in a browser. You should see the heading text slide in from the right, grow larger, and remain large. Compare your work to Figure 11.13 and chapter11/11.8/step4.html in the student files.

Figure 11.13 The animation has been applied

5. Just for fun, lets, add another keyframe to the animation. Locate the `@keyframes` rule and add a keyframe at 50% of the duration that sets font-size to 250% and margin-left to 50%, as indicated below:

```
@keyframes slideme {
    from { margin-left: 100%;
           width: 300%;    }
    50% { margin-left: 50%;
          font-size: 250%; }
    to  {  font-size: 300%;
           margin-left: 0%;
           width: 100%; }
}
```

6. Save your file and display it in a browser. You should see the heading text slide in from the right and increase in size. Then, when the heading begins at about 50% in, the animation will slow and then speed up again as the heading continues to slide and grow larger. The change in speed is due to the default value (ease) of the `animation-timing-function` property. Compare your work to chapter11/11.8/step5.html.

7. To cause the animation to run at a constant speed, locate the h1 element selector within the media query and set the `animation-timing-function` to `linear` as indicated below

```
h1 {    animation-duration: 5s;
        animation-name: slideme;
        animation-fill-mode: forwards;
        animation-timing-function: linear; }
```

Save your file and display it in a browser. You should see the heading text slide in from the right in a smooth fashion. Compare your work to chapter11/11.8/index.html in the student files.

### Explore CSS Animation

This section provided an introduction to animation with CSS. To get started exploring this topic further, check out the following resources:

- https://developer.mozilla.org/en-US/docs/Web/CSS/CSS_Animations
- https://daneden.github.io/animate.css/
- https://medium.freecodecamp.org/a-simple-css-animation-tutorial-8a35aa8e87ff

# 11.6 Details and Summary Elements

The details element and summary element are used together to configure an interactive widget that will hide and show information.

## Details Element

The purpose of the **details** element is to configure the browser to render an interactive widget which contains one summary element and detailed information (which can be a combination of text and HTML tags. The details element begins with the `<details>` tag and ends with the `</details>` tag.

## Summary Element

The **summary element** is coded within the details element. The purpose of the summary element is to contain the text summary shown in the interactive widget. The summary element begins with the `<summary>` tag and ends with the `</summary>` tag.

## Details & Summary Widget

Figures 11.14 and 11.15 show the details and summary elements in action. Figure 11.14 shows the initial display of the web page with each summary item (in this case the terms Repetition, Contrast, Proximity, and Alignment) visible and displayed next to a triangle rendered automatically by the Chrome browser.

In Figure 11.15, the visitor has selected the first summary item (Repetition) which caused browser to display the detailed information for that item. The visitor can select the same summary item again to hide the details or can select another summary item to also show its corresponding detailed information.

Browsers that do not support the details and summary elements display all the information immediately and do not provide interactivity.

Figure 11.14   Initial browser display

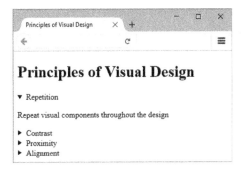

Figure 11.15   Detailed information displays

## Hands-On Practice 11.9

In this Hands-On Practice you will configure an interactive widget with the details and summary elements as you create the page shown in Figures 11.14 and 11.15. Create a new folder named ch11details. Launch a text editor and open chapter11/template.html in the student files. Save the file as index.html in your ch11details folder. Modify the file to configure a web page as indicated:

1. Configure the text, Principles of Visual Design, within an h1 element and within the title element.

2. Code the following in the body of the web page:

```
<details>
  <summary>Repetition</summary>
  <p>Repeat visual components throughout the design</p>
</details>
<details>
  <summary>Contrast</summary>
  <p>Add visual excitement and draw attention</p>
</details>
```

```
<details>
  <summary>Proximity</summary>
  <p>Group related items</p>
</details>
<details>
  <summary>Alignment</summary>
  <p>Align elements to create visual unity</p>
</details>
```

Save your file and test your page in Firefox or Chrome. The initial display should be similar to Figure 11.15. Try selecting or clicking on one of the terms or arrows to display the information you coded within the details element. If you select the term "Repetition" your browser should be similar to Figure 11.15.

If you are using a browser that does not support the details and summary elements, your display will be similar to Figure 11.16.

A suggested solution is in the student files chapter11/11.9 folder. Visit http://caniuse.com/#feat=details to check the current level of browser support for the details and summary elements.

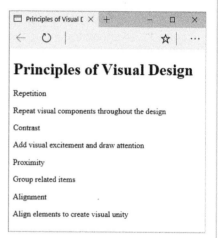

**Principles of Visual Design**

Repetition

Repeat visual components throughout the design

Contrast

Add visual excitement and draw attention

Proximity

Group related items

Alignment

Align elements to create visual unity

**Figure 11.16** Display in a nonsupporting browser. ©2018 Google LLC, used with permission. Google and the Google logo are registered trademarks of Google LLC.

## Checkpoint 11.2

**1.** What is the purpose of the transform property?

**2.** What is a keyframe?

**3.** What is the purpose of the details and summary elements?

# 11.7 JavaScript

Although some interactivity on web pages can be achieved with CSS, JavaScript powers much of the interactivity on the Web. **JavaScript**, developed initially by Brendan Eich at Netscape, is an object-based, **client-side scripting** language interpreted by a web browser. JavaScript is considered to be **object-based** because it's used to manipulate the objects associated with a web page document: the browser window, the document itself, and elements such as forms, images, and hyperlinks.

JavaScript statements can be coded directly in a web page within an HTML script element or placed in a separate file (with a .js extension) that is accessed by a web browser. The purpose of the **script element** is to either contain scripting statements or to indicate a file that contains scripting statements. Some JavaScript also can be coded within HTML tags. In all cases, the web browser interprets the JavaScript statements. Because JavaScript is interpreted by a browser, it is considered to be a client-side scripting language.

JavaScript can be used to respond to events such as moving the mouse, clicking a button, and loading a web page. This technology is also often utilized to edit and verify information on HTML form controls such as text boxes, check boxes, and radio buttons. Other uses for JavaScript include pop-up windows, image slideshows, animation, date manipulation, and calculations. Figure 11.18 shows a web page (found in the student files at chapter11/date.html) that uses JavaScript to determine and display the current date. The JavaScript statements are enclosed within an HTML script element and coded directly in the .html file. The code sample is below:

Figure 11.17 JavaScript in action

```
<h2>Today is
<script>
var myDate = new Date()
var month = myDate.getMonth() + 1
var day = myDate.getDate()
var year = myDate.getFullYear()
document.write(month + "/" + day + "/" + year)
</script>
</h2>
```

There is an introduction to coding JavaScript in Chapter 14. An important part of working with JavaScript is manipulating the **Document Object Model (DOM)**. The DOM defines every object and element on a web page. Its hierarchical structure can be used to access page elements and apply styles to page elements. A portion of a basic DOM that is common to most browsers is shown in Figure 11.18.

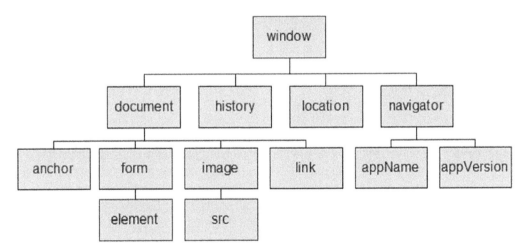

Figure 11.18 The Document Object Model (DOM)

## JavaScript Resources

There is a lot to learn about JavaScript, but there are many free resources for JavaScript code and JavaScript tutorials on the Web. Here are a few sites that offer free tutorials:

- JavaScript Tutorial: http://echoecho.com/javascript.htm
- Mozilla Developer Network JavaScript Guide: https://developer.mozilla.org/en-US/docs/Web/JavaScript/Guide
- JavaScript Tutorial: http://www.w3schools.com/JS

Once you are comfortable with HTML and CSS, the JavaScript language is a good technology to learn as you continue your studies. Try some of the resources listed and get your feet wet. See Chapter 14 for a more detailed introduction to JavaScript. The next section introduces Ajax, a technology that uses JavaScript.

# 11.8  Ajax

The term **Ajax** stands for Asynchronous JavaScript and XML. These technologies are not new, but recently have been used together to provide a better experience for web visitors and create interactive web applications. The technologies utilized in Ajax to provide a better experience for web visitors and create interactive web applications are as follows:

- Standards-based HTML and CSS
- The Document Object Model
- XML (and the related XSLT technology)
- Asynchronous data retrieval using XMLHttpRequest
- JavaScript

Some of these technologies may be unfamiliar to you. That's okay at this point in your web development career. You're currently creating a strong foundation in HTML and CSS and may decide to continue your studies in the future and learn additional web technologies. Right now, it's enough to know that these technologies exist and what they can be used for.

Ajax is a web development technique for creating interactive web applications. Recall the client/server model discussed in Chapters 1 and 9. The browser makes a request to the server (often triggered by clicking a link or a submit button), and the server returns an entire new web page for the browser to display. Ajax pushes more of the processing on the client (browser) using JavaScript and XML and often uses behind-the-scenes asynchronous requests to the server to refresh a portion of the browser display instead of the entire web page. The key is that when using Ajax technology, JavaScript code (which runs on the client computer within the confines of the browser) can communicate directly with the server, exchanging data and modifying parts of the web page display without reloading the entire web page. For example, as soon as a website visitor types a zip code into a form, the value could be looked up in a zip code database and the city/state automatically populated using Ajax—and all of this takes place while the visitor is entering the form information before they click the submit button. The result is that the visitor perceives the web page as being more responsive and has a more interactive experience.

## Ajax Resources

Although you'll probably want to become familiar with scripting before you tackle Ajax, there are many resources and articles available. Some helpful sites are listed here:

- Getting Started with Ajax: https://www.alistapart.com/articles/gettingstartedwithajax
- Ajax Tutorial: http://www.tizag.com/ajaxTutorial

# 11.9 jQuery

You're already aware that JavaScript is a client-side scripting language that adds interactivity and functionality to web pages. Web developers need to configure the same type of common interactive features (such as slideshows, form validation, and animation) on web pages. One approach is for each person to write their own JavaScript code and test it in a wide variety of browsers and operating systems. As you might guess, this can become quite time consuming. John Resig developed the free, open-source **jQuery** JavaScript library to simplify client-side scripting.

An **application programming interface (API)** is a protocol that allows software components to communicate—Interacting and sharing data. The jQuery API can be used to configure many interactive features, including:

- image slideshows
- animation (moving, hiding, fading)
- event handling (mouse movements and mouse clicking)
- document manipulation
- Ajax

Many web developers and designers have found that jQuery is easier to learn and work with than writing their own JavaScript, although a basic understanding of JavaScript is needed to be efficient when using jQuery. An advantage of the jQuery library is its compatibility with all current browsers.

jQuery is an open source library, so anyone can extend the jQuery library by writing a new plugin that provides a new or enhanced interactive feature. For example, the jQuery Cycle plugin (http://jquery.malsup.com/cycle) supports a variety of transition effects. Figure 11.19 (see https://webdevfoundations. net/jquery/index.html) shows an example of using jQuery and the Cycle plugin to create an image slideshow. Chapter 14 includes a brief introduction to working with jQuery.

**jQuery Slideshow Example**

Figure 11.19 jQuery is used to configure a slideshow

## jQuery Resources

There are many free resources and tutorials that can help you learn about jQuery. If you'd like to find out more about jQuery, visit the following resources:

- jQuery Tutorials for Web Designers: https://webdesignerwall.com/tutorials/jquery-tutorials-for-designers
- jQuery Fundamentals: http://jqfundamentals.com/chapter/jquery-basics
- How jQuery Works: https://learn.jquery.com/about-jquery/how-jquery-works/

**FAQ**   **Is jQuery the only JavaScript library or API?**

No. jQuery was one of the first JavaScript libraries and is still used on websites today. Other JavaScript APIs include React (https://reactjs.org), Vue (https://vuejs.org), and Angular (https://angularjs.org).

# 11.10 HTML5 APIs

You've already been introduced to the term, application programming interface (API), which is a protocol that allows software components to communicate—interacting and sharing data. A variety of APIs that are intended to work with HTML5, CSS, and JavaScript have been developed and approved by the W3C. We'll explore some of the new APIs in this section, including geolocation, web storage, progressive web applications, and two-dimensional drawing.

## Geolocation

The **geolocation** API (http://www.w3.org/TR/geolocation-API/) allows your web page visitors to share their geographic location. The browser will first confirm that your visitor wants to share their location. Then, their location may be determined by the IP address, wireless network connection, local cell tower, or GPS hardware depending on the type of device and browser. JavaScript is used to work with the latitude and longitude coordinates provided by the browser. Visit https://developers.google.com/maps/documentation/javascript/examples/map-geolocation for an example of geolocation in action.

## Web Storage

Web developers have traditionally used the JavaScript cookie object to store information in key-value pairs on the client (the website visitor's computer). The **Web Storage** API (http://www.w3.org/TR/webstorage) provides two new ways to store information on the client side: local storage and session storage. An advantage to using web storage is the increase in the amount of data that can be stored (5MB per domain). The **localStorage** object stores data without an expiration date. The **sessionStorage** object stores data only for the duration of the current browser session. JavaScript is used to work with the values stored in the localStorage and sessionStorage objects. Visit http://webdevfoundations.net/storage and http://html5demos.com/storage for examples of web storage.

## Progressive Web Application

You've most likely used native applications (apps) for mobile phones. A native app must be built and distributed specifically for the platform it will be installed on. If your client would like a native mobile app for both an iPhone and an Android, you would need to create two different apps! In contrast, a web application can be written with HTML, CSS, and JavaScript and can run in any browser—as long as you are online. **A progressive web application (PWA)** offers a rich experience similar to a native app on a mobile device—the user can choose to add the website's icon to the home screen, and the website has some level of functionality even when the device is not connected to the Internet.

An early approach to progressive web applications (https://www.w3.org/TR/2011/WD-html5-20110525/offline.html) utilized an application cache that informed the browser about files to automatically download and update, fallback files to display when a resource has not been cached, and files that are only available online. However, there were issues with this approach and the W3C is developing a combination of new APIs to power PWAs including Manifest and Service Workers.

The **Manifest API** (https://www.w3.org/TR/appmanifest) contains information about the PWA; including the data needed for the PWA's icon to be added to the home screen of a device. The **Service Workers API** (https://www.w3.org/TR/service-workers-1/) provides a way for websites to perform persistent background processing such as push notifications and background data syncing. A service worker is JavaScript that runs in the background, separate from a web page, and listens for events such as install, activate, message, fetch, sync, and push. To provide more security, service workers must run over HTTPS.

For more information about PWAs, visit the following resources:

- https://developer.mozilla.org/en-US/docs/Web/Apps/Progressive/Introduction

- https://developers.google.com/web/progressive-web-apps/

- https://medium.com/samsung-internet-dev/a-beginners-guide-to-making-progressive-web-apps-beb56224948e

- https://docs.microsoft.com/en-us/microsoft-edge/progressive-web-apps/get-started

## Drawing with the Canvas Element

The HTML5 **canvas element** is a container for dynamic graphics. The canvas element begins with the **`<canvas>`** tag and ends with the `</canvas>` tag. The canvas element is configured with the Canvas 2D Context API (http://www.w3.org/TR/2dcontext2), which provides a way to dynamically draw and transform lines, shapes, images, and text on web pages. If that wasn't enough, the canvas API also provides for interaction with actions taken by the user, like moving the mouse. The canvas offers methods for two-dimensional (2D) bitmap drawing, including lines, strokes, arcs, fills, gradients, images, and text. However, instead of drawing visually using a graphics application, you draw programmatically by writing JavaScript statements. A very basic example of using JavaScript to draw within the canvas element is shown in Figure 11.20 (see chapter11/canvas.html in the student files). The code is

Figure 11.20  The canvas element

```
<!DOCTYPE html>
<html lang="en">
<head>
<title>Canvas Element</title>
<meta charset="utf-8">
<style>
canvas { border: 2px solid red; }
</style>
```

```
<script type="text/javascript">
function drawMe() {
  var canvas = document.getElementById("myCanvas");
  if (canvas.getContext) {
    var ctx = canvas.getContext("2d");
    ctx.fillStyle = "rgb(255, 0, 0)";
    ctx.font = "bold 3em Georgia";
    ctx.fillText("My Canvas", 70, 100);
    ctx.fillStyle = "rgba(0, 0, 200, 0.50)";
    ctx.fillRect(57, 54, 100, 65);
 }
}
</script>
</head>
<body onload="drawMe()">
<h1>The Canvas Element</h1>
<canvas id="myCanvas" width="400" height="175">
My Canvas</canvas>
</body>
</html>
```

If some of the code looks like a foreign language to you, don't worry: JavaScript IS a different language than CSS and HTML; it has its own syntax and rules. Here's a quick overview of the code:

- The red outline was created by applying CSS to the canvas selector.

- The JavaScript function drawMe() is invoked when the browser loads the page. JavaScript looks for a canvas element assigned to the "myCanvas" id. JavaScript tests for browser support of canvas and, if true, performs the following actions:

  - Sets the canvas context to 2D.

  - Draws the "My Canvas" text.

  - Uses the fillStyle attribute to set the drawing color to red.

  - Uses the font attribute to configure font weight, font size, and font family.

  - Uses the fillText method to specify the text to display, followed by the x-value (pixels in from the left) and y-value (pixels down from the top).

  - Draws the rectangle.

  - Uses the fillStyle attribute to set the drawing color to blue with 50% opacity.

  - Uses the fillRect method to set the x-value (pixels in from the left), y-value (pixels down from the top), width, and height of the rectangle.

The promise of the canvas element is that it can be used to provide sophisticated interactions. Experience virtuoso examples of the canvas element in action at https://davidwalsh.name/canvas-demos.

## FAQ  What is SVG?

SVG (Scalable Vector Graphics) is a markup language that describes vector-based, two-dimensional graphics in XML (https://www.w3.org/Graphics/SVG/). Vector graphic shapes, images, and text objects can be included in an SVG, which can scale to increase or decrease in size without losing clarity. Advantages of using SVG images include scalability and small file size. SVG content is stored in the .svg file extension and can be interactive and animated.

You can write the XML code for an SVG yourself, but it's common to use a vector graphics editor, such as Adobe Illustrator, Adobe Animate CC, open-source Inkscape (https://inkscape.org), or the online app http://editor.method.ac to generate an SVG file.

There are several methods commonly used to display an SVG on a web page: an img element with an .svg file as the src attribute value, a CSS background image, and an svg element that contains the XML code for the SVG graphic. See the chapter11/svg folder in the student files for examples of SVG in use.

To learn more about SVG visit the following resources:

- https://developer.mozilla.org/en-US/docs/Web/SVG/Tutorial
- https://css-tricks.com/using-svg
- https://css-tricks.com/lodge/svg/06-using-svg-svg-background-image

## HTML5 API Resources

This section provided a brief overview of several of HTML5 APIs. Visit the following resources for more information, tutorials, and demos.

- https://bestvpn.org/html5demos/
- https://developers.google.com/web/progressive-web-apps/
- https://blog.bitsrc.io/what-is-a-pwa-and-why-should-you-care-388afb6c0bad

## Checkpoint 11.3

**1.** What are two uses of JavaScript?

**2.** Describe some features of a PWA.

**3.** What is the purpose of the HTML5 canvas element?

# 11.11 Multimedia, Animation, and Interactivity Accessibility Issues

**Focus on Accessibility**

Multimedia, animation, and interactivity can help to create a compelling, engaging experience for your website visitors. Please keep in mind that not every web visitor will be able to experience these features, so incorporate the following into your website:

- Text descriptions and equivalent content (such as captions) of audio and video will provide access for those with hearing challenges and will also assist visitors using mobile devices or slow Internet connections.

- When you work with multimedia developers and software developers to create animations for your site, request features that provide accessibility, such as keyboard access, text descriptions, and so on.

- WCAG 2.1 Success Criterion 2.2.2 recommends providing a way to pause, stop and/or hide moving, blinking, or scrolling information if it begins automatically and lasts more than five seconds. A further recommendation is to provide a way to pause, stop or hide auto-updating information if it begins automatically and is presented along with other content (https://www.w3.org/WAI/WCAG21/quickref/#pause-stop-hide). The duration of the animation you created in Hands-On Practice 11.8 was set to five seconds in order to meet this success criterion.

- WCAG 2.1 Success Criterion 2.3.1 recommends that a web page not contain any item that flashes more than three times per second (https://www.w3.org/WAI/WCAG21/quickref/#three-flashes-or-below-threshold). The purpose of this guideline is to prevent optically induced seizures. You may need to work with your animation developer to ensure that dynamic effects perform within a safe range.

- If you use JavaScript, be aware that some visitors may have JavaScript disabled or are unable to manipulate the mouse. A website should be functional at a basic level, even if your visitor's browser does not support JavaScript. A site using Ajax to redisplay a portion of the browser window may have issues when accessed using an assistive technology or text browser. The importance of testing cannot be over-emphasized. The W3C has developed ARIA (Accessible Rich Internet Applications), which is a protocol that supports accessibility for scripted and dynamic content, such as the web applications created using Ajax. See WAI-ARIA Overview (https://www.w3.org/WAI/standards-guidelines/aria/) for more information about ARIA.

When you design multimedia, animation, and interactivity with accessibility in mind, you help those visitors who have physical challenges, as well as those who are using low bandwidth or who may be missing plug-ins on their browser. As a last resort, consider creating a separate text-only version of the page if the multimedia, animation, and/or interactivity used on a page cannot comply with accessibility guidelines.

# Chapter Summary

This chapter introduced technologies to add media and interactivity to web pages. HTML techniques used to configure sound and video were discussed. JavaScript, Ajax, and HTML5 APIs were introduced. You configured an interactive CSS menu, an interactive CSS image gallery, a widget with the details and summary elements, and explored the CSS transition, transform, and animate properties. Accessibility and copyright issues related to these technologies were addressed. Visit the textbook website at https://www.webdevfoundations. net for examples, the links listed in this chapter, and updated information.

## Key Terms

.aiff
.au
.av1
.avi
.class
.m4a
.m4v
.mid
.mov
.mp3
.mp4
.mpg
.ogg
.ogv
.swf
.wav
.webm
.wmv
`<audio>`
`<canvas>`
`<details>`

`<script>`
`<source>`
`<summary>`
`<video>`
`@keyframes` rule
Ajax
animation property
application programming interface (API)
audio element
canvas element
client-side scripting
codec
container
copyright
Creative Commons license
details element
Document Object Model (DOM)
fair use
geolocation
interactivity

JavaScript
jQuery
keyframe
`localStorage`
manifest
media
object-based
progressive web application
`rotate()` transform
`scale()` transform
script element
sessionStorage
service worker
source element
summary element
`transform` property
`transition` property
video element
web storage

## Review Questions

### Multiple Choice

1. Which property provides a way for you to rotate, scale, skew, or move an element?

   a. display

   b. transition

   c. transform

   d. relative

2. Which code provides a hyperlink to an audio file called hello.mp3?

   a. `<audio data="hello.mp3"> </audio>`

   b. `<a href="hello.mp3">Hello (Audio File)</a>`

   c. `<canvas data="hello.mp3"></canvas>`

   d. `<link src="hello.mp3">`

3. What type of files are .wav, .aiff, .mid, and .au?
   a. audio files
   b. video files
   c. both audio and video files
   d. image files

4. Which of the following should you do to provide for usability and accessibility?
   a. Use video and sound whenever possible.
   b. Supply text descriptions of audio and video files that appear on your web pages.
   c. Never use audio and video files.
   d. none of the above

5. What happens when a browser does not support the video or audio element?
   a. The computer crashes.
   b. The web page does not display.
   c. The fallback content, if it exists, will display.
   d. The browser closes.

6. Which of the following is an object-based, client-side scripting language?
   a. JavaScript
   b. HTML
   c. CSS
   d. API

7. Which is an HTML API that stores information on the client?
   a. web storage
   b. geolocation
   c. canvas
   d. client storage

8. Which of the following is an open-source video codec?
   a. Theora
   b. Vorbis
   c. MP3
   d. Wave

9. Which elements can be used to configure an interactive widget?
   a. hide and show
   b. details and summary
   c. display and hidden
   d. title and summary

10. Which of the following can describe Ajax?
    a. It is an object-based scripting language.
    b. It is a useful HTML element.
    c. It is a web development technique for creating interactive web applications.
    d. It is a CSS property.

## Fill in the Blank

11. A(n) _____ is a protocol that allows software components to communicate—interacting and sharing data.

12. Use of a copyrighted work for purposes such as criticism, reporting, teaching, scholarship, or research is called _____.

13. The file extensions .webm, .ogv, and .m4v indicate types of _____ files.

14. CSS animations provide a way to animate the values of _____ over time.

15. The _____ defines every object and element on a web page.

## Short Answer

16. List at least two reasons not to use audio or video on a web page.

17. Describe a type of copyright license that empowers the author/artist to grant some, but not all, rights for using his or her work.

# Apply Your Knowledge

1. **Predict the Result.** Draw and write a brief description of the web page that will be created with the following HTML code:

```html
<!DOCTYPE html>
<html lang="en">
<head>
<title>CircleSoft Designs</title>
<meta charset="utf-8">
<style>
body { background-color: #FFFFCC; color: #330000;
       font-family: Arial,Helvetica,sans-serif; }
#wrapper { width: 80%; }
</style>
</head>
<body>
<div id="wrapper">
<h1>CircleSoft Design</h1>
<div><strong>CircleSoft Designs will </strong>
<ul>
  <li>work with you to create a Web presence that fits your
company</li>
  <li>listen to you and answer your questions</li>
  <li>utilize the most appropriate technology for your website</li>
</ul>
<p><a href="podcast.mp3" title="CircleSoft Client
Testimonial">Listen to what our clients say</a>
</p>
</div>
</div>
</body>
</html>
```

2. **Fill in the Missing Code.** This web page should display a details and summary widget. Some HTML element names, indicated by **<_>** and **</_>**, are missing. Fill in the missing code.

```html
<!DOCTYPE html>
<html lang="en">
<head>
<title>Fill in the Missing Code</title>
<meta charset="utf-8">
</head>
<body>
<_>
<_>Transition Property</_>
<p>A CSS transition provides for changes in property values to
display in a smoother manner over a specified time.</p>
</_>
</body>
</html>
```

3. **Find the Error.** The purpose of the following web page is to display a video. The video does not display on the Safari browser. Why?

```
<!DOCTYPE html>
<html lang="en">
<head>
<title>Find the Error</title>
<meta charset="utf-8">
</head>
<body>
<video controls="controls" width="160" height="150">
    <source src="sparky.webm" type="video/webm">
    <p>You are missing a great video.</p>
</video>
</body>
</html>
```

## Hands-On Exercises

1. Write the HTML for a hyperlink to a video called sparky.mov on a web page.

2. Write the HTML to allow a web visitor to control the playback of an audio file named lesson1.mp3.

3. Write the HTML to play a video on a web page. The video source files are prime.m4v, prime.ogv, and prime.webm. The dimensions of the video are 213 pixels wide by 163 pixels high.

4. Write the HTML to display a details and summary widget with three items on a web page.

5. Create a web page about your favorite movie or music CD that plays an audio file (use Windows Sound Recorder or a similar program to record your voice) and includes your review and recommendation. Remember to consider accessibility and provide a transcript of your audio file. Choose to either include the transcript text directly on the page or provide access to it with a hyperlink. Place an e-mail link to yourself on the web page. Save the page as audio11.html.

6. Create a web page about your favorite movie or music CD that plays a video file (use a digital camera, smartphone, or one of the applications listed in this chapter to record yourself) and includes your review and recommendation. Remember to consider accessibility and either provide a transcript of your video file or caption the video file. Place an e-mail link to yourself on the web page. Save the page as video11.html.

## Web Research

1. Issues related to copyright law were discussed in this chapter. With the resources provided as a starting point, search for additional information related to copyright law and the Web. Create a web page that provides five helpful facts about copyright law and the Web. Provide the URLs of the websites you used as resources. Place a media console on the page to allow visitors to play an audio file while they read your web page. Include an audio file (soundloop.mp3) from this chapter, record your own, or find an appropriate sound file on the Web. Place your name in an e-mail link on the web page.

2. Choose one of the following to research: JavaScript, jQuery or Progressive Web Applications. Use the resources listed in the chapter as a starting point, but also search the Web for additional resources on the topic you have chosen. Create a web page that lists at least five useful resources along with a brief description of each. Organize your web page with a list that provides the name of the site, the URL, a brief description of what is offered, and a recommended page (such as a tutorial or free script) for each resource. Place your name in an e-mail link on the web page.

3. Choose one of the following to research: JavaScript, Canvas Element API, or jQuery. Use the resources listed in the chapter as a starting point, but also search the Web for additional resources on the topic you have chosen. Find either a tutorial or a free download that uses the method of web interactivity you are researching. Create a web page that uses the code or download that you found. Describe the effect and list the URL of the resource on the web page. Place your name in an e-mail link on the web page.

## Focus on Web Design

There are web design usability and accessibility issues associated with HTML5 video. Visit the following sites to become aware of these issues:

- https://developer.mozilla.org/en-US/docs/Learn/Accessibility/Multimedia
- https://developer.mozilla.org/en-US/docs/Learn/Tools_and_testing/Cross_browser_testing/Accessibility
- http://www.afb.org/blog/afb-blog/an-accessible-html5-video-player-from-the-american-foundation-for-the-blind/12

Write a one-page report that describes HTML5 Video usability issues that web designers should be mindful of. Cite the URLs of the resources you used.

 # WEBSITE CASE STUDY
## Adding Multimedia

Each of the following case studies continues throughout most of the text. This chapter adds media and interactivity to the websites.

### JavaJam Coffee Bar

See Chapter 2 for an introduction to the JavaJam Coffee Bar case study. Figure 2.32 shows a site map for the JavaJam website. Use the Chapter 9 JavaJam website as a starting point for this case study. You have three tasks in this case study:

1. Create a new folder for this JavaJam case study.

2. Modify the style sheet (javajam.css) to configure style rules for an audio element.

3. Configure the Music page (music.html) to play audio files. Figure 11.21 shows the Music page with the audio players.

**Figure 11.21** The audio element on the Music page

## Hands-On Practice Case Study

**Task 1: The Website Folder**. Create a folder called javajam11. Copy all the files from your Chapter 9 javajam9 folder into the javajam11 folder. Copy the files from the chapter11/starters/javajam folder in the student files and save them to your javajam11 folder.

**Task 2: Configure the CSS**. Modify the external style sheet (javajam.css). Open javajam.css in a text editor. Code an audio element selector above the media queries with block display and 1em of top margin. Save the javajam.css file.

**Task 3: Update the Music Page.** Open music.html in a text editor. Modify music.html so that two HTML5 audio controls display (see Figure 11.21). Refer to Hands-On Practice 11.2 when you create the audio control. Configure an audio control within the div about Melanie to play the melanie.mp3 or melanie.ogg file and provide a hyperlink to the melanie.mp3 file as a fallback if the audio element is not supported. Configure an audio control within the div about Greg to play the greg.mp3 or greg.ogg file and provide a hyperlink to the greg.mp3 file as a fallback if the audio element is not supported. Save the web page. Check your HTML syntax using the W3C validator (https://validator.w3.org). Correct and retest if necessary. Display the page in different browsers and play the audio files.

# Fish Creek Animal Clinic

See Chapter 2 for an introduction to the Fish Creek Animal Clinic case study.
Figure 2.36 shows a site map for the Fish Creek website. Use the Chapter 9 Fish Creek
website as a starting point for this case study. You have three tasks in this case study:

1. Create a new folder for this Fish Creek case study.

2. Modify fishcreek.css to configure an animated page heading and the placement of
   an audio control.

3. Add an audio control to the Ask the Vet page (askvet.html). See Figure 11.22 for a
   sample screenshot.

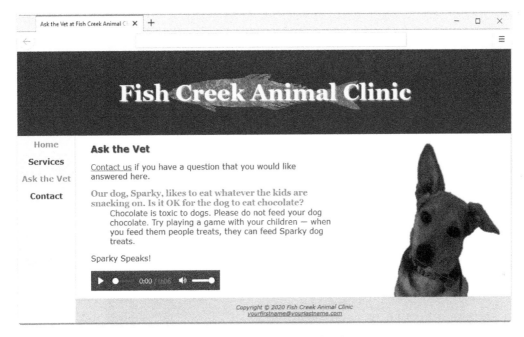

Figure 11.22  Fish Creek Ask the Vet page with an audio element

## Hands-On Practice Case Study

**Task 1: The Website Folder**.  Create a folder called fishcreek11. Copy all the files from your
Chapter 9 fishcreek9 folder into the fishcreek11 folder. Copy the files from the chapter11/
starters/fishcreek folder in the student files and save them to your fishcreek11 folder.

**Task 2: Configure the CSS**.  Modify the external style sheet (fishcreek.css). Open
fishcreek.css in a text editor. First, configure the animation style rules above the media
queries. Code a @keyframes rule named `fadein` that begins with opacity set to 0 and
ends with opacity set to 1. Code a style rule for the h1 element selector that configures the
`fadein` animation with a five second duration and ease-out timing. Next, prepare for a new
flex item on the Ask the Vet page. Locate the first media query and add a style rule for the
article element selector that configures `flex: 2`. Save the fishcreek.css file.

**Task 3: Configure an Audio Control on the Ask the Vet Page.** Launch a text editor and edit the Ask the Vet page (askvet.html). Add the text "Sparky Speaks!" within an h3 element below the description list. Configure an audio control (sparky.mp3 and sparky.ogg files) to display below the h3 element. Use the HTML5 audio and source elements. Code an article element that contains the description list, h3, and audio elements. Check your HTML syntax using the W3C validator (https://validator.w3.org). Correct and retest if necessary. Save your web page and test it using several browsers.

## Pacific Trails Resort

See Chapter 2 for an introduction to the Pacific Trails Resort case study. Figure 2.40 shows a site map for the Pacific Trails website. Use the Chapter 9 Pacific Trails website as a starting point for this case study. You have three tasks in this case study:

1. Create a new folder for this Pacific Trails case study.

2. Modify pacific.css to configure the placement of a video.

3. Add a video to the home page (index.html). See Figure 11.23 for a sample screenshot.

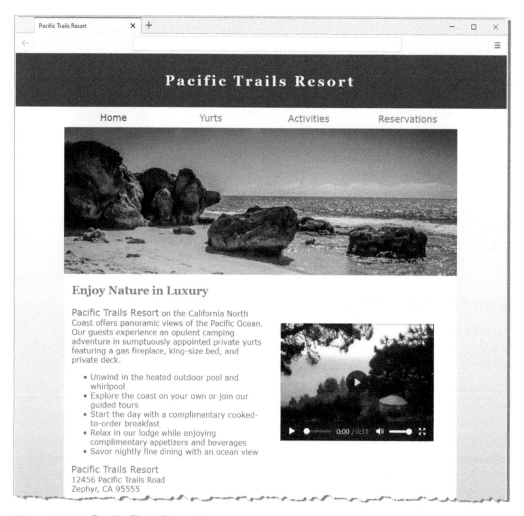

Figure 11.23  Pacific Trails Resort home page

## Hands-On Practice Case Study

**Task 1: The Website Folder.** Create a folder called pacific11. Copy all of the files from your Chapter 9 pacific9 folder into the pacific11 folder. Copy the files from the chapter11/starters/pacific folder in the student files and save them in your pacific11 folder.

**Task 2: Configure the CSS.** Modify the external style sheet (pacific.css). Open pacific.css in a text editor. Edit the CSS and configure a new video element selector above the media queries with style declarations to float to the right and margin set to 2em. Save the pacific.css file.

**Task 3: Configure the Video.** Launch a text editor and open the home page (index.html). Code the HTML5 video control below the h2 element and above the paragraph. Configure the video, and source elements to work with the following files: pacific.mp4, pacific.ogv, and pacific.jpg. The dimensions of the video are 320 pixels wide by 240 pixels high. Save the file. Check your HTML syntax using the W3C validator (https://validator.w3.org). Launch a browser and test your new Home page (index.html). It should look similar to Figure 11.23.

## Path of Light Yoga Studio

See Chapter 2 for an introduction to the Path of Light Yoga Studio case study. Figure 2.44 shows a site map for the Path of Light Yoga Studio website. Use the Chapter 9 Path of Light Yoga Studio website as a starting point for this case study. You have three tasks:

1. Create a new folder for this Path of Light Yoga Studio case study.

2. Modify yoga.css to configure the placement of an audio element.

3. Configure the Classes page (classes.html) to display an audio control.

## Hands-On Practice Case Study

**Task 1: The Website Folder.** Create a folder called yoga11. Copy all of the files from your Chapter 9 yoga9 folder into the yoga11 folder. Copy the files from the chapter11/starters/yoga folder in the student files and save them in your yoga11 folder.

**Task 2: Configure the CSS.** Modify the external style sheet (yoga.css). Open yoga.css in a text editor. Edit the CSS and code a new audio element selector above the media queries with block display and 1em margins. Save the yoga.css file.

**Task 3: Configure the Audio.** Open the Classes page (classes.html) in a text editor. Modify classes.html so that a heading, a paragraph, and an HTML5 audio control displays below the div assigned to the id named `flow` (see Figure 11.24). Use an h2 element to display the text "Relax Anytime with Savasana". Add a paragraph that contains the following text:

"Prepare yourself for savasana. Lie down on your yoga mat with your arms at your side with palms up. Close your eyes and breathe slowly but deeply. Sink into the mat and let your worries slip away. When you are ready, roll on your side and use your arms to push yourself to a sitting position with crossed legs. Place your hands in a prayer position. Be grateful for all that you have in life. Namaste."

Refer to Hands-On Practice 11.2 when you create the audio control. Configure the audio and source elements to work with the following files: savasana.mp3 and savasana.ogg. Configure a hyperlink to the savasana.mp3 file as a fallback if the audio element is not supported. Save the file. Check your HTML syntax using the W3C validator (https://validator.w3.org). Correct and retest if necessary. Launch a browser and test your new Classes page (classes.html). It should look similar to Figure 11.24.

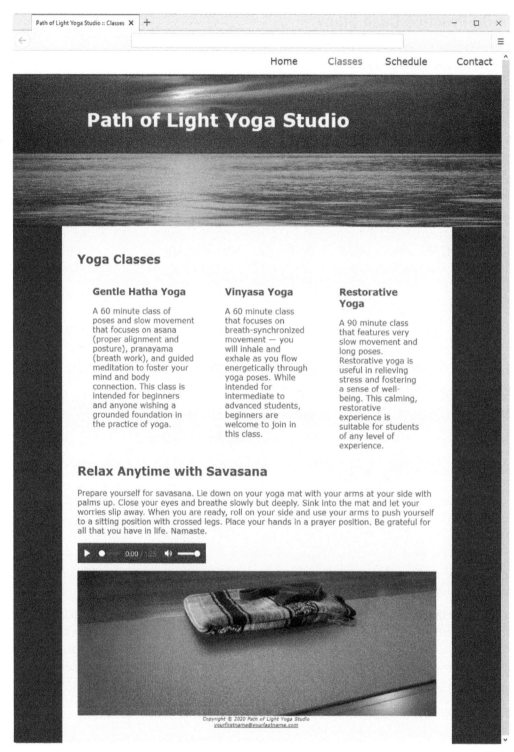

**Figure 11.24** The classes page displays an HTML5 audio control

# Web Project

See Chapter 5 for an introduction to the Web Project case study. Review the goals of your website and determine whether the use of media or interactivity would add value to your site. If so, you will add either media and/or interactivity to your project site. Check with your instructor regarding the required use of any specific media or technology that supports interactivity in your web project.

Select one or more from the following:

1. Media: Choose one of the examples from the chapter, record your own audio or media file, or search the Web for royalty-free media.

2. CSS image gallery: Create or locate images that relate to your web project. Using Hands-On Practice 11.7 as an example, configure a CSS image gallery.

3. Details & Summary Widget: Choose a web page in your project that contains definitions or descriptions of items that could be enhanced with a details and summary widget. Using Hands On Practice 11.9 as an example, configure a details and summary widget.

4. Decide where to apply the media and/or interactive technology to your site. Modify, save the page(s), and test in various browsers.

# 12

# E-Commerce Overview

## Chapter Objectives    In this chapter, you will learn how to . . .

- Define e-commerce
- Identify the benefits and risks of e-commerce
- Describe e-commerce business models
- Describe e-commerce security and encryption
- Define Electronic Data Interchange (EDI)
- Identify trends and projections for e-commerce
- Describe issues related to e-commerce
- Describe options for order and payment processing

**E-commerce is the buying and selling of goods** and services on the Internet. Whether business-to-business, business-to-consumer, or consumer-to-consumer, websites that support e-commerce are everywhere. This chapter provides an overview of this topic.

# 12.1  What Is E-Commerce?

A formal definition of **e-commerce** is the integration of communications, data management, and security technologies, which allows individuals and organizations to exchange information related to the sale of goods and services. The major functions of e-commerce include the buying of goods, the selling of goods, and the performance of financial transactions on the Internet.

## Advantages of E-Commerce

There are a number of advantages for both businesses and consumers when engaging in e-commerce. For businesses, the many advantages include the following:

- **Reduced Costs.** Online businesses can stay open 24 hours a day without the overhead of a brick-and-mortar facility. Many businesses establish a website before attempting e-commerce. When they add e-commerce functions to their website, the site becomes a source of revenue and, in many cases, pays for itself in short order.

- **Increased Customer Satisfaction.**  Businesses can use their websites to improve communication with customers and increase customer satisfaction. E-commerce sites often contain a page for frequently asked questions (FAQs). The availability of customer service representatives by e-mail, discussion forums, or even online chats (see LivePerson at http://www.liveperson.com) can improve customer relations.

- **More Effective Data Management.**  Depending on the level of automation, e-commerce sites can perform credit card verification and authorization, update inventory levels, and interface with order fulfillment systems, thereby managing the organization's data more efficiently.

- **Potentially Higher Sales.**  An e-commerce store that is open 24 hours a day, 7 days a week and is available to everyone on the planet has the potential for higher sales than a traditional brick-and-mortar storefront.

Businesses aren't the only beneficiaries of e-commerce; consumers see some advantages as well, including the following:

- **Convenience.**  Consumers can shop at any time of the day. There is no travel time to get to the store. Some consumers prefer website shopping over traditional catalog shopping because they can view additional images and join discussion forums about the products.

- **Easier Comparison Shopping.**  There is no driving from store to store to check the price of an item. Customers can easily surf the Web to compare prices and value.

- **Wider Selection of Goods.**  Because it is convenient to shop and compare, consumers have a wider selection of goods available for purchase.

As you can see, e-commerce provides a number of advantages for both businesses and consumers.

# Risks of E-Commerce

There are risks involved in any business transaction and e-commerce is no exception. The possible risks for businesses include the following:

- **Loss of Sales if Technology Fails.** If your website isn't available or your e-commerce form processing doesn't work, customers may not return to your site. It is always important to have a user-friendly, reliable website, but when you engage in e-commerce, reliability and ease of use are critical factors in the success of your business.

- **Fraudulent Transactions.** Fraudulent credit card purchases or crank orders placed by vandals (or 13-year-olds with time on their hands) are risks that businesses need to deal with.

- **Customer Reluctance.** Although more and more consumers are willing to purchase on the Web, the target market of your business may not be. However, by offering incentives such as free shipping or a "no questions asked" returns policy, your business may be able to attract these consumers.

- **Increased Competition.** Because the overhead for an e-commerce site can be much lower than that of a traditional brick-and-mortar store, a company operating out of a basement can be just as impressive as a long-standing business if its website looks professional. Because it is much easier to enter the marketplace with an e-commerce store, your business will have increased competition.

Businesses are not alone in needing to deal with the risks associated with e-commerce. Consumers may perceive the following risks:

- **Security Issues.** Later in this chapter, you will learn how to determine whether a website uses a Secure Sockets Layer (SSL) protocol for the encryption and security of information. The general public may not know how to determine whether a website is using this encryption method and be wary of placing a credit card order. Another, possibly more important, issue is what the site does with information after it is transmitted over the Internet. Is the database secure? Are the database backups secure? These questions are difficult to answer. It's a good idea to purchase only from sites that you consider to be reputable.

- **Privacy Issues.** Many sites post privacy policy statements. These describe what the site will do (or will not do) with the information they receive. Some sites use the data for internal marketing purposes only. Other sites sell the data to outside companies. Websites can and do change their privacy policies over time. Consumers may be leery of purchasing online because of the potential lack of privacy.

- **Purchasing Based on Photos and Descriptions.** There is nothing like holding and touching an item before you purchase it. Consumers run the risk of purchasing a product that they will not be happy with because they are making purchasing decisions based on photographs and written descriptions. If an e-commerce site has a generous returns policy, consumers will feel more confident about making a purchase.

- **Returns.** It is often more difficult to return an item to an e-commerce store than to a brick-and-mortar store. Consumers may not want to risk this inconvenience.

# 12.2 E-Commerce Business Models

Both businesses and consumers are riding the e-commerce wave. There are four common e-commerce business models: business-to-consumer, business-to-business, consumer-to-consumer, and business-to-government.

- **Business-to-Consumer (B2C).** Most of the business-to-consumer selling takes place at online stores. Some, like Amazon.com (http://www.amazon.com), are online only. Others are click-and-mortar—electronic storefronts for well-known brick-and-mortar stores such as Sears (http://www.sears.com).
- **Business-to-Business (B2B).** E-commerce between two businesses often takes the form of exchanging business supply chain information among vendors, partners, and business customers. Electronic Data Interchange (EDI) is also included in this category.
- **Consumer-to-Consumer (C2C).** Individuals are selling to each other on the Internet. The most common format is that of the auction. The most well-known auction site is eBay (http://www.ebay.com), which was founded in 1995.
- **Business-to-Government (B2G).** Businesses are selling to the government on the Internet. There are very strict usability standards for businesses that target governmental agencies. Section 508 of the Rehabilitation Act requires that electronic and information technology (including web pages) used by federal agencies is accessible to people with disabilities. See http://www.section508.gov for more information.

Businesses began exchanging information electronically using EDI many years before the Web came into existence.

# 12.3 Electronic Data Interchange (EDI)

**Electronic Data Interchange (EDI)** is the transfer of structured data between companies over a network. This facilitates the exchange of standard business documents, including purchase orders and invoices. EDI predates the Internet and has been in existence since the 1960s. Organizations that exchange EDI transmissions are called trading partners.

The Accredited Standards Committee X12 (ASC X12) is chartered by the American National Standards Institute (ANSI) to develop and maintain EDI standards. These standards include transaction sets for common business forms, such as requisitions and invoices. This allows businesses to reduce paperwork and communicate electronically.

EDI messages are placed in transaction sets, which consist of a header; one or more data segments, which are strings of data elements separated by delimiters; and a trailer. Newer technologies such as XML and web services are allowing trading partners virtually unlimited opportunities to customize their information exchange over the Internet.

Now that you are aware of the possibilities of e-commerce and the types of business models, you may be wondering where the most money is being made. The next section discusses some statistics related to e-commerce.

# 12.4 E-Commerce Statistics

Although e-commerce growth stalled during the recent economic downturn, it is again demonstrating growth. Statista reports that worldwide retail e-commerce sales are expected to grow from $2.3 trillion in 2017 to $4.9 trillion in 2021 (https://www.statista.com/statistics/379046/worldwide-retail-e-commerce-sales/).

You may be wondering what people are buying online. A report compiled by the U.S. Census Bureau (https://www2.census.gov/programs-surveys/arts/tables/2016/supecommerce4541.xlsa) indicated that the top eight categories for online retail sales in 2016 (the most recent year reported) were the following:

1. General merchandise ($27.3 billion)

2. Electronics and appliances ($22.3 billion)

3. Clothing and accessories ($21.2 billion)

4. Building material and garden supplies ($7.6 billion)

5. Furniture and home furnishings ($7 billion)

6. Sporting goods, hobby, musical instruments, and books ($5.8 billion)

7. Health and personal care ($3.2 billion)

8. Food and beverage ($1.4 billion)

Now that you know what is selling the best online, who are your potential online consumers? A survey by the PEW Internet and American Life Project (https://www.pewresearch.org/fact-tank/2018/03/14/about-a-quarter-of-americans-report-going-online-almost-constantly/) indicated that 39% of Americans aged 18-29 go online "almost constantly." Table 12.1 shows an excerpt from this research.

Table 12.1 Americans online "almost constantly" Data from Pew Research Center Internet Project Survey.

| Category | Percentage Online "Almost Constantly" |
|---|---|
| U.S. Adults | 26% |
| Men | 25% |
| Women | 27% |
| Age: 18–29 | 39% |
| Age: 30–49 | 36% |
| Age: 50–64 | 17% |
| Age: 65 and older | 8% |
| Household Income: Less than $30,000 | 24% |
| Household Income: $30,000 to $49,999 | 27% |
| Household Income: $50,000 to $74,999 | 23% |
| Household Income: $75,000 or higher | 35% |
| Education: High school graduate | 20% |
| Education: Some college | 28% |
| Education: College graduate | 34% |

# 12.5 E-Commerce Issues

Doing business on the Internet is not without its problems. The following are some common issues:

- **Intellectual Property.** There has been some recent controversy regarding intellectual property rights and domain names. **Cybersquatting** is the practice of registering a domain name that is a trademark of another entity in the hopes of profiting by selling the domain name to the entity. The Internet Corporation for Assigned Names and Numbers (ICANN) sponsors the Uniform Domain Name Dispute Policy (https://www.icann.org/resources/pages/help/dndr/udrp-en), which can be used to combat cybersquatters.

- **Security.**  Security is a constant issue on the Internet. Distributed denial of service (DDoS) attacks, which are malicious attempts to make a website unavailable by flooding it with requests from multiple computers, have shut down popular e-commerce sites.

- **Fraud.**  Fraudulent websites that ask for credit card numbers without any intent of delivering products or with fraudulent intent are an understandable source of concern for consumers.

- **Taxation.**  State governments and local municipalities use sales tax to fund education, public safety, health, and many other essential services. When an item is purchased at a retail store, the sales tax is collected from the purchaser by the seller at the time of the sale and periodically remitted by the seller to the state in which the sale occurred.

  When an item is purchased on the Internet and the seller does not have a physical presence in the consumer's state, the seller often does not collect and remit the sales tax. In this situation, many states require that consumers file a use tax and pay the amount that would have been collected. In reality, few consumers do this and few states attempt to enforce it. Nolo.com provides information on Internet sales tax laws for each state (https://www.nolo.com/legal-encyclopedia/50-state-guide-internet-sales-tax-laws.html). A 2018 U.S. Supreme Court ruling (https://www.supremecourt.gov/opinions/17pdf/17-494_j4el.pdf) upheld a law enacted in the State of South Dakota, which requires sellers that engage in over 200 transactions or $100,000 in sales within South Dakota to collect and remit sales tax.

- **International Commerce.** Websites that target a global audience have additional concerns. If a site will be offered in multiple languages, there are options of automatic translation solutions such as SYSTRAN (http://www.systransoft.com) and companies that provide customized website translation services such as WorldLingo (http://www.worldlingo.com). Be aware that the graphical user interface (GUI) that works with English may not work with other languages. For example, comparable words and phrases often take quite a few more letters in German than in English. If your GUI has minimal white space in the English version of the site, how will it look in the German version?

  How will your international customers pay you? If you accept credit cards, the credit card company will perform the currency conversion. What about the culture of your target international audience? Have you studied the target countries and made certain that your site is appealing and not offensive? Another issue related to international commerce is the cost of shipping and the availability of delivery to remote destinations.

Now that you are familiar with e-commerce concepts and terms, let's take a closer look at encryption methods and security. The next section introduces encryption methods, SSL, and digital certificates.

# 12.6 E-Commerce Security

## Encryption

Encryption is used to ensure privacy within an organization and on the Internet. **Encryption** is the conversion of data into an unreadable form, called a **ciphertext**. Ciphertext cannot be easily understood by unauthorized individuals. **Decryption** is the process of converting the ciphertext into its original form, called plain text or **clear text**, so that it can be understood. The process of encryption and decryption requires an algorithm and a key. An **algorithm** involves a mathematical calculation. A **key** is a numeric code that should be long enough so that its value cannot easily be guessed.

Encryption is important on the Internet because information in a packet can be intercepted as it travels the communications media. If a hacker or business competitor intercepts an encrypted packet, he or she will not be able to use the information (such as a credit card number or business strategy) because it cannot be read.

A number of types of encryption are commonly used on the Internet, including symmetric-key encryption and asymmetric-key encryption.

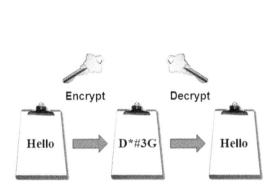

**Figure 12.1** Symmetric-key encryption uses a single key

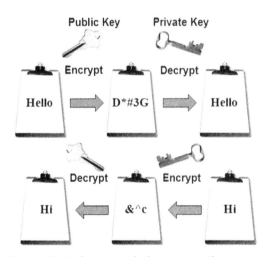

**Figure 12.2** Asymmetric-key encryption uses a key pair

### Symmetric-Key Encryption

**Symmetric-key encryption**, shown in Figure 12.1, is also called single-key encryption because both the encryption and decryption use the same key. Because the key must be kept secret from others, both the sender and the receiver must know the key before communicating using encryption. An advantage of symmetric-key encryption is speed.

### Asymmetric-Key Encryption

**Asymmetric-key encryption** is also called public-key encryption because there is no shared secret. Instead, two keys are created at the same time. This key pair contains a public key and a private key. The public key and the private key are mathematically related in such a way that it is unlikely that anyone would guess one of the pair even with knowledge of the other. Only the public key can decrypt a message encrypted with the private key and only the private key can decrypt a message encrypted with the public key (see Figure 12.2). The public key is available via a digital certificate (more on that later). The private key should be kept secure and secret. It is stored on the web server (or other computer) of the key owner. Asymmetric-key encryption is much slower than symmetric-key encryption.

## Integrity

The encryption methods described above help to keep the contents of a message secret. However, e-commerce security is also concerned with making sure that messages have not been altered or damaged during transmission. A message is said to have **integrity** if it can be proven that is has not been altered. **Hash functions** provide a way to ensure the integrity of messages. A hash function, or hash algorithm, transforms a string of characters into a usually shorter, fixed-length value or key, called a **digest**, which represents the original string.

These security methods—especially the techniques of symmetric-key and asymmetric-key encryption—are used as part of SSL, the technology that helps to make commerce on the Internet secure. The next section introduces this technology.

## Secure Sockets Layer (SSL)

**Secure Sockets Layer (SSL)** is a protocol that allows data to be privately exchanged over public networks. It was developed by Netscape in 1994 to encrypt data sent between a client (usually a web browser) and a web server. SSL utilizes both symmetric and asymmetric keys.

**Transport Layer Security (TLS)** was later developed and implemented as an improvement and replacement for Secure Sockets Layer. However, the acronym SSL is commonly used to indicate encrypted secure communication between a web browser and a web server.

SSL provides secure communication between a client and a server by using the following:

- Server and (optionally) client digital certificates for authentication
- Symmetric-key cryptography with a "session key" for bulk encryption
- Public-key cryptography for transfer of the session key
- Message digests (hash functions) to verify the integrity of the transmission

You can tell that a website is using SSL by the protocol in the web browser address text box—it shows https instead of http. When a URL begins with https://, it indicates that the browser is using **HTTPS**, which stands for **Hypertext Transport Protocol Secure**. HTTPS combines HTTP with SSL. In addition to displaying the https protocol, browsers typically display a lock icon or other indicator of SSL, as shown in Figure 12.3.

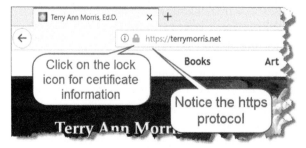

**Figure 12.3** The browser indicates that SSL is being used. Screenshots of Mozilla Firefox. Courtesy of Mozilla Foundation.

**FAQ**   **When some websites are displayed in a browser, there is a color bar in the address area. What's up?**

If a website displays a color bar in the address area of the browser in addition to the lock icon in the status bar, you know that it is using **Extended Validation SSL (EV SSL).** EV SSL signifies that the business has undergone more rigorous background checks to obtain its digital certificate, including verification of the following:

- The applicant owns the domain.
- The applicant works for the organization.
- The applicant has the authority to update the website.
- The organization is a valid, recognized place of business.

## Digital Certificate

SSL enables two computers to communicate securely by posting a digital certificate for authentication. A **digital certificate** is a form of an asymmetric key that also contains information about the certificate, the holder of the certificate, and the issuer of the certificate. The contents of a digital certificate include the following:

- The public key
- The effective date of the certificate
- The expiration date of the certificate
- Details about the certificate authority (the issuer of the certificate)
- Details about the certificate holder
- A digest of the certificate content

VeriSign (https://www.verisign.com), Thawte (https://thawte.com), and Entrust (https://entrustdatacard.com) are well-known certificate authorities.

To obtain your own certificate, you will need to generate a certificate signing request (CSR) and a private/public key pair (see https://www.digitalocean.com/community/tutorials/how-to-install-an-ssl-certificate-from-a-commercial-certificate-authority) for an overview of this process. Next, you request a certificate from a certificate authority, pay the application fee, and provide your CSR and public key. The certificate authority verifies your identity. There may be a waiting period, and you will need to pay an annual fee. After verification, the certificate authority signs and issues your certificate. You store the certificate in your software, such as a web server, web browser, or e-mail application. When linking to your secure web pages, use "https" instead of "http" on your absolute hyperlinks.

### FAQ   **Do I have to apply for a certificate?**

If you are accepting any personal information on your website such as credit card numbers, you should be using SSL. Using SSL not only improves the security of your website, it may also help with marketing your website. Google's PageRank algorithm ranks secure pages higher than nonsecure pages. However, you may not need to apply for your won certificate; other options exist. Cloudflare (https:/www.cloudflare.com/ssl/) offers an online content delivery network (CDN) service that will route copies of your web pages through their servers and encrypt via SSL. There are several levels of service plans at varying costs, including a free starter plan. Also, many web hosts offer basic SSL with their web hosting packages. Check with your web host provider to determine if they offer this feature.

## SSL and Digital Certificates

A number of steps are involved in the SSL authentication process. The web browser and web server go through initial handshaking steps, exchanging information about the server certificate and keys. Once trust is established, the web browser generates and encrypts the session key (symmetric key) that will be used for the rest of the communication. From this point on, all data is encrypted through the session key. Table 12.2 shows this process.

**Table 12.2**  SSL encryption process overview

| Browser | → | "hello" | → | Server |
|---|---|---|---|---|
| Browser | ← | "hello" + server certificate (with public key) | ← | Server |
| *The browser now verifies the identity of the web server. It obtains the certificate of certificate authority (CA) that signed the server's certificate. Then the browser decrypts the certificate digest using the CA's public key (held in a root CA certificate). Next, the browser authenticates the server's certificate and checks the expiration date of the certificate. If all is valid, the next step occurs.* | | | | |
| Browser | → | The browser randomly generates a session key encrypted with server's public key. | → | Server |
| | | *Server decrypts the session key with private key.* | | |
| Browser | ← | The server sends a message that is encrypted with the session key. | ← | Server |
| | | *All future transmissions between the browser and the server are encrypted with the session key.* | | |

At this point, you have a general idea of how SSL works to protect the integrity of information on the Internet, including the information exchanged in e-commerce transactions. The next section takes a closer look at order and payment processing in e-commerce.

## Checkpoint 12.1

1. What are three advantages of e-commerce for an entrepreneur who is just starting a business?

2. What are three risks that businesses face when engaging in e-commerce?

3. Define SSL. How can an online shopper tell that an e-commerce site is using SSL.

# 12.7 Order and Payment Processing

In B2C e-commerce, the products for sale are displayed in an online catalog. On large sites, these catalog pages are dynamically created using server-side scripts to access databases. Each item usually has a button or image that invites visitors to "Buy Me" or "Add to Cart". Items selected are placed in a virtual shopping cart. When visitors are finished shopping, they click a button or image link which indicates that they want to "Check Out" or "Place Order". At this point, the items in their shopping cart are usually displayed on a web page with an order form.

Secure ordering is facilitated through the use of SSL. Once an order is placed, there are a number of commonly used payment methods by which to pay for the merchandise or service, including credit card, stored-value card, digital wallet, and digital cash.

## Credit Card

Credit card payment processing is a very important component of an e-commerce website. Funds from the customer need to be transferred to the merchant's bank. In order to accept credit cards, the site owner must apply for a merchant account and be approved. A **merchant account** is a type of business bank account that allows a business to accept credit card payments. You may also need real-time credit card verification using a payment gateway or third party such as Authorize.Net (https://www.authorizenet.com). While merchant accounts can be expensive, PayPal (https://www.paypal.com) offers a low-cost solution. Originally intended for consumer-to-consumer credit card sales, PayPal now offers credit card and shopping cart services for business website owners. You can add an online shopping experience to your website in a day with a PayPal shopping cart (https://www.paypal.com/us/webapps/mpp/shopping-cart).

## Stored-value Card

A **stored-value card**, such as a gift card for a major department store, holds information, including cash. Magnetic stripe stored-value cards can hold a limited amount of information. A stored-value **smart card** has an integrated circuit embedded within and offers more capacity to store information. Smart cards are widely used in Europe, Australia, and Japan. Visit Smart Cart Alliance (http://www.smartcardbasics.com/smart-card-overview.html) for more information about smart cards.

## Digital Wallet

A **digital wallet**, also called an e-wallet, is a virtual wallet that can be used for mobile or online payments. A digital wallet may store information about one or more credit cards along with personal identification and contact information. Examples of this popular technology include Visa Checkout (https://www.v.me/), Google Pay (https://pay.google.com), and Apple Pay (https://www.apple.com/apple-pay). **Near field communication (NFC)** is described by Techspot (http://www.techspot.com/guides/385-everything-about-nfc/) as a short-range wireless communication that uses a radio frequency to share information between NFC devices in close proximity, such as an NFC-equipped smartphone and an NFC-ready credit card readers or NFC-ready ticket gate. Purchasers using the Apple Pay and Google Pay digital wallets only have to tap their phone on a compatible NFC device to share information and complete a purchase.

## Digital Cash

**Digital cash** serves as a substitute for government-issued currency. A currently popular digital cash provider is **Bitcoin** (http://bitcoin.org), which is not a company, but can be described as a peer-to-peer payment network for digital money with no central authority. No single person owns or controls Bitcoin. Government-issued currency is not deposited or exchanged. Instead, the currency is bitcoins. Bitcoin is easy to use – a Bitcoin user can send or receive bitcoins using a mobile app or digital wallet. A public ledger, called the blockchain, is kept of all Bitcoin transactions. Bitcoins are accepted at a growing number of businesses, including Overstock.com and Dell.

# 12.8 E-Commerce Technology Solutions

You have probably shopped at online stores and found some easy to work with and others difficult. A large problem for e-commerce sites is abandoned shopping carts—visitors who begin to shop but never place an order. This section explores types of e-commerce technology solutions and shopping carts. A number of different options are available to business owners and web developers. They range from a simple, instant online storefront supplied by another website to a sophisticated e-commerce platform. This section examines some of the options.

## Instant Online Storefront

You supply the products, the **instant online storefront** does the rest. There is no need to install software. All you do is use your web browser to point and click your way to a virtual store. You use a template provided by the online storefront and choose features, configure settings, and add your products, uploading images, descriptions, prices, and captions.

There are some disadvantages to this approach. You are limited to the templates offered by the online storefront provider. The number of products that you can sell may also be limited. Your store may have a look and feel that is similar to the other instant stores hosted by the provider. However, this method provides a low-overhead, low-risk approach for a small business owner who has limited technical expertise. The storefront provider will often offer merchant accounts and payment automation.

Some instant storefront solutions are free, with limited service or a limited number of products. Others are fee-based and may charge hosting fees, processing fees, and monthly fees. Two popular instant storefront solutions are Shopify (https://www.shopify.com) and BigCommerce (https://www.bigcommerce.com). Artists and crafters have found a home on Etsy (https://www.etsy.com) to create instant e-storefronts to display and sell their wares.

There are also a number of free shopping cart scripts available on the Web. Check out JustAddCommerce (http://www.richmediatech.com) and Mal's e-commerce (https://www.mals-e.com) for some alternate solutions. The level of difficulty and the exact processing of these solutions vary. Each website has instructions and documentation for its product. Some may require you to register before they provide you with specific HTML. Others may require you to download and install the scripts on your own web server. PayPal (https://www.paypal.com) offers a shopping cart and payment verification for businesses at a very low cost. PayPal writes the code that you need to place on your web pages in order to interface with them. You only need to copy and paste it in. Budget-wise solutions such as PayPal, Mal's e-commerce, or JustAddCommerce work best for businesses that fit the standard business model and do not require special processing needs.

## Shopping Cart Software

With this approach, software that provides a standardized set of e-commerce features is purchased, installed on your web server, and customized. Many web host providers offer this option, which usually includes a shopping cart, order processing, and optional credit card payment processing. **Shopping cart software** provides an online catalog where your visitors can browse, add items to their virtual shopping cart, and check out through an order form when they are ready to make a purchase. Popular options offered by web host providers are AgoraCart (http://agoracart.com), osCommerce (https://oscommerce.com), and ZenCart (https://www.zen-cart.com).

## E-Commerce Platform

Custom building a large-scale e-commerce website entirely from scratch usually requires expertise, time, and a sizable budget! The advantage is that you get exactly what you need. Software development tools for a custom-built site include development tools such as Adobe Dreamweaver or Microsoft Visual Studio, a database management system (DBMS), and server-side scripting. An **e-commerce platform** is a software application that provides sophisticated features needed for B2C or B2B e-commerce, including website management, product management, customer management, order management, shopping cart, shipping and tax calculations. Two well-known e-commerce platforms are Microsoft Azure Commerce (https://azure.microsoft.com/en-us/solutions/ecommerce/) and Adobe Commerce Cloud (https://www.adobe.com/commerce/magento.html).

 **Checkpoint 12.2**

1. Name three payment methods that are commonly used on the Web.

2. Have you made purchases online? If so, think about the last item that you purchased. Why did you purchase it online instead of at a store? Did you check to see if the transaction was secure? Why or why not? How will your shopping habits be different in the future?

3. Describe three types of available e-commerce solutions. Which one provides the easiest entry to e-commerce? Why?

# Chapter Summary

This chapter introduced basic e-commerce concepts and implementation. Consider taking an e-commerce course to continue your study of this dynamic and growing area of web development. Visit the textbook website at https://www.webdevfoundations.net for examples, the links listed in this chapter, and updated information.

## Key Terms

asymmetric-key encryption
Bitcoin
Business-to-Business (B2B)
Business-to-Consumer (B2C)
Business-to-Government (B2G)
ciphertext
clear text
Consumer-to-Consumer (C2C)
cybersquatting
decryption
digest
digital cash

digital certificate
digital wallet
e-commerce
e-commerce platform
Electronic Data Interchange (EDI)
encryption
Extended Validation SSL (EV SSL)
hash functions
Hypertext Transfer Protocol Secure
  (HTTPS)
instant online storefront
integrity

international commerce
key
merchant account
near field communication
  (NFC)
Secure Sockets Layer (SSL)
shopping cart software
smart card
stored-value card
symmetric-key encryption
taxation
Transport Layer Security (TLS)

## Review Questions

### Multiple Choice

1. Which of the following acronyms refer to the business-to-consumer e-commerce business model?
   a. B2B
   b. BTC
   c. B2C
   d. C2B

2. What is a short-range wireless communication that uses a radio frequency to share information between electronic devices?
   a. NFC
   b. SSL
   c. EDI
   d. FTP

3. For businesses, which is a potential risk of using e-commerce?
   a. increased customer satisfaction
   b. the possibility of fraudulent transactions
   c. lower overhead costs
   d. none of the above

4. For businesses, which is an advantage of using e-commerce?
   a. the potential for fraudulent transactions
   b. reduced costs
   c. using shopping carts
   d. increased costs

5. Which of the following options best describes how a website owner can obtain a digital certificate?
   a. Digital certificates are automatically created when you register for a domain name.
   b. Contact a certificate authority and apply for a digital certificate.
   c. Digital certificates are automatically created when you are listed in a search engine.
   d. none of the above

6. Which of the following issues are uniquely related to international e-commerce?
   a. language and currency conversion
   b. browser version and screen resolution
   c. bandwidth and Internet service provider
   d. none of the above

7. Which of the following is a major function of e-commerce?
   a. using SSL to encrypt orders
   b. adding items to a shopping cart
   c. buying and selling goods
   d. none of the above

8. Which of the following is a disadvantage of an instant online storefront?
   a. The store is based on a template and may look very similar to other online stores.
   b. The store can be ready in minutes.
   c. The store cannot accept credit cards.
   d. none of the above

9. Which of the following include(s) an online catalog, a shopping cart, and a secure order form?
   a. web host providers
   b. shopping cart software
   c. web server software
   d. shopping cart script

10. Which of the following is true?
    a. A merchant account allows you to use SSL on your website.
    b. A digital wallet is a virtual wallet that can be used for mobile or online payments.
    c. Instant storefronts are what most large-scale e-commerce sites use.
    d. none of the above

## Fill in the Blank

11. _____ is a protocol that allows data to be privately exchanged over public networks.

12. _____ can be described as the transfer of structured data between different companies using networks.

13. A digital certificate is a form of a(n) _____ that also contains additional information about the entity holding the certificate.

14. An encryption method that uses a single, shared private key is _____.

## Short Answer

15. List one option for a website that needs to reach audiences that speak different languages.

# Hands-On Exercises

1. In this Hands-On Exercise, you will create an instant storefront. Choose one of the following websites that offer free trial online stores: InstanteStore (https://www.instantestore.com), Shopify (https://www.shopify.com), and BigCommerce (https://www.bigcommerce.com). Websites are constantly changing their policies, so these sites may no longer offer free trials when you do this assignment. If this is the case, check the textbook's website for updated information, ask your instructor for assistance, or search the Web for free online storefronts or trial stores. If you are certain that you have found a website that offers a free trial store, continue with this exercise and create a store that meets the following criteria:

   - Name: Door County Images
   - Purpose: To sell fine quality prints of Door County scenery
   - Target Audience: Adults age 40+ who have visited Door County; are middle to upper class; and who enjoy nature, boating, hiking, cycling, and fishing

- Item 1: Print of Ellison Bay at Sunset, Size: 11 inches by 14 inches, Price: $19.95
- Item 2: Print of Ellison Bay in Summer, Size: 11 inches by 14 inches, Price: $19.95

Create a folder called doorcounty. Copy the following images from the chapter 12 folder in the student files to your doorcounty folder: summer.jpg, summer_small.jpg, sunset.jpg, and sunset_small.jpg. Once you are organized, visit the website you have chosen to host your free store. You will have to log in, choose options, and upload your images. Follow the instructions provided. Most free online store sites have an FAQ section or technical support to help you. Figure 12.4 shows a page from an instant storefront. After you have completed your store, print out the browser view of the home page and catalog page.

Figure 12.4 An instant store

## Web Research

1. Just how popular is e-commerce? How many of your friends, family members, coworkers, and classmates purchase on the Web? Survey at least 20 people. Determine the following:

   a. How many have purchased an item online?

   b. How many have shopped but not purchased online?

   c. How many purchase online once a year? Once a month? Once a week?

   d. What is their age range (18–25, 26–39, 40–50, or over 50)?

   e. What is their gender?

   f. What is their level of education (high school, some college, college graduate, or graduate school)?

   g. What is their favorite online shopping site?

Create a web page that illustrates your findings. Also comment on the results and draw some conclusions. Search the Web for statistics that support your conclusions. Use the Pew Internet and American Life Project (https://pewinternet.org), eMarketer (https://www.emarketer.com/Articles), ClickZ (https://www.clickz.com), and E-Commerce Times (https://www.ecommercetimes.com) as starting points for your research. Place your name in an e-mail link on the web page.

2. This chapter provided a number of resources for e-commerce shopping cart and ordering systems. Use them as a starting point. Search the Web for additional resources. Find at least three shopping cart systems that you feel would be easy to use. Create a web page that reports your findings. Organize your page and list the information along with the URLs of the websites you used as resources. Include information such as the product name, a brief description, the cost, and the web server requirements (if any). Place your name in an e-mail link on the web page.

## Focus on Web Design

Visit the following sites as a starting point as you explore the web design topic of shopping cart usability:

- E-commerce Shopping Cart Usability Research Findings: https://www.uxteam.com/blog/e-commerce-shopping-cart-usability-research-findings/
- Dos and Don'ts of Mobile Shopping Cart Design: https://www.growcode.com/blog/mobile-shopping-cart-design/
- New E-Commerce Checkout Research: https://baymard.com/blog/ecommerce-checkout-usability-report-and-benchmark
- 10 Best Practices for Shopping Cart Page Optimization: https://www.abtasty.com/blog/shopping-cart-optimization/
- Optimizing Shopping Cart Page Design and Usability: http://www.ecommerceillustrated.com/optimizing-shopping-cart-pages-reducing-cart-abandonment/

Write a one-page report that describes shopping cart usability issues that web designers should be aware of. Cite the URLs of the resources you used.

# WEBSITE CASE STUDY
## Adding a Catalog Page for an Online Store

Each of the following case studies has continued throughout most of the text. This chapter adds a catalog page for an online store to the websites. This catalog page will connect to a placeholder shopping cart page on the textbook website at https://www.webdevfoundations.net.

## JavaJam Coffee Bar

See Chapter 2 for an introduction to the JavaJam Coffee Bar case study. Use the Chapter 9 JavaJam website as a starting point for this case study. As frequently happens with websites, the client, Julio Perez, is pleased with the response to the site and has an idea about a new use for it—selling JavaJam gear, such as T-shirts and coffee mugs. This new page, gear.html, will be part of the main navigation of the site. All pages should link to it. A revised site map is shown in Figure 12.5.

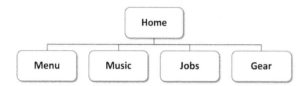

Figure 12.5   Revised JavaJam site map

The Gear page should contain a description, image, and price for each product. It should link to a shopping cart system when the visitor wants to purchase an item. You may access a placeholder page provided by the textbook's website. If you have access to a different shopping cart system, check with your instructor and ask if you can use it instead.

You have four tasks in this case study:

1. Create a new folder for this JavaJam case study.

2. Modify the main navigation on each page to include a link to the new Gear page.

3. Modify the javajam.css external CSS file.

4. Create the new Gear page (gear.html) shown in Figure 12.6.

## Hands-On Practice Case Study

**Task 1: The Website Folder**. Create a folder called javajam12. Copy all of the files from your Chapter 9 javajam9 folder into the javajam12 folder. Copy the javamug.jpg, javashirt.jpg, and herocouch.jpg images from the chapter 12 folder in the student files and save them to your javajam12 folder.

**Task 2: Update the Navigation on Each Page**. Launch a text editor and open the home page (index.html). Add a new list item and hyperlink in the main navigation area that displays the text "Gear" and links to the file gear.html. See Figure 12.6 for an example of the navigation area. Save the file. Edit the Menu (menu.html), Music (music.html), and Jobs (jobs.html) pages in a similar manner and save each file.

**Task 3: Configure the CSS**. Launch a text editor and open javajam.css. Configure the following styles above the media queries.

a. Add a new style rule to configure a class named `item` that has a `#FAF9F7` background color, 1em margin, 1em padding, and set the overflow property to auto.

b. Add a new style rule to configure the img elements within the item class to float to the right.

c. Configure a new id named `#herocouch` with 300px height that displays the herocouch.jpg image in 100% of the background. Use the `#heroguitar` id as a guide as you code the styles.

Save your javajam.css file.

Figure 12.6 New JavaJam Gear page

**Task 4: Create the New Gear Page**. One way to be productive is to create pages based on your earlier work. Launch a text editor and open the Menu page (menu.html). Save the file as gear.html. This will give you a head start and ensure that the pages on the website are similar. Perform the following modifications:

a. Change the page title to an appropriate phrase.

b. Locate the div assigned to the `heromugs` id. Assign to an id named `herocouch`.

c. Change the text within the h2 element to "JavaJam Gear".

d. Delete the existing paragraph and place each sentence below in a separate paragraph:

JavaJam gear not only looks good, it's good to your wallet, too.

Get a 10% discount when you wear a JavaJam shirt or bring in your JavaJam mug!

e. Locate the div assigned to the id named `flow`. Delete all the HTML elements and their contents within this div. You will code the shopping cart items in this area.

f. Configure a div element assigned to the class named `item`. Code the following img, h3, and paragraph tags in the div.

   1. Configure an img element to display the javashirt.jpg graphic.

   2. Configure the text "JavaJam Shirt" within an h3 element.

   3. Configure the following text in a paragraph: "JavaJam shirts are comfortable to wear to school and around town. 100% cotton. XL only. $14.95"

g. Configure a div element assigned to the class named `item`. Code the following img, h3, and paragraph tags in the div.

1. Configure an img element to display the javamug.jpg graphic.

2. Configure the text "JavaJam Mug" within an h3 element.

3. Configure the following text in a paragraph: "JavaJam mugs carry a full load of caffeine (12 oz.) to jump-start your morning. $9.95".

h. Each item for sale has an "Add to Cart" button, which is contained within a form with an action attribute set to https://webdevbasics.net/cart.html, a placeholder shopping cart page.

To place the shopping cart button for the T-shirt, add the following code below the paragraph that describes the T-shirt and above the closing div tag.

```
<form method="post"
    action="https://webdevbasics.net/cart.html">
    <input type="submit" value="Add to Cart">
</form>
```

The process for adding the shopping cart button for the mug is the same. Add the following code below the paragraph that contains the description of the mug.

```
<form method="post"
    action="https://webdevbasics.net/cart.html">
    <input type="submit" value="Add to Cart">
</form>
```

Save your page and test it in a browser. It should look similar to the one shown in Figure 12.6. Click the Add to Cart buttons for one of the items. The placeholder shopping cart will display and your screen should look similar to the one shown in Figure 12.7.

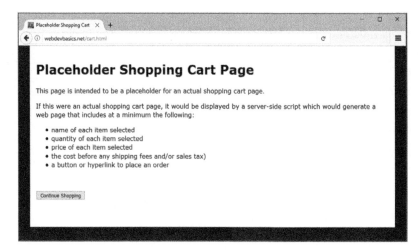

Figure 12.7  A placeholder shopping cart page

## Fish Creek Animal Clinic

See Chapter 2 for an introduction to the Fish Creek Animal Clinic case study. You will use the Chapter 9 fishcreek9 folder as the starting point for this case study.

After a site is initially created, it's typical for a client to think of new ideas for the website. The owner of Fish Creek, Magda Patel, is pleased with the response to the site and has a new use for it—selling sweatshirts and tote bags with the Fish Creek logo. She already has these materials for sale at her front desk in the animal hospital and her customers seem to like them. This new Shop page (shop.html) will be part of the main navigation of the site. All pages should link to it. A revised site map is shown in Figure 12.8.

**Figure 12.8** Revised Fish Creek site map

The Shop page should contain the description, image, and price of each product. It should link to a shopping cart system when the visitor wants to purchase an item. You may access a placeholder page provided by the textbook's website. If you have access to a different shopping cart system, check with your instructor and ask if you can use it instead.

You have four tasks in this case study:

1. Create a new folder for this Fish Creek case study.
2. Modify the main navigation on each page to include a link to the new Shop page.
3. Modify the fishcreek.css external CSS file.
4. Create the new Shop page (shop.html) shown in Figure 12.9.

Figure 12.9  New Fish Creek Shop page

## Hands-On Practice Case

**Task 1: The Website Folder**. Create a folder called fishcreek12. Copy all of the files from your Chapter 9 fishcreek9 folder into the fishcreek12 folder. Copy the fishtote.gif and fishsweat.gif images from the chapter12 folder in the student files and save them to your fishcreek12 folder.

**Task 2: Update the Navigation on Each Page**. Launch a text editor and open the home page (index.html). Add a new list item and hyperlink in the main navigation area that displays the text "Shop" and links to the file shop.html. See Figure 12.9 for an example of the navigation area. Save the file. Edit the Services (services.html), Ask the Vet (askvet.html), and Contact (contact.html) pages in a similar manner. Save each file.

**Task 3: Configure the CSS**. Launch a text editor and open the fishcreek.css file. Configure the following styles above the media queries.

  a. Configure a class named `shop` with a 1px solid #AEC3E3 border and white background.

  b. Add a style rule for the img elements within the shop class. Configure right float.

  c. Add a style rule for the form elements within the shop class. Set clear to right.

Save your fishcreek.css file.

**Task 4: Create the New Shop Page**. One way to be productive is to create pages based on your earlier work. Launch a text editor and open the home page (index.html). Save the file as shop.html. This will give you a head start and ensure that the pages on the website are similar. Perform the following modifications:

  a. Change the page title to an appropriate phrase.

  b. Change the text within the h2 element to "Shop at Fish Creek Animal Clinic".

  c. Delete the paragraph element and its content.

  d. Delete the contents of the first section element. Assign the section element to the class named `shop`. The section will contain an h3, an image, a description and a form that will process the Add to Cart button. Code an h3 element with the text "Fish Creek Tote Bag". Configure the fishtote.gif image below the h3. You will configure the description below the image. Type the following descriptive text in a paragraph: "Carry your pet supplies and accessories in a special tote from Fish Creek. 100% cotton. $14.95".

  e. Delete the contents of the second section element. Assign the section element to the class named `shop`. The section will contain an h3, an image, a description and a form that will process the Add to Cart button. Code an h3 element with the text "Fish Creek Sweatshirt". Configure the fishsweat.gif image below the h3. You will configure the description below the image. Type the following descriptive text in a paragraph: "A Fish Creek sweatshirt will warm you up on cool morning walks with your pet. 100% cotton. Size XL. $29.95".

  f. Delete the third section element and its contents.

  g. Delete the div assigned to the `address` class and its contents.

  h. Next, we will add a shopping cart button to each item for sale. This shopping cart button is placed in a form after the paragraph in each section. The action for the form is https://webdevbasics.net/cart.html, a placeholder shopping cart page.

To place the shopping cart button for the tote, add the following code below the paragraph with the tote's description and above the closing section tag:

```
<form method="post"
action="https://webdevbasics.net/cart.html">
  <input type="submit" value="Add to Cart">
</form>
```

The process for adding the shopping cart button for the sweatshirt is the same. The HTML is

```
<form method="post"
action="https://webdevbasics.net/cart.html">
    <input type="submit" value="Add to Cart">
</form>
```

Save your page and test it in a browser. It should look similar to the one shown in Figure 12.9. Click the Add to Cart button for the tote. The placeholder shopping cart will display and your screen should look similar to the one shown in Figure 12.7.

## Pacific Trails Resort

See Chapter 2 for an introduction to the Pacific Trails case study. You will use the Chapter 9 pacific9 folder as the starting point for this case study.

As often happens with websites, the client, Melanie Bowie, is pleased with the response to the site and has an idea about a new use for it—selling books that she's written about yoga and hiking at Pacific Trails Resort. She already has these for sale at the resort front desk and her customers seem to like them. This new Shop page (shop.html) will be part of the main navigation of the site. All pages should link to it. A revised site map is shown in Figure 12.10.

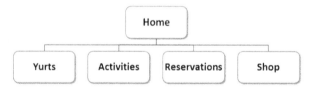

**Figure 12.10** Revised Pacific Trails site map

The Shop page should contain the description, image, and price of each book. It should link to a shopping cart system when the visitor wants to purchase an item. You may access a placeholder page provided by the textbook's website. If you have access to a different shopping cart system, check with your instructor and ask if you can use it instead.

You have four tasks in this case study:

1. Create a new folder for this Pacific Trails case study.
2. Modify the main navigation on each page to include a link to the new Shop page.
3. Modify the pacific.css external CSS file.
4. Create the new Shop page (shop.html) shown in Figure 12.11.

### Hands-On Practice Case Study

**Task 1: The Website Folder**. Create a folder called pacific12. Copy all of the files from your Chapter 9 pacific9 folder into the pacific12 folder. Copy the psunset.jpg, trailguide.jpg, and yurtyoga.jpg images from the Chapter12 folder in the student files and save them to your pacific12 folder.

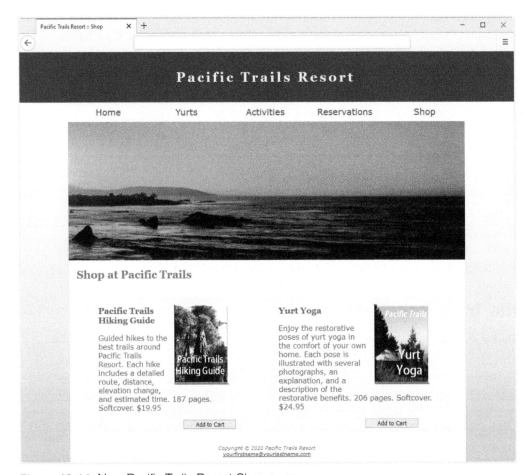

**Figure 12.11** New Pacific Trails Resort Shop page

**Task 2: Update the Navigation on Each Page.** Launch a text editor and open the home page (index.html). Add a new list item and hyperlink in the main navigation area that displays the text "Shop" and links to the file shop.html. See Figure 12.11 for an example of the navigation area. Save the file. Edit the Yurts (yurts.html), Activities (activities.html), and Reservations (reservations.html) pages in a similar manner. Save each file.

**Task 3: Configure the CSS.** Launch a text editor and open the pacific.css file. Configure the following styles above the media queries.

a. Configure a style rule for an id named `shophero` that displays psunset.jpg as a background image. Use the `#trailhero` style rule as a guide.

b. Configure a style rule for a class named `shop` with 1em margin and background color set to #F4F4F4.

c. Configure a style rule for img elements contained within a class named shop that sets right float and 1em padding.

d. Configure a style rule for form elements within a class named shop that clears right float.

Locate the first media query and add a style rule that configures the `shophero` id selector with background-size set to 100% 100%.

Save your pacific.css file.

**Task 4: Create the new Shop page**. One way to be productive is to create pages based on your earlier work. Launch a text editor and open the Activities page (activities.html). Save the file as shop.html. This will give you a head start and ensure that the pages on the website are similar. Perform the following modifications:

a. Change the page title to an appropriate phrase.

b. Change the text within the h2 element to "Shop at Pacific Trails".

c. Locate the div assigned to the `trailhero` id. Assign it to an id named `shophero`.

d. Delete the contents of the first section element. The section will contain an img, h3, paragraph, and shopping cart form. Assign the section element to a class named `shop`.

e. Write the HTML to display the trailguide.jpg image.

f. Configure an h3 element to display "Pacific Trails Hiking Guide".

g. Code a paragraph that will display the text description: "Guided hikes to the best trails around Pacific Trails Resort. Each hike includes a detailed route, distance, elevation change, and estimated time. 187 pages. Softcover. $19.95"

h. Each item for sale has an "Add to Cart" button, which is contained within a form with an action attribute set to https://webdevbasics.net/cart.html, a placeholder shopping cart page. To add the shopping cart button for the Hiking Guide book below the description paragraph, write the following code:

```
<form method="post"
  action="https://webdevbasics.net/cart.html">
  <input type="submit" value="Add to Cart">
</form>
```

i. Delete the contents of the second section element. The section will contain an img, h3, paragraph, and shopping cart form. Assign the section element to a class named `shop`.

j. Write the HTML to display the yurtyoga.jpg image.

k. Configure an h3 element to display "Yurt Yoga".

l. Code a paragraph that will display the text description: "Enjoy the restorative poses of yurt yoga in the comfort of your own home. Each pose is illustrated with several photographs, an explanation, and a description of the restorative benefits. 206 pages. Softcover. $24.95"

m. Configure the Add to Cart button by writing the following HTML for the form with the shopping cart button:

```
<form method="post"
  action="https://webdevbasics.net/cart.html">
  <input type="submit" value="Add to Cart">
</form>
```

n. Delete the third section element and its contents.

Save your page and test it in a browser. It should look similar to the one shown in Figure 12.11. Click the Add to Cart button for one of the books. The placeholder shopping cart will display and your screen should look similar to the one shown in Figure 12.7.

# Path of Light Yoga Studio

See Chapter 2 for an introduction to the Path of Light Yoga Studio case study. You will use the Chapter 9 yoga9 folder as the starting point for this case study.

The owner, Ariana Starrweaver is thrilled with the new website and would like to add an online store to sell her preferred yoga mats, blankets, and blocks. The new Store page (store.html) will be part of the main navigation of the site. All pages should link to it. A revised site map is shown in Figure 12.12.

**Figure 12.12** Revised Path of Light Yoga Studio site map

The Store page, shown in Figure 12.13, should display a photo and provide information about the two yoga sets available for purchase (with the description and price of each set). You may access a placeholder page provided by the textbook's website. If you have access to a different shopping cart system, check with your instructor and ask if you can use it instead.

You have four tasks in this case study:

1. Create a new folder for this Path of Light Yoga Studio case study.

2. Modify the main navigation on each page to include a link to the new Store page.

3. Modify the yoga.css external CSS file.

4. Create the new Store page (store.html) shown in Figure 12.13.

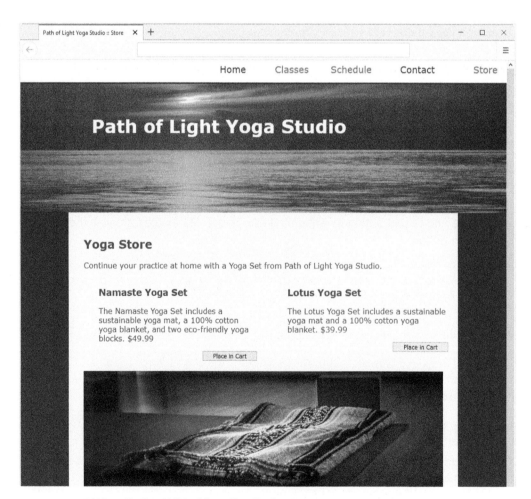

**Figure 12.13** New Path of Light Yoga Studio Store page

## Hands-On Practice Case Study

**Task 1: The Website Folder**. Create a folder called yoga12. Copy all of the files from your Chapter 9 yoga9 folder into the yoga12 folder. Copy the store.jpg image from the Chapter12 folder in the student files and save it to your yoga12 folder.

**Task 2: Update the Navigation on Each Page**. Launch a text editor and open the home page (index.html). Add a new list item and hyperlink in the main navigation area that displays the text "Store" and links to the file store.html. See Figure 12.13 for an example of the navigation area. Save the file. Edit the Classes (classes.html), Schedule (schedule.html), and Contact (contact.html) pages in a similar manner. Save each file.

**Task 3: Configure the CSS**. Launch a text editor and open the yoga.css file. Configure the following styles above the media queries.

a. Configure an id named `storehero` that displays store.jpg as a background image. Use the CSS for `#loungehero` as a guide.

b. Code a style rule that configures 1em bottom padding for form elements contained within section elements.

Locate the first media query and configure the `#storehero` id in the same way as the other hero images.

Save your yoga.css file.

**Task 4: Create the New Store Page**. One way to be productive is to create pages based on your earlier work. Launch a text editor and open the Classes page (classes.html). Save the file as store.html. This will give you a head start and ensure that the pages on the website are similar. Perform the following modifications:

a. Change the page title to an appropriate phrase.

b. Scroll down the page. Assign the div above the closing main tag to the id named `storehero`.

c. Locate the h2 at the top of the main element. Change the Yoga Classes heading to Yoga Store.

d. Place your cursor on the line after the Yoga Store heading. Create a paragraph with the following text:

"Continue your practice at home with a Yoga Set from Path of Light Yoga Studio."

e. Locate the first section element. The section element will contain an h3, a paragraph and a form. Configure the h3 element to display the text "Namaste Yoga Set".

f. Configure the paragraph with the following text: "The Namaste Yoga Set includes a sustainable yoga mat, a 100% cotton yoga blanket, and two eco-friendly yoga blocks. $49.99"

g. Next, we will add a shopping cart button. The action on the form is https://webdevbasics.net/cart.html, a placeholder shopping cart page.

To place the shopping cart button for the Namaste Yoga Set, add the following code below the paragraph:

```
<form method="post"
action="https://webdevbasics.net/cart.html">
    <input type="submit" value="Place in Cart">
</form>
```

h. Locate the second section element. The section element will contain an h3, a paragraph and a form. Configure the h3 element to display the text "Lotus Yoga Set".

i. Configure the paragraph with the following text: "The Lotus Yoga Set includes a sustainable yoga mat and a 100% cotton yoga blanket. $39.99"

j. Configure the shopping cart button for the Lotus Yoga Set. The HTML is

```
<form method="post"
action="http://webdevbasics.net/cart.html">
   <input type="submit" value="Place in Cart">
</form>
```

k. Delete the third section element and its contents.

Save your page and test it in a browser. It should look similar to the one shown in Figure 12.13. Click the Place in Cart button for the Lotus Yoga Set. The placeholder shopping cart will display and your screen should be similar to the one pictured in Figure 12.7.

## Web Project

See Chapter 5 for an introduction to the Web Project. Review the goals of your website and determine whether they include an e-commerce component. If so, you will add this component to your web project.

### Hands-On Practice Case Study

Revise the site map as needed to include the e-commerce component. Perhaps you will add a Products page to your website. Perhaps the Products page already exists and you are just adding functionality to the page. In either case, make sure that the site map and content sheets reflect the new processing.

There are a number of free or low-cost shopping cart providers on the Web. Some are provided in the following list. Your instructor may have additional resources or suggestions. Choose one of the providers from the list in order to add a shopping cart to your website. When you subscribe or sign up for these services, be sure to note any potential costs.

- Mal's e-commerce (free and low-cost service): https://www.mals-e.com

- PayPal (there is a cost per transaction for this service): https://www.paypal.com

- JustAddCommerce (free trial): http://www.richmediatech.com

Save and test your page. Experiment with the shopping cart. Welcome to the world of e-commerce!

# 13

# Web Promotion

**Chapter Objectives**    In this chapter, you will learn how to . . .

- Identify commonly used search engines and search indexes
- Describe the components of a search engine
- Design web pages that are friendly to search engines
- Submit a website for inclusion in a search engine
- Monitor a search engine listing
- Describe other website promotion activities
- Use the iframe element to create an inline frame

You've built it—now what can you do to attract visitors to your website? Once you have visitors, how do you encourage them to return? Getting listed on search engines, site affiliations, and banner ads are some of the topics that are discussed in this chapter.

# 13.1 Search Engine Overview

What do you do when you need to find a website? Using a **search engine** is a popular way to navigate the Web and find websites.

A search engine listing helps customers find your site and increases the chances that they will make a purchase. Search engine listings can be an excellent marketing tool for your business. To harness the power of search engines, it helps to know how they work.

# 13.2 Popular Search Engines

According to NetMarketShare (https://www.netmarketshare.com/search-engine-market-share.aspx?qprid=4&qpcustomd=0), Google was the most popular search engine during a recent month. Google was reported to have an overwhelming desktop market share of 76%, while the closest competitors were Baidu (9.64%), Bing (8.59%), and Yahoo! (3.16%). Google's popularity has continued to grow since it was founded in the late 1990s.

# 13.3 Components of a Search Engine

Search engines have the following components:

- Robot
- Database
- Search form

## Robot

A **robot** (sometimes called a spider or bot) is a program that automatically traverses the hypertext structure of the Web by retrieving a web page document and following the hyperlinks on the page. It moves like a robot spider on the Web, accessing and documenting web pages. The robot categorizes the pages and stores information about the website and the web pages in a database. Various robots may work differently, but, in general, they access and may store the following sections of web pages: title, meta tag descriptions, and some of the text on the page (usually either the first few sentences or the text contained in heading tags). Visit Web Robots Pages (https://www.robotstxt.org) if you'd like more details about web robots.

## Database

A **database** is a collection of information which is organized so that its contents can easily be accessed, managed, and updated. A database management system (DBMS), such as Oracle, SQL Server, MySQL, or IBM DB2, is used to configure and manage the database. The web page that displays the results of your search has information from the database accessed by the search engine site. According to Bruce Clay (https://www.bruceclay.com/searchenginerelationshipchart.htm), some search engines receive portions of their content from other search engines. For example, Yahoo! receives its primary search results from Google.

## Search Form

The **search form** is the component of a search engine that you are most familiar with. You have probably used a search engine many times but haven't thought about what goes on "under the hood." The search form is the graphical user interface that allows a user to type in a word or phrase to search for. It is usually simply a text box and a submit button. The visitor to the search engine types in words (called keywords) related to his or her search into the text box. When the form is submitted, the data typed into the text box is sent to a server-side script that searches the database using the keywords entered. The **search results** (also called a result set) are a list of information, such as the URLs for web pages, that meets your criteria. This result set is formatted with a link to each page, along with additional information which might include the page title, a brief description, the first few lines of text, or the size of the page. The type of additional information varies by search engine. Next, the web server at the search engine site sends the **search engine results page (SERP)** to your browser for display.

The order in which the pages are displayed may depend on paid advertisements, alphabetical order, and link popularity (more on this later). Each search engine has its own policy for ordering the search results. Be aware that these policies can change over time.

The components of a search engine (robot, database, and search form) work together to obtain information about web pages, store information about web pages, and provide a graphical user interface to facilitate searching for and displaying a list of web pages that are relevant to the given keywords. Now that you are aware of the components of search engines, let's get to the most important part: how to design your pages to promote your website.

# 13.4 Search Engine Optimization

If you have followed recommended web design practices, you've already designed your website so that the pages are appealing and compelling to your target audience. How can you also make your site work with search engines? This section provides some suggestions and hints on designing your pages for search engines—a process called **search engine optimization (SEO)**.

## Keywords

Spend some time brainstorming about terms and phrases that people may use when searching for your site. Make a list of them. These terms or phrases that describe your website or business are your **keywords**.

## Page Titles

A descriptive page title (the text between the `<title>` tags), which includes your company and/or website name, will help your site market itself. It's common for search engines to display the text in the page title in the SERP. The page title is also saved by default when a visitor bookmarks your site and is often included when a visitor prints a page of your site. Avoid using the exact same title for every page; include keywords in the page title that are appropriate for the page. For example, instead of just "Trillium Media Design," configure the page title to include both the company name and the purpose of the page: "Trillium Media Design: Custom E-Commerce Solutions."

## Heading Tags

Use structural tags, such as `<h1>`, `<h2>`, and so on, to organize your page content. If it is appropriate for the web page content, also include some keywords in the text contained within the heading tags. Some search engines will give a higher list position if keywords are included in a page title or heading. Also include keywords, as appropriate, within the page text content. However, avoid spamming keywords—that is, do not list them over and over again. The programs behind search engines are becoming more sophisticated all the time and you can actually be prevented from being listed if it is perceived that you are not being honest or are trying to cheat the system.

## Description

What is special about your website that would make someone want to visit? With this in mind, write a few sentences about your website or business. This description should be inviting and interesting so that a person searching the Web will choose your site from the list provided by a search engine. Some search engines will display your description in their search engine results. You might be wondering how these are applied to the actual web pages. The description is placed on a web page by adding an HTML meta tag to the head section.

## Description Meta Tag

A meta tag is a self-contained tag that is placed in the head section of a web page. You've been using a meta tag to indicate character encoding. There are a number of other uses for meta tags. We'll focus here on providing a description of a website for use by search engines. The **description meta tag** content is displayed on the SERP by some search engines, such as Google. The `name` attribute indicates the use of the meta tag. The `content` attribute indicates the values needed for that specific use. The `description` value for the `name` attribute indicates that the use of the meta tag is to provide a description. For example, a description meta tag for a website about a web development consulting firm called Acme Design could be configured as follows:

```
<meta name="description" content="Acme Design, a premier web consulting
group that specializes in e-commerce, web design, web development, and
website redesign.">
```

 **FAQ   What if I do not want a search engine to index a page?**

Sometimes there will be pages that you do not want indexed, perhaps test pages or pages only meant for a small group of individuals (such as family or coworkers). Meta tags can be used for this purpose also. To indicate to a search engine robot that a page should not be indexed and the links should not be followed, do not code a description meta tag in the page. Instead, add a **robots meta tag** to the page as follows:

```
<meta name="robots" content="noindex, nofollow">
```

## Linking

Verify that all hyperlinks are working. Each page on your website should be reachable by a text hyperlink. The text should be descriptive (avoid phrases like "More info" and "Click here") and should include keywords as appropriate. Inbound links (sometimes called incoming links) are also a factor in SEO; see the link popularity section later in this chapter.

## Images and Multimedia

Be mindful that search engine robots do not "see" the text embedded within your images and multimedia. Configure meaningful alternate text for images. Include relevant keywords in the alternate text.

## Valid Code

Search engines do not require that your HTML and CSS code pass validation tests. However, code that is valid and well structured is likely to be more easily processed by search engine robots. This may help with your placement in the search engine results.

## Content of Value

Probably the most basic, but often overlooked, component of SEO is providing content of value contained within a website that follows web design best practices (see Chapter 5). Your website should contain high-quality, well-organized content that is of value to your visitors.

## HTTPS Protocol

As part of Google's support for security on the Web, the search engine has begun to consider the HTTPS protocol (see Chapter 12) in its page rank algorithms. You may consider adopting HTTPS for your website.

# 13.5  Submitting your Website to a Search Engine

Although search engines bring visitors to your website, it is not always easy to get listed in a search engine. Before you even *think* about submitting your website to a search engine, be sure that it is complete and that you have followed basic SEO techniques (as described in the previous section). Once you're confident that your website is ready, it is time to submit your site for consideration by a search engine.

Back in the day, all you needed to do to submit your website to Google or Bing was to anonymously fill out a form on their website. Now, the process is more complex.

To work with Google, visit https://search.google.com/search-console. Sign in with your Google account and look for the "add property" option. You'll provide the URL of your website and follow instructions provided by Google to verify that you are the actual site owner. Once verified, visit https://www.google.com/webmasters/tools/submit-url and follow the instructions to either submit a Sitemap or use the Fetch as Google tool.

To work with Bing, visit https://www.bing.com/toolbox/webmaster. Sign in with an account of your choice (Microsoft, Google, or Facebook). You'll provide the URL of your website and follow instructions provided by Bing to verify that you are the actual site owner. Once verified, you will be able to submit URLs to Bing (in the Dashboard, select "Configure My Site" and "Submit URLs") by filling out a form. You can also submit a Sitemap to Bing using the Dashboard.

After you submit your URL, it's time to wait for the search engine's spider or bot to visit your website. This may take several weeks. Try to be patient.

Several weeks after you submit your website, check the search engine to see if your site is listed. If it is not listed, review your pages and check whether they are optimized for search engines (see the previous section) and display in common browsers.

If the website is for a business, you may want to consider paying for preferential placement in search engine displays (called sponsoring or advertising), and paying each time a visitor clicks the search engine's link to your site. Many businesses regard payment for these types of services as another marketing expense, such as paying for a newspaper ad.

 **FAQ**   **Is advertising on a search engine worth the cost?**

It depends. How much is it worth to your client to appear on the first page of the search engine results? You select the keywords that will trigger the display of your ad. You also set your monthly budget and the maximum amount to pay for each click. While costs and charges vary by search engine, at this time, Google charges are based on cost per click—you'll be charged each time a visitor to Google clicks on your advertisement. Visit https://ads.google.com/home/ for more information about their program.

If you explore the paid advertising programs that search engines offer, you'll encounter a number of acronyms related to marketing. The most common are listed below:

- **CPC: Cost per click**

  CPC (also referred to as PPC, pay per click) is the price you are charged if you have signed up for a paid sponsor or ad program and a visitor clicks on a link to your website.

- **CPM: Cost per thousand impressions**

  CPM is your cost for every 1,000 times that your ad is displayed on a web page (whether or not the visitor clicks on your ad).

- **CTR: Click-through rate**

  CTR is the ratio of the number of times an ad is clicked on to the number of times an ad is viewed. For example, if your ad was shown 100 times and 20 people clicked on it, your CTR would be 20/100, or 20%.

## Map Your Site

Google's Webmaster Guidelines describe two types of site maps that are useful for SEO:

- An HTML site map is a web page with a map of the site that contains a hierarchical list of hyperlinks to the major pages in your website. For an example, view the site map web page at https://webdevbasics.net/sitemap.html. The information on the site map page is not only helpful for your website visitors, but also may assist search engine robots as they follow hyperlinks on your site.

- An XML **Sitemap** is an XML file that is used by search engines, but it is not accessed by your web page visitors. A Sitemap provides information to a search engine, such as Google, about your website and is essentially a list of pages, along with the following information: date that each page was last modified, an indicator of how frequently each page changes, and a priority level for each page. See https://www.sitemaps.org/protocol.html for more information about manually coding a Sitemap. An excerpt from a Sitemap file (sitemap.xml) is shown below:

```
<url>
  <loc>http://webdevfoundations.net/</loc>
  <lastmod>2018-07-03T08:10:09+00:00</lastmod>
  <changefreq>monthly</changefreq>
  <priority>1.00</priority>
</url>
<url>
  <loc>http://webdevfoundations.net/index.html</loc>
  <lastmod>2018-07-03T08:10:09+00:00</lastmod>
  <changefreq>monthly</changefreq>
  <priority>1.00</priority>
</url>
<url>
  <loc>http://webdevfoundations.net/8e/chapter1.html</loc>
  <lastmod>2018-08-22T15:09:07+00:00</lastmod>
  <changefreq>monthly</changefreq>
  <priority>0.800</priority>
</url>
```

Online Sitemap generators, such as https://www.xml-sitemaps.com will automatically create a Sitemap file, named sitemap.xml, for you. You will need to upload the Sitemap to your website and notify Google and/or Bing of its URL. Visit https://support.google.com/webmasters/answer/183668?hl=en for more information about Sitemaps.

 **Checkpoint 13.1**

**1.** Describe the three components of a search engine.

**2.** What is the purpose of the description meta tag?

**3.** Is it beneficial for a business to pay for preferential listing? Why or why not?

# 13.6  Monitoring Search Listings

Although you may want your website to appear instantaneously in search engines, some time may be required before your site appears in the SERPs. Also, be mindful that there is no guarantee when you submit your site that it will be listed; however, it is rare that a quality website with content of value is not indexed and included in search engine listings.

As your sites get listed, it becomes important to determine which keywords are working. Usually, you need to fine-tune and modify your keywords over time. Here are a few methods for determining which keywords are working:

- **Manual Checking**. Visit search engines and type in the keywords. Assess the results. You might consider keeping a record of the search engine, keyword(s), and page ranking.

- **Web Analytics**. Every visitor to your website, including those who were referred by search engines, is recorded in your website log files. A **website log** consists of one or more text files that record each visit to your site, capturing information about your visitors and about referring websites. You can discover whether your keywords are successful and which search engines are being used by analyzing your log. You can also determine the days and times that your site is visited, the operating systems and browsers being used, the paths that visitors take through the site, and much more. The log is a rather cryptic text file. See Figure 13.1 for a partial log.

Web analytics software can analyze your log file and create easy-to-use charts and reports to provide you with information to help you improve and optimize your website for your target visitor. If you have your own website and domain name, many web host providers allow free access to the log and may even run web analysis reports as part

```
#Software: Microsoft Internet Information Services 7.0
#Version: 1.0
#Date: 2018-07-13 09:50:57
#Fields: date time s-sitename s-computername s-ip cs-method cs-uri-stem
cs-uri-query s-port cs-username c-ip cs-version cs(User-Agent) cs
(Referer) cs-host sc-status sc-substatus sc-win32-status sc-bytes cs-
bytes time-taken
2018-07-13 09:50:57 W3SVC724 ORF-PREMIUM11B 65.182.100.116 GET
/chapter5/index.htm - 80 - 74.6.73.82 HTTP/1.0 Mozilla/5.0+(compatible;
+Yahoo!+Slurp;+http://help.yahoo.com/help/us/ysearch/slurp) -
webdevfoundations.net 304 0 0 232 256 78
#Software: Microsoft Internet Information Services 7.0
#Version: 1.0
#Date: 2018-07-13 10:16:55
#Fields: date time s-sitename s-computername s-ip cs-method cs-uri-stem
cs-uri-query s-port cs-username c-ip cs-version cs(User-Agent) cs
(Referer) cs-host sc-status sc-substatus sc-win32-status sc-bytes cs-
bytes time-taken
2018-07-13 10:16:55 W3SVC724 ORF-PREMIUM11B 65.182.100.116 GET
/fireworks8/page3.10.gif - 80 - 65.55.212.239 HTTP/1.0 msnbot-media/1.0
+(+http://search.msn.com/msnbot.htm) - webdevfoundations.net 200 0 0
28665 283 406
```

Figure 13.1 A website log file contains useful information, but can be difficult to read.

of the monthly hosting fee. By checking information in the log, you can determine not only what keywords are working, but also which search engines your visitors are using. See Figure 13.2 for information from a log analysis report listing the top 10 keywords used by actual web visitors when searching Google to find a particular website.

| Keyword | Visits | Pages Per Visit | Average Time on Site |
|---|---|---|---|
| web design best practices | 27,097 | 1.75 | 00:01:17 |
| web design best practice | 21,773 | 6.08 | 00:07:32 |
| web development and design foundations | 15,751 | 5.71 | 00:04:56 |
| basics of web design: HTML5 & CSS3 | 14,346 | 5.96 | 00:05:43 |
| html5 basics | 6,859 | 5.32 | 00:04:05 |
| basic html5 template | 4,943 | 5.98 | 00:06:24 |
| basic html5 page | 4,023 | 8.20 | 00:05:23 |
| html5 basic code | 3,198 | 4.17 | 00:05:02 |
| basic html5 tags | 3,141 | 5.06 | 00:04:46 |
| html5 basics pdf | 3,120 | 4.94 | 00:04:27 |

Figure 13.2 Partial log file analysis report

Website log analysis is a powerful marketing tool because you can determine exactly how visitors are finding your site. This lets you know which keywords are working and which are not. Perhaps the developers of this website might consider adding additional content related to the popular keywords.

Google offers a free web analytics service at https://marketingplatform.google.com/about/analytics/. The type of information provided includes:

- Audience (including a geographical map and browser information)
- Traffic Sources (such as referring sites, keywords, and AdWords)
- Content (including landing pages, paths through the site, and exit pages)
- Conversions (tracks business objectives)

# 13.7 Link Popularity

**Link popularity** is a rating determined by a search engine based on the number of sites that link to a particular website and the quality of those sites. For example, a link from a well-known site such as Oprah Winfrey's website (http://www.oprah.com) would be considered a higher quality link than one from your friend's home page on a free web server. The link popularity of your website can determine its order in the search engine results page. One way to check which sites link to yours is to analyze your log file. Another method is to visit particular search engines and check for yourself. At Google, type "link:yourdomainname. com" into the search box and the sites that link to yourdomainname.com will be listed. Search engines are not the only tools you can use to bring visitors to your website. The next section looks at some other options.

# 13.8 Social Media Optimization

Reach out to your current and potential website visitors with **social media optimization (SMO)** by creating content of value that is easily sharable. The benefits of SMO include increased awareness of your brand and/or site, along with an increase in the number of inbound links (which can help with SEO). Social bookmarking sites such as Digg (https://digg.com), Reddit (https://reddit.com), and Pinterest (https://pinterest.com) provide a way for people to store, share, and categorize website content. Make it easy for your visitors to add your site to social bookmarking sites and social networking sites like Twitter and Facebook. You can code hyperlinks to these yourself or use a content-sharing service such as AddThis (https://www.addthis.com).

Visit the following resources for more information about SMO:

- The Beginners Guide to Social Media:
  https://moz.com/beginners-guide-to-social-media

- The 5 NEW Rules of Social Media Optimization (SMO):
  http://www.rohitbhargava.com/2010/08/the-5-new-rules-of-social-media-optimization-smo.html

- Free Tools for Social Media Optimization:
  http://www.socialmediaexaminer.com/social-media-seo/

## Blogs

Chapter 1 introduced blogs, which are easily updatable and readily available journals on the Web. The power of the blog to share information and elicit comments is being used by businesses of various types (ranging from Nike to Adobe) to build and expand customer relationships. Popular blog hosting sites include Google's Blogger (http://blogger.com) and WordPress (http://wordpress.com). To see a blog in action, visit this textbook's blog at http://webdevfoundations.blogspot.com.

## Social Networking

Join groups on social networking sites such as Facebook (https://www.facebook.com) or LinkedIn (https://www.linkedin.com) to find and connect with current and potential visitors. Create portable content that promotes your website and publish it on

YouTube (https://www.youtube.com), SlideShare (https://www.slideshare.net), Instagram (https://www.instagram.com), and other similar sites. Think of your own use of social media—you are probably more likely to follow a post that includes a photo or a video. Hubspot.com (http://bit.ly/wdadf1) kept track of their video posts and found that the following lengths generated the most visitor engagement: two minute videos on YouTube, one minute videos on Facebook, and 30 second videos on Instagram. Animito (https://animoto.com) and Adobe Spark (https://spark.adobe.com) are easy to use to quickly generate promotional videos.

Be active on microblogging sites such as Twitter (https://twitter.com). Twitter is not limited to personal use. The business world has also discovered the marketing reach that Twitter can provide. Visit https://business.twitter.com/basics for insights on how to use Twitter to promote your business and communicate with customers. Let viral marketing go to work for you as current and potential visitors find and share your content, which should increase awareness and bring new and returning visitors to your site.

# 13.9  Other Site Promotion Activities

There are a number of other ways you can promote your website, including **Quick Response (QR) codes**, affiliate programs, banner ads, banner exchanges, reciprocal link agreements, newsletters, personal recommendations, traditional media advertising, and placement of the URL on all promotional materials.

## Quick Response (QR) Codes

A QR code is a two-dimensional barcode in a square pattern that is readable by a smartphone camera scan application or a QR barcode reader. The data encoded can be text, a telephone number, or even the URL of a website. There are many free online QR code generators, including https://qrcode.kaywa.com and https://www.qrstuff.com. Free apps, such as ScanLife and QR Code Scanner, are available for smartphones that use the camera feature to scan the QR code, typically a URL for a website, which is then displayed by the smartphone's web browser. QR codes are useful for promoting a website; include it on your business card or even a T-shirt! The QR code in Figure 13.3 displays the home page of the textbook's website (http://webdevfoundations.net).

Figure 13.3 QR code for http:// webdevfoundations .net

## Affiliate Programs

The essence of **affiliate programs** is that one website (the affiliate) promotes another website's products or services (the merchant) in exchange for a commission. Both websites benefit from this association. Amazon.com reportedly began the first affiliate marketing program and its Amazon.com Associates program is still going strong. By joining this program, your website can feature books and other products with a link to the Amazon website. If one of your visitors makes a purchase, you get a commission. Amazon benefits because you have delivered an interested visitor who may buy items now or in the future. Your site benefits from the prestige of being affiliated with a known site such as Amazon and the potential for income from the program.

View the CJ Affiliate website (https://www.cj.com) to see a program that matches websites with potential affiliate programs. Their service allows publishers (website owners and developers) to choose from a wide range of advertisers and affiliate programs. The benefits to web developers include the opportunity to partner with leading advertisers, earn additional revenue from website visitors or ad space, and view real-time tracking and reporting. Visit AssociatePrograms.com (https://www.associateprograms.com) for a directory of affiliate, associate, and referral programs.

## Banner Ads

A **banner ad** is typically a graphic image that is used to announce and advertise the name or identity of a site. Banner ads are image hyperlinks that display the advertised site when clicked. You probably see them many times as you surf the Web. They've been around for quite some time; *HotWired*, the first commercial web magazine, introduced the first banner ad in 1994 to promote AT&T.

There is no official size for a banner ad. However, the Interactive Advertising Bureau (IAB) provides guidelines for standard ad dimensions. Dimensions have traditionally been pixel-based, such as a leaderboard (728 × 90 pixels) and a wide skyscraper (160 × 600 pixels). The IAB is overhauling the standards and planning to move to aspect-ratio sizes that work well on multiple devices (https://www.iab.com/newadportfolio). The cost to display your banner ad can vary. Some websites charge by the impression (usually in terms of cost per thousand impressions, or CPM). Others charge for click-throughs only (when the banner ad is clicked). Most search engines sell ads and will display your ad on a results page for a keyword that relates to your site.

## Banner Exchange

While the details of **banner exchange** programs vary, the idea is that you agree to show banners from other sites and they will show your banner. Information on banner exchanges may be found at The Banner Exchange (http://www.thebannerexchange.com). Banner exchanges can be beneficial to all parties because of the free advertising.

## Reciprocal Link Agreements

A **reciprocal link agreement** is usually between two sites with related or complementary content. You agree to link to each other. The result should be more visitors for each site. If you find a site that you'd like to set up a reciprocal link agreement with, contact its webmaster (usually by e-mail) and ask! Because some search engines partially determine rankings based on the number of quality links to a website, a well-placed reciprocal link can help both sites.

## Newsletters

A **newsletter** can bring return visitors to your site. The first step is to collect e-mail addresses. Allow website visitors to opt-in to receive your newsletter by filling out a form that typically collects the visitor's name and e-mail address.

Offer your visitors some perceived value—timely information on a topic, discounts, and so on. Send out the newsletter with fresh, compelling content regularly. This helps to remind your previous visitors about your site. They may even forward the newsletter to a colleague and bring a new visitor to your site.

## Sticky Site Features

Updating your website often and keeping your content fresh will encourage visitors to return to your site. How can you keep them there? Make your website sticky. **Stickiness** is the ability to keep visitors at your site. Display your interesting and compelling content along with features that encourage stickiness, such as news updates, polls and surveys, and chats or message boards.

## Personal Recommendations

While forwarding a newsletter is a form of **personal recommendation**, some sites make it even easier to tell a friend about them. They offer a link that is used with a phrase such as "E-mail this article", "Send this page to a friend", or "Tell a colleague about this site". This personal recommendation brings a new visitor who is likely to be interested in the content of your site.

## Website Forum Postings

Subscribe to forums related to your website content. Do not reply to postings with an advertisement of your site. Instead, reply to postings when your response can offer assistance or advice. Include a signature line with your website URL. Be subtle! You can get banned from some forums if the moderator perceives that you are merely advertising. However, by offering friendly, helpful advice in a forum you can market your website in a subtle, positive manner at no cost other than your Internet connection.

## Traditional Media Ads and Existing Marketing Materials

Don't forget to mention your website in any print, TV, or radio ads that your organization runs. Include the URL of your website on all brochures, stationery, and business cards. This will help make your website easy to find by your current and potential customers. Depending upon your target audience, also consider including a QR code for your website on printed materials.

 **Checkpoint 13.2**

**1.** Are the results returned by various search engines really different? Choose a place, music group, or movie to search for. Enter the same search terms, such as "Door County" into the following three search engines: Google, Yahoo!, and Bing. List the URLs of the top three sites returned by each. Comment on your findings.

**2.** How can you determine whether your website has been indexed by a search engine? How can you determine which search engines are being used to find your site?

**3.** List four website promotion methods that do not use search engines. Which would be your first choice? Why?

# 13.10  Serving Dynamic Content with Inline Frames

How does a website display a banner ad on its home page that is hosted and controlled by another organization? How can a web page easily display a variety of multimedia clips? How are the potential customer referrals provided by the Amazon.com Associates program initiated and tracked? How does Google facilitate Ad Sense advertisement displays and click-throughs on third-party websites? At the time this was written, the answer to all of these questions is inline frames. Inline frames are widely used on the Web for a variety of marketing and promotional purposes, including displaying banner ads, playing multimedia that may be hosted on a separate web server, and serving content for associate and partner sites to display. The advantage is separation of control. The dynamic content—such as the banner ad or multimedia clip—can be changed by a project team without allowing them access to change the rest of the website. For example, in the case of the banner ad, a third-party organization (such as DoubleClick) has control over the ad content, but is prevented from updating the other items on the page. This is accomplished by configuring the dynamic content (in the form of banner ads) within an inline frame. Let's explore how inline frames are configured.

## Iframe Element

An **inline frame**, also called a floating frame, can be placed on the body of any web page, similar to the way you would place an image on a web page. The **iframe element** configures an inline frame that displays the contents of another web page within your web page document, which is referred to as *nested browsing*. The iframe element begins with the **<iframe>** tag and ends with the </iframe> tag. Fallback content that should be displayed if the browser does not support inline frames (such as a text description or hyperlink to the actual web page) should be placed between the tags. Figure 13.4 shows the use of an inline frame (chapter13/dcwildflowers/index.html in the student files). The white background area is the inline frame; it displays another web page that contains the image of the flower and a text description.

**Figure 13.4** The white scrolling area on the page is an inline frame that displays a separate web page

The code for the inline frame that creates this effect is

```
<iframe src="trillium.html" title="Trillium Wild Flower"
  height="160" width="350" name="flower">
  Description of the lovely Spring wild flower, the
  <a href="trillium.html" target="_blank">Trillium</a>
</iframe>
```

The screenshots shown in Figure 13.5 are of the same web page with different pages displayed in the inline frame area.

Figure 13.5 The same page with different content in the inline frame area

Table 13.1 lists iframe element attributes. Commonly used attributes are shown in bold.

Table 13.1 Commonly used iframe element attributes

| Attribute | Description |
| --- | --- |
| **src** | URL of the web page to be displayed in the inline frame |
| **height** | Inline frame height in pixels |
| **width** | Inline frame width in pixels |
| id | Optional; text name, alphanumeric, beginning with a letter, no spaces; the value must be unique and not used for other id values on the same web page document |
| name | Optional; text name, alphanumeric, beginning with a letter, no spaces; this attribute names the inline frame |
| sandbox | Optional; disallow/disable features such as plug-ins, scripts, forms |
| title | Optional; specifies a brief text description that may be displayed by browsers or assistive technologies |

## Video in an Inline Frame

YouTube (https://www.youtube.com) is a popular website for sharing videos for both personal and business use. When a video is uploaded to YouTube, the creator can choose to share their video with others. It's easy to display a YouTube video on your web page; just select Share and then copy and paste the HTML into your web page source code. The code uses an iframe element to display a web page file within your web page. YouTube detects the browser and operating system of your web page visitor and serves the content in an appropriate video format.

## Hands-On Practice 13.1

VideoNote
*Configure an Inline frame*

In this Hands-On Practice, you will launch a text editor and create a web page that displays a YouTube video within an iframe element.

This example embeds the video found at https://youtu.be/2CuOug8KDWI. You can choose to display this video or select a different video. The process is to visit the YouTube page for the video, select Share, and copy the URL provided. Take note of the video identifier, which is after the / symbol. In this example, the video identifier is 2CuOug8KDWI.

Use the chapter13/template.html file as a starting point and configure a web page with the heading "Inline Frame" and an iframe element that displays the video. Code the src attribute to display http://www.youtube.com/embed/ followed by the video identifier. In this example, set the src attribute to the value http://www.youtube.com/embed/2CuOug8KDWI. Configure a hyperlink to the YouTube video page as fallback content. The code to display the video is

```
<iframe src="http://www.youtube.com/embed/2CuOug8KDWI" width="640"
height="395">
  View the <a
href="https://youtu.be/2CuOug8KDWI">YouTube Video</a>
</iframe>
```

Save your page as iframe.html and display it in a browser. Test your page in several browsers. Compare your work to chapter13/13.1/iframe.html in the student files.

# Chapter Summary

This chapter introduced concepts related to promoting your website. The activities involved in submitting websites to search engines were discussed, along with techniques for optimizing your website for search engines. Other website promotion activities, such as social media optimization, QR codes, banner ads, and newsletters, were also introduced. At this point, you should have an idea of what is involved in the other side of website development—marketing and promotion. You can help the marketing staff by creating websites that work with search engines by following the suggestions in this chapter. For examples, chapter links, and updated information visit the textbook website at https://webdevfoundations.net.

## Key Terms

`<iframe>`
affiliate programs
banner ad
banner exchange
click-through rate (CTR)
cost per click (CPC)
cost per thousand impressions (CPM)
database
description meta tag
iframe element

inline frame
keywords
link popularity
meta tag
newsletter
personal recommendation
Quick Response (QR) codes
reciprocal link agreement
robot
robots meta tag
search engine

search engine optimization (SEO)
search engine results page (SERP)
search form
search results
Sitemap
social media optimization (SMO)
stickiness
web analytics
website log

## Review Questions

### Multiple Choice

1. Which of the following contains information about which keywords are bringing visitors to your website?
   a. web position log
   b. website log
   c. search engine file
   d. none of the above

2. In which section of a web page should meta tags be placed?
   a. head
   b. body
   c. comment
   d. CSS

3. What is a first step for search engine optimization?
   a. Join an affiliate program.
   b. Start a blog.
   c. Add a description meta tag to each page.
   d. Create a QR code.

4. In which of the following does one website promote another site's products or services in exchange for a commission?
   a. newsletter
   b. affiliate program
   c. search engine optimization
   d. stickiness

5. Which of the following is a collection of information which is organized so that its contents can easily be accessed, managed, and updated?
   a. SERP
   b. database
   c. robot
   d. QR Code

**6.** Which of the following is a rating determined by a search engine based on the number of links to a particular site and the qualities of those links?

a. line checking

b. reciprocal linking

c. link popularity

d. social media optimization

**7.** Which of the following is the most popular search engine?

a. Iframe

b. Yahoo!

c. Google

d. Bing

**8.** Which of the following is a promotion method whose main purpose is to bring return visitors to your website?

a. newsletter

b. banner exchange

c. TV ad

d. none of the above

**9.** Which of the following is a term for creating content that is easily sharable?

a. search engine optimization

b. social media optimization

c. link popularity

d. search engine optimization

**10.** Typically, how long can it take between the time you submit your website and the time it is listed in a search engine?

a. several hours

b. several weeks

c. several months

d. a year

## Fill in the Blank

**11.** The ability to keep web page visitors at your site is called _____.

**12.** Use _____ to indicate that you do not want a web page to be indexed.

**13.** Frequently used information research resources are _____.

**14.** In addition to a search engine listing, a website can be promoted by _____.

**15.** Two-dimensional barcodes that can be scanned by smartphones to access a website are called _____ codes.

## Hands-On Exercises

**1.** Practice writing description meta tags. For each scenario described here, write the HTML to create an appropriate meta tag that includes keywords which may be used by visitors to search for the business.

a. Lanwell Publishing is a small independent publisher of English as a second language (ESL) books used for secondary school and adult continuing education learners. The website offers textbooks and teacher's manuals.

b. RevGear is a small specialty truck and auto repair shop in Schaumburg, Illinois. The company sponsors a local drag racing team.

c. Morris Accounting is a small accounting firm that specializes in tax return preparation and accounting for small businesses. The owner, Greg Morris, is a CPA and Certified Financial Planner.

**2.** Choose one of the company scenarios listed in Hands-On Exercise 1 (Lanwell Publishing, RevGear, or Morris Accounting). Create a home page for the site that includes a description meta tag, appropriate page titles, and keywords used appropriately in headings. Place an e-mail link to yourself on the web page. Save the page as scenario.html.

3. Choose one of the company scenarios listed in Hands-On Exercise 1. Create a web page that lists at least three possible activities that could be used to promote the site in addition to search engine submission. For each activity, explain why it could be helpful for the website. Place an e-mail link to yourself on the web page. Save the page as promotion.html.

4. Write the HTML and CSS to create a page named inline.html that is configured to display the heading "Web Promotion Techniques", an inline frame that is 400 pixels wide and 200 pixels high, and an e-mail link with your name. Code a web page named marketing.html that lists your three favorite web promotion techniques. Configure the inline frame to display the marketing.html file.

## Web Research

1. This chapter discussed a number of website promotion techniques. Choose one technique described in the chapter to research. Obtain information from at least three different websites about the promotion technique you chose. Create a web page that lists at least five hints or facts about the promotion method, along with helpful links that provide additional information on the hint or fact. Provide the URLs of the websites that you used as resources. Place your name in an e-mail link on the web page.

2. Using a single page website for a small business or an event is trendy but offers challenges for search engine optimization. Visit the following resources as a starting point as you search for three recommendations for single page website SEO:

   - https://www.awwwards.com/seo-tricks-for-one-page-websites.html
   - https://yoast.com/one-page-website-seo/
   - https://www.99signals.com/single-page-websites-seo/
   - https://www.popwebdesign.net/popart_blog/en/2018/05/
     how-to-optimize-a-one-page-website/

Create a web page that describes your findings. Provide URLs of the websites you used as resources. Place your name in an e-mail link on the web page.

## Focus on Web Design

Explore how to design your website so that it is optimized for search engines (search engine optimization, or SEO). Visit the following sites as a starting point as you search for three SEO tips or hints:

   - Old Skool Search Engine Success, Step-by-Step:
     https://www.sitepoint.com/article/skool-search-engine-success
   - The 10 Most Important SEO Tips You Need to Know:
     https://neilpatel.com/blog/10-most-important-seo-tips-you-need-to-know/
   - The Definitive Guide to SEO in 2019:
     https://backlinko.com/seo-this-year

Write a one-page report that describes three tips which you found interesting or potentially useful. Cite the URLs of the resources that you used.

# WEBSITE CASE STUDY
# Meta Tags to Promote Websites

Each of the following case studies continues throughout most of the text. This chapter case study focuses on description meta tags.

## JavaJam Coffee Bar

See Chapter 2 for an introduction to the JavaJam Coffee Bar case study. Use the Chapter 9 JavaJam website as a starting point for this case study. You have three tasks in this case study:

1. Create a new folder for this JavaJam case study.
2. Write a description of the JavaJam Coffee Bar business.
3. Code a description meta tag on each page in the website.

### Hands-On Practice Case Study

**Task 1: The Website Folder**. Create a folder called javajam13. Copy all of the files from your Chapter 9 javajam9 folder into the javajam13 folder.

**Task 2: Write a Description**. Review the JavaJam pages that you created in earlier chapters. Write a brief paragraph that describes the JavaJam site. Edit the paragraph down to a description that is only a few sentences and less than 25 words in length.

**Task 3: Update Each Page**. Open each page in a text editor and add a description meta tag to the head section. Save the files and test them in a browser. They will not look different, but they are much friendlier to search engines!

## Fish Creek Animal Clinic

See Chapter 2 for an introduction to the Fish Creek Animal Clinic case study.
Use the Chapter 9 Fish Creek website as a starting point for this case study. You have three tasks in this case study:

1. Create a new folder for this Fish Creek case study.
2. Write a description of the Fish Creek Animal Clinic business.
3. Code a description meta tag on each page in the website.

### Hands-On Practice Case Study

**Task 1: The Website Folder**. Create a folder called fishcreek13. Copy all of the files from your Chapter 9 fishcreek9 folder into the fishcreek13 folder.

**Task 2: Write a Description**. Review the Fish Creek pages that you created in earlier chapters. Write a brief paragraph that describes the Fish Creek site. Edit the paragraph down to a description that is only a few sentences and less than 25 words in length.

**Task 3: Update Each Page**. Open each page in a text editor and add a description meta tag to the head section. Save the files and test them in a browser. They will not look different, but they are much friendlier to search engines!

## Pacific Trails Resort

See Chapter 2 for an introduction to the Pacific Trails Resort case study. Use the Chapter 9 Pacific Trails website as a starting point for this case study. You have three tasks in this case study:

1. Create a new folder for this Pacific Trails case study.

2. Write a description of the Pacific Trails Resort business.

3. Code a description meta tag on each page in the website.

### Hands-On Practice Case Study

**Task 1: The Website Folder**. Create a folder called pacific13. Copy all of the files from your Chapter 9 pacific9 folder into the pacific13 folder.

**Task 2: Write a Description**. Review the Pacific Trails pages that you created in earlier chapters. Write a brief paragraph that describes the Pacific Trails site. Edit the paragraph down to a description that is only a few sentences and less than 25 words in length.

**Task 3: Update Each Page**. Open each page in a text editor and add a description meta tag to the head section. Save the files and test them in a browser. They will not look different, but they are much friendlier to search engines!

## Path of Light Yoga Studio

See Chapter 2 for an introduction to the Path of Light Yoga Studio case study. Use the Chapter 9 Path of Light Yoga Studio website as a starting point for this case study. You have three tasks in this case study:

1. Create a new folder for this Path of Light Yoga Studio case study.

2. Write a description of the Path of Light Yoga Studio business.

3. Code a description meta tag on each page in the website.

### Hands-On Practice Case Study

**Task 1: The Website Folder**. Create a folder called yoga13. Copy all of the files from your Chapter 9 yoga9 folder into the yoga13 folder.

**Task 2: Write a Description**. Review the Path of Light Yoga Studio pages that you created in earlier chapters. Write a brief paragraph that describes the Path of Light Yoga Studio site. Edit the paragraph down to a description that is only a few sentences and less than 25 words in length.

**Task 3: Update Each Page**. Open each page in a text editor and add a description meta tag to the head section. Save the files and test them in a browser. They will not look different, but they are much friendlier to search engines!

## Web Project

See Chapter 5 for an introduction to the Web Project case study. Your task is to add an appropriate description meta tag to each page in the website.

### Hands-On Practice Case Study

1. Review the Project Topic Approval document that you created in the Chapter 9 case study. Take a moment to view the pages that you created in earlier chapters. Write a brief paragraph that describes the Web Project website.

2. Launch a text editor and edit the web pages in the project folder. Add a description meta tag to each page. Save your pages and test them in a browser. They will not look different, but they are now friendlier to search engines!

# 14

# A Brief Look at JavaScript and jQuery

## Chapter Objectives    In this chapter, you will learn how to . . .

- Describe common uses of JavaScript in web pages
- Describe the purpose of the Document Object Model (DOM) and list some common events
- Code JavaScript methods, properties, event handlers, and event listeners
- Use JavaScript variables, operators, and the if control structure
- Create a basic JavaScript form data validation script
- Describe common uses of jQuery
- Describe how to obtain jQuery
- Use jQuery selectors and methods
- Configure an image gallery with jQuery
- Describe the purpose of jQuery plugins

**If a popup window mysteriously appears while you are surfing the Web,** you're experiencing the effects of JavaScript. JavaScript is a scripting language and JavaScript commands can be included in an HTML file. Using JavaScript, you can incorporate techniques and effects that will make your web pages come alive! You can display an alert box containing an important message for the user. You can display an image when a user moves the mouse pointer over a link and much more. jQuery is a JavaScript library that provides an easier way to code interactive effects with JavaScript. This chapter introduces JavaScript and jQuery while providing some examples that you can build on to create your own web pages.

# 14.1 Overview of JavaScript

There are a variety of methods for adding interactivity to a web page. As you learned in Chapter 6, CSS can be used to achieve a hover effect as you position your mouse pointer over a hypertext link. CSS can also be used for interactive effects, including an image gallery and the new CSS3 transitions and transforms. In Chapter 11, you saw examples of how JavaScript can be used to add interactivity and functionality to web pages.

So, what is JavaScript? It's an object-based, client-side scripting language interpreted by a web browser. JavaScript is considered to be **object-based** because it's used to work with the objects associated with a web page **document**: the browser window, the document itself, and elements such as forms, images, and links. Because JavaScript is interpreted by a browser, it is considered to be a client-side scripting language. A **scripting language** is a type of programming language, but no need to worry! You don't have to be a computer programmer to understand this.

Let's review clients and servers. In Chapter 10, we discussed hosting a website on a web server. As you learned, a web host provider allows you to transfer your files to the web server and stores your website. Visitors to your site (also called users) are able to point their web browsers to your website using the URL provided by your web host provider. As you may recall, the user's web browser is called a client.

JavaScript is interpreted by the client. This means that the JavaScript code, embedded in the HTML document, will be rendered by the browser. The server's job is to provide the HTML document. The web browser's job is to interpret the code in the HTML file and display the web page accordingly. Because all the processing is performed by the client (in this case, the web browser), this is referred to as **client-side processing**. There are programming languages that are executed on the server, which are referred to as server-side programming languages. **Server-side processing** may involve sending e-mail, storing items in a database, or tracking items in a shopping cart. In Chapter 9, you learned how to set the action of a form to point to a server-side script.

In summary, JavaScript is an object-based, client-side scripting language interpreted by a web browser. The JavaScript code is embedded in the HTML file and the web browser interprets it and displays the results as needed.

# 14.2 The Development of JavaScript

There is a popular misconception that Java and JavaScript are the same. Java and JavaScript are completely separate languages with very little in common. Java is a robust object-oriented programming language that can be used to build large applications for businesses, such as inventory control systems and payroll systems. Sun Microsystems developed Java in the 1990s and designed the language to run on an operating system such as Windows or Unix. JavaScript, developed initially by Brendan Eich at Netscape, was originally called LiveScript. When Netscape collaborated with Sun Microsystems on modifications to the language, it was renamed JavaScript. However, JavaScript is not the same as the Java programming language. JavaScript is much simpler than Java. The two languages have more differences than similarities.

# 14.3 Popular Uses for JavaScript

The uses of JavaScript range from providing some "bells and whistles," such as simple animation and fancy menus, to functionality, such as popping up a new window that contains product information and detecting errors in a form. Let's look at some examples of some of these uses.

## Alert Message

An alert message is a popular technique used to draw the user's attention to something that is happening. For instance, a retail website may use an alert message to list errors in an order form or remind the user about an upcoming sale. Figure 14.1 illustrates an alert message that thanks the user for visiting the page. This alert message is displayed when the user is leaving the website and going to a new site.

Figure 14.1 Alert message is displayed when the user leaves the website

Notice that the user must click the OK button before the next page will load. This effectively grabs the user's attention, but it quickly becomes annoying if it is overused.

## Popup Windows

And speaking of annoying, a **popup window** is a web browser window that may appear when you interact with a web page by clicking on an image or hovering over a page area, or it may seem to appear somewhat mysteriously. This technique has some legitimate uses, such as popping up an information window that contains a larger picture and description of a product when the user clicks on the product in the main window. Unfortunately, the use of popup windows has been so abused that most browsers allow users to disable popup windows. This also means that the useful popup windows are not displayed. Figure 14.2 shows a popup window that appears when the user clicks the link on the main page.

Figure 14.2 The smaller popup window appears when the user clicks on the link in the larger window. Screenshots of Mozilla Firefox. Courtesy of Mozilla Foundation.

## Jump Menus

JavaScript can also be used to create **jump menus** based on a select list as introduced in Chapter 9. The user can select a web page from a select list and click a button to load the selected Web page. Figure 14.3 shows this technique.

Figure 14.3 Jump menu that shows the selection of the Contact Information menu option

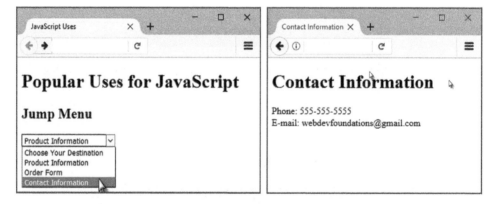

In this example, the user selected the Contact Information option from the select list. The Contact Information page will load in the browser window.

## Mouse Movement Techniques

JavaScript can be used to perform a task based on mouse movement in the browser window. One popular technique is to display a submenu when the user hovers the mouse pointer over a menu item. Figure 14.4 shows this technique.

Figure 14.4 The submenu is displayed when the user hovers over the Products menu item

The window on the left shows the main menu and the window on the right shows the submenu displayed when the user hovers the mouse pointer over the Products menu item. When the user moves the mouse away from the Products menu item, the submenu disappears. Mouse movements also trigger **image swapping**, often referred to as rollover images. An image is displayed on the web page when the page initially loads. When the user positions the mouse pointer on top of the image, the original image is swapped for a new image. When the user moves the mouse away from the image, the original image reappears. Figure 14.5 shows the image-swapping technique. For many years, this technique was commonly used for navigation button bars. However, modern web developers typically use CSS to configure similar effects with the `:hover` pseudo-class, such as changing the background color or background image of an element.

Figure 14.5 The original image is on the left and the swapped image is on the right with the mouse pointer hovering on the image

In this chapter, we will touch on some of the highlights and concepts involved in using JavaScript. We will create some scripts to demonstrate the use of the alert message, mouseovers, and some of the techniques involved in checking a form for input errors. This chapter offers just a taste of JavaScript, but it will give you on overview of how some of the techniques are developed.

# 14.4 Adding JavaScript to a Web Page

JavaScript code is embedded in an HTML web page and is interpreted by the web browser. This means that the web browser is capable of understanding the code and running it. Most modern browsers include developer options that provide JavaScript error messages generated when running the code. The examples in this textbook use the Mozilla Firefox browser. If you have not already installed Mozilla Firefox on your computer, visit https://www.mozilla.com/firefox for a free download.

## Script Element

When JavaScript code is embedded in an HTML document, it needs to be contained, or encapsulated, in a script element. The JavaScript is typed between the opening **`<script>`** tag and the closing `</script>` tag. Web pages are rendered by the browser from top to bottom. The impact on our scripts is that they will execute wherever they are located in the document. The script element can be coded within the head element or the body element.

## Alert Message Box

The alert message box is displayed using the **alert()** method. The structure is

```
alert("message to be displayed");
```

Each JavaScript command line generally ends with a semicolon (;). Also, JavaScript is **case-sensitive**, which means that there's a difference between uppercase and lowercase characters and it will be important to be precise when typing JavaScript code.

## Hands-On Practice 14.1

In this Hands-On Practice, you will create a simple script with an alert message box. Launch a text editor and type the following HTML and JavaScript code. Note that alert() does not contain a space between alert and the opening parenthesis.

```html
<!DOCTYPE html>
<html lang="en">
<head>
  <title>JavaScript Practice</title>
  <meta charset="utf-8">
</head>
<body>
<h1>Using JavaScript</h1>
<script>
alert("Welcome to my web page!");
</script>
<h2>When does this display?</h2>
</body>
</html>
```

Save this file as alert.html. Display your file in a browser. Notice that the first heading appears and then the alert message pops up (see Figure 14.6). After you click the OK button, the second heading appears. This illustrates the top-down processing of the web page and the embedded JavaScript. The JavaScript block is between the headings and that's where the alert message appears as well.

Figure 14.6 JavaScript displays the alert message box (alert.html)

## Practice with Debugging

Sometimes your JavaScript code does not work the first time you test it. When this happens, you'll need to **debug** the code—find the errors and correct them.

Let's look at a debugging technique. Edit the JavaScript alert to introduce a typing error:

```
aalert("Welcome to my web page!");
```

Save the file and view it in the browser. Notice that the alert box does not display this time. Firefox will point out some errors in JavaScript code, but we need to open the Web Console in order to see them.

In Firefox, select the top right menu icon > Web Developer > Web Console. The Web Console panel will display and the error message will appear (see Figure 14.7).

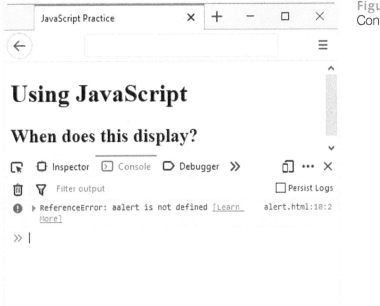

Figure 14.7 The Web Console displays an error

Notice that the error is displayed, along with the file name and line number where the error was detected. It's useful to create your documents in a text editor that displays the line numbers, but it's not necessary. If you are using Notepad, make use of the Go To feature in the Edit menu. This will allow you to specify a line number and the insertion point will be positioned at the beginning of that line.

Edit the alert.html file to correct the error and test it in the browser. This time the alert box should display after the first heading. Compare your work to chapter14/14.1/alert.html in the student files.

 **FAQ** **Will the Firefox Web Console display all of the errors in my JavaScript code?**

The Web Console will display the syntax errors, which include things like missing quotes and items that it does not recognize. Sometimes the error is above the line indicated, particularly if there is a missing parenthesis or quote. The errors displayed indicate that there is something wrong and they serve as a guide as to where the error might be located. Start by looking at the line indicated; if that line looks correct, look at the lines above it.

 **Checkpoint 14.1**

**1.** Describe at least three popular uses for JavaScript.

**2.** How many JavaScript code blocks can be embedded in an HTML document?

**3.** Describe a method that can be used to find an error in a JavaScript code block.

# 14.5 Document Object Model Overview

JavaScript can manipulate the elements of an HTML document, such as container tags like paragraphs, spans, and div elements. Elements also include images, forms, and individual form elements such as text boxes and select lists. In order to access these elements, we need to understand a little bit about the Document Object Model (DOM).

In general, an **object** is an entity or a "thing". When using the DOM, the browser window, web page document, and any HTML element are considered to be objects. The browser window is an object. When a web page loads in the browser, the web page is considered to be a document. The document itself is an object. The document can contain objects such as images, headings, paragraphs, and individual form elements such as text boxes. The objects may have properties that can be detected or manipulated. For example, a property of the document is its title. Another property of the document is its background color.

There are actions that can be performed on some objects. For example, the **window object** can display the alert message box or a prompt box. This type of action is called a **method**.

The command to display an alert message is referred to as a method of the window object. The DOM is the collection of objects, properties, and methods. JavaScript uses the DOM to detect and manipulate the elements in the HTML document.

Let's look at this system of objects, properties, and methods differently. Let's say that your car is an object. It has properties such as color, manufacturer, and year. Your car has elements such as the hood and trunk. The hood and trunk can be opened and closed. If we were to use a programming language to open and close the hood and trunk, the commands might look something like the following:

```
car.hood.open()
car.hood.close()
car.trunk.open()
car.trunk.close()
```

If we wanted to know the color, year, and manufacturer of the car, the commands might look something like the following:

```
car.color
car.year
car.model
car.manufacturer
```

When we use the values, `car.color` might be equal to "silver", `car.manufacturer` might be equal to "Nissan", and `car.model` might be equal to "370Z". We might be able to change the values or only read them without changing them. In this example, car is an object and its properties are hood, trunk, color, year, model, and manufacturer. Hood and trunk could be considered properties as well. Open and close are methods of hood and are also methods of trunk.

With respect to the DOM, we can write to the document using the **write()** method of the document object. The structure is

```
document.write("text to be written to the document");
```

We can use this in JavaScript to write text and HTML tags to a document and the browser will render it. The `alert()` method used in the previous Hands-On Practice is a method of the window object. It can be written as

```
window.alert("message");
```

The window object is assumed to exist and can be omitted. If the window doesn't exist, the script doesn't exist either.

One property of the document is `lastModified`. This property contains the date on which the file was most recently saved or modified and we can access it using `document.lastModified`. This is a read-only property that we can display in the browser window or use for some other purpose.

**Hands-On Practice 14.2**

In this Hands-On Practice, you will practice using the `write()` method of the document and the `lastModified` property of the document. You will use `document.write()` to add text and some HTML tags to an HTML document. You will also use `document.write()` to write the date the file was last saved to the document.

Open the alert.html file (found at chapter14/14.1/alert.html in the student files) and edit the code as indicated:

```
<!DOCTYPE html>
<html lang="en">
<head>
  <title>JavaScript Practice</title>
  <meta charset="utf-8">
</head>
<body>
<h1>Using JavaScript</h1>
<script>
document.write("<p>Using document.write to add text</p>");
document.write("<h2>Notice that we can add HTML tags too!</h2>");
</script>
<h3>This document was last modified on:
<script>
document.write(document.lastModified);
</script>
</h3>
</body>
</html>
```

Save this file as write.html and view it in the browser. The text should display (see Figure 14.8). If the text does not display, open the Web Console and correct any errors that appear.

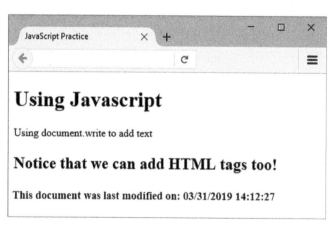

**Figure 14.8** The Firefox browser displays write.html

JavaScript can be seen in the source code. To confirm this, select the top right menu icon > Web Developer > Page Source to see the source code. Close the source code window when you have finished viewing the code. A suggested solution is located at chapter14/14.2/write.html in the student files.

**FAQ** **Why would I use `document.write` when I can just type the HTML code by itself?**

In practice, you typically wouldn't use `document.write` to generate your web page if you could just type the HTML code by itself. You would use `document.write` in conjunction with other techniques. For instance, you might use JavaScript to detect the time of day and, if it is before noon, use `document.write` to write "Good morning" to the document. If it is afternoon, write "Good afternoon" to the document, and if it is after 6:00 p.m., write "Good evening" to the document.

# 14.6 Events and Event Handlers

As the user is viewing a web page, the browser detects mouse movement and events. An **event** is an action taken by the web page visitor, such as clicking the mouse, loading pages, or submitting forms. For instance, when you move your mouse pointer over a hypertext link, the browser detects a mouseover event. Table 14.1 lists a few of the events and their descriptions.

Table 14.1 Events and their descriptions

| Event | Description |
|-------|-------------|
| click | The user clicks on an item. This could be an image, hypertext link, or button. |
| load | The browser displays a web page. |
| mouseover | The mouse pointer hovers over an item. The mouse pointer does not have to rest on the object. This could be a hypertext link, image, paragraph, or another object. |
| mouseout | The mouse pointer is moved away from an item that it had previously hovered over. |
| submit | The user clicks the submit button on a form. |
| unload | The web page unloads in the browser. This event occurs just before a new web page loads. |

When an event occurs, this can trigger some JavaScript code to execute. One widely used technique is to detect the mouseover and mouseout events and swap images or display a menu.

We need to indicate which events will be acted upon and what will be done when an event occurs. We can use an **event handler** to property indicate which event to target. An event handler is embedded in an HTML tag as an attribute and indicates some JavaScript code to execute when the event occurs. Event handlers use the event name with the prefix "on". Table 14.2 shows the event handlers that correspond to the events described in Table 14.1. For example, the **onload** event is triggered when browser renders (loads) a web page. When you move your mouse pointer over a text hyperlink, a **mouseover** event occurs and is detected by the browser. If that hyperlink contains an **onmouseover** event handler, the JavaScript code indicated by the event handler will execute. This code might pop up an alert message, display an image, or display a menu. Other event handlers such as **onclick** and **onmouseout** can cause JavaScript code to execute when their corresponding event occurs.

Table 14.2 Events and event handler properties

| Event | Event Handler |
|-------|---------------|
| click | onclick |
| load | onload |
| mouseover | onmouseover |
| mouseout | onmouseout |
| submit | onsubmit |
| unload | onunload |

## Hands-On Practice 14.3

Let's practice using the onmouseover and onmouseout event handlers and alert messages to indicate when the event handler has been triggered. We will use simple hypertext links and embed the event handlers in the anchor tags. We will not need the <script> block because event handlers are placed as attributes within the HTML tags. We'll place the hypertext links in an unordered list so that there's a lot of room in the browser window to move the mouse pointer and test our script.

Open a text editor and enter the code shown below. Note the use of the double and single quotes in the onmouseover and onmouseout event handlers. We need quotes around the message in the alert() method and we need quotes that encapsulate the JavaScript for the event handler. HTML and JavaScript will allow us to use either double quotes or single quotes. The rule is that they must match in pairs. So when you have a situation where you need two sets of quotes, you can use both double and single quotes. Use double quotes for the outer set and single quotes for the inner set. In the anchor tag, the # symbol is used for the href value because we don't need the functionality of loading another web page. We need the hypertext link to sense mouseover and mouseout events.

```
<!DOCTYPE html>
<html lang="en">
<head>
  <title>JavaScript Practice</title>
  <meta charset="utf-8">
</head>
<body>
<h1>Using JavaScript</h1>
<ul>
  <li><a href="#" onmouseover="alert('You moused over');">Mouseover
  test</a></li>
  <li><a href="#" onmouseout="alert('You moused out');">Mouseout
  test</a></li>
</ul>
</body>
</html>
```

Save this file as mouse.html and load it in the browser. Move your mouse on top of the Mouseover test link. As soon as your mouse touches the link, the mouseover event occurs and the onmouseover event handler is triggered. This displays the alert box (see Figure 14.9).

Click the OK button and position your mouse pointer over the Mouseout test link. Notice that nothing happens. This is because the mouseout event has not occurred yet.

Move the mouse pointer away from the link. As soon as the mouse pointer is no longer on the link, the mouseout event occurs and the onmouseout event handler is triggered. This displays the alert box (see Figure 14.10). A suggested solution can be found in the student files (chapter14/14.3/mouse.html).

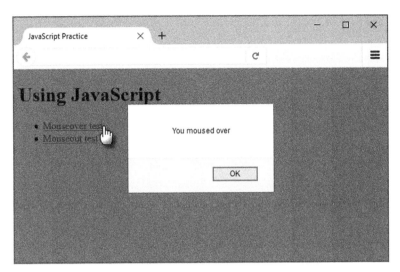

Figure 14.9 Demonstration of onmouseover

Figure 14.10 Demonstration of onmouseout

 Checkpoint 14.2

**1.** When referring to objects, describe the difference between a property and a method. Feel free to use words like thing, action, description, attribute, and so on.

**2.** What is the difference between an event and an event handler?

**3.** Where are event handlers placed in the HTML document?

# 14.7 Variables

Sometimes we need to be able to collect information from the user. A simple example is prompting the user for a name and writing the name to the document. We would store the name in a **variable**. You probably took a math course at some point and used *x* and *y* as variables in equations as placeholders for values. The same principle applies when using variables in JavaScript. (We won't do any tricky math here, so relax!) JavaScript variables are also placeholders for data and the value of the variable can change. Robust programming languages like C++ and Java have all kinds of rules for variables and their data types. JavaScript is very loose that way. We won't have to worry about what type of data is contained in a variable.

 FAQ   **Are there any tips for creating variable names?**

Creating the name of a variable is really something of an art form. First of all, you want to create a variable name that describes the data it contains. The underscore, or an uppercase character, can be used for readability to indicate more than one word. Do not use other special characters, though. Stick to letters and numbers. Be careful not to use a JavaScript **reserved word** or keyword, such as `var`, `return`, `function`, and so on. Visit https://webplatform.github.io/docs/javascript/reserved_words/ for a list of JavaScript keywords. The following are some variable names that could be used for a product code:

- `productCode`
- `prodCode`
- `product_code`

## Writing a Variable to a Web Page

Before we use a variable, we can declare it with the JavaScript **var** keyword. This step isn't necessary, but it is good programming practice. We can assign data to a variable using the assignment operator, the equal sign (=). A variable can contain a number or a string. A **string** is encapsulated in quotes and can contain alphabetic characters, spaces, numbers, and special characters. For instance, a string can be a last name, e-mail address, street address, product code, or paragraph of information. Let's do a practice exercise that assigns data to a variable and writes it to the document.

 Hands-On Practice 14.4

In this Hands-On Practice, you will declare a variable, assign string data to it, and write it to the document.

Open a text editor and type the following:

```
<!DOCTYPE html>
<html lang="en">
<head>
  <title>JavaScript Practice</title>
  <meta charset="utf-8">
</head>
```

```
<body>
<h1>Using JavaScript</h1>
<h2>Hello
<script>
var userName;
userName = "Karen";
document.write(userName);
</script>
</h2>
</body>
</html>
```

Notice that the `<h2>` tag is placed before the script block and the `</h2>` tag is placed after the script block. This renders the value of `userName` in the `<h2>` heading format. There is also a single space after the "o" in "Hello". If you miss this space, you'll see the `userName` value displayed right after the "o".

Notice that the variable is mixed case. This is a convention used in many programming languages to make the variable readable. Some developers might use an underscore, like user_name. Selecting a variable name is somewhat of an art form, but try to select names that indicate the contents of the variable.

Also notice that the `document.write()` method does not contain quotes. The contents of the variable will be written to the document. If we had used quotes around the variable name, the variable name itself would be written to the document and not the contents of the variable.

Save this document as var.html and load it in the browser. Figure 14.11 shows the var.html file in the browser. Compare your work to chapter14/14.4/var.html in the student files.

Figure 14.11 Browser with var.html displayed

Chopping up the `<h2>` heading so that it is placed before and after the script is a bit cumbersome. We can combine strings using the plus (+) symbol. You'll see later in this chapter that the plus symbol can also be used to add numbers. The practice of combining strings using the plus symbol is called **concatenation**. Let's concatenate the `<h2>` information as a string with the `userName` value and the `</h2>` tag.

Edit the var.html document as follows:

```
<!DOCTYPE html>
<html lang="en">
<head>
  <title>JavaScript Practice</title>
  <meta charset="utf-8">
</head>
```

```
<body>
<h1>Using JavaScript</h1>
<script>
var userName;
userName = "Karen";
document.write("<h2>Hello " + userName + "</h2>");
</script>
</body>
</html>
```

Be sure to remove the `<h2>` and `</h2>` information above and below the script block. Save the file as var2.html and display it in the browser window. You should not see any difference in the document in the browser. Compare your work to chapter14/14.4/var2.html in the student files.

## Collecting Variable Values Using a Prompt

To demonstrate the interactive aspect of JavaScript and variables, we can use the `prompt()` method to request data from the user and write this data to the web page. For example, we will build on Hands-On Practice 14.4 and prompt the user for a name rather than hard code this data in the userName variable.

The `prompt()` method is a method of the window object. We could use `window.prompt()`, but the window object is assumed, so we can write this simply as `prompt()`. The `prompt()` method can provide a message to the user. This method is generally used in conjunction with a variable so that the incoming data is stored in a variable. The structure is

```
someVariable = prompt("prompt message");
```

When this command executes, a prompt box pops up that displays the message and an input box for data entry. The user types in the prompt box, clicks the OK button, and the data is assigned to the variable. Let's add this feature to the var2.html file.

 ## Hands-On Practice 14.5

In this Hands-On Practice, you will use the `prompt()` method to gather data from the user and write it to the document.

Edit your file from Hands-On Practice 14.4 (also found in the student files at chapter14/14.4/var2.html) as follows:

```
<script>
var userName;
userName = prompt("Please enter your name");
document.write("<h2>Hello " + userName + "</h2>");
</script>
```

Only the `userName` variable assignment command has changed. The data typed by the user will be assigned to the variable `userName`.

Save the file as var3.html and display it in the browser. The prompt box will appear and you can type a name in the input box and click the OK button (see Figure 14.12). The name should appear in the browser window. Compare your work to chapter14/14.5/var3.html in the student files.

Figure 14.12 The prompt box is displayed in the browser when the web page is loaded. The visitor types their name and clicks OK. Next, the browser accepts the input and writes a welcome message on the page.

Let's do a variation on this and allow the user to type a color name. The user's preference will be used as the background color of the document. We will use the `bgColor` property of the document object and set it to the user's color preference. Be sure that an upper-case C is used when typing `bgColor`.

Edit the var3.html document as follows and save it as var4.html:

```
<script>
var userColor;
userColor = prompt("Please type the color name blue or red");
document.bgColor = userColor;
</script>
```

We are prompting the user to type the color name "blue" or "red". You know from your HTML experience that there are more options for color names. Feel free to experiment!

Save the document and display it in the browser. The prompt box will appear and you can type a color name and click the OK button. You should notice the background color change immediately. Compare your work to chapter14/14.5/var4.html in the student files.

# 14.8 Introduction to Programming Concepts

Until now, we have used the DOM to access properties and methods for the window and document. We have also used some simple event handlers. There is another aspect of JavaScript that is more like programming. In this section, we'll touch on just a small part of this to get a feel for the power of using programming concepts and build on this later to test input on a form.

## Arithmetic Operators

When working with variables, it is often useful to be able to do some arithmetic. For instance, you may be creating a web page that calculates the tax on a product. Once the user has selected a product, you can use JavaScript to calculate the tax and write the result to the document. Table 14.3 shows a list of **arithmetic operators**, descriptions, and some examples.

Table 14.3 Commonly used arithmetic operators

| Operator | Description | Example | Value of Quantity |
| --- | --- | --- | --- |
| = | Assign | quantity = 10 | 10 |
| + | Addition | quantity = 10 + 6 | 16 |
| – | Subtraction | quantity = 10 – 6 | 4 |
| × | Multiplication | quantity = 10 × 2 | 20 |
| / | Division | quantity = 10 / 2 | 5 |

Programming languages differ greatly in capabilities, but they all have a few things in common. They all allow the use of variables and have commands for decision making, command repetition, and reusable code blocks. Decision making would be used when different outcomes are required, depending on the input or action of the user. In the next Hands-On Practice, we will prompt the user to enter a number and write different text on the web page document based on the value entered. Repetition of commands comes in handy when performing a similar task many times. For instance, it is tedious to create a select list containing the numbers 1 through 31 for the days of the months. We can use JavaScript to do this with a few lines of code. Reusable code blocks are handy when you want to refer to a block of code in an event handler rather than typing many commands in the HTML tag's event handler. Because this chapter is meant to be a very brief introduction, it is beyond our scope to elaborate further. We will touch on decision making and reusable code in the Hands-On Practice.

## Decision Making

As we've seen, we can use variables in JavaScript. We may wish to test the value of a variable and perform different tasks based on the value of the variable. For instance, perhaps an order form requires that the user enter a quantity greater than 0. We could test the quantity input box to verify that the number entered is greater than 0. If the quantity is not greater than 0, we could pop up an alert message that instructs the user to enter a quantity greater than 0. The `if` control structure will be

```
if (condition) {
... commands to execute if condition is true
} else {
... commands to execute if condition is false
}
```

Notice that there are two types of grouping symbols used: parentheses and brackets. The parentheses are placed around the condition and the brackets are used to encapsulate a block of commands. The `if` statement includes a block of commands to execute if the condition is true and a block of commands to execute if the condition is false. The brackets are aligned so that you can easily see the opening brackets and closing brackets. It's very easy to miss a bracket when you're typing and then you would have to hunt for the missing bracket. Aligning them makes it much easier to track them visually. As you are typing JavaScript code, remember that parentheses, brackets, and quotes always are used in pairs. If a script isn't working as intended, verify that each of these items has a "partner."

If the condition evaluates as true, the first command block will be executed and the else block will be skipped. If the condition is false, the first command block will be skipped and the else block will execute.

This overview should give you a sense of how conditions and the `if` control structure can be useful. The condition must be something that can be evaluated as either true or false. We can think of this as a mathematical condition. The condition will generally make use of an operator. Table 14.4 lists commonly used **comparison operators**. The examples in Table 14.4 could be used as conditions in an `if` control structure.

Table 14.4 Commonly used comparison operators

| Operator | Description | Example | Sample Values of a Quantity that Would Result in True |
|---|---|---|---|
| == | Double equal signs (equivalent); "is exactly equal to" | quantity == 10 | 10 |
| > | Greater than | quantity > 10 | 11, 12 (but not 10) |
| >= | Greater than or equal to | quantity >= 10 | 10, 11, 12 |
| < | Less than | quantity < 10 | 9, 8 (but not 10) |
| <= | Less than or equal to | quantity <= 10 | 10, 9, 8 |

FAQ **What can I do when my JavaScript code doesn't seem to be working?**

You can try the following debugging techniques:

- Open the Web Console in Firefox (Tools > Web Developer > Web Console) to see if there are any errors. Common errors include missing a semicolon at the end of a line and typing errors in commands.

- Use `alert()` to print variables to verify the contents. For instance, if you have a variable named quantity, try `alert(quantity);` to see what is contained in the variable.

- Ask a classmate to look at your code. It's difficult to edit your own code because you tend to see what you think you wrote rather than what you actually wrote. It's easier to edit someone else's code.

- Try to explain your code to a classmate. Often, talking through the code will help you uncover errors.
- Verify that you are not using any JavaScript reserved words as variable names or function names.

## Hands-On Practice 14.6

In this Hands-On Practice, you will code the quantity example described earlier. The user will be prompted for a quantity and must enter a quantity greater than 0. We will assume that the user will enter a number. If the user enters a value of 0 or a negative number, there will be an error message displayed. If the user enters a value greater than 0, a message will be displayed thanking the user for the order. We will use a prompt and will write messages to the document.

Open a text editor and enter the following:

```
<!DOCTYPE html>
<html lang="en">
<head>
  <title>JavaScript Practice</title>
  <meta charset="utf-8">
</head>
<body>
<h1>Using JavaScript</h1>
<script>
var quantity;
quantity = prompt("Type a quantity greater than 0");
if (quantity <= 0) {
    document.write("<p>Quantity is not greater than 0.</p>");
    document.write("<p>Please refresh the web page.</p>");
} else {
    document.write("<p>Quantity is greater than 0.</p>");
}
</script>
</body>
</html>
```

Save this document as quantityif.html and display it in a browser. If the prompt box does not appear, remember to check the Web Console for errors. When the prompt box appears, type the number 0 and click the OK button. You should see the error message you have created in the browser window (see Figure 14.13).

Now, refresh the page and enter a value greater than 0 (see Figure 14.14). Compare your work to chapter14/14.6/if.html in the student files.

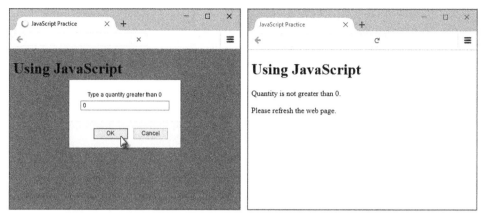

Figure 14.13 The browser on the left shows the prompt box with input of 0 and the browser on the right shows the result

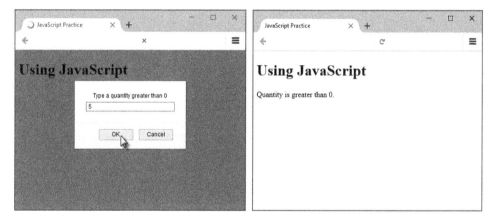

Figure 14.14 The browser on the left shows the prompt box with an input value that is greater than 0 and the browser on the right shows the result

## Functions

In Hands-On Practice 14.6, you coded a prompt box that pops up as soon as the page loads. What if we prefer to allow the user to decide when a particular script should be interpreted or run by the browser? Perhaps we could use an onmouseover event handler and run the script when the user moves the mouse pointer over a link or image. Another method, perhaps more intuitive for the user, is to make use of a button and direct the user to click the button to run the script. The web page visitor doesn't need to be aware that a script will run, but can click a button to initiate some sort of functionality.

Form submit and reset buttons were introduced in Chapter 9:

- A submit button, `<input type="submit">`, is used to submit a form.
- A reset button, `<input type="reset">`, is used to clear values entered on a form.

In this section, we will use the `button` element and the `onclick` event handler to run JavaScript. The sample HTML is

```
<button onclick="alert('Welcome');">Click to see a message</button>
```

In this sample, the button will display the text "Click to see a message". When the user clicks the button, the click event occurs and the `onclick` event handler executes the `alert('Welcome!');` statement. The message box appears. This method is very effective when there is only one JavaScript statement to execute. It quickly becomes unmanageable when there are more statements to execute. When that happens, it makes sense to place all JavaScript statements in a block and somehow point to the block to execute. If the statement block has a name, we can execute the block by pointing to the name. In addition to providing a shortcut name, this code is also easily reused. We can provide a name for a statement block by creating a function.

A **function** is a block of JavaScript statements with a specific purpose that can be run when needed. A function can contain a single statement or a group of statements and is defined as

```
function function_name() {
...  JavaScript statements
}
```

The function definition starts with the keyword `function` followed by the name of the function. The parentheses are required and more advanced functions make use of them. You can choose a name for the function just like you choose a name for a variable. The function name should indicate the purpose of the function. The statements are contained within the brackets. The block of statements will execute when you **invoke**, or call, the function.

Here's an example of a function definition:

```
function showAlerts() {
  alert("Please click OK to continue.");
  alert("Please click OK again.");
  alert("Click OK for the last time to continue.");
}
```

The function can be invoked using

```
showAlerts();
```

Now, we could include the `showAlerts()` function call in a button as

```
<button onclick="showAlerts();">Click to see alerts</button>
```

When the user clicks the button, the `showAlerts()` function will be called and the three alert messages will appear one after the other. Try out the example in the student files (chapter14/function.html) to see this in action.

Function definitions are typically placed in the head section of the HTML document. This loads the function definition code, but it does not execute or run until it is invoked. This ensures that the function definition is loaded and ready to use before the function is called. Another feature of a function is that variables declared within the function are only available within that function; they have limited **scope** and are not available outside of the function. In contrast, variables that are declared outside of functions have global scope and can be available to all JavaScript associated with the page. Limiting scope prevents conflicts with variable names when using JavaScript libraries such as jQuery.

 ## Hands-On Practice 14.7

In this Hands-On Practice, you will edit your file from Hands-On Practice 14.6 (found in the student files at chapter14/14.6/if.html) to move the prompting script into a function and call it with an `onclick` event handler. There are a few things to note. The script has been moved into the head section and is included in a function definition. The `document.write()` methods have been changed to `alert()` methods and the messages have been altered slightly. The `document.write()` methods will not work well after the page has already been written, as is the case in this exercise. Also, there have been some comments added to the end brackets for the `if` statement and the function definition. These comments can help you keep track of the code blocks within the script. The indentation of the code blocks also helps to identify which brackets begin and end various statements. Launch a text editor and edit the if.html file as follows:

```html
<!DOCTYPE html>
<html lang="en">
<head>
  <title>JavaScript Practice</title>
  <meta charset="utf-8">
<script>
function promptQuantity() {
    var quantity;
    quantity = prompt("Please type a quantity greater than 0");
    if (quantity <= 0) {
        alert("Quantity is not greater than 0.");
    } else {
        alert("Thank you for entering a quantity greater than 0.");
    } // end if
} // end function promptQuantity
</script>
</head>
<body>
<h1>Using JavaScript</h1>
<button onclick="promptQuantity();">Click to enter quantity</button>
</body>
</html>
```

Save the document as if2.html and display it in a browser. Open the Web Console to check whether there are typing errors when you run the script.

Click the button to test the script. If the prompt box does not appear, check the Web Console and correct any errors. Figure 14.15 shows the browser and the prompt box after the button has been clicked, as well as the resulting alert box. Be sure to test for a value larger than 0 and a value of 0 or less. Compare your work to chapter14/14.7/if2.html in the student files.

**Figure 14.15** The browser on the left shows the prompt box and input; the browser on the right shows the alert box displayed after the input

As you've been working with JavaScript, you may have noticed that you have been coding event handlers, such as onclick, directly in the HTML tags. In the next section, you'll be introduced to a more modern approach that avoids embedding JavaScript within HTML tags.

## The addEventListener Method

In section 14.6 you began to work with events (such as `click` and `mouseover`) and coded event handler properties (such as `onclick` and `onmouseover`) directly within HTML tags. While this technique works, there are disadvantages: you are limited to only one event handler for an element (if you happen to write more than one event handler for the same element, only the last one will run) and the JavaScript code is mixed in with the HTML code, which could increase the complexity of maintenance. A more modern approach is to code an **event listener**, using the **addEventListener method** in the JavaScript block. The event listener will wait (or listen) for an event (such as click and mouseover) and cause code to be run, typically calling a function. When using this coding technique, the script element is typically placed before the closing body tag.

The syntax for an event listener uses the document object model and precisely identifies the id of the target element, the event, and the name of the function to be run when the event occurs. For example, the following JavaScript configures an event listener for a `click` event that occurs on an element assigned to the `myB` id and calls a function named `showMe`.

```
document.getElementById("myB").addEventListener("click",showMe);
```

The function is listed below.

```
function showMe() {
    alert("Thank you for clicking the button");
}
```

When the user clicks the button, the `showMe()` function will be called and the alert message will appear. Try out the example in the student files (chapter14/listen.html) to see this in action.

## Hands-On Practice 14.8

In this Hands-On Practice, you will use your file from Hands-On Practice 14.7 (found in the student files at chapter14/14.7/if2.html) and revise the code to use an event listener. There are a few things to note. The script has been moved into the body section before the closing body tag. The button element in the HTML has been modified: the onclick has been removed and the myB id was assigned. The event listener was added. Note that a variable was used so that the addEventListener statement would fit on this page. Launch a text editor and modify the if.html file as shown below.

```
<!DOCTYPE html>
<html lang="en">
<head>
<title>JavaScript Practice</title>
<meta charset="utf-8">
</head>
<body>
<h1>Using JavaScript</h1>
<button id="myB">Click to enter quantity</button>
<script>
var myButton = document.getElementById("myB");
myButton.addEventListener("click",promptQuantity);
function promptQuantity() {
   var quantity;
   quantity = prompt("Please type a quantity greater than 0");
   if (quantity <= 0) {
     alert("Quantity is not greater than 0.");
   } else {
     alert("Thank you for entering a quantity greater than 0.");
   } // end if
} // end function promptQuantity
</script>
</body>
</html>
```

Save the document as if3.html and display it in a browser. Open the Web Console to check whether there are typing errors when you run the script. Click the button to test the script. If the prompt box does not appear, check the Web Console and correct any errors. Figure 14.15 shows the browser and the prompt box after the button has been clicked, as well as the resulting alert box. Be sure to test for a value larger than 0 and a value of 0 or less. Compare your work to chapter14/14.8/if3.html in the student files.

## Checkpoint 14.3

**1.** Describe a method that can be used to gather a piece of data such as the user's age.

**2.** Write the JavaScript code to display an alert message for users who are under 18 years old and a different alert message for users who are 18 years or older.

**3.** What is a function definition?

# 14.9 Form Handling

As you discovered in Chapter 9, the data from a web form can be submitted to a CGI or a server-side script. This data can be added to a database or used for some other purpose; therefore, it is important that the data submitted by a user is as accurate as possible. When the user enters information in a form, there is always a chance that the information will be incorrect or inaccurate. Often, the form data is checked for invalid data before it is submitted. Form data validation can be done by the server-side script, but it can also be done client-side, using JavaScript. Again, this topic is simplified here, but we can get a sense of how this might be done.

When the user clicks the form's submit button, the submit event occurs. We can use the **onsubmit** event handler or an event listener to call a function that tests form data for validation. This technique is referred to as **form handling**. The web developer can validate all form input, some input, or just one form input. Examples of items that might be validated include:

- Required fields such as name and e-mail address
- A required check box to acknowledge a license agreement
- A radio button that indicates a method of payment or a delivery option
- A value entered that is numeric and must be within a particular range

When the user clicks the submit button, the onsubmit event handler invokes a function that tests all of the appropriate form elements for valid data. Then the validation function confirms that the data is valid (true) or not valid (false). The form is submitted to the URL indicated in the form action attribute if the data is valid (true). The form would not be submitted if the data is not valid (false) and some indication to the user regarding errors would be displayed. The overall structure of the web page code related to declaring the function and handling the onsubmit event is

```
...   HTML begins the web page
function validateForm() {
   ...   JavaScript commands to test form data go here
   if form data is valid
      return true
   else
      return false
}
...   HTML continues
<form method="post" action="URL" onsubmit="return validateForm();">
...   form elements go here
<input type="submit" value="submit form">
</form>
...   HTML continues
```

A new concept with regard to functions is indicated here. A function can encapsulate a group of statements, but it can also send a value back to where it was invoked, or called. This is referred to as "returning a value" and the JavaScript keyword `return` is used in the JavaScript code to indicate the value that will be sent back. Our example will return a value of true if the data is valid and a value of false if the data does not pass our validation tests. Notice that the onsubmit event handler also contains the keyword `return`. It works like this: If the validateForm() function returns a value of true, the onsubmit event handler becomes return true and the form is submitted. If the validateForm() function returns a value of false, the onsubmit event handler becomes return false and the form is not submitted. Once a function returns a value, it is finished executing, even if there are more statements in the function.

## Hands-On Practice 14.9

In this Hands-On Practice, you will create a form with inputs for name and age, and use JavaScript to validate: verify data in the name field and a value for age of 18 or greater. If there is nothing in the name field, an alert message will be displayed that indicates an error. If the age value entered is less than 18, an alert message will be displayed that indicates an error. If all data is valid, an alert message will be displayed indicating that the data is valid and the form will be submitted.

Let's start by creating the form. Open a text editor and type the HTML below. Notice that the `onsubmit` form handler is embedded in the `<form>` tag and we will add the JavaScript code later. CSS is used to align and add space around the form elements.

```
<!DOCTYPE html>
<html lang="en">
<head>
  <title>JavaScript Practice</title>
  <meta charset="utf-8">
<style>
input { display: block;
        margin-bottom: 1em;
}
label { float: left;
        width: 5em;
        padding-right: 1em;
        text-align: right;
}
input[type="submit"] { margin-left: 7em; }
</style>
</head>
<body>
<h1>JavaScript Form Handling</h1>
<form method="post"
      action="https://webdevbasics.net/scripts/demo.php"
      onsubmit="return validateForm();">
<label for="userName">Name: </label>
<input type="text" name="userName" id="userName">
<label for="userAge">Age: </label>
<input type="text" name="userAge" id="userAge">
<input type="submit" value="Send information">
</form>
</body>
</html>
```

Save the file as form.html and view it in the browser. Figure 14.16 shows the form in the browser.

Feel free to click the submit button. You will notice that the inputs will be submitted. For the moment, we have not coded the `validateForm()` function, so the form simply submits.

Figure 14.16 The form.html file displayed in the browser

Accessing form inputs is a little tricky. The form is a property of the document object. Each form element is a property of the form object. A property of a form element can be a value. So, the HTML for accessing the contents of an input box could look something like this:

```
document.forms[0].inputbox_name.value
```

The form is identified by `forms[0]` to indicate which form will be used. An HTML document can contain multiple forms. Note that there is an `s` in `forms[0]`. The first form is `forms[0]`. To access the value in the `userAge` input box, we will need to use `document.forms[0].userAge.value`. This is a mouthful, for sure.

Also, notice that the values `true` and `false` are not enclosed in quotes. This is important because `true` and `false` are not strings, they are JavaScript reserved words, or key-words, and represent special values. If you add quotes to them, they become strings and this function will not work properly.

Let's start by adding the code to validate the age. Edit the form.html file to add the following script block in the head section above the `</head>` tag:

```
<script>
function validateForm() {
if (document.forms[0].userAge.value < 18) {
    alert ("Age is less than 18. You are not an adult.");
    return false;
} // end if
alert ("Age is valid.");
return true;
} // end function validateForm
</script>
```

The validateForm() function will check the age in the `userAge` input box. If it is less than 18, the alert message will be displayed and a value of false will be returned and the function will finish executing. The onsubmit event handler will become return false and the form will not be submitted. If the value for age is 18 or greater, the statements in the `if` structure will be skipped and the `alert("Age is valid.");` will execute. After the user clicks the OK button in the alert message, the statement `return true;` will execute and the onsubmit event handler will become return true; thus, the form will be submitted. Let's test this out!

Type a value less than 18 in the `userAge` input box and click the submit button. If the form submits right away, there is likely an error in the JavaScript code. If this happens, open the Error Console and correct the errors indicated. Figure 14.17 shows the alert message displayed after clicking the submit button.

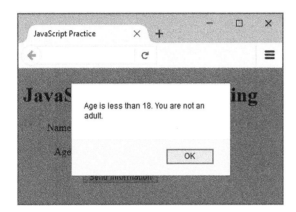

Figure 14.17 The form.html file displayed in a browser with input for age that is less than 18 (notice the alert message)

Click the OK button and type a value for age that is 18 or greater in the `userAge` input box. Click the submit button. Figure 14.18 shows the alert message and the resulting web page after the form has been submitted.

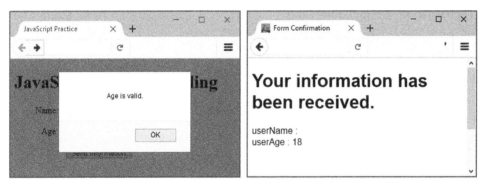

Figure 14.18 The form.html file displayed in a browser with input for age greater than or equal to 18 (notice the alert message); the browser on the right shows the resulting web page after the form is submitted

Now, let's add another if statement to validate the name. To ensure that something has been entered in the `userName` input box, we will test to see if the value of the input box is empty. The **null** string (no characters) is represented by two double quotes ("") or two single quotes ('') without a space or any other character in between. We can compare the value of the `userName` text box to the null string. If the value of the `userName` box is equal to the null string, then we know that the user did not enter any information in this box. In our example, we will be sending only one error message at a time. If the user does not have a name in the `userName` box and also does not have an appropriate age in the `userAge` box, the user will only see the `userName` error message displayed. After the user corrects the name and resubmits the information, the user will see the `userAge` error message displayed. This is very basic form processing, but it gives you an idea of how form handling might be accomplished. More sophisticated form processing would verify each form field and indicate all errors each time the form is submitted.

Let's add the code to validate the `userName` data. Edit the formvalidation.html file and modify the following script block. Note that two equal signs represent equivalency in the `if` statement. Some students find it helpful to read the two equal signs (==) as "is exactly equal to".

```
<script>
function validateForm() {
if (document.forms[0].userName.value == "") {
    alert("Name field cannot be empty.");
    return false;
} // end if
if (document.forms[0].userAge.value < 18) {
    alert("Age is less than 18. You are not an adult.");
    return false;
} // end if
alert("Name and age are valid.");
return true;
} // end function validateForm
</script>
```

Save the document and refresh it in the browser window. Click the submit button without entering data in the Name or Age input boxes. Figure 14.19 shows the alert message displayed when no data has been input and the submit button has been clicked.

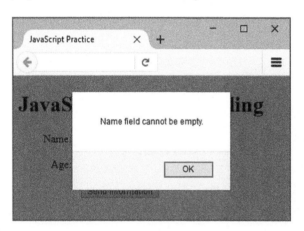

Figure 14.19 The form.html file displayed in the browser without input in the Name and Age boxes; the alert message appears after the form is submitted

Click the OK button, enter some text in the Name input box, and submit the form again. Figure 14.20 shows data in the Name input box and the alert message that appears as a result of validating the age when no value for age is entered.

Figure 14.20 The form.html file displayed in the browser with input in the Name box and without input in the Age box; the alert message appears after the submit button is clicked

Click the OK button and enter a value for age that is 18 or greater. Click the submit button. Figure 14.21 shows data in the Name and Age input boxes and the alert message that displays after the submit button has been clicked. It also shows the resulting web page after successful submission when all data is valid. Compare your work to chapter14/14.9/form.html in the student files.

**Figure 14.21** The form.html file displayed in the browser with valid input in the Name and Age boxes and alert message; the browser on the right shows the web page displayed after valid input has been submitted

## Checkpoint 14.4

1. What is meant by the term "form data validation"?

2. Give three examples of form data that may require validation.

3. An HTML document contains the `<form>` tag as follows:

```
<form method="post"
action="https://webdevbasics.net/scripts/demo.php"
onsubmit="return validateForm();">
```

What happens when the user clicks the submit button?

# 14.10 Accessibility and JavaScript

The interactivity and functionality that JavaScript can add to a web page is exciting. However, be aware that some visitors may have JavaScript disabled, may not be able to see your visual effect, or may be unable to manipulate the mouse. WCAG 2.1 and Section 508 require that your site is functional at a basic level, even if your visitor's browser does not support JavaScript. If you use JavaScript to handle mouse events in your site navigation, you should also provide plain-text navigation that does not require a mouse and can be easily accessed by a screen reader. If you use JavaScript for form validation, provide an e-mail address to allow physically challenged visitors to contact your organization and obtain assistance.

**Focus on Accessibility**

## 14.11 JavaScript Resources

This chapter has barely scratched the surface regarding the uses of JavaScript in web development. You may wish to do further research using some of the following online resources:

- JavaScript Tutorial: https://www.w3schools.com/JS

- JavaScript Tutorial: http://echoecho.com/javascript.htm

- Mozilla Developer Network JavaScript Reference: https://developer.mozilla.org/en-US/docs/Web/JavaScript/Reference

- Mozilla Developer Network JavaScript Guide: https://developer.mozilla.org/en-US/docs/Web/JavaScript/Guide

## 14.12  Overview of jQuery

Many websites use jQuery to provide interaction and dynamic effects on web pages. The free, open-source **jQuery** JavaScript library was developed by John Resig in 2006 to simplify client-side scripting. The jQuery Foundation is a volunteer organization that contributes to the continued development of jQuery and provides jQuery documentation at http://api.jquery.com.

So, what can you do with jQuery? The jQuery API (application programming interface) works along with JavaScript and provides easy ways to dynamically manipulate the CSS properties of elements, detect and react to events (such as mouse movements), and animate elements on a web page, such as image slideshows. And there's more—the jQuery JavaScript library has been thoroughly tested and is compatible with all current browsers. Many web developers and designers have found that jQuery is easier to learn to work with than trying to write and test their own complex JavaScript interactions. However, a basic understanding of JavaScript is useful when working with jQuery.

## 14.13  Adding jQuery to a Web Page

The jQuery library is stored in a .js JavaScript file. There are two ways to access the jQuery library. You can either download the jQuery JavaScript library file and save it to your hard drive or you can access a version of the jQuery JavaScript library file online through a Content Delivery Network (CDN).

### Download jQuery

Visit http://jquery.com/download to download one of the jQuery library .js files. There are several versions of jQuery to choose from. When you visit the download page, right click on "Download the compressed, production jQuery 3.4.1" and save the file with the name of jquery-3.4.1.min.js in your website folder. You can make jQuery available to your web page by adding the following script tag to the head section of your web page document:

```
<script src="jquery-3.4.1.min.js"></script>
```

## Access jQuery via a Content Delivery Network

Google, Microsoft, Amazon, and Media Temple have created free **Content Delivery Network (CDN)** repositories of frequently used code and scripts, such as jQuery. There is no cost for you or your web page visitor to use a CDN. An advantage of using a CDN is that your pages may load faster because your visitor's browser most likely has accessed the CDN in the past and already saved the file in its cache. A disadvantage of using a CDN is that you will always need to have a live Internet connection when you are coding and testing your pages. We'll use Google's CDN in this chapter. To access the jQuery library that is stored in Google's Content Delivery Network (CDN), add the following script tag in the head section of your web page document:

```
<script
src="https://ajax.googleapis.com/ajax/libs/jquery/3.4.1/jquery.min.js">
</script>
```

## The Ready Event

You need to inform the jQuery library when your web page's Document Object Model (DOM) has been completely loaded by the browser. A jQuery statement referred to as the **ready event** is used for this purpose. A jQuery statement consists of a jQuery alias, a selector, and a method in the following format:

```
$(selector).method()
```

The **jQuery alias** is your choice of either the text "jQuery" or the $ character. Most people use the $ character because it is shorter. The **selector** indicates the DOM element(s) that jQuery will work with. The method is an action that jQuery can take. The ready() method indicates the code the browser should execute when the DOM is fully loaded.

In this case, the selector is the document itself, so the syntax for the ready event is as follows:

```
$(document).ready(function() {
    Your JavaScript statements and other jQuery statements go here
});
```

Place your JavaScript statements and additional jQuery statements after the opening line in the ready event. For example, to display an alert box when the DOM is ready for jQuery, code the following:

```
$(document).ready(function() {
  alert("Ready for jQuery");
});
```

**FAQ**    **What's the `function()` part of the ready event?**

The `function()` creates an unnamed, anonymous function that defines a block of code, and, for example, limits the scope of variables declared within the code block. This prevents conflicts, such as those caused by duplicate variable names, that can occur when you are using multiple libraries of code.

## Hands-On Practice 14.10

Let's practice using the jQuery ready event. Open a text editor and enter the code shown below.

```html
<!DOCTYPE html>
<html lang="en">
<head>
<title>JavaScript Practice</title>
<meta charset="utf-8">
<script
src="https://ajax.googleapis.com/ajax/libs/jquery/3.4.1/jquery.min.js">
</script>
<script>
$(document).ready(function() {
  alert("Ready for jQuery");
});
</script>
</head>
<body>
<h1>Using jQuery</h1>
</body>
</html>
```

Save this file as ready.html and open it in the browser. If you are connected to the Internet, the jQuery library at the CDN will be accessed and the alert message will display (see Figure 14.22) when the web page's DOM is fully loaded by the browser. Compare your work with the solution in the student files chapter14/14.10/ready.html.

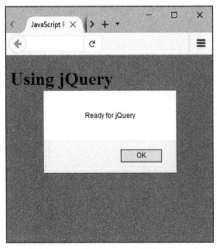

**Figure 14.22** Ready for jQuery

# 14.14 jQuery Selectors

Configure a **jQuery selector** to indicate which DOM elements jQuery will affect. There are a wide variety of selectors—similar to the types of selectors you can configure in CSS. A wildcard selector will cause jQuery to act upon all elements. You could also specify a class, id, or html element selector. In addition, filters, such as `:first` and `:odd` can be applied to selectors. A complete list of jQuery selectors is available at http://api.jquery.com/category/selectors. Table 14.5 shows examples of some commonly used jQuery selectors and their purpose.

Table 14.5 Commonly used jQuery selectors

| Selector | Purpose |
|---|---|
| `$('*')` | wildcard—selects all elements |
| `$('li')` | HTML element selector—selects all li elements |
| `$('.myclass')` | Class selector—selects all elements assigned to the class named myclass |
| `$('#myid')` | Id selector—selects the element assigned to the id named myid |
| `$('nav a')` | HTML element selector—selects all anchor elements contained within the nav element |
| `$('#resources a')` | Id selector and HTML element selector—selects all anchor elements contained within the id named resources |
| `$('li:first')` | Positional selector that selects the first element of that type on the page |
| `$('li:odd')` | Positional selector—selects every other li element on the page |

# 14.15 jQuery Methods

Configure a **jQuery method** to act upon the DOM element(s) you have selected. There are several categories of methods including methods that work with CSS, Effects, Events, Forms, Traversing, Data, Ajax, and Manipulation. The jQuery documentation at http://api.jquery.com provides a somewhat overwhelming list—it takes a while to explore the methods available in the jQuery library. Table 14.6 lists some commonly used jQuery methods.

Table 14.6 Commonly used jQuery methods

| Method | Purpose |
|---|---|
| `attr()` | Gets or sets attributes for the selected element(s) |
| `click()` | Binds a jQuery event handler to the JavaScript click event |
| `css()` | Sets the specified CSS property for the selected element(s) |
| `fadeToggle()` | Displays or hides the selected element(s) by animating their opacity |
| `hover()` | Binds a jQuery event handler to the JavaScript onmouseover event |
| `html()` | Gets or sets HTML contents for the selected element(s) |
| `slideToggle()` | Displays or hides the selected element(s) with a sliding motion |
| `toggle()` | Displays or hides the selected element(s) |

Let's start by delving into the `css()` and `click()` methods. Use the **css()** method to set a CSS property for the selector. The `css()` method accepts a pair of string expressions that indicate the CSS property and value. For example, the following script, found in the student files (chapter14/color.html), will select all li elements on a page and configure them with a text color of red, use the $('li') selector along with the css() method to set the color property to #FF0000.

```
$(document).ready(function(){
     $('li').css('color','#FF0000');
  });
```

Use the **click()** method to bind, or associate, a JavaScript click event for the selected element(s) with an event handler action in jQuery. jQuery will execute the event handler when the event occurs. The web page shown in Figure 14.23 (see the student files chapter14/changeme.html) demonstrates the click event. The click event has been bound to the anchor element and causes the text color of every other li element to change when the click event fires. The script is as follows:

```
$(document).ready(function() {
$('a').click(function(){
     $('li:even').css('color','#006600');
     });
});
```

Figure 14.23 The changeme.html file displayed in a browser; the browser on the right shows the resulting web page after the "Click Me" hyperlink is clicked.

## Hands-On Practice 14.11

The best way to learn to use jQuery is to practice coding. You'll work with the click() and toggle() methods in this Hands-On Practice. You'll configure CSS to initially hide a block of text by setting the display property to none. Then, you'll use jQuery to bind a click event to an event handler that invokes the **toggle()** method to swap back and forth between displaying and hiding a block of text. Open a text editor and enter the code shown below.

```
<!DOCTYPE html>
<html lang="en">
<head>
<title>jQuery Toggle Practice</title>
<meta charset="utf-8">
<style>
#details { display: none; }
</style>
```

```
<script
src="https://ajax.googleapis.com/ajax/libs/jquery/3.4.1/jquery.min.js">
</script>
<script>
$(document).ready(function() {
    $('#more').click(function(){
        $('#details').toggle();
    });
});
</script>
</head>
<body>
<h1>jQuery</h1>
<p>Many websites, including Amazon and Google, use jQuery, to provide
interaction and dynamic effects on web pages. <a href="#"
id="more">More</a></p>
<div id="details"><p>The jQuery API (application programming
interface) works along with JavaScript and provides easy ways to
dynamically manipulate the CSS properties of elements, detect and
react to events (such as mouse movements), and animate elements on a
web page, such as image slideshows.</p>
</div>
</body>
</html>
```

Save this file as toggle.html and open it in the browser. As shown in Figure 14.24, the second paragraph does not initially display. Click on the "More" hyperlink to display the second paragraph. Next, click on the "More" hyperlink again to hide the second paragraph. The "More" hyperlink works as a toggle to hide and show the div assigned to the id details. Compare your work with the solution in the student files chapter14/14.11/toggle.html.

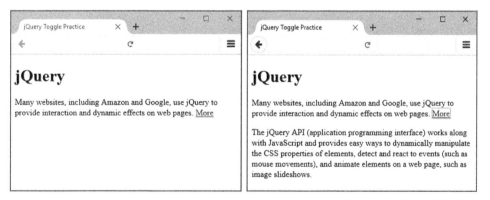

**Figure 14.24** The toggle.html file displayed in a browser; the browser on the right shows the resulting web page after the "More" hyperlink is clicked.

Experiment with the **fadeToggle()** and **slideToggle()** methods. You can control the speed of the effect of these methods by passing a duration parameter—valid values are `'slow'`, `'fast'`, and a number indicating the milliseconds. Configure the duration of the `fadeToggle()` to be 1000 milliseconds. Open your file in a text editor and replace the `$('#details').toggle();` statement with the following:

```
$('#details').fadeToggle(10000);
```

Test in a browser. Did you notice the text fade in? Feel free to experiment with other values for the duration parameter.

Next, open your file in a text editor and replace the `fadeToggle()` method with the `slideToggle()` method with slow duration as follows:

```
$('#details').slideToggle('slow');
```

Test in a browser. Did you notice the text slide in? Feel free to experiment with other values for the duration parameter.

You can find out more about these methods at http://api.jquery.com/fadeToggle and http://api.jquery.com/slideToggle.

# 14.16 jQuery Image Gallery

You created an interactive image gallery with CSS in Chapter 11. In the next Hands-On Practice you'll explore using jQuery and JavaScript along with CSS to create three versions of the image gallery (shown in Figure 14.25) with different interactions.

**Figure 14.25** Image gallery with jQuery interactions

You'll work with some jQuery methods you have already used, the `click()`, `css()`, and `fadeToggle()` methods. You'll also explore the `hover()`, `html()`, and `attr()` methods. Use the **hover()** method to bind, or associate, the jQuery **mouseenter** and **mouseleave** events for the selected element(s) with an event handler action in jQuery. jQuery will execute the event handler when the event occurs.

The **html()** method allows you to dynamically configure the content of an HTML element. You'll use the html() to change the text that is displayed within a figcaption element. The **attr()** method allows you to configure the value of HTML attributes. You'll use the attr() method to change the src and alt attributes of the large gallery image.

## Hands-On Practice 14.12

Create a new folder called gallery14. Copy all the images from the chapter14/starters/ gallery folder in the student files to the new gallery14 folder. Launch a text editor and modify the chapter14/template.html file to configure a web page as indicated:

1. Configure the text, "Image Gallery", within an h1 element and within the title element.

2. Code a div element assigned to the id named gallery. This div will consist of an unordered list and a figure element. The unordered list will contain the thumbnail image links. The figure element will contain the large gallery image and a figcaption element.

3. Configure an unordered list within the div. Code six li elements, one for each thumbnail image. The thumbnail images will function as image links. Each anchor tag will include a title attribute with a descriptive text title. An example of the first li element is

```
<li>
<a href="photo1.jpg" title="Golden Gate Bridge"><img
src="photo1thumb.jpg" width="100" height="75" alt="Golden
Gate Bridge"></a>
</li>
```

4. Configure all six li elements in a similar manner. Substitute the actual name of each image file for the href and src values in the code. Write your own descriptive text for each image. Use photo2.jpg and photo2thumb.jpg in the second li element. Use photo3.jpg and photo3thumb.jpg in the third li element, and so on for all six images. Save the file as index.html in the gallery14 folder.

5. Configure a figure element below the unordered list within the div. The figure element will contain an img tag that displays photo1.jpg and a figcaption element that contains the text "Golden Gate Bridge".

6. Code a style element in the head section of your document. Configure embedded CSS as follows:

   a. Configure the body element selector with a dark background color (#333333) and a light gray text color (#EAEAEA).

   b. Configure the gallery id selector. Set the width to 800px.

   c. Configure the unordered list within the #gallery with a width of 300 pixels, no list marker, and left float.

   d. Configure the list item elements within the #gallery with inline display, left float, and 16 pixels of padding.

   e. Configure the img elements within the #gallery to not display a border.

   f. Configure the figure element selector with 30 pixels of top padding and center text alignment.

   g. Configure the figcaption element selector with bold font and 1.5em font size.

**7.** Code a script element in the head section of your document that accesses the Google jQuery CDN.

```
<script
src="https://ajax.googleapis.com/ajax/libs/jquery/3.4.1/jquery.min.js">
</script>
```

**8.** Code jQuery and JavaScript statements in the head section of your document that determine when a mouse is placed over a thumbnail image link and change the gallery image and description.

   a. Code a pair of script tags that contain the jQuery ready event.

```
<script>
$(document).ready(function(){

});
</script>
```

   b. Add the following code within the ready event to listen for the hover event on anchor elements in the `#gallery` div.

```
$('#gallery a').hover(function(){

});
```

   c. Code JavaScript statements within the hover method's function to store href value and title value from the anchor tag in JavaScript variables. The Javascript keyword `this` indicates that the attributes refer to the current selector.

```
var galleryHref = $(this).attr('href');
var galleryAlt = $(this).attr('title');
```

   d. Use the jQuery `attr()` method to set the `src` and `alt` attributes on the large gallery image. Add the following statement below the variable assignment.

```
$('figure img').attr({ src: galleryHref, alt: galleryAlt });
```

   e. Use the jQuery `html()` method to change the text displayed within the figcaption element: Add the following statement below the `attr()` method statement.

```
$('figcaption').html(galleryAlt);
```

   f. The entire jQuery code block is

```
<script>
$(document).ready(function(){
  $('#gallery a').hover(function(){
     var galleryHref = $(this).attr('href');
     var galleryAlt = $(this).attr('title');
   $('figure img').attr({ src: galleryHref, alt: galleryAlt });
     $('figcaption').html(galleryAlt);
   });
});
</script>
```

9. Save your file in the gallery14 folder as hover.html and display it in a browser. The large gallery image will change when you hover on an image link. Compare your work with the student files (chapter14/14.12/hover.html).

10. Next, create a new version of the image gallery that will change the large gallery image and description when a web page visitor clicks on a thumbnail image instead of placing the mouse over a thumbnail image. Launch a text editor and open hover.html. Save the file with a new name: click.html. Edit the jQuery code block. Replace hover with click. By default, the hyperlink will open the larger image in a new window. To prevent this from happening, code return false; after the html() method statement. The entire jQuery code block is:

```
<script>
$(document).ready(function(){
  $('#gallery a').click(function(){
     var galleryHref = $(this).attr('href');
     var galleryAlt = $(this).attr('title');
     $('figure img').attr({ src: galleryHref, alt: galleryAlt });
     $('figcaption').html(galleryAlt);
     return false;
  });
});
</script>
```

11. Save your file in the gallery14 folder and display it in a browser. The large gallery image will change when you click on an image link. Compare your work with the student files (chapter14/14.12/click.html).

12. Now, let's experiment with a slightly different jQuery interaction for the image gallery, using the fadeToggle() method, which either displays or hides selected elements. In order to force the fadeToggle() method to always fade in and display the large gallery image when a thumbnail image is clicked, you need to hide the figure element before invoking fadeToggle(). Launch a text editor, open the click.html, save the file with a new name: toggle.html, and add two new statements to the jQuery code block as shown below:

```
<script>
$(document).ready(function(){
    $('#gallery a').click(function(){
       var galleryHref = $(this).attr('href');
       var galleryAlt = $(this).attr('title');
       $('figure').css('display','none');
       $('figure img').attr({ src: galleryHref, alt: galleryAlt });
       $('figcaption').html(galleryAlt);
       $('figure').fadeToggle(1000);
       return false;
    });
});
</script>
```

13. Save your file in the gallery14 folder and display it in a browser. When you click on a thumbnail image link, the large gallery image area will briefly fade to black and then fade in with the new gallery image. Experiment with different duration values for the fadeToggle. Compare your work the student files (chapter14/14.12/toggle.html).

# 14.17 jQuery Plugins

jQuery is open-source and designed for continued enhancement and extension. An experienced web developer can create a new jQuery method and build a **plugin** that extends the functionality of jQuery. There are many jQuery plugins available, providing interactions and functionality such as slideshows, tooltips, and form validation. Visit the jQuery Plugin Registry at http://plugins.jquery.com/ for a list. You can also find jQuery plugins by searching the Web.

When you find a plugin that you think you may want to use, check the plugin documentation which will explain the purpose of the plugin, describe how to work with the plugin, and often provide examples of using the plugin. Check the documentation to verify that it is compatible with the version of jQuery you are using. Verify the terms of the license for use of the plugin—many plugins use an MIT license (https://opensource.org/licenses/MIT), which freely allows use and distribution of both noncommercial and commercial work. Also, search the Web and see what types of comments and/or questions others have written about the plugin. If there are a lot of people struggling with using a plugin, you may want to choose a different one! You'll work with two popular jQuery plugins in the following Hands-On Practice exercises.

 Hands-On Practice 14.13

In this Hands-On Practice you'll create the web page shown in Figure 14.26 as you work with the very easy to use fotorama plugin for jQuery (https://fotorama.io), which configures a slideshow.

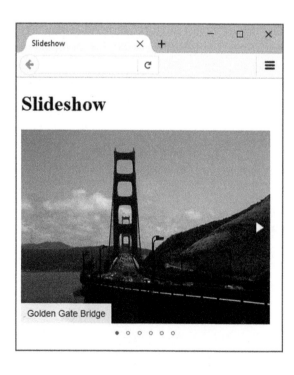

Figure 14.26 jQuery plugin slideshow

Create a new folder called slideshow. Copy the following images from the chapter14/ starters/gallery folder in the student files to the new slideshow folder: photo1.jpg, photo2.jpg, photo3.jpg, photo4.jpg, photo5.jpg, and photo6.jpg. Launch a text editor and modify the chapter14/template.html file to configure a web page as indicated:

1. Configure the text, "Slideshow," within an h1 element and within the title element.

2. Code a div element assigned to the class named fotorama below the h1 element. The slideshow will not automatically play by default. The plugin's documentation specifies that adding the `data-autoplay="true"` attribute to the fotorama div element will configure automatic play. Code the opening div tag as follows:

   ```
   <div class="fotorama" data-autoplay="true">
   ```

3. Code an img tag for each photograph within the div. Configure both the `alt` and the `data-caption` attribute with a description of the image. The plugin requires the `data-caption` attribute to display a caption for the image in the slideshow. An example of the first img element is

   ```
   <img src="photo1.jpg" data-caption="Golden Gate Bridge"
   alt="Golden Gate Bridge">
   ```

   Configure the other images in a similar manner.

4. Code the following link tag in the head section of your document to access the CSS needed by the fotorama plugin:

   ```
   <link href="https://cdnjs.cloudflare.com/ajax/libs/fotorama/4.6.4/fotorama.css"
   rel="stylesheet">
   ```

5. Code the following script element in the head section of your document to access the jQuery library:

   ```
   <script src=
   "https://ajax.googleapis.com/ajax/libs/jquery/3.4.1/jquery.min.js">
   </script>
   ```

6. Code the following script element in the head section of your document to access the fotorama library:

   ```
   <script src=
   "https://cdnjs.cloudflare.com/ajax/libs/fotorama/4.6.4/fotorama.js">
   </script>
   ```

7. That's all there is to it! Save your file with the name index.html in the slideshow folder and display it in a browser. The slideshow will automatically start to play. Place your mouse over the image to trigger the caption and side arrows to appear. Select the side arrow or bottom image indicator to move directly to a specific image. Compare your work with the student files (chapter14/14.13/index.html).

## Hands-On Practice 14.14

In this Hands-On Practice you'll work with the jQuery validation plugin (https://jqueryvalidation.org), which performs basic form validation. This plugin has many features listed in its documentation. For example when you configure a form control, such as an input element, with one of class names specified in the documentation, the plugin will automatically perform the corresponding edit. In addition the plugin is configured to assign the class named error to the error messages it generates. A partial list of class names supported by the plugin for data validation is shown in Table 14.7.

Table 14.7 Selected jQuery validate plugin class names and actions

| Class Name | Action |
|---|---|
| required | Verifies whether data is entered |
| email | Verifies whether data is in e-mail format |
| digits | Verifies whether data is a positive integer |
| url | Verifies whether data is in url format |

To get started, create a new folder called jform. You'll work with the web page shown in Figure 14.27. Launch a text editor and open the chapter14/formstarter.html file. Edit the code as indicated:

Figure 14.27 Newsletter signup form

1. Style error messages. Edit the embedded CSS and configure styles for a class named error with a 1em left margin and red, italic, .90em size, Arial or sans-serif font typeface:

```
.error { font-family: Arial, sans-serif;
         font-style: italic; font-size: .90em;
         color: #FF0000; margin-left: 1em; }
```

2. Code the following script element in the head section of your document to access the jQuery library:

```
<script src=
"https://ajax.googleapis.com/ajax/libs/jquery/3.4.1/jquery.min.js">
</script>
```

3. Code the following script element in the head section of your document to access the Validate plugin:

```
<script src=
"https://cdnjs.cloudflare.com/ajax/libs/jquery-validate/1.19.0/
jquery.validate.js">
</script>
```

4. Code script tags, the jQuery ready event, and a jQuery statement that will invoke form validation in the head section of the document:

```
<script>
$(document).ready(function(){
$('form').validate();
});
</script>
```

5. Edit the HTML to configure the form validation. The Name is required. The e-mail address is required and should be in e-mail format.

   a. Add `class="required"` to the input tag for the Name textbox.
   b. Add `class="required email"` to the input tag for the e-mail textbox.

6. Save your file with the name index.html in the jform folder and display it in a browser. Try clicking the Sign Up button without entering any data. The jQuery Validation plugin will check for the errors you specified and it will display two error messages as shown in Figure 14.28.

Figure 14.28 jQuery validate plugin error messages

7. Next, enter information in both textboxes but do not enter a correct e-mail address. The jQuery Validation plugin will display an error message as shown in Figure 14.29.

Figure 14.29 jQuery validate plugin e-mail error message

8. Finally, submit the form with both a name and a valid e-mail address entered. With all specified edits passed, the browser will send the form information to the server-side script configured in the form's action attribute and you'll see a confirmation page display. Compare your work with the student files (chapter14/14.14/index.html).

# 14.18 jQuery Resources

This chapter has just touched on some of the power and functionality of jQuery. There is so much more to learn! You may wish to do further research using some of the following online resources:

- jQuery

  http://jquery.com

- jQuery Documentation

  http://docs.jquery.com

- How jQuery Works

  http://learn.jquery.com/about-jquery/how-jquery-works

- jQuery Fundamentals

  http://jqfundamentals.com/chapter/jquery-basics

- jQuery Tutorials for Web Designers

  https://webdesignerwall.com/tutorials/jquery-tutorials-for-designers

 **Checkpoint 14.5**

1. Describe the two ways the web developers can obtain the jQuery JavaScript Library.

2. Explain the purpose of the `css()` method.

3. Describe the purpose of the ready event.

# Chapter Summary

This chapter introduced the use of JavaScript as a client-side scripting language in web pages. You learned how to embed script blocks in web pages, display an alert message, use an event handler, and validate a form. Visit the textbook web site at https://www.webdevfoundations.net for examples, the links listed in this chapter, and updated information.

## Key Terms

| | | |
|---|---|---|
| `alert()` | Content Delivery Network (CDN) | object |
| `attr()` | debug | object-based |
| `click()` | document | `onclick` |
| `css()` | event | `onload` |
| `hover()` | event handler | `onmouseout` |
| `html()` | event listener | `onmouseover` |
| `fadeToggle()` | form handling | `onsubmit` |
| `prompt()` | function | plugin |
| `slideToggle()` | image swapping | popup window |
| `toggle()` | invoke | `ready` event |
| `<script>` | jQuery | reserved word |
| `write()` | jQuery alias | scripting language |
| arithmetic operators | jQuery method | scope |
| case-sensitive | jQuery selector | server-side processing |
| client-side processing | jump menus | string |
| comments | method | `var` |
| comparison operators | mouseover | variable |
| concatenation | `null` | window object |

## Review Questions

### Multiple Choice

1. Which of the following is a technique for creating reusable JavaScript code?
   a. define a function
   b. create a script block
   c. define an if statement
   d. use an onclick event handler

2. When the user positions the mouse pointer on a link, the browser detects which one of these events?
   a. mouseon
   b. mousehover
   c. mouseover
   d. mousedown

3. When the user moves the mouse pointer away from a link it had been hovering over, the browser detects which one of these events?
   a. mouseoff
   b. mouseout
   c. mouseaway
   d. mouseup

4. Which method of the window can be used to display a message to the user?
   a. `alert()`
   b. `message()`
   c. `status()`
   d. `display()`

5. Which of the following will assign the value 5 to the variable `productCost`?

   a. `productCost => 5;`

   b. `productCost <= 5;`

   c. `productCost == 5;`

   d. `productCost = 5;`

6. A condition (`productCost > 5`) is used in an if statement. Which of the following values of `productCost` will result in this condition being evaluated as true?

   a. 4

   b. 5

   c. 5.1

   d. none of the above

7. Which of the following can describe JavaScript as used in a web page?

   a. a scripting language

   b. a markup language

   c. an easy form of Java

   d. a language created by Microsoft

8. Which of the following is the code for accessing the contents of an input box named `userData` on a form?

   a. `document.forms[0].userData`

   b. `document.forms[0].userData.value`

   c. `document.forms[0].userData.contents`

   d. `document.forms[0].userData.data`

9. Which of the following is the code to invoke a function called `isValid()` when the user clicks the submit button?

   a. `<input type="text" onmouseout="isValid();">`

   b. `<input type="submit" onsubmit="isValid();">`

   c. `<form method="post" action="URL" onsubmit="return isValid();">`

   d. `<form method="post" action="URL" onclick="return isValid();">`

10. A web page document is considered to be which of the following in the Document Object Model?

    a. object

    b. property

    c. method

    d. attribute

11. What does the jQuery code snippet `$('div')` select?

    a. the element assigned to an id named div

    b. all div elements

    c. the first div element

    d. the last div element

## Fill in the Blank

12. The comparison operator that checks for the exactly equal to condition is _____.

13. Use the _____ jQuery method to configure the value of HTML attributes.

14. The _____ object is assumed to exist and it is not necessary to include it as an object when referring to its methods and properties.

15. The jQuery _____ is triggered when the DOM of a web page is completely loaded by a browser.

16. A form control button can be used with a(n) _____ event handler to run a script when the user clicks a button.

17. jQuery is a(n) _____ library.

18. Use the _____ jQuery method to configure CSS styles.

## Short Answer

19. Describe at least three popular uses for JavaScript.

20. Describe how you could debug JavaScript code when it is not working properly.

## Apply Your Knowledge

1. **Predict the Result.** Given the following code, what will happen when the user clicks the button?

```
<!DOCTYPE html>
<html lang="en">
<head>
<title>JavaScript Practice</title>
<meta charset="utf-8">
<script>
function mystory() {
    alert('hello');
}
</script>
</head>
<body>
<h1>Using JavaScript</h1>
<button onclick="mystory()">Click Me</button>
</body>
</html>
```

2. **Fill in the Missing Code.** This web page should prompt the user for the name of a song and print the song name in the document. The missing code is indicated by "_". Fill in the missing code.

```
<!DOCTYPE html>
<html lang="en">
<head>
<title>JavaScript Practice</title>
<meta charset="utf-8">
</head>
<body>
<h1>Using JavaScript</h1>
<script>
var userSong;
userSong = _("Please enter your favorite song title.");
document._(_);
</script>
</body>
</html>
```

3. **Find the Error.** When this page is loaded in the web browser, it is supposed to display an error message if the user has not typed any data in the Name input box. It is not working properly, so the form is submitted regardless of the missing input. Fix the errors so that the form does not submit if there is no information in the Name input box. Correct the errors and describe the process you followed.

```
<!DOCTYPE html>
<html lang="en">
<head>
<title>JavaScript Practice</title>
<meta charset="utf-8">
```

```
<script>
function validateForm() {
if (document.forms[0].userName.value == "" ) {
    aert("Name field cannot be empty.");
    return false;
} // end if
aert("Name and age are valid.");
return true;
} // end function validateForm
</script>
</head>
<body>
<h1>JavaScript Form Handling</h1>
<form method="post"
action="http://webdevbasics.net/scripts/demo.php"
    onsubmit="return validateUser();">
  <label>Name: <input type="text" name="userName"></label>
  <br>
  <input type="submit" value="Send information">
</form>
</body>
</html>
```

## Hands-On Exercises

1. Practice writing event handlers.

   a. Write the HTML tag and event handler to pop up an alert message that says "Welcome" when the user clicks a button.

   b. Write the HTML tag and event handler to pop up an alert message that says "Welcome" when the user moves the mouse pointer over a hypertext link that says "Hover for a welcome message".

   c. Write the HTML tag and event handler to pop up an alert message that says "Welcome" when the user moves the mouse pointer away from a hypertext link that says "Move your mouse pointer here for a welcome message".

2. Practice writing jQuery selectors:

   a. Write the jQuery selector that will select all anchor tags in the main element.

   b. Write the jQuery selector that will select the first div on a web page.

3. Create a web page that will pop up an alert message that welcomes the user to the web page. Use a script block in the head section for this task.

4. Create a web page that will prompt the user for a name and age, and write a message using the name and age in the message. Use the `prompt()` method and variables to accomplish this.

5. Create a web page that will prompt the user for a color name. Use this color name to write the text "This is your favorite color!". The `fgColor` property of the document changes the text color of all text in a document. Use the `fgColor` property to accomplish this task.

6. Continue with Hands-On Practice 14.9. Add a text box for the user's city. Ensure that this text box is not empty when the form is submitted. If the city text box is empty, pop up an appropriate alert message and do not submit the form. If the city text box is not empty and the other data is valid, submit the form.

7. Using Hands-On Practice 14.12 as a guide, create an image gallery web page with your own favorite photos. Remember to optimize each photo for web display.

8. Using Hands-On Practice 14.13 as a guide, create a slideshow web page with your own favorite photos. Remember to optimize each photo for web display. If the jQuery plugin is not available for some reason, search for and use an alternate jQuery slide-show plugin.

## Web Research

1. Use the resources listed in this chapter as a starting point, but also search the Web for additional resources on JavaScript. Create a web page that lists at least five useful resources, along with a brief description of each. Organize your web page with a list that provides the name of the site, the URL, a brief description of what is offered, and a recommended page (such as a tutorial, free script, and so on) for each resource. Place your name in an e-mail link on the web page.

2. Use the resources listed in the chapter as a starting point, but also search the Web for additional resources on JavaScript. Find either a tutorial or a free download that uses JavaScript. Create a web page that uses the code or download that you found. Describe the effect and list the URL of the resource on the web page. Place your name in an e-mail link on the web page.

3. Use the resources listed in the chapter as a starting point, but also search the Web for additional resources on jQuery. Locate a jQuery plugin that is appealing and/or useful to you. Create a web page that uses the jQuery plugin. Describe the purpose of the plugin and list the URL of the plugin documentation on the web page. Place your name in an e-mail link on the web page.

# WEBSITE CASE STUDY

## Adding JavaScript

Each of the following case studies has continued throughout most of the text. This chapter adds JavaScript to selected web pages from each of the case studies.

## JavaJam Coffee Bar

See Chapter 2 for an introduction to the JavaJam Coffee Bar case study. Figure 2.32 shows a site map for the JavaJam website. The pages were created in earlier chapters. You have three tasks in this case study:

1. Create a new folder for this JavaJam case study.

2. Add the date that the document was last modified to the bottom of the Home page (index.html).

3. Add an alert message to the Menu page (menu.html).

## Hands-On Practice Case Study

**Task 1: The Website Folder.** Create a folder called javajam14. Copy all the files from your Chapter 9 javajam9 folder into the javajam14 folder.

**Task 2: Add a Date to the Home Page.** Launch a text editor and open the index.html file. You will add the date that the document was last modified to the bottom of the index.html page.

You have the option to complete this task with JavaScript or to complete this task with jQuery.

**Option 1: Using JavaScript.** Modify the page as follows:

- In the footer area after the e-mail link, add a script block contained within a div element that will write the following message to the document:

  "This page was last modified on: date"

- Use the `document.lastModified` property to print the date.

Save the index.html page and test it in the browser. You should see the new information in the footer area below the e-mail address.

**Option 2: Using JavaScript and jQuery.** Modify the page as follows:

- In the footer area after the e-mail link, code a div element.

- Add a script tag in the head section to access a jQuery CDN.

- Code a jQuery script block that includes the ready event and uses the `html()` method to display the message "This page was last modified on:" and the `document.lastModified` value within the new div.

Save the index.html page and test it in the browser. You should see the new information in the footer area below the e-mail address.

**Task 3: Display an Alert Message on the Menu Page.** Launch a text editor and open the menu.html file. You will add JavaScript to the menu.html page so that an alert message will pop up when the user places the mouse over the phrase "Mug Club". The alert message will indicate "JavaJam Mug Club Members get a 10% discount on each cup of coffee!"

You have the option to complete this task with JavaScript or to complete this task with jQuery.

**Option 1: Using Javascript.** Modify the page as follows:

- Add a hypertext link to the first paragraph with an onmouseover event handler as follows:

  ```
  <a href="#" onmouseover=
  "alert('JavaJam Mug Club Members get a 10% discount on each cup
  of coffee!');">Mug Club</a>
  ```

Save the menu.html page and test it in the browser. Figure 14.30 shows the alert message when users place their mouse pointer over the hyperlinked phrase.

**Option 2: Using JavaScript and jQuery.** Modify the page as follows:

- Configure a hyperlink in the paragraph for the text "Mug Club".

- Code # as the value of the href attribute in the anchor tag.

- Add a script tag in the head section to access a jQuery CDN

- Code a jQuery script block that includes the ready event.

- Code a jQuery statement to listen for the hover event on anchor tags in the main element. Code JavaScript to display an alert box with the message "JavaJam Mug Club Members get a 10% discount on each cup of coffee!" when the hover occurs.

Save the menu.html page and test it in the browser. Figure 14.30 shows the alert message when users place their mouse pointer over the hyperlinked phrase.

Figure 14.30 JavaJam Menu page with the mouseover alert

## Fish Creek Animal Clinic

See Chapter 2 for an introduction to the Fish Creek Animal Clinic case study. Figure 2.36 shows a site map for the Fish Creek website. The pages were created in earlier chapters. You have three tasks in this case study:

1. Create a new folder for this Fish Creek case study.

2. Add the date last modified to the Home page (index.html).

3. Add an alert message to the Ask the Vet page (menu.html).

### Hands-On Practice Case Study

**Task 1: The Website Folder.** Create a folder called fishcreek14. Copy all the files from your Chapter 9 fishcreek9 folder into the fishcreek14 folder.

**Task 2: Add a Date to the Home Page.** Launch a text editor and open the index.html file. You will add the date that the document was last modified to the bottom of the index.html page.

You have the option to complete this task with JavaScript or to complete this task with jQuery.

**Option 1: Using JavaScript.** Modify the page as follows:

- In the page footer section after the e-mail link, add div element that contains a script block that will write the following message to the document:

  "This page was last modified on: date"

- Use the `document.lastModified` property to print the date.

Save the index.html page and test it in the browser. You should see the new information in the footer area below the e-mail address.

**Option 2: Using JavaScript and jQuery.** Modify the page as follows:

- In the footer area after the e-mail link, code a div element.
- Add a script tag in the head section to access a jQuery CDN.
- Code a jQuery script block that includes the ready event and uses the `html()` method to display the message "This page was last modified on:" and the `document.lastModified` value within the new div.

Save the index.html page and test it in the browser. You should see the new information in the footer area below the e-mail address.

**Task 3: Display an Alert Message on the Ask the Vet Page.** Launch a text editor and open the askvet.html file. You will configure the askvet.html page so that an alert message will pop up when the page is displayed in the browser.

You have the option to complete this task with JavaScript or to complete this task with jQuery.

**Option 1: Using JavaScript.**

- Edit the body tag as follows:

```
<body onload="alert('Send in your question to Ask the Vet and
receive a 10% discount');">
```

- The load event occurs when the web page begins to load in the browser. The `onload` event handler in this case pops up an alert message.
- Save the file and test it in the browser. Your display should be similar to Figure 14.31.

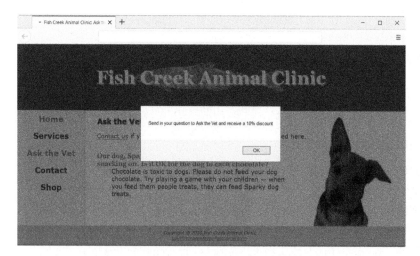

**Figure 14.31** Fish Creek Animal Hospital Ask the Vet page

**Option 2: Using JavaScript and jQuery.** Modify the page as follows:

- Add a script tag in the head section to access a jQuery CDN.
- Code a jQuery script block that includes the ready event. Code JavaScript within the ready event to display an alert box with the message, "'Send in your question to Ask the Vet and receive a 10% discount!".
- Save the file and test it in the browser. Your display should be similar to Figure 14.31.

## Pacific Trails Resort

See Chapter 2 for an introduction to the Pacific Trails case study. Figure 2.40 shows a site map for the Pacific Trails Resort website. The pages were created in earlier chapters. You have three tasks:

1. Create a new folder for this Pacific Trails case study.

2. Add an alert message that displays a message when the browser renders the Yurts page (yurts.html).

3. Add the date that the document was last modified to the bottom of the Home page (index.html).

### Hands-On Practice Case Study

**Task 1: The Website Folder.** Create a folder called pacific14. Copy all of the files from your Chapter 9 pacific9 folder into the pacific14 folder.

**Task 2: Display an Alert Message on the Yurts Page.** Launch a text editor and open the yurts.html file. You will configure the yurts.html page so that an alert message will pop up when the page is displayed in the browser.

You have the option to complete this task with JavaScript or to complete this task with jQuery.

**Option 1: Using JavaScript.**

- Edit the body tag as follows:

```
<body onload="alert('Today only - 10% off on a weekend - coupon code ZenTen');">
```

- The load event occurs when the web page begins to load in the browser. The `onload` event handler in this case pops up an alert message.

Save the file and test it in the browser. Your display should be similar to Figure 14.32.

Figure 14.32 A message displays when the Yurts page is loaded by the browser

**Option 2: Using JavaScript and jQuery**. Modify the page as follows:

- Add a script tag in the head section to access a jQuery CDN.

- Code a jQuery script block that includes the ready event. Code JavaScript within the ready event to display an alert box with the message, "Today only—10% off on a weekend—coupon code ZenTen".

Save the file and test it in the browser. Your display should be similar to Figure 14.32.

**Task 3: Add a Date to the Home Page**. Launch a text editor and open the index.html file. You will add the date that the document was last modified to the bottom of the index.html page.

You have the option to complete this task with JavaScript or to complete this task with jQuery.

**Option 1: Using JavaScript.**

- In the footer area after the e-mail link, add a script block contained within a div element that will write the following message to the document: "This page was last modified on: date"

- Use the `document.lastModified` property to print the date.

- Save the index.html page and test it in the browser. You should see the new information in the footer area below the e-mail address.

**Option 2: Using JavaScript and jQuery**. Modify the page as follows:

- In the footer area after the e-mail link, code a div element.

- Add a script tag in the head section to access a jQuery CDN.

- Code a jQuery script block that includes the ready event and uses the `html()` method to display the message "This page was last modified on:" and the `document.lastModified` value within the new div.

- Save the index.html page and test it in the browser. You should see the new information in the footer area below the e-mail address.

## Path of Light Yoga Studio

See Chapter 2 for an introduction to the Path of Light Yoga Studio case study. Figure 2.44 shows a site map for the Path of Light Yoga Studio website. The pages were created in earlier chapters. You have three tasks in this case study.

1. Create a new folder for this Path of Light Yoga Studio case study.

2. Add the date last modified to the footer section of the Schedule page (schedule.html).

3. Add an alert message that displays a message when the browser renders the Classes page (classes.html).

### Hands-On Practice Case Study

**Task 1: The Website Folder.** Create a folder called yoga14. Copy all the files from your Chapter 9 yoga9 folder into the yoga14 folder.

**Task 2: Add a Date to the Schedule Page.** Launch a text editor and open the schedule.html file. You will add the date that the document was last modified to the bottom of the schedule.html page. You have the option to complete this task with JavaScript or to complete this task with jQuery.

**Option 1: Using JavaScript.** Modify the page as follows:

- In the page footer section after the e-mail link, add a div element containing a script block that will write the following message to the document:

  "This page was last modified on: date"

- Use the `document.lastModified` property to print the date.

Save the file and test it in a browser.

You should see the new information in the footer area below the e-mail address.

**Option 2: Using JavaScript and jQuery.** Modify the page as follows:

- In the footer area after the e-mail link, code a div element.

- Add a script tag in the head section to access a jQuery CDN.

- Code a jQuery script block that includes the ready event and uses the `html()` method to display the message "This page was last modified on:" and the `document.lastModified` value within the new div.

Save the schedule.html page and test it in the browser. You should see the new information in the footer area below the e-mail address.

**Task 3: Display an Alert Message on the Classes Page.** Launch a text editor and open the classes.html file. You will configure the classes.html page so that an alert message will pop up when the page is displayed in the browser.

You have the option to complete this task with JavaScript or to complete this task with jQuery.

**Option 1: Using JavaScript.**

- Edit the body tag as follows:

  ```
  <body onload="alert('Yin Yoga classes begin next month!');">
  ```

- The load event occurs when the web page begins to load in the browser. The `onload` event handler in this case pops up an alert message.

- Save the file and test it in the browser. Your display should be similar to Figure 14.33.

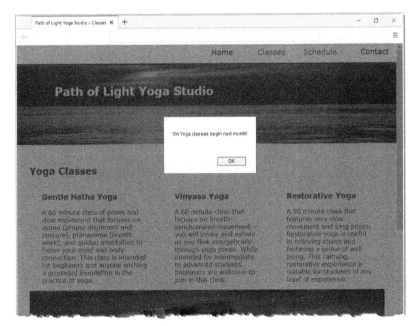

Figure 14.33 A message displays when the Classes page is loaded by the browser. Copyright © 2016 Path Of Light Yoga.

**Option 2: Using JavaScript and jQuery.** Modify the page as follows:

- Add a script tag in the head section to access a jQuery CDN.

- Code a jQuery script block that includes the ready event. Code JavaScript within the ready event to display an alert box with the message, "Yin Yoga classes begin next month!".

- Save the file and test it in the browser. Your display should be similar to Figure 14.33.

## Web Project

See Chapter 5 for an introduction to the Web Project case study. Review the goals of your website and determine whether the use of JavaScript in order to add interactivity would add value to your site. If so, add it appropriately. Check with your instructor regarding the required use of interactivity (with or without jQuery) in your Web project.

Select one or more from the following:

- Choose one of the examples from the chapter to add an alert message to grab the user's attention with regard to important information.

- Choose one of the examples from the chapter to add data validation to a form on your website.

- Display a slideshow of images using a jQuery plugin

- Locate a JavaScript or jQuery tutorial on the Web and adapt the code for your web project

Decide where to apply the interactive technology to your site. Modify the page(s), save the page(s), and test it in a browser.

# Web Developer's Handbook

In the following Appendices you will find a variety of resources that can help you be a more productive web developer.

## APPENDIXES

Appendix A. HTML5 Quick Reference contains a list of commonly used HTML5 elements and attributes

Appendix B. Special Entity Characters contains a list of codes needed to display symbols and other special characters on web pages

Appendix C. CSS Property Reference contains a list of commonly used properties and values

Appendix D. WCAG 2.1 Quick Reference lists the WCAG 2.1 accessibility principles and the textbook chapters that discuss related coding or design techniques

Appendix E. Landmark Roles with ARIA

Appendix F. FTP Tutorial provides a brief introduction to using File Transfer Protocol

Appendix G. The Web-Safe Color Palette provides examples of each color along with hexadecimal and decimal RGB values

# HTML5 Quick Reference

## Commonly Used HTML5 Elements

| Element | Purpose | Commonly Used Attributes |
|---------|---------|--------------------------|
| `<!-- -->` | Comment | *Not applicable* |
| `<a>` | Anchor tag: configures hyperlinks | accesskey, class, href, id, name, rel, style, tabindex, target, title |
| `<abbr>` | Configures an abbreviation | class, id, style |
| `<address>` | Configures contact information | class, id, style |
| `<area>` | Configures an area in an image map | accesskey, alt, class, href, hreflang, id, media, shape, style, tabindex, target |
| `<article>` | Configures an independent section of a document as an article | class, id, style |
| `<aside>` | Configures tangential content | class, id, style |
| `<audio>` | Configures an audio control native to the browser | autoplay, class, controls, id, loop, preload, src, style, title |
| `<b>` | Configures bold text with no implied importance | class, id, style |
| `<blockquote>` | Configures a long quotation | class, id, style |
| `<body>` | Configures the body section | class, id, style |
| `<br>` | Configures a line break | class, id, style |
| `<button>` | Configures a button | accesskey, autofocus, class, disabled, form, formaction, formenctype, formmethod, formtarget, formnovalidate, id, name, type, style, value |
| `<canvas>` | Configures dynamic graphics | class, height, id, style, title, width |
| `<caption>` | Configures a caption for a table | align (obsolete), class, id, style |
| `<cite>` | Configures the title of a cited work | class, height, id, style, title, width |
| `<code>` | Configures a fragment of computer code | class, id, style |
| `<col>` | Configures a table column | class, id, span, style |
| `<colgroup>` | Configures a group of one or more columns in a table | class, id, span, style |

*(Continued)*

647

| Element | Purpose | Commonly Used Attributes |
|---|---|---|
| `<command>` | Configures an area to represent commands | `class, id, style, type` |
| `<data>` | Provides a machine-readable format for text content | `class, id, style, value` |
| `<datalist>` | Configures a control that contains one or more option elements | `class, id, style` |
| `<dd>` | Configures a description area in a description list | `class, id, style` |
| `<del>` | Configures deleted text (with strikethrough) | `cite, class, datetime, id, style` |
| `<details>` | Configures a widget to provide additional information to the user on demand | `class, id, open, style` |
| `<dfn>` | Configures the definition of a term | `class, id, style` |
| `<dialog>` | Configures a dialog box | `class, id, open, style` |
| `<div>` | Configures a generic section or division in a document | `align` (obsolete)`, class, id, style` |
| `<dl>` | Configures a description list (formerly called a definition list) | `class, id, style` |
| `<dt>` | Configures a term in a description list | `class, id, style` |
| `<em>` | Configures emphasized text (usually displays in italics) | `class, id, style` |
| `<fieldset>` | Configures a grouping of form elements with a border | `class, id, style` |
| `<figcaption>` | Configures a caption for a figure | `class, id, style` |
| `<figure>` | Configures a figure | `class, id, style` |
| `<footer>` | Configures a footer area | `class, id, style` |
| `<form>` | Configures a form | `accept-charset, action, autocomplete, class, enctype, id, method, name, novalidate, style, target` |
| `<h1> ... <h6>` | Configures headings | `align` (obsolete)`, class, id, style` |
| `<head>` | Configures the head section | Not applicable |
| `<header>` | Configures a header area | `class, id, style` |
| `<hr>` | Configures a horizontal line; indicates a thematic break in HTML5 | `class, id, style` |
| `<html>` | Configures the root element of a web page document | `lang, manifest` |
| `<i>` | Configures italic text with no particular emphasis or importance | `class, id, style` |
| `<iframe>` | Configures an inline frame | `class, height, id, name, sandbox, src, style, title, width` |
| `<img>` | Configures an image | `alt, class, height, id, ismap, longdesc, name, sizes, src, srcset, style, usemap, width` |
| `<input>` | Configures an input control: text box, email text box, URL text box, search text box, telephone number text box, scrolling text box, submit button, reset button, password box, calendar control, slider control, spinner control, color-well control, or hidden field form control | `accesskey, autocomplete, class, checked, disabled, form, id, list, max, maxlength, min, name, pattern, placeholder, readonly, required, size, step, style, tabindex, type, value` |

| Element | Purpose | Commonly Used Attributes |
|---|---|---|
| `<ins>` | Configures text that has been inserted into a document | `cite, class, datetime, id, style` |
| `<kbd>` | Configures a representation of user input | `class, id, style` |
| `<keygen>` | Configures a control that generates a public-private key pair or submits the public key | `autofocus, challenge, class, disabled, form, id, keytype, style` |
| `<label>` | Configures a label for a form control | `class, for, form, id, style` |
| `<legend>` | Configures a caption for a fieldset element | `class, id, style` |
| `<li>` | Configures a list item in an unordered or ordered list | `class, id, style, value` |
| `<link>` | Associates a web page document with an external resource | `class, href, hreflang, id, rel, media, sizes, style, type` |
| `<main>` | Configures the main content area of a web page | `class, id, style` |
| `<map>` | Configures an image map | `class, id, name, style` |
| `<mark>` | Configures text as marked (or highlighted) for easy reference | `class, id, style` |
| `<menu>` | Configures a list of commands | `class, id, label, style` |
| `<meta>` | Configures metadata | `charset, content, http-equiv, name` |
| `<meter>` | Configures a visual gauge of a value | `class, id, high, low, max, min, optimum, style, value` |
| `<nav>` | Configures an area with navigation hyperlinks | `class, id, style` |
| `<noscript>` | Configures content for browsers that do not support client-side scripting | |
| `<object>` | Configures an embedded object | `classid, codebase, data, form, height, name, id, style, title, tabindex, type, width` |
| `<ol>` | Configures an ordered list | `class, id, reversed, start, style, type` |
| `<optgroup>` | Configures a group of related options in a select list | `class, disabled, id, label, style` |
| `<option>` | Configures an option in a select list | `class, disabled, id, selected, style, value` |
| `<output>` | Configures the results of a calculation | `class, for, form, id, name, style` |
| `<p>` | Configures a paragraph | `class, id, style` |
| `<param>` | Configures a parameter for plug-ins | `name, value` |
| `<picture>` | Configures display of different images depending on specific | `class, id, style` |
| `<pre>` | Configures preformatted text | `class, id, style` |
| `<progress>` | Configures a visual progress indicator | `class, id, max, style, value` |
| `<q>` | Configures quoted text | `class, id, style` |
| `<rp>` | Configures a ruby parenthesis | `class, id, style` |
| `<rt>` | Configures ruby text component of a ruby annotation | `class, id, style` |
| `<ruby>` | Configures a ruby annotation | `class, id, style` |
| `<s>` | Configures text that is no longer accurate or relevant | `class, id, style` |
| `<samp>` | Configures sample output from a computer program or system | `class, id, style` |

*(Continued)*

| Element | Purpose | Commonly Used Attributes |
|---|---|---|
| `<script>` | Configures a client-side script (typically, JavaScript) | async, charset, defer, src, type |
| `<section>` | Configures a section of a document | class, id, style |
| `<select>` | Configures a select list form control | class, disabled, form, id, multiple, name, size, style, tabindex |
| `<small>` | Configures a disclaimer in small text size | class, id, style |
| `<source>` | Configures a media file and MIME type | class, id, media, sizes, src, srcset, style, type |
| `<span>` | Configures a generic section of a document with inline display | class, id, style |
| `<strong>` | Configures text with strong importance (typically displayed as bold) | class, id, style |
| `<style>` | Configures embedded styles in a document | media, scoped, type |
| `<sub>` | Configures subscript text | class, id, style |
| `<summary>` | Configures text as a summary, caption, or legend for a details control | class, id, style |
| `<sup>` | Configures superscript text | class, id, style |
| `<table>` | Configures a table | class, id, style, summary |
| `<tbody>` | Configures the body section of a table | class, id, style |
| `<td>` | Configures a table data cell in a table | class, colspan, id, headers, rowspan |
| `<textarea>` | Configures a scrolling text box form control | accesskey, autofocus, class, cols, disabled, id, maxlength, name, placeholder, readonly, required, rows, style, tabindex, wrap |
| `<tfoot>` | Configures the footer section of a table | class, id, style |
| `<th>` | Configures a table header cell in a table | class, colspan, id, headers, rowspan, scope, style |
| `<thead>` | Configures the head section of a table | class, id, style |
| `<time>` | Configures a date and/or time | class, datetime, id, style |
| `<title>` | Configures the title of a web page document | |
| `<tr>` | Configures a row in a table | class, id, style |
| `<track>` | Configures a subtitle or caption track for media | class, default, id, kind, label, src, srclang, style |
| `<u>` | Configures text conventionally styled with an underline | class, id, style |
| `<ul>` | Configures an unordered list | class, id, style |
| `<var>` | Configures text as a variable or placeholder | class, id, style |
| `<video>` | Configures a video control native to the browser | autoplay, class, controls, height, id, loop, poster, preload, src, style, width |
| `<wbr>` | Configures a line-break opportunity | class, id, style |

# Special Entity Characters

The table that follows lists a selection of special entity characters in order of numeric code. The most commonly used special characters are shown in bold. The W3Cs list of special characters is found at http://www.w3.org/MarkUp/html-spec/html-spec_13.html.

| Entity Name | Numeric Code | Descriptive Code | Character |
|---|---|---|---|
| **Quotation mark** | **&#34;** | **&quot;** | " |
| **Ampersand** | **&#38;** | **&amp;** | & |
| Apostrophe | &#39; | | ' |
| **Less than sign** | **&#60;** | **&lt;** | < |
| **Greater than sign** | **&#62;** | **&gt;** | > |
| Vertical bar | &#124; | | \| |
| **Left single quotation mark** | **&#145;** | **&lsquo;** | ' |
| **Right single quotation mark** | **&#146;** | **&rsquo;** | ' |
| **Nonbreaking space** | ** ** | ** ** | a blank space |
| Inverted exclamation | &#161; | &iexcl; | ¡ |
| Cent sign | &#162; | &cent; | ¢ |
| Pound sterling sign | &#163; | &pound; | £ |
| General currency sign | &#164; | &curren; | ‡ |
| Yen sign | &#165; | &yen; | ¥ |
| Broken vertical bar | &#166; | &brvbar; | ¦ |
| Section sign | &#167; | &sect; | § |
| Umlaut | &#168; | &uml; | ¨ |
| **Copyright symbol** | **&#169;** | **&copy;** | © |
| Feminine ordinal | &#170; | &ordf; | ª |
| Left angle quote | &#171; | &laquo; | << |
| Not sign | &#172; | &not; | ¬ |
| Soft hyphen | &#173; | &shy; | - |
| **Registered trademark symbol** | **&#174;** | **&reg;** | ® |

*(Continued)*

| Entity Name | Numeric Code | Descriptive Code | Character |
|---|---|---|---|
| Macron | `&#175;` | `&macr;` | ¯ |
| Degree sign | `&#176;` | `&deg;` | ° |
| Plus or minus | `&#177;` | `&plusmn;` | ± |
| Superscript two | `&#178;` | `&sup2;` | 2 |
| Superscript three | `&#179;` | `&sup3;` | 3 |
| Acute accent | `&#180;` | `&acute;` | ´ |
| Micro (Mu) | `&#181;` | `&micro;` | µ |
| Paragraph sign | `&#182;` | `&para;` | ¶ |
| Middle dot | `&#183;` | `&middot;` | · |
| Cedilla | `&#184;` | `&cedil;` | ¸ |
| Superscript one | `&#185;` | `&sup1;` | 1 |
| Masculine ordinal | `&#186;` | `&ordm;` | º |
| Right angle quote | `&#187;` | `&raquo;` | » |
| Fraction one-fourth | `&#188;` | `&frac14;` | ¼ |
| Fraction one-half | `&#189;` | `&frac12;` | ½ |
| Fraction three-fourths | `&#190;` | `&frac34;` | ¾ |
| Inverted question mark | `&#191;` | `&iquest;` | ¿ |
| Small e, grave accent | `&#232;` | `&egrave;` | è |
| Small e, acute accent | `&#233;` | `&eacute;` | é |
| En dash | `&#8211;` | `&ndash;` | – |
| **Em dash** | `&#8212;` | `&mdash;` | — |

# CSS Property Reference

## Commonly Used CSS Properties

| Property | Description |
|---|---|
| align-items | Configures the way the browser displays extra space along the cross-axis of the container. Value: `baseline, center, flex-end, flex-start, stretch` |
| animation | Shorthand property that describes the way an pre-configured animation is applied. Value: List the value for `animation-name` and `animation-duration` separated by spaces (required). Other animation property values are optional. |
| animation-delay | Delay before beginning animation Value: Default value 0s configures an immediate animation; a numeric value specifies delay time in seconds or milliseconds |
| animation-direction | Configures if animation should play forward, backwards or alternating Value: `normal` (default), `reverse, alternate, alternate-reverse` |
| animation-duration | Length of animation Value: Default value 0s configures no animation; a numeric value specifies length of animation in seconds or milliseconds |
| animation-fill-mode | Configures what CSS properties apply when the animation is not running Value: `none` (default), `forwards, backwards, both` |
| animation-iteration-count | Configures the number of times to repeat the animation; Value: 1 (default), positive number, `infinite` |
| animation-name | Indicates the associated @keyframes rule for the animation Value: name of a @keyframes rule |
| animation-play-state | Indicates if animation is playing or paused Value: `running` (default), `paused` |
| animation-timing-function | Configures changes in the speed of the animation by describing how intermediate property values are calculated Value: `ease` (default), `linear, ease-in, ease-out, ease-in-out` |
| background | Shorthand to configure all the background properties of an element Value: `background-attachment background-clip background-color background-image background-origin background-position background-repeat background-size` |

*(Continued)*

| Property | Description |
|---|---|
| background-attachment | Configures a background image as fixed in place or scrolling<br>Value: scroll (default), fixed, or local |
| background-clip | Configures the area to display the background<br>Value: border-box, padding-box, or content-box |
| background-color | Configures the background color of an element<br>Value: Valid color value |
| background-image | Configures a background image for an element<br>Value: url(*file name or path to the image*), none (default)<br>Optional functions: linear-gradient() and radial-gradient() |
| background-origin | Configures the background positioning area<br>Value: padding-box, border-box, or content-box |
| background-position | Configures the position of a background image<br>Value: Two percentages, pixel values, or position values (left, top, center, bottom, right) |
| background-repeat | Configures how the background image will be repeated<br>Value: repeat (default), repeat-y, repeat-x, or no-repeat |
| background-size | Configures the size of the background images<br>Value: Numeric value (px or em), percentage, contain, cover |
| border | Shorthand to configure the border of an element<br>Value: border-width border-style border-color |
| border-bottom | Configures the bottom border of an element<br>Value: border-width border-style border-color |
| border-collapse | Configures the display of borders in a table<br>Value: separate (default) or collapse |
| border-color | Configures the border color of an element<br>Value: Valid color value |
| border-image | Configures an image in the border of an element<br>See http://www.w3.org/TR/css3-background\#the-border-image |
| border-left | Configures the left border of an element<br>Value: border-width border-style border-color |
| border-radius | Configures rounded corners<br>Value: One to four numeric values (px or em) or percentages that configure the radius of the corners. If a single value is provided, it configures all four corners. The corners are configured in order of top left, top right, bottom right, and bottom left.<br>Related properties: border-top-left-radius, border-top-right-radius, border-bottom-left-radius, and border-bottom-right-radius |
| border-right | Configures the right border of an element<br>Value: border-width border-style border-color |
| border-spacing | Configures the space between table cells in a table<br>Value: Numeric value (px or em) |
| border-style | Configures the style of the borders around an element<br>Value: none (default), inset, outset, double, groove, ridge, solid, dashed, or dotted |
| border-top | Configures the top border of an element<br>Value: border-width border-style border-color |
| border-width | Configures the width of an element's border<br>Value: numeric pixel value (such as 1px), thin, medium, or thick |
| bottom | Configures the offset position from the bottom of a containing element<br>Value: Numeric value (px or em), percentage, or auto (default) |

| Property | Description |
| --- | --- |
| box-shadow | Configures a drop shadow on an element<br>Values: Three or four numerical values (px or em) to indicate horizontal offset, vertical offset, blur radius, spread distance (optional), and a valid color value. Use the `inset` keyword to configure an inner shadow. |
| box-sizing | Alters the default CSS box model that calculates widths and heights of elements<br>Values: `content-box` (default), `padding-box, border-box` |
| caption-side | Configures the placement of a table caption<br>Value: `top` (default) or `bottom` |
| clear | Configures the display of an element in relation to floating elements<br>Value: `none` (default), `left, right, or both` |
| color | Configures the color of text within an element<br>Value: Valid color value |
| column-gap | Configures the space between grid columns<br>Value: Numeric length or percentage |
| display | Configures how and whether an element will display<br>Value: `inline, none, block, flex, grid, inline-flex, list-item, table, table-row, or table-cell` |
| flex | Configures proportional size and flexibility of a flex item<br>Values: numeric value sets the proportional flexible size of the item. See http://www.w3.org/TR/css3-flexbox/#flex-common |
| flex-basis | Configures the initial dimension along the main axis of the flex item<br>Value: content, auto,numeric or percentage |
| flex-direction | Configures direction of flex items within a flex container<br>Values: `row` (default), `column, row-reverse, column-reverse` |
| flex-grow | Determines the growth of the flex item relative to other items in the flex container<br>Value: 0 (default), positive number |
| flex-shrink | Determines how much the flex item will shrink relative to the other items in the flex container<br>Value: 1 (default), positive number |
| flex-wrap | Configures whether flex items are displayed on multiple lines within a flex container<br>Value: `nowrap` (default), `wrap, wrap-reverse` |
| float | Configures the horizontal placement (left or right) of an element<br>Value: `none` (default), `left, or right` |
| font-family | Configures the font typeface of text<br>Value: List of valid font names or generic font family names |
| font-size | Configures the font size of text<br>Value: Numeric value (px, pt, em) percentage value, `xx-small, x-small, small, medium` (default), `large, x-large, xx-large, smaller, or larger` |
| font-stretch | Configures a normal, condensed, or expanded face from a font family<br>Value: normal (default), `wider, narrower, condensed, semi-condensed, expanded, or ultra-expanded` |
| font-style | Configures the font style of text<br>Value: normal (default), `italic,` or `oblique` |
| font-variant | Configures whether text is displayed in small-caps font<br>Value: `normal` (default) or `small-caps` |
| font-weight | Configures the weight (boldness) of text<br>Value: normal (default), `bold, bolder, lighter, 100, 200, 300, 400, 500, 600, 700, 800, or 900` |

*(Continued)*

| Property | Description |
|---|---|
| grid-area | Associates a grid item with a named area of the grid<br>Value: Name of a grid area |
| grid-column | Configures one or more columns in the grid for an item or area<br>Value: See https://www.w3.org/TR/css-grid-1/#typedef-grid-row-start-grid-line |
| grid-column-gap | Configures the space between grid columns<br>Value: Numeric length or percentage |
| grid-gap | Configures the space between grid columns and grid rows<br>Value: Numeric length or percentage |
| grid-row-gap | Configures the space between grid rows<br>Value: Numeric length or percentage |
| grid-row | Configures one or more rows in the grid for an item or area<br>Value: See https://www.w3.org/TR/css-grid-1/#typedef-grid-row-start-grid-line |
| grid-template | Shorthand property that combines the grid-template-areas, grid-template-rows, and grid-template-columns properties<br>Value: A series of strings for each row that indicate placement of named grid areas; the last row describes the columns widths<br>See https://www.w3.org/TR/css-grid-1/#propdef-grid-template |
| grid-template-areas | Visually indicates the placement of the named grid areas on the grid<br>Value: A series of strings for each row that indicate placement of named grid areas<br>See https://www.w3.org/TR/css-grid-1/#grid-template-areas-property |
| grid-template-columns | Specifies how much space to reserve for each column in the grid<br>Value: Numeric pixels, percentage, auto, and fr units;<br>see https://www.w3.org/TR/css-grid-1/#propdef-grid-template-columns |
| grid-template-rows | Specifies how much space to reserve for each row in the grid<br>Value: Numeric pixels, percentage, auto, and fr units;<br>see https://www.w3.org/TR/css-grid-1/#propdef-grid-template-rows |
| height | Configures the height of an element<br>Value: Numeric value (px or em), percentage, or auto (default) |
| justify-content | Configures how the browser should display any extra space that may exist in the flex container<br>Values: flex-start (default), flex-end, center, space-between, space-around |
| left | Configures the offset position from the left of a containing element<br>Value: Numeric value (px or em), percentage, or auto (default) |
| letter-spacing | Configures the space between text characters<br>Value: Numeric value (px or em) or normal (default) |
| line-height | Configures the line height of the text<br>Value: Numeric value (px or em), percentage, multiplier numeric value, or normal (default) |
| list-style | Shorthand to configure the properties of a list<br>Value: list-style-type list-style-position list-style-image |
| list-style-image | Configures an image as a list marker<br>Value: url(*file name or path to the image*) or none (default) |
| list-style-position | Configures the position of the list markers<br>Value: inside or outside (default) |
| list-style-type | Configures the type of list marker displayed<br>Value: none, circle, disc (default), square, decimal, decimal-leading-zero, georgian, lower-alpha, lower-roman, upper-alpha, or upper-roman |
| margin | Shorthand to configure the margin of an element<br>Value: One to four numeric values (px or em) or percentages, auto, or 0 |

| Property | Description |
| --- | --- |
| margin-bottom | Configures the bottom margin of an element<br>Value: Numeric value (px or em), percentage, auto, or 0 |
| margin-left | Configures the left margin of an element<br>Value: Numeric value (px or em), percentage, auto, or 0 |
| margin-right | Configures the right margin of an element<br>Value: Numeric value (px or em), percentage, auto, or 0 |
| margin-top | Configures the top margin of an element<br>Value: Numeric value (px or em), percentage, auto, or 0 |
| max-height | Configures the maximum height of an element<br>Value: Numeric value (px or em), percentage, or none (default) |
| max-width | Configures the maximum width of an element<br>Value: Numeric value (px or em), percentage, or none (default) |
| min-height | Configures the minimum height of an element<br>Value: Numeric value (px or em), percentage, or none (default) |
| min-width | Configures the minimum width of an element<br>Value: Numeric value (px or em), percentage, or none (default) |
| opacity | Configures the transparency of an element and its child elements<br>Value: Numeric value between 1 (fully opaque) and 0 (completely transparent) |
| order | Display the flex items or grid items in a different order than they are coded<br>Value: Numeric value |
| outline | Shorthand to configure an outline of an element<br>Value: outline-width, outline-style, outline-color |
| outline-color | Configures the outline color of an element<br>Value: Valid color value |
| outline-style | Configures the style of the outline around an element<br>Value: none (default), inset, outset, double, groove, ridge, solid, dashed, or dotted |
| outline-width | Configures the width of an element's outline<br>Value: Numeric pixel value (such as 1px), thin, medium, or thick |
| overflow | Configures how content should display if it is too large for the area allocated<br>Value: visible (default), hidden, auto, or scroll |
| padding | Shorthand to configure the padding of an element<br>Value: One to four numeric values (px or em) or percentages, or 0 |
| padding-bottom | Configures the bottom padding of an element<br>Value: Numeric value (px or em), percentage, or 0 |
| padding-left | Configures the left padding of an element<br>Value: Numeric value (px or em), percentage, or 0 |
| padding-right | Configures the right padding of an element<br>Value: Numeric value (px or em), percentage, or 0 |
| padding-top | Configures the top padding of an element<br>Value: Numeric value (px or em), percentage, or 0 |
| page-break-after | Configures the page break after an element<br>Value: auto (default), always, avoid, left, or right |
| page-break-before | Configures the page break before an element<br>Value: auto (default), always, avoid, left, or right |
| page-break-inside | Configures the page break inside an element<br>Value: auto (default) or avoid |
| position | Configures the type of positioning used to display an element<br>Value: static (default), absolute, fixed, relative, or sticky |

*(Continued)*

| Property | Description |
|---|---|
| right | Configures the offset position from the right of a containing element<br>Value: Numeric value (px or em), percentage, or auto (default) |
| text-align | Configures the horizontal alignment of text within an element<br>Value: left (default), right, center, or justify |
| text-decoration | Configures the decoration added to text<br>Value: none (default), underline, overline, line-through, or blink |
| text-indent | Configures the indentation of the first line of text<br>Value: Numeric value (px or em) or percentage |
| text-outline | Configures an outline around text displayed within an element<br>Value: One or two numerical values (px or em) to indicate thickness and (optionally) blur radius, and a valid color value |
| text-shadow | Configures a drop shadow on the text displayed within an element<br>Values: Three or four numerical values (px or em) to indicate horizontal offset, vertical offset, blur radius, or spread distance (optional), and a valid color value |
| text-transform | Configures the capitalization of text<br>Value: none (default), capitalize, uppercase, or lowercase |
| top | Configures the offset position from the top of a containing element<br>Value: Numeric value (px or em), percentage, or auto (default) |
| transform | Configures change or transformation in the display of an element<br>Value: A transform function such as scale(), translate(), matrix(), rotate(), skew(), or perspective() |
| transition | Shorthand property to configure the presentational transition of a CSS property<br>Value: List the value for the transition-property, transition-duration, transition-timing-function, and transition-delay, separated by spaces; default values can be omitted, but the first time unit applies to transition-duration |
| transition-delay | Indicates the beginning of the transition<br>Value: 0 (default) configures no delay; otherwise use a numeric value to specify time (usually in seconds) |
| transition-duration | Indicates the length of time to apply the transition<br>Value: 0 (default) configures an immediate transition; otherwise use a numeric value to specify time (usually in seconds) |
| transition-property | Indicates the CSS property that the transition applies to<br>Value: A list of applicable properties is available at http://www.w3.org/TR/css3-transitions |
| transition-timing-function | Configures changes in the speed of the transition by describing how intermediate property values are calculated<br>Value: ease (default), linear, ease-in, ease-out, or ease-in-out |
| vertical-align | Configures the vertical alignment of an element<br>Value: Numeric value (px or em), percentage, baseline (default), sub, super, top, text-top, middle, bottom, or text-bottom |
| visibility | Configures the visibility of an element<br>Value: visible (default), hidden, or collapse |
| white-space | Configures white space inside an element<br>Value: normal (default), nowrap, pre, pre-line, or pre-wrap |
| width | Configures the width of an element<br>Value: Numeric value (px or em), percentage, or auto (default) |
| word-spacing | Configures the space between words within text<br>Value: Numeric value (px or em) or auto (default) |
| z-index | Configures the stacking order of an element<br>Value: Numeric value or auto (default) |

# WCAG 2.1 Quick Reference

Web Content Accessibility Guidelines (WCAG) 2.1 reached W3C Recommendation status in June 2018. WCAG 2.1 includes all WCAG 2.0 success criteria. WCAG 2.1 also introduces new success criteria.

## Perceivable

- **1.1 Text Alternatives:**  Provide text alternatives for any nontext content so that it can be changed into other forms people need, such as large print, Braille, speech, symbols, or simpler language. *You configure images* (Chapter 4) *and multimedia* (Chapter 11*) on web pages and provide for alternative text content.*

- **1.2 Time-Based Media:**  Provide alternatives for time-based media. *You don't create time-based media in this textbook, but keep this option in mind for the future if you create animation.* You create a jQuery slideshow in Chapter 14, which includes an option for the user to manually advance or reverse the slide display.

- **1.3 Adaptable:**  Create content that can be presented in different ways (for example, simpler layout) without losing information or structure. In Chapter 2, you use *block elements (such as headings, paragraphs, and lists) to create single-column web pages.* You create multicolumn web pages in Chapter 6 and Chapter 7. You use HTML tables in Chapter 8 to configure information.

- **1.4 Distinguishable:**  Make it easier for users to see and hear content, including separating foreground from background. *You are aware of the importance of good contrast between text and background.*

# Operable

- **2.1 Keyboard Accessible:** Make all functionality available from a keyboard. In Chapter 6, you configure hyperlinks to named fragment identifiers on a web page. The label element is introduced in Chapter 9.

- **2.2 Enough Time:** Provide users enough time to read and use content. Provide a way to pause, stop and/or hide moving, blinking, or scrolling information if it begins automatically and lasts more than five seconds. In Chapter 11, you limit the duration of animation to five seconds.

- **2.3 Seizures:** Do not design content in a way that is known to cause seizures. *Be careful when you use animation created by others; web pages should not contain elements that flash more than three times in a one-second period.*

- **2.4 Navigable:** Provide ways to help users navigate, find content, and determine where they are. *In Chapter 2, you use block elements (such as headings and lists) to organize web page content. In Chapter 6, you learn to structure navigation links within an unordered list and you configure hyperlinks to named fragment identifiers on a web page.*

- **2.5 Input Modalities:** Design to support input via other devices than a keyboard. *In Chapter 7, you create responsive web pages that work well on both desktop and mobile devices.*

# Understandable

- **3.1 Readable:** Make text content readable and understandable. You explore techniques used in writing for the Web in Chapter 5.

- **3.2 Predictable:** Make web pages appear and operate in predictable ways. *The web pages you create are predictable, with clearly labeled and functioning hyperlinks.*

- **3.3 Input Assistance:** Help users avoid and correct mistakes. You learn to use *HTML form controls in* Chapter 9 *that cause a supporting browser to validate basic form information and display error messages. In Chapter 14, you configure client-side scripting to edit web page forms and provide additional feedback to users.*

# Robust

- **4.1 Compatible:** Maximize compatibility with current and future user agents, including assistive technologies. *You provide for future compatibility by writing code that follows W3C Recommendations (standards).*

*The How to Meet WCAG 2 (Quick Reference) (https://www.w3.org/WAI/WCAG21/quickref/) entries are copyright © 2019 World Wide Web Consortium, (MIT, ERCIM, Keio, Beihang). https://www.w3.org/Consortium/Legal/2002/ipr-notice-20021231.*

# Resources

Web Content Accessibility Guidelines (WCAG) 2.1 reached W3C Recommendation status in June 2018. WCAG 2.1 includes all WCAG 2.0 success criteria. WCAG 2.1 also introduces new success criteria, described at https://www.w3.org/WAI/standards-guidelines/wcag/new-in-21/. You'll find the most up-to-date information about WCAG 2.1 at the following resources:

- Web Content Accessibility Guidelines (WCAG) 2.1    https://www.w3.org/TR/WCAG21/
- Understanding WCAG 2.1    https://www.w3.org/WAI/WCAG21/Understanding/
- How to Meet WCAG 2    https://www.w3.org/WAI/WCAG21/quickref/

# Landmark Roles with ARIA

The W3C's Web Accessibility Initiative (WAI) has developed a standard to provide for additional accessibility, called **Accessible Rich Internet Applications (ARIA).** ARIA provides methods intended to increase the accessibility of web pages and web applications by identifying the role or purpose of an element on a web page (https://www.w3.org/WAI/intro/aria).

We'll focus on ARIA landmark roles in this appendix. A **landmark** on a web page is a major section such as a banner, navigation, main content, and so on. **ARIA landmark roles** allow web developers to configure semantic descriptions of HTML elements using the **role attribute** to indicate landmarks on the web page. For example, to indicate the landmark role of main on an element containing the main content of a web page document, code `role="main"` on the opening tag.

People visiting a web page with a screen reader or other assistive technology can access the landmark roles to quickly skip to specific areas on a web page (watch the video at https://www.youtube.com/watch?v=IhWMou12_Vk for a demonstration). Visit https://www.w3.org/TR/wai-aria-practices/#landmark-roles for a complete list of ARIA landmark roles.

Commonly used ARIA landmark roles include:

- `banner` (a header/logo area)
- `navigation` (a collection of navigation elements)
- `main` (the main content of a document)
- `complementary` (a supporting part of the web page document, designed to be complementary to the main content)
- `contentinfo` (an area that contains information about the content such as copyright)
- `form` (an area that contains a form)
- `search` (an area of a web page that provides search functionality)

The code for the body section of sample web page with the banner, navigation, main, and contentinfo roles configured is shown below. Notice that while the role attribute will not change the way the web page displays, it offers additional information about the document that can be used by assistive technologies.

```
<body>
  <header role="banner">
    <h1>Heading Logo Banner</h1>
  </header>
  <nav role="navigation">
     <a href="index.html">Home</a> <a href="contact.html">Contact</a>
  </nav>
  <main role="main">
      This is the main content area.
  </main>
  <footer role="contentinfo">
      Copyright &copy; 2020 Your Name Here
  </footer>
</body>
```

# FTP Tutorial

## Publish with File Transfer Protocol (FTP)

Once you obtain your web hosting space, you'll need to upload your files. Although your web host may offer a web-based file manager application for client use, a common method of transferring files is to use File Transfer Protocol (FTP). A protocol is a convention or standard that enables computers to speak to one another. FTP is used to copy and manage files and folders over the Internet. FTP uses two ports to communicate over a network—one for the data (typically port 20) and one for control commands (typically port 21). See https://www.iana.org/assignments/service-names-port-numbers/service-names-port-numbers.xhtml for a list port numbers used on the Internet.

### FTP Applications

There are many FTP applications available for download or purchase on the Web, including the following:

- **Filezilla**
  - Windows, Mac, Linux Platform
  - https://filezilla-project.org
  - Free download
- **SmartFTP**
  - Windows
  - https://www.smartftp.com
  - Free download
- **CuteFTP**
  - Windows, Mac
  - https://www.globalscape.com/cuteftp
  - Free trial download, academic pricing available

## Connecting with FTP

Your web host will provide you with the following information along with any other specifications, such as whether the FTP server requires the use of active mode or passive mode:

FTP Host: Your FTP Host

Username: Your Account Username

Password: Your Account Password

## Overview of Using an FTP Application

This section focuses on FileZilla, a free FTP application with versions for the Windows, Mac, and Linux platforms. A free download of FileZilla is available at https://filezilla-project.org/download.php. After you download an FTP application of your choice, install the program on your computer, using the instructions provided.

### Launch and Login

Launch Filezilla or another FTP application. Enter the information required by your web host (such as FTP host, username, and password) and initiate the connection. An example screenshot of FileZilla after a connection is shown in Figure F.1

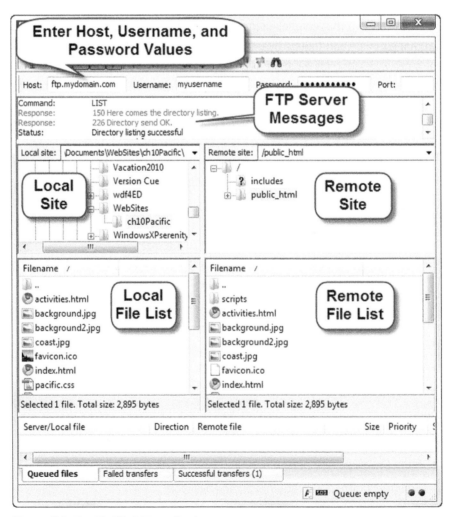

Figure F.1  The FileZilla FTP application. Terry Felke-Morris

As you examine Figure F.1, notice the text boxes near the top of the application for the Host, Username, and Password information. Under this area is a display of messages from the FTP server. Review the area to confirm a successful connection and the results of file transfers. Next, notice that the application is divided into a left panel and a right panel. The left panel is the local site—it displays information about your local computer and allows you to navigate to your drives, folders, and files. The right panel is the remote site—it displays information about your website and provides a way to navigate to its folders and files.

## Uploading a File

It's really easy to transfer a file from your local computer to your remote website: Just select the file with your mouse in the left panel (local site list) and drag it to the right panel (remote site list).

## Downloading a File

If you need to download a file from your website to your local computer, just drag the file with your mouse from the right panel (remote site list) to the left panel (local site list).

## Deleting a File

To delete a file on your website, right-click on the file name (in the right panel) and select Delete from the context-sensitive menu.

## And There's More!

Feel free to explore the other functions offered by FileZilla (and most FTP applications). Right-click on a file in the remote site list to display a context-sensitive menu with several options, including renaming a file, creating a new directory (also known as a folder), and viewing a file.

# Web-Safe Color Palette

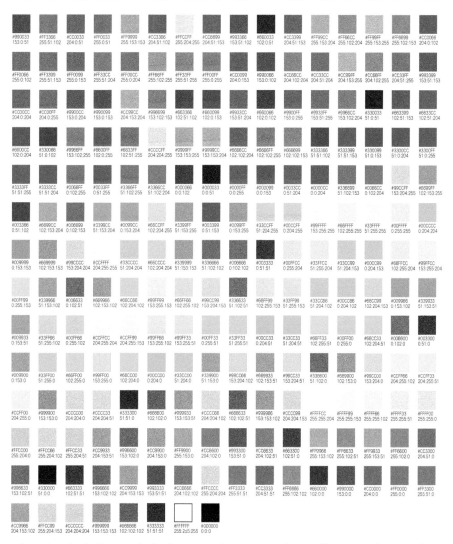

Web-safe colors look the most similar on various computer platforms and computer monitors. Back in the day of eight-bit color it was crucial to use web-safe colors. Since most modern video drivers support millions of colors the use of web-safe colors is now optional. The hexadecimal and decimal RGB values are shown for each web-safe color in the palette above.

# Answers

## Chapter 1

### Checkpoint 1.1

1. The Internet is a public, globally connected network of computer networks. The Web is a graphical user interface to information stored on computers running web servers connected to the Internet. The Web is a subset of the Internet.

2. The commercialization and exponential growth of the Internet that began in the early 1990s was due largely to a convergence of technologies, including the development of personal computers with graphical operating systems, widespread availability of Internet connection services, the removal of the restriction of commercial use on NSFnet, the development of the World Wide Web by Tim Berners-Lee at CERN, and the development of a graphical browser (called Mosaic) at the NCSA. These events combined to provide the commercial incentive and an easy way to share and access information in a manner that had never been experienced.

3. Universal design is a very important concept for web developers because the websites that they create should be usable by all people. Not only is this the right thing to do, but in developing websites for the government or for educational institutions, access to technology (including websites) is mandated by law.

### Checkpoint 1.2

1. An example of a web client is a computer running a browser software application such as Internet Explorer. Typically, the computer is connected to the Internet only when needed. The web browser software uses HTTP to request web pages and related resources from a web server. A web server is a computer that is continually connected to the Internet and that runs some type of web server software application. It uses the HTTP protocol to receive requests for web pages and related resources. It responds to these requests and sends the resources.

**2.** In this chapter, several protocols are discussed that use the Internet but not the Web. E-mail messages are transmitted via the Internet. SMTP (Simple Mail Transfer Protocol) is used to send e-mail messages. POP (Post Office Protocol) and IMAP (Internet Message Access Protocol) can be used to receive e-mail messages. FTP (File Transfer Protocol) can be used to exchange (send and receive) files with a computer connected to the Internet.

**3.** A URL (Uniform Resource Locator) represents the address of a resource that is available on the Internet. A URL consists of a protocol, a domain name, and the hierarchical location of the file or resource. An example of a URL is http://www.webdevfoundations.net/9e/chapter1.html. A domain name locates an organization or other entity on the Internet and is associated with a unique numeric IP address. A domain name is part of a URL. An example of a domain name is webdevfoundations.net.

## Review Questions

**1.** b

**2.** b

**3.** c

**4.** a

**5.** a

**6.** True

**7.** True

**8.** False

**9.** False

**10.** True

**11.** HTML

**12.** subdomain

**13.** SGML

**14.** microblogging

**15.** TCP

# Chapter 2

## Checkpoint 2.1

**1.** HTML (Hypertext Markup Language) was developed by Tim Berners-Lee at CERN, using SGML. HTML is the set of markup symbols or codes placed in a file intended for display on a web browser. HTML configures a platform-independent display of information. Each markup code is referred to as an element (or tag).

**2.** No expensive software is required to create and code web pages. You can use a Windows or Mac text editor application that is part of the operating system. Free text editors and web browsers are also available for download.

**3.** The head section is located between the `<head>` and `</head>` tags on a web page. This area is used to contain information that describes the web page, such as the title of the page that will display in the menu bar of the browser window. The body section is located between the `<body>` and `</body>` tags. This area is used to code text and tags that show directly in the browser's display of the web page. The purpose of the body section is to describe the contents of the web page.

## Checkpoint 2.2

1. The heading element is used to display headings and subheadings of documents. The size of the heading is configured with the particular heading level used—ranging from 1 to 6. `<h1>` is the largest heading. `<h6>` is the smallest heading. Text contained between heading tags will be displayed in a bold font and will have a line break above and below.

2. Ordered lists and unordered lists can be used to organize information on a web page. Unordered lists display a small symbol or bullet in front of each item. Use the `<ul>` tag to configure an unordered list. By default, ordered lists display a sequence of numbers in front of each item. Use the `<ol>` tag to configure an ordered list. Configure individual items in both ordered and unordered lists using the `<li>` tag.

3. The purpose of the blockquote element is to format a long quotation by indenting a section of text on a web page. Empty space is placed above and below the text contained in the blockquote element. The text is indented from both the left and right margins.

## Checkpoint 2.3

1. Special characters are used to display items such as quotation marks, greater than (>), less than (<), and the copyright symbol © on a web page. These special characters, sometimes called entity characters, are interpreted by the browser when the page is rendered.

2. Use an absolute link to display a web page document from a website other than your own. The http protocol is used in the href value. Example:
   `<a href = "http://www.google.com">Google</a>`

3. Use a relative link to display a web page document from your website. The http protocol is not used in the href value.

## Review Questions

1. b
2. c
3. c
4. a
5. b
6. c
7. d
8. b
9. b
10. b
11. strong
12. article
13. describe a characteristic of a web page, such as the character encoding.
14.  
15. em
16. It is good practice to place the e-mail address both on the web page and within the anchor tag. Not everyone has an e-mail program configured with his or her browser. By placing the e-mail address in both places, you increase usability for all your visitors.

# Chapter 3

## Checkpoint 3.1

1. Reasons to use CSS on a web page include the following: greater control of typography and page layout, separation of style from structure, potentially smaller web page documents, and easier site maintenance.

2. Because visitors may set their browsers to certain colors, it is a good idea when changing a text or background color to configure both the text color and the background color properties to provide good contrast between text and background.

3. Embedded styles are coded once in the header section of the web page and apply to the entire page. This practice is more efficient than using inline styles to code individual styles on HTML elements.

## Checkpoint 3.2

1. Embedded styles can be used to configure the text and color formatting for an entire web page. Embedded styles are placed in the head section of a web page. The `<style>` tag is used to contain the CSS selectors and properties that configure the embedded styles.

2. External styles can be used to configure the text and color formatting for some or all of the pages on a website in one file. This single file can be changed, and all the web pages associated with it will display the new styles the next time they are rendered in a browser. External styles are placed in a separate text file that uses a .css file extension. Web pages use the `<link>` tag to indicate that they are using an external style sheet.

3. `<link rel="stylesheet" href="mystyles.css">`

## Review Questions

| | | | |
|---|---|---|---|
| 1. | b | 9. | a |
| 2. | b | 10. | b |
| 3. | a | 11. | c |
| 4. | c | 12. | span |
| 5. | c | 13. | text-align |
| 6. | c | 14. | text-indent |
| 7. | d | 15. | font-weight |
| 8. | d | | |

# Chapter 4

## Checkpoint 4.1

1. It is reasonable to code pages that look similar on various browsers; it is not reasonable to try to code pages that look exactly the same on various browsers and operating systems. Modern web developers code pages to look satisfactory in

commonly used browsers and may add enhancements that are applied by the most recent browser versions. This approach is called "progressive enhancement." Look for more web design tips in Chapter 5.

2. The first style rule is missing an ending semicolon (;).

3. True. CSS can be utilized to configure color, text, and even visual elements such as rectangular shapes (with the background-color property) and lines (with the border property).

## Checkpoint 4.2

1. The CSS background-image property configures the file that is displayed. The CSS background-repeat property configures the way the image is displayed on the page.

Suggested solution:

```
h1 { background-image: url(circle.jpg);
     background-repeat: no-repeat;
}
```

2. The CSS background-image property configures the file that is displayed. The CSS background-repeat property configures the way the image is displayed on the page.

Suggested solution:

```
body { background-image: url(bg.gif);
       background-repeat: repeat-y;
}
```

3. The browser will display the background color immediately. Then, the browser will render the background image and repeat the image as specified in the CSS. The background color will appear in areas not covered by the background image.

## Checkpoint 4.3

1. Answers will vary with the site that you choose to review. There should be good contrast between the navigation text and image background. Alt attributes should be descriptive and contain the text displayed in the image. A row of plain text navigation links in the footer section of the web page could help provide for accessibility.

2. The image, map, and area elements work together to create a functioning image map. The `<img>` tag configures the image that will be used for the map and contains a usemap attribute whose value corresponds to the id value on the `<map>` tag associated with the image. The `<map>` tag is a container tag and surrounds one or more `<area>` tags. There is one self-contained `<area>` tag for each clickable hotspot on the image map.

3. False. There is a trade-off between the quality of the image and the file size. The goal should be to save images that use the smallest file size which provides acceptable display quality.

## Review Questions

1. d
2. b
3. b
4. b
5. a
6. c
7. d
8. b
9. c
10. d
11. tiled
12. text links
13. thumbnail
14. box-shadow
15. meter

# Chapter 5

## Checkpoint 5.1

1. The four basic principles of design are repetition, contrast, proximity, and alignment. Descriptions of school home pages and how these principles are applied will vary.

2. Answers will vary. Best practices for writing for the Web include the following: short paragraphs, bullet points, common fonts, white space, multiple columns if possible, bold or emphasized important text, and correct spelling and grammar. The chosen best practice, URL of each example website, and description of how the website exemplifies the best practice will vary.

3. https://www.walmart.com is an e-commerce site. It is designed to appeal to the general public–note the white background and high contrast and the use of tabbed navigation, product hierarchy, and site search. This design meets the needs of its target audience: teen and adult shoppers. https://www.sesamestreet.org/art-maker is geared toward young children and their parents. It is bright and colorful with much interactivity and animation, all of which is appealing to the target audience. http://www.willyporter.com is a musician's site designed to appeal to everyone. The home page features a compelling photo of the musician along with a grouping of small sections that point you to the new album, gigs, and related social media sites. This site appeals to its audience.

## Checkpoint 5.2

1. Answers will vary.

2. Answers will vary.

3. Best practices for using graphics on web pages include the following: careful choice of colors, use of necessary images only, use of images optimized for display on web pages, a usable site even if images are not displayed, and use of the alt attribute to configure text descriptions for images. Recommendations for school home pages will vary.

## Review Questions

1. d
2. b
3. b
4. b
5. c
6. d
7. c
8. a
9. c
10. b
11. hierarchical
12. do not
13. Web Accessibility Initiative (WAI)
14. Student answers will vary. Issues to be aware of in designing for the mobile web include small screen size, low bandwidth, awkward controls, limited processor and memory, and reduced support of font typefaces and color.
15. Student answers will vary. The four principles that are essential to complying with WCAG 2.0 are as follows: **P**erceivable, **O**perable, **U**nderstandable, and **R**obust.

    1. Content must be **P**erceivable
    2. Interface components in the content must be **O**perable
    3. Content and controls must be **U**nderstandable
    4. Content should be **R**obust enough to work with current and future user agents, including assistive technologies

# Chapter 6

## Checkpoint 6.1

1. The components of the box model, from innermost to outermost, are the content, padding, border, and margin.
2. The purpose of the float property is to shift the display of an element to the right or left side of the container element outside of normal flow.
3. The clear property and the overflow property can be used to "clear" a float.

## Checkpoint 6.2

1. Web page areas can be configured specifically for hard copy. For example, navigation areas can be hidden, page breaks can be configured, font typeface can configured in serif fonts. In addition, other properties can be adjusted such as margin, padding, width, and float, for the printed hard copy.
2. Advantages of using CSS sprites on a website include reduced bandwidth (a condensed sprite image typically will have lower file size than multiple individual images will have), reduced number of http requests by the browser (only one request must be made for the sprite image, instead of multiple requests for individual image files), and quick display of individual images in the sprite, which are configured to display in response to mouse movement.

3. Configure CSS for the element that should remain at the top of the browser viewport with the position property set to the value fixed or the value sticky, top set to 0, left set to 0, and z-index set to a high positive integer.

## Review Questions

| | |
|---|---|
| **1.** a | **9.** d |
| **2.** a | **10.** b |
| **3.** b | **11.** id attribute |
| **4.** b | **12.** left |
| **5.** d | **13.** margin |
| **6.** c | **14.** :hover |
| **7.** b | **15.** z-index |
| **8.** c | |

# Chapter 7

## Checkpoint 7.1

1. Use the CSS display property to configure a CSS selector as a grid container (display: grid;) or a flexbox container (display: flex;).

2. The justify-content property set to the value "center" causes the flex items to be centered in the flex container along the main axis with equal empty space before the first flex item and after the last flex item. The justify-content property set to the value "space-between" causes the flex items to be evenly distributed in the flex container along the main axis. The first item begins at the start of the flex container. The last item is placed at the end of the flex container. The justify-content property set to the value "space-around" causes the flex items to be evenly distributed in the flex container along the main axis with space before the first flex item and space after the last flex item.

3. The grid-template property is a shorthand property that combines the grid-template-areas, grid-template-rows, and grid-template-columns properties. The grid-template property can be used to indicate the location of named grid areas on each row, the height of each row, and the width of each column.

## Checkpoint 7.2

**1.** The Mobile First process begins by first configuring a page layout that works well in smartphones (you can test with a small browser window). This provides the quickest display for mobile devices. Next, resize the browser viewport to be larger until the design "breaks" and needs to be reworked for a pleasing display—this is the point where you need to code a media query. If appropriate,continue resizing the browser viewport to be larger until the design breaks and code additional media queries.

**2.** There are so many different types of devices and viewport sizes that there are no values that "must" be used in media queries. When following mobile first strategy, you configure the CSS for a narrow viewport. Then, increase the size of the viewport. When the design looks awkward (or "breaks") it is time for a media query.

**3.** Use the following well-supported techniques to configure flexible images with CSS:

**a.** Remove the height and width attributes from the HTML

**b.** Set the CSS max-width property to 100%

**c.** Set the CSS height property to auto

Other techniques available to configure responsive images include using the picture element (and companion source element) and configuring the img element with the sizes and srcset attributes.

## Review Questions

1. a
2. a
3. c
4. b
5. c
6. a
7. b
8. c
9. c
10. b

11. grid-template
12. media queries
13. justify-content, align-items
14. flex-flow
15. srcset

# Chapter 8

## Checkpoint 8.1

1. Tables are often used to organize tabular information on a web page.
2. The default browser rendering of the text contained within a th element is bold and centered.
3. Coding a caption element with a relevant description and configuring headers for columns or rows are among the various coding techniques that improve the accessibility of a table.

## Checkpoint 8.2

1. Using CSS properties instead of HTML attributes to configure table characteristics provides for flexibility and easier maintenance.
2. The thead, tbody, and tfoot elements are used to group table rows.

## Review Questions

| | | | |
|---|---|---|---|
| 1. b | | 9. b | |
| 2. c | | 10. a | |
| 3. c | | 11. border | |
| 4. d | | 12. vertical-align | |
| 5. c | | 13. rowspan | |
| 6. b | | 14. headers | |
| 7. d | | 15. caption | |
| 8. b | | | |

# Chapter 9

## Checkpoint 9.1

1. Although either solution would be appropriate, the solution that uses three input boxes (first name, last name, and e-mail address) is the more flexible solution. These separate values could be stored in a database by server-side processing, where they could easily be selected and placed into personalized e-mail messages. This approach provides the most useful functionality of the collected information in future manipulations.

2. There are a number of possible solutions for this design question. If the responses are short and of about equal length, perhaps a group of radio buttons would be appropriate. If the responses are lengthy or of widely varying lengths, a select list would be a good choice. Radio button groups can accept only one response per group. By default, select lists accept only one response. Check boxes would not be appropriate because they allow more than one response to be selected.

3. False. In a radio button group, the name attribute is used by the browser to process separate elements as a group.

## Checkpoint 9.2

1. The fieldset element creates a visual border around the elements contained within the fieldset. The border can help to organize form elements and increase the usability of the form. The legend element is used to provide a text description of the area bounded by the fieldset element, further increasing the usability of the form for visitors using browsers that support these tags.

2. The accesskey attribute allows a visitor to select an element immediately by using the keyboard instead of a mouse. This approach improves the accessibility of the page and can be very helpful to mobility-impaired visitors. The W3C recommends providing a visual cue of an underlined letter, bold letter, or message that indicates the hot keys to press to activate an element.

3. The web designer and client decide which is used: standard submit button, image button, or button tag. However, it makes sense to use the simplest possible technology that provides the needed functionality. In most cases, this is the standard submit button. Visually challenged visitors using a screen reader will hear that a submit button has been encountered. Submit buttons automatically invoke the server-side processing configured in the form tag.

An image button will also automatically invoke the server-side processing configured for the form and can be more accessible if configured with the alt and accesskey attributes. Unless there is a very good reason or a very insistent client, avoid the button element for standard web forms. Avoid choosing a complex solution when a basic submit button can be used.

## Checkpoint 9.3

1. A web browser requests web pages and their related files from a web server. The web server locates the files and sends them to your web browser. Then the web browser renders the returned files and displays the requested web pages. Server-side processing is required to save and handle information entered by web page visitors. The action attribute on a form element specifies the script or program that the web server should invoke and pass the form data to. The script or program returns a result (often a web page) that is sent from the web server to the browser for display.

**2.** The server-side script developer and the web page designer must work together to get both parts of the form processing—the front-end web page and the back-end server-side script—working together. They need to communicate regarding the method (get or post) to be used by the form and the location of the server-side script. Because the names of the form elements are often used by the server-side script as variable names, the form element names are usually specified at this time.

## Review Questions

1. b
2. a
3. a
4. b
5. b
6. d
7. c
8. c
9. a
10. d
11. d
12. maxlength

13. fieldset
14. name
15. The following form controls could provide a way for a web page visitor to select a color: an input text box for free-form entry of a color value, an HTML5 datalist with one option element for each color choice, a radio button group with one radio button for each color choice, a select list with one option element for each color choice, and an HTML5 color-well form control (although this is not yet well supported by browsers and will usually result in the display of an input text box).

# Chapter 10

## Checkpoint 10.1

1. The project manager directs the website development process—creating the project plan and schedule. He or she must keep the big picture in mind while communicating with the staff and coordinating team activities. The project manager is accountable for meeting project milestones and producing results.

2. A large-scale web project is much more than brochure-ware–it is often a complex information application that the company depends on. Such an application needs the special talents of a wide variety of individuals—including experts in graphics, organization, writing, marketing, coding, database administration, and so on—one or two people simply cannot fulfill all these roles and create a quality website.

3. Answers will vary. Different testing techniques include the unit testing done by individual web developers, automated testing performed by link checker programs, code testing and validation performed by code validation programs, and usability testing achieved by watching typical web visitors use a website to perform tasks.

## Checkpoint 10.2

1. A virtual web host that offers reliability and scalability would meet the needs of a small company for its initial web presence. The web host chosen should offer higher-end packages with scripting, database, and e-commerce capabilities to allow for future growth.

2. A dedicated web server is owned and supported by the web host company. The client company may choose to administer it or may pay the web host company to perform this task. A co-located server is owned by the client company and housed at the web host provider. This configuration offers both the advantage of a reliable Internet connection at the web host and full control of the administration and support of the web server.

3. If your website is down and your web host is not responding to technical support requests, it doesn't matter that you are saving $5.00 per month. When comparing web host plans, check prices to know the currently prevailing fees. If the charges of a particular Web host seem abnormally low, the company is probably cutting corners. Do not base your choice on price alone.

## Review Questions

1. a
2. a
3. c
4. b
5. d
6. d
7. d
8. a
9. a
10. c
11. usability testing
12. graphic designer
13. UNIX and Linux
14. A careful review of your competitor's web presence helps you design a site that will stand out from the rest and be more appealing to your shared customer base. Note both the good and bad components of your competitors' sites.

15. Contacting technical support can give you a general idea of the responsiveness of the web host provider to issues and problems. If the technical support staff is slow getting back to you at this point, don't be surprised if you get the same type of service when you have a problem and need immediate help. While not fail-safe, a quick response to a simple question at least gives the appearance of a well-organized, professional, and responsive technical support staff.

# Chapter 11

## Checkpoint 11.1

1. Use the HTML video and source elements to configure a video to play on a web page. It's a good idea to code multiple source elements and offer multiple versions of the video in various formats. Also include text or a hyperlink to the video to

display if the browser cannot play the video. This is coded after the source elements but before the closing video tag.

2. The poster element configures an image to display before the video is downloaded by the browser. This avoids an awkward empty area while waiting for a video to play.

3. Fair use is the use of a copyrighted work for purposes such as criticism, reporting, teaching, scholarship, or research. So, while students can use resources found on the Web, they need to be sure to comply with fair use: educational, factual (not creative such as passing off someone else's photograph as your own), a small portion, and use does not impede the original work's marketability. Also the source of the original work should be cited. If the original work has been granted a Creative Commons license by the originator, then the student must comply with the specific license requirements (see https://creativecommons.org).

## Checkpoint 11.2

1. The purpose of the transform property is to provide a means to change the display of an element with functions that can rotate, scale, skew, and reposition an element.

2. When working with animation, a keyframe is a point of change. The purpose of the @keyframes rule is to define an animation – naming the animation and grouping the keyframes.

3. The details element and summary element are used together to configure an interactive widget that will hide and show information.

## Checkpoint 11.3

1. JavaScript can be used to add a wide range of interactive effects to a web page, including form validation, popup windows, jump menus, message boxes, image rollovers, status message changes, calculations, and so on.

2. A PWA is a Progressive Web Application, which is configured as web page and "lives" in a browser, but has features associated with native smartphone apps, such as offering some offline functionality and the ability to be added to the device home screen. PWAs use the Manifest API and ServiceWorkers API. PWAs use the HTTPS protocol.

3. The HTML5 canvas element provides an API to web developers that allows them to configure dynamic graphics with JavaScript.

## Review Questions

1. c

2. b

3. a

4. b

5. c

6. a

7. a

8. a

9. b

10. c

11. application programming interface (API)

12. fair use

13. video

14. CSS properties

15. Document Object Model (DOM)

16. Answers will vary but may include the following: large file size to download, accessibility issues, and the time, talent, and software required to create audio or video content.

17. Creative Commons at https://creativecommons.org provides a free service that allows authors and artists to register a type of a copyright license. The Creative Commons license informs others exactly what they can and cannot do with the creative work.

# Chapter 12

## Checkpoint 12.1

1. There are many advantages to engaging in e-commerce, especially for a small business owner who must watch costs carefully. Advantages include very low overhead, 24/7 business hours, and global sales potential.

2. There are risks in any business venture, including e-commerce. Risks associated with e-commerce include increased competition, fraudulent transactions, and security issues.

3. SSL (Secure Sockets Layer) is a protocol that allows data to be privately exchanged over public networks such as the Internet. SSL has been replaced by the TLS (Transport Layer Secure) protocol, but the term "SSL" remains in common use to describe secure transfer of information on the Web. An online shopper can check the following to determine whether SSL is being used:

   - The https protocol, rather than http, will display in the browser address bar.

   - The browser may display a lock icon. If this icon is clicked, information about the digital certificate and encryption level being used will display.

## Checkpoint 12.2

1. Commonly used payment methods include credit card, stored-value card, digital wallet, and digital cash.

2. Answers will vary. People make online purchases for many reasons, including the following: convenience, lower cost, and ease of shipping. If you did not check for SSL the last time you purchased an item on the Web, most likely you'll look for it in the future.

3. E-commerce solutions include instant storefronts, off-the-shelf shopping cart software that you or your web host installs, and e-commerce platforms. The easiest entry to e-commerce is an instant storefront. Although this solution does not provide the most flexibility, you can get a store up and running in an afternoon.

## Review Questions

1. c

2. a

3. b

4. b

5. b

6. a

7. c

8. a

9. b

10. b

11. Secure Sockets Layer (SSL)

12. EDI

13. asymmetric key

14. symmetric encryption

15. The website developers may use an automatic translation program or other customized web translation service.

# Chapter 13

## Checkpoint 13.1

1. Three components of a search engine are the robot, database, and search form. The robot is a special program that "walks" the Web and follows links to sites. The robot updates the search engine's database with the information it finds. The search form is the graphical user interface that is used to request a search by a visitor to the search engine site.

2. Use the description meta tag to provide a brief description of the website. The information in the description meta tag may be used by search engines when they index your website. Some search engines, such as Google, display the description meta tag information on the search engine results page (SERP).

3. Yes, it may be beneficial for a business to pay for preferential listing. If your business is listed in the first page of search results, visitors are more likely to find your site than if you are in the hundredth page of search results. Paid programs for preferential listing such as Google's AdWords should be carefully considered and may be a good match for the marketing goals of an organization.

## Checkpoint 13.2

1. Answers will vary. In most cases, the top three sites returned for a particular search phrase will not be the same. Consider optimizing your site so that currently the most popular search engine displays the site as high as possible in its results list.

2. A brute force method is to experiment by visiting a search engine, typing in keywords, and checking for your site in the search results. If your web site host provides you with web log reports, you can easily tell by examining the reports. You'll see the names of the robot/spider programs—Googlebot is the name of Google's spider (see https://www.robotstxt.org for more information on search engine robots). The web log reports will also itemize both the search engines used by visitors and the keywords used to locate your site.

3. Answers will vary. Website promotion methods that do not use search engines include the following: affiliate programs, banner ads, banner exchanges, reciprocal link agreements, newsletters, sticky site features such as polls, forums, surveys, QR codes, personal recommendations, newsgroup/listserv postings, social media marketing techniques, blog postings, traditional media ads, and existing paper marketing materials. Any of these are valid as a first choice—depending on the needs of the organization.

The newsletter technique is an interesting promotion method. Place a form on a web page to allow visitors to opt into your newsletter. Send them a periodic e-mail with information of value related to your site (possibly even special offers). This approach encourages visitors to return to your site. They may even forward your e-mail to a friend.

*Note:* Be sure to provide a way for visitors to opt out of the newsletter. For example, newsletters sent by TechLearning News include the following message:

"UNSUBSCRIBE

To unsubscribe from this type of e-mail, please reply to this message. unsubtechlearning@news.techlearning.com"

## Review Questions

1. b
2. a
3. c
4. b
5. b
6. c
7. c
8. a
9. b
10. b
11. stickiness

12. ```
    <meta name="robots"
        description="noindex,
        nofollow">
    ```

13. search engines

14. a variety of methods, including affiliate programs, banner ads, banner exchanges, reciprocal link agreements, blog posting, RSS feeds, newsletters, personal recommendations, social bookmarking, and traditional media advertising, or including a URL or QR code on all promotional materials

15. QR codes

# Chapter 14

## Checkpoint 14.1

1. JavaScript can be used for rollover images, form data validation, popup windows, interactivity such as alert messages and prompts, and mathematical calculations for tasks such as determining tax.

2. There is no limit to the number of script blocks that can be embedded in an HTML document.

3. You can use the JavaScript Console in Firefox to find an error. You could also look through your code, paying particular attention to names of objects, properties, methods and statements, and missing semicolons.
    ```

## Checkpoint 14.2

1. An object is a thing, a property is an attribute, and a method is an action.

2. An event is an occurrence such as clicking a mouse, loading a page, or placing the mouse over an area on the page. An event handler is an attribute embedded in an HTML tag such as onclick, onload, and onmouseover, that points to JavaScript code to execute when the corresponding event occurs.

3. Event handlers are embedded in HTML tags and are not placed in separate script blocks.

## Checkpoint 14.3

1. The `prompt()` method could be used to gather a piece of data such as the user's age. The prompt () method should be used in conjunction with a variable so that the data will be stored in the variable.

2. The code might look something like the following:

```
if (userAge < 18) {
  alert("You are under 18");
} else {
  alert("You are 18 or older");
}
```

3. A function definition begins with the keyword `function`, followed by the name of the function and some JavaScript statements. It defines a function, and calling that function results in the execution of the statements within it.

## Checkpoint 14.4

1. Form data validation refers to checking form input against validation rules and not allowing the form to be submitted if the data does not conform to the rules.

2. Answers may vary, but may include required fields such as name, e-mail address, and phone number. Numeric fields may require validation to ensure that they are within particular bounds—for example, order quantity greater than 0 and age between 1 and 120.

3. When the user clicks the submit button, the submit event occurs and the onsubmit event handler executes the `return validateForm()` statement. The `validateForm` function runs and tests the form data for validation. If the data is valid, `validateForm()` returns the value of true, and the form is submitted. If the data is not valid, `validateForm()` returns the value of false and the form is not submitted.

## Checkpoint 14.5

1. You can either download the .js file for the jQuery library from http://jquery.com/download or you can access the jQuery library stored at a CDN using a script tag with the src value set to the URL of the jQuery CDN.

**2.** The `css()` method allows you to set css properties dynamically within jQuery.

**3.** The ready event is a jQuery statement that determines when the Document object model (DOM) has been completely loaded by the browser.

## Review Questions

1. a

2. c

3. b

4. a

5. d

6. c

7. a

8. b

9. c

10. a

11. b

12. = =

13. attr()

14. window

15. ready event

16. onclick

17. JavaScript

18. css()

19. Common uses for JavaScript include rollover images, form data validation, popup windows, interactivity such as alert messages and prompts, and mathematical calculations.

20. The following techniques can be used in debugging JavaScript: Check the JavaScript code carefully for syntax errors. Verify that quotation marks, braces, and parentheses are used in pairs. Check for missing semicolons. Verify that your code uses the correct case (uppercase and lowercase characters) in variable, object, property, and method names. Use the Console to help with debugging—it will provide some information about the error. Use an `alert()` to display the values of variables or to display messages as your script is running.

# Index